D0741901

IN PATRIA

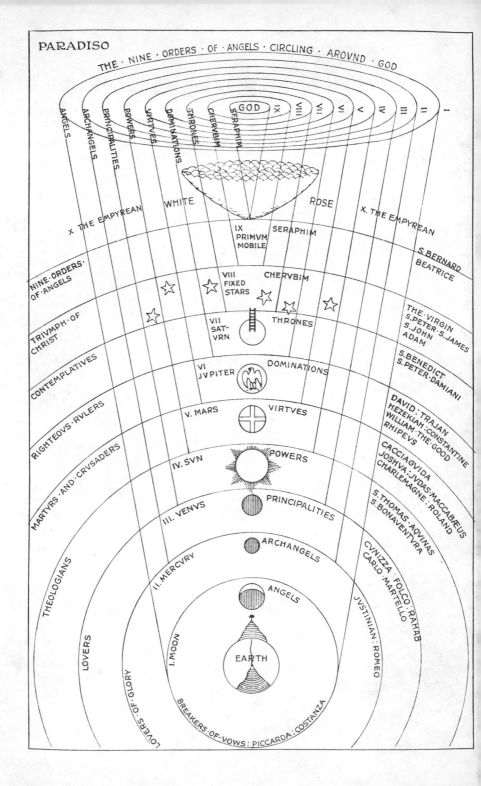

PARADISO

THE · NINE · ORDERS · OF · ANGELS · CIRCLING · AROVND · GOD

GOD

ANGELS
ARCHANGELS
PRINCIPALITIES
POWERS
VIRTVES
DOMINATIONS
THRONES
CHERVBIM
SERAPHIM

I II III IV V VI VII VIII IX

X · THE EMPYREAN — WHITE — ROSE — X. THE EMPYREAN

IX PRIMVM MOBILE — SERAPHIM

S. BERNARD
BEATRICE

NINE · ORDERS · OF · ANGELS

VIII FIXED STARS — CHERVBIM

THE · VIRGIN
S. PETER · S. JAMES
S. JOHN
ADAM

TRIVMPH · OF CHRIST

VII SAT-VRN — THRONES

CONTEMPLATIVES

VI JVPITER — DOMINATIONS

S. BENEDICT
S. PETER · DAMIANI

RIGHTEOVS · RVLERS

V. MARS — VIRTVES

DAVID : TRAJAN
HEZEKIAH · CONSTANTINE
WILLIAM · THE GOOD
RHIPEVS

MARTYRS · AND · CRVSADERS

IV. SVN — POWERS

CACCIAGVIDA
JOSHVA : JVDAS · MACCABÆVS
CHARLEMAGNE · ROLAND

III. VENVS — PRINCIPALITIES

S. THOMAS · AQVINAS
S. BONAVENTVRA

THEOLOGIANS

II. MERCVRY — ARCHANGELS

CVNIZZA · FOLCO · RAHAB
CARLO · MARTELLO

I. MOON — ANGELS

JVSTINIAN · ROMEO

LOVERS

EARTH

LOVERS · OF · GLORY

BREAKERS · OF · VOWS : PICCARDA · COSTANZA

In Patria

AN EXPOSITION OF

DANTE'S PARADISO

BY THE REV.

JOHN S. CARROLL, M.A., D.D.

KENNIKAT PRESS
Port Washington, N. Y./London

Turn you to the strong hold, ye prisoners of hope.

Zech. ix. 12.

La bontà infinita ha sì gran braccia,

Che prende ciò che si rivolge a lei.

Purg. iii. 122, 123.

IN PATRIA

First published in 1911
Reissued in 1971 by Kennikat Press
Library of Congress Catalog Card No: 73-130327
ISBN 0-8046-1386-9

Manufactured by Taylor Publishing Company   Dallas, Texas

TO

SOULS IN VIA AND IN PATRIA

WHO TAUGHT MY HOPE TO CLIMB

THE LONGER STAIRWAY

O sodalizio eletto alla gran cena
Del benedetto Agnello!

PEACE

My Soul, there is a Countrie
  Afar beyond the stars,
Where stands a winged Sentrie
  All skilfull in the wars.
There, above noise and danger,
  Sweet peace sits crown'd with smiles,
And One born in a Manger
  Commands the Beauteous files.
He is thy gracious friend
  And (O my Soul awake !)
Did in pure love descend,
  To die here for thy sake.
If thou canst get but thither,
  There growes the flowre of peace,
The Rose that cannot wither,
  Thy fortresse, and thy ease.
Leave then thy foolish ranges ;
  For none can thee secure,
But One, who never changes,
  Thy God, thy Life, thy Cure.
                    HENRY VAUGHAN.

PREFACE

In this volume I complete, as far as lies within my
power, my exposition of the *Divina Commedia*; and
those who have ever attempted the task will best
understand the sense of inevitable shortcoming with
which I close a labour pursued for many years with
the remnants of time and strength left by exacting
duties which had the first claim on both. If any
critic regrets that Dante's warning in the second Canto
of the *Paradiso* to those who would follow in his wake
did not nip this exposition in the bud, the author
assures him it is a regret he has often had occasion to
share: not once or twice he was tempted to turn his
'picciolotta barca' and make for the ease and safety
of the familiar shore of earth and time. It had perhaps been wiser to let the temptation have its way;
certainly nothing but the fear of Virgil's scorn held
him to the Divine adventure:

> 'L'anima tua è da viltate offesa.'

Let it be counted to him for righteousness that he is at
least not ignorant of the distance at which his little
bark follows ' the daring prow' of the great galleon.

In one respect it must be admitted that the *Paradiso* stands in contrast to the other divisions of the
poem: it does not flow so directly out of Dante's own
life and experience. The women of Verona were not
altogether in error when they pointed to the little dark

figure in the streets, and whispered that it had been in hell. The *Inferno* and the *Purgatorio* came straight out of the poet's character and experience of the moral life : he had been in both. But it is different with the *Paradiso*, as he himself seems to acknowledge in his Epistle to Can Grande. The materials out of which he built his Paradise were of necessity drawn largely from the systems and experiences of the theologians and saints whom he loved and studied. Any exposition of the *Paradiso*, therefore, demands some acquaintance with these sources. This, of course, has its drawbacks. No attempt, for example, has been made in the present volume to bring out directly the marvellous beauty of the *Paradiso* : for marvellous its beauty is, in spite of what many regard as dreary wastes of scholastic physics and metaphysics. As Dr. Hettinger says : 'In the theology of the *Divina Commedia* we must distinguish its matter, method, and form. Its matter is the theology of the Catholic Church, as contained in writings and tradition. Its method is that of the thirteenth century, consequently the scholastic, and more especially the system of St. Thomas. Its form is that of a poem stored with Christian, mythological, and historical imagery ; but, in the main, the poet's creation.' As an expositor my work has of necessity been much more occupied with the doctrinal matter and the scholastic method than with the poetic form. Yet the three are so inextricably woven together that no true perception of the beauty of the poetry is possible save through some clear and definite knowledge of the philosophy and theology which form the warp and woof of the

Paradiso. Doubtless even the most casual reader
can scarcely fail to catch here and there broken
glimpses of a vivid and piercing loveliness; but to see
the beauty of the conception as a whole, a foundation
of definite and positive knowledge appears to me
absolutely indispensable. In short, my apology, if
apology is needed, is that I follow the principle on
which Dante expressly based the *Paradiso* itself: that
we must know before we love and enjoy. It had been
easy to rhapsodize over the poetic beauty; but I have
generally found that such rhapsody is in inverse ratio
to the writer's knowledge of the actual thought in the
poet's mind.

This necessary foundation of knowledge, then, I have
striven, however imperfectly, to supply. I have
drawn the material largely from such theologians
as Aquinas, Bonaventura, and Bernard, and have
preferred as far as possible to give their words,
instead of a mere paraphrase of my own. If this has
been carried to excess, it is a fault which, in an
expositor, leans to virtue's side; Dante's meaning
ought surely to become clearer when we see the
sources of his thought. In spite of every effort after
simplicity, however, the inherent difficulties of the task
make perfect clearness hard to attain: the antiquated
system of Astronomy, the Dionysian chain of Angelic
Orders, the procession of the Divine virtue from rank
to rank and from sphere to sphere, the mystic symbolism rising through veil beyond veil to the ineffable
Vision, and the scholastic terminology for which there
frequently exists no accepted modern equivalent. I
can only hope that when such difficulties are taken

into account, the reception of the book may be not less kindly than that given to its predecessors.

While I have been careful to acknowledge as far as possible my obligations in the footnotes, my special thanks are once more due to such Dante scholars as Dr. Moore, Dr. Toynbee, and Mr. Vernon. I am also much indebted to Father Joseph Rickaby, who may be truly called an expert in Scholasticism. Mr. Edmund G. Gardner's beautiful study of the *Paradiso*, 'Dante's Ten Heavens,' seemed to me on first reading to render another exposition almost a work of supererogation. On further consideration, however, I saw that our points of view were different, not to speak of methods and emphasis; but I cannot close without expressing my gratitude for much helpful suggestion.

To one I owe another kind of debt, beyond the repayment of words, for the patience of hope which never failed during the long years since first I set hand to the labour of love, and without which I had 'in thinking consumed the emprise':

'O Donna, in cui la mia speranza vige!'

JOHN S. CARROLL.

INNISFAIL, NEWLANDS, GLASGOW,
October 1911.

CONTENTS

xi

CONTENTS

CONTENTS XV

CONTENTS

DIAGRAMS

INTRODUCTION

Hierarchy is, in my judgment, a sacred order and science and operation, assimilated, as far as attainable, to the likeness of God, and conducted to the illuminations granted to it from God, according to capacity, with a view to the Divine imitation.

Dionysius, *The Heavenly Hierarchy*, iii. 1.

I saw the concourse of the Sons of God,
The Hosts Celestial, passing in their number
Perchance all atoms of all visible worlds ;
Images of God's beauty ; bodily beings
Compared with Him ; spiritual with us compared ;
Fed from His Heart with knowledge and with power
Their everlasting Eucharistic Feast ;
Intuitive in Intellect, with their gaze
Ever on Beatific Vision fixed,
Yet active here below, even as man's soul,
Then most in Reason rests while works his hand.
That Faculty Intuitive, their dower,
Passed on to me through sympathy. I saw them,
And knew their nature, even as Adam knew,
When at God's will God's creatures passed before him,
The end of each. Plainly on every grade
Some Attribute divine had pressed its seal,
Its character engraved ;—three Hierarchies,
Three Choirs in each.

Aubrey de Vere, *Saint Dionysius, the Areopagite.*

INTRODUCTION

THE *Paradiso* is based, physically, on the Ptolemaic system of Astronomy, and, spiritually, on the *Celestial Hierarchy* of Dionysius the Areopagite.[1] According to the former, the Earth is the fixed centre of the universe, around which the heavenly bodies revolve in nine concentric spheres. Each of the eight innermost of these spheres has a heavenly body or bodies embedded, so to speak, in its crystalline substance, which it carries round the earth in its revolutions. To these eight, it became necessary to postulate a ninth, in order to account for their movements, and this was called the Primum Mobile, the revolution of which, from East to West, is the swiftest, being completed in rather less than twenty-four hours. The Christian religion added a tenth Heaven, the Empyrean, itself immovable, but the source of motion to the Primum Mobile, and through it to all the lower spheres, whose speed diminishes in proportion to their nearness to the motionless centre, Earth. In the *Convito* (ii. 4) Dante describes the system thus: 'The order of their position is this, that the first which is enumerated is that where the Moon is; the second is that where Mercury is; the third is that where Venus is; the fourth is that where the Sun is, the fifth is that where Mars is; the sixth is that where Jupiter is; the seventh is that where Saturn is; the eighth is that of the Fixed Stars; the ninth is

---

[1] It is impossible in this Introduction to avoid a certain amount of repetition, but even this may have its use. Dante himself, indeed, is constantly doubling back on his own thoughts; and the general framework and much of the detail are so foreign to our modern minds that some repetition is almost necessary to render them familiar. At all events, it is hoped that this preliminary section will furnish an outline which will make it much easier to follow the exposition in detail.

that which is not perceptible by sense, save by the movement which was spoken of above, which many call the Crystalline Heaven, that is, the diaphanous, or all transparent. But, outside of all these, the Catholics place the Empyrean Heaven, which is as much as to say the Heaven of Flame, or the Luminous Heaven; and they hold it to be immovable, because it has in itself, in relation to every part, that which its matter wills. And this is the cause of the Primum Mobile having the swiftest movement, because through the most fervent longing which every part of that ninth Heaven, which is next to it, has to be united to every part of that Divinest and tranquil Heaven, it revolves within it with so great desire that its velocity is almost beyond comprehension. And quiet and peaceful is the place of that Supreme Deity, who alone perfectly sees Himself. This is the place of the blessed spirits, according to Holy Church which cannot lie; and Aristotle also seems to think so, to him who well understands him, in the first *Of the Heaven and the World*. This is the sovran edifice of the world, in which all the world is included, and outside of which is nothing; and it is not in space, but was formed only in the First Mind, which the Greeks call Protonoë. This is that magnificence, of which the Psalmist spoke, when he says to God: "Thy magnificence is exalted above the heavens." [1]

It will be noticed that this description of the corporeal Heavens overflows, so to speak, into the spiritual significance, which was, indeed, the principal thing in Dante's regard. To understand it, we must make some acquaintance with the *Celestial Hierarchy*

---

[1] In *Conv.* ii. 14, 15, the ten Heavens have a quite different symbolism from that in the *Paradiso*. The seven planetary Heavens stand for the seven liberal arts of the Trivium and Quadrivium: the Moon for Grammar; Mercury for Dialectic; Venus for Rhetoric; the Sun for Arithmetic; Mars for Music; Jupiter for Geometry; and Saturn for Astrology (or Astronomy). The Starry Heaven represents Physics and Metaphysics; the Primum Mobile, Ethics; the unmoved Empyrean, Theology. The correspondences are worked out with much fanciful ingenuity.

of Dionysius the Areopagite, whom Dante sets in the
Fourth Heaven and describes as

> ' that taper
> Which in the flesh below saw most within
> The angelic nature and its ministry.' [1]

In common with all theologians of his age, Dante
believed this mystical work to have been written by
that Dionysius the Areopagite, who was one of the
few converts made by St. Paul's preaching in Athens.
He became, as one says, 'the mythical hero of mysticism,'
and legends gravitated to his name. At the time of the
crucifixion, he was a student in Heliopolis in Egypt,
and when he saw the darkness which was over the
earth for three hours he said to his friend and fellow-
student, Apollophanes : 'The God of Nature suffers,
or the fabric of the world is broken up.' [2] After his
conversion he became the first Bishop of Athens ; and
St. Paul was believed to have revealed to him the
mysteries of the Angelic world, as he had seen them
when he was caught up to the third heaven. [3] The
legend goes on to identify him with St. Denis, the
patron saint of France. After St. Paul's martyrdom,
Pope Clement, the successor of St. Peter, sent him
to evangelize Gaul, and at Paris he sealed his testi-
mony with his blood under Domitian, or, according to
some, Trajan. The extraordinary series of mystical
writings attributed to him, belonging probably to the
fifth century, [4] exercised a most marvellous influence
on mediæval theology. Translated into Latin in

---

[1] *Par.* x. 115-117. See below, p. 188.

[2] See Westcott, *Relig. Thought in the West*, 155. In Fra Angelico's
famous fresco of the Crucifixion in San Marco, Florence, Dionysius is
introduced in the framework among the O. T. prophets who foretold
the death of the Messiah. On his scroll are the words, '*Deus naturae
patitur.*' Mrs. Jameson (*Sacred and Legendary Art*, ii. 716) says she
saw an old French print which represented the saint at Heliopolis on a
tower, contemplating the crucifixion of Christ in the far distance, *through
a telescope !*   [3] *Par.* xxviii. 136-139. See p. 440 below.

[4] The first mention of them is at a conference at Constantinople in
A.D. 532. The Severians, a Monophysite sect, quoted them in support of
their views, and their opponents denied their genuineness on the ground
that they were unknown to Cyril, Athanasius, etc. See Westcott, *Relig.
Thought in the West*, 147 ff. ; Smith and Wace's *Dict. of Christian Biog.*
i. 841 ff.

the ninth century by Johannes Scotus Erigena, they coloured the entire current of scholastic theology with Neoplatonism. 'When the text was once accessible, numerous commentaries followed ; as that of Hugo of St. Victor on 'The Heavenly Hierarchy' (c. 1120), of Robert Grosseteste on all the books (c. 1235), of Thomas Aquinas on 'The Divine Names' (c. 1255), of Albertus Magnus (c. 1260), of Dionysius Carthusianus (c. 1450) ; and in almost every mediæval writing on theology the authority of the Areopagite is quoted as decisive.'[1]

It is, then, this unknown Neoplatonist, this Pseudo-Dionysius, who dictated to Dante the spiritual form of the *Paradiso*. According to his conception, the Angelic world consists of nine Orders, divided into three Hierarchies, which form the heavenly antitype of the three orders of the Ecclesiastical Hierarchy on earth —Bishops, Priests, Deacons. God, the Fountain of all Being, is thrown into a distant and awful glory, to be approached through a long chain of Angelic mediators, whose function is to act as mirrors, receiving in themselves, and transmitting to all around them and beneath, the Eternal and Uncreated Light, according to their several capacities to see it: 'The purpose, then, of Hierarchy is the assimilation and union, as far as attainable, with God, having Him Leader of all religious science and operation, by looking unflinchingly to His most Divine comeliness, and copying, as far as possible, and by perfecting its own followers as Divine images, mirrors most luminous and without flaw, receptive of the primal light and the supremely Divine ray, and devoutly filled with the entrusted radiance, and again, spreading this radiance ungrudgingly to those after it, in accordance with the supremely Divine regulations.'[2] Three movements of this general function are distinguished—purifying, illumination, and perfecting.[3]

(1) The work of *perfecting* is specially assigned to the

---

[1] Westcott, *Relig. Thought in the West*, 151.
[2] *De Coel. Hier*. iii. 2 (Parker's trans.).
[3] For the corresponding human functions, see Dion. *De Eccles. Hier*.

highest Hierarchy, which consists, in the order of their nearness to God, of Seraphim, Cherubim, and Thrones. The Seraphim remain for ever in the Divine presence, and receive their name from the fire of Eternal Love which glows through them, burning away every possibility of evil. This fire of Love is transmitted by them to the second Order, the Cherubim, in whom it shines in the special form of knowledge—that immediate knowledge which comes from the direct vision of God, without that 'manifold texture of sacred veils' or symbols, which hides so much of the Divine from human eyes. This wisdom the Cherubim in turn pass on to the third Order, the Thrones, in whom it assumes the form of calmness and stability in Divine truth and power, by which they become the seats of the Divine decrees and judgments.[1]

(2) The virtue which this First Hierarchy thus receives from God it communicates to the Second, according to the power of the receptivity of its three Orders—Dominations, Virtues, Powers, whose special function is *illumination*. The work of the three is thus discriminated by Westcott (who, however, calls the Virtues *Powers*, and the Powers *Authorities*): 'The Dominations, with the spirit of generous freedom, strive towards a likeness to the true dominion, regardless of all vain attractions; the Powers with masculine and unshaken courage seek to carry out every divine motion: the Authorities, with clear and well-ordered sway, to bring everything into right subjection to the source of all authority.' To the Powers, Aquinas attributes the function of repelling evil spirits; and to the Virtues, that of working miracles.[2]

(3) This emanation of Divine power flows down into the Third Hierarchy—Principalities, Archangels, Angels—to whom is assigned the work of *purifying*. Through them the knowledge and goodness of God,

---

[1] *De Coel. Hier.* vii. 1. For Dante's view of how the three Hierarchies contemplate the different Persons of the Trinity, see *Conv.* ii. 6.

[2] *Summa*, i. q. cviii. a. 5. The doctrine of Angels in all its aspects is discussed in qq. l.-lxiv; cvi-cxiv.

which they have received through the mediation of the higher Hierarchies, are finally communicated to the human race. The Principalities, being an image of the Principality of God, seek to draw all Princes into that same image. The Archangels and Angels, as their names imply, are messengers,—the former carrying the greater messages of God to the nation or the race, the latter the minor messages to individuals, over whom they exercise a certain Divine guardianship.

It is at this point that the necessity arises of a threefold Hierarchy of men to carry on this great communication of Divine things through the Angelic Hierarchies. The human Hierarchy consists of the three Orders of Bishops, Priests, Deacons, to whom are assigned the three functions respectively of perfecting, illuminating, and purifying. This great chain is completed, apparently, by the Incarnation. It is by the Divine Word—the Eternal Idea, begotten of the Father —that all the Angelic Hierarchies are enlightened with the knowledge of the whole Trinity; but it is by the Word made flesh that the human Hierarchies are rendered able to receive the revelation. 'There proceeds,' says Dean Colet, 'a diffusion of the Deity from order to order, from hierarchy to hierarchy, and from better creatures to worse, according to each one's capacity, for the rendering godlike of all; "to the praise," in St. Paul's words, " of the glory of the grace of God." In this allotted task moreover are men, that they may be refashioned in a hierarchy representative of God. And when, in reducing them to order the angels were wearied out, then did Jesus Christ, who is Himself Order, and the incarnate beauty of God, "fairer than the children of men," come to their aid, establishing in Himself three hierarchies, and in each one of these the threefold virtues of purifying, illuminating, perfecting; in order that men also, being fellow-workers in Christ for the glorifying of God, may at length form a finished hierarchy on earth, to be made equal hereafter to the angels in heaven.'[1] It was

---

[1] Rev. J. H. Lupton's *Dean Colet on the Hierarchies of Dionysius*, p. 15.

because he always saw this ideal hierarchy of men continuous with the Angels, that Dante never ceased to
believe in the Divine authority and function of the
Church, in spite of its manifold corruptions.

This then, in general outline, is the scheme of thought
by which Dante and the theologians of his day sought
to make clear to their minds the procession of the
Power, Wisdom, and Love of that God who, by His
very being, was lifted above man into an infinite distance of burning and unapproachable glory. The next
step was to blend this scheme with the Ptolemaic
system of astronomy, which lent itself easily to the
union. Each of the nine Orders of Angels was conceived of as the motive power of one of the nine
spheres, its ruler and mover under God. This power
to move is independent of all physical contact, since
Angels are pure spiritual subsistences, apart from
matter. It is the operation of intellect, and intellect
alone: hence all Angels are called Intelligences, as par-
taking of intellect in a super-eminent degree; and as
the whole meaning of the *Paradiso* hangs on intellect,
it may be well to see something of what it means.
Aristotle's teaching, as we shall see, is that all motion
originates in the Divine Mind; and the power to move
in creatures is in proportion to their participation in
that Mind. Now, the knowledge of Angels differs
from that of man chiefly in this, that it requires no
mediation of 'sensible species' or 'phantasms,' to use
scholastic terms,—that is, images drawn from things of
sense, on which the mind can work. Human knowledge is a *process*, and the process works thus. First,
an image or phantasm of a material thing enters the
senses. Then the intellect issues forth, seizes on this
image of sense, abstracts it from its individual qualities,
and thus forms a universal concept of it, in which the
intellect penetrates to the 'substance' as distinguished
from its 'accidents'—the thing as it exists *per se*. Now,
the Angelic intellect needs to pass through no such
process. Being pure spirit, Intelligence separate from
body, it has, and can have, no sensible image or

phantasm of anything. By means of 'intelligible species'—that is, images of things implanted in the intellect in the very act of its creation—it penetrates direct, without any preliminary process of reasoning and abstraction, to the substance and the universal in everything. When intellect reaches this sublime height, its likeness to the Divine Intellect gives it power to move even the vast spheres of Heaven. The Seraphim as the highest created Intelligences govern the greatest sphere, the Primum Mobile, pouring out on it, so to speak, the full volume of the Power, Wisdom, and Love which they receive from the Trinity, and thereby causing it to revolve with almost the same inconceivable velocity with which they themselves circle round God. This Ninth Heaven thus contains implicitly the totality of the being of the universe—the 'potency' of the entire creation, and this passes through the Cherubim to the Eighth Heaven over which they are set as governors, that of the Fixed Stars, by means of the multitude of which it is broken up 'through diverse essences.' These essences then pass down to the seven lower Heavens, each ruled by its own Angelic Order, and are by them distributed and directed to their various ends, according to their nature. Thus the Nine Heavens are, in Dante's phrase, 'the organs of the world,' informed by the Divine Mind, flowing down through the intellect of the various Orders of Angels who are their appointed movers.[1] Each Heaven receives the Divine virtue from those above it, and transmits it to those beneath, until it reaches the Earth lying motionless in the centre. It is, in short, as one says, a species of celestial feudalism : the devolution of power and authority from the Eternal Emperor through a vast gradation of ranks and orders in a feudal system of the universe.[2]

This, it may be noted in passing, gives us the solution of that peculiar belief in the influence of the stars over human life which meets us so often in Dante's writings.

---

[1] *Par.* ii. 112-148. For exposition see below, p. 73 f.
[2] See Father Rickaby's *Of God and His Creatures*, p. 248 n.

It is not, as we are apt to imagine, a superstitious belief in the power of the stars to fix human destiny or to bind the human will. It was simply Dante's way of conceiving the manner in which the Divine virtue descended into human life, from Order to Order of Angels and from sphere to sphere of Heaven; and, so far was it from binding man in a chain of necessity, that the freedom of the will was the first and greatest gift which God, through this influence of the stars, bestowed upon mankind.[1]

Having now the physical and spiritual structure of Dante's Paradise before us, we may proceed to examine his distribution of the souls of the Redeemed throughout the various Heavens. In the first place, he warns us that these Heavens are not allotted really and locally to the souls of the Blessed. If some are shown to him in the Moon, others in Mercury, and so on, they meet him in these different spheres for certain symbolic reasons: partly, perhaps, to indicate the sphere that most influenced a soul; but chiefly to mark by these 'many mansions' the various degrees of beatitude, according to the quality and measure of each soul's sanctity. As we shall see, each Heaven has some symbolic correspondence to the spiritual state of the souls that appear in it: the inconstancy of the Moon, the smallness of Mercury, the epicycle of Venus, and so on, representing certain differences in the quality of their holiness. But we are expressly told that in reality all souls are in the Tenth Heaven, the Empyrean, the Heaven of the Divine Peace, where Dante at the end of his Pilgrimage sees them all once more, gathered together in their eternal rank and order in the great White Rose which represents the Church Triumphant.

This Tenth Heaven demands some special notice, because it is at once the beginning and the end of that motion which is one of the chief symbolic elements of the *Paradiso*. It is called the *Empyrean* from the fire of holy love wherewith it is ever burning.[2] Its only place, as we have seen, is the Divine Mind, in

<hr>

[1] *Par.* v. 19-24.   [2] *Epis.* x. 24.

which saints and Angels have their abode. Beatrice describes it as

> 'the Heaven which is pure light,
> Light intellectual fulfilled of love,
> Love of true good fulfilled of joy,
> Joy which transcendeth every sweetness.' [1]

Its absolute perfection renders it incapable of motion: containing within itself everything that its own being demands, it has no unsatisfied yearning to make it restless. When God, the final and absolute Truth, is seen, every desire is fulfilled in a 'peace which passeth all understanding.' It is just this perfection of the Empyrean, however, which is the source of the motions of all the other Heavens which it enfolds: they revolve, swifter or slower, according to the strength of their yearning for the Fountain of their being. It is on this principle that the movements of the Angels are to be accounted for: Dante saw the nine Orders revolve round God in the form of nine concentric circles of fire,—the Seraphim, as nearest to the Source, moving with the greatest swiftness, and the speed of the rest diminishing in proportion to their distance from the centre. This is also the explanation of the movements of the Redeemed in the various spheres. It provokes a smile, perhaps, when we read of grave theologians and doctors in the Heaven of the Sun circling in the dance, and their movement compared to the revolutions of a millstone; but the incongruity disappears when we remember that all through the *Paradiso* motion is the symbol of yearning for a more perfect union with God, the final rest of the intellect in the absolute Truth. By a beautiful inconsistency Dante represents saints and Angels as existing in both conditions of motion and rest. As he ascends through the nine Heavens he finds everywhere the movement of desire for God; yet he assures us that all the time the happy spirits are in the Empyrean, the motionless Heaven of Divine Peace, where every desire is satisfied.

[1] *Par.* xxx. 39-42. See below, p. 463.

Their motion *is* their rest : the longing for God for ever satisfies, because it for ever creates new longing.

Motion is one of the three elements out of which Dante builds up his conception of Paradise. The other two are Music and Light. On rising with Beatrice from the Earthly Paradise, the harmony of the eternal world breaks upon his ear. There is no need to trace this to any heathen source, such as Cicero's *Dream of Scipio*, in which a music too grand for mortal ears is produced by the rush of the spheres through space. The thought is a most natural one to any Christian mind. The songs and hymns of Paradise represent partly the joy and gratitude of the Redeemed breaking forth in praise to the God of their salvation; and partly that harmony which binds into one the various powers and experiences of the blessed spirits, as, for example, when the voices of Theologians are compared to the chimes of Church bells calling 'the Spouse of God' to her matin songs.[1] A hymn is heard in every Heaven save one: in Saturn no music breaks the rapt silence of the contemplative saints, lest Dante should be overpowered by its sweetness.[2] Doubtless every hymn has some special appropriateness to the Heaven in which it is heard, as when the Emperor Justinian sings Osanna to the Lord of Hosts, and Theologians hymn the Trinity, and the Soldiers of the Cross in Mars chant their battle-song, 'Arise and conquer.' The first hymn, sung by Piccarda in the lowest Heaven, and the last, sung by Gabriel in the highest, is the *Ave Maria*: the obvious intention being to honour the Virgin as the means by which salvation in all its forms and degrees flowed to the human race through the Incarnation. And always Motion and Music are united, the song passing into the dance or the dance into the song.

It is, however, Light on which Dante's mind loves most to dwell; and, considering the apparent simplicity of this element, it is marvellous to mark the variety he contrives to impart to it in order to carry out his

[1] *Par*. x. 139-148. [2] *Par*. xxi. 55-63.

symbolism. The Moon, like a pearly cloud; Mercury, veiling itself in the sun's rays; Venus, with the bright beauty of morning and evening star; the Sun, whose light, 'unbroken of the prism,' is the truest image of Deity; Mars, whose blood-red shield is quartered by the white cross of Christ; the silver shining of temperate Jupiter; the crystal coldness of Saturn, down which gleams the golden stairway of Contemplation; the endlessly varied lights of the Fixed Stars; the diaphanous shell of the Crystalline Heaven; and these all giving way at last to the pure intellectual light of the Empyrean. No one who did not love light in all its wonders, changes, surprises, could thus have conceived the universe as if it were one vast precious stone with layer upon layer of varying colour and clearness.

For the most part the souls of the Blessed are clothed in light. In the two lowest Heavens Dante sees them in their own proper forms; whereas in the remaining spheres up to the ninth, they are concealed in a radiance of light, and appear in the form of stars. The symbolic reason for the difference seems to lie in the various degrees of holiness. In the lowest Heavens the souls have not completely lost themselves in the light and knowledge of God—so much of their old earthly infirmity clings to them, that they appear in their own personal forms; whereas in the higher spirits the personal self is entirely hidden in a halo of Divine radiance. That this is the symbolic purpose seems certain because, when the same souls are shown in the Empyrean, gathered into the unity of the White Rose, Dante sees them clad by anticipation in their resurrection bodies,—the great Flower glowing in the *Lumen gloriae* from above, and mirrored in the sea of light which forms its golden heart.

Paradise is divided into three parts: within the shadow of Earth, beyond the shadow, and up the Golden Stairway; and the entire Pilgrimage will become much easier if we see clearly at the outset the reason for this division.

I. Within Earth's Shadowy Cone.

The three lowest Heavens—the Moon, Mercury, Venus—lie within the shadow which the Earth casts out into space. Venus is described as

> 'this heaven where ends the shadowy cone
> Cast by your world.'[1]

The symbolic meaning is that some frailty of the earthly life clings to the souls in these Heavens and lies like a shadow on their beatitude: in the Moon, inconstancy of will which broke religious vows; in Mercury, love of their own glory; in Venus, some unworthy love of earth which disputed the heart with God. It has often been pointed out that each of these groups of souls failed more or less in one of the three theological virtues. The inconstant souls of the Moon were weak in Faith. Those in Mercury failed somewhat in Hope: the hope of the glory of God being dimmed by the seeking of their own glory. The souls in Venus failed in Love, dividing their hearts between God and man.

II. Beyond Earth's Shadow.

The next four Heavens—the Sun, Mars, Jupiter, Saturn—lie entirely beyond the shadow of Earth, in the full cloudless light of God. All the souls here have the three theological virtues in which the lower spirits partially failed; but they receive the light and vision of God according to the *cardinal* virtue in which they excelled on earth. Thus Prudence, being an intellectual virtue, is that specially appropriate to the Theologians in the Sun. The Martyrs and Crusaders of Mars were eminent in Fortitude. Justice is the obvious virtue of the Righteous Rulers of Jupiter. And Temperance is as obviously that of the Ascetics and Contemplatives of the cold planet Saturn.

---

[1] *Par.* ix. 118, 119. Comp. Milton's *Par. Lost*, iv. 776,
  Now had Night measured with her shadowy cone
  Half-way up-hill this vast sublunar vault,

III. Up the Golden Stair.

The Golden Stairway of Contemplation is let down into the sphere of Saturn; hence the remaining Heavens above this planet—the Fixed Stars, the Primum Mobile, and the Empyrean—are, so to speak, the upper steps of the Ladder, the subjects of mystical contemplation to which it leads: the Triumph of Christ in His Church, in the Heaven of the Fixed Stars; the doctrine of Angels, in the Primum Mobile; and the Beatific Vision, in the Empyrean.

What the Beatific Vision meant to Dante and the mystics of his time is discussed elsewhere; meantime the fundamental thing to remember is that it is always regarded as a direct intellectual knowledge. The Aristotelian doctrine followed by Aquinas is that the intellect is the proper nature of man, and that therefore the satisfaction of the intellect is his final beatitude. This satisfaction is found in the contemplation of God, the Absolute Truth. Hence beatitude is the intellectual vision of the Divine Essence, directly and immediately, as a man sees his friend face to face. There is, of course, no question of bodily sight: God being absolutely incorporeal remains for ever invisible to the eye of the flesh.

Two questions, however, arise. The first is whether this vision is possible to man's own unaided natural powers. Is the human intellect, as it comes to us in the mere order and process of nature, able to penetrate to direct contemplation of the very Essence of the Eternal Intellect? The answer of Dante and his Church is in the negative. The mere natural intellect, through study of the creatures of God, may gather by means of sense, reason, and inference some knowledge of the excellence of the invisible Creator, and thus attain what kind and measure of beatitude is possible within the limits of the order of Nature. But for the direct vision, without any medium of creature or sense or discourse of reason—for knowledge of the Divine

Essence as immediately as it is known to God Himself —nothing avails but a supernatural elevation of the natural intellect by an infusion into it of the Divine Intellect by grace. This infusion of the Eternal Light, by which the human intellect is raised above itself, and made capable of seeing the Essence of God and all things directly and immediately in Him, is what the scholastics call the *Lumen gloriae.* This is not a light of glory shining *on* the saints from the outside like sunshine, but shining *in* them by an infusion of the Divine light into the intellect, whereby is formed, as Aquinas says, 'that disposition by which a created intelligence is raised to the intellectual vision of the Divine substance.'[1] The entire poem may be regarded as one long climbing through creatures and reason and symbolic veils, in preparation for this final elevation of human nature above itself.

The second question referred to is whether the source and principle of the Beatific Vision is Love or Knowledge. The former view is taken by Duns Scotus, who held that 'beatitude is an act of the will by which it loves God with the love of friendship'; but Aquinas contends for the priority of knowledge, and this is the view adopted by Dante and applied consistently throughout the poem. Joining together the various passages, we find that the experiences of the saints in bliss pass through the following order : first comes the intellectual knowledge of God in His Essence; then born of this, and in proportion to its fulness, love to God, since we love only what we know ; this love in turn creates joy, and the joy radiating outward from the soul forms a garment of light, whose brightness is in exact proportion to the knowledge, love, and joy. Neither Aquinas nor Dante means that knowledge is in itself superior to love, but that it is its necessary condition.[2]

---

[1] *Cont. Gent.* iii. 53.

[2] *Summa*, i. q. cviii. a. 6: 'Knowledge exists, according as the things known are in him who knows ; but love, according as he who loves is united to the object loved. But higher things exist in a more noble mode in themselves than in those that are beneath ; while the lower exist in a

The mention of the *Lumen gloriae* a little ago suggests the advisability of explaining Dante's usage in the matter of words connected with light—a usage from which I think he never varies, and on which the exact meaning of many passages in the *Paradiso* depends. The usage, as Dr. Wicksteed points out, is derived from Aquinas, who 'distinguishes between *lux, lumen, radius,* and *splendor.* *Lux* is light at its source; *lumen* is the general luminosity of the diaphanous medium through which the light travels; *radius* is the direct line of the passage of light from its source to the object it strikes, and *splendor* is the reflected ray.' Throughout the *Paradiso* Dante uses the corresponding Italian words in accordance with this discrimination. God is the 'prima *luce,*' 'eterna *luce,*' 'somma *luce*': the *fons et origo* of all light. This primal light creates around itself a luminous atmosphere, so to speak, which is distinguished by the name of *lume*; and by this word *lume* Dante, I think, often means to indicate the Divine light supernaturally infused as the *lumen gloriae* into the created intellect, as when he speaks of

'ciò che ne dona
Di *gratuito lume* il Sommo Bene';[1]

and again,

Lume è lassù, che visibile face
Lo Creatore a quella creatura,
Che solo in lui vedere ha la sua pace.[2]

The *raggio* (*radius*, ray) is defined in the *Convito* (iii. 14) as the light 'in so far as it exists in the medium, between its source and the first body by which it is arrested';[3] while, finally, the *splendore* (splendour) is

more noble mode in higher things than in themselves. And therefore the knowledge of things beneath us excels the love of them; but the love of what is above us, and especially of God, excels the knowledge of them.' See below, p. 442 f.

[1] *Par.* xiv. 46, 47.

[2] *Par.* xxx. 100-102.

[3] Comp. *Conv.* ii. 7: 'The rays (*raggi*) of each heaven are the path by which descends their virtue into these things here below. . . . Rays are no other than a light (*lume*) which comes from the origin of the light (*luce*) through the air even to the thing illumined.'

the light 'as it is thrown back on some other part which it illuminates.' In this sense it may be said that everything capable of reflecting the Divine light in any measure is a 'splendour.' The Nine Angelic Orders are called 'mirrors' receiving and transmitting the Eternal Light according to their various powers. The spirits of the Seventh Heaven are 'splendours' of the Life Contemplative. St. Dominic is a 'splendour of cherubic light,' because he reflects on the world the light of God as it was transmitted to him from the mirror of the Cherubim who excel in wisdom. And the whole host of the Redeemed in the Empyrean form one single 'splendour' by whose reflected light Dante is enabled to see 'the lofty Triumph.' It is perhaps impossible to say that this use of these four words is never departed from, especially as in the *Convito* (iii. 14) the explanation seems to be slightly varied; but, from a careful examination of many passages, I have come to the conclusion that in the *Paradiso* these meanings were always before Dante's mind. Take, e.g., the following *terzina* concerning the illumination of the Angelic nature, in which three of the forms of light are certainly named:

> 'La prima *luce*, che tutta la *raia*
> Per tanti modi in essa si recepe,
> Quanti son gli *splendori* a che s'appaia':[1]

'The primal *light* (*luce*, God), which *rays* (*raia* = *raggia*) upon it all (the entire Angelic nature), is received into it by as many modes as are the *splendours* (*splendori*, i.e., the individual Angels, regarded as mirrors to reflect the Divine rays to other parts of the universe) with which it pairs itself.' The passage shows the clear discrimination made by Dante of the various words relating to light, according as it exists in its source, or passes through a medium, or is reflected from creature to creature.

There remain to be considered certain symbolic correspondences which run throughout the various spheres.

---

[1] *Par.* xxix. 136-138.

I. The first is the relation of the different ranks of the Blessed to the several Heavens in which Dante sees them. Each Heaven is a figure and symbol of their spiritual state. The Moon, with its changing phases, its spots, and the slowness of its motion, is an image of the inconstancy which broke religious vows. Mercury, as the smallest star, is the fit symbol of the smallness of the heaven which lovers of fame create for themselves; while its hiding of itself in the Sun's rays teaches them that man's true glory is to lose himself in the glory of God. Venus, with the duplex movement to which Dante draws attention, one round the Earth in its cycle, the other round the Sun in its epicycle, represents that twofold motion of love by which the souls of this star divided their hearts between God and man. These three, as we saw, lie within earth's shadowy cone, the earthly frailty dimming the brightness of their celestial bliss.

The Sun, being the highest sensible image of the Divine Light, is the natural 'mansion' of Theologians, the subject of whose study is God Himself. Equally natural is it that Soldiers of the Faith should appear in Mars, which shines like a great crusader's shield, quartered by the white cross. Jupiter is the white temperate star, the realm of Righteous Rulers,—its whiteness representing probably the purity of their justice, and its temperateness, as Dante explains, its mid-position between the fiery temper of Mars and the cold ascetic spirits of Saturn, who, dead to the world, retire from the active life which is proper to rulers. Thus, in a certain symbolic sense the souls return to the stars which have had the greatest influence on them, though Dante is careful to guard against the idea that this involves any necessity imposed upon their wills.[1]

II. This brings us to a second correspondence—that between the Nine Orders of Angels and the souls in the Nine Heavens of which they are the movers under God. Mr. Gardner, following Prof. Lubin, works out

---

[1] *Par.* iv. 49-63. See below, p. 85.

this correspondence as well, perhaps, as it is possible to do it. There can be no doubt that it existed in Dante's mind, and existed probably with great symbolic exactness. But I confess that after reading the *Celestial Hierarchy* of Dionysius many times, I fail—doubtless through some defect in myself—to distinguish clearly the functions assigned to the various Orders. The author of this strange book has a style which has been truly called 'verbose and turgid.' 'He piles epithet on epithet, throws superlative on superlative, hyperbole on hyperbole,' flinging them out in a vain effort to capture the infinite in a net of words. The discrimination of Angelic functions, therefore, often seems to be verbal and unreal; and the plain truth about these Celestial Choirs appears to be that, in the words of a Catholic theologian, 'nothing is truly known concerning them beyond their names : nothing can be known except by revelation, and it seems that no revelation has been given.'[1] This is the true reason why neither Dionysius nor his commentators manage to convey any clear idea of the functions of the various Orders, and why their correspondence to the Nine Heavens over which they rule is difficult to trace. Such as it is, however, let us see what can be made of it.

(1) The lowest Order, the Angels, being nearest Earth, are the direct link of communication between it and Heaven, and are regarded as the guardians of *individual souls*. Hence in the Moon, which is their sphere, Dante sets souls that dedicated themselves to their own individual salvation, and questions are discussed here which gather round this—Free Will, Vows, etc. Mr. Gardner thinks this is also the reason why the souls here 'appear in the likeness of the human form.'[2] But this is not confined to the Moon, and I have given reasons elsewhere for believing that it has another meaning.

(2) The function of the Second Order—the Archangels, counting upwards—is to bear to earth the most im-

---

[1] Father Hunter, *Outlines of Dogmatic Theology*, ii. 282.
[2] *Dante's Ten Heavens*, 21.   For the guardianship of the lowest Order of Angels over individuals, see *Summa*, i. q. cxiii.

portant and sacred messages, and to act as guardians of *nations*. Hence in Mercury, over which they preside, are discussed the great doctrines of the Incarnation and Atonement; and Mr. Gardner makes the ingenious suggestion that 'the Emperor Justinian plays the same part towards the Roman people that Michael did for the Jews.'[1] This view is based on the doctrine commonly received in Dante's day, that the places left vacant by the fallen Angels were to be filled up by the Redeemed, who would then fulfil their functions.

(3) The third Order, the Principalities, have a more universal superintendence of the nations of earth: 'they are able,' says St. Bernard, 'to change and vary kingdoms and dignities at their will—to dispose of men and of things, making the last to be first, and the first last; putting down the mighty from their seat, and exalting the humble and meek.'[2] It is perhaps for this reason that it is in their sphere of Venus the general question is discussed as to whether the Heavens transmit the various human powers which are necessary for the existence and welfare of society. Mr. Gardner connects them specially with the love with which Princes ought to rule their subjects—a matter which is also discussed in this Heaven.

(4) The work of the Powers, the rulers of the Sun, is, naturally, to restrain the powers of darkness and evil: by them, says Aquinas, evil spirits are held in check, as evil-doers are by 'the powers that be' on earth. Hence in this Heaven are praised St. Francis and St. Dominic, who rescued the Church from the powers of evil; and the great Theologians are shown who scattered the powers of darkness with the sunlight of Divine Truth.

(5) The Virtues, who rule Mars, may be described in the words of Dionysius himself, partly because the quotation will give a fair example of his extraordinary style: 'The appellation of the Holy Powers denotes

---

[1] *Dante's Ten Heavens*, 21. The guardianship of Archangels over nations is founded on Dan. x. 13, xii. 1. See *Summa*, i. q. cxiii. a. 3, 8.
[2] *Cantica Canticorum*, Serm. xix. Comp. *De Consideratione*, v. 4.

courageous and unflinching virility, for all those Godlike energies within them—not feebly weak for the
reception of any of the Divine illuminations vouchsafed
to it—vigorously conducted to the Divine imitation,
not forsaking the Godlike movement through its own
unmanliness, but unflinchingly looking to the superessential and powerful-making power, and becoming
a powerlike image of this, as far as is attainable, and
powerfully turned to this, as Source of Power, and
issuing forth to those next in degree [i.e. the Order
beneath it], in gift of Power, and in likeness to God.'[1]
This courage and fortitude are imaged in the souls of
Martyrs and Crusaders, who form themselves into the
similitude of the Cross of Christ. Another function
attributed to the Virtues was that of working miracles
or portents; and a passage in the *Convito* (ii. 14) shows
that this may have been in Dante's mind when he drew
the Cross upon the face of Mars. He connects a portent
of a similar image in the heavens with this planet and
the downfall of his native city : 'And in Florence, at
the beginning of its ruin, was seen in the air, in the
figure of a cross, a great quantity of these vapours
that follow the star of Mars.' In this sphere the poet's
ancestor Cacciaguida discusses the ruin of Florence,
whose first patron was Mars, and attributes it to the
decay of that 'courageous and unflinching virility'
which is the special characteristic of the Virtues, and
without which neither individuals nor cities can with-
stand the powers of evil.

(6) The Dominations, who govern Jupiter, are
described by Dionysius as the image of the true
lordship or dominion in God—ever seeking to reach it
themselves, and to draw all lordships of heaven and
earth into its likeness. They dwell in a lofty freedom
far above all tyranny and cruelty. 'Therefore,' says
Mr. Gardner, 'in the heaven of Jupiter the souls of
just kings and emperors appear; and they form the
imperial Eagle, the emblem of the universal and
absolute form of dominion divinely ordained.'[2] To

[1] *De Coel. Hier.* viii. 1 (Parker).   [2] *Dante's Ten Heavens*, 23.

this we may add that in this Heaven are fittingly
discussed the mysterious decrees of Divine justice in
the salvation of men, which is the foundation of the
Eternal Empire, and kings and Popes who subvert
justice are sternly denounced.

(7) The next Order is the Thrones, the rulers of
Saturn. They are God's seat of judgment, fixed in a
peace which passeth all understanding. They know,
says Aquinas, the reasons of things in God; and Dante
speaks of them as mirrors reflecting the Divine judgments to all the lower spheres.[1] The tranquillity of
the Thrones is reflected in the quiet of the Contemplative Saints to whom this Heaven is assigned; and
their Divine judgments are echoed in the cry as of
thunder uttered by these saints against unfaithful
bishops.

(8) The correspondence of the Eighth Order is one
of the clearest. 'The appellation of the Cherubim,'
writes Dionysius, 'denotes their knowledge and their
vision of God, and their readiness to receive the
highest gift of light, and their power of contemplating
the super-Divine comeliness in its first revealed power,
and their being filled anew with the impartation which
maketh wise, and their ungrudging communication
to those next to them, by the stream of the given
wisdom.'[2] The revelation of the Heaven of the Fixed
Stars over which they preside corresponds to this
wisdom of the Cherubim. A vision of Christ, the
Wisdom of God, is given in His saints. Through
Dante's examination in Faith, Hope and Love, the
Apostles draw forth wisdom and impart it to the
world; and Adam, who had been created originally
in a marvellous wisdom, shares his knowledge with the
poet.

(9) The Ninth and highest Order, the Seraphim,
who excel in Love, set in motion the Heaven of the
First Movement. The word 'seraph' was believed to
mean burning. 'The appellation of Seraphim,' according to Dionysius, 'plainly teaches their ever moving

[1] *Par.* ix. 61, 62. [2] *De Coel. Hier.* vii. 1 (Parker).

around things Divine, and constancy, and warmth, and keenness, and the seething of that persistent, indomitable, and inflexible perpetual motion, and the vigorous assimilation and elevation of the subordinate, as giving new life and rekindling them to the same heat; and purifying through fire and burnt-offering, and the light-like and light-shedding characteristic which can never be concealed or consumed, and remains always the same, which destroys and dispels every kind of obscure darkness.'[1] In this Heaven, where begins the movement of the entire universe in the. fire of the Seraphic Love, it is fittingly explained to Dante how the Angelic Hierarchies and their Orders were created by the Love of God, whose one motive in creation is to impart as much of His own being to all His creatures as they are severally able to receive.[2]

III. In the foregoing discussion two correspondences have been mentioned incidentally—the relation of the theological doctrines, and of the denunciations, to the Heavens in which they occur; and it may be well to examine these more particularly.

Almost the entire scheme of Christian Theology as accepted by the Church, is discussed in the *Paradiso*, and it would be quite at variance with the poet's usage to fling the several doctrines promiscuously into this Heaven or that without order. Each has some natural link of connection with the sphere in which it occurs, with its inhabitants, or with its Angelic Movers.

(1) In the lowest Heaven, the Moon, comes that dry

---

[1] *De Coel. Hier.* vii. 1 (Parker).

[2] Mr. Gardner (*Dante's Ten Heavens*, 24) says Aquinas thinks no member of this Ninth Order fell. The passage to which he refers (*Summa*, i. q. lxiii. a. 7) does not bear out the statement. Aquinas holds the 'more probable' opinion to be that 'the highest angel among those who sinned was the highest among all'—that is, not only a Seraph, but the highest of the Order : which is certainly Dante's view (*Purg.* xii. 25; *Par.* xix. 47). What Aquinas does say is this. The *name* of Seraph could be no longer applied to one who fell from this Order, because it indicates the *fire of love*, which of course cannot exist with mortal sin. The name of a lower Order, as the Cherubim who excel in *knowledge*, may be applied to fallen Seraphim, since their intellectual powers remain even after their fall..

discussion of the cause of the moon-spots which has exposed Dante to no little ridicule. Yet his chief motive in introducing it is to explain the scholastic doctrine of ' Forms,' or Ideas existing originally in the Divine Mind, and the distribution of these throughout the universe by means of the Heaven of the Fixed Stars. The discussion of broken vows is intimately bound up with Dante's doctrine of Free Will, on which depend the merits which win different degrees of bliss in Paradise.

(2) In Mercury, the Heaven of men like Justinian, who did great and good deeds out of a heart divided between God's glory and their own, the long review of Roman history leads up to the doctrines of the Incarnation and the Atonement,—the underlying suggestion being the contrast between the self-glorying of these spirits and the absolute humility and generosity of God in emptying Himself to become man, and taking on Himself the penalty of human sin.

(3) The principal doctrine discussed in Venus is the influence of the Heavens on the constitution of Society. If heredity alone were at work, each man would be a facsimile of his father, and the variety of powers necessary for society would not exist. Hence special Divine gifts are bestowed on man at birth which secure this variety. This may refer to the Principalities who preside over this Heaven. It is their function to exercise guardianship over society in general upon earth; and part of their work therefore may be to secure this diversity of human powers without which society must fall to pieces.

(4) The Heaven of Theologians, the Sun, is the natural image of God, the great subject of their study. No direct exposition of the doctrine of God, however, is given here. The Trinity is referred to in the hymns sung by the spirits, in their triple dances, and in the three circles of theology revealed to Dante; but the immediate vision of the Trinity is reserved for the Empyrean. Meantime God is expounded in His creatures: in His care of His Church by such men as

St. Francis and St. Dominic; in His creative power; and in the resurrection of the body. And all this by 'discourse of reason,' as is proper to Theologians, not by the intuitive glance of contemplative saints.

(5) If there is any Heaven in which there may be said to be no exposition of doctrine, it is that of Mars, on which shines the Cross of Christ. The only exposition of the Cross is that which comes through bearing it :

> Whoso doth take his cross and follow Christ
> Will yet forgive me what I leave unsaid,
> When in that white dawn he sees Christ lighten.[1]

And in accordance with this Dante's ancestor, Caccia-guida, warns him not to shrink from his share in the fellowship of Christ's sufferings, first, in the sorrows of his exile, and second, in speaking the truth about the great ones of the earth, no matter what hatred and persecution it may rouse against him.

(6) In Jupiter the correspondence we are tracing is clear. The spirits of Just Rulers form themselves into an Eagle, symbol of the Empire of Divine and Eternal Justice. This Justice as it works in human salvation is therefore the doctrine expounded in this sphere, and the mysterious way in which it is hidden in the Divine wisdom and goodness.

(7) In Saturn, the sphere of Contemplation, this mystery is further dwelt on in the impenetrable doctrine of Predestination. The soul most enlightened by the ecstasy of contemplation, the Seraph who has his eye most fixed on God, is powerless to pierce that burning darkness.

(8) In the Heaven of the Fixed Stars, Dante is examined by Peter, James, and John on Faith, Hope, and Love respectively—the three supernatural virtues without which the vision of God is impossible. The last human soul with whom Dante holds converse before entering the superhuman sphere of the Angelic life, is Adam, probably because it was through his fall

[1] *Par.* xiv. 106-108.

the three theological virtues were lost to the human race.

(9) The Primum Mobile being the first Heaven moved by the Angels, Dante receives there from Beatrice an exposition of the doctrine of Angels—their creation, knowledge, functions—based, of course, on the Areopagite.

(10) Finally, in the Empyrean, the motionless abode of God, Dante receives all he is capable of comprehending of the Beatific Vision: the beatitude of the Redeemed; the universe in its substance and accidents, as it exists in the Divine Mind; the Trinity in the unity of the substance and the distinction of the Persons; and the final mystery of the Incarnation.

It is, perhaps, not easy for non-theological readers to interest themselves in these long discussions of doctrine, or to find much poetry in the scholastic form into which they are thrown; but they are of the essence of the *Paradiso*, of the essence also of Dante's soul, and neither he nor it can be known without a serious effort to understand them. It is obvious, I think, that he intends us to see some real correspondence, such as the above, between the various Heavens and the doctrines discussed in them.

IV. The remaining correspondence—that of Denunciations—need not detain us so long.

(1) In the Moon, the sphere of broken vows, a woe is pronounced on ecclesiastics who encourage the breaking of vows by granting an easy pardon.

(2) In Mercury, Justinian after recounting the achievements of the Roman standard, the Eagle, denounces the Guelphs for opposing to it the Lilies of France, and the Ghibellines for degrading it into the ensign of a faction.

(3) Venus being ruled over by the Principalities, the denunciation here is levelled against Princes who neglect and ruin their dominions: the house of Anjou for its tyranny in Sicily, and the Pope for abandoning the Holy Land to the infidel—Palestine being regarded as rightfully under the dominion of the Pope.

(4) In the Sun, the Mendicant Orders are denounced for their departure from the rule and example of their founders, thereby darkening the light which Francis and Dominic had shed upon the world.

(5) Mars is governed by the Virtues through whose fortitude men gain courage to bear the cross; and here Cacciaguida denounces the present effeminacy of Florence as compared with the old simple heroic days.

(6) In Jupiter, the Heaven of Just Kings, woes are pronounced against unjust rulers, Popes and Kings, still living or but recently dead.

(7) In Saturn, the ascetic saint Peter Damiani, himself a Cardinal and Bishop, denounces Prelates of the Church for their pomp and luxury, and St. Benedict laments that Contemplation is dead in his Order. In the system of Dionysius the Thrones, who rule this sphere, represent, along with the Cherubim and Seraphim, the Order of Bishops on earth; and the denunciation means that the earthly Hierarchy has ceased to be a true mirror of the heavenly.

(8) In the Eighth Heaven St. Peter as the first Pope pronounces woe on his successors who had turned his tomb, the Vatican, into a sewer of filth and blood. Their true function is to act as mirrors of the Divine Wisdom shed upon them by the Cherubim of this sphere; whereas they darken Heaven itself with shame for their wickedness, even as earth was darkened with eclipse at the death of Christ.

(9) The denunciation of this Heaven—the Primum Mobile—is that of preachers who for the Gospel substitute their own empty speculations and irreverent jests, to win the applause and laughter of the crowd. Their proper work is that of the Nine Circles of Angels revealed in this Heaven, namely, to impart the light and truth of God; and this is how they fulfil their angelic function.

(10) Even in the Heaven of the Divine Peace there is a woe. The last words Beatrice utters are a woe on Italy for her rejection of Henry VII., God's representative on earth in things temporal, and on His

representative in spiritual things, Clement v., for degrading them to matters of merchandise. The connection of this woe with this Heaven over which God Himself presides, is obvious.

The time of Dante's ascent from the Earthly Paradise is matter of much dispute, but there is little doubt that here as elsewhere he follows the symbolism of time in the *Convito*. At nightfall he had descended into Hell, and at sunrise risen into the new life on the shore of the Purgatorial Mount; and it is natural to suppose that for his ascent to the Celestial Paradise he would choose the hour of noon, which he calls the noblest of the day.[1] His rising from Heaven to Heaven is of a marvellous swiftness. There is, however, nothing miraculous about it: sin is a weight which binds one to the earth, and having worked it out of his nature on Mount Purgatory, his ascension was as natural as the rising of flame to the sphere of fire to which it belongs.

His guide is Beatrice. Now at last he gives glorious fulfilment to his promise in the *Vita Nuova* 'to say of her what was never said of any woman.' There is, of course, much controversy as to her symbolic significance, and no doubt it is, as Dr. Moore says, complex, as is everything in Dante. 'Beatrice often symbolizes Theology, not as a scientific system, but rather in its aspect of Revelation, or Revealed Truth. Further, as the Church is the "keeper and witness" of Revelation, which is guarded and dispensed by Ecclesiastical Authority, that embodiment of Authority is sometimes represented by Beatrice. Following on from this to a still more definite and concrete symbol, she sometimes stands . . . as the representative of the ideal Papacy, which guides and governs humanity on its spiritual side as the Emperor does on its temporal side.'[2] Perhaps we shall best see her significance if we bear in mind what she was to Dante at the close of the *Purgatorio*. There she first descends as the Spirit of Revelation into the Chariot of the Church. Then a harlot

---

[1] *Conv.* iv. 23.   See below, p. 50 f.
[2] *Studies in Dante*, 3rd series, 188.

takes her place in the Chariot—the outward and visible
organization of the Church—which is torn violently
from the Tree of Empire, and dragged away by a Giant.
This is the 'Babylonish captivity' of the Church—the
transference of the servile Papacy to Avignon by Philip
the Fair of France. Beatrice is then left, with the
Seven Virtues, alone under the Imperial Tree. For
Dante this meant the annihilation for the time of the
Church as a Divine institution in the world—'it was,
and is not.' What then was left? If we care to say
the Ideal Church, or the Revelation of which the faithless Church ought to have been the guardian, the
practical meaning is the same for Dante. He feels that
he has no guide to eternal beatitude save that Spirit
of Revelation which once descended on the Chariot—
no visible Church on earth, only the Ideal of that
Church as it exists in the Mind of God. If there is no
further mention of the handmaidens of Beatrice, the
Seven Virtues, it is because they have now returned to
their celestial form of stars,—the stars to which he is
about to rise. As he ascends from star to star, the increasing beauty of the eyes and smile of this Divine
Wisdom is the sign that he has entered a higher
Heaven, and sees with clearer eyes 'the living Light
Eternal.' In the final Heaven, Beatrice suddenly disappears, and Dante finds in her stead St. Bernard
of Clairvaux, who points her out in her place in the
third rank of the great White Rose of the Redeemed,
seated beside Rachel, the symbol of Contemplation.
The reason for this change of guides is much disputed,
and must be more carefully examined afterwards; but
I cannot accept the theory that it was because the
power of Beatrice to lead failed at this point. The first
and obvious reason is that Dante wishes now to drop
the symbolic veil and set Beatrice the woman in her
appointed place among the saints. It is natural to
suppose that Bernard is chosen to take her place because he is, in Dante's regard, the best representative
of that Divine Wisdom for which she stands,—perhaps
because of the marvellous union in him of Action and

Contemplation.　Even Bernard, however, cannot reveal
the final vision : he can but pray that she whose face is
likest Christ will grant him grace to make his eyes
clear and strong to see God 'face to face.'

The beautiful figure of a White Rose as the similitude
of the Church Triumphant grew like a flower out of the
poet's deep and tender veneration for the Virgin.　She
was the *Rosa Mystica* of the Litany, 'the Rose of Sharon '
of the Song of Songs, the highest, holiest symbol of
the Church redeemed by her Son.　To picture the great
multitude of the Blessed in the form of the most beautiful
of her flowers, was the most loving and reverential
acknowledgment of what Dante devoutly believed to
be her share in the glorious work of man's salvation.
The colour of the Rose is that of her virgin purity, and
in Art was given to her in pictures of the Assumption.
To Dante's mystical imagination it probably had
another meaning, peculiarly appropriate to the saints
absorbed in the vision of God.　In a curious passage of
the *Convito* (iv. 22) whiteness is interpreted as symbolic
of Speculation or Contemplation.　The words of the
Angel after the Resurrection of Christ: 'He goeth
before you into Galilee ' (Matt. xxviii. 7), are taken
mystically as meaning: '*Beatitude* will go before them
into Galilee, that is, into *Speculation.　Galilee* is as
much as to say *whiteness*: and whiteness is a colour
full of corporeal light more than any other; and in
like manner Contemplation is more full of spiritual
light than aught else that is here below.'[1]　The whiteness of the Rose therefore is at once the purity and
the power of contemplation which purity gives:
'Blessed are the pure in heart, for they shall see God.'
Other symbolisms spring from the very nature of a
flower.　For a flower is a living and organic unity,
every part of which is necessary to the beauty of the

---

[1] Dr. Toynbee (*Dante Dict.* p. 259) says this interpretation of 'Galilaea'
is derived from Isidore of Seville through the *Magnae Derivationes* of
Uguccione da Pisa, who says: '*Gala* grece, latine dicitur lac . . . item a
gala haec *Galilea* regio Palestinae, sic dicta quia gignat candidiores
homines quam alia regio Palestinae, et hinc *galileus, -a, -um.*'

whole. Such a living and organic unity was the host of the Redeemed to the poet's mind. The Rose of the Church Triumphant springs from two roots, Adam and Peter, the natural and the spiritual. The one eternal life flows through every petal. The very symmetry of its plan which at first sight seems artificial,—the Old Testament saints and the New, the souls of children and of the full-grown, balancing each other —springs from Dante's desire to work out and emphasize this living and organic unity of the Eternal Flower, ' the unity of the Spirit in the bond of peace,' which makes all saints one for ever in the life and love and joy of God.

WITHIN EARTH'S SHADOWY CONE

Cantos I-IX

De parte vero esecutiva, quae fuit divisa iuxta totum prologum, nec dividendo nec sententiando quidquam dicetur ad praesens; nisi hoc, quod ibi procedetur ascendendo de coelo in coelum, et recitabitur de animabus beatis inventis in quolibet orbe, et quod vera illa beatitudo in sentiendo veritatis principium consistit; ut patet per Iohannem ibi: 'Haec est vera beatitudo, ut cognoscant te Deum verum,' etc.; et per Boetium in tertio *De Consolatione* ibi: 'Te cernere finis.' Inde est quod ad ostendendum gloriam beatitudinis in illis animabus, ab eis, tamquam videntibus omnem veritatem, multa quaerentur quae magnam habent utilitatem et delectationem. Et quia, invento principio, seu primo, videlicet Deo, nihil est quod ulterius quaeratur, quum sit A et O, id est principium et finis, ut visio Iohannis designat; in ipso Deo terminatur tractatus, qui est benedictus in saecula saeculorum.

Epistle to Can Grande, 33.

> Questo cielo, in cui l'ombra s'appunta
> Che il vostro mondo face.

Par. ix. 118, 119.

> Anzi è formale ad esto beato *esse*
>   Tenersi dentro alla divina voglia,
>   Per ch' una fansi nostre voglie stesse.
> Sì che, come noi sem di soglia in soglia
>   Per questo regno, a tutto il regno piace,
>   Com' allo re ch' a suo voler ne invoglia:
> E la sua volontate è nostra pace;
>   Ella è quel mare al qual tutto si move
>   Ciò ch' ella crea, e che natura face.

Par. iii. 79-87.

CHAPTER I

ASCENT FROM THE EARTHLY TO THE HEAVENLY PARADISE

IN the Epistle in which he dedicates the *Paradiso* to his friend and patron, Can Grande della Scala, Lord of Verona, Dante gives an exposition of the first twelve lines of the opening Canto, which, he says, form part of the Prologue to this third division of the *Commedia*.[1] After a few words about the invocation which begins at the thirteenth line, he suddenly breaks off with a pathetic confession of poverty: 'This is the meaning of the second part of the Prologue in general; but in detail I will not expound it at present, for narrow household circumstances so press upon me that these and other things profitable for the common weal, I am forced to relinquish. But I hope of your magnificence that means may be otherwise provided of proceeding to a profitable exposition.'[2] If we are ever tempted to wish that we had Dante's own commentary on the entire poem, this fragment may partly reconcile us to the loss. The greatest lover of Dante must surely confess that it is dry and scholastic in the extreme, and itself stands in need of a commentary. The subject of the *Paradiso*, he says, is 'man, in so far as by meriting he is liable to rewarding justice': Heaven

---

[1] Following Aristotle's *Rhetoric* (iii. 14), he says 'the *proem* is the beginning in a rhetorical oration, as the *prologue* is in poetry, and the *prelude* in flute-playing.' I assume the genuineness of the Epistle to Can Grande. The subject is fully and, to my mind, convincingly discussed in Dr. Moore's *Studies in Dante*, 3rd series, pp. 284-369. The references throughout are to Dr. Moore's Oxford edition of Dante's works.

[2] *Epis.* x. 32. For Dante's meaning of 'magnificence,' see *Conv.* iv. 17.

being regarded as the just reward of human merit.[1]
The end of this as of the other parts of the poem is 'to
remove those living in this life from the state of
misery and lead them to the state of felicity.' His aim
in the Prologue is to render his readers sympathetic,
attentive, and teachable: *sympathetic*, because of the
profitableness of the subject, the joys of Paradise for
which all men long ; *attentive*, because of the marvellous tidings he brings of the nature of the Kingdom
of Heaven; and *teachable*, because the things he saw
are possible to others, who ought therefore to be willing to learn.   The exposition of the Prologue, which
begins at this point, is carried on after Dante's manner
by an appeal first to reason and then to the authority
of Holy Scripture. A paraphrase of the lines com-
mented on may make it easier to follow the exposition
in detail: 'The light of God shines throughout the
entire universe, according to the power of the various
creatures to receive it. I, Dante, have been in the
Empyrean, the Heaven which receives it in greatest
fulness.   For that very reason, power fails me to
relate the things I saw ; for the nearer we approach
God, the end of all desire, the more the intellect
engulfs itself, and memory becomes powerless to
recall the full and final vision. But whatsoever of
the Holy Kingdom my mind has been able to treasure
up will now be the matter of my song.' One is tempted
to content one's self with this paraphrase, were it not
that Dante's own exposition of the lines may form a
slight introduction to certain forms of scholastic and
mystical thought which pervade the entire Cantica.
The opening *terzina* runs thus :

> The glory of Him who moveth everything
> Penetrates through the universe, and shines back
> In one part more, and in another less.

What underlies this is the Aristotelian conception of
God as the unmoved Mover of the universe. As we

---

[1] It is to be remembered that, according to the teaching of the Church,
human merit is in no sense independent of Divine grace : without grace
meritorious works are impossible.   See below, p. 402.

saw in the Introduction, to a Divine Being motion is impossible, because motion implies want, and God wants nothing. Possessing in His own being everything essential to perfect blessedness, He remains for ever at rest in the contemplation of Himself. 'Everything that is moved,' says Aquinas, 'by its motion acquires something, and attains to that to which formerly it had not attained. But God, since He is infinite, comprehending in Himself the entire plenitude of the perfection of all that is, cannot acquire anything, nor extend Himself to anything to which He had not formerly attained. Therefore in no manner does motion pertain to Him. And thence is it that certain of the ancients, as if forced by truth itself, laid it down that the First Principle is immovable.'[1] It is this Divine unchangeable 'plenitude of perfection' which sets the entire wheel of Nature in motion with longing for union with itself.

Also, it is the glory of this First Mover which is reflected in all things, more or less according to their nature, just as stone, gold, diamond receive and render back the sunlight in diverse modes.[2] In the *De Vulgari Eloquentia* (i. 16) Dante says that God 'is more perceptible in a man than in a brute, in an animal than in a plant, in a plant than in a mineral, in a mineral than in fire, in fire than in earth.' The idea is dwelt on in many passages, and in the Epistle to Can Grande is established by the double authority of reason and Scripture. A good example of Dante's scholastic method is the subtle interpretation of the words in l. 2, *penetra e risplende*—'penetrates and shines back' : 'Well therefore is it said, when it says that the Divine ray, or the Divine glory, through the universe *penetrates and shines back*. *Penetrates* as to essence (*essentia*); *shines back* as to being (*esse*).'[3] It is safe to say that this is a significance which no modern commentator would ever have guessed ; and it is by no means easy to know what Dante understood by it. In scholastic phraseology, the essence of a thing is its inmost being

---

[1] *Summa*, i. q. ix. a. i.   [2] *Conv.* iii. 7.   [3] *Ep.* x. 23.

whereby it is what it is; and the conception of it is
reached by the intellect abstracting it from all the
accidental qualities of the thing. For instance, the
essence of *man* is not a fair or dark complexion,
tallness or shortness, youth or age, or any of the
accidental qualities which are found in individuals.
The essence is the something which we call humanity,
the something which is common to all individuals of
the species, and which the intellect reaches by abstraction from their individualizing qualities. On the
other hand, the *esse* or being of anything is just its
existence as an individual, with all the qualities which
make it an individual. When, therefore, Dante says
that the glory of God *penetrates* as to essence he is
giving expression to one of the profoundest of his
metaphysical convictions, that the mysterious something which constitutes the nature of each species of
creatures is a ray of the light of God ; and when he
says that it *shines back* as to *esse* or being, he means
that this essential light comes reflected back through
the individual creature as such, through the accidental
qualities which make him an individual. It is perhaps
scarcely worth while occupying so much space with
an explanation which may prove to be none and only
weary the reader. But the time may not be wasted if
it shows us how, in the first place, Dante under what
seem mere poetic phrases often conceals profound
philosophical and religious meanings; and, in the
second place, how he conceived of the entire universe,
essence and being, species and individual, substance
and accident, as an emanation and a mirror of the
Divine glory. The best commentary on the *penetra e
risplende* of the Prologue is the mysteriously beautiful
vision of the universe in God which he sees in the
Eternal Light of the highest Heaven :

> I saw that in its depth far down is lying,
> Bound up with love together in one volume,
> What through the universe in leaves is scattered ;
> Substance and accidents and their operations,
> All interfused together in such wise

> That what I speak of is one simple light.
> The universal form of this knot
> Methinks I saw, since more abundantly
> In saying this I feel that I rejoice.[1]

Dante proceeds in his exposition to explain what he means when he says that he had been in the Heaven which receives most of the light of God—the supreme Heaven, 'containing all the bodies of the universe and contained by none.' 'It is called the *Empyrean*, which is the same as the heaven glowing with fire or heat; not because there is in it material fire or heat, but spiritual, which is holy love or charity.' The principal proof that it receives most of the Divine light is 'its eternal quiet or peace.' The argument rests on the scholastic doctrine explained above, that motion implies defect: 'Everything that moves, moves on account of something which it has not, and which is the goal of its motion.' The absolute rest of the Empyrean is the proof of its perfection; 'and since all perfection is a ray of the First, which exists in the highest degree of perfection, it is manifest that the first Heaven receives more of the light of the First, which is God.'[2]

In the last place, Dante proceeds to explain what he means when he says that he is powerless to relate the things he saw in this highest Heaven:

> I saw things which to re-tell
> Nor knows, nor can, who from above descends;
> Because, in drawing near to its desire,
> Our intellect engulfs itself so far
> That after it the memory cannot go.

Dante's exposition of these lines rests on the conception of the Beatific Vision as explained in the Introduction.[3] It is the sight of God face to face, as friend sees friend. The organ of vision is the intellect, that

---

[1] *Par.* xxxiii. 85-93. See p. 526 f. below.

[2] *Ep.* x. 24-26. The idea which underlies this argument is that the intellect cannot rest until it sees the full light of God; therefore the Heaven which is perfect rest must be that which receives the largest measure of that light.

[3] See p. 16 f.

part of us which is nearest God, and which can never be satisfied until it pass behind all second causes to the First Cause, behind all symbols to the Truth, all accidents to the Eternal Substance. But this is possible only by man rising above himself, transcending the natural limits of his being by the supernatural illumination of grace. It follows that the intellect having sunk itself profoundly in a *supernatural* life, when it returns to the old limits of the *natural*, the memory fails to bridge the almost infinite gulf between the two worlds of experience.[1] As instances of this failure of memory he gives the visions of St. Paul, of the three disciples on the Mount of Transfiguration, and of the prophet Ezekiel. And then he adds an interesting passage which reveals some of the sources of his own vision, and at the same time hints not obscurely at the sneers which were probably flung at him and it by some of his contemporaries : 'And wherein these examples do not suffice for the invidious, let them read Richard of Saint Victor, in the book *De Contemplatione* ; let them read Bernard, in the book *De Consideratione* ; let them read Augustine, in the book, *De Quantitate Animae*, and they will be invidious no longer. But if they should rail at the assignment of so great an exaltation on account of the sin of the speaker, let them read Daniel, where they will find that even Nabuchodonosor by Divine means saw certain things against sinners, and committed them to oblivion. For "He who maketh his sun to rise on the evil and on the good, and sendeth rain on the just and on the unjust," sometimes

---

[1] Cf. Augustine's *Confessions*, Book x. in which he dwells on the wonderful power of memory, yet declares that he must go beyond memory to find God : 'Great is the power of memory, a fearful thing, O my God, a deep and boundless manifoldness; and this thing is the mind, and this am I myself. . . . What shall I do then, O Thou my true life, my God? I will pass even beyond this power of mine which is called memory: yea, I will pass beyond it, that I may approach unto Thee, O sweet Light.' (Pusey's translation.) Compare Tennyson's trance in *In Memoriam*, xcv. :

> Vague words ! but ah, how hard to frame
> In matter-moulded forms of speech,
> Or even for intellect to reach
> Thro' memory that which I became.

in compassion, for their conversion, sometimes in severity, for their punishment, manifests His glory more or less, as He wills, to those who live never so evilly.'[1] One can well believe that there were not lacking among Dante's contemporaries those who found it easier to believe that he had visited Hell, than that he had been in the Heaven which receives most of the Divine Light. Dante himself never doubted that, sinful man as he was, he had been as divinely chosen and inspired for this Vision as any of the prophets of ancient Israel.

The exposition ends with the reason for his saying that he who returns to earth from that highest Heaven 'neither knows, nor can' retell the vision. 'He *knows not*, because he has forgotten; he *cannot*, because even if he remember and retain the substance, nevertheless language fails: for by the intellect we see many things for which the vocal signs are wanting; which Plato sufficiently suggests in his books by the adoption of metaphors: for by intellectual light he saw many things which he was unable to express in the language proper to them.'[2]

The exposition, as we saw, breaks off suddenly with a pathetic appeal for help, and Dante closes the Letter with a general statement of what is contained in the 'executive part'—that is from line 37 of the Canto to the end of the poem: 'There will be a process of ascension from heaven to heaven, and the narrative will tell of the blessed souls found in each orb, and that true blessedness consists in knowing the Source of Truth, as is evident by John where he says: "This is true blessedness, that they may know thee, the true God,'" etc.; and by Boethius in the third of *De Consolatione*, where he says: "To see thee is the end." Hence it is

[1] *Ep.* x. 28.
[2] Cf. *Inf.* xxviii. 4; *Conv.* iii. 4: 'A limit is set to our intelligence, in each of its operations, not by us, but by universal Nature; and therefore it is to be known that the boundaries of the intelligence are wider in thought than in speech, and wider in speech than in signs.' Dante adds that man is not responsible for these limitations, since they are not of his making.

that, in order to show forth the glory of blessedness in
those souls, many things which have great profit and
delight will be asked of them, as of those who see all
truth.   And because, when the Source or First, namely
God, is found, there is nothing to be sought beyond,
since He is Alpha and Omega, that is, the Beginning
and the End, as the vision of John denotes, the treatise
ends in God Himself, who is blessed *in saecula
saeculorum*.'

From this point onward we are left to our own
guidance, and it may be well to remind ourselves of the
poet's warning in the beginning of the Second Canto—
if, indeed, we are of the chosen few ' who lift their
necks betimes to the bread of the angels '—to keep the
furrow of his keel in front of our little bark, lest losing
him we lose ourselves.   Nothing is easier than to lose
him on those high seas of eternity, especially if we seek
to read into his words a meaning of our own, instead
of being content to learn his.

A comparison of the invocation in the *Paradiso* with
those in the preceding Cantiche will show us that
Dante felt he had now come to the final and supreme
labour of his life.   In the *Inferno* he regards 'the
memory which errs not' as sufficient to the task of
describing sin and its punishments, and therefore he
invokes simply the Muses, the spirit of Genius, and the
natural human powers :

> O Muses, O lofty Genius, now assist me !
> O Memory, that didst write down what I saw,
> Here thy nobility shall be made manifest ! [1]

In the *Purgatorio*, which deals with a more sacred
theme, his invocation is to the Holy Muses, and in
especial to Calliope, the Muse of Epic poetry.[2]   In the
Paradiso, however, where the subject rises so far
beyond the mere natural powers that memory fails, he
appeals to the loftiest supernatural power: ' O good
Apollo !'—the Sun-god standing in Dante's mind for the

[1] *Inf.* ii. 7-9.   [2] *Purg.* i. 9.

inspiration of the true Eternal Light.[1] As he says in
the Epistle to Can Grande (§ 18), poets 'have need of a
great invocation, since something beyond the common
scope of men is to be sought from the higher substances:
a certain gift almost divine.' In the Second Canto
(ll. 8, 9) he feels that his prayer is answered :

> Minerva breathes, and pilots me Apollo,
> And Muses nine point out to me the Bears,—

the polar stars, by which to steer his course across
an unknown sea.[2] The reference in lines 16-18 of the
present Canto to the two yokes of Parnassus, though
obscure, indicates Dante's sense of the greatness of this
his 'last labour,' his 'final arena.'[3] It is impossible to
say with certainty what exactly he meant by the two
yokes, about which much confusion existed among post-
classical writers. From his reference to 'Cirra' in l. 36,
the probability is that he was following Isidore of
Seville, whose *Origines* he must have known, in which
the two peaks are named Cirra and Nisa, the former, it
is said, being dedicated to Apollo, the latter to Liber or
Bacchus.

From Mr. Tozer's full and clear note, which I take
the liberty of quoting below, there is no ground for
this division of the two peaks between these divinities,
or between Apollo and the Muses ;[4] and it is impossible

---

[1] *Par.* i. 13. A parallel case is *Purg.* vi. 118, where Christ is addressed
as 'sommo Giove,' 'supreme Jove.' In *Conv.* iii. 12, God is called 'the
spiritual Sun, accessible to the intellect.' 'No object of sense in all the
universe is more worthy to be made the symbol of God than the sun,
which enlightens, with the light of sense, first itself, and then all the
celestial and elemental bodies ; and in like manner God illuminates first
Himself with intellectual light, and then the celestial and other creatures
accessible to the intellect' (Wicksteed's transl.).

[2] I follow Dr. Moore's reading '*nove* Muse,' *nine* Muses, rather than
'*nuove*,' *new*. The chief point in favour of the latter is that as Dante is
sailing over a new, untravelled sea, he needed new Muses to point him to
the stars; 'but on the other hand,' as Butler says, 'no one has explained
why new Muses should be required, but not a new Minerva or Apollo.'

[3] Landino says: '*Aringo* in Tuscan signifies pulpit, and an elevated
place, from which we say *ringhiera* (platform or balcony). Then by
similitude the yoke is called *aringo*.'

[4] 'It is well to notice the origin of the idea concerning the summits of
Parnassus, from which Dante's metaphorical language is drawn. That
mountain rises to a single conspicuous summit; and when the Greek

to suppose that Dante invokes Bacchus for inspiration to recall to memory the Beatific Vision. We are forced to content ourselves with the general idea that for this final task he felt his need of a double portion of Divine inspiration; or perhaps, more specifically, that up to this point in the poem the natural faculties had sufficed, but that now a supernatural power must lift the natural man above himself. This, indeed, may be the meaning of the mysterious prayer to Apollo:

> Enter thou into my breast, and breathe,
> Even as when Marsyas thou didst draw
> From out the scabbard of his limbs.[1]

The reference is to the fate of Marsyas, the Phrygian satyr. Having presumptuously challenged Apollo to a contest in music, the god after conquering him tied him to a tree and flayed him alive. It is possible to find here, as some do, a veiled warning to the poet's rivals—the 'invidious' of the Epistle to Can Grande—that the fate of Marsyas will be theirs; but a pride so scornful is inconsistent with the hope expressed a few lines further on, that the little spark of his poem may

poets speak of its two summits (Soph. *Ant.* 1126; Eurip. *Bacch.* 307; cp. *Ion.* 86-8) they mean, not the real summit of the mountain, but the two peaks that rise above Delphi, which are several thousand feet lower. These expressions were misunderstood by the Roman poets, who regularly describe Parnassus as rising to two summits; e.g. Ov. *Met.* i. 316, "Mons ibi verticibus petit arduus astra duobus, Nomine Parnassus"; Lucan, v. 72, "Parnassus gemino petit aethera colle." Dante followed them, and naturally fell into the same mistake. Then, as Parnassus is the representative of poetic inspiration, he quaintly regards the two summits as a double portion of that inspiration. There is no sufficient ground for saying, as some commentators do, that one peak was sacred to Apollo, the other to Bacchus and the Muses; and that when the two peaks are named it is implied that Dante, who has hitherto invoked the Muses, now invokes Apollo also. Great confusion existed in the minds of post-classical writers about these two (supposed) peaks of Parnassus, and by some— e.g. Servius (on *Aen.* vii. 641 and x. 163) and Isidore (*Orig.* xiv. 8)—they were identified with Helicon and Cithaeron. But the two divinities to whom they were regarded as being sacred were Apollo and Bacchus; and no writer, so far as we know, with whom Dante was acquainted, regarded one peak as dedicated to Apollo and the other to the Muses' (*English Commentary*, 405-6). The fact remains, of course, that while the Muses are invoked in the *Inferno* and *Purgatorio*, this is the first invocation to Apollo.

[1] *Par.* i. 19-21.

kindle a great flame, and that better prayers will gain
an answer from Cirrha, the peak regarded as sacred to
Apollo.[1] A truer and deeper meaning is suggested in
the MS. note of Coleridge in Cary's Dante in the British
Museum : 'He asks for an evacuation or exinanition
of all self in him, like the unsheathing of Marsyas, that
so he may become a mere vessel or wine-skin of the
Deity,' a meaning which would certainly fit in with the
'transhumanize' of line 70, the transcending of the
limits of humanity.

There is something pathetic in the peculiar mingling
of pride and humility in Dante's longing for the laurel
crown. It breaks out even in the Stellar Heaven,
where he consoles himself with the thought that, while
his own 'fair sheepfold' held him in cruel exile and
refused the honour, Peter himself, the chief Shepherd,
on hearing the confession of his faith, did not disdain
to make of his own starry light a better crown for his
fast-whitening brow.[2] One remembers too how, in
his first Eclogue to Giovanni del Virgilio (ll. 42-4) he
puts aside his friend's offer of the crown from Bologna,
too proud to take from another what his 'ancestral
Arno' denied him. The hope, however, seems never
to have died out of his heart; in the passage before us
he thinks that if in this final Cantica he is able to give
even 'the shadow of the blessed realm,' it must bring
him the much longed-for garland. And then, with a
sudden humility as deep as his pride, he ends with the

---

[1] It cannot be without purpose, however, that a similar myth is referred
to in the invocation to the 'Holy Muses,' in *Purg.* i. 7-12, where Dante
prays Calliope to 'rise somewhat,'

> Accompanying my song with that sound
> Of which the miserable Magpies felt
> The blow so great that they despaired of pardon.

The reference is to the nine daughters of Pierus, King of Emathia,
in Macedon, who, on challenging the Muses to a contest and being
defeated, were changed into magpies. It is certainly strange that Dante
could not invoke aid for himself as a poet without thinking of the defeat
and punishment of proud, presumptuous singers. Perhaps it was his
way of avoiding a similar pride.

[2] *Par.* xxiv. 151-xxv. 12.   See p. 395.

hope that his little spark may kindle a great flame, and
the laurel fall upon some worthier brow.[1]

We come now to the ascent through the Sphere of
Fire to the Heaven of the Moon.   Line 37, which begins
what Dante calls ' the executive part,' must be regarded as a direct continuation of the closing words of
the *Purgatorio*.   It is a mistake to assume any interval
of time : certainly none is even hinted at.   The last
note of time given is in *Purg.* xxxiii. 103, 104, where
Dante tells us that ' the sun was holding the meridian
circle' when a draught of the River Eunoë made
him 'pure and disposed to mount unto the stars.'   To
say, as many do, that he did not ascend till the following morning at sunrise, leaves a period of eighteen
hours entirely unaccounted for, and destroys the mystic
parallelism of time which obviously runs through the
whole poem.   There is no justification for this beyond
the mention of 'morning' in l. 43, which is assumed
to mean the *following* morning.   An examination of
the passage will show the true meaning.   It runs as
follows :

> To mortal men by passages diverse
> Uprises the world's lamp ; but by that one
> Which circles four uniteth with three crosses,
> With better course and with a better star
> Conjoined it issues, and the mundane wax
> Tempers and stamps more after its own fashion.
> Almost that passage had made morning there
> And evening here, and there was wholly white
> That hemisphere, and black the other part,
> When Beatrice towards the left-hand side
> I saw turned round, and gazing at the sun ;
> Never did eagle fasten so upon it.[2]

---

[1] *Par.* i. 22-36.   Compare *Inf.* iv. 79-102, where Dante ranks himself
with those whom he regarded as the five greatest poets, Homer and
Virgil, Horace, Ovid, and Lucan.   Boccaccio in his Life of Dante has a
curious digression in which he finds good reason for Dante's longing for
the laurel in three properties of that plant : (1) it never looses its verdure,
and is therefore a symbol of enduring fame ; (2) it is never found to have
been struck with lightning—the lightning, in the figurative sense, of
envy and the thunderbolt of time ; (3) it is very sweet smelling, as are
the works of all great poets.   No wonder, he thinks, that Dante longed
to be worthy of such a crown.
[2] *Par.* i. 37-48.

Dante's general purpose in this difficult passage is to
tell us that his ascent to Paradise took place *at the
most auspicious time*, when all the powers of heaven
and earth conspired to make his journey prosperous.
First of all, it was the most gracious season of the
year.   In the circle of the year the sun rises at various
points; but there is one passage—that of the vernal
equinox—in which a happy conjunction of celestial
forces gives it its noblest power over earthly things.
It is then in Aries, 'a better star,' because it ushers in
the spring and begins 'a better course.' This passage,
which the sun was 'almost' at (*quasi* in l. 44 refers
to the fact that the vernal equinox was slightly past [1]),
is described as that which 'unites four circles with
three crosses.' These, in the literal sense, are the circles
of the equator, the ecliptic, and the equinoctial colure,
which, by intersection with one another and with the
fourth circle of the horizon, make three crosses.   There
can be no doubt that to Dante, who saw in the sun the
sensible image of God, and in the conjunctions of the
Heavens the means by which He stamps His image on
'the mundane wax,' all this had a deep symbolic meaning.   The four circles and the three crosses are, allegorically, the four cardinal and the three theological
virtues—changed now from the form of nymphs in
which he saw them in the Earthly Paradise to their
celestial equivalents.   The full allegorical meaning,
then, seems to be: when the four cardinal virtues in
full circle intersect, so to speak, in human life and
character with the three theological, then God, the
Eternal Sun, coming to man by the passage of this
conjunction, is able most clearly to impress His image
as a seal on wax.   It is, indeed, precisely the greater or
less perfection of this conjunction of the seven virtues
which constitutes the various degrees of blessedness of
the seven lower Heavens into which Dante is about to
enter.[2] If any one cares to see, with Mr. Gardner, the
further meaning, that since the cardinal virtues are

[1] Mr. Tozer says, 'it was now April 13, and the vernal equinox was on
March 21.'   [2] See above, p. 15.

more closely connected with the Empire, and the theological with the Church, Dante may have meant that,
'in that age of conflicting claims of Pope and Emperor,
God shone most upon a soul prepared to fulfil the duty
of rendering to Caesar the things that are Caesar's and
to God the things that are God's,' there is certainly
much to justify it in Dante's ideal of Church and
Empire. But only in his *ideal*. We must not forget
that to him the actual Empire was the despoiled Tree
which he pictures in the Earthly Paradise, and the
Church the ruined Chariot which he saw torn from it
into captivity : nothing is now left to him but Beatrice,
the ideal Heavenly Wisdom, and her handmaidens.

We naturally expect that the hour of the day will
have a nobility corresponding to that of the season ;
and we know that Dante regarded noon as the most
noble of the twenty-four. In the *Convito* (iv. 23) he
says expressly that 'the sixth hour, that is, noon, is
the most noble of the whole day, and has the most
virtue,' and for this reason was the hour, according to
Luke, at which our Lord died. It was also the hour,
says Bonaventura, at which He ascended to Heaven ;
and he emphasizes the sacredness of it by representing
it as the hour at which the exulting praise of the Angels
passed on and up from choir to choir of the Nine
Orders: 'For the Ascension of the Lord was at the
sixth hour. . . . Although all those in the Fatherland
(*in patria*) made exultation beyond the power of words
to tell, yet from the first day (i.e. the day of the Ascension) to the sixth hour of the day following, the Angels
in especial kept festival. . . . On the second day the
Archangels did likewise, on the third the Principalities,
on the fourth the Powers, on the fifth the Virtues, on
the sixth the Dominations, on the seventh the Thrones,
on the eighth the Cherubim, on the ninth the Seraphim,
which are the Nine Orders of Angels.'[1] Bearing all
this in mind, we ought to be careful not to break the
mystic correspondence of time between Dante and his
Lord which runs through the *Commedia*: at *sunset*

[1] *Meditationes Vitae Christi*, ch. xcviii.

Dante descended with Christ into Hell; at *sunrise* he rose with Him into the new life; at *mid-day* he ascended to the Heaven to which He ascended.

The chief difficulty of this interpretation is the mention of 'morning' in l. 43: 'such a passage had made morning on that side' (*di là*, i.e. on Mount Purgatory), 'and evening on this' (*di qua*, i.e. in the north hemisphere, in which Dante is writing). Doubtless if 'morning' is taken in the strict sense of sunrise, the other interpretation would hold; but Dante's words immediately after make this strict sense impossible: 'there was *wholly* white that hemisphere' (the one in which Mount Purgatory was), 'and black the other part' (the north hemisphere). This could not be the case at sunrise: the Purgatorial hemisphere then would be only partially illuminated, and the north hemisphere only partially darkened. As Dr. Moore says, 'noon is involved in the statement that the *whole* of the south hemisphere was light, the mountain of Purgatory being its central point, just as Jerusalem was of the north hemisphere, the *whole* of which was consequently dark.'[1]

We come now to the beginning of the Ascension. Dante and Beatrice, it must be remembered, are still standing on the bank of Eunoë in the Earthly Paradise. The very memory of sin has been blotted out. God, in His highest natural symbol, the Sun, is shining on Dante in meridian fulness, through the conjunction of the four natural with the three supernatural virtues. In other words, Dante being now in the Garden of Eden, 'the place made as proper to the human race' (ll. 56,

---

[1] *Studies in Dante*, 3rd series, 62 n. Dr. Moore here retracts the view expressed in his *Time References* (53 n.), that the hour was sunrise. It may seem a small matter to spend so much time over, but to Dante himself it was of great importance. Mr. Gardner has stated clearly the reasons for the noon hour (*Dante's Ten Heavens*, 34-37). Mr. Tozer's note is valuable: 'The difficulty of this passage arises from the Poet having introduced into one sentence two times of day, viz. sunrise—which is mentioned in connexion with the preceding six lines in order to determine the season of the year—and midday, which is the time intended in the narrative. This difficulty disappears, if we give due weight to the tenses of the verbs, pluperfect and imperfect respectively' (*Eng Comm.* 408).

57), has returned, as far as return is possible, to the original righteousness and powers of the first man.[1] The ideal situation, therefore, is that he is now starting from the state from which Adam would have started, had he retained his integrity. By nature Adam had the four cardinal virtues, and by grace the three theological, without which he could not see God;[2] and Dante's long climb up the purifying Mount had simply undone the Fall and brought him back to the state of virtue which the First Father lost. From this necessary standing-ground of nature and grace, the ascent begins. Beatrice, turning on her left side,[3] fixes her eyes like an eagle on the sun; and her attitude, like a ray of light, reflects itself in Dante by turning his eyes upward in the same gaze of contemplation. The virtues of Eden, now restored, gave him a power of looking at the sun far surpassing that of the fallen world below; yet even there his eyes were able to bear the brightness only long enough to see the sun's circumference break out into sparks like iron issuing from the fire. And then

> Of a sudden it seemed that day to day
> Was added, as if He who has the power
> Had with another sun the heaven adorned.[4]

This represents the vast increase of knowledge which

---

[1] 'The head and aim of all the Christian mysteries is my perfection and restoration and return to the first Adam' (St. Gregory of Nazianzus, quoted in Father Hunter's *Outlines of Dogmatic Theology*, ii. 374).

[2] The much debated question whether Adam received grace in the first instant of his creation or at some later time before his Fall, is left open by the Church. The former view was that of Aquinas, and is the received teaching of the Church at the present time. It follows that Adam had all the virtues, natural and supernatural (*Summa*, i. q. xcv. a. 1, 3).

[3] This left-hand movement may surprise us, the left being the direction in the Inferno, and the right in Purgatory. The physical reason is plain : at noon in the south hemisphere the sun would be northward, and Beatrice who had been facing the east, of necessity turned on her left side to see the sun. If any symbolism is meant it may be connected with the fact that the left is the side of the heart.

[4] *Par*. i. 61-63. 'The light of the moon shall be as the light of the sun, and the light of the sun shall be sevenfold, as the light of seven days, in the day that the Lord bindeth up the hurt of his people, and healeth the stroke of their wound' (Is. xxx. 26).

would have come to Adam had he remained in his first
estate, and which Dante receives because he has regained it,—not the direct vision of the Divine Essence,
but power to see the sparks which it flung forth—its
operations and effects in creation.[1] This knowledge
even of the sparks of the Divine Being added day to
day, doubled the light of all his seeing. In short, what
Dante sees up to this point is simply what is natural
to man in his original state, the knowledge which
would have come to him from his natural powers,
quickened by grace, and directed to the effects and
operations of God in the natural world.[2]

This, however, is not the end for which man was
made, and therefore Dante turns from the sparks of
the Divine Light in creation to Beatrice. Mr. Gardner
thinks this turning to Beatrice was necessary because
'she is invested with the ecclesiastical authority
appointed by God to lead mankind to eternal life in
accordance with revelation, and by means of theology
to interpret the mysteries which would otherwise
dazzle our intellectual eyesight';[3] but we must bear
in mind, as already pointed out, that for Dante no
'ecclesiastical authority' now exists. 'The first Peter'
declares that his place is vacant 'in the presence of the

---

[1] In *Par.* xxviii. 88-90, Dante uses the same figure of the sparks of
molten iron to indicate the individual Angels of the nine concentric
circles of fire which represent the Nine Orders.

[2] Perhaps one ought rather to say that it represents the knowledge
Adam actually had before the Fall, in which Dante here shares. In
Summa, i. q. xciv, Aquinas says the first man did not see the essence of
God, else sin had been impossible; 'he saw God in an ænigma, because he
saw God by means of the created effect.' At the same time his knowledge
was far clearer than ours; 'the first man was not hindered by exterior
things (as we are) from clear and firm contemplation of intelligible effects,
which he perceived by irradiation of the Primal Truth, either by knowledge natural or of grace.' He adds that he had knowledge of all things
naturally knowable, and of supernatural things in so far as they were
necessary for the supernatural end for which he was created—things
which we can know only by revelation and faith. The interpretation
given above is substantially that of Landino, though he does not connect
it with man's original state: 'The allegorical sense is that the purified
mind can contemplate God, but not in such manner that it knows His
essence, but it has knowledge of the sparks which come from the sun,
that is, of the effects which proceed from God, because we know the
cause through the effects, and not the effects through the cause.'

[3] *Dante's Ten Heavens*, p. 38.

Son of God.'[1] The church 'was, and is not.'[2] If, then, Beatrice represents any ecclesiastical authority it must be as it exists, like Plato's ideas, in the Divine Mind, and not as it was embodied in the Church of the poet's day. It comes nearer the truth to say that she stands for the Spirit of the grace and wisdom and revelation of God, apart from all ecclesiastical forms—that direct inspiration which Adam enjoyed in his unfallen state, and which, had that state continued, would have rendered the mediation of the Church unnecessary.[3]

Turning then to Beatrice, and finding her absorbed in contemplation of 'the eternal wheels,' Dante fixed his eyes upon her with so rapt a gaze that there was wrought within him the beginning of the great mysterious change and exaltation of the natural into the supernatural, by which man becomes 'partaker of the Divine nature':[4]

> In her aspect such I inwardly became
> As became Glaucus in the tasting of the herb,
> That made him peer in the sea of the other gods.
> To signify by words 'transhumanize'
> Impossible were: let the example then suffice
> Him for whom grace the experience reserves.
> If I was only that of me which Thou the last
> Createdst, O Love that rulest heaven,
> Thou knowest, who didst lift me with Thy light.[5]

---

[1] *Par.* xxvii. 22-24.   [2] *Purg.* xxxiii. 34-36.

[3] *De Mon.* iii. 4: 'If man had remained in the state of innocence in which he was made by God he would have had no need of such directive regimens [as Church and Empire]. Such regimens, then, are remedial against the infirmity of sin.' For a further discussion of this question, I may be allowed to refer to my exposition of the *Purgatorio*, *Prisoners of Hope*, pp, 394, 395.

[4] 2 Peter i. 4.

[5] *Par.* i. 67-75. Plato in the *Republic* (x. 611) has a curious passage in which he uses Glaucus for just the opposite purpose—as a figure of the degradation of the human soul in the ocean of this present world, in which her condition 'may be compared to that of the sea-god Glaucus, whose original image can hardly be discerned because his natural members are broken off and crushed and in many ways damaged by the waves, and incrustations have grown over them of seaweed and shells and stones, so that he is liker to some sea-monster than to his natural form.' In spite of the apparent contrast, Plato's meaning is substantially the same as that of Dante, for he proceeds to say that the soul must be 'borne by a divine impulse' out of this world-ocean, and freed from its incrustations and defilements, before her true nature and beauty can be seen.

Here Dante, after his well-known custom, gives parallel
examples, one from profane, the other from holy writ.
Glaucus is the Bœotian fisherman who ate of a herb
sown by Saturn, and was transformed into a sea-god.
The Scriptural example is only hinted at: Dante was
too humble to set his vision on a level with Paul's,
though he applies to himself the Apostle's doubt:
' whether in the body, I cannot tell; or whether out of
the body, I cannot tell: God knoweth.'[1] It would, of
course, be folly to try to explain what Dante declares
can be known only by experience; but there is a
passage in the *Dialogues* of St. Gregory which attempts
to put in words what he left folded up in 'transhumanize': ' All creatures be, as it were, nothing, to
that soul which beholdeth the Creator: for though it
see but a glimpse of that light which is in the Creator,
yet very small do all things seem that be created: for
by means of that supernatural light the capacity of the
inward soul is enlarged, and is in God so extended that
it is far above the world: yea and the soul of him that
seeth in this manner is also above itself; for being rapt
up in the light of God, it is inwardly in itself enlarged
above itself; and when it is so exalted, and looketh downward, then doth it comprehend how little all that is
which before in former baseness it could not comprehend.'[2] It is the beginning of this light which now
breaks in a flood of music upon the astonished soul:

> When the wheel which Thou dost make eternal
> Through desire for Thee, made me attentive to it,
> By the harmony Thou dost blend and separate,
> Then seemed to me so much of heaven enkindled
> By the sun's flame, that neither rain nor river
> E'er made a lake so widely spread abroad.[3]

---

[1] 2 Cor. xii. 2. Comp. *Inf.* ii. 32, where Dante shrinks from the vision:
> I not Aeneas am, I am not Paul,
> Nor I, nor others, think me worthy of it.

When Dante says (ll. 73-75) he did not know whether he was only that
which God created last, he means whether it was only his *soul* that
ascended to Paradise. According to the doctrine of Creationism, the
soul is a direct creation by God; and it is created last—after the body has
reached a certain point in embryo (*Purg.* xxv. 61-75).

[2] *The Dialogues of St. Gregory the Great : An Old English Version*,
p. 113.   [3] *Par.* i. 76-81.

The sea of flame into which Dante has now entered,
is, in the literal sense, the Sphere of Fire, which,
according to the ideas of the time, was believed to
encircle the earth immediately underneath the moon.[1]
In the allegorical sense, it is the Divine light which is
kindled only when the 'transhumanized' soul is drawn
by contemplation to the highest Heaven, the wheel
which the desire for God makes eternal. This wheel
is the Empyrean, the Heaven of the Fire of Love,
which, as explained in the Introduction, itself eternally
at rest, moves all the other spheres with ceaseless
longing for union with it. Dante's meaning seems to
be that this lower Sphere of Fire which he has now
reached, is kindled by the fire of the Empyrean. That
which drew his mind so high was, he tells us, the harmony of the nine spheres which revolve between these
two fiery confines—the *flammantia moenia mundi*, as it
were, of Lucretius. Aristotle and Aquinas rejected the
Platonic idea of the music of the spheres; but Dante,
for symbolic reasons, prefers to follow a passage in
Cicero's *Vision of Scipio* : 'The melody which you hear,
and which, though composed in unequal time, is nevertheless divided into regular harmony, is effected by the
motion and impulse of the spheres themselves, which,
by a happy temper of sharp and grave notes, regularly
produces various harmonic effects.'[2] Probably Dante
took the idea in its symbolic sense. What he means to
tell us is that it was his perception of the unity and
balance of the nine spheres which led his mind up

---

[1] The four elemental spheres—in order downward from the moon, fire,
air, water, earth—were, as Dr. Moore says, 'a continuation of the system
of the ten heavens.' 'The way in which one element is enveloped by
another is graphically compared by Bede to the constituent parts of
an egg. Earth is like the yolk in the centre, water surrounds it like
the white of the egg; air corresponds with the membrane round the
white ; and fire with the shell that includes the whole. (From Beazley,
Dawn of Geography, p. 371)'—*Studies in Dante*, 3rd series, p. 31.

[2] Edmonds' translation. Plato in the vision of Er (*Rep.* x. 617) speaks
of 'the spindle of Necessity,' on which, as on an axis, the eight spheres
of heaven revolve. 'The spindle turns on the knees of Necessity ; and on
the upper surface of each circle is a siren, who goes round with them,
hymning a single sound and note. The eight together form one harmony.'
The idea, derived from Pythagoras, was expressly rejected by Aristotle
(*De Coelo*, ii. 9) and Aquinas (on Job xxxviii. 37 as in Vulg.).

to the tenth—each with its distinct note, and all
blended together as in a harmony of sweet music.
It is obviously meant to stand in contrast to the
sounds which greeted him on his entrance to the other
two realms. The wailings of the lost broke him down
into tears. On entering Purgatory Proper, the hoarse
grating of the long-disused Gate mingled with the
sweet music of the *Te Deum laudamus*. But here all
discord is laid to rest: the harmony is, in Milton's
words,

> That undisturbèd song of pure concent,
> Aye sung before the sapphire-coloured throne
> To him that sits thereon.

Not knowing that he has left the earth, Dante is
thrown into a great eagerness to learn the cause of the
strange sound and light, and Beatrice rebukes him for
his ignorance. Had he shaken his soul free from the
'false imagining' of the gross earth below, he would
have known that he was now returning to the Sphere
of Fire, the proper home of lightning, more swiftly
than lightning flash ever left it [1]—returning, because
his soul is but going to the God from whom it came.
This error, however, is slight and natural, and therefore Beatrice takes the edge off her rebuke with a
smile (l. 95); but Dante's next perplexity draws from
her a sigh of pity and a look such as a mother casts on
a delirious child. He is in amaze how he 'transcends
these light bodies,' the spheres of air and fire through
which he is passing. The question shows Beatrice that
he does not yet understand the fundamental doctrine
of the order of the universe; and not to understand
it is a species of delirium. As this, therefore, lies at the
root of all that earth and heaven are, Beatrice begins
with it her first great theological discourse. The
passage is important:

---

[1] The Sphere of Fire was regarded as the source of the lightning,
and indeed of all fire. Hence fire is always rising, in an effort to regain
its natural home. 'Fire cannot be trained to sink downwards' (Arist.
Ethics, ii. 1). The idea occurs often in Dante, as in *Par.* i. 139-141; xxiii.
40-42; *Conv.* iii. 3.

> ' All things whate'er they be
> Have order among themselves, and this is *form*,
> Which makes the universe resemble God.
> Here do the high creatures see the footprints
> Of the Eternal Goodness, which is the end
> Whereto the law aforesaid has been made.
> In the order that I speak of are inclined
> All natures, by their destinies diverse,
> More or less near unto their origin ;
> Hence they move onward unto ports diverse,
> O'er the great sea of being ; and each one
> With instinct given it which bears it on.
> This bears away the fire towards the moon ;
> This is in mortal hearts the motive power ;
> This binds together and unites the earth.
> Nor only the created things that are
> Without intelligence this bow shoots forth,
> But those that have both intellect and love.
> The Providence that regulates all this
> Makes with its light the heaven for ever quiet,
> Wherein that turns which has the greatest haste ;
> And thither now, as to a site decreed,
> Bears us away the virtue of that cord
> Which aims its arrows at a joyous mark.' [1]

In these few lines Beatrice has condensed the substance of many passages of Aquinas. The scholastic word *form* in l. 104 means the 'idea' or pattern existing in the Divine mind, according to which each created thing receives its essence or substantial being. But there is a 'form' or Divine idea not merely for each separate thing, but for the universe as a whole; and this 'form' or Divine idea is the mutual order by which the several parts are so bound together that they constitute an organic unity. It is this mutual order, impressed by the Divine idea on the totality of created things, which makes the universe a similitude of God. 'Since the world,' says Aquinas, 'was not made by chance, but was made by God by the agency of intellect, it is necessary there be in the Divine mind *form*, in the similitude of which the world was made.' [2] So close is

---

[1] *Par.* i. 103-126 (Longfellow's transl. slightly altered).

[2] *Summa*, i. q. xv. a. 1. The word *form* has so changed its meaning that it is almost impossible to make its scholastic sense clear to our modern minds. We speak of a thing as being 'a *formality*,' 'a *formal* thing,' 'a mere matter of *form*,' meaning a thing of no great importance. To

this similitude that elsewhere he argues confidently from the unity of the world to the unity of its Maker. And not His unity alone, but His Eternal Goodness (*eterno valore*, l. 107), the end for which this law of order has been impressed on the universe. For, by the very inequalities of things 'God has communicated His goodness in such a way that one creature can transmit to others the good which it has received. To take away order from creation is to take away the best thing that there is in creation: for while individual things in themselves are good, the conjunction of them all is best by reason of the order in the universe: for the whole is ever better than the parts and is the end of the parts.'[1] Men and Angels—'the high creatures' of l. 106—trace in this order the footsteps of that Eternal Goodness which is its final end.

For the preservation of this order and the attaining of the unity and goodness which are the similitude of God, Beatrice continues, their Maker has infused into all creatures an inclination or instinct which impels them to seek for some good, in various ways, according to the greater or less nearness of their natures to the Source of their being. 'Since all things proceed from the Divine will, all things in their own way are inclined by appetite toward good, but the ways vary. For some are inclined to a good by natural disposition alone, without knowledge, as plants and inanimate bodies; and such an inclination is called *natural* appetite. But some are inclined to a good with a certain amount of knowledge; not so, however, that they know the rational ground of good, but that they

the scholastics *form* was of the last importance—it meant, as one writer says, 'the *last complement of reality*, the *final determination*, or *complete realization of being*.' Perhaps it will help us to understand this and some other things if we borrow this author's illustration of Aristotle's four kinds of causes by means of a statue. 'The *material* principle is the iron, bronze, or stone—the stuff out of which the particular statue is wrought. The *formal* principle is the determining figure or shape, by which the statue is made to represent Napoleon or Nelson. The *efficient* cause is the sculptor, his hammer, chisel, etc. The *final* cause is the satisfaction, fame, or money which the artist has in view in the production of the work' (Father Maher's *Psychology*, 555-560).

[1] *Contra Gentiles*, iii. 69 (Father Rickaby's transl.).

know some particular good : as the sense knows sweet
and white, and things of this kind. Inclination then
which follows this sort of knowledge is called *sensitive* appetite. But some are inclined to good with a
knowledge by which they recognize the rational
conception of good itself, which is the property of the
intellect. And these are inclined to the good in the
most perfect way; not as if merely directed to the
good by another, like the things that lack knowledge ;
nor to a particular good only, as those in which sensitive knowledge alone exists, but as if inclined to
universal good itself ; and this inclination is called *will.*'[1]
In the present passage Beatrice gives examples of each
of these three classes. (1) The mere *natural* appetite
' bears the fire toward the moon ': that is, the fire, by
the unconscious law of its nature impressed on it by
God from without, rises in the direction of the sphere
of fire to which it belongs. The same natural appetite
—the law of gravitation—' binds together and unites
the earth.' (2) The *sensitive* appetite is ' the motive
power in mortal hearts '—that is, the lower animals,
moved by mere instinct.[2] (3) The *rational* appetite is
that which inclines ' those that have both intellect
and love '—men and Angels, who can rise to the conception of a universal good. It is just in this last,
Beatrice admits, that a flaw in the order of the universe
may arise—the matter may be ' deaf to respond ' to
' the intention of the art.' Intellect and love imply
will, and will has power to swerve aside to a ' false
pleasure.' The nearer to God any nature is, the greater
is its power of self-determination : the stone has no
option, the man has a wide range of choice. In one
thing, indeed, neither man nor Angel has any choice :
they have by the very constitution of their nature

[1] *Summa*, i. q. lix. a. 1.
[2] Butler is certainly wrong in translating *nei cuor mortali* ' in the
hearts of men.' The next *terzina* shows clearly that Dante is here thinking of ' creatures that are without intelligence.' In the *Conv.* (ii. 9) he
says ' many things that live are entirely mortal, such as the brute
animals,' but this, he holds, separates them from men, who have the hope
of immortality.

the general conception of the good—the universal *bonum*—which they cannot but seek. Their freedom is that the will has power to direct itself to this particular object or that, which may seem to partake of the universal good, and thus the possibility of error arises: 'false pleasures' may persuade the soul to rest in some good lower than the highest, or even in some evil which presents itself as good. When this happens, 'the clay is marred in the hand of the potter.'[1]

Dante, however, is now in no danger of thus breaking the Divine order of the universe. His will is 'free, upright and sane'; 'false pleasures' have lost their power; his long climb out of sin, the stern discipline of Terrace after Terrace, the draughts of Lethe and Eunoë by which the memory of sin vanished and that of good revived—all had left him 'pure and disposed to mount unto the stars.' And therefore Beatrice tells him they are now flying up to the heaven of peace, as to their appointed site, borne by the bowstring of the Divine will, which never shoots, save at 'a joyful mark.' Freed from the weight and impediment of sin, it was as natural for him to rise as for a torrent to fall down a lofty mountain; and it had been as marvellous a thing for him to settle down below, as for fire to remain quiet on the earth and refuse to ascend to its native sphere. And then Beatrice fulfils her own teaching:

> Thereon toward heaven she turned back her face.

---

[1] Jer. xviii. 4. In *Conv.* iv. 12, the soul is compared to a pilgrim on the pathway of this life, never before travelled by it, and therefore mistaking every house it sees for its true inn, on its way home to the God from whom it came. The conception of the universal good with which it is born impels it onward, but its inexperience leads it into the error of identifying that highest good with this trivial object and that.

CHAPTER II

1. *Symbolism of the Moon-Spots*

THE more thorough and serious our study of the *Paradiso*, the better will we understand the necessity of the warning to those who would follow in his wake,[1] with which Dante opens the second Canto. He has been accused of showing here 'a pretentious and proud ostentation of wisdom'; but the general neglect and misunderstanding of the *Paradiso*, as compared with the other two divisions of the poem, prove that he was speaking the simple fact. The true affectation would have been to pretend that no difficulty exists. Dante knew well that

> the sacred poem
> To which both heaven and earth have set a hand,
> So that it many a year hath made me lean,[2]

was not going to be understood by every one who chose to follow his ship in 'a tiny boat' (*piccioletta barca*)—the slender equipment of knowledge possessed by men who never 'lifted the neck' to Divine Wisdom, 'the bread of angels.' The theme even of the *Purgatorio* was so much nearer the level of the human mind that Dante felt the need for it of nothing but 'a little ship' (*navicella*)—the same, indeed, as the passage implies, in which he had sailed the 'cruel sea' of the *Inferno*.[3] Now, however, that he is out upon the high seas of that knowledge of God which is eternal life, nothing less than a great ship (*legno*, l. 3, *navigio*, l. 14)

---

[1] Not imitators, as Butler suggests, but readers and commentators. Dante must have known that the latter were a necessary evil.

[2] *Par.* xxv. 1-3. [3] *Purg.* i. 1-3.

can venture into waters never thus crossed before.[1]
In ll. 8, 9 he tells us what his own equipment is:

> Minerva breathes, and pilots me Apollo,
> And Muses nine point out to me the Bears.

We may surely see in these words something more
definite than vague general allusions to pagan myths.
If, as we saw in the first Canto, Apollo stands for God
and the light of His grace, Minerva may well stand for
Beatrice, the Divine Wisdom, who carries him up from
Heaven to Heaven. The nine Muses may correspond
to the nine Orders of Angels which send down through
the nine Heavens the powers and virtues poured out
upon them by God; or perhaps the nine Sciences which
in the *Convito* (ii. 14) he connects with the nine Heavens
—Grammar, Logic, Rhetoric, Arithmetic, Music, Geometry, Astrology, Natural Science, and Moral Science.
The Tenth Heaven represents Divine Science, already
included in Minerva and Apollo. These, or such as
these, form that 'bread of the angels' to which Dante
lifted up his neck betimes. We are reminded of the
famous fresco in the Spanish Chapel in Florence, in
which Dante's chief master in theology, Thomas
Aquinas, is seated in the midst of the sacred writers
and of the virtues poured out on him by the Spirit of
God: the theological nearest heaven, the cardinal a
little lower, and underneath him the intellectual
virtues in the form of the various sciences in which
he had proved himself a master. Some such equipment
for this, his crowning labour, Dante here claims to
possess; and, without some measure of it, they who
attempt to follow in his wake may remain lost on that
ocean of the infinite. This does not necessarily imply
lack of intellect or of education in other directions.
As Plumptre says, the warning seems 'addressed
prophetically to those who, like Voltaire and Goethe,

---

[1] The idea is repeated in *Par.* xxiii. 67-69, when Dante comes to the
Triumph of Christ in the Eighth Heaven:

> It is no passage for a little boat,
> That which the daring prow cleaves as it goes,
> Nor for a helmsman who spares himself.

Leigh Hunt and Savage Landor, have turned away in
weariness and disgust from the philosophy and theology
of the *Paradiso*.' It is just this philosophy and theology
which, to Dante's mind, constitute 'the bread of the
angels'; and he knows that few indeed are the souls
that lift the neck to this celestial food. Even these
few must keep close in his wake, for, if they lag too far
behind, the waters ploughed by his keel will return to
the level, the subject fall back into its ancient trackless
mystery. He pledges himself that the chosen few
shall see a greater marvel than did the Argonauts
when Jason was turned into a ploughman at Colchis.
It is difficult to see the point of the comparison.
Aeëtes, the Colchian king, promises to give Jason the
golden fleece on condition that he yoke to a brazen
plough two brazen-hoofed, fire-breathing bulls, plough
with them the field of Ares, sow the furrows with
dragons' teeth, and conquer the mail-clad warriors
who would spring out of them. Landino suggests the
idea that if Jason's task was 'against nature,' Dante's
work is 'so hidden in the secrets of nature, that it does
not seem natural.' Perhaps we should be content with
the general idea that the few who are fit to follow
Dante to the end of his journey will see him transcend
the limits of nature in a way more wonderful than that
of Jason in his marvellous feat.[1]

A short narrative of the portion of the poem covered
in this chapter will help us to follow the exposition
with greater ease. 'The concreated and perpetual
thirst for the deiform realm'—the world made according to the Divine 'forms' or ideas—bore Dante and his
guide in an instant from the Sphere of Fire to the
Moon. This lowest Heaven received them as into a
cloud, 'lucid, close, solid and polished.' If his body
entered into it, he cannot explain how body can penetrate body, any more than meantime he can understand
what shall yet be clear—how humanity and Deity are
one in Christ. After thanks to God for uniting him
with the first star, Beatrice explains the true cause of

---

[1] The story of Jason's ploughing is told in Ovid, *Met.* vii. 104-121.

the spots on the Moon. Some of the souls belonging to this Heaven now appear, and one of them, Piccarda, a dear friend of Dante's in the earthly life, explains why all ranks of the Redeemed are contented with their several degrees of beatitude, and points out the soul of the Empress Constance. Beatrice tells him that they are the spirits of those who had not been able to keep their religious vows with perfect faithfulness.

Before passing on to examine the symbolic correspondence of the Moon with its inhabitants,[1] there is a *terzina* so compact of scholastic thought concerning beatitude, that it may repay a few minutes spent upon it. Dante is uncertain whether his body entered into the cloudy substance of the Moon. If it did, then our present inability to conceive how two bodies can exist together in the same space should quicken in us the longing to see the Divine Essence in which we shall see the great mystery of the Incarnation, 'how our nature and God were unified.' Now, it is the word *see* which suggests the *terzina* referred to (ii. 43-45):

There (in the Divine Essence) shall be seen that which we hold by faith,
Not demonstrated, but known of itself (*per sè noto*),
In fashion of the first truth that man believes.

'The first truth' here is that known as the Principle of Contradiction: *Nothing can both be and not be.* This being the most universal and fundamental of axioms or necessary truths, it is received by the human mind with a direct, immediate vision which has no need of argument or demonstration.[2] It is this direct, immediate vision of the union of the Divine and human in Christ, as of an axiomatic or necessary truth, which is given in the Divine Essence, and which Dante after-

---

[1] As we shall see, they are not really its inhabitants, but the word is convenient. See p. 86.

[2] '*Necessary truths* were termed by the Schoolmen *per se notae*' (Father Maher's *Psychology*, 289), which is exactly the *per sè noto* of l. 44. Mr. Tozer thinks Dante means 'such primary truths as the sense of personality, of right and wrong, etc., which come to us without any conscious process of reasoning'; but to an Aristotelian 'the first truth' would certainly be the axiom of contradiction as above.

wards receives in a lightning flash of insight as the
very crown of his beatitude.[1] In this *terzina* he sets it
in contrast with *faith* and *demonstration*. The truths
of revelation must meantime be received by faith just
because they are not yet known in this direct and
axiomatic way,—if they were thus known, obviously
revelation and faith would be alike unnecessary.
Again, demonstration, in the scholastic sense, gives a
very imperfect knowledge of a thing. For, according
to Aquinas, it proceeds by negations, removing this
attribute and that, in order to separate the thing from
other objects. Demonstration therefore can show
what a thing is *not*, but what it *is* remains unknown.
But it is just what it is that the beatified soul sees, as
it sees a necessary truth, in the Divine Essence.[2] The
passage is a good example of the ease with which
Dante condenses a whole theology into a single *terzina*.
It shows also the necessity there is for the warning
with which this Canto opens.

We come now to the symbolic correspondences
between the Moon and the souls whom Dante finds
there. As we shall see, the souls are not really and
locally in the Moon or any of the nine lower spheres,
as in their eternal 'mansion.' They manifest themselves in the various spheres for two reasons : first,

[1] *Par.* xxxiii. 127-141. See p. 535 f.
[2] For this scholastic sense of *demonstration*, see *Contra Gentiles*, iii.
39, in which Aquinas decides that 'happiness does not consist in the
knowledge of God which is to be had by Demonstration' : 'Demonstration removes from Him (God) many attributes, by the removal of which
the mind discerns God standing apart from other beings. Thus
demonstration shows God to be unchangeable, eternal, incorporeal,
absolutely simple, one. A proper knowledge of an object is arrived at,
not only by affirmations, but also by negations. . . . But between these
two modes of proper knowledge there is this difference, that when a
proper knowledge of a thing is got by affirmations, we know both what
the thing is and how it is distinct from others ; but when a proper knowledge of a thing is got by negations, we know that a thing is distinct from
other things, but what it is remains unknown. Such is the proper knowledge of God which we have by demonstrations. But that is not sufficient
for the final happiness of man' (Father Rickaby's translation). Applied
to what Dante is here discussing, this means that at present our knowledge of the union of the Divine and human in Christ is largely negative
—knowledge of what it is *not*, rather than what it *is*. The latter is part of
the final beatitude.

as an accommodation to human weakness, coming down out of the Empyrean, their true abode, to make themselves more easily intelligible to one like Dante who is not yet pure intellect; and second, to indicate by figures the various degrees of blessedness of the saints—each sphere having certain symbolic correspondences to the souls in it, which make it 'a sign' to Dante of their spiritual condition and reward.

The first of these correspondences is that the Moon lies deepest within the shadowy cone which the earth casts out as far as Venus, the third Heaven.[1] This, as we saw in the Introduction,[2] represents the shadow of an earthly frailty which rests, and rests for ever, on the blessedness of these spirits, dimming the light of their eternal joy. The frailty here is a certain vacillation and inconstancy of the will, which hindered them from fulfilling with perfect faithfulness their religious vows. Thus on the outskirts of the three realms of the other world Dante sets souls in whom the will is weak in varying forms and degrees: immediately inside the Gate of Despair, the Neutrals, too weak to choose a side and hold to it, for good or for evil; at the foot of Mount Purgatory, souls whose wills have been so weakened by years of sin that they are powerless yet to face the purifying pain; and here, in the lowest Heaven, spirits of an inconstant will, who gave themselves to God sincerely, yet faltered somewhat under the strain of strong temptation. Of this inconstancy the ever-changing Moon, in its waxing and waning, is a natural symbol; and it is not unlikely that the moon-spots, the cause of which is discussed at great length, have some figurative reference to the broken light of the beatitude which flows from this wavering of the will. The idea assumes another form in the similes Dante uses to describe the Moon—cloud, adamant, and pearl:

> It seemed to me a cloud did cover us,
> Luminous, dense, consolidate and polished
> As adamant on which the sun doth strike.

---

[1] *Par.* ix. 118, 119.   [2] Pp. 15, 20.

> Within itself did the eternal pearl
> Receive us, even as water doth receive
> A ray of light, remaining still unbroken.[1]

This seems to imply a peculiar combination of brightness and obscurity—a pearly cloudiness with the brilliance of the diamond in it, which may well symbolize the spiritual condition of these souls, half splendour and half cloud. The final correspondence is that the Moon, being the lowest is also the slowest of the Heavens.[2] We saw that the rate of speed indicates the strength of the desire for God. It is partly the cause and partly the effect of the breaking of their vows, that these spirits have the least yearning for God of all the ranks of the Blessed.

And all this, Dante tells us, is mirrored in the souls themselves. He compares them to faces reflected dimly in smooth transparent glass or calm clear water. Their shadowy images come to the eye as slowly as 'a pearl on a white brow'—the pearl-like souls almost invisible against the pearly background of the Moon. 'Mirrored semblances,' he calls them, and is so certain they are reflections in a mirror that he instinctively turns round to see who cast them. Whereupon Beatrice with a smile rebukes him for his childish thought, which, according to its wont, ever turns him round on vacancy. The obvious meaning is that inconstancy of will can never create a clear, firm, and, as it were, solid character and personality. The inconstancy is reflected in their forms, they remain for ever shadowy images and 'mirrored semblances' of souls.[3]

Also it is to be noticed that, along with those in Mercury, the next Heaven, they are the only spirits that are seen in their own proper forms;[4] and, this

---

[1] *Par.* ii. 31-36. Probably Dante in this passage had in his mind the 'bright cloud' (Vulg. *nubis lucida*, Matt. xvii. 5) which overshadowed the three disciples on the Mount of Transfiguration, and the cloud which received Christ when he ascended from the Mount of Olives (Acts, i. 9).

[2] *Par.* iii. 51. [3] *Par.* iii. 10-28.

[4] It is true that all the souls are seen in the White Rose of the Em-

strange to say, is a sign of the diminution of their
vision and their joy. The souls in the higher spheres
are 'covered with light as with a garment'; and the
law of heavenly beatitude is that the clearer the vision
of God the greater the love, and the greater the love
the loftier the joy which burns outward like a robe of
light, in which all thought of self is for ever hidden and
lost. The mere fact that the souls in the two lowest
Heavens are visible in their own proper forms is the
proof that self is not completely lost in the vision and
love and joy of God.[1]

Another curious hint is given which may be easily
missed. Piccarda after her conversation with Dante
is said to vanish 'as through deep water something
heavy.'[2] This indicates a certain comparative slowness of motion, in contrast, for example, with the swift
movement of the souls in the next Heaven, which
Dante compares to the sudden rush of fishes to their
food.[3] We have seen that motion, whether in spheres
or Angels or human souls, is swift or slow according
to the strength of the yearning after God. Hence the
comparatively slow movement of these spirits of the
Moon is the sign that their yearning is the least of all
the souls in Paradise. Their old infirmity of will still
subjects them to the earthly law of gravitation, and
they sink into the pearly substance of their inconstant
planet as a heavy body in deep waters. Indeed, if it
were not for fear of the besetting sin of commentators,
over-subtlety, one might be tempted to find in the
frequent mention of water another reference to this
instability of will. Dante sees the souls as faces in
water; he is received into the dense cloud of the Moon
as water receives a ray of light; Piccarda vanishes like
something heavy in deep water. It is probably only a
fancy, but it almost looks as if the figure of the restless

pyrean in their proper forms (see Canto xxii. 58-63); but, for the symbolic
reasons explained above, those in the Moon and Mercury alone are not
clothed with light.

[1] For this law of beatitude, to which the Angels also are subject, see
Par. xiv. 37-42; xxviii. 106-111; xxix. 130-141.

[2] *Par.* iii. 123.   [3] *Par.* v. 100-105.

wavering water was all the time half unconsciously in the background of the poet's imagination.[1]

Nevertheless these 'mirrored semblances' of souls have a white mysterious pearly beauty of their own, the outraying of their inner joy. Piccarda's brother, Forese Donati, told Dante when he met him on Mount Purgatory, that he knew not which was greater, his sister's beauty or her goodness.[2] Now her earthly beauty, whatever it was, is so far surpassed that Dante, who had known her well, fails at first to recognize her, just as for the opposite reason he had failed to recognize Forese himself.[3]

> ' In your wondrous aspects
> Shines back I know not what of the divine,
> Which doth transmute you from the first conceptions.' [4]

The vague ' I know not what of the divine' hints that their beauty is the reflection of something undefined in their own character ; yet the lowest beauty of Paradise far transcends the highest of earth.

We come now to that curious discussion concerning the Moon-spots which, it must be confessed, is apt to try the patience even of the poet's lovers. It seems at first sight little more than an old dry mediæval problem dragged in without rhyme or reason. There is no harm in admitting the existence of a little human weakness even in Dante, as, for instance, an eagerness to air his new scientific theory; but I think we shall find that his final reason is to withdraw an old theory based on mere sense-perceptions for a spiritual one, in which all phenomena of the heavenly bodies are traced to the government of the Angelic Orders.

Let us now trace the course of the discussion with what patience we can. Almost immediately on arrival in the Moon, Dante asked Beatrice the cause of the dark marks upon it which give rise to the legend of

---

[1] I do not, of course, press this; but we may compare Gen. xlix. 4, 'Unstable as water, thou shalt not excel,' or, as it stands in the Vulgate, ' Effusus es sicut aqua, non crescas.'

[2] *Purg.* xxiv. 13-15.   [3] *Purg.* xxiii. 37-60.

[4] *Par.* iii. 58-60.

Cain and the thorns.[1] She turns the question on himself: what is his own opinion ? In reply he repeats the
explanation which he had already given in the *Convito*
(ii. 14), that the spots are due to variations in the
density of the Moon's substance: 'If the moon be
rightly examined two special things are perceived in
her which are not perceived in the other stars; the one
is the shadow upon her which is nought else than the
rarity of her substance, whereon the rays of the sun
may not be stayed and thrown back, as from her other
parts; the other is the variation of her luminosity,
which now shines from the one side and now from the
other, according as the sun looks upon her.'[2] In
refutation of this Beatrice enters into an elaborate
argument in true scholastic fashion. She smiles at the
fable of Cain as an example of the errors into which
men fall when they have only 'the key of sense' to
unlock mysteries; and Dante's own theory is proof
that even reason, when it follows the senses, 'has
short wings.' Her arguments will show how far his
thought was sunk in falsity.

(1) In the first place, turn to the Eighth Sphere, the
Stellar Heaven. There you find a multitude of starry
lights, which are plainly seen to be diverse in quality
and quantity. If such diversities were produced by

---

[1] This legend is referred to in *Inf.* xx. 124-6. It is familiar in English
literature : see *Tempest*, Act ii. sc. 2 ; *Midsummer Night's Dream*, Act iii.
sc. 1 ; Act v. sc. 1, etc. According to one form of the story, the thorns
are those which Cain threw on the body of Abel to conceal his crime. For
some curious variations of the tale, see C. G. Leland, *Legends of Florence*,
254-271.

[2] Wicksteed's translation, Temple Classics. Dr. Toynbee in his *Dante
Studies and Researches* (78-86) traces this theory to Averroës, but Dr.
Moore (*Studies in Dante*, 2nd series, p. 362) thinks Dante probably took
it from Ristoro d' Arezzo's *La Composizione del Mondo*, written in 1282.
Milton's theory as given by the Archangel Raphael is apparently that of
Averroës, that the spots are vapours which the moon draws to herself for
her own nourishment :

Of Elements
The grosser feeds the purer : Earth the Sea ;
Earth and the Sea feed Air ; the Air those Fires
Ethereal, and, as lowest, first the Moon ;
Whence in her visage round those spots, unpurged
Vapours not yet into her substance turned.

Par. Lost, v. 415-420.

rarity and density, as Dante's theory of the Moon would require, then it would follow that there was but one virtue in the universe distributed thus unequally. But in point of fact there are many virtues or powers, and these are the effects of as many 'formal principles.' The 'formal principle' of anything is that reality in its complete substance which constitutes its essential nature according to a Divine 'form' or idea. Beatrice explains in a little how these 'formal principles,' through the medium of the fixed stars, distribute the heavenly 'virtues' or influences in various forms to the seven planetary spheres and the earth. On Dante's theory there could exist only one formal principle and one virtue flowing from it.[1]

(2) Again, if rarity were the cause of the darkness, one of two things would happen: either the rarity would go right through, thus causing an opening in the substance of the moon; or the dense and the rarer layers must alternate with one another like the leaves of a book or the arrangement of fat and lean in a body. The former is disproved by the fact that during an eclipse the light of the sun does not shine through, as it would do if there was a hole in the moon. The latter is disproved by a simple experiment. The sun's rays are reflected from the dense layers of the moon; and since these layers are some on the surface and some deeper within, Dante might think that the sunlight reflected from the latter was somewhat darkened by being cast back from a greater distance. An experiment would free him from this error. Take two mirrors and set them at an equal distance from you. Between them, but farther away, set a third. Cause a light from behind you to fall on the three, and you will find that the distant mirror sends as bright a reflection as the nearer ones, though of a lesser area. The inference is that the shadows in the moon are not caused by the reflections from the more distant layers of her denser substance.[2]

(3) Having thus cleared away his errors, Beatrice

---

[1] *Par.* ii. 64-72.   [2] *Par.* ii. 73-105.

proceeds to show Dante the truth. It consists of a combination of the Ptolemaic system of astronomy and the doctrine of Dionysius the Areopagite concerning Angels. The highest sphere is 'the Heaven of the Divine Peace,' the Empyrean, which sets in motion within it

> a body in whose virtue
> Lies the being of all that it contains.[1]

This 'body' is the Primum Mobile, and 'all that it contains' is the rest of the heavenly circles, the Stellar Heaven and the seven planetary spheres, with the earth at the centre of them. The entire being of all these is contained in the Primum Mobile. It receives this from the Heaven of the Empyrean above it, and transmits it to the Stellar Heaven below. This is the Heaven of the Fixed Stars; and through these as 'diverse essences' (l. 116) the totality of being is broken up and distributed to the circles beneath, the seven planetary spheres. These in their turn dispose these distinctions, thus lodged in their nature, through various differences, to the ends for which they were made and the seeds and effects they were designed to bear. Thus 'these organs of the world' go from grade to grade, each receiving from above and working downwards.[2]

At this point Beatrice interrupts the discourse in order to impress on Dante the critical importance of the next stage of the argument, that afterward he may know how ' to hold the ford alone.'[3] 'The ford' is, apparently, the transition from a mechanical theory of the universe to a spiritual one. All that she has said up to this point might mean nothing more than that the universe is a mere material machine working on of itself blindly and unconsciously; and it is possible, from the urgency of the warning, that Dante had been

---

[1] *Par.* ii. 112-114. The Nine Heavens within the Empyrean are regarded as material. Hence here the Primum Mobile is called 'a body' (*un corpo*), and in *Par.* xxx. 39, 'the greatest body' (*il maggior corpo*). Comp. *Par.* xxviii. 64.

[2] *Par.* ii. 112-123. Cf. xxviii. 127-129. [3] *Par.* ii. 124-126.

tempted at some time to adopt this view. The saying of Aquinas, 'the heavenly spheres are the instruments of spirit,'[1] may be taken as the text of the remainder of the discourse. As the hammer derives its art, not from itself, but from the smith who wields it, so 'the holy spheres' receive their motion and virtue from the breathing of 'the blessed movers,' the various orders of Angels appointed for the government of the different Heavens. In particular the Eighth Heaven, 'which so many lights make beautiful,' is moved by 'the profound mind' of the Order of the Cherubim, of which it receives the image which it then stamps as with a seal on the innumerable stars with which it is adorned. Thus the Cherubic Intelligence, while preserving its own unity, diffuses its excellence multiplied through the stars, as the human soul within our dust pervades the various members and their faculties.[2] The different virtues thus diffused make different alloys with the heavenly bodies which they quicken, and in which they are bound up, as life is in ourselves. Thus this diffused virtue is mingled, the Cherubim with the several spheres which bear the impress of their ' deep mind,' and both of these with 'the joyful nature' which is their source, namely, God; and this Divine joy it is which shines through each heavenly body as through a human eye. This brings us to the cause of the moon-spots. They are not due to density and rarity of the planet's substance,

---

[1] *Cont. Gent.* iii. 24: 'The heavenly spheres (*coelum*) are the cause of sublunary motions by virtue of their own motion, which is impressed upon them by a spirit. It follows that the heavenly spheres are the instrument of spirit. Spirit then is the prime agent, causing and intending the forms and motions of sublunary bodies; while the heavenly spheres are the instruments of the same' (Rickaby).

[2] Comp. *Aen.* vi. 724-727:

'Principio coelum, ac terras, camposque liquentes,
Lucentemque globum Lunae, Titaniaque astra,
Spiritus intus alit : totamque infusa per artus
Mens agitat molem, et magno se corpore miscet.'

It is a mistake to say without qualification, as is sometimes done, that the basis of Latin theology is the remoteness of God from the world. Aquinas assuredly teaches the Divine immanence : 'God is in all things by *power*, because all are subject to Him ; He is in all things by *essence*, because He created all immediately ; and He is in all things by *presence*, because He knows all' (*Summa*, i. q. viii. a. 3).

as Dante thought when reason followed sense.   Let
reason follow spirit and he will see that the differences
between light and light in all the heavenly bodies, the
moon included, are caused by this mingling with them
of the Divine joy and the Angelic intelligence, flowing
down from Heaven to Heaven :

> ' From this proceeds whate'er from light to light
> Appeareth different, not from dense and rare :
> This is the formal principle that produces,
> Conformably to its goodness, dark and bright.' [1]

There, then, is the long, difficult, and to us obscure explanation which Beatrice gives of the moon-spots.   It
seems a trivial subject on which to spend so much time ;
but Dante's reason for giving it such prominence seems
to be, as already suggested, that it gave him the
opportunity of substituting for a mere physical view
of the universe a spiritual one.   In the *Contra Gentiles*
(iii. 23) Aquinas argues in the same way against a
mechanical view of the movements of the heavenly
bodies ; they are 'the instruments of spirit,' kept in
motion by intelligence.   Arguing as a philosopher, he
is willing to leave it an open question whether the
intelligence is that of God directly, or of Angels as
mediators, or of a living soul in the heavenly bodies
themselves : 'It makes no difference,' he says, 'to our
present purpose, whether the heavenly sphere is moved
by a subsistent intelligence united with it as a soul, or
by an intelligence subsisting apart (i.e. an Angel) ; and
whether each of the heavenly spheres is moved by God,
or whether none of them is moved by Him immediately,
but they are moved mediately through created spirits ;
or whether the first alone (the Primum Mobile) is
moved immediately by God, and the others through
the medium of created spirits ; provided it be held that
the movement of the heavens is the work of spirit.'

Another meaning is suggested by Dean Plumptre.
' The text of the " two great lights " (*Gen*. i. 16) was the
favourite argument of the Popes who claimed authority
over the Empire.   The sun and the moon were symbols

[1] *Par*. ii. 127-148.

of the Church and the State, and the moon derived
its light from the sun. "No," is Dante's answer. "I
admit the symbolism, but I deny the fact. The moon
shines by its own light. The Empire has its own
independent rights."' The question is discussed in *De
Monarchia*, iii. 4. Dante admits, indeed, that part of
the moon's light comes from the sun; but maintains
that 'for its being, the moon in no way depends on the
sun, nor for its power, nor for its working, considered
in itself. Its motion comes from its proper mover, its
influence is from its own rays. For it has a certain
light of its own, which is manifest at the time of an
eclipse; though for its better and more powerful working it receives from the sun an abundant light, which
enables it to work more powerfully.'[1] His inference is
that similarly the temporal power is not dependent on
the spiritual power for its being, its authority, or its
working, though 'the light of grace which the benediction of the Supreme Pontiff bestows on it' enables it
to work more effectively. If in the discussion of the
moon-spots Dante had this political purpose in view,
the independence of the moon (and therefore of the
temporal power) is established by showing that the
light and virtue of the moon come from the same source
as those of the sun and the other spheres—the Divine
power poured out on the Primum Mobile, and distributed
by the fixed stars of the Eighth Heaven throughout the
universe, according to each creature's power to receive
it. When we remember Dante's love of many meanings, this interpretation is by no means impossible; but
the principal purpose must be, as stated above, to show
that the movement and light of the heavens are the
work of spiritual intelligence, and not the blind action
of an unconscious mechanism.

This long scholastic discussion throws into relief the
beautiful incident of the poet's meeting with one who
seems to have been very dear to him in the earthly life.
It is characteristic of Dante that in each of the three
realms the first soul he holds converse with is one with

[1] Church's transl.

whom he had some kindly personal relations here
below: in the lost world, Francesca da Rimini;[1] on the
shore of Purgatory, Casella of Florence; and in the
Celestial Paradise, Piccarda Donati, a kinswoman of
his own by marriage, and, like Dante's own daughter
Beatrice,[2] a nun of the Franciscan Order of St. Clara.
She was a sister, as we saw, of that Forese Donati
whom Dante met on the Sixth Terrace of Purgatory,
and of Corso Donati, who was one of the chief agents
in procuring the poet's banishment.[3] So much of the
Divine shone in the pearly whiteness of her shade that
Dante, not recognizing her, asks to know her name and
lot and 'the web through which she did not draw the
shuttle to the end'—that is, how she had failed in her
vow. Her answer is:

> ' I was in the world a virgin Sister;
> And if thy mind do well regard me,
> The being more fair will not hide me from thee,
> But thou wilt recognize I am Piccarda,
> Who, placed here with these other blessed,
> Am blessed in the sphere that slowest moves . . .
> A perfect life and merit high enheaven
> A lady higher up,' she said, ' unto whose rule
> In your world below they vest and veil themselves,
> That even till death, they may keep watch and sleep
> With that Spouse who every vow accepteth
> Which charity conformeth to His pleasure,
> From the world, to follow her, while still a girl
> I fled, and in her habit closed myself,

---

[1] I omit the Limbo of the Unbaptized and take the Circle of the
Sensual, in which Francesca is, as virtually the First. Although the
dates render impossible Carlyle's pretty picture : 'Francesca herself may
have sat upon the Poet's knee, as a bright innocent little child' (she was
married in 1275 when Dante was a boy of ten), and it is probable he did
not know her personally, yet his friendship with his host, her nephew
Guido Novella, lord of Ravenna, helped to invest the unhappy lady with
a most pathetic personal interest in his eyes.

[2] During the closing years of her father's life she was with him in
Ravenna as a nun of the Convent of Santo Stefano dell' Uliva.

[3] In *Purg.* xxiv. 82-87 Corso's doom is foretold—his place is ' the valley
where is never forgiveness.' Thus, after a way Dante has, members of
the same family are often distributed throughout the three realms of the
other world. The Empress Constance in this Heaven, her son Frederick II.
in the City of Dis, and her grandson Manfred at the base of Mount
Purgatory, form another notable example.

> And undertook the pathway of her order.
> Thereafter men more used to evil than to good
> Tore me away forth of the sweet cloister :
> God knows what after that my life became.' [1]

The story, as told by the *Ottimo*, is that her brothers had promised her in marriage to a Florentine gentleman, Rossellino della Tosa. During her brother Corso's absence as Podestà of Bologna, Piccarda entered the convent of Santa Chiara in Florence. When the news reached him, he straightway returned, tore her violently out of the cloister, and forced her into the promised marriage. The line, 'God knows what after that my life became,' is one of those mysterious veils by which Dante knew so well how at once to quicken and to baffle the imagination. It gave rise to legends that Christ, in reply to her prayers, fulfilled her vow of chastity by smiting her with leprosy, or, according to another story, by a wasting sickness which soon ended her earthly life. The probability is, as Casini says, that the line is a veil drawn over the unhappy lady's fate in order to leave to the reader's imagination the moral tortures of having to live at the side of a man she did not love, intensified with the agony of having failed in her sacred vows. The words, however, sound like an appeal to God against human judgment—He and He alone knows how, as she says afterward about Constance, 'the veil from the heart was never loosened.'

This Constance is the 'splendour' shining with 'all the light of our sphere,' whom Piccarda now points out on her right as having suffered the same fate :

> 'This is the light of the great Costanza,
> Who of the second wind of Suabia
> Bore the third, and the last power.' [2]

The first 'wind of Suabia' was Frederick Barbarossa, the second Henry VI., the third Frederick II., and, according to some of the old commentators, they are

---

[1] *Par*. iii. 46-51 ; 97-108.   [2] *Par*. iii. 118-120.

called 'winds' because their worldly glory passed
away like the wind and the family became extinct.
Frederick II. is also called 'the last power,' not simply
because his house virtually died out in him, but
because in Dante's view he was the last Roman
Emperor.[1] There can be little doubt that one principal
purpose of the poet was to defend the Empress
Constance and her son Frederick II. from the
calumnies of their Guelph enemies. The historical
facts are these. William II. of Sicily being without
heir, the throne on his death would descend to his
aunt Constance, daughter of Roger I. Frederick
Barbarossa, who was engaged in a struggle with the
Papacy for the territory of the Countess Matilda, by
a stroke of diplomatic strategy secured the kingdom
of Sicily through the marriage of his son Henry to
Constance. This was one of the heaviest defeats the
Roman policy could suffer. 'The kingdom of Sicily
was thus, instead of a place of refuge for the Pope
against the Emperor, now an imperial territory;
the King [Henry was King of Italy], instead of a
vassal holding his realm as an acknowledged fief of
the Papacy, the Pope's implacable antagonist. The
Pope was placed, at Rome, between two fires.'[2] In
order to discredit the marriage and its offspring, a
number of Guelph legends were commonly believed
in Dante's day. Villani's account is that William, the
brother of Constance, in consequence of a prophecy
that she should rule over Sicily in ruin and desolation,
resolved to put her to death, but was persuaded by
his friends to consign her to the cloister. 'And so it
came to pass that the said Constance was preserved
from death, and she, not of her own will, but
through fear of death, lived in the guise of a nun in

---

[1] *Conv.* iv. 3. Dante was not the only one who believed this. 'Even in
his old age, Salimbene (d. 1288) attributes the death of Popes Gregory x.
and Honorius iv., in part at least, to their flying in the face of Providence by attempting to set up new Emperors after Frederick's death, for
it had been prophesied "by some Sibyl, as men say," that the Empire
should end with him' (Coulton, *From St. Francis to Dante*, p. 244).

[2] Milman's *Latin Christianity*, Bk. viii. ch. ix.

a certain convent of nuns.' On the death of William, the throne was seized by Tancred against the will of the Church; and a discord having broken out between him and the Archbishop of Palermo, the latter received instructions from the Pope to transfer the kingdom from Tancred by removing Constance from the cloister and marrying her to Henry VI. According to Villani, she was at this time 'perhaps fifty years old,' 'a nun in her body but not in her mind.' In reality she was about thirty-two, although her son Frederick II. was not born till some nine years after. It is plain that the object was to throw opprobrium on Frederick as one born against natural and spiritual law alike: ' And it was not without Divine occasioning and judgment that such a baneful heir must needs be the issue, being born of a holy nun, and she more than fifty-two years old, when it is almost impossible for a woman to bear a child; so that he was born of two contradictions—against spiritual laws, and, in a sense, against natural laws.'[1] Dante, it is obvious, regards all this as a Guelph calumny; and in this passage he sets himself to vindicate the character of 'the great Costanza.' The mere fact that she is in Paradise at all is her vindication. If she is in the lowest Heaven, at all events she shines with ' *all* the light' of that sphere: partly because she voluntarily exchanged her high rank for that of a simple 'sister'; and partly because when, 'against her will and against good usage,' she was turned back to the world she had left, 'from the heart's veil she was never loosened.'[2]

When Piccarda revealed herself to Dante, she told him that she and her companions were quite happy even in this slowest Heaven, because their place is part of that order of the universe ordained by the

[1] Villani's *Chronicle*, iv. 20; v. 16. Villani's chief charge against Constance is that she was 'the mother—we shall not say of Frederick II. who was long king of the Roman Empire,—but rather of Frederick who brought the said Empire to destruction, as will appear fully in his deeds' (Miss Selfe's translation). To the Joachimites Frederick was the Antichrist, and they and the Guelphs felt that there was some 'mystery of iniquity' about his birth. See Coulton, *From St. Francis to Dante*, 76, 241. [2] *Par.* iii, 109-120.

Holy Spirit, through whom their affections are enkindled.[1] This contentment is beyond Dante's understanding: it seems almost a natural instinct to long
for a loftier degree of blessedness, and he puts the
question to Piccarda:

> 'But tell me, ye who in this place are happy,
>   Are you desirous of a higher place,
>   To see more, or to make yourselves more friends?'[2]

'To see more' refers to the 'essential beatitude' of the
Redeemed, the vision of God, which grows clearer the
nearer the soul comes to His presence. 'To make
yourselves more friends' refers to their 'accidental
beatitude.' Aquinas says that 'if there were only one
soul enjoying God, it would be happy without having
any neighbour to love'; but he admits 'that friendship
is a concomitant of perfect beatitude,' and quotes
St. Augustine: 'The only aid to happiness in spiritual
creatures is intrinsic from the eternity, truth, and
charity of the Creator: but if they are to be said to
receive any extrinsic aid at all, perhaps it is in this
alone, that they see one another and enjoy one
another's company.'[3] Dante is much more certain
that the communion of saints is an element in the
bliss of Paradise; and in this passage he seems to
believe that the power to make friends increases the
nearer the soul approaches God.[4]

---

[1] *Par.* iii. 46-57.

[2] *Par.* iii. 64-66. Another interpretation is often given : ' Do you desire
a higher place in order to see more of your friends who are farther up, or
to make yourselves more dear to God?' This seems to me quite away
from Dante's idea, though it is supported by great names.

[3] *Summa,* i-ii. q. iv. a. 8. Father Rickaby, whose translation is here
quoted, questions the view of Aquinas : 'The actual state of the blessed
is one of social happiness in "the holy city Jerusalem" (Apoc. xxi. 10), as
the way leading to it is life in the society of the Church on earth. The
blessed in Heaven and the faithful upon earth are essentially a body,
consisting of Christ the Head with His members. Hence we should
hesitate to pronounce the "communion of saints" a mere accidental
element in happiness. Cf. Aristotle, *Eth.cs,* ix. ix. 10' (*Aquinas Ethicus,*
i. 31 n.).

[4] The words 'to make yourselves more friends' (*per più farvi amici,*
l. 66) seem to be taken from the *facite vobis amicos* of the Vulgate of
Luke xvi. 9. Aristotle (*Ethics,* ix. 10) discusses whether it is a duty to
make the largest possible number of friends, and decides : 'Perhaps it is

Piccarda's answer is one of those beautiful passages of the poem which haunt the memory like a strain of heavenly music. The joy of her perfect contentment broke forth in a smile and a radiance so vivid that 'she seemed to burn in the first fire of love'—the joy of the virgin heart that knows no love but God's. The very essence of beatitude, she says, is charity, and the nature of charity is to conform joyfully to the Divine will. This creates a great unity of all wills in Paradise, and makes envy of one another's lot impossible:

> ' Nay, 'tis essential to this blest existence
> To hold itself within the will Divine,
> Whereby our own wills are themselves made one.
> So that, as we are from threshold unto threshold
> Throughout this realm, to all the realm 'tis pleasing,
> As to the King, who to his will en-wills us:
> And his will is our peace; it is that sea
> Whereunto everything is moving on,
> That which it createth, and which nature makes.' [1]

Dante now sees clearly ' how everywhere in Heaven is Paradise,' in spite of the varying degrees of blessedness. It is all part of that universal order by which everything, according to its nature, is drawn by the power of Love into union with that Will from which it sprang. In such a universe of love, envy is inconceivable. 'As now,' says St. Augustine, 'the angels do not envy the archangels, so the lower spirits will not envy those higher. For no one will wish to be what he has not received, though bound in fetters of union with him who has received; just as in the body the finger does not seek to be the eye, though both members take their place harmoniously in the complete body. And thus along with his gift, greater or

---

well not to try to have the largest possible number of friends, but to have only so many as are sufficient for community of life, as it would seem to be impossible to be a devoted friend to a number of people ' ; but, of course, he is discussing friendship in the present life.

[1] *Par.* iii. 70-87. The distinction drawn in the last line is between what the Divine will *creates* directly and immediately—as the first matter and the Nine Heavens, the Angels and the human soul—and *what nature makes*, the seeds and fruits and issues that come through second causes.

less, each shall receive the further gift to desire no more than he has.'[1]

[1] *De Civitate Dei*, Book xxii. 30. Cf. St. Gregory (*Dialogues*, IV. ch. xxxv.) : 'If there were not inequality of rewards in the everlasting felicity of Heaven, there were not many mansions, but rather one, wherefore there be many mansions in which divers orders and degrees of God's Saints be distinguished, who in common do all rejoice in the society and fellowship of their merits ; and yet all they that laboured receive one penny, though they remain in distinct mansions ; because the felicity and joy which there they possess is one, and the reward which by divers and unequal good works they receive is not one but divers.'

CHAPTER III

2. *The Ethics of Vows*

WHEN Piccarda, singing the *Ave Maria*, vanished 'like something heavy in deep water,' Dante turned his eyes on Beatrice, only to find himself blinded as by a lightning-flash. The cause is, in the literal sense, the contrast between the pale moonlight of the faces of Piccarda and her companions and the sunlit radiance of one who belonged to a far loftier Heaven; and, in the allegorical sense, that the very brightness of the Divine Wisdom threw into deeper darkness two great doubts which now possessed his mind. In true scholastic fashion, he compares himself, in his uncertainty which to attempt first, to a starving man between two foods equally distant from him and equally attractive; or to a lamb in an equipoise of terror between two wolves; or to a dog between two does. The comparison is taken from Aquinas in his discussion of the problem of the freedom of the will. An opponent urges that the will has no freedom: it simply obeys the strongest motive, and when motives are perfectly balanced, it is para-lysed.[1] The simile is recalled to Dante's mind by the fact that it is this same problem of the freedom of the will which underlies both his doubts, and which he is now about to discuss. Beatrice divines and answers the questions which Dante was powerless to put in words:

[1] *Summa*, i-ii. q. 13, a. 6: 'If any two things are absolutely equal, a man is not moved to the one more than to the other; just as a starving man, if he has food equally appetizing in different directions and at an equal distance, is not moved to the one more than to the other.'

> 'Thou arguest: If the good will endureth,
> By what reason does another's violence
> Decrease the measure of desert in me?
> Again, it gives thee cause for doubting
> That the souls seem to return to the stars,
> According to the sentiment of Plato.' [1]

Beatrice quickly solves Dante's hesitation between these two doubts by taking first 'that which has the most of gall.' This is the opinion attributed to Plato in the *Timaeus*:

> 'He saith the soul unto its star returns,
> Believing that from thence it was dissevered,
> When nature for a form did give it.' [2]

The reference is to a Platonic myth of creation. The Creator, having mingled the elements and 'the soul of the universe' in a cup, 'divided the whole mixture into souls equal in number to the stars, and assigned each soul to a star.' They were then sent forth to inhabit mortal bodies on earth, and 'he who lived well during his appointed time was to return to the star which was his habitation and there he would have a blessed and suitable existence.' [3] The inference Dante draws from this passage is that it involves the denial of free-will: the star to which the soul belonged originally draws it back to itself as by the power of destiny. Now, it is perfectly clear that Dante believed in some great influence of the stars over human fate. When he reached the sign of Gemini in which the sun was when he was born, he broke into a cry of praise:

> O glorious stars, O light impregnated
> With great virtue, from which I recognize
> All of my genius, whatsoe'er it be. [4]

---

[1] *Par.* iv. 19-24.

[2] *Par.* iv. 52-54.   Cf. *Summa*, ii-ii. q. clxiv. a. 1: 'the *form* of man is the rational soul'; and Spenser's *Hymne in Honour of Beauty*: 'For soule is forme, and doth the bodie make.'

[3] *Timaeus*, 41, 42 (Jowett's transl.).   The passage proceeds that if the soul live ill, it will be transformed into a woman, then into some brute like it in its evil ways, and so on through many transformations, until reason overcome the irrational elements, and the soul return to its first and better nature.   In *Conv.* iv. 21 Dante says: 'Plato and others hold that they (souls) proceeded from the stars and were more or less noble according to the nobility of their star.'

[4] *Par.* xxii. 112-114.

Nevertheless, he strenuously opposes the idea that the influence of the stars has any power to over-ride free-will, destroy human merit and demerit, and thus break up the very foundations of moral responsibility. To impart genius is one thing, to control the will is another. One of the souls in Purgatory tells Dante that it is part of the blindness of the world from which he came to trace everything to the compulsion of the stars:

> ' Ye who are living every cause refer
> Up to the heavens alone, as if all things
> They of necessity moved with themselves.
> If this were so, in you would be destroyed
> Free will, nor any justice would there be
> In having joy for good, or grief for evil.' [1]

This is why Beatrice regards this doctrine of Plato as having more of poison than Dante's other doubt: by reducing all to necessity, it denies the existence of free-will, and therefore of human responsibility, merit or demerit, on which the rewards and punishments of the world to come are based. It thus leads away from Beatrice, that is, from the Divine Wisdom.

This doubt had risen from the fact that the souls of Piccarda and her companions had appeared to Dante in the Moon; and Beatrice now assures him that they are not really and locally there, and therefore do not return to their star, as Plato seemed to teach. From lowest saint to highest Angel, all are in the Empyrean, the Heaven of the Divine Peace:

> ' He of the Seraphim most absorbed in God,
> Moses, and Samuel, and whichever John
> Thou mayst select, I say, and even Mary,
> Have not in any other heaven their seats,
> Than have those spirits that just appeared to thee,
> Nor of existence more or fewer years;
> But all make beautiful the primal circle,
> And have sweet life in different degrees,
> By feeling more or less the eternal breath.' [2]

If, then, they are in 'the primal circle,' why are the saints shown to Dante in the various spheres? As an

---

[1] *Purg.* xvi. 67-72.   [2] *Par.* iv. 28-36.

accommodation to his human weakness; or perhaps simply to the essential union in him of soul and body. This union means that all knowledge begins with an image of an object received by the senses. 'This sensible image excites the phantasy, "the faculty that ministers discourse to reason" (*Purg.* xxix. 49), and furnishes it with the material on which it works.'[1] The result is that Dante, being unable by the power of pure intellect to rise to the vision of these souls in the Empyrean of the Divine Mind, receives, as it were, a series of sense-perceptions or symbols of their state by means of the various spheres in which they are made visible to him. It is the same principle on which Holy Scripture uses corporeal images to express spiritual realities, as when it attributes feet and hands to God, 'and means something else.'[2] Similarly, Holy Church represents the Archangels, Gabriel, Michael, and Raphael, under human forms. It is a Divine condescension to our faculties; as Aquinas says: 'It befits Holy Scripture to teach Divine and spiritual things under the similitude of corporeal things. For God provides for all creatures according to the nature of each. But it is natural to man to come to things of the intellect through things apprehended by the senses; because all our knowledge has its beginning from sense. Hence in Holy Scripture

---

[1] Hettinger, *Dante's Divina Commedia*, 270, 277. Father Maher in his *Psychology* (p. 311) thus summarizes the scholastic theory of knowledge: 'An object produces an impression on a sensitive faculty. This results in a sensuous phantasm in the imagination, and here the work of the lower power ends. Since, however, in man the sensuous faculties of cognition have their source in a soul also endowed with intellectual aptitudes, the latter now issue into action. The presence of the phantasm forms the condition of rational activity, and the intellect abstracts the essence; that is, by its own active and passive capabilities generates the concept which expresses in the abstract the essence of the object. By a further reflective act it views this abstract concept as capable of representing any member of the class, and thus constitutes it a formally universal idea.' The appearance of souls in the stars corresponds to 'the sensuous phantasm in the imagination' on which afterwards the intellect works.

[2] *Summa*, i. q. i. a. 10: 'The literal sense is not the figure itself, but that which is figured. For when Scripture names the arm of God, the literal sense is not that there is in God a bodily member of this kind, but that which is signified by this member, to wit, operative power.' Comp. St. Bernard on Canticles, Sermon iv.

spiritual things are fittingly conveyed to us under metaphors of corporeal things. And this is what Dionysius says : It is impossible that the Divine ray should otherwise illumine us, except in so far as it is enveloped in a diversity of holy veils.'[1]

Beatrice proceeds to suggest another and worthier meaning of Plato's words—not that the souls themselves return to the stars, but the honour and the blame of the influences which they shower down on men. It is not easy to see the precise thought that was in Dante's mind ; but we may perhaps connect it with the teaching of Aquinas concerning the 'accidental reward' of the Angels, who are the movers of the stars. Their proper and 'essential reward' is the beatitude to which the good Angels were raised for their cleaving to God when the evil fell away. But in addition to this, they have an accidental reward, in the increase of their joy 'by reason of the salvation of those whom they have induced to do meritorious works.'[2] Thus 'the honour and the blame' may return to the stars and their Angelic Movers—as, for example, the mingling of light and shadow in the three lowest Heavens.

Beatrice winds up the discussion of this first doubt by declaring the origin of the heathen worship of the stars :

> 'This principle ill understood once warped
> The whole world nearly, till it went astray
> Invoking Jove and Mercury and Mars.'[3]

---

[1] *Summa*, i. q. i. a. 9 ; Dion. *Heavenly Hierarchy*, ch. i. Dionysius acutely remarks that it is better that a similitude be not too like the reality, lest it be mistaken for it. E.g. There is less likelihood of our falling into error about angels when they are represented under animal forms (Ezek. i.), than when they appear as men. The very incongruity in the former case protects our minds ; whereas in the latter, we may fall into the mistake of imagining 'that the Heavenly Beings are certain creatures with the appearance of gold, and certain men with the appearance of light, and glittering like lightning, handsome, clothed in bright shining raiment, shedding forth innocuous flame, and so with regard to all the other shapes and appropriate forms, with which the Word of God has depicted the Heavenly Minds' (Parker's transl.).

[2] *Summa*, Suppl. q. lxxxix. a. 8. Cf. Job, xxv. 5, 'Behold, even the moon hath no brightness, and the stars are not pure in his sight.'

[3] *Par*. iv. 61-63.

'This principle' is taken by many commentators to mean this Platonic doctrine of the return of souls to the stars from which they issued; which is an impossible meaning when we remember that Beatrice has just shown its falseness. The principle is obviously that which forms the main subject of her discourse, namely, that God 'condescends to our faculties,' teaching truth by signs which appeal to the senses. The very stars are signs (iv. 38), according to the words in Gen. i. 14, 'Let them be for signs.' Aquinas, discussing the creation of luminaries on the Fourth Day, says that they were set as signs to measure times and foretell seasons, lest man should be deceived into adoring them as gods.[1] It is, says Beatrice, because 'this principle' of teaching by signs was ill understood, that the heathen fell into the error of thinking each star an actual deity, with power to stamp its own character irrevocably on the souls of men.

We come now to Dante's second doubt: if the will remains firm, why should the violence of others diminish the merit of these souls, and thus consign them to the lowest of the Heavens?[2] This doubt, says Beatrice, has 'less of poison,' and cannot lead away from her; and for this she gives a reason which has led to much controversy:

> 'That our justice should appear unjust
> In the eyes of mortals, is an argument
> Of faith, and not of heretic iniquity.'[3]

---

[1] *Summa*, i. q. lxx. a. 2.

[2] Plumptre finds in the discussion which follows, and which 'seems to us at first to belong to the dreariest regions of casuistry,' a personal element which redeems it. 'What if Dante found in his own life a parallel to that of Piccarda? What if, behind the memory of Beatrice and the cord of the Tertiary Order, not in itself binding to celibacy, there had been an inward purpose, half-formulated into a vow, of which the celibate life would have been the natural outcome, and his friends had pressed marriage upon him, marriage with a Donati, as Corso Donati had pressed it on Piccarda? They had urged the pleas of health, wealth, worldly prosperity, and he had yielded, without "the gold or silver key," without consulting his spiritual director.' I think this personal element exists in every one of the Heavens; but in the Moon may it not be precisely the opposite of what Plumptre conjectures—a profound thankfulness that he had *not* taken vows of religion, which he had now good reason to know he would have been powerless to keep?   [3] *Par.* iv. 67-69.

Scartazzini reduces the various interpretations, ancient and modern, to the three following: (1) That in some particular case the divine justice appears unjust is proof of faith in this justice in general (i.e. the exception proves the rule); (2) that the divine justice seems unjust is a question of faith, which faith itself must solve, and not human reason; and (3) that the divine justice seems to us unjust, is a motive for us to believe in it (*i.e.* take it on faith). It seems possible to suggest another meaning. What Dante wishes to convey is that there is a doubt which, so far from springing from 'heretic iniquity,' has its roots in our very faith in God. Had we no ideal of Divine justice in our souls, nothing would ever seem to violate justice. The very existence of the doubt, therefore, is proof or 'argument of faith': without faith, doubt is impossible. Towards the end of this Fourth Canto (ll. 130-132), after Beatrice has explained the difficulty, he throws the idea into figurative form: doubt is like a shoot which the tree of truth, by its very vitality, sends forth:[1]

> ' Well do I see that never sated is
> Our intellect, unless the Truth illume it,
> Outside of which no truth expands itself.
> It rests therein as wild beast in its lair,
> When it attains it; and attain it can—
> Else each desire would frustrate be.
> Through that is born, in fashion of a shoot,
> The doubt at the foot of truth : and it is nature,
> Which to the top thrusts us from ridge to ridge.'

The intellect of man is so made that it cannot rest

[1] All the interpretations which turn on the contrast between Faith and Reason seem to me mistaken. The contrast is not between Faith and Reason, but between Faith and Heresy. Perhaps Job and his friends will best help us to understand the idea. The Patriarch, storming Heaven with wild accusations of its injustice, seems a heretic past hope; but when he cries, ' Though he slay me, yet will I trust in him,' we see that it is his very faith which creates his doubts, and that his 'heresy' has infinitely more faith in it, than the dead orthodoxy of his friends who are so shocked by it. It is, of course, possible that Dante is thinking of the fact that the Church had made no pronouncement on the subject of this doubt, and therefore left it open; whereas the subject of the previous doubt—the Platonic doctrine of the return of souls to their stars—had been condemned as a heresy by the Council of Constantinople in the year 540. For opinions which can be held without heresy, see *Summa*, i. q. xxxii. a. 4.

short of the final Truth, God Himself. This final Truth can be reached, else, desire remaining for ever unsatisfied, man could never attain the beatitude for which he was created, 'the good of the intellect.' This frustration of the highest 'natural desire,' as Aquinas calls it, is impossible. Hence Nature herself takes means to ensure that the intellect do not rest in any intermediate truth, but is driven on and up 'from ridge to ridge,' till it reach the summit, the final Truth which contains every truth, and is contained by none. Now, the means by which Nature secures this is *doubt*. Truth itself throws forth doubts from its foot, as a tree sends forth shoots :—from its foot, because it is at the beginning of the search for truth that doubts are most prolific. Hence we reach these three profoundly important conclusions, which I have no doubt were in Dante's mind : (1) it is the very vitality of truth which throws forth the shoots of doubt—the more eager the search, the more vigorous the rush of questions that assail the mind at the outset; (2) the doubts are not alien to the truth, but of its own substance, as the shoots are of the very nature and substance of the tree; (3) this rank growth of doubts at the foot of truth is Nature's device to give the intellect of man no rest until it rest in God. This, in Dante's philosophy, is based on Aristotle's definition of 'Nature' as 'the first principle of motion and of rest' : of motion, since all things seek an end, a *bonum*; of rest, since, the end being attained, rest follows.[1]

Beatrice now explains the difficulty about the justice of God in setting these spirits here in the lowest Heaven. They suffered violence, indeed, inasmuch as they were dragged from the cloister; but also they

---

[1] See Cornoldi, *The Physical System of St. Thomas*, chaps. iv. and xvi. 'By "movement" Aristotle, as well as St. Thomas, understands *all* forms of change, whether subjective or objective—not merely external sensible movement as many modern writers imagine' (Maher's *Psychology*, 374 n.). It includes, says Aquinas, 'any movement in our soul, according, for example, to the succession of cognitions and imaginations.' Hence the above definition of Nature as 'the first principle of motion,' etc., covers the human intellect, of which Dante is here thinking : though, of course, Nature cannot reach its end without Grace.

aided the violence by not returning to 'the holy place,' the moment the force was withdrawn : unlike fire, for instance, which seeks its upward way though turned aside by violence a thousand times. The will in its very nature is inviolable. 'As regards the proper act of the will itself,' says Aquinas, 'no violence can be done it.' Nothing external to itself can force it. A perfectly firm will, such as held St. Lawrence on the gridiron and made Mutius thrust his hand into the fire, would have compelled them to go back; hence there must have been some flaw in their wills, some consenting to the violence.

This, however, only leads to another difficulty. Beatrice had assured Dante that he might implicitly believe whatever these spirits told him (iii. 31-33); and Piccarda had declared that the Empress Constance never gave up her love for the veil (iii. 115-117). How, then, can this be reconciled with what Beatrice has just said? The answer is that Piccarda was speaking of 'the will absolute,' while Beatrice was speaking of the will according to certain circumstances. Constance and her companions had yielded to force through fear of the consequences of resistance; and, in so far as fear entered in, the action became voluntary. The absolute will is the will considered in the abstract and apart from such circumstances of fear, and this absolute will never faltered. The distinction is taken from Aristotle and Aquinas, both of whom use an illustration which makes the meaning clear—the case of throwing goods overboard during a storm at sea: 'for although nobody would voluntarily make such a sacrifice in the abstract (that is, by the 'absolute will'), yet every sensible person will make it for his own safety and the safety of his fellow passengers'—in which case the action becomes a voluntary one in face of the danger. Hence Piccarda and Beatrice do not contradict one another: the two statements taken together constitute the full truth.[1]

---

[1] *Ethics*, iii. 1; *Summa*, i-ii. q. vi. a. 6. The definition of *Violence* in iv. 73, 74 is taken direct from Aristotle : 'An action is compulsory if its origin is external to the agent, *i.e.* if the person who is the subject of

Dante is so perfectly satisfied with this answer that he is encouraged to seek the solution of a third difficulty: whether compensation can be made for broken vows:

> ' I wish to know if man can satisfy you
> For broken vows with other good deeds, so
> That in your balance they will not be light.' [1]

Beatrice, after warmly expressing her joy in Dante's spiritual progress,[2] replies to the effect that a vow is the offering to God of our free-will, and since free-will is the most precious of all things we possess, there exists no possible equivalent for it:

> ' The greatest gift which in his largess God
> Made in creating, and to his own goodness
> Most conformed, and that which he doth prize
> The most, was the freedom of the will,
> Wherewith the creatures of intelligence,
> Both all and only, were and are endowed.' [3]

In other words, the peculiar dignity of free-will is that it is the image within us of the Divine goodness, which is absolutely free. The nearer in nature anything is to God, the greater is this inner power of self-determination bestowed upon it; so that, while stones, plants, animals are under laws of necessity, ' the creatures of intelligence,' men and Angels, and they alone, have something of this Divine power of freely determining their own being. When this highest gift of the Creator is offered back to him in a vow, and the vow then broken, man has nothing of equal value to render as a substitute in satisfaction. And that for three reasons which are stated in three lines:

> ' For, in confirming between God and man the compact,
> A victim is made of this same treasure,
> Such as I say, and made with its own act.' [4]

The first reason here is that it is a ' compact' between

compulsion is in no sense contributory to the action.' It is to this definition Aquinas refers in his discussion of the subject: ' In what is done through force or violence, the inner will is quiescent, but in what is done through fear the will is active. And therefore in the definition of violence, it is not merely affirmed that "the violent is that, the origin whereof is from without," but it is added, "without any concurrence on the part of him to whom the force is applied."'

[1] *Par.* iv. 133-138.   [2] *Par.* v. 1-12.   [3] *Par.* v. 19-24.   [4] *Par.* v. 28-30.

God and man, and therefore a more solemn thing than a compact between man and man. The second, that this infinitely precious thing is made 'a victim,' the will being thus declared dead to itself, as a victim offered in sacrifice is dead. The third is that all this is done by the will's own act—it is the priest as well as the victim. For all these reasons there is no adequate satisfaction for a broken vow. To think that we can use the will which we offered and drew back for some other good end, is to use ill-gotten gains for the doing of good deeds: as if, in Dante's words about another matter, one should steal the cloth from the altar to spread it on the table at which he feasts his friends.[1]

This decision, however, seems to be contradicted by the fact that Holy Church grants dispensations from vows, and to this difficulty Beatrice now addresses herself. She draws a distinction between the matter of a vow, and the compact or agreement itself, the latter of which, as the previous discourse showed, could never be cancelled, save by being fulfilled. Even the Hebrews had still to offer, though sometimes the thing offered was allowed to be changed. Among Christians the surrender of the will in a vow must still be made, but in certain cases the 'matter' of the vow may be exchanged for something else. This commutation, however, is to take place under the strictest conditions. First of all, no man is at liberty to shift the burden at his own pleasure: since the vow is to God, only God's representative can alter it—'both the white key and

---

[1] *Par.* v. 25-33; *Conv.* iv. 27. Butler thinks that the argument in this passage is Dante's own, no trace of it being found in *Summa*, ii-ii. q. lxxxviii. where the subject of vows is fully discussed. If, however, we turn to q. clxxxvi. of the same division of the *Summa*, we find the following argument: 'Religion' means a state of perfection; perfection consists of poverty, chastity and obedience; to these three things religious perfection demands that a man be bound by a vow, thus offering himself as a holocaust to God; and finally, of the three, the vow of obedience is the chief, because by it '*a man offers something greater to God, namely, his own will*, which is a better gift than his own body, which he offers by continence, and than exterior things, which he offers by the vow of poverty.' The meaning is that in these three vows, a man offers his entire being to God, the most precious part of which is the will; and this involves Dante's inference that, for the will, there exists no equivalent which can take its place.

the yellow' must turn in the lock, the knowledge and
the authority of the Church. Even the Church, in the
second place, ought not to commute the 'matter' of
a vow save for something else of greater value. In the
Mosaic law, the increase of value was assessed at one-
fifth ; Dante raises it to one-half—the proportion is to
be as four to six. It follows from this, in the next
place, that there are some things of such supreme value
that this exchange of a half more is impossible ; and
in this case there can be no commutation, far less
dispensation.[1] It is commonly assumed that Dante is
here referring to the vow of chastity, which 'draws
down every scale,' and can have no equivalent. The
question is carefully discussed by Aquinas, who holds
that even the Papal authority has no power to cancel
this vow. It can, indeed, grant a dispensation to one
in Holy orders, because to these continence is not
annexed essentially, but only by statute of the Church.
But in the state of religion, which is a renunciation
of the world, marriage included, continence is an
essential, and not even when the common good and the
peace of a country demand the marriage of certain
persons under this vow, is a dispensation lawful. That
would be to convert things that belong to God to
human use. 'Those who have professed religion are
dead to the world, and live to God, hence they are not
to be recalled to human life by occasion of any event
whatsoever.' It is to be noted that while Aquinas starts
from the vow of chastity, his argument runs back to
the religious state as a whole, and he says expressly,
'the Pope cannot make that he who has professed
religion, be not a religious; though some jurists ignor-
antly say the contrary.'[2] It is not likely, therefore, that
Dante, any more than Aquinas, is confining himself to
the vow of chastity : he has the whole state of religion
in view. That state is founded on the vow of obedience,

---

[1] *Par.* v. 43-63.
[2] *Summa*, ii-ii. q. lxxxviii. a. 11. Aquinas founds the impossibility of
commuting a vow of chastity on the Vulgate of Ecclus. xxvi. 20 : 'Omnis
ponderatio non est digna animae continentis,' though the context seems
to me to refer to the married woman rather than to cloistered nuns.

which, as Aquinas says, 'contains under itself the other vows'; the vow of obedience is a sacrifice of the will; and the will being the most precious thing man can offer to God, dispensation, or even commutation, is impossible.

It is in the light of all this that we must read what Aquinas says as to the power of the Church to commute and dispense in the case of other vows. No man has this power in himself—he must submit the case to a Prelate of the Church, as the representative of God, who may rule that 'in this particular case the matter is not proper matter for a vow,' or not proper for that particular person. 'And therefore, when a Prelate of the Church dispenses from a vow, he does not dispense from any precept of natural or divine law; but he rules a point, which was become matter of obligation through the resolve of a human will, wherein the person who so made up his mind was not able at the time to see all round the circumstances of the case.' The whole discussion may indeed seem, in Plumptre's words, to belong to 'the dreariest regions of casuistry'; but the Spiritual Franciscans found this question of the Papal power a matter of life and death. Not many years after Dante wrote this passage, these unhappy men were being burned in batches all over the south of France for denying that Pope John XXII. had power to cancel their vows of poverty and chastity.[1]

The discussion ends with certain practical exhortations against taking vows in a trifling spirit, or without seeing clearly what they may involve.[2] Of this second class Beatrice gives two examples: the vows of Jephthah and Agamemnon, which it had been better to break, since they involved the slaying of their innocent daughters in sacrifice. She warns Christians that

---

[1] Lea, *A History of the Inquisition*, iii. 77.

[2] 'A person vowing makes in a certain way a law for himself, binding himself to something that is ordinarily and for most cases good. But it may happen that in a particular case the thing proves either simply evil, or useless, or a hindrance to greater good; which is against the idea of what falls under a vow. And therefore it is necessary to have it ruled in such a case that the vow is not to be observed' (*Summa*, ii-ii. q. lxxxviii. a. 10).

they must neither vow on every slight occasion, as if
they were feathers moved by every breath of wind;
nor, having vowed, imagine that the guilt of unfaithfulness can be lightly washed away with a few drops of
holy water. Nay, she hints plainly enough that vows
are not necessary for salvation:

> 'Ye have the Old and the New Testament,
>   And the Shepherd of the Church who guideth you:
>   Let this suffice you unto your salvation.'

We may compare with this the passage in the *Convito*
(iv. 28) in which, with special reference to marriage,
Dante declares religious vows unnecessary for salvation: 'Not he alone turns to religion who makes
himself in habit and life like St. Benedict and St.
Augustine and St. Francis and St. Dominic, but also
it is possible to turn to a good and true religion whilst
remaining in matrimony, for God wishes nothing
religious of us but the heart. And therefore St. Paul
says to the Romans: "He is not a Jew, which is one
outwardly; neither is that circumcision which is outward in the flesh: but he is a Jew which is one
inwardly; and circumcision is that of the heart, in the
spirit, not in the letter; whose praise is not of men but
of God."' Aquinas, of course, held equally that religious
vows, while essential to perfection, are not necessary
to salvation; but it is evident that on the question of
the superior ethical power of vows, Dante parts
company with his master. It is difficult to believe that
he would have accepted the following: 'The same
work done with a vow is better and more meritorious
than without a vow, for three reasons. First, because
to vow is an act of religion, which is the chief of the
moral virtues. . . . And therefore the acts of the other
moral virtues, as of abstinence and of chastity, are
better and more meritorious for being done by vow,
because thus they come to belong to divine worship
as sacrifices offered to God. Secondly, because he who
both vows a thing and does it accordingly, subjects
himself to God more thoroughly than another, who

simply does the thing; for he subjects himself to God,
not only as to the act, but also as to the power, because
henceforth he has it not in his power to act otherwise:
as he who should give a man the tree with the fruit,
would give more than another who gave the fruit only.
Thirdly, because by a vow the will is clamped fast to
good; but to do a thing with a will, firm set on good,
belongs to the perfection of virtue, as obstinacy in sin
is an aggravation of the sin.'[1]   At all events, Dante
appeals to Christians to be on their guard against the
wicked greed which will tell them that the Old and the
New Testament and the Shepherd of the Church are
not sufficient to salvation, and induces them to take
vows under promise of an easy absolution for the
breaking of them.   The reference is said to be to the
Friars of St. Anthony, popularly known as *fratres de
campanella*, who for a trifling payment absolved from
all vows.[2]   The very Jews, who had only the one guide,
the Old Testament, and kept their vows better, mocked
at such laxity.   Christians who were guilty of it are
like a silly and wanton lamb which leaves his mother's
milk to fight with his own self for his own pleasure:
'the mother's milk' is the true guidance to salvation
which has just been pointed out; and the 'fighting
with his own self' well describes the pastime of lightly
making and lightly breaking vows—the will fighting
against the will.[3]

[1] *Summa*, ii-ii. q. lxxxviii. a. 6 (Rickaby's transl.). If Dante, as is not
improbable, ever contemplated joining the Franciscan Order, the casting
away of the Cord in *Inf*. xvi. 106-114 may be taken as corroboration of his
distrust of vows for salvation. The subject is discussed in my *Exiles of
Eternity*, 254-259, and *Prisoners of Hope*, 16-20. In the latter, the Cord
which he cast away is contrasted with the rush with which Virgil girt
him on the shore of Mount Purgatory.

[2] *Par*. v. 64-81. '*They eat up the sin of my people* (Hosea iv. 8), as if
He said: "They exact the price of sins for their own profit, but for the
sinners they do not take the care which is due." Whom will you find
among those who are set over the government of the Church who is not far
more intent upon emptying the purses of those under his authority than of
rooting up their sins?' (St. Bernard on the Canticles, Sermon lxxvii.
Eales' transl.). The evil was not confined to an obscure order of friars.

[3] *Par*. v. 82-84.

CHAPTER IV

SECOND HEAVEN—MERCURY : LOVERS OF GLORY

1. *The Emperor Justinian and the Code*

TURNING now to 'that part where the world is most living,' Beatrice by her silence and changed look checked the new questions that were rising in Dante's mind. In a moment, like an arrow that strikes the mark before the bowstring ceases to quiver, they find themselves in Mercury, the second Heaven.[1] The joy of his Lady on entering was so greatly increased that the planet grew more luminous for her presence; and, says Dante, with one of his swift flashes of light upon himself,

> If the star itself was changed and smiled,
> What then did I, who by my very nature am
> Susceptible to change through every guise![2]

It is not improbable that we have here a hint of Dante's belief in the astrology of his day. Elsewhere he tells us that his genius, whatever it was, came from Gemini, the sign under which he was born; and, according to the astrologers, Gemini is the 'house' of Mercury.[3]

[1] It is to be noted that Dante follows all the ancient systems of Astronomy in transposing the true position of Mercury and Venus relatively to the earth and the sun. Dr. Moore traces this error to the periods of their orbital motions : 'It was not unnaturally assumed that their relative proximity [to the earth] was proportionate to their periods of apparent revolution round the earth. Thus (1) the moon, one month ; (2) Mercury, c. 88 days (sidereal) or c. 116 (synodical); (3) Venus, c. 225 (sidereal), c. 584 (synodical), and so on.' When Dante looks down from the sign of Gemini on the solar system, he sees Mercury and Venus in the same transposed order (*Par.* xxii. 139 ff.). See Dr. Moore, *Studies in Dante*, 3rd series, 27-29.   [2] *Par.* v. 97-99.

[3] *Par.* xxii. 112-120: see below, p. 359. Comp. R. A. Proctor's *Myths and Marvels of Astronomy*, chap. i., in which a short popular account of Astrology is given. 'Gemini is the house of Mercury. The native of Gemini will have a sanguine complexion and tall, straight figure, dark eyes quick and piercing, brown hair, active ways, and will be of exceedingly ingenious intellect' (p. 23). For the limitations of Dante's belief in the stars, see above, pp. 10, 85.

From this, therefore, came a certain 'mercurial' temperament—not mere fickleness, but an openness to impressions, to rapid movements of the mind and alternations of emotion. The words are perhaps an expression of his sympathy with the spirits of this star : he shares with them the quick mercurial temperament which responds to every change of praise and censure. Another meaning may be found in the mutual joy of Beatrice and the planet. In the *Convito* (ii. 14) Mercury stands for the science of Dialectics. The joy of Beatrice or Theology as she enters Mercury may well be the delight of the theologian in the application of dialectic to the subject of his study, a delight in which, as the whole poem shows, Dante had his full share. On the other hand, the entrance of Beatrice gave a new brightness to the planet : a symbolical way of saying that dialectic gains clearness and beauty when applied to theology, the highest subject of human thought. To quote Landino, 'Mercury has influence on doctrine and eloquence. . . . Beatrice, that is to say, Christian theology, causes Mercury to shine; because in no other religion is its influence more apparent than in ours. And, according to the astrologers, it has a great part in the Christian religion, because in the nativity of our Redeemer, the infrangible and immutable rock on which is built the Christian Church, Mercury was found in Gemini its mansion, and in the ninth house, which is the house of religion and of faith : through the influence of which our doctors, both by wisdom and by eloquence, have conquered all the writers of every other religion.'

It is necessary now to have an outline of the narrative clearly before our minds. The moment the Pilgrims enter the planet, 'more than a thousand splendours' flash towards them. One of these reveals himself as the great Emperor Justinian, who, after a short account of his own life and work, enters into a long narration of the victorious march of the Roman Eagle from the day when Pallas died to give it empire, to the time when Charlemagne defended Holy Church from the Lombards. The object of this historical review is to show the Guelphs and Ghibellines their sin in their different attitudes to 'the standard sacrosanct,' to which God had given this long unbroken career of victory. Justinian then points out the spirit of Romeo, whose services had been so ill requited by his master, Raymond Berenger IV. of Provence. When the splendours vanish like swift sparks, Beatrice instructs Dante on certain theological mysteries which arise out of Justinian's discourse, and, in particular, the Atonement.

Let us now proceed to gather out of this narrative the symbolic correspondences between these spirits and their Heaven. Like the Moon, Mercury lies within the shadowy cone of Earth, though not so deeply; and this implies, as we have seen, that some earthly frailty falls like a shadow on its blessedness. The frailty is a certain love of their own glory with which these spirits dimmed their desire for the glory of God. They wrought great and good deeds, but with a divided heart. In Justinian's words,

'This little star doth furnish forth herself
With the good spirits who have active been,
That honour and fame should wait upon them;
And whensoever the desires mount thither,
Thus deviating, it is but meet the rays
Of the true love should mount up with less life.' [1]

Their activity, in contrast with the slow movements of the cloistered virtue of the Moon, is set forth in various figures. The eagerness with which they rush to meet Dante is like that of fishes in a clear and tranquil pool,

---

[1] *Par.* vi. 112-117. If Boccaccio is to be believed, this very alloy of vainglory was what drew Dante himself into the strife of politics in Florence which proved his ruin. 'When he saw that his labour was in vain [in trying to reconcile the factions], and perceived that the minds of his hearers were hardened, supposing it to be a judgment of God he at first purposed utterly to withdraw himself from every public office, and live in private to himself; but afterward, drawn on by the sweetness of glory, and the vain favour of the people, and further by the persuasions of his elders, and beside all this thinking that should the occasion come he would be able to do far more good for his city if he were a great power in public affairs than as a mere private man, far removed from public place,—oh foolish longing for human splendours, how far mightier is thy strength than he who has not tried it would believe! this man, in his mature age, brought up, nourished, and instructed in the bosom of Philosophy, having before' his eyes the fall of ancient kings and modern, the desolation of kingdoms, provinces and cities, the furious rushes of fortune which aim only at exalted things, yet had not the wit or had not the power to resist thy sweetness!' (*Life of Dante*, Wicksteed's Transl.).

when something falls which they think may be their
food;[1] and when they depart, it is like swiftest sparks
of fire which veil themselves from his sight 'by
sudden distance,' in obvious contrast to the way in
which Piccarda vanished slowly, like a heavy body
sinking in deep water.[2] Justinian is taken as a typical
instance of this activity: Gibbon, indeed, regards his
perpetual diligence as a danger to the Empire: 'His
repasts were short and frugal: on solemn fasts, he contented himself with water and vegetables; and such
was his strength, as well as fervour, that he frequently
passed two days and as many nights without tasting
any food. The measure of his sleep was not less
rigorous: after the repose of a single hour, the body
was awakened by the soul, and, to the astonishment of
his chamberlains, Justinian walked or studied till the
morning light. Such restless application prolonged
his time for the acquisition of knowledge and the dis-
patch of business; and he might seriously deserve the
reproach of confounding, by minute and preposterous
diligence, the general order of his administration. The
emperor professed himself a musician and architect,
a poet and philosopher, a lawyer and theologian; and,
if he failed in the enterprise of reconciling the Christian
sects, the review of the Roman jurisprudence is a noble
monument of his spirit and industry.' Yet much of
this untiring diligence had its root in his own glory.
'The love of fame,' continues Gibbon, 'was deeply implanted in his breast, but he condescended to the poor
ambition of titles, honours, and contemporary praise;
and, while he laboured to fix the admiration, he forfeited the esteem and affection, of the Romans.'[3]

---

[1] *Par.* v. 100-105.   [2] *Par.* vii. 7-9.
[3] *Decline and Fall*, ch. xliii. In *Summa*, ii-ii. q. cxxxii., Aquinas
discusses the subject of Vainglory. The seeking after glory in itself is
not necessarily a vice: it becomes so when the seeking is for vain or
empty glory. Glory becomes vain in three ways: (1) when the endow-
ment for which we seek glory is unworthy of glory; (2) when the judgment of the man from whom we seek it is worthless; (3) when the seeking is not directed to the due end—the honour of God or the salvation of
men. Vainglory is not necessarily inconsistent with charity, and therefore may not be a mortal sin.

The effects of this vainglory are seen in Mercury in three symbolic forms. The first is that already named, the earthly shadow which rests for ever on this Heaven; or, as Justinian states it without the figure, the desire for honour and fame arrests the rays of the true love, the love of God and man, and makes them mount up with a less living fire. The second is that Mercury is a 'small star'—indeed, 'the smallest star of heaven,' as Dante calls it in the *Convito* (ii. 14). The symbolic meaning is that men who are lovers of their own glory pursue it under the delusion that they are creating for themselves a great heaven, a wide and ample beatitude. In reality, they are narrowing their heaven, dooming themselves to a far lower quality and degree of blessedness than if they had been able to lose themselves in 'the glory of Him who moveth all.' And finally, Mercury is 'the sphere that veils itself to mortals with another's rays.' 'It is more veiled by the rays of the sun,' says the *Convito* (ii. 14), 'than any other star'—the proximity of Mercury to the Sun making it very difficult to see. The meaning turns on the words 'to mortals.' Just as the Heaven of these spirits is made small by their ambition, so also is it veiled even to their fellowmen on earth. In other words, when men see the vainglorious motive shining through a great and good career, they refuse to give the very honour for which the career is run—it grows dim even in their eyes, 'by reason of the glory that excelleth.' They instinctively feel that all human glory is as nothing and vanity beside that of Him who is the Eternal Sun. Thus in both worlds these spirits lose the self-glory for which they toiled.[1]

The visible aspect of Justinian and his companions bears the likeness of their spiritual state. Like the

---

[1] It is a mistake to say the sun means fame, and that these souls therefore lost themselves in the fame of their cause, as Mercury is veiled in the sun's rays (see W. T. Harris, *The Spiritual Sense of Dante's Divina Commedia*, p. 86). The sun is always to Dante the greatest natural symbol of God. He is thinking of the way in which the glory of God quenches the small star of their own glory, for which these men had lived.

souls in the Moon, they are seen by Dante in their
own proper forms, even to the sparkling of their eyes.[1]
This, as we saw, is the sign that they have not lost
themselves completely in the light and love and joy of
God. Nevertheless, though some of the effects of their
vainglory remain in their souls for ever, they are
raised far above the old earthly condition, as Dante
indicates by the variation in the play of light within
and around them.

> ' By the light which through all the heaven is spread
> We are enkindled,' [2]

says Justinian significantly : they no longer draw any
of their light from men. When they first come near,
they are called 'splendours' for the same reason, that
they now reflect the Divine rays; and the change is
heard in the words with which they welcome Dante :
' Lo ! one who shall increase our *loves*,' not our *glories*,
as they would once have said or thought.[3] It is the
same change which is implied in Dante's words to
Justinian :

> ' I see well how thou dost nest thyself
> In thine own light, and drawest it from thine eyes,
> Because they sparkle when thou smilest.' [1]

This is in contrast to the time when he drew his light
from the eyes of others, and nested in the light of
glory which they gave him. Now the light is his own,
drawn from his own eyes, which sparkle with the
inner joy; and in that light he rests content, even as a
bird within her nest.[4] And then comes the last and
greatest change of all, the entire concealment of his
form in light. When Dante asks the Emperor who he
is and why he is in this Heaven, the inner light breaks
forth for very joy and covers him 'with its own ray'
as with a garment—the joy, obviously, of losing
himself in the glorious achievements of the Roman

---

[1] *Par.* v. 124-126.   [2] *Par.* v. 118, 119.   [3] *Par.* 100-105.
[4] Cf. Gal. vi. 4 : 'But let every man prove his own work, and then
shall he have his glorying in regard of himself alone, and not of his
neighbour' (R.V.).

Eagle, 'the bird of God,' of which he proceeds to speak. The time was when the Empire existed for his glory; now the thought that it exists for the glory of God shines through him, until, to use Dante's simile, like the sun it burns away all mists and vapours of self, and hides itself in its own excess of light. But this height of self-forgetfulness is intermittent: in rare and radiant moments these Mercurial spirits are capable of this lofty rapture in which all self is hidden, but their usual condition is that in which Dante first met them. There is, however, no murmuring at the lowness of their Heaven. As Piccarda had peace in the Divine Will, they have joy in the Divine Justice:

> ' But in the commensuration of our wages
> With our desert is portion of our joy,
> Because we see them neither less nor greater.
> Herein doth the Living Justice sweeten so
> Affection in us, that for evermore
> It cannot warp to any wickedness.
> Divers voices make sweet notes below:
> So divers seats in this our life
> Render sweet harmony among these wheels.' [1]

Justinian, in reply to Dante's question, now reveals his identity in a passage which shows the poet's great power of idealizing the facts of history in the interests of his theory of Church and State:

> ' After that Constantine the eagle turned
> Against the course of heaven, which it had followed
> Behind the ancient who Lavinia took, [2]
> A hundred and a hundred years and more

---

[1] *Par.* vi. 118-126.

[2] Aeneas, who married Lavinia, daughter of Latinus, King of Latium. She and her father are named among the heroes of antiquity in *Inf.* iv. 125, 126. For other references see *Purg.* xvii. 34-39; *De Mon.* ii. 3. ' Against the course of heaven' is from west to east; but the idea beneath is that in the founding of Constantinople and the turning back the course of empire, Constantine was going against the will of heaven which had brought the eagle out of that very quarter in order to found the empire at Rome. In *Par.* xx. 55-57, he is described as one who,

> Under a good intent which bore ill fruit
> To give place to the Pastor *made himself a Greek*—

i.e. an enemy of the Trojan race from which Rome sprang (see p. 312 n.).

The bird of God in the extreme of Europe
Held itself, nigh to the mountains whence it issued first ;
And under the shadow of the sacred plumes
It governed the world there from hand to hand,
And, changing thus, upon mine own alighted.[1]
Caesar I was, and am Justinian,
Who, by will of the First Love, whom I feel,
Drew from the laws the redundant and the vain ; [2]
And ere unto the work I was attent,
One nature to exist in Christ, not more,
Believed, and with such faith was I contented.
But the blessed Agapetus, he who was
The chief shepherd, unto the pure faith
Pointed me out the way by his discourse.
Him I believed, and what was in his faith
I now see clearly, even as thou dost see
Each contradiction to be false and true.[3]
So soon as with the Church I moved my feet,
It pleased God of His grace to inspire in me
The lofty labour, and all to it I gave me ;
And to my Belisarius I committed arms,
To whom the right hand of Heaven was so joined
That 'twas a signal that I ought to rest.'[4]

There can be no doubt that this is an adaptation of historical facts—honestly believed in, of course—in

It was probably a point in Justinian's favour that by the victories of Belisarius he had restored Italy to the Empire. Scartazzini notes the anachronism of making the Eagle the Roman standard in the time of Aeneas: it was Marius who first made it the standard of the army. According to a legend, it was an eagle flying from the opposite shore that indicated to Constantine the site of his new capital. Among the places he had thought of was Troy itself.

[1] The seat of Empire was removed to Byzantium in A.D. 324, and Justinian succeeded as Emperor in A.D. 527, just beyond the 200 years here mentioned. The Eagle is here named ' the bird of *God*,' because the Empire became Christian under Constantine ; but when Dante is speaking of its Pagan days when it persecuted the Church, he calls it 'the bird of *Jove*' (*Purg.* xxxii. 112).

[2] Like Buonconte da Montefeltro (*Purg.* v. 88), Justinian feels that all earthly titles pass, and only the naked soul remains. His love of titles was part of his vainglory, and now, in the humility of heaven he lays aside the greatest of them. It belongs also to this humility that in the lines which follow he attributes the glory of his great work on the Laws to the inspiration of the Church, and of his wars to Belisarius.

[3] That is, in every pair of contradictories (e.g. 'all men are mortal'— ' some men are not mortal') if one is true, the other must be false. In the same axiomatic way, Justinian now sees the Divine and human natures in Christ, which seem to contradict one another. See p. 65, on *Par.* ii. 40-45. The reference to Pope Agapetus and Justinian's conversion from the Monophysite heresy is dealt with below.

[4] *Par.* vi. 1-27.

order to show what Dante regarded as the true ideal
relation between Pope and Emperor. 'The blessed
Agapetus' came to Constantinople with no claim of
temporal power or jurisdiction over the Emperor. He
was there indeed on a political errand, as peacemaker between Justinian and the Arian king of the
Ostrogoths, Theodatus. The Patriarch of Constantinople at the time was Anthimus, who was deeply
tainted, like the Empress Theodora who had raised
him to the chair, with the Monophysite heresy that
Christ had but one composite nature—the humanity
being 'a mere accident of the immutable divine
substance.' The Pope refused to communicate with
him, and Anthimus was summoned before the Emperor,
convicted of heresy, and degraded from his see. In
this Dante sees the conversion of Justinian himself
from the same error; and affirms that it was not until
his feet moved with the Church that he was inspired
by Divine grace to his great task of simplifying the
laws, and the right hand of heaven gave success to his
arms. This, to the poet's mind, represents the true
relation between the temporal power and the spiritual.
On the one hand, the Pope exercises his spiritual
knowledge and authority as 'the chief shepherd,' to
lead the Emperor out of heresy into 'the pure faith.'
On the other, the Emperor, humbly accepting the
teaching of his spiritual Father, finds his power of
fulfilling his Divinely appointed task of government
thereby greatly increased, as is promised in the closing
words of the *De Monarchia*: 'Let, therefore, Caesar
be reverent to Peter, as the first-born son should be
reverent to his father, that he may be illuminated
with the light of his father's grace, and so may be
stronger to lighten the world over which he has been
placed by Him alone, who is the ruler of all things
spiritual as well as temporal.'[1]

Unfortunately for the poet's theory, neither dates
nor facts support it. It was the year 536 when
Agapetus came to Constantinople, and therefore

[1] Church's translation.

Justinian's conversion from Monophysitism could not have taken place earlier. But 'the lofty labour' of reducing the wilderness of laws to simplicity, striking out of them 'the superfluous and the useless,' had been accomplished more than two years before, and so could not possibly be the result of the Emperor's conversion to orthodoxy. The work was begun almost immediately after his accession to the throne in A.D. 527. The *Code* was finished in April, 529, after fourteen months' labour. The *Pandects* or *Digest*, a much heavier task, occupied three years, 530-533.[1]

Further, the Emperor's heresy had no existence at the time of the visit of Agapetus to Constantinople. As Neander says, he 'meant to be considered a zealous champion of the Chalcedonian orthodoxy,' and therefore he abhorred the Monophysite party, to which, however, the Empress was as passionately attached. His laborious foible of acting the great theologian and ecclesiastical statesman, made him an easy tool in his wife's hands for the furtherance of her party. He was under the conviction that Anthimus was orthodox, and when Agapetus revealed how he had been fooled, he was furious with indignation and deposed him.[2] The curious thing is that this imperial champion of orthodoxy fell at the very end of his life into the extreme form of the Monophysite heresy known as Aphthartodocetism—that the body of Christ was incorruptible, that, 'even during His earthly life, it was not subjected, by any necessity of nature, to sensuous affections and wants, such as hunger, thirst, and pain; but that, by a free determination of His own will, he subjected Himself to all these things for the salvation of man.' Justinian was preparing to force this heresy upon his people by persecution, and his people to resist, when his opportune death at the age of eighty-three

---

[1] As Gibbon says, ten years had been a short time for such a labour. 'Two thousand treatises were comprised in an abridgment of fifty books; and it has been carefully recorded that three millions of lines or sentences were reduced, in this abstract, to the moderate number of one hundred and fifty thousand' (*Decline and Fall*, chap. xliv.).

[2] Neander, *Church History*, iv. 244-246 (Bohn).

saved the Church from a bitter and sanguinary conflict.[1]

The affectionate reference to 'il mio Bellisar' can be understood only on the supposition that a deep draught of Lethe had washed from Justinian's memory his abominably ungrateful treatment of the great general who had saved the Byzantine Empire from being dismembered by Persians, Vandals and Goths. He held in check Persia, the ancient enemy of Rome; restored to the Empire North Africa from the Straits of Gibraltar to the Syrtes, Sicily, and Italy; and beat back almost from the walls of Constantinople itself the hordes of Bulgarian savages. Yet for these services of forty years he was repaid by his master with a constant suspicion and envy. Twice the wealth which his campaigns had accumulated was confiscated. His refusal at the age of thirty of the offer of the Western Empire, did not save him at sixty from being thrown into prison on suspicion of conspiring against his master's life. If we must set aside as legendary the story that his eyes were put out and the veteran reduced to beg his bread in the streets of the capital, 'Give Belisarius an obolus!' the very existence of such a legend is proof of the ingratitude with which his services were paid. After all this, it is, to say the least, a curious lapse of memory of his own conduct, which allows Justinian to point out the spirit of Romeo as one 'whose beautiful and great work was so ill requited' by his master.[2]

It is not easy to see why this Romeo is in this Heaven at all, his love of glory certainly not lying on the surface. Dante follows the legend current in his day as it is given by Villani. It is uncertain if Romeo was his proper name: Villani takes it as equivalent to a

---

[1] Neander, *Church History*, iv. 267, 268 ; *Decline and Fall*, chap. xlvii.

[2] It is, of course, possible that this is Dante's way of telling us the change which Heaven has wrought in Justinian : he sees now what he did not see on earth—the baseness of rewarding a faithful servant with suspicion and ingratitude. Only one wishes that the *amende* had been made more directly to ' il mio Bellisar ' ! See Finlay, *Greece under the Romans* (2nd ed.), 293, 294 ; 523-525.

pilgrim in general. In the *Vita Nuova* (§ 41) Dante
gives the word the specific meaning of a pilgrim to
Rome.[1] This Romeo, according to Villani, was a
pilgrim who, returning from the shrine of St. James
of Compostella, hearing of the goodness of Raymond,
the last Count of Provence, remained at his court, and
rose into such favour that the Count 'made him master
and steward of all that he had.' The choice proved a
wise one. The Pilgrim increased his master's revenue
threefold; by his wisdom and the treasure he had
accumulated, made him victorious in his war with the
Count of Toulouse; and married the Count's four
daughters to four kings.[2] This 'work, beautiful and
great,' as Justinian calls it, wrought Romeo's ruin. 'It
came to pass afterwards, through envy, which destroys
all good, that the barons of Provence accused the good
Romeo that he had managed the Count's treasure ill,
and they called upon him to give an account[3]; the
worthy Romeo said, "Count, I have served thee long
while, and raised thy estate from small to great, and
for this, through the false counsel of thy people, thou
art little grateful: I came to thy court a poor pilgrim,
and I have lived virtuously here; give me back my
mule, my staff, and my scrip, as I came here, and I
renounce thy service." The Count would not that he
should depart; but for nought that he could do would
he remain; and as he came, so he departed, and no one
knew whence he came or whither he went. But many
held that he was a sainted soul.'[4] In all this it is not

---

[1] 'There are three separate denominations proper unto those who
undertake journeys to the glory of God. They are called *Palmers* who
go beyond the seas eastward, whence often they bring palm-branches.
And *Pilgrims*, as I have said, are they who journey unto the holy House
of Gallicia [i.e. the shrine of St. James at Compostella in the N.W. of
Spain]; seeing that no other apostle was buried so far from his birthplace
as St. James. And there is a third sort who are called *Romers* (*Romei*);
in that they go whither these whom I have called pilgrims went: which
is to say, unto Rome' (Rossetti's translation).

[2] Margherita to Louis IX. of France ; Eleonora to Henry III. of England;
Sanzia to Richard, Earl of Cornwall, afterwards King of the Romans ; and
Beatrice to the brother of Louis IX., Charles of Anjou, who became King
of Sicily and Naples.

[3] Dante says he gave the Count 'seven and five for ten' (vi. 138).

[4] Villani's *Chronicle*, vi. 90 (Miss Selfe's transl.).

easy to find any trace of self-glorying under Romeo's 'beautiful and great work.' Scartazzini sees it in the words with which Justinian ends the story:

> ' Then he departed poor and stricken in years ;
> And if the world could know the heart he had,
> In begging crust by crust his livelihood,—
> Much it praises him—and more would praise.'

It is in this praise of men for his stooping from his comparative affluence to beg his bread that we are to find, according to this commentator, his love of glory— the pride of his humility. The difficulty of this is that this stooping to beggary is not 'the beautiful and great work' so often referred to. I find the love of glory rather in the wounded pride which refused to pardon his master's suspicions and indignantly renounced his service. It was the wounded pride of a man who could not do without praise and appreciation. Perfect humility is independent of praise and blame alike, and finds its satisfaction in the doing of duty for its own sake.[1]

[1] Many commentators rightly find in this passage the poet's sympathy with one whose fate had been so like his own. Both had served ungrateful masters, Provence and Florence ; both had been accused of breach of trust and embezzlement of public moneys ; both had been reduced to begging their bread. If the world knew what it was for a man to do this for the sake of uprightness, it could not withhold its praise. This is the man's true glory.

CHAPTER V

2. *The Roman Eagle and the Atonement*

WHEN Justinian, in answer to Dante's question, had revealed his identity, he added that the 'condition' or nature of his reply made it necessary to say something more; whereupon he enters on a long historical review of the rise and progress of the Roman Empire. The necessity sprang from the evil and unworthy attitude assumed towards 'the standard sacrosanct' by the two great political parties of Dante's day. The Ghibellines appropriated to themselves as a faction the Eagle which was the ensign of universal empire; the Guelphs opposed to it 'the yellow lilies' of France, borne by the house of Anjou; and Dante knows not which have the greater sin.[1] To reveal the iniquity of both, he sets forth the great deeds accomplished by the Roman Eagle, as the sign and proof of its Divine election and mission. The present passage is the third in which this subject is treated, the others being the *Convito*, iv.

---

[1] This is an echo of the Emperor Henry VII.'s repudiation of both parties. Dante's contemporary, Albertino Mussato of Padua, in his *De Gestis Henrici VII. Caesaris*, gives us Henry's indignant refusal to be made a party leader: 'Or has God, the supreme teacher of what is just and right, laid upon me any more venerable command than that I should love my neighbour as myself? Is there any distinction or difference to be made amongst Christians as to who that neighbour is? Is it the German, the Frenchman, the Spaniard, the Suabian, the Lombard, the Tuscan? Is there any one of you who would dare to answer, "It is the Ghibelline"? O infamy! Whereto did I come? Whereto was I sent? . . . Was it to stir again the divisions now waxing feeble? Did Clement, who occupies the seat of God upon earth, incite my expedition for this? Did he seal the commission that I was to subject the Guelfs to the Ghibellines or the Ghibellines to the Guelfs? What is the meaning of this rivalry? The one brings hatred on the name of the Empire and the other on the name of the Church by using them as blinds, at the instigation of that Lucifer who fell' (quoted in Wicksteed and Gardner's *Dante and Giovanni del Virgilio*, p. 14).

4, 5, and the *De Monarchia*, in particular, Book ii.
Perhaps the best introduction to Justinian's historical
review is Dante's conception of the Roman Empire as
it is given in the treatise last named.

In the *De Monarchia* the following three principles
are developed: (1) that universal monarchy—i.e. the
Empire—is necessary for the well-being of the world;
(2) that this universal monarchy belongs by right to
the Roman people, and through them to the emperor;
and (3) that the authority of the emperor comes
directly from God, and not from His vicar the Pope.
Now, it is the second of these principles which underlies
Justinian's survey of Roman history. The argument
is characteristic. By the just will of God, the Roman
people received the office of monarchy over all mankind,
as the noblest people under heaven. The proofs of this
nobility are these. First, the nobility of the father of
the race, Aeneas, in his own virtue and courage, in his
ancestors, and in his marriages. Next, the Divine
miracles wrought for this people. Third, the unselfish
and beneficent policy which made Rome, in Cicero's
words, 'a Protectorate of the whole world,'[1] and the
splendid self-sacrifice of individual citizens for the
public good. In the fourth place, her very success in
gaining empire: many strove for the primacy—she
alone won it, and won it by the ordeal of battle,
individual against individual, nation against nation.
And finally, her relation to the Christian faith: Christ
willed to be born under a decree of Augustus, and
thereby declared the decree just and the jurisdiction
which issued it legal; and also to die under a regular
judge, for if the judge was not appointed by an empire
with jurisdiction over all mankind, then the sin of all
mankind was not punished in Christ. The birth and
the death of our Lord, therefore, are proofs of the
Divine right of Rome to universal empire.

Now, it is the last two of these arguments on which
Justinian bases his review. Rome won the prize of
monarchy by the ordeal of battle, an ordeal in which

---

[1] *Offices*, ii. 8.

'Heaven's right hand' gave her victory for well-nigh two thousand years.[1] The keynote of sacrifice is struck in the death of Pallas, son of Evander, who gave his life in single combat with Turnus, that the Eagle might bear sway.[2] Justinian then passes in rapid review the chief periods of the great struggle by which Rome proved her right to universal empire: the three hundred years and more at Alba Longa; the seven kings and their conquests; the wars of the Republic against Brennus, Pyrrhus, Hannibal, and other foes. Then comes the culminating period when the Republic, passing into the Empire, prepared the way for the time of peace in which the Saviour of the race chose to be born. Under Caesar the Eagle swept in victory from Spain to Troy, from Gaul to 'the hot Nile.' Augustus, the next 'standard-bearer,' brought the world into so profound a peace that the temple of Janus was closed. Then came the crowning glory which made past and future seem small and dim— marvellous to say, the crucifixion of Christ under Tiberius, 'the third Caesar'!

> 'The living Justice which inspireth me
> Granted it, in the hand of him I speak of,
> The glory of doing vengeance for His wrath.'

With Titus it did 'vengeance on the vengeance of the ancient sin,' in the destruction of Jerusalem. And finally, seven hundred years later, Charlemagne, under the Eagle's wings, protected Holy Church from the attacks of the Lombard barbarians.[3]

Nothing could be a greater mistake than to see in

---

[1] Dante (*Conv.* iv. 5) regards David and Aeneas as practically contemporaries. The passage is quoted below, p. 306.

[2] 'Pallas, who was fighting on the side of Aeneas, was slain by Turnus. His death led to that of Turnus, because Aeneas would have spared the latter's life, had he not seen the belt of Pallas, which he was wearing (*Aen.* xii. 940-50). By Turnus' death Aeneas became possessed of Lavinia, and of the kingdom of Latinus. Thus the death of Pallas ultimately caused the eagle to obtain the sovereignty' (Tozer, *English Commentary*).

[3] Mr. Tozer points out that there is here a slight error. The date of Charlemagne's victory over Desiderius, King of the Lombards, was 774; and since he was not crowned Emperor of the West until 800, Charles was not at that time fighting under the wings of the Roman Eagle. 'Dante's error here,' adds Mr. Tozer, 'is of a part with his more serious mistake in *De Mon.* iii. 11, ll. 1-7, where he says Charles was crowned emperor by

this age-long trial by combat any glorification of war for its own sake. To the poet's stern mind it is the dread means used by the Eternal Justice to secure among the nations the survival of the fittest to rule. Once this is secured, the end is peace—peace by the administration of just laws under one imperial head. This is why Justinian is chosen as the representative spirit here : the victories of Belisarius had their chief value in that they secured for the Emperor peace to labour at the laws which should strengthen and extend the *pax Romana* throughout the world. 'The vain titles of the victories of Justinian,' says Gibbon, ' are crumbled into dust; but the name of the legislator is inscribed on a fair and everlasting monument. Under his reign, and by his care, the civil jurisprudence was digested in the immortal works of the *Code*, the *Pandects*, and the *Institutes*; the public reason of the Romans has been silently or studiously transfused into the domestic institutions of Europe; and the laws of Justinian still command the respect or obedience of independent nations. Wise or fortunate is the prince who connects his own reputation with the honour and interest of a perpetual order of men.'[1] This is undoubtedly Dante's conception of the Roman Empire: its long career of war has for its chief end the promulgation of Roman law and the securing thereby of the peace of the world. It is the conception he had learned from Virgil in the famous passage which he quotes in the *De Monarchia* (ii. 7) :

> Excudent alii spirantia mollius aera,
> Credo equidem ; vivos ducent de marmore vultus :
> Orabunt causas melius ; coelique meatus
> Describent radio ; et surgentia sidera dicent:
> Tu regere imperio populos, Romane, memento ;
> Hae tibi erunt artes, pacisque imponere morem,
> Parcere subiectis et debellare superbos.[2]

Adrian I. while the emperor Michael was on the throne of Constantinople —whereas in reality he was crowned by Leo III. during the reign of Irene.' See also Toynbee's *Dante Dictionary* under ' Carlo Magno.'

[1] *Decline and Fall*, chap. xliv.

[2] *Aen.* vi. 847-53. ' Others, I well believe, shall beat out more delicately the breathing bronze ; shall draw from the marble the living features;

Further, in Dante's regard, Rome was as surely chosen of God for the promulgation of Roman law as Israel for the diffusion of the Gospel. In the birth and crucifixion of Christ the two elect peoples met, the Atonement was made, and the Empire became the temporal home and protector of the Church. All this is undoubtedly what Dante saw, and meant to say, in the long survey of Roman history which he puts into the lips of the great Emperor of the East, who thus serves himself heir to the glories of the Western Empire. It is this Eagle, thus chosen and approved of God as the agent of His 'vengeance on the ancient sin' and the protector of His Church, which the Guelphs opposed, and the Ghibellines degraded to the standard of a faction.

After pointing out the soul of Romeo, Justinian sang a hymn of praise to God, and, 'revolving to his own note,' passed with his companions suddenly out of sight, 'like swiftest sparks.' The hymn is a curious mingling of Latin, the language of the Christian Church, and Hebrew, that of the Jewish:

> 'Osanna sanctus Deus Sabaoth,
> Superillustrans claritate tua
> Felices ignes horum malachoth!'[1]

---

plead causes better; describe with the rod the movements of the sky; and tell the rising stars: remember thou, Roman, to rule the peoples with empire; these shall be thy Arts: to impose the custom of peace, to spare the humbled and fight down the proud.' A modern poet applies these words in a fine passage to England:

> 'Yet ever remembering
> The precepts of gold,
> That were written in part
> For the great ones of old—
> " Let other hands fashion
> The marvels of art;
> To thee fate has given
> A loftier part.
> To rule the wide peoples;
> To bind them to thee "
> By the sole bond of loving,
> That bindeth the free.'

(Lewis Morris, *Songs of Two Worlds*, 2nd series, 'The Organ Boy'). The state of Ireland, however, is a curious commentary on such words.

[1] *Par.* vii. 1-3: 'Hosannah! holy God of Hosts, illuming by thy brightness from above the happy fires of these kingdoms.' The note in Toynbee's

It is natural for the great Emperor who had been the master of armies to address the Highest as 'the God of Hosts'; and the reference to His illumination of the spirits in all the realms of Paradise is his confession that there is no glory but that which makes blessed with His light. Justinian has risen for ever above the desire to shine by his own glory.

We come now to the chief theological discourse in the *Paradiso*, its subject being the Atonement, on which all human salvation hangs. It arises from the passage in Justinian's review which relates to the three Roman Emperors—Augustus, Tiberius, Titus—whom Dante connects in a peculiar way with the birth and crucifixion of Christ. The general idea is that through these three 'the Living Justice' wrought 'vengeance on the ancient sin'—the original sin of the race, and then vengeance on that vengeance; and Beatrice [1] explains this marvellous paradox of justice. To understand her exposition, it is necessary to have clearly in mind Dante's view of these three Emperors as set forth in the *De Monarchia*.

That which Justinian specially emphasizes in the victorious career of the Eagle in the hand of Augustus, is the state of peace it secured :

' With him it set the world in so great peace,
That unto Janus was his temple locked ' [2]

Now, although Dante does not here follow out the idea, yet in the First Book of the *De Monarchia* he regards this peace as one Divinely ordained for the birth of Christ. He argues at length that only under a monarch can there exist social unity, freedom, justice, and peace,

---

Dante Dictionary (s.v. 'Deus') is : Dante introduces three Hebrew words here, two of which occur in the Vulgate ('Hosanna,' *Matt.* xxi. 9, 15; *Mark* xi. 9, 10; *John* xii. 13; 'Sabaoth,' *James* v. 4); the third, 'malachoth,' which is a misreading (found apparently in all the MSS. of the Vulgate) for 'mamlachot,' occurs in the Preface to the Vulgate by St. Jerome, known as 'Hieronymi Prologus Galeatus.'

[1] Dante hesitates to ask Beatrice for this explanation. His reverence for even a fragment of her name *Be* or *Ice*—its beginning or ending—hinders him. Some think the reference is to the familiar name 'Bice' which he uses in *Vita Nuova* § 24, and Sonnet xxxii., but the connection here makes this familiarity very improbable.

[2] *Par.* vi. 80, 81.

and that this is confirmed by the condition of peace when Christ was born: 'For if, from the fall of our first parents, which was the turning-point at which all our going astray began, we carry our thoughts over the distribution of the human race and the order of its times, we shall find that never but under the divine Augustus, who was sole ruler, and under whom a per- fect Monarchy existed, was the world everywhere quiet.' This peace of the perfect Monarchy was, he says, 'the fulness of the times' of which Paul writes, 'which the Son of God, when, for the salvation of man, He was about to put on man, either waited for, or, at the moment when He willed, Himself so ordered.' In Book II. 12, he argues, as we have already seen, that the birth of Christ under an edict of the Roman Empire was His acknowledgment of the rightful authority of the Empire: 'I say, then, that if the Roman empire did not exist by right, Christ in being born pre-supposed and sanctioned an unjust thing. . . . But Christ, as Luke, who writes His story, says, willed to be born of the Virgin Mary under an edict of Roman authority, so that in that unexampled census of mankind, the Son of God, made man, might be counted as man: and this was to carry out that edict. . . . Therefore Christ, by His action, enforced the justice of the edict of Augustus, who then wielded the Roman power. And since to issue a just edict implies jurisdiction, it necessarily follows that He who showed that He thought an edict just, must also have showed that He thought the juris- diction under which it was issued just; but unless it existed by right it were unjust.'

This may help us to understand Justinian's words concerning the crowning glory of the Eagle under Tiberius—the crucifixion of Christ:

> 'But what the ensign that doth make me speak
> Had done before, and after was about to do,
> Throughout the mortal realm which to it is subject,
> Becometh in appearance small and dim,
> If in the third Caesar's hand 'tis looked at
> With eye unclouded and affection pure;

Because the Living Justice that inspires me
Granted it, in his hand of whom I speak,
The glory of doing vengeance for His wrath.' [1]

The wrath is the just anger of God against the human
race for its sins; and the 'doing of vengeance' is the
death of Christ, regarded as the bearing of the punishment inflicted by that anger. The extraordinary thing
is that Dante regards the crucifixion as the supreme
glory of Roman justice, inasmuch as it was the agent
by which 'the Living Justice' 'did vengeance for His
wrath.' In the *De Monarchia* (ii. 13) he argues, as we
saw above, that 'if the Roman Empire did not exist by
right, the sin of Adam was not punished in Christ. . . .
It is convenient that it should be understood that
punishment is not merely penalty inflicted on him who
has done wrong, but that penalty inflicted by one who
has penal jurisdiction. And therefore a penalty should
not be called punishment, but rather injury, except
where it is inflicted by the sentence of a regular
judge. . . . If therefore Christ had not suffered by the
sentence of a regular judge, the penalty would not
properly have been punishment; and none could be a
regular judge who had not jurisdiction over all mankind; for all mankind was punished in the flesh of
Christ, who "hath borne our griefs and carried our
sorrows," as saith the Prophet Isaiah. And if the
Roman Empire had not existed by right, Tiberius
Caesar, whose vicar was Pontius Pilate, would not
have had jurisdiction over all mankind.' This astonishing view seems peculiar to Dante. Aquinas refuses
thus to transfigure the greatest of crimes into the most
glorious act of Roman justice. Discussing the guilt of
the various actors in the tragedy, he distinguishes
three degrees: that of the elders of the Jews who knew
that Jesus was the Christ, but were ignorant of His
Divinity (1 Cor. ii. 8); that of the Jewish people who,
less versed in the mysteries of Scripture, did not fully
know Him to be either the Son of God or the Messiah;
that of the Gentiles (in this case, of course, the Romans),

[1] *Par.* vi. 82-90.

whose sin was more excusable in that they were
ignorant of the Law and the Scriptures. Dante, in the
interests of his political theory of the Roman Empire,
transforms this minor degree of guilt into a triumph
of justice.[1]

This brings us to the source of Dante's perplexity—
what the Eagle wrought in the hand of the Emperor
Titus :

> ' Later it ran with Titus to do vengeance
> Upon the vengeance on the ancient sin.'

The reference, as we have seen, is to the destruction of
Jerusalem, by which God took vengeance on the Jews
for the sin of crucifying Christ. But the crucifixion
being itself a just vengeance on the ancient sin, where
is the justice of avenging it?[2] It is one of those

---

[1] *Summa*, iii. q. xlvii. a. 4, 5, 6. It is to be noted that, while all the
chief Jewish agents in the crucifixion are set in the Inferno—Annas,
Caiaphas, Judas—Pilate is not named in any of the Circles. In my
Exiles of Eternity (58-60) I have argued for his identification with 'the
shade of him who made through cowardice the great refusal' (*Inf.* iii.
59, 60). I am glad to find this identification supported in a recent book
by Signor Giovanni Rosadi, *The Trial of Jesus*, chap. xvi : 'To him and
to no others pointed the poet as

colui
Che fece per viltate il gran rifiuto ;

to him, the prototype of that long train of those who were never quite
alive, who vainly sought glory in this world, vainly dreaded infamy; who,
ever wavering betwixt good and evil, washed their hands; who, like the
neutral angels of the threshold, were neither faithful nor rebellious; who
are equally despised by pity and justice; who render themselves

A Dio spiacenti ed ai nemici sui.

And what man other than Pilate was ever placed so typically, in such
accordance with the idea of the poet, between the Son of God and His
enemies, between justice and mercy, between right and wrong, between
the Emperor and the Jews, and has refused either issue of the dilemma?'
(Translation edited by Dr. Emil Reich.) His political theory may compel
Dante to prove the lawful jurisdiction of Rome in the crucifixion, but his
true judgment of the Roman governor is seen in his calling Philip the
Fair 'the new Pilate' for his outrage on Boniface at Anagni (*Purg.* xx.
86-93).

[2] Dante appears to have derived the idea from the *Historiae adversum
Paganos* of Paulus Orosius (see p. 189 below), who says that in the destruction of Jerusalem Titus 'had been ordained by the judgment of God for
the avenging of the blood of the Lord Jesus Christ' (Toynbee's *Dante
Studies and Researches*, 134). Compare the curious apocryphal fragment
of the seventh or eighth century, *The Avenging of the Saviour*, in which
Titus, 'a prince under Tiberius in the region of Equitania, in a city of
Libia which is called Burgidalla,' in gratitude for the cure of a cancer in
his face by the power of Christ, resolves to execute vengeance on His
enemies (*Ante-Nicene Christian Library*, vol. xvi. p. 245).

dialectical paradoxes in which the scholastic mind delighted; and Beatrice cuts the knot by drawing a distinction in Christ between the human nature and the Divine Person—a distinction which may be possible to thought, but could have no existence in the world of reality. Adam, 'that man who was not born,' refused to endure the rein which God put upon his will for his own good—the *frenum concupiscentiae*, as the school-men called that supernatural grace of original justice by which the senses were kept subject to the reason,—and thereby condemned himself and his offspring. In this estrangement the human race lay sick for many an age, until it pleased the Word of God to descend to earth and, by act of His own love alone, unite with Himself in person the very nature which had thus departed from its Maker. So long as it had remained united with its Maker, this nature had no alloy of evil; but turning aside from 'the way of truth and of its own life,' it became self-exiled from Paradise. Hence arises a twofold and apparently contradictory aspect of the crucifixion. Looked at in relation to the nature assumed which fell away from God in self-will, the penalty of the Cross was the perfection of justice. Looked at in relation to the Person who assumed and suffered[1]—the Word of God—there never was so great an injury. Hence also it had the most diverse issues: it pleased both God and the Jews,—God, as the fulfilment of His justice; the Jews, as the expression of their malice. The earth trembled at it in the earthquake, and by it Heaven was opened from 'its long interdict.' This is the way in which it can be said with truth that

[1] From Dante's words in C. vii. 44, 45, we might think that only the Divine Person suffered in the crucifixion. This, of course, is not the meaning. In *Summa*, iii. q. xlvi. a. 12, Aquinas discusses the question whether the Passion of Christ is to be attributed to His Divinity, and replies that Passion is not to be attributed to it by reason of itself, the Divine Nature being impassible, but by reason of the passible Human Nature united with it, in the One Person of the Eternal Word. That is why Dante speaks here of

'the Person who suffered,
In whom there was contracted such a nature,'
i.e. the Human Nature which made the suffering possible.

'a just vengeance
By a just court was afterwards avenged.'[1]

This solution, while it satisfies Dante, only raises another difficulty, namely, 'why God willed for our redemption this mode and no other,' of the Incarnation and the Cross. Might there not have been other ways? The general meaning of the answer of Beatrice is that God chose that mode which gave the greatest scope for the revelation of His goodness. And it is just here that we see the fitness of this discourse to this Heaven. It is the Heaven of those who did great and good things for their own glory. God also does great and good things for His own glory, and chooses that one mode which will best display it. But His glory is His goodness, and the one mode which shares it most widely with sinful man is the humiliation of His Son to the flesh and to the cross. The false glory and the true are therefore set here face to face.

Beatrice begins her discourse by declaring that the condition of understanding the mystery is Love, and Love in its maturity. For this reason, it is much discussed, but little discerned. The necessity for Love in those who would understand it, rises from the fact that the choice of this mode of salvation before all others springs from the pure love of God. The Divine goodness, spurning all envy, sends out from its own inner light such sparkles of its glory as best display 'the eternal beauties.' This out-sparkling of Himself begins in creation, in which, as Aquinas says, 'God willed to communicate to creatures, as much as possible, the perfection of His Goodness.'[2] Now, the

---

[1] *Par.* vi. 91-93; vii. 49-51.

[2] Comp. *Timaeus*, 29: 'Let me tell you why the creator created and made the universe. He was good, and no goodness can ever have any jealousy of anything. And being free from jealousy, he desired that all things should be as like himself as possible. . . . God desired that all things should be good and nothing bad in so far as this could be accomplished' (Jowett's transl.). In *Summa*, iii. q. i. a. 1, Aquinas argues the fitness of the Incarnation from the very nature of the Divine goodness. It pertains to the conception of goodness that it communicates itself to others; and therefore to the conception of the Highest Goodness that it communicates itself in the highest mode, and the highest mode is the Incarnation in which the Divine and human are united.

greatest communication of this goodness takes place
in the case of those beings which are created by the
immediate hand of God, and without the intervention
of second causes. Such is man who, as the direct
creation of God, received from the Divine goodness
three great gifts of likeness to Itself—first, the seal
of immortality; second, freedom from subjection to
second causes, or, as Beatrice calls them, 'the new
things,' because of their later creation ; and third, the
image of the Divine Love, which shines most in that
which most resembles it. These three constitute the
nobility of man in his original state as he left the hand
of God, and if any one of them fails the nobility is lost.
The failure took place in the free-will, which by sin lost
much of its original freedom :

> ' 'Tis sin alone which doth disfranchise him,
> And render him unlike the Good Supreme,
> So that he little with its light is brightened.' [1]

Human nature, thus sinning as a whole 'in its seed,'
the First Parent,[2] lost Paradise, and can recover its
original dignities in one way alone, by filling up the
void which sin has made in the justice of the universe,
by means of a just penalty equivalent to the evil
delight. The only possible alternative to this would be
that God, 'of His sole courtesy,' should grant a free
pardon. Anselm, in his *Cur Deus Homo?* from which
much of the argument here seems to be taken, argues
that to pass sin by without a satisfaction would be to
sanction an irregularity in the order and beauty of the
universe, and to set wicked and righteous on the same

---

[1] *Par.* vii. 79-81.

[2] *Par.* vii. 85-87. The fall of human nature *as a whole* 'in its seed'
constitutes another impossibility in the redemption of man by himself.
'No mere man was able to satisfy for the sin of all mankind, since
every mere man is something less than the whole multitude of mankind.
For the deliverance then of mankind from their common sin, it was
requisite for one to make satisfaction, who was at once man, so that satisfaction should be expected of him, and something above man, so that his
merit should be sufficient to satisfy for the sin of the whole human
race ' (*Contra Gentiles*, iv. 54, Rickaby's transl.). Dante's idea throughout
the present passage is that Christ assumed human nature in its entirety,
and therefore was able to satisfy for the whole race.

level; and the very perfection of God forbids this.
Since, therefore, a satisfaction is absolutely necessary,
has fallen man the power to render it? Beatrice
replies that the very nature of the sin makes this
impossible. It was a sin of pride, and pride which
aimed at the highest — 'to be as gods.' The only
adequate satisfaction would be for man to humble himself as far in the opposite direction—a humiliation
impossible within the limits of his human nature. As
he had sought to soar above his humanity into Divinity,
to restore the moral balance it would be necessary to
stoop into some form of existence which would degrade
him beneath his humanity. Hence God Himself must
undertake the satisfaction by the exact reversal of
Adam's pride. Man aimed at becoming God; God fills
up the moral breach by becoming man. The humiliation of the second Adam is the exact counterpoise of
the pride of the first.[1]

In the rendering of this satisfaction by which man
is reinstated in his full original life, the Divine goodness resolved 'to proceed by all its ways,' in order the
better to reveal the love of the Heart from which it
flowed. The reference is to Psalm xxv. 10: *Universae
viae Domini misericordia et veritas*, 'All the paths of
the Lord are mercy and truth,' or *justice*, as Aquinas
interprets *veritas*: 'The justice of God is fittingly called
truth, because it constitutes the order in things which
conforms to the idea of His wisdom, which is His law.'[2]
It is on these two feet of mercy and justice, to borrow
St. Bernard's quaint figure,[3] that, in the Incarnation,

---

[1] *Par.* vii. 97-102. Compare Augustine quoted in *Summa*, iii. q. i. a. 2:
'The pride of man, which is the greatest hindrance to his cleaving to
God, can be rebuked and healed by the so great humility of God'—i.e. in
the Incarnation. So far as I can see, there is no trace in the passage of
the familiar mediæval idea that the pride of man, being an outrage on
the honour of an infinite Being, requires an infinite satisfaction. 'The
sin being committed against God,' says Aquinas, 'has a certain infinity
from the infinity of the Divine Majesty: for the gravity of the offence is
greater in proportion to the greatness of the person outraged. Hence for
condign satisfaction it needs that the act of him who satisfies should have
an infinite efficacy' (*Summa*, iii. q. i. a. 2).

[2] *Summa*, i. q. xxi. a. 2.

[3] On the Song of Songs, Serm. vi.

God goes forth to the great process of salvation. The Incarnation is a greater revelation of Divine mercy than a mere free pardon, for two reasons: it costs God something, it is the generous giving of Himself; and it enables man 'to uplift himself' to his original state, by the restoration of the gift of grace through which he attains to merit salvation by good works. On the other hand, it secures the Divine justice, in that the humility of the Son of God in becoming man repairs the breach in the moral order caused by the pride of man in seeking to be as God.[1] It is the argument used by Aquinas: 'That man be set free by the Passion of Christ was fitting both to His mercy and to His justice. To justice on the one hand, because by His Passion Christ made satisfaction for the sin of the human race, and thus man by the justice of Christ was set free; to mercy on the other, because since man by himself had no power to satisfy for the sin of the whole of human nature, God gave His Son to make satisfaction, according to the passage (Rom. iii. 24): *Being justified freely by his grace through the redemption that is in Christ Jesus: whom God hath set forth to be a propitiation, through faith, in his blood:* and this was a more abundant mercy than if he had remitted the sins without satisfaction.'[2] In another passage Aquinas states that while God, by virtue of His omnipotence, might have restored mankind in many other ways, that of the Incarnation was the best fitted to secure our salvation by giving us a foundation for *faith*, a ground of *hope*, and an incentive to *charity*—the virtues without which man can never receive the Beatific Vision.[3]

We come now to a final question rising out of a passage in the preceding discourse. In vii. 67-69 Beatrice, speaking of the Divine goodness, had said:

---

[1] *Par.* vii. 103-120. In *Summa*, iii. q. xlix. a. 6, Aquinas says that 'Christ in His Passion humbled Himself beneath His dignity in four respects: (1) as to His Passion and death, to which He was not a debtor; (2) as to place, since His body was laid in the tomb, and His soul in Hell; (3) as to the confusion and opprobrium which He bore; (4) in that He was delivered into the power of man.'

[2] *Summa*, iii. q. xlvi. a. i.

[3] *Summa*, iii. q. i. a. 2.   See below on *Par.* xxxiii. 127-141, p. 535 f.

'Whatso from It immediately distils
Thereafter hath no end, for never removed
Is Its imprint, whene'er It sets the seal.'[1]

In other words, what God creates without any intervening medium is for that reason immortal and
incorruptible: how can this be true when we see fire,
air, earth, and all the compounds of them 'come to
corruption and endure but little'? Are these things
not 'creatures,' and if so, why are they not secure
against corruption? Beatrice replies by explaining
that creation properly so-called is when a thing is
brought into existence in its entire being 'even as it is'
—that is, without transformation from previously
created substances, or through previously created
agencies. The Angels and the Heavens ('the pure
country in which thou art,' ll. 130, 131) are examples
of this immediate creation—creation proper out of
nothing. But the elements and all their compounds
are informed by a power which was itself created: the
prima materia of the elements and the virtue in the
stars which gives to this first matter its specific 'forms';
and these are the immediate incorruptible creations out
of which the corruptible elements issue. Similarly, the
souls of brutes and plants—the 'sensitive' and 'vegetative' souls—are drawn into existence, not immediately by God, but by the stars, 'the ray and movement
of the holy lights,'[2] acting on what Beatrice calls
complession potenziata, 'potentiated constitution' or
'temperament' — that is, a temperament with a
potency to become sensitive and vegetative souls, and
therefore subject to corruption. But it is otherwise
with the rational human soul, which is immortal
because inbreathed immediately by the Highest Goodness, which enamours it with a never-ending yearning
for Itself. From this principle that whatever is
immediately created by God is incorruptible, Beatrice
invites Dante to draw the inference of the resurrection
of the body. The flesh of the First Parents came with-

---

[1] *Par.* vii. 67-69. See p. 219 f.
[2] 'The *rays* of each heaven are the way by which their virtue descends
on things here below' (*Conv.* ii. 7). See above, p. 18.

out medium from the hand of God,[1] and is therefore
imperishable; and Dante apparently regards the bodies
of their descendants as sharing in the same imperishable nature. It is not easy to reconcile this with the
doctrine of the Church, or with Dante's own words in
this Canto. According to Aquinas, the bodies of the
First Parents, though created immediately by God, had
no inherent immortality by nature : immortality was
a distinct gift of grace, bestowed in the act of creation.
On account of sin this gift was withdrawn, and their
bodies lapsed back to their natural liability to corruption; and it is only by the restoration of grace through
the Incarnation and Passion of Christ, that the resurrection becomes possible.[2] This, indeed, seems to be

[1] In *Summa*, i. q. xci. a. 2, Aquinas says 'the first formation of the
human body could not be by any created virtue, but immediately by God,'
to whom alone belongs the power to create form without any natural
precedent form. Hence the first man must have been created by God,
since there existed then no other from whom by means of generation a
like species could have originated. He adds that 'there may have been
some ministry of Angels in this formation of the first human body, as
there may be afterwards in the resurrection. In *Summa*, q. xcii. a. 4,
he adds that woman was also formed immediately by God, since, being
made of other matter than that from which man is usually generated,
she could have been made by no other.

[2] In *Summa*, i. q. xcvii. a. 1, Aquinas says that man in a state of innocence would have been immortal, not because his body possessed any
inherent power of incorruptibility, but because of a supernatural gift
bestowed on his soul by which the body would have been preserved from
corruption so long as he remained subject to God. Although Adam after
the Fall recovered grace and the power of meriting glory, he did not
immediately recover his lost immortality. That comes only through the
resurrection of Christ, which is the source and model of ours. A passage
in *Contra Gentiles* (iv. 81) may be quoted: 'In the first creation of
human nature God endowed the human body with an attribute over and
above what was due to it by the natural principles of its constitution,
namely, with a certain imperishability, to adapt it to its *form*, that as the
life of the soul is perpetual, so the body might perpetually live by the soul.
Granting that this imperishability was not natural in regard to its active
principle [i.e. the "organism" of the body, as Father Rickaby, whose
version I quote, explains it], still it may be called natural in regard of the
end, taking the end of matter to be proportioned to its natural form.
When then, contrary to the order of its nature, the soul turned away from
God, there was withdrawn from the body that God-given constitution
which made it proportionate to the soul; and death ensued. Considering
then how human nature was actually constituted to begin with, we
may say that death is something which has accidentally supervened upon
man through sin. This accident has been removed by Christ, who by the
merit of His passion and death has destroyed death. Consequently that
same divine power, which originally endowed the body with incorruption,
will restore the body again from death to life.'

Dante's own view in the passage expounded above; [1]
yet here he appears to assume another source of the
resurrection of the body—the immediacy, namely, of its
creation by God. His meaning, however, may be that
this immediacy forms the very ground and possibility
of the restoration of physical immortality : had man's
body come from any other than God's own hand, even
the Resurrection of Christ might have been powerless
to rescue it from the bondage of its own natural
corruption.

[1] *Par.* vii. 67-120.

CHAPTER VI

THIRD HEAVEN—VENUS: LOVERS

1. *Cycle and Epicycle.   Carlo Martello*

THE only sign by which Dante was made aware that
he had risen to Venus, the third Heaven,[1] was the
increase of beauty in his Lady.   A circle of spirits in
the form of lights suspend their dance and flash
toward the newcomers more swiftly than the lightning.   One soul reveals himself as the poet's friend,
Carlo Martello,[2] eldest son of Charles II. of Naples,
who tells him of the vast dominion over which he
would have ruled had he been spared.   In reply to
Dante's question he explains how degenerate children
may spring from noble parents.   Then Cunizza, sister
of the tyrant Ezzelino III. da Romano, points out the
soul of Folco the troubadour of Marseilles, and he in
turn that of Rahab the harlot, the name of whom
rouses Dante's indignation against the Pope and the
Cardinals for their abandonment of Holy Land to the
infidels.

We have now to trace the symbolic correspondences
of the star to the souls whom Dante sees in it.   It
represents the Heaven possible to those who on earth
divided their hearts between two diverse loves: the

[1] For the transposition of Mercury and Venus, see note on p. 99.

[2] Mr. Vernon complains that commentators do not warn their readers
that this Charles Martel is not the famous Duke of Austrasia who, in
A.D. 732, gained the great victory over the Saracens between Tours and
Poitiers.   The omission is not unnatural : it may surely be taken for
granted that a contemporary of Dante in the thirteenth century is not a
man who lived in the eighth.   The *Martel* here, Mr. Vernon reminds us,
does not mean a *Hammer* as in the case of the earlier Charles, but is
'merely a common mediæval form for *Martin*.'

love of God, else there had been no heaven for them;
and the unworthy love of some fellow-creature, else
their heaven had been higher. It is essential to
understand clearly what this unworthy love is. It is
a mistake to identify it, as is sometimes done, with
the simple, natural human love of family and friends.
It is the heaven of lovers, says one writer, 'and includes the conjugal, the parental, the filial, and the
fraternal, as well as the love of friends. Terrestrial
love is connected with a limitation,—devoted to a
special object, parent, child, husband, wife, brother,
sister, or friend. Such love is of the same nature
fundamentally as celestial love or Divine Charity.
But there is a particular limitation in the former
which prevents its complete identity. . . . It is allied
to selfishness in the fact that it is thus limited to those
near it, or connected by natural ties.'[1] The entire
passage which treats of this Heaven shows that Dante
was thinking of a far different love. The opening
lines of Canto viii. strike the keynote by their
reference to 'the beautiful Cyprian,' the goddess
Venus, whose star was believed by the ancient world
'in its peril' to ray down 'mad love,' the lust which
overflows the limits of the wise love of nature and
reason. The classical example given is Dido, in whose
lap Cupid, the son of Venus, sat in the form of
Ascanius, the son of Aeneas; and Dido is placed in the
Circle of the Sensual in the Inferno.[2] If any doubt
remained, it would be dispelled by a glance at the souls
whom Dante singles out for mention. There might
be some uncertainty about Charles Martel, but there
is none whatever about Cunizza, Folco, and Rahab.
It is this sensual love which lies like the shadow of
earth upon their Heaven: a heart which has thus
yielded itself to an impure love can never be
illuminated as it might have been with the unclouded light of Him who is the Eternal Love and
Purity. Nevertheless, it is to be noted that Venus is

---

[1] W. T. Harris, *The Spiritual Sense of Dante's Divina Commedia*,
p. 88.   [2] *Inf.* v. 85.

the Heaven in which the shadowy cone of earth 'comes to a point':[1] evil as such love is, it does not, in Dante's view, sink the soul so deeply into the shadow as what might seem the lighter sins of Mercury and the Moon.

Now, the planet Venus corresponds to this twofold power of love in a peculiar way to which Dante draws special attention when he says that it 'revolves in the third epicycle.'[2] 'On the summit of this circle in the Heaven of Venus,' he says in the *Convito* (ii. 4), 'is a small sphere which revolves of itself in that Heaven; the circle of which the astrologers call an *epicycle*.' Now, it is important to understand the cycle and epicycle of Venus, because they represent in the poet's symbolism that twofold movement of the human heart already spoken of—one round God, and one round some unworthy object of earth. 'Epicycle' is a term of the Ptolemaic system of astronomy, according to which the heavenly bodies, as explained in the Introduction, revolve round the Earth as the fixed centre of the universe. The Sun, for example, goes round the Earth in a simple circle or cycle. Venus also goes round the Earth, but not in a mere cycle: by another motion she appears sometimes as morning star, sometimes as evening star,—in Dante's words, she

Wooes the sun now from behind, now from before.[3]

This is her epicyclic motion—a motion like that of a

<hr />

[1] *Par.* ix. 118, 119.

[2] I take the liberty of borrowing this diagram from Toynbee's *Dante Dictionary* (p. 530), adapting it to the case before us. S, the Sun, revolves round E, the Earth, the fixed centre of the universe, carrying V, Venus, with it, so that the cycle of the Sun involves also the cycle of Venus. But as Venus is thus carried round in her *cycle*, she is all the time revolving round the Sun in the smaller circle, which is her *epicycle*. As Toynbee says, this theoretical movement of the planet with regard to the Earth in the Ptolemaic system is 'similar to the actual movement of the Moon, as the satellite of the Earth, about the Sun in our solar system.'

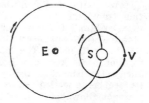

[3] *Par.* viii. 12.

satellite round the Sun. It may be said that Dante did not conceive of Venus as such a satellite; but I am not so sure of this. When from the height of the Heaven of the Fixed Stars he looks down on the seven spheres, he tells us that he saw the Sun,

> and how there move
> *Around and near to him* Maia and Dione,[1]

Maia and Dione being Mercury and Venus named after their mothers; and this certainly seems to imply that he conceived of these inferior planets as virtually satellites of the Sun. If so, then the movements are these. First, the Sun makes his revolution round the Earth, carrying Venus with him as a satellite, so that his *cycle* is also hers. But in addition she performs a revolution of her own round him, and this constitutes her *epicycle*. Translating all this into its spiritual equivalent, the meaning appears to be: as Venus had one movement round the Earth and another round the Sun, so these souls had two movements of the heart, cyclic and epicyclic, one round some earthly centre, the other round God, of whom the Sun is the natural symbol. This divided and twofold life of theirs is again hinted at in the passage in which Dante compares them to a spark within a flame, and a voice within a voice:

> And as within a flame a spark is seen,
> And as within a voice a voice discerned,
> When one is steadfast, and one goes and comes,
> Within that light beheld I other lamps
> Move in a circle, speeding more and less
> In measure, I believe, of their eternal vision.[2]

---

[1] *Par.* xxii: 142-144. Butler, however, following a different punctuation, translates: 'how he (the Sun) moves around, and Maia and Dione near to him.' I follow the pointing of the Oxford edition. See Dr. Moore's *Studies in Dante*, 3rd series, p. 40, note.

[2] *Par.* viii. 16-21. The reference of *voce ferma* in ll. 17, 18 is to the form of music known in Italian as *canto fermo*, firm or fixed song, 'the ancient traditional vocal music of the Christian church : so called because, its form being settled and its use prescribed by ecclesiastical authority, it was not allowable to alter it in any manner. It was originally sung in unison, or in octave only, and in its strictest form one note was assigned to each syllable of the words. After the third century it was allowable to add other parts in harmony with the canto fermo, which was then assigned to the tenor voice and sung without change, the other parts

It adds much to the probability and the interest of this interpretation that it is based on Dante's own experience, as he hints in the line of one of his poems which he makes his friend Charles Martel quote:

' Ye who by intellect the third heaven move.' [1]

This is the opening line of Canzone I. of the *Convito*, and is addressed to the Angelic Intelligences that move the sphere of Venus as an appeal to rescue him from this very conflict of two loves within his heart. One draws him heavenward to Beatrice:

> The life of my sad heart is wont to be
> One gentle thought the which would take its way
> Full many a time even to your Sire's feet,
> Where a Lady it beheld in glory,
> Of whom it spoke to me so sweetly
> That my soul said, ' I, too, would go !'

This Godward movement of his heart, however, is immediately followed by another in a different direction:

> Now appeareth one who putteth it to flight,
> And lords it over me with so great power
> The trembling of my heart appears without.

The story of this struggle is told in the closing sections of the *Vita Nuova*, in which, after the death of Beatrice, he curses his eyes that he cannot withhold them from another lady.[2] The veil of allegory which

moving above and below it in counterpoint more or less free. . . . These additional parts, being more elaborate and ornamental than the canto fermo, were called, in contradistinction to it, *canto figurato*' (*Century Dictionary*).

[1] *Par.* viii. 37.

[2] See especially § xxxviii.: 'At length, by the constant sight of this lady, mine eyes began to be gladdened overmuch with her company; through which thing many times I had much unrest, and rebuked myself as a base person: also, many times I cursed the unsteadfastness of mine eyes, and said to them inwardly: "Was not your grievous condition of weeping wont one while to make others weep? And will ye now forget this thing because a lady looketh upon you? who so looketh merely in compassion of the grief ye then showed for your own blessed lady. But whatso ye can, that do ye, accursed eyes! many a time will I make you remember it! for never, till death dry you up, should ye make an end of your weeping"' (Rossetti's translation).

he draws over this in the *Convito* cannot hide the
true original meaning.   Probably therefore the whole
conception of this Heaven of Venus as the only
Paradise of the divided heart, had its root in Dante's
own experience : he felt himself circling round some
earthly love unworthy of him ; yet he was conscious
all the time that his soul had never really forgotten
Beatrice, but was moving round her in an epicycle of
true heavenly love.

We turn now to the symbolic forms by which Dante
indicates the celestial condition and blessedness of
these spirits of Venus, and the way in which the
higher love now rules their life.   Almost the first
thing he marks in them is the swiftness of their
motion as they draw near to him, singing *Hosanna* :

> From a cold cloud never descended winds,
> Or visible or not, with so great swiftness,
> That they would not appear restrained and slow
> To any one who had those lights divine
> Seen come toward us, leaving the circling
> Whose first beginning is in the high Seraphim.[1]

The 'winds or visible or not' are hurricanes or lightnings, lightnings being, according to Aristotle, winds
made visible by ignition.[2]   The comparison indicates
the eager, swift, mysterious movements of love, as in
the passage Canticles viii. 6, which was probably in
Dante's mind : 'the flashes thereof are flashes of fire,
a very flame of the Lord.'[3]   It is now the eagerness of
unselfish love which suspends the circling of its own
joy to increase the joy of the strangers : 'We are all
ready to thy pleasure that thou mayest have joy of
us,' are the first words of Carlo Martello.

It is to be noted too that the spirits of this star, unlike
those of the Moon and Mercury, are invisible to Dante
in their own proper forms.   His friend, Charles Martel,

---

[1] *Par.* viii. 22-27.
[2] *Meteor.* II. ix. ; III. i.   See Moore, *Studies in Dante*, 1st series, **p.**
132.
[3] Revised Version.   Dante would read it in the Vulgate : 'lampades
eius lampades ignis atque flammarum.'

explains that it is the intensity of his joy which hides
him with its light, like a silkworm in its cocoon:

> 'My gladness keepeth me concealed from thee,
>   Which rayeth round about me, and doth hide me,
>   Like an animal in its own silk enswathed.'[1]

It is a mistake to say, as is sometimes done, that this
is a mere temporary concealment due to the sudden
increase of joy caused by this meeting with his friend.
Doubtless there was this increase of joy, and therefore
of light, for Dante expressly says so;[2] but from the
very first he describes them as 'lamps' and 'sparks'
within a flame.   There is no indication that at any
time he saw them in their own proper forms.   The
reason, as already explained,[3] is that the souls in this
and the remaining Heavens have lost *self*: their greater
vision creates greater love, and greater love greater
joy, joy which rays round them an aureole of conceal-
ing light:

> By joy up there is brightness won,
>   Even as a smile down here.[4]

The idea is virtually that of Tennyson's well-known
lines, except that Dante is thinking of a higher love:

> 'Love took up the harp of Life, and smote on all the chords
>   with might;
>   Smote the chord of Self, that, trembling, pass'd in music
>   out of sight.'[5]

The music is here too: the souls flash toward Dante
singing *Hosanna*, for love and joy cannot but fulfil
themselves in praise.

Further, Dante tells us that these souls, though they

---

[1] *Par*. viii. 52-54.   [2] *Par*. viii. 46-48.   [3] See pp. 14, 68, 104.
[4] *Par*. ix. 70, 71.   I am not using the word 'aureole' here in its
theological sense.   Aquinas uses it for a certain accidental reward superadded to the essential bliss of Paradise for some excellent victory gained
during the earthly warfare.   There are three aureoles—of virgins, of
martyrs, of doctors and preachers.   'Virgins have triumphed with special
glory over the flesh ; martyrs, over the world, which persecuted them to
death ; preachers, over the devil, whom they have driven, not only from
their own hearts, but also from those of others' (Addis and Arnold's
Catholic Dictionary).   The subject is discussed at great length in *Summa*,
Supp., q. xcvi.   Obviously the aureole in this sense could not be given
to the souls in Venus.   [5] *Locksley Hall.*

must bear for ever the spiritual consequences of their cyclic and epicyclic love, have nevertheless escaped from that duplicity of movement, and attained to the peace of one single revolution around God. This is undoubtedly the general meaning, although it is not easy to work it out in detail. The first hint of this unity of motion is the circling in which Dante finds them engaged on his arrival, and which they suspend in order to speak to him. It is 'the circling first begun in the high Seraphim'; and since the Seraphim are the Order of Angels nearest God, burning with His Love, and revolving most swiftly with longing for Him, the obvious meaning is that these spirits of Venus are now being swept in that one single movement of the Highest Love which turns all the spheres. Charles Martel by a threefold repetition emphasizes this unity of movement, in relation to the Order of the Principalities which rules this third sphere:

> ' We turn around with the celestial Princes
> In one circle, and one circling, and one thirst,
> To whom thou in the world of old didst say :
> *Ye who by intellect the third heaven move.*' [1]

This line, as we have just seen, is the beginning of the first Canzone of the *Convito*, and is addressed to the Angelic Movers of this Heaven of Venus, not, as Plumptre suggests, because Dante had 'a paternal fondness' for it, but because, as I have shown, it is his own personal experience which fills these Cantos. When he wrote it his heart was divided between a higher and a lower love ; and now these souls tell him that they, after the same struggle, have attained to peace, and turn 'in one circle, and one circling, and one thirst' with the Movers of this Heaven, to whom once he had addressed his prayer. There seems also to be a pathetic reason for putting this line in the mouth

---

[1] *Par.* viii. 34-37. In l. 35, the 'one circle' (*un giro*) seems to mean this special sphere of Venus in its revolution; the 'one circling' (*un girare*), the one same rate of motion with the Principalities; and the 'one thirst' (*una sete*), the same intensity of longing for God which produces the 'circling.' The point of the emphasis is the *unity* of their motion now—the double movement of the divided heart is for ever past.

of Charles Martel. From a comparison of the dates
mentioned in *Convito* ii. 2, at the beginning, and 13,
ll. 49-69, it is inferred that this Canzone was written in
March, 1294, the precise time when Charles, as we shall
see, visited Florence. ‘Can we doubt,’ asks Mr. Vernon,
‘that Dante then communicated it to his royal friend,
who probably expressed his admiration of it? The
death of Charles occurred within the year, and the
friends do not appear to have met again. It is a touching incident that their first greeting in Paradise should
recall the words of the song which was associated with
their last intercourse on earth!’[1]

There is, however, some difficulty in reconciling
Charles Martel’s words here with Dante’s in the *Convito*.
The Intelligences invoked in the line quoted are not the
Princes, or Principalities, of whom Charles speaks, but
the *Thrones*, which, says Dante, ‘taking their nature
from the love of the Holy Spirit, make their operation
connatural thereto, to wit the movement of that heaven
which is full of love.’[2] As we have seen in the Introduction, Dante in the *Paradiso* (xxviii. 97-139) follows
the order of the Angelic Hierarchy as laid down by the
Pseudo-Dionysius, according to which the Thrones
preside over the movements of Saturn. They are
referred to in the present Heaven as mirrors up above,
which reflect to all the lower spheres the Divine judgments.[3] It is in accordance with the same Dionysian
doctrine that the Principalities are now regarded as
the Intelligences who move this third Heaven; and in
this there is a certain symbolic appropriateness to the
discourse which follows by a prince and concerning
princes. To Dante’s mind this sphere of Venus, ruled
over by ‘the heavenly Princes,’ represents the love

[1] Vernon, *Readings on the Paradiso*, p. 255 note. Comp. Moore,
Studies in Dante, 3rd series, pp. 42, 43. It is possible that it is for some
similar personal reason Dante puts into the lips of his friend Casella the
song, ‘*Love that in my mind discourseth to me*,’ the second Canzone in
the *Convito* (*Purg.* ii. 112).

[2] *Conv.* ii. 6.

[3] *Par.* ix. 61-63. According to Dionysius, every Order is a mirror to
those beneath. The Thrones mirror and reflect in particular the Divine
judgments. See pp. 6, 24 above. Comp. *Epis.* x. 21.

with which earthly princes must rule their subjects, if their kingdoms are to endure. There is a passage in the *De Monarchia* (i. 11) in which this conviction is applied to the monarch, the head and ruler of princes: 'Moreover, just as greed, though it be never so little, clouds to some extent the disposition of justice, so does charity or right love sharpen and brighten it. In whomsoever therefore right love has the greatest power of inhering, in him justice may take the most commanding place. The monarch is such; therefore when he exists justice is most powerful, or at any rate may be so. Now, that right love has the action I have said, may be shown thus. Greed, scorning the intrinsic significance of man, seeks other things; but charity, scorning all other things, seeks God and man, and consequently the good of man. And since, amongst the other blessings of man, living in peace is the chief, and justice is the chiefest and mightiest accomplisher of this, therefore charity will chiefly give vigour to justice; and the stronger she is, the more.'[1] It is the function of the celestial Princes of Venus to inspire earthly princes with this 'right love' which 'sharpens and brightens' justice; and when these reject this inspiration, it becomes the duty of the Principalities to place their dominion in hands that may prove worthier. 'By their government and wisdom,' says St. Bernard, 'all rule on earth is established, ruled, limited, transferred, curtailed, changed.'[2] This is why in the discourse which follows Charles Martel tells how the tyranny of his grandfather Charles of Anjou lost Sicily to his house, and warns his brother Robert of Naples of the disasters which his greed as a prince will drag upon him.

This Charles Martel is the only member of the house of Anjou whom Dante's soul could tolerate. The two probably met in Florence on the occasion of the young king's visit in 1294, when he was awaiting the return of his father, who had gone to France to receive his

---

[1] Wicksteed's translation in *The Latin Works of Dante*, Temple Classics.   [2] *De Consideratione*, v. 4.   See also above, p. 22.

VIII.] CARLO MARTELLO 139

three sons whom he had left as hostages in Aragon.
Villani tells how he came to the city 'with his company
of 200 knights with golden spurs, French and Provençal
and from the Kingdom, all young men, invested by the
king with habits of scarlet and dark green, and all with
saddles of one device, with their palfreys adorned with
silver and gold, with arms quarterly, bearing golden
lilies and surrounded by a bordure of red and silver,
which are the arms of Hungary. And they appeared
the noblest and richest company a young king ever
had with him. And in Florence he abode more than
twenty days, awaiting his father, King Charles, and
his brothers; and the Florentines did him great
honour, and he showed great love to the Florentines,
wherefore he was held in high favour with them all.'[1]
A warm affection sprang up between the poet and the
prince, to which Charles here alludes:

> 'Much didst thou love me, and thou hadst good cause;
> For had I been below, I should have shown thee
> Something beyond the leafage of my love.'[2]

His death within the year at the age of twenty-four
left unfulfilled the great hopes Dante had formed of
him, both from his character and from the vastness
of the realms over which he would ultimately have
reigned. Charles goes over the count of them, not in
pride, but to show the evils he might have prevented
had he lived. Through his grandmother Beatrice, he
would have been Count of Provence (viii. 58-60). On
his father's death, he would have succeeded to the
throne of Apulia, 'that horn of Ausonia' (ll. 61-63).
Through his mother, Mary, daughter of Stephen v. of
Hungary, he had already been crowned king of that
country (ll. 64-66). Above all, had not the 'evil lordship' of his grandfather Charles of Anjou provoked the
'Sicilian vespers,' 'beautiful Trinacria'[3] would have
been ruled over by his descendants, whom he signifi-

---

[1] *Chronicle*, viii. 13 (Miss Selfe's transl.). [2] *Par.* viii. 55-57.
[3] Trinacria is the name given to Sicily by Virgil (*Aen.* iii. 384, 440, etc.)
and others, from, it is said, its triangular shape. When Frederick II. of
Aragon wrested the island from Charles II. of Naples, he took the title of
'King of Trinacria,' to distinguish his kingdom from that of the two
Sicilies, Naples and Apulia, which remained in the hands of Charles.

cantly describes as 'born through me from Charles and
from Rudolph' (ll. 67-75). In 1291 Charles Martel
married Clemence of Hapsburg, daughter of the
Emperor Rudolph, in the hope, as Villani suggests,[1] that
the alliance would unite the Guelph and Ghibelline
factions. The discourse closes with a warning to his
younger brother, Robert, third son of Charles the
Lame. Since the poem is written from the standpoint
of the year 1300, and Robert did not succeed till his
father's death in 1309, the warning is prophetic. The
lawful heir to the kingdom of Naples was Charles
Martel's son, Carobert, whom his uncle by a successful
appeal to Pope Clement V. ousted from his rights. In
the opening of the Ninth Canto Dante addresses
Clemence, Charles Martel's wife, and assures her that
her and her son's wrongs will be avenged: *how* he is not
at liberty to say, the spirit of her husband having bound
him to silence.[2] Meantime this unscrupulous Prince—
the avaricious son of a liberal sire—was preparing to
ruin his realm with the horde of greedy Catalan adven-
turers whom he had gathered round him during his
captivity in Aragon—their rapacity, if he could but see
it, only giving less scope for his own.[3] This denunciation may not be unconnected with the fact that Robert,
as head of the Guelphs, was the bitter enemy of the
Emperor, Henry VII., around whom all Dante's hopes
had gathered. It may be noted too that it was Robert's
vicar in Florence who in 1315 renewed the sentence of
death against Dante, extending it also to his two sons.

Toynbee is no doubt right in thinking that the use of the name Trinacria
here is meant to give an additional sting to Charles Martel's rebuke of his
house for the misgovernment which lost the fair island to Frederick.

[1] *Chron.* vii. 55.

[2] Robert based his claim on his father's will. I assume that the Clemence here meant is the wife of Charles, and not his daughter who bore
the same name. To me it is inconceivable that a writer so careful as
Dante would ever speak to a daughter of her father as 'thy Charles.'
Dante writes from the ideal standpoint of the year 1300, and although
Charles's wife died in 1301, we have no grounds for assuming that this
standpoint is here abandoned. The *intention* of the passage is to
encourage the wronged family with the promise of justice on the usurper.
Commentators seem fairly divided between Clemence the wife and Clemence the daughter, but 'thy Charles' seems to me quite decisive.

[3] *Par.* viii. 76-84.

The reference to the contrast between Robert and his father, Charles the Lame, suggests the question ' how from sweet seed bitter can issue forth.' We are somewhat surprised to hear Dante call Charles II. liberal. From *Par.* xix. 127-129, this must be his one solitary virtue, for there he declares that his goodness is marked by an I, and his contrary qualities by an M, a thousand. Liberality was one of the virtues attributed to him by Villani; but this one solitary goodness, according to Dante, is lacking in his son.[1]

This problem of heredity, or rather the failure of heredity, has been already discussed in *Purg.* vii. 115-132, and in precisely the same connection. In the Valley of the Princes the same contrast between father and son rises in Dante's mind, and he accounts for it by the very nature of virtue. Virtue is a personal thing into which the will must go : it can be had only by claiming it from God. In the passage before us, however, he traces it to the nature of society. Society requires men of various gifts, and provision for this variety must be made somewhere in the laws of birth. Charles Martel's argument is as follows. The providence of God, like a well-directed arrow, never fails to strike the end it has in view. This end is threefold : first, the individual nature of each thing; second, their relations to each other; and third, their salvation or preservation. If this threefold end is not attained, nature fails : the Heavens, the Angelic intellects which work through them, nay, the Primal Intellect which ought to have made them perfect, all have failed, and produce not works of art but ruins : which is impossible. Now, according to Dante's master, Aristotle, the nature and preservation of man imply citizenship, since, apart from the relations of society, the individual cannot reach his true nature and well-being ; and citizenship implies diversity of individual powers and faculties.[2]

---

[1] It is strange to find liberality attributed to Charles the Lame in face of *Purg.* xx. 79-84, where he is accused of selling his daughter in marriage through avarice. Villani admits that Robert grew avaricious in his old age, but seems to regard this as his one vice (*Chron.* xii. 10).

[2] Aristotle, *Pol.* ii. 2 : ' Not only does a State consist of a number of indi-

Hence one is born Solon, a lawgiver; another Xerxes,
a soldier; a third, Melchizedek, a priest; a fourth,
Daedalus, an artificer. If no power intervened, these
diversities would be impossible—like would produce
like in endless sameness. The intervening power is
'revolving Nature,' the stars in their courses. The star
under which a man is born sets its stamp upon him,
according to its own virtue, and not according to the
character or faculties of his parents: as Dante puts it,
it does not distinguish one inn, or house, or family,
from another. This is why even twin-brothers differ as
widely as Esau and Jacob; why Quirinus (a name for
Romulus), whose father was utterly unknown, was
attributed to Mars, so impossible did it seem that so
great a warrior should spring from some obscure root.
We are reminded of the 'audacious fiction' which
Socrates in the *Republic* (iii. 415) proposes 'to communicate gradually, first to the rulers, then to the soldiers,
and lastly to the people.' 'Citizens, we shall say to
them in our tale, you are brothers, yet God has framed
you differently. Some of you have the power of command, and these he has composed of gold, wherefore
also they have the greatest honour; others of silver, to
be auxiliaries; others again who are to be husbandmen
and craftsmen he has made of brass and iron; and the
species will generally be preserved in the children. But
as you are of the same original family, a golden parent
will sometimes have a silver son, or a silver parent a
golden son. And God proclaims to the rulers, as a first
principle, that above all they should watch over their
offspring, and see what elements mingle in their nature;
for if the son of a golden or silver parent has an
admixture of brass and iron, then nature orders a
transposition of ranks, and the eye of the ruler must

viduals, but the individuals are different in kind. It is impossible to form
a State all the members of which are alike.' In iii. 4 he says : ' Since the
members of the State are dissimilar, and, as an animal e.g. consists of soul
and body, soul of reason and appetite, and a household of husband and
wife, master and slave, so too a State consists of all these and of other
dissimilar elements besides, it follows that the virtue of all the citizens
can no more be one and the same than the virtue of a leader and a subordinate member of a chorus' (Welldon's transl.). Comp. *Conv.* iv. 4.

not be pitiful towards his child because he has to descend in the scale and become a husbandman or artisan,
just as there may be others sprung from the artisan
class who are raised to honour, and become guardians
and auxiliaries. For an oracle says that when a man
of brass or iron guards the State, it will then be
destroyed. Such is the tale ; is there any possibility of
making our citizens believe in it ? '[1]

Charles Martel ends with a ' corollary,' which is substantially the same as Plato's conclusion in the above
quotation, namely, that each man's function in the
State should be determined by the faculties with which
he is endowed by Nature — Nature being, as just
explained, the power of God which, working through
the starry spheres, stamps each soul with a separate
and individual quality, beyond the operation of a mere
mechanical heredity. He gives two examples of the
confusion caused by the violation of Nature's inten-
tions :

> ' But ye to a religious order wrench aside
> Such as was born to gird him with the sword,
> And make a king of one who is for preaching ;
> Wherefore your track is outside of the road.' [2]

There is little doubt that Charles is referring to two of
his own brothers. Louis, the next to himself in age,
almost immediately after his release from captivity in
Aragon, renounced his hereditary rights, joined the
Franciscan Order, and was made Bishop of Toulouse.[3]
This renunciation of the sword, for which Dante
evidently thought him better fitted, gave the throne to
his younger brother Robert, who had in him more of
the preacher than the king. Villani says of him : ' This
King Robert was the wisest king that had been among
Christians for five hundred years, both in natural
ability and in knowledge, being a very great master in
theology and a consummate philosopher.' [4]

[1] Jowett's translation.
[2] *Par.* viii. 137-148.
[3] Louis died in 1297, and was canonized in 1311.
[4] *Chronicle*, xii. 10. Robert was surnamed ' the Wise.' Petrarch, who

The discussion provokes one inevitable criticism, that it explains nothing of the difficulty from which it sprang, namely, how a covetous son could be descended from a liberal father.   This is the problem of the origin of the *moral* differences between parents and children.   It is certainly no explanation of these to point out the source of those differences of *natural* gift and ability which are necessary for the service of the State.   Obviously to explain how one is born a law-giver and another a soldier is an entirely different thing from telling us how a son is born with a vice from which his father is comparatively free.   It is the only case known to me in which Dante wanders into a discussion not strictly revelant to the point at issue.

regarded him as the king of philosophers and poets, submitted to be examined by him for the space of two days and a half, in the presence of the entire Court, on every known branch of learning.   Gregorovius sweeps aside Robert's claims to wisdom with contempt: 'The King enjoyed an undeserved reputation as a lover of learning, and was himself the author of tedious lucubrations on religious and profane questions.' His character reminds us of James, 'the British Solomon,' who held that 'a sovereign ought to be the most learned clerk in his dominions,' and took himself seriously as a great theologian.   Dante probably would have agreed with Plato (*Rep.* v. 473) that only philosophers should be kings, provided they be lovers of wisdom indeed.   In *De Mon.* iii. 16 he lays it down as the function of the Emperor 'to guide mankind to happiness in this world, *in accordance with the teaching of philosophy.*'   The tomb of Robert in Sta. Chiara, Naples, unites the secular and the religious vocations.   On a throne above, Robert sits as king with crown and sceptre and royal robes: the inscription being: *Cernite Robertum Regem Virtute Refertum.*   At the foot of the pedestal he lies in the humble garb of a Franciscan friar, and barefooted; but even in death the friar retains his crown and sceptre.   See engraving in D'Agincourt's *History of Art*, vol. ii., Plate xxx.

CHAPTER VII

THIRD HEAVEN—VENUS: LOVERS

2. *Cunizza, Folco, Rahab*

WHEN Charles Martel at the close of his discourse turned to the Sun that now fulfilled his entire being, another of the 'splendours' of this star drew near to Dante, brightening outwardly in token of its will to please him. Receiving liberty from the eyes of Beatrice, the poet asked the 'blessed spirit' to give him proof of its power to reflect his thought by answering his unspoken wish—the wish being, as the answer shows, to know the soul's identity. It turns out to be that of Cunizza, youngest daughter of Ezzelino II. da Romano, the most famous of whose many lovers was Sordello of Mantua, who acts as guide to Dante and Virgil in the Valley of the Princes on Mount Purgatory.[1] In Browning's *Sordello*, Cunizza is the heroine under the name of Palma.[2]

She describes herself as having been born 'out of one root' with the 'torch' of the Trevisan March, the torch being the infamous tyrant Ezzelino III. da Romano, whom Dante, for his horrible bloodshed and cruelties, plunges up to the eyebrows in the River of Blood in the Seventh Circle of the Inferno:

[1] *Purg.* vi. 58 f.

[2]   'Palma, Dante spoke with in the clear
        Amorous silence of the Swooning-sphere,—
        Cunizza, as he called her!' (Bk. v.).

Browning tells how to the young Sordello she sat 'conspicuous in his world of dreams':
        'How the tresses curled
    Into a sumptuous swell of gold and wound
    About her like a glory! even the ground
    Was bright as with spilt sunbeams' (Bk. I.).

> 'That forehead there which has the hair so black
>   Is Azzolino.'[1]

He is called a torch in reference apparently to the story of his mother's dream that she had given birth to a blazing firebrand. So intolerable did his lust for blood and torture grow that the Pope proclaimed a crusade against him, as 'a son of perdition, a man of blood, the most inhuman of the children of men, who, by his infamous torture of the nobles and massacre of the people, has broken every bond of human society, and violated every law of Christian liberty.'[2] It is not without purpose that Cunizza describes herself as born 'out of one root' with this destroying firebrand. It is another example of those inscrutable differences in members of the same family of which Charles Martel had just been speaking. Born of the same root, the sister is here in Paradise, the brother in the heart of Hell. This mysterious separation of families seems to have taken strong hold of the poet's imagination; again and again he takes a family group and separates its members throughout the three divisions of the other world, to indicate, apparently, that nothing but spiritual kinship prevails at last.

This contrast of destiny grows more mysterious when we remember that Cunizza seems to have been not much better in her love adventures than her brother in his cruelties. Even at the risk of being classed among the 'vulgar herd' to whom Dante refers (ix. 36), one can scarcely refrain from wondering why she is not in the same Circle as Paolo and Francesca. Probably Dean Plumptre's explanation is correct, that Dante

---

[1] *Inf.* xii. 109.

[2] For his cruelties, see Villani, vi. 72. 'I believe in truth,' says Salimbene, 'that no such wicked man has been from the beginning of the world unto our own days: for all men trembled at him as a rush quivers in the water, and not without cause : for he who lived to-day was never sure of the morrow. The father would seek out and slay his son, and the son his father, or any of his kinsfolk, to please this man : he would submit ladies to the foulest mutilations, and cast them into prison with their sons and daughters to perish of hunger' (Coulton, *From St. Francis to Dante*, 246). Cunizza describes Romano as lying between the Rialto (Venice) and the springs of the rivers Brenta and Piave (ix. 25-27).

knew something of her repentance in her last days, a repentance which seems to have shown some genuine kindness of heart. After the death of her brothers, he says, 'she found a retreat in Florence. The last fact known of her is that she made her will in that city (1265) in the house of Cavalcante dei Cavalcanti, father of Dante's friend Guido (*Inf.* x. 53). . . . Her latter days at Florence were said to have been marked by piety and charity. Even before that, she was said to have relieved, as far as she could, the victims of Ezzelin's oppression. By her will she gave freedom to her serfs. The date of her death is unknown. It is possible that Dante himself may have had early memories of the gracious penitent lady, still retaining much of the fascination of her former beauty, or may have heard of such memories, and of the romance of her love for the great Mantuan poet from Guido Cavalcanti, who was sixteen years older than himself. Anyhow, he believed that she had repented, and therefore did not shrink from placing her in Paradise. He remembered, it may be, the story of a certain woman who also had had five husbands (*John* iv. 18), of a woman whose sins, that were many, were forgiven her because she loved much (*Luke* vii. 47).'

Cunizza points out at her side the soul of Folco of Marseilles, troubadour and Bishop, dwelling on his fame in order to rebuke 'the present rabble' which inhabited her native province for their indifference to the excellence which adds life to life. Scourged by tyrants, their misery has failed to lead them to repentance. Hence she foretells three judgments which will soon fall upon them—judgments which she sees in the mirror of the Thrones above.[1] The first is a judgment on Padua and Vicenza for their stubbornness against duty —the duty of obedience to the Emperor Henry VII.

> 'But soon shall be that Padua at the marsh
> Will change the water that Vicenza bathes,
> Because the folk are stubborn against duty—'[2]

---

[1] *Par.* ix. 61-63.   [2] *Par.* ix. 46-48.

that is, the river Bacchiglione, which runs through Vicenza, will be dyed with the blood shed in the war between these two cities. It is impossible to enter into the almost interminable disputes as to the particular incident meant, to which this passage has given rise. In 1265, a few years after she had shaken off the yoke of the tyrant Ezzelino, Padua made war upon Vicenza and conquered her. When Henry VII. crossed the Alps into Italy, the Vicentines, with the aid of the Imperial Vicar, Can Grande of Verona, threw off the Paduan yoke, exchanging one tyranny for another. The reference in the present passage is perhaps to the general course of the war which followed, and which consisted for the most part of a long series of marauding expeditions into one another's territories. The struggle ended in 1314, when Can Grande with a mere handful of men drove the whole Paduan army out of Vicenza, which it had just captured and treacherously sacked. 'Strings of bound captives whom the prisons of Vicenza would not hold were driven through the pitiless rain to Verona. Fugitives wandered over all the hills. Day after day they were hunted with hounds in the forest, and the more fortunate ones straggled home in twos and threes, stripped of all they had and overwhelmed with shame.'[1] It is possible, however, that the mention of 'the water that bathes Vicenza' has reference to a matter which occurred some time prior to this defeat. The Vicentines in time of war with Padua were in the habit of damming up the river Bacchiglione in order to divert the water from the city of their enemies—the overflow forming 'the marsh' (*il palude*) of line 46. Mr. Vernon, giving a digest of a monograph by the Abbate Bortolan, says that the Paduans when negotiating for the surrender of their

---

[1] Wicksteed and Gardner, *Dante and Giovanni del Virgilio*, p. 33. Comp. Villani, ix. 63; and the line (28) in his first Eclogue in which del Virgilio suggests this war with Can Grande as a more fitting subject for Dante's pen than the *Commedia*:

'Tell of the Phrygian does torn by the stag-hound's tooth,'—the 'stag-hound' being Can Grande, and the 'Phrygian does' the Paduans: *Phrygian*, because they traced their descent to Antenor of Troy; and *does*, because of the cowardice with which they fled.

city to Henry VII. expressly stipulated as a condition
that the Emperor order the Vicentines to restore the
waters of the river to their ancient bed. The latter
refused to obey the Emperor, the war broke out afresh,
and the territories of the two wretched cities were
devastated with fire and sword. Both were stubborn
against their duty to the Emperor, and their blood
dyed the water of the river for which they fought.[1]

The second judgment foreseen by Cunizza is that
which fell on Riccardo da Cammino, Lord of Treviso,
in the year 1312. Various accounts are given of 'the
net' that was being woven to catch him. He was
assassinated while playing chess in his own palace by
one of his servants who was bribed to do the deed.
According to one story, the chief agent was Riccardo's
brother, who wished to seize his lordship; according to
another, a husband who thus avenged his wife's honour;
while a third account traces the murder to a conspiracy
of citizens to secure their country's liberty. It is quite
possible that 'the net,' as is common in such cases, was
woven of all these threads of mixed motive.[2]

The third judgment foretold is the wailing of the
city of Feltro for 'the crime of its impious pastor,'
Bishop Alessandro Novello of Treviso. In 1314 a number
of Ferrarese Ghibellines, having conspired against Pino
della Tosa, King Robert's Vicar in Ferrara, which he
held for the Church, fled to Feltro and placed themselves under the protection of its bishop. Alessandro,
as an act of courtesy to the Guelph party to which he
belonged, treacherously delivered them up to the Vicar,
who immediately had them executed in Ferrara to the
number of thirty. Such courteous gifts of human blood
from spiritual to temporal ruler, says Cunizza, are in
harmony with her country's way of living; and no
greater criminal than this bishop ever entered Malta—
probably the prison of that name in Viterbo in which

---

[1] *Readings on the Paradiso*, i. 300-2.
[2] *Par.* ix. 49-51. Gherardo, the father of this Riccardo, is named in
Conv. iv. 14 as a man of conspicuous nobility of character. Giovanna,
daughter of Nino Visconti of Pisa (*Purg.* viii. 70-3) was Riccardo's wife.

the Pope confined ecclesiastical offenders. According to Benvenuto, Alessandro was beaten to death by sandbags by Riccardo da Cammino, but as Riccardo had been assassinated two years before, this is impossible. Feltro passed into the tyrannous hands of the Cammino family, and doubtless had cause enough to bewail the treachery of its courteous pastor.[1]

We turn now to Cunizza's nearest neighbour, Folco or Folquet of Marseilles, whom she has already pointed out to Dante. She dwells on the great fame as a troubadour which 'this shining and dear jewel of our heaven' has left behind on earth, and prophesies that five hundred years more will not exhaust it. Dante probably did not know that his own mention of him would be his chief claim on the memory of after ages. It is, indeed, a characteristic weakness of Dante that the love of fame should slip out instinctively even here, just as higher up he cannot repress his pride in the nobility of his blood.[2] In the preceding Heaven, as we saw, the love of fame lies like the shadow of earth upon the soul for ever.

The story of Folco's life is not the most pleasant reading. The son of a rich Genoese merchant settled in Marseilles,[3] he spent his youth in dissipation. As a troubadour he frequented the courts of such princes as

---

[1] *Par.* ix. 52-60. Malta has been identified with several other prisons, such as that which the older commentators say existed at the south end of the Lake of Bolsena, and a tower of that name built by Ezzelino in the castle of Cittadella, between Vicenza and Treviso. Some commentators are inclined to think that Dante's chief reason for setting Cunizza in this Heaven was to make her the mouthpiece of this denunciation of her native province, the Trevisan March.

[2] *Par.* xvi. 1-6. See p. 249.

[3] In ll. 82-93 Folco gives a curious description of the situation of his native place, Marseilles. (1) By a roundabout process he indicates that the sun travels through 90° from the East end of the Mediterranean to the Pillars of Hercules—the geographers of his day giving it more than twice its true length (Moore, *Studies*, 3rd series, 126). (2) Marseilles is midway between the rivers Ebro in Spain and Macra, the boundary between Genoa and Tuscany. (3) In his native place sunrise and sunset have almost the same time as in Buggea or Bougie in the North of Africa —that is, the two have the same longitude. The reason for this roundabout description is that Folco is telling the situation of Marseilles from the planet Venus: he sees the whole Mediterranean valley spread out beneath him, as Dante saw the earth from the Starry Heaven (*Par.* xxii. 151).

Alphonso VIII. of Castile, Raymond V., Count of Toulouse, and Barral, Viscount of Marseilles. It is to
Adelaide, the wife of the last named, that most of his
songs were written, though his court was by no means
confined to her. In his confession to Dante he hides
nothing of his wickedness:

> 'Folco that people called me, unto whom
> My name was known; and now with me this heaven
> Imprints itself, as I did once with it;
> For more the daughter of Belus never burned,
> Offending both Sichaeus and Creüsa,
> Than I, so long as it became my locks;
> Nor yet that Rhodopeian, who deluded
> Was by Demophoön, nor yet Alcides,
> When Iolë he in his heart had locked.'[1]

It is amazing to find that Dante passes by in absolute
silence the life and deeds of Folco after his repentance.
To many minds his conversion certainly seems to have
been from one form of evil to a worse. On the death
of the Lady Adelaide and the princes named above, he
became a Cistercian monk, and rose to be Abbot of a
monastery, and finally Bishop of Toulouse. And then
his whole nature flung itself in almost incredible
cruelty into the crusade of the Church against the
Albigenses. Milman calls him 'the ecclesiastical de
Montfort of the crusade,' and says: 'There is no act of
treachery or cruelty throughout the war in which
the Bishop of Toulouse was not the most forward,

---

[1] *Par.* ix. 94-102. 'The daughter of Belus' is Dido, her love for Aeneas
being regarded as an offence to the shade of his wife Creüsa and to that
of her own husband, Sichaeus (comp. *Inf.* v. 61-2; *Aen.* iv. 552). The
'Rhodopeian' is Phyllis, daughter of Sithon, King of Thrace: Demo-
phoön, son of Theseus and Phaedra, having, on his way home from Troy,
won her love, promised to marry her after settling his affairs in Attica;
and on his return after a long delay he found that, thinking herself forgotten, she had put an end to her life. Alcides is Hercules who fell in
love with Iolë, daughter of Eurytus, King of Oechalia. To win back his
love, his wife Deïaneira sent him a white garment steeped in the
poisonous blood of the Centaur Nessus, and thereby unwittingly caused
his death. It has been suggested that the mention of Dido, Phyllis, and
Iolë is an allusion to the three ladies whom Folco had loved on earth,
Adelaide, wife of Barral, Laura, his sister, and Eudoxia, daughter of the
Emperor Manuel Comnenus, and wife of William VIII. of Montpellier
(Toynbee, *Dante Dictionary*, 'Folco'). Whether this is so or not, it is
the intensity of his passion he specially wishes to indicate, and the fact
that it lasted far on into his life.

sanguinary, unscrupulous.'[1]   'A nightingale turned
hawk, a shepherd allying himself with the wolves, he
made his early sins look white by the blackness of his
later virtues, and made religion odious by faithfully
serving the Church. . . . It was Folquet who persuaded
Count Raimon, with lying words of good-will and
affection, to invite Montfort and the legate of the Pope
to Toulouse, and give them possession of the citadel:
"a great sin," says the Provençal historian, "which
cost the lives of many thousands of men." It was
Folquet who urged hardest that the son of his friend
and benefactor [Raymond v. of Toulouse] should be
deprived of his estates. It was Folquet who travelled
through northern France enlisting aid against the
heretics and especially against the count, "the worst
wretch of them all." It was Folquet who introduced St. Dominic to the Pope, and established
the Inquisition in Languedoc. It was Folquet who
would not permit the crusaders to spare Toulouse
when they felt that the count and his people had
suffered enough. It was Folquet who ordered all the
clergy to leave the city and carry with them the Holy
Sacrament, inflicting on many thousands of the faithful the terrible dread of dying as heathen. It was
Folquet who appeared at the Lateran Council (1215) as
the implacable enemy of the count, and Folquet who
was twice charged there with causing the death of ten
thousand persons in his own episcopal city.

---

[1] *Latin Christianity*, Bk. IX. chap. viii. 'Never in the history of man,'
says Milman in the same chapter, 'were the great eternal principles of
justice, the faith of treaties, common humanity so trampled under foot
as in the Albigensian war. Never was war waged in which ambition,
the consciousness of strength, rapacity, implacable hatred, and pitiless
cruelty played a greater part. And throughout the war it cannot be dis-
guised that it was not merely the army of the Church, but the Church
itself in arms. Papal legates and the greatest prelates headed the host,
and mingled in all the horrors of the battle and the siege. In no instance
did they interfere to arrest the massacre, in some cases urged it on.
"Slay all, God will know His own," was the boasted saying of Abbot
Arnold, Legate of the Pope, before Béziers. Arnold was the captain-
general of the army.' The Albigenses were charged with holding the
Manichean heresy of a good and evil principle in the world : the Church
gave them full proof in their own blood of at least the latter half of their
heresy.

But this was not enough; the flames were not yet quenched. Once more he roused Montfort to take vengeance on Toulouse, and bade him strip its inhabitants of all they had. On the approach of the army he exhorted the people to go out and make their peace with the enemy, promising they should be well received, while Montfort, as had been arranged, put them in irons as fast as they came. Folquet himself then began the pillage of the city, and Montfort came up and set it on fire : Béziers was to be outdone. With the energy of despair the citizens drove out the crusaders; but Folquet gave them asylum in his cathedral and palace. Then, by an understanding with Montfort, he went out through the streets declaring that he had persuaded Simon to surrender his prisoners and pardon the city if the people would go to their homes and give up their arms. No sooner was this done than Simon, by Folquet's advice, exiled his prisoners instead of surrendering them, and announced that the city would be sacked unless it engaged to pay an almost impossible ransom. When the people dared to promise the ransom he declared that if the last penny were not ready at the appointed time he would kill every one of them. And after the money was paid,—the city was pillaged none the less.'[1]

I have given this somewhat long quotation that we may see more clearly the kind of saint Dante sets here in Paradise. Although he says nothing of this part of Folco's life, he must have known the facts perfectly well. So far from condemning what seems to us a most inhuman cruelty, it was doubtless this very zeal for the Church against heretics which proved to Dante's mind the reality of Folco's repentance, and therefore his right to heaven. It certainly gives us a shock to find a noble spirit like Dante's so subdued to the colour and temper of its time that deeds which sink Ezzelino

---

[1] Prof. Justin H. Smith, *The Troubadours at Home*, I. 388, 403-5. 'It was natural that Simon de Montfort, a soldier by trade, should represent the violence of the Albigensian crusade; but it was monstrous that Folquet de Marseilla, a poet and a priest, should represent its fury and sin.'

to perdition exalt Folco to Paradise, because done in the name of Christ and by authority of His Vicar.

Returning, however, from this digression, let us now trace some of the ways in which Dante indicates the changes this Heaven has wrought in Folco from his old troubadour days. When Dante, for example, turned to speak to him, his joy brightened 'like a fine ruby which the sun strikes through.'[1] According to Longfellow, quoting King's *Antique Gems*, 'the *Balais Ruby* represses vain and lascivious thoughts'; and if, as seems probable, Dante was thinking of this virtue of the gem, the comparison implies that Folco is now entirely beyond the old earthly passions, and that his joy shines through a pure heart. Further, this purity of heart gives him so clear a vision of all things in God that he is able, like Cunizza, to read Dante's unspoken wish to know who he is:

> 'God seeth all, and into Him thy sight so enters,
> Blest spirit,' said I, 'that no wish
> Hath power to steal itself away from thee.'[2]

For the same reason his voice has taken a higher range. The earthly love which made him sing his troubadour songs has given way to the inspiration of the highest celestial love, that of the Seraphim, who ever burn with the Love before which they veil themselves with their wings:

> 'Thy voice, that for ever makes the heavens
> Glad, with the singing of those holy fires
> Which of their six wings make themselves a cowl.'[3]

The reference here is probably to St. Bonaventura's work *De sex alis Seraphim*, in which he spiritualizes the well-known passage in Isaiah vi.[4] The six wings of

---

[1] *Par.* ix. 69. The word Dante uses is *balascio*—the balas ruby, rose-pink in colour, which gets its name from the country in Central Asia where it is found—Badakshan, variously spelt Badascian, Balakshan, Balashan, Balasian (Marco Polo), etc. Probably all Dante's references to precious stones have some symbolic meaning.

[2] *Par.* ix. 73-5.   [3] *Par.* ix. 76-8.

[4] 'Above him stood the seraphim : each one had six wings ; with twain he covered his face, and with twain he covered his feet, and with twain he did fly.' One cannot help wondering whether the word 'cowl' has any reference to the fact that Folco was monk as well as bishop, especially

the Seraphim are the six virtues which ought to adorn
the Prelates of the Church, who, according to Dionysius, correspond on earth to the loftiest Hierarchy of
Heaven. The two which cover the head are zeal of
justice and piety or fraternal compassion; the two
which cover the body and feet are patience and an
exemplary life; and the two by which they fly are
circumspection and devotion to God. By saying that
the voice of Folco unites with the song of the Seraphim
who covered themselves with their six wings, Dante
means to imply that as a bishop of the Church he was
adorned with these six virtues. This, apparently, was
how his conduct in the Albigensian Crusade impressed
the poet. Yet for all his virtues he administers a slight
rebuke for forcing him to request an answer at all—
the seraphic love ought to have inspired his voice to
answer his wish before ever it was spoken.[1]

But by far the most interesting change in such souls
as Folco and Cunizza is the mysterious relation in
which they now stand to their earthly sins. In the
Earthly Paradise Dante drank of two rivers—Lethe,
for oblivion of his sins; and Eunoë or Good-Mind, for
the revival in memory of his good deeds.[2] Is, then, the
forgetfulness of sins absolute in Paradise? Obviously,
it is not, since both Cunizza and Folco remember them
in some sense. The mysterious thing is that the
memory carries no sting of grief or repentance—
nothing but a great gratitude to God who can use even
sin for man's salvation. Cunizza knows that this is a
hard saying for the crowd: after confessing the sin
which fixed her eternal lot in this star, she says:

'But gladly do I pardon to myself
The cause of this my lot, and it grieves me not,
Which would haply seem hard saying to your vulgar.'[3]

---

when one remembers that in the Dionysian system the Seraphim belong
to the highest Celestial Hierarchy, the Bishops to the highest Earthly
Hierarchy, and the Monks to the highest order of the 'initiated.'

[1] In *Conv.* i. 8 Dante says it is a mark of 'prompt liberality' to give
without being asked. Comp. *Purg.* xvii. 59-60:

'For he who awaits the prayer and sees the need,
Malignly leans already towards refusal.'

[2] *Purg.* xxxi. 91-102; xxxiii. 127-145.   [3] *Par.* ix. 32-36.

And Folco's words are more explicit :

> ' Yet here is no repenting, but we smile,
> Not at the fault, which comes not back to mind,
> But at the Power which ordered and foresaw.
> Here we gaze back into the art which beautifies
> Its own so great effect, and we discern the good
> Whereby to the world above returns that below.' [1]

The idea runs back to St. Augustine's distinction between intellectual and experimental knowledge. ' The soul then shall have an intellectual remembrance of its past ills, but so far as regards sensible experience they shall be wholly forgotten. For a skilled physician knows indeed professionally all diseases, but experimentally only those from which he has himself suffered. As, then, the knowledge of evil is twofold, the one by mental insight, the other by sensible experience, in two ways also it can be forgotten. The skilled and learned (physician), through neglect of his profession, may forget sufferings; the patient, through escape from them. And in this latter way will the saints forget their past ills, for their deliverance from them will be so complete, that they will be entirely blotted out of their experience. But their intellectual knowledge, which will be great, will keep them acquainted not only with their own past woes, but with the eternal sufferings of the lost. Were they indeed to become unconscious of their past miseries, how could they, as the Psalmist says (lxxxviii. 2), sing for ever the mercies of God? . . . In that City of God there will be free will, one in all and indivisible in each, freed from all evil and filled with all good, enjoying indefectibly the sweetness of eternal bliss, oblivious of sins, oblivious of sufferings, yet not so oblivious of its deliverance as to be ungrateful to its Deliverer.' [1] Aquinas, discussing the question whether after the Resurrection every one will have knowledge of the sins he has committed, replies that since the general judgment proceeds on the record of each man's con-

---

[1] *Par.* ix. 103-108. A friend puts the difficulty with a happy humour : the saints must have a great deal of trouble ' remembering to forget' their sins.   [2] *City of God*, xxii. 30. See Hettinger, p. 204 n.

science, this knowledge is indispensable. The objection is stated that since in this life our sorrow for remembered sins is in proportion to the increase of our charity, and since in the risen saints charity is perfect, this sorrow would be at its maximum in Paradise; and this being impossible the very memory of sin must be blotted out. To this Aquinas replies that 'although charity is now a cause of grieving for sin, yet the saints in the Father-land (*in patria*) will be so flooded with joy that grief can have no place in them: and so they will not grieve for sins, but rather rejoice in the Divine mercy by which they have been released from their sins; even as now the angels rejoice in the Divine justice, where-by those over whom they are guardians, when forsaken by grace, fall into sin; for whose salvation, nevertheless, they solicitously watch.'[1] It is, of course, impossible to say what change death may work in the human soul; but the idea that the memory of sin remains in the intellect alone in order to provide material for gratitude for salvation to the rest of the nature, carries no sense of reality, either psychological or moral. If, for example, this intellectual knowledge, as St. Augustine in the above quotation declares, keeps the saints *in patria* 'acquainted with the eternal suffer-ings of the lost,' and if among the lost be some victim of a libertine like Folco in his unregenerate days, it is surely a strange species of justice which allows him to smile gratefully for his own salvation, without one twinge of conscience for the eternal sufferings of which he knows himself to be one chief cause.

In order to fulfil all the desires which this sphere quickened in Dante, Folco points out the light in which Rahab[2] had her peace—it being necessary for full

---

[1] *Summa*, iii. *Suppl.* q. lxxxvii. a. 1. In this article Aquinas says that demerits which are destroyed by penitence will remain in the memory of that penitence, so that there will be in every man something by means of which he will be able to recall his works to memory.

[2] Butler thinks Rahab may have been introduced here in order to indicate that the invective against the court of Rome which follows was spoken just over Babylon, thus bringing it into correspondence with the denunciations of Cantos xviii. and xxvii., pronounced over Jerusalem and Rome respectively. He gets the connection from Ps. lxxxvii. 4, 'I will

understanding of this Heaven to know whether any of the outcast class to which she belonged had ever been admitted to its bliss.   The sequel shows a harlot not only admitted, but exalted to the place of honour:

> ' when to our order she was joined,
> With her *in the highest grade* it sealed itself.'[1]

doubtless in fulfilment of Paul's words: 'where sin abounded, grace did much more abound.'[2]   The purity she has now attained is compared to the sparkling of a sunbeam in pure water.   This comparison and the likening of her in l. 121 to a palm seems to me a good example of the way in which Dante drew his similes and figures out of the heart of the subject he was dealing with.   Rahab called up before his imagination Jericho, 'the city of palm trees,' and the innumerable streams of her plain, sparkling in the eastern sun as they pursue their way to the Jordan a few miles distant.[3] It is this picture in his imagination which dictates these figures of the palm and the sunlit water.   Dante sets her as near the eternal Sun as he can by connecting her with the ending of the shadowy cone of earth (ll. 118, 119).   She stands as it were on the borderland between the first three Heavens on which the shadow of earthly frailty rests, and the higher purer Heavens which revolve in the unclouded light of God, and is

make mention of Rahab and Babylon to them that know me,' where, however, Rahab means Egypt.   Another suggestion is that Rahab and Folquet are conjoined because of a certain parallelism in their histories. 'As Rahab was in relation to Joshua and Jericho, so was Folquet to Simon de Montfort and Toulouse and other places; and the military operations of the crusade, according to the historians of the time, are not without resemblance to Joshua's capture of Jericho in such an instance as the storming of Lavaur, when the assailants advanced with the Cistercian monks at their head, sang the *Veni creator*, and the walls of the fortress fell forthwith' (Chaytor, *Troubadours of Dante*, 167).*

[1] *Par.* ix. 116-7.   We may wonder why there is no mention of Mary Magdalene.   The only reference to her is *Conv.* iv. 22, where she is allegorized into the type of the Epicurean school!

[2] Rom. v. 20.

[3] Deut. xxxiv. 3; Judges i. 16, iii. 13, etc.   Stanley speaks of the great forest which surrounded Jericho in the days of Joshua.   It 'did not then consist, as now, merely of the picturesque thorn, but was a vast grove of majestic palms, nearly three miles broad, and eight miles long.   Even the solitary relic of the palm-forest, seen as late as 1838, has now disappeared' (*Sinai and Palestine*, 307).

therefore the point of transition from the one to the other.

What, then, is the reason for the lofty place thus assigned to Rahab? Doubtless her position in the New Testament as an example of the union of faith and works had much to do with it; but behind this lies the peculiar reverence which gathered round this woman from very early times. In the genealogy of Christ given by Matthew (i. 5), her name occurs as one of the ancestresses of our Lord, and this of itself was enough to make her sacred to every Christian. Further, she was believed to have been a prophetess of the sufferings of Christ upon the cross, by faith in which she was finally saved. In his first Epistle to the Corinthians, St. Clement of Rome after narrating the story of the spies adds: 'And moreover they gave her a sign, that she should hang out from her house a scarlet thread, thereby showing beforehand that through the blood of the Lord there shall be redemption unto all them that believe and hope on God. Ye see, dearly beloved, not only faith, but prophecy, is found in the woman.' This interpretation of the scarlet thread was adopted by the Apostolic Fathers,[1] and was doubtless in Dante's mind when he called Rahab 'a palm'

> 'of the high victory
> Which was achieved with the one and the other palm,'

that is, of the two hands of Christ upon the cross— a trophy of the victory by which He won the heavenly Canaan, as Joshua did the earthly one. For this reason she is regarded as an Old Testament type of the Christian Church, as Joshua himself is of Christ; and

> 'Because she favoured the first glory
> Of Joshua upon the Holy Land,'

---

[1] Irenæus (*Against Heresies*, iv. chap. 20) takes the scarlet thread as symbolic of the Passover and Exodus; but since these in turn are types of the death of Christ and His deliverance of His people, the meaning is the same: 'Rahab the harlot was preserved, when all was over [*in ultimis*], together with all her house, through faith of the scarlet sign; as the Lord also declared to those who did not receive His advent,—the Pharisees, no doubt, nullify the sign of the scarlet thread, which meant the passover, and the redemption and exodus of the people from Egypt,— when He said, "The publicans and the harlots go into the kingdom of heaven before you"' (Rambaut's transl.).

and was herself the first-fruits of that glory, therefore she was the first of all souls to be rescued from Limbo and taken up to this star in the Triumph of Christ.[1] And now, as Mr. Gardner says, she is 'the last soul who appears within the earth's shadow, as a type of the Church which should guide men beyond that shadow.'[2]

The memory of the conquest of Canaan rouses Folco into a passion of indignation against Pope and Cardinals for their indifference to the fate of the Holy Land. He had flung himself, as we have seen, into the crusade for the rescue of Languedoc from the heretics, and he could not understand how the Head of the Church could basely abandon to the infidel the sacred soil on which the Church's Lord was born. For favouring Joshua in his first struggle for that land, Rahab is set 'in the highest grade' of this third Heaven; yet that Church of which she was but the type lifts no finger to rescue it from the Saracens. Boniface VIII., the reigning Pope in 1300, the ideal date of the poem, undertook no crusade.[3] His successors Clement V. and John XXII. raised money throughout Europe for a crusade to rescue Holy Land, but it went no farther than the papal coffers. Dean Plumptre tells us that the Register of his own Cathedral of Wells contains records of money raised for a crusade in obedience to Clement V., and an order

---

[1] *Par.* ix. 118-125. I have followed the generally received interpretation of 'the one and the other palm.' Scartazzini, Casini, and others hold that the reference is to 'the high victory' of Joshua in the taking of Jericho, and the taking of it by prayer—the holding up of the two palms to heaven (comp. Exod. xvii. 10-13). They quote the eulogy pronounced on Joshua in Ecclus. xlvi., in particular v. 2: 'How great glory gat he *when he did lift up his hands* (*in tollendo manus suas*), and stretched out his sword against the cities.' There is no need to set the two interpretations against each other. Joshua, whose very name in the Vulgate is Jesus (Acts vii. 45; Heb. iv. 8), was a recognized type of Christ, and his victory of Christ's victory. The lifting up of Joshua's hands, therefore, would almost inevitably suggest the lifting up of our Lord's hands upon the cross. It is useless to object that *all* the souls of the blessed are 'palms' of the high victory of Christ as well as Rahab's: the point is that she was the *first-fruits* of His Triumph (ll. 119, 120). The two interpretations run into and complete each other.

[2] *Dante's Ten Heavens*, p. 88.

[3] Comp. *Inf.* xxvii. 85-90, where Boniface, 'the Prince of the new Pharisees,' is represented as carrying on a war against neither Saracens nor Jews, but against Christians—the great rival house of the Colonnas.

from John XXII. to reserve for this and other pious uses 'the incomes of forty-six of the best livings in the diocese.' 'Fancy that kind of thing,' he exclaims, 'going on through the length and breadth of Western Europe!'[1] No wonder Dante lays the blame on 'the accursed flower' made and spread by that city which was planted by Satan—the gold florin of Florence which was stamped with the *fleur-de-lys*. For its sake the shepherd is changed into a wolf, the Gospel and the great Doctors are deserted for the Decretals,[2] and the Pope and Cardinals do not allow so much as their *thoughts* to go to Nazareth, to which the Archangel Gabriel did not disdain to make a journey from Heaven itself. The name Nazareth contains an allusion which, so far as my reading goes, has remained unnoted. 'Nazareth' is frequently derived from *Netser*, the word in Isaiah xi. 1, translated in the Authorized Version, 'a *Branch* shall grow out of his roots.' Jerome in the Vulgate translates, '*Flos* de radice eius ascendet,' and Aquinas says, 'Nazareth *flos* interpretatur.'[3] There is every probability that Dante was familiar with this meaning, and that he set the two flowers against one

---

[1] Plumptre's *Dante*, i. pp. cxiii, cxvi. For the enormous wealth amassed by these two Popes, see Milman, *Latin Christianity*, Bk. XII. chaps. vi, vii. 'The brother of Villani the historian, a banker, was ordered to take the inventory [of John's treasure]. It amounted to eighteen millions of gold florins in specie, seven millions in plate and jewels. "The good man," observes the historian, "had forgotten that saying, 'Lay not up your treasures upon earth'; but perhaps I have said more than enough—perhaps he intended this wealth for the recovery of the Holy Land."' For the ingenious and unscrupulous expedients by which this enormous treasure was wrung out of Christendom, see Lea's *History of the Inquisition of the Middle Ages*, III. 67, 68.

[2] For Dante's view of the Decretals and Scripture, see *De Mon.* iii. 3; *Epis.* viii. 7, etc. Yet Gratian, founder of the science of canon law, is in the next Heaven (x. 103).

[3] *Summa*, iii. q. xxxv. a. 7. St. Bernard (*On Cant.*, Serm. lviii.) calls Jesus the first Flower of the Resurrection : 'He is the first and chiefest Flower of the human race which has ever appeared on earth. For the Christ is called *the first-fruits of them that slept* (1 Cor. xv. 20). Jesus, I say, is the Rose of Sharon, and the Lily of the valleys (ii. 1). He who was supposed the Son of Joseph, He who was Jesus of Nazareth, which itself means a flower [or branch]. He then appeared as the first Flower of the Resurrection.' In his *De Laudibus Virginis* (Hom. i. 3) Bernard weaves similar fancies round this interpretation of 'Nazareth,' in connection with the Annunciation.

another in intentional contrast : 'the accursed flower'
of Florence which turned the shepherd into a very wolf
of avarice, and the blessed Flower of Nazareth, who
there lived a life of poverty in a humble home.   We
shall see in a later Canto the keen irony with which
the image of the Baptist on the other side of the same
coin is used in denunciation of another aspect of this
insatiable papal greed.[1]

The Canto closes with a prophecy the form of which
gains a peculiar force when we remember the Heaven
in which it is uttered :

> ' But Vatican and the other parts elect
> Of Rome, which have a cemetery been
> Unto the soldiery that followed Peter,
> Shall soon be freed from the adultery.'

The reference may be to the ignominious death of
Boniface VIII. in 1303, or the removal of the Papal Court
two years later to Avignon, or, more generally, that
hope of a Deliverer from the oppressions of the Church
which breathes through many a passage of the *Commedia*.   But the word of special significance is 'adultery.'
In this star various forms of sensual love are redeemed
and purified ; but Dante declares in effect that there is
a spiritual adultery which is beyond redemption, and
for which nothing remains but judgment.   St. Paul
calls covetousness idolatry, and idolatry in the Old
Testament is regarded as spiritual unfaithfulness on
the part of Israel to her Divine Husband.   The translation in the Vulgate of 'Thou shalt not covet' by
'Non concupisces,' and of 'coveting' by 'concupiscentia,'
undoubtedly strengthened the association of the two
sins in men's minds.[2]   It was natural, therefore, that
in this Heaven of Venus Dante's thought should pass
from the carnal to the spiritual form of the sin.   The
Church was the Spouse of God, and her covetous
idolatry of wealth was to his mind a spiritual infidelity

---

[1] *Par.* xviii. 133-6.   See p. 291.
[2] Rom. vii. 7 : 'Peccatum non cognovi nisi per legem ; nam concupis-
centiam nesciebam nisi lex diceret : Non concupisces.'

to her Divine Husband, of far deeper heinousness than
any mere lust of the flesh.[1]

[1] The idea runs everywhere through Dante's works. Simony is a pros-
titution of 'the things of God which ought to be espoused to goodness'
(*Inf.* xix. 1); the Church is the 'dishevelled harlot' that sold herself to
Philip the Fair and allowed herself to be dragged into captivity in Avignon
(*Purg.* xxxii. 148-160)—in shameful contrast to Rahab, her Old Testament
type. Nay, lower still, in his letter to Henry VII. Dante calls Florence
'this abandoned and impious Myrrha,' the imputation being that, by
yielding herself so completely to Boniface, she was guilty of a species of
spiritual incest with her spiritual Father (*Epis.* vii. 7 ; *Inf.* xxx. 37-40).

BEYOND THE SHADOW

Cantos X-XXII

O insensata cura dei mortali,
  Quanto son difettivi sillogismi
  Quei che ti fanno in basso batter l'ali!
Chi dietro a iura, e chi ad aforismi
  Sen giva, e chi seguendo sacerdozio,
  E chi regnar per forza o per sofismi,
E chi rubare, e chi civil negozio,
  Chi nel diletto della carne involto,
  S'affaticava, e chi si dava all' ozio;
Quando da tutte queste cose sciolto,
  Con Beatrice m'era suso in cielo
  Cotanto gloriosamente accolto.

Par. xi. 1-12.

I saw Eternity the other night
Like a great Ring of pure and endless light,
  All calm, as it was bright;
And round beneath it, Time in hours, days, years,
  Driv'n by the spheres
Like a vast shadow mov'd, in which the world
  And all her train were hurl'd.

.   .   .   .   .   .

One whispered thus,
This Ring the Bride-groome did for none provide,
  But for His bride.

HENRY VAUGHAN.

CHAPTER VIII

1. *The Three Circles of Theology*

WE have now emerged from the last shadow of earthly stain or weakness into the cloudless light of God, and it may be well to remind ourselves of the nature of the change which this involves. The souls in the three Heavens within the shadow failed somewhat in the three theological virtues—the inconstant spirits of the Moon in Faith, the ambitious spirits of Mercury in Hope, and spirits of Lovers in Venus in Love. The souls in the unclouded Heavens on which we now enter have these three virtues in their fulness; and, in addition, each of the next four Heavens is specially endowed with one of the four cardinal virtues—the theologians of the Sun with Prudence; the soldiers of Mars with Fortitude; the righteous rulers of Jupiter with Justice; and the contemplatives of Saturn with Temperance.[1]

A brief outline of the four and a half Cantos which the Heaven of the Sun occupies will help us to follow more intelligently the long and difficult discussion of the symbolism which lies before us. After praising God for his arrival in the Sun, which is His sensible image, Dante finds himself and Beatrice surrounded by a circle of twelve spirits in the form of starry lights of such brilliancy that they shine out clearly even against the dazzling background of the Sun. One of them, St. Thomas Aquinas the Dominican, Dante's chief authority in moral and theological questions, names his companions in his circle, pronounces a great eulogy

[1] See Introduction, p. 15.

on St. Francis, and bewails the degeneracy of his own
Order. On his resuming silence, a second circle, also
of twelve stars, appears outside the first, fitting harmoniously into its dance and song; and the friend of
Aquinas, St. Bonaventura the Franciscan, acts as its
spokesman, pronouncing a eulogy on St. Dominic,
naming the souls in his circle, and lamenting the corruption of his own Order. And finally, after a discourse by Solomon on the Resurrection body, far out
beyond these two arises a third circle like a horizon
clearing up; 'new subsistences' appear in it like stars
scarce seen in the first fall of evening; and then suddenly it flashes out into such burning brightness that
Dante's eyes are unable to bear it, and he can only
exclaim:

O true sparkling of the Holy Spirit!

It may conduce to clearness if I state here at the
outset the interpretation of the three circles which I
hope to establish in the detailed exposition. The fact
that Aquinas is the spokesman of the first circle implies
that it represents, on the whole, the Dominican type
of theology—the type which has its chief source in the
intellect, and of which St. Thomas himself is the leading exponent. Similarly, the choice of the Franciscan
St. Bonaventura as the mouthpiece of the second
circle means that it stands for the Franciscan type
of theology — a type represented by Bonaventura
himself, 'the Seraphic Doctor,' with a much stronger
infusion of mysticism, and greater reliance on the
instincts of the heart than on the arguments of the
intellect. The two are not antagonistic: it is one of
Dante's chief aims to show that they are complementary
and necessary to each other. Yet even the union of
them is not the final type of theology: there is a
knowledge of God—the 'true sparkling of the Holy
Spirit'—far out on the horizon of the future, wider in
its scope than anything Aquinas or Bonaventura had
reached, and too bright yet for mortal eyes. I wish to
connect this third circle with the prophecies of the last

soul named in the Franciscan circle—Joachim the
Calabrian Abbot, whose doctrine of the third era of the
world, that of the Holy Spirit, was creating in Dante's
day such widespread division and persecution in the
Franciscan Order itself. Dante, in short, wishes to
indicate the amount of truth he believed to be contained
in this Joachimite doctrine of the era of the Holy
Ghost. It is also possible, though I cannot feel so
sure, that the first two circles correspond in some way
to the eras of the Father and of the Son. As we shall
see, these Cantos overflow with allusions to the Trinity,
and it is almost impossible to conceive of Dante's setting three such circles in this Heaven of Theologians,
without intending them to correspond in some fashion
to the three Persons of the Godhead.

We turn now to the detailed exposition. Dante was
no more aware of his ascent to the Sun than a man is
of his first thought before it comes. Beatrice, who
represents Theology in its widest sense, and the souls
of Theologians, who constitute 'the fourth household
of the High Father,' shine so brightly that he saw
them, not by their colour, but by their light, light
visible even against the brilliance of the Sun. The
meaning is best seen by contrasting this with the seven
streamers which, in the Earthly Paradise, flow from
the Golden Candlestick back over the whole Procession
of the sacred writers: the light of Revelation broken
up into the seven colours of the rainbow.[1] Here in the
Celestial Paradise the broken hues of Revelation are
blended back into their original unity—the white light
of the Eternal Truth. We shall soon see that this unity
of truth is one of the leading ideas of this Heaven.

On his arrival, Beatrice calls on Dante to praise God
for his ascent to this nobler sphere:

> 'Give thanks, give thanks
> To the Sun of the Angels, who to this
> Sensible sun hath raised thee by His grace.'[2]

'No object of sense in all the universe,' says Dante in

---

[1] *Purg.* xxix. 43-150.   [2] *Par.* x. 52-54.

the *Convito,* ' is more worthy to be made the symbol of
God than the Sun, which enlightens with the light of
sense, itself first, and then all the celestial and
elemental bodies ; and in like manner God illuminates
first Himself with intellectual light, and then the
celestial and other creatures capable of intellect'[1]—
that is, Angels and men. In other words, Dante knows
that even yet he is only in the 'sensible sun' which is
but a symbol of that Sun who is the light of all Intelligences; and therefore that the theology which the Sun
represents is not the final vision, the direct immediate
knowledge of God. Yet, though he is still in a world
of symbols, his gratitude was so filled with devotion
and love to God, that for a moment he forgot Beatrice
herself. Whereat she smiled : Theology, which she
represents, has fulfilled its chief end when it raises
the soul beyond itself into an ecstasy of love and praise.
Then 'the splendour of her smiling eyes' divided his
mind, rapt into this unity of devotion, among the many
souls of this Heaven and the many forms of theological
thought for which they stand.[2]

The Sun thus symbolizing God, it is the appropriate
'mansion' of Theologians ; and the Trinity forming the
great subject of their study, these Cantos overflow with
allusions to this doctrine, some of which I may here
point out and explain. The opening lines of Canto x.
strike this Trinitarian keynote at the very outset :

> Looking into His Son with the Love
> Which the one and the other breathe eternally,
> The Primal and unutterable Power
> Whate'er through mind or space doth circle
> With so great order made, that whoso sees it
> Cannot remain without some taste of Him.

This is the doctrine that Creation is the act of the
whole Trinity. 'To create,' says Aquinas, 'pertains to
God according to His being, which is His essence, which
is common to the three Persons. Hence creation is not
proper to any one Person, but is common to the entire
Trinity. . . . God the Father wrought the creature

---

[1] *Conv.* iii. 12.   [2] *Par.* x. 59-63.

through His Word, which is His Son; and through His
Love, which is the Holy Spirit. . . . To the Father is
attributed and appropriated *Power*, which is specially
manifested in creation, and therefore to be creator is
attributed to the Father. To the Son is appropriated
Wisdom, through which every one who acts by intellect operates; and therefore it is said of the Son: *All
things were made by him* (John i. 3). To the Holy Spirit
is appropriated *Goodness* (*bonitas*), to which belongs
government leading things to their proper ends, and
the giving of life.'[1] We must also note the care with
which Dante states the doctrine of the Double Procession—the going forth of the Holy Spirit, not, as the
Greeks held, from the Father alone, but from both
Father and Son. It was the addition by the Latin
Church of the *filioque* clause to the Nicene Creed, which
was one chief cause of the Great Schism between East
and West which became final in 1054. The Greeks held
that to derive the Procession of the Spirit from both
Father and Son implied two Principles in the Godhead.
Aquinas replies that the Spirit necessarily proceeds
from the Son, else there would be no real distinction of
Person between them, and the Trinity would be denied.[2]
Probably Dante had here a special interest in asserting
the orthodox doctrine, because the two chief spokesmen of this Heaven were summoned to defend it
against the Greek deputies at the Council of Lyons
in 1274. Aquinas died on the way, and Bonaventura
during the sitting of the Council. The two sides agreed
upon a form of words which united them for the
moment: the Holy Ghost proceeds from the Father and
the Son, yet 'not as from two Principles, but as from
one Principle; not by two Spirations, but by one
Spiration.' The Prelates of East and West chanted the
Nicene Creed in their respective tongues, with the
filioque added; but the agreement was a purely verbal
one, and the old Schism soon prevailed. It is, then,
this mystery of the Trinity, thus fought over by the
Church on earth, which is now clearly revealed to this

[1] *Summa*, i. q. xlv. a. 6.   [2] *Summa*, i. q. xxxvi. a. 2.

> fourth family
> Of the high Father, who forever sates it,
> Showing how he doth *breathe*, and how *beget*.[1]

In connection with this doctrine of creation by the
Trinity, there is a passage about the motions of the Sun
of great difficulty.[2] It seems to be given as a supreme
example of the *order* of creation. Dante asks the reader
to lift his eyes to 'the high wheels' at that point
'where the one motion on the other strikes'—that is
the equinoctial point, where the ecliptic, 'the oblique
circle which bears the planets,' crosses the circle of the
Equator. The reference is to the annual revolution of
the Sun. Its *daily* motion is from east to west, and
parallel to the Equator; but its *annual* motion is from
west to east, and along the Zodiac at a certain angle to
the Equator. Dante now supposes two things. (1)
There might have been no such angle—the Zodiac, the
pathway of the planets, might have run parallel with
the Equator, in which case,

> Much virtue in the heaven would be in vain,
> And almost every potency down here were dead.

Or (2) if the angle at which the Zodiac branches off
from the Equator were greater or less than it is, much
would be wanting in the order of the universe both
above and below. All this sounds unintelligible to
many readers, yet Dante's meaning is simple. It is
contained in x. 32, 33, where he speaks of the Sun, 'the
greatest minister of Nature,' as

> *circling through the spirals*
> In which ever earlier he presents himself.

This is explained in *Convito* iii. 5. Dante pictured the
way in which, from the Spring equinox onward, the
sun rises earlier morning by morning till it reaches its
highest point and begins to descend, as the spirals of
the screw of a press. Along these spirals it rises north
of the Equator *earlier* each morning for ninety-one
days and a little more. Then the spiral movement is

---

[1] *Par.* x. 49-51. See below, p. 531 f. on xxxiii. 115-120.
[2] *Par.* x. 7-27.

reversed for the same length of time, the sun rising *later* each morning. The same then takes place on the south side of the Equator. Now, it is by this annual spiral movement of the sun, caused by the obliquity of the ecliptic, that every part of the earth, says Dante, receives in the full round of the year an equal distribution of light and darkness. If, for example, the sun moved on a circle parallel with the Equator, and directly above it, the equatorial regions would be scorched, the present temperate zones would have no summer, and the Arctic regions would lie in a perpetual winter. If, on the other hand, the obliquity of the ecliptic were either greater or less, there would result some disturbance of the proper distribution of sunlight, and therefore of the seasons on which human life depends. The probability is that Dante was thinking not of the seasons alone, but of the entire influences which descend through the planets, and in particular that distribution of Divine light which is necessary for the salvation of the world. Hence in this passage he urges his reader to feed himself with this heavenly food which he has set before him; and in the *Convito* he breaks into praise of the Divine wisdom: 'Wherefore it may be seen that, by divine provision, the world is so ordained that when the sphere of the sun has revolved and returned to any point, this ball, on which we are placed, has received in its every region an equal time of light and of darkness. Oh, unutterable wisdom that didst thus ordain, how poor is our mind to comprehend thee; and ye for whose behoof and delight I am writing, in what blindness do ye live, not lifting up your eyes to these things but keeping them fixed upon the mire of your folly!'[1]

---

[1] *Conv.* iii. 5 (Wicksteed's transl.). It is curious to compare this with Milton's view. But for sin, the sun had circled directly above the equator, and perpetual spring, equal in day and night, had smiled upon the earth. On the Fall, God gave the Angels charge to alter the world to bring it into keeping with the fallen state by extremes of heat and cold, storms and droughts, and baleful influences of the planets. This was accomplished by the obliquity of the ecliptic, which was brought about in one of two ways—either the earth was pushed askew, or the sun's course was altered, Milton cannot say which:

I.

Before entering on the narrative it may be well to gather out some characteristics of the two Circles of Theologians, which may help us to understand better their relations to one another.

(1) They are spoken of as garlands surrounding Beatrice. The inner one is called

> 'this garland which encircles with delight
> The beauteous Lady who strengthens thee for heaven';

and when the second forms beyond it, Dante says

> Of those sempiternal roses
> The garlands twain encompassed us about.[1]

The meaning is obvious. In the first place, theologians are many, theology is one. However these spirits may have differed from one another in the great subject of their study here below, in that heavenly world they are woven together into crowns for Beatrice, the Divine Wisdom; and the crowns themselves, as we shall see immediately, are so vitally related that they are not two but one. In the second place, they are Dante's garland as well as his Lady's: the theologians whom he sets in these two Circles are undoubtedly those whom he wishes us to regard as his chief teachers and guides in theology. This is obvious in the case of the two spokesmen. The influence of Aquinas pervades the entire poem, and when Dante

> 'Some say he bid his Angels turn askance
> The poles of Earth twice ten degrees and more
> From the Sun's axle; they with labour pushed
> Oblique the centric Globe: some say the Sun
> Was bid turn reins from the equinoctial road
> Like distant breadth' (*Par. Lost*, x. 649 ff.).

However grotesque this sounds, it is only an attempt to show that Nature shared in the Fall of Man; and Dante has substantially the same idea when he makes the storms and variations of weather cease at St. Peter's Gate on Mount Purgatory, and perpetual Spring reign in the Eden on the top (*Purg.* xxi. 40-57). To Dante, however, the obliquity of the ecliptic was an original part of the order of the universe, and a supreme proof of the Divine wisdom and goodness.

[1] *Par.* x. 91-93; xii. 19, 20.

hears Bonaventura's voice he turns to it as the needle to the pole.[1]

(2) Their own proper shape is invisible; they appear in the form of stars, the brightest in the sky,[2] partly to indicate that all self is lost in the light of God, the joy of knowledge glowing round them ; and partly in fulfilment of the words of Daniel (xii. 3): 'They that be wise shall shine as the brightness of the firmament ; and they that turn many to righteousness as the stars for ever and ever.' They are still 'fires living and conquering'[3]—conquering not merely our eyes, or the brightness of the sun, as some think, but the darkness and evil of this lower world. As already pointed out, they have no colour, for colour is only a fragment of light: the pure white light of Divine truth in its unity shines through them.

(3) Their movements are also significant. They dance and sing, partly in joy of their vision of God, and partly in yearning for a deeper vision : for we must never forget that motion means the longing of the soul for its Highest Good. The subject of their song is the Trinity and the Incarnation, three times repeated in the threefold circling of the dance :

> That One and Two and Three who ever liveth,
> And reigneth ever in Three and Two and One,
> Not circumscribed and all things circumscribing,
> Three several times was chanted by each one
> Among those spirits, with such melody
> That for all merit it were just reward.[4]

And again :

> There did they sing, not Bacchus and not Paean,
> But in the divine nature Persons Three,
> And in one Person the divine and human—

for the Incarnation is the last and crowning mystery of theology.[5]

(4) Their knowledge of these high mysteries is pro-

---

[1] *Par.* xii. 28-30.   [2] *Par.* xiii. 1-24.
[3] *Par.* x. 64.   [4] *Par.* xiv. 28-33.
[5] *Par.* xiii. 25-27. The Incarnation is the last flash of the Beatific Vision seen by Dante himself (xxxiii. 127-142).

gressive. Dante indicates this by comparing the
garland of theologians to ladies who pause in the
dance waiting for the music of a new movement :

> Ladies to me they seemed, not from the dance released,
> But who do pause, in silence listening
> Until that they have gathered the new notes.

Casini says the simile is drawn from the pauses in the
singing and dancing of the *ballata* in Dante's day,
especially in Tuscany; and while indeed this adds
vividness to the comparison, it was not for mere
vividness it was made. The spiritual idea is that in
Paradise there is an endless growth in the knowledge
of God which is eternal life : joy in what is already
known, expressed in song ; longing for fuller vision,
symbolized in the circling of the dance ; and the silent
pause of meditation necessary for the new knowledge,
represented by the ladies waiting to catch 'the new
notes' of the next movement of the dance.[1]

(5) But, as already hinted, Dante's chief interest
gathers round the unity of all types and shades of
true theology—a unity which is a passion with him,
and which he seeks to bring out in a great variety of
ways. Let us look first at the two distinct theological
types represented by the two inner circles. Thomas
Aquinas the Dominican is the chief speaker of the
first; Bonaventura the Franciscan, of the second. We
have a right, therefore, to infer that Dante meant the
circles to stand respectively for the Dominican and
Franciscan types of theology; and the distinction
between the two is indicated in the contrast Aquinas

---

[1] *Par.* x. 79-81. Of course, one is quite prepared to hear that this
interpretation is one of the over-subtleties of commentators; but if the
motion of these spirits means, as it certainly does, yearning for fuller
vision of God, it is reasonable to suppose that their *pause* has also its
symbolic sense. The truth is that commentators are not subtle enough,
or subtle in the wrong places ; they often content themselves with the
mere surface and pictorial aspect of a simile instead of penetrating to its
symbolic core. Critics should remember that it is quite as bad an error
of exegesis *not* to see a symbolic meaning where the poet meant it, as to
see one where he did not mean it. In the *De Mon.* (iii. 4) he says 'there
are two ways of going wrong as to the mystic sense, either by looking for
it where it is not, or by taking it as it ought not to be taken.' There is a
third way—never suspecting that it is there at all.

draws between the Founders of the two Orders—the 'two Princes' ordained of God to guide the Church 'on this side and on that':

> ' The one was all seraphical in ardour,
> The other by his wisdom upon earth
> A splendour was of light cherubical,' [1]

The first is St. Francis, 'the Seraphic Father.' The Seraphim are the highest Order of Angels, nearest God, and burning with His Love. This therefore indicates the type of the Franciscan theology— theology of the heart rather than of the head, of intuition rather than of discourse of reason. And although, in spite of the warnings of St. Francis that books and knowledge would be the ruin of the Order, many of his followers became learned men, like Bonaventura himself, yet something of the Founder's spirit clung to them which gave a distinct colour to Franciscan theology—a touch of mystical seraphic ardour, which trusted more to the affections of the heart than to the colder speculations of the head.

St. Dominic, on the other hand, is 'a splendour of cherubic light'—the Cherubim being the second Order of Angels, who shine with the knowledge of God, as the Seraphim burn with His love. St. Dominic was the reflected 'splendour' upon earth of that cherubic knowledge and wisdom in Heaven. Hence the Dominican type of theology is prevailingly intellectual. Unlike his great Italian brother, Dominic was from the first a man of learning and the schools. His chief aim being to combat heretics, and learning being a weapon to smite them with, his followers became frequenters of the universities. Thus a certain character was stamped on Dominican theology—a clear, learned, intellectual impress, which is seen at its highest in 'the Angelic Doctor' who acts as the spokesman of the first circle. It is scarcely possible to imagine a more perfect specimen of the pure

[1] *Par.* xi. 37-39.

scholastic intellect than Thomas Aquinas—perfect clearness, perfect knowledge according to his time, perfect calmness of statement. Milman draws his intellectual portrait with too little atmosphere perhaps, yet the likeness is unmistakable to any one who knows Aquinas at all: 'He approaches more nearly than most philosophers, certainly than most divines, to pure embodied intellect. He is perfectly passionless; he has no polemic indignation, nothing of the Churchman's jealousy and suspicion; he has no fear of the result of any investigation; he hates nothing, hardly heresy; loves nothing, unless perhaps naked, abstract truth.'[1] When he adds, ' God must be revealed by syllogistic process,' Milman falls into the not uncommon error of drawing too sharp a line between the scholastic and the mystical intellect. For, as Harnack shows, there is a very real sense in which 'Mysticism is the presupposition of Scholasticism,' because the ' syllogistic process' of a man like Aquinas rested upon personal piety, and personal piety was conceived of as *contemplation* of the relation of the soul to God, accompanied by an ascetic discipline of life. Hence ' Mystic theology and Scholastic theology are one and the same phenomenon, which only present themselves in manifold gradations, according as the subjective or objective interest prevails '—that is, according as the soul within, or the world without, in their relation to God, predominates. ' The former interest was so little lacking even to the most distinguished Schoolmen that their whole theology can be unhesitatingly described as *also* Mystic theology—for Thomas, Mysticism is the starting-point and practical application of Scholasticism—and, on the other hand, there are theologians who are described as Mystics, but who, in the strength of their desire to know the *world*, and to understand in a systematic way the Church doctrine, are not a whit behind the so-called Schoolmen.'[2]

---

[1] *Latin Christianity*, Bk. xiv. chap. iii.
[2] *History of Dogma*, vi. pp. 26, 27 (Eng. transl.).

II.

Subject, then, to this qualification, we may describe the two circles as the Scholastic and the Mystical, or the Aristotelian and the Platonic the latter distinction certainly indicating the difference between Aquinas and Bonaventura.[1] Within this general character of each circle are names of men whom we might be inclined to class otherwise; but I have no doubt whatever that Dante selected the names with the utmost care, and discriminated the two groups according as, in his regard, there prevailed in them the cherubic or the seraphic, the wisdom of the head or the ardour of the heart. Having thus distinguished them, Dante is at still greater pains to show their Divine and heavenly unity.

(1) Take, for example, the way in which he indicates the unity of the various elements which compose the first circle, the Dominican or Scholastic. The mere fact that it *is* a circle implies this unity, the circle being the most perfect form, the complete round of truth so far as the intellect can compass it. We have seen also how the separate flowers of the circle are woven into a garland for Beatrice, the symbol of Theology. But there is another figure by which Dante beautifully suggests at once the unity and the differences without which the unity could not exist. He compares the dance and song of the first circle to the movements and music of a horologe, whose sweet chimes ring the faithful to matins:

---

[1] Father Rickaby (*Scholasticism*, 24) says Bonaventura differed from Aquinas 'by making more of the will than of the understanding; by being conservative rather than an innovator in philosophy; by not allowing the angels to be pure forms; by allowing a plurality of substantial forms, one, however, dominant over the rest, in the same being; by ascribing to primordial matter some radical predispositions of its own; by denying the reality of the distinction between essence and existence in existing creatures; by making the principle of individuation to be matter and form together; by not allowing the philosophic possibility of creation from all eternity.' Philosophically, Dante was much more of a disciple of Aquinas than of Bonaventura.

> Then, like a horologe that calleth us
> What hour the Bride of God rises to sing
> Matins to her Spouse, that he may love her,
> Wherein one part the other draws and thrusts,
> ' Ting ting ' forth sounding with so sweet a note
> That the well-disposèd spirit swells with love :
> So did I see the glorious wheel revolve
> And render voice to voice in harmony
> And in sweetness which may not be known,
> Save there where joy doth make itself eternal.[1]

The significant words are 'one part the other *draws and thrusts*.' The harmony and sweetness are produced by the very differences of the theologians forming this circle, the attraction and repulsion of their various views issuing in songs of praise for what each adds to each, and setting them all in motion with longing for still greater knowledge.[2]

(2) There is a corresponding relation of harmony between the two circles in song and motion. They are compared to 'two rainbows parallel and like in colour'; to voice and its echo; to the movements of the eyelids ' which must needs together shut and lift themselves.' When the second circle, the Franciscan, first appeared outside the other, we are told that it took its movement and its song from the circle within;[3] and in a later passage we learn the precise way in which it did so. Take, says the poet, fifteen of the brightest stars scattered throughout the heavens; add to these seven from the Great Bear and two from the Little Bear; imagine the twenty-four arranged in two circles like Ariadne's Crown,

> And the one within the other to have its rays,
> And both to whirl themselves in such a manner
> That one should forward go, the other backward.[4]

---

[1] *Par.* x. 139-148. Plumptre thinks the comparison is drawn from 'one of the mediæval clocks, of which the Cathedrals of Strasburg and Wells furnish examples, and in which, as the clock struck the hours, figures came forth and wheeled round and round, as in a dance'; but I am doubtful of this. For the difficulties of ascertaining the hours at night in monasteries before the invention of clocks in the twelfth century, see Dr. Moore's *Studies in Dante*, 3rd series, 103.

[2] The idea is repeated in *Par.* xiv. 19, where the souls are '*thrust and drawn* by greater gladness.' We are reminded of Hegel's unity of opposites, the reaching of truth through antagonisms.

[3] *Par.* xii. 1-27.

[4] *Par.* xiii. 16-18.

This last line I have translated as I have finally decided, after much hesitation, to interpret it; but it is necessary to give the alternative version accepted by many Dante scholars. The line in the original stands:

Che l'uno andasse *al prima* e l'altro *al poi*,

and many render it:

That the one should go *first* and the other *after*.

According to this translation the two circles revolve *in the same direction*, but it is the inner circle (the Dominican) which *begins* the movement, and the other *follows*. If this is the idea, the meaning is substantially the same as when Dante compared the two circles to a voice and its echo—'the one without born of the one within.'[1] This gives a perfectly good meaning, and one which pervades the *Paradiso*. The inner circle of knowledge sets in motion the outer circle of love. According to Aquinas, love springs from knowledge and is proportioned to it—as the poor sinful Queen said,

'We needs must love the highest *when we see it.*'

This view is expressly stated in Canto xxviii. 109-111:

'Hence may be seen how the being blessed
Is founded on the act which seeth,
Not on that which loves, *which follows after.*'

Those, then, who take this translation have much to say for it.[2] Dante is here taking his side in the controversy as to whether love sprang from knowledge or

---

[1] *Par.* xii. 13.

[2] In point of fact, so far as my reading goes, commentators say nothing for their different translations of this line. They do, indeed, state their preference for this rendering or that; but they seem to have no idea that, *whichever rendering we adopt,* the question remains,—what did Dante mean by it? For it is inconceivable that he took all this trouble to put the motions of the four-and-twenty stars before our eyes, and then meant nothing by it. Whether he says the two circles began their movements *at different times,* or that they moved *in different directions,* in either case it is an expositor's duty to suggest an interpretation or frankly confess his ignorance.

knowledge from love. Aquinas held the former, Duns
Scotus the Franciscan, the latter.[1]

I take the other translation, which means that the
two circles go *in opposite directions*, partly because of
the figure which, I think, was before Dante's eyes. He
pictured the two circles very much, if I may use a
mechanical illustration, as if they were two cog-wheels,
the teeth of which fitted into and drove one another in
opposite directions. The teeth are the rays which each
had, says Dante, 'within the other.' When we remember that they are the rays in the one case of knowledge, in the other of love, we will not wonder at their
contrary movements. In this world, at least, head and
heart often seem to move, even in religion, in opposite
directions, to have different methods of work, and to
arrive at conclusions hard to reconcile. In the world
above, the great reconciliation takes place: the contrary movements of head and heart, knowledge and
love, fit into and even produce one another, as by the
'kiss of toothèd wheels.' If this interpretation is correct,
nothing could better show Dante's conviction that these
two types of theology belong together and complete
each other—their rays fit into one another, and their
apparent contradictions produce that swift movement
which means intense yearning for a still deeper knowledge and love of God.

(3) Again, Dante takes pains to rebuke the unholy
rivalry which existed in his day between the two
Orders by showing their original friendship and their
present unity in the world of light and love. In the
first place, however Francis and Dominic differed, and
indeed just because they differed, 'their works were to
one end'—the raising of the Church out of the living
death into which it had sunk. Its two great enemies
were its own worldliness, and the almost innumerable
heretical growths for which that worldliness was
largely responsible. The former evil was met by the
'*doing*' of St. Francis, his active life of Christian love;
and the latter by the '*word*' of St. Dominic, the teach-

---

[1] On this controversy, see below, p. 442 f.

ing by which he protected the people from heresies.[1]
For this twofold service they were raised up by God :
two Champions to gather together by word and deed,
to increase, consolidate, and encourage, the army of the
Church which was moving 'slow, suspicious and few '; [2]
two Pilots to guide 'the barque of Peter' across the
high seas 'by the right sign,' the Cross; [3] two wheels
of the Chariot of the Church, Love and Knowledge,
on which it moves into battle against foes within and
without.[4] If then God thus united these two men,
using their diverse gifts for this one great end, how
evil must be the present hatred and rivalry of their
followers ! To emphasize this rebuke, Dante puts the
praise of St. Francis into the mouth of Aquinas the
Dominican, and of St. Dominic into that of Bonaventura
the Franciscan : each feeling that to speak of one is to
speak of both.[5]

(4) One interesting note of unity remains : the clearing away in Paradise of the old theological rivalries
and misunderstandings of earth. An example is given
in each of the two circles. In the Dominican, the soul
next to Aquinas on the left is that of a certain Sigieri,
believed to be Siger of Brabant, a professor of Philosophy in the University of Paris in the thirteenth
century, with whom Thomas came into collision. 'It
appears,' says Toynbee, 'that Siger took a prominent
part in the violent disputes which arose between the
lay members of the University of Paris and the friars
of the mendicant orders concerning the liberty of
teaching; and that in 1266 he and Guillaume de St.
Amour were publicly refuted by St. Thomas Aquinas,

---

[1] *Par.* xii. 43-45.   [2] *Par.* xii. 37-39.

[3] *Par.* xi. 118-120. *Per dritto segno* is generally translated 'towards
the right sign,' but I take it ' by the right sign,' and understand the only
right sign for the Church to be the Cross.

[4] *Par.* xii. 106-111.

[5] 'These Religious Orders still maintain this reciprocal courtesy. The
Franciscans officiate in the Dominican Church on St. Dominic's Feast.
. . . On St. Francis' Day the Dominicans officiate for the Franciscans'
(Note by Father Bowden in his edition of Hettinger's *Dante's Divina Com-
media*, 308). In Dante's day ' this reciprocal courtesy,' it is to be feared,
was confined to Paradise.

the champion of the Dominicans.' He is said to have
been executed at the Papal Court at Orvieto in 1283 or
1284. It is this old opponent of Aquinas who is now
his left hand neighbour in Paradise.[1] That this is no
mere accident is proved by a precisely similar arrangement in the Franciscan circle. The spirit immediately
on Bonaventura's left is ' the Calabrian abbot Joachim,'
with whom personally indeed he had nothing to do since
the abbot was dead some twenty years before his birth.
But Bonaventura had much to do, as we shall see, with
Joachim's theology which, in the form of prophecy,
spread rapidly among the 'Spiritual' Franciscans.
When Bonaventura became General of the Order, he
dealt severely with these 'Spirituals' or Joachimites
as being virtually heretics; and now the very man
against whose theology he fought on earth shines at
his side in the same circle in Paradise. Dante's meaning is clear: the man whom on earth we regard as a
heretic may be our nearest neighbour in that world of
light where we know as we are known.[2]

[1] *Par.* x. 133-138. See below, p. 191. According to Ueberweg, however,
Siger ' passed over from a type of doctrine akin to Scotism to Thomism'
(*History of Philosophy*, i. 457).

[2] *Par.* xii. 140. It is not meant that Joachim himself was regarded as
a heretic, though he narrowly escaped this fate through his eagerness to
prove heresy against another. He charged Peter the Lombard (one of
the souls in the inner circle here) with holding a Quaternity in God,
instead of the Trinity he professed to teach. The tract in which Joachim
brought this accusation was itself condemned by the great Lateran Council
in 1215, thirteen years after his death; and he himself escaped only
because shortly before his death he had professed himself a good Catholic
and submitted his writings to the judgment of Rome. The relation of
his theology to the Franciscan Order is more fully discussed in chap. xi.
The reconciliation of opposing theologians is parallel to that of kings in
the valley of the Princes in *Purg.* vii., where Princes who on earth were
sworn enemies are seen sitting side by side, singing the same Christian
hymn, and comforting one another during their exile from the Fatherland.

DOMINICAN·AND
FRANCISCAN
CIRCLES·OF
THEOLOGY

KNOWLEDGE
AND·LOVE

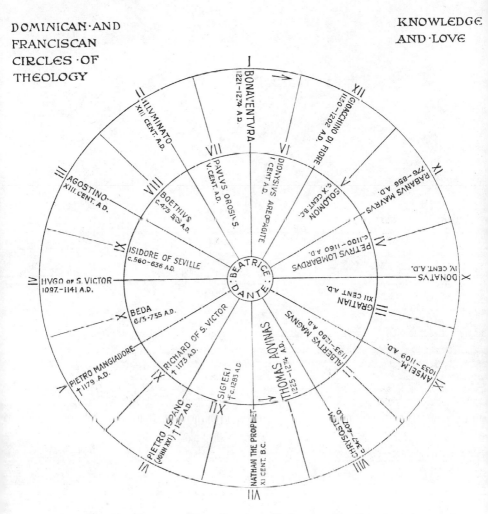

According to the exposition, the two Circles, representing two types of Theology, revolve in opposite directions, the inner (the Dominican) to the right, the outer (the Franciscan) to the left. Their rays, of Knowledge and Love respectively, fit into one another in their revolutions after the manner of the teeth of cog-wheels (*Par.* xiii. 16-18). The mechanical illustration, of course, must not be pressed too far.

CHAPTER IX

FOURTH HEAVEN—THE SUN: THEOLOGIANS

2. *The Dominican Circle*: *Aquinas*

WE turn now to the narrative. St. Thomas Aquinas, when his circle had ceased from the threefold song and dance with which it welcomed Dante and his Guide, revealed the names of the twelve spirits that composed it. He begins reverently with his 'brother and master,' 'Albert of Cologne,' known to us as Albertus Magnus —'brother,' because he belonged to the same Order, and 'master,' because Aquinas was his pupil. The twenty-one folio volumes which he left on almost every subject then known—logic, metaphysics, psychology, natural science, ethics, theology, chemistry, botany, and others —justify his title of 'Universal Doctor.' He was almost the first to Christianize Aristotle [1]—to apply his systematic methods to the construction of that vast scientific organism of the Christian faith which his pupil, with greater keenness and precision, wrought out in the *Summa Theologiae*. For this, the name of 'the Ape of Aristotle' was flung at him in contempt, and he was accused of allotting to a Pagan 'the principal seat in the middle of Christ's temple.' In Dante's regard, Aquinas triumphantly vindicated his master's work and method.[2]

---

[1] See note on Alexander of Hales on p. 214 below.

[2] Albert is the true fountain-head of the *Summa*, and therefore of the ethics and theology of the greater part of the *Commedia*. His proper title to fame is, as Milman says, that, like the Franciscan Roger Bacon, he applied himself to physical science and advocated experimental methods of research. 'He was great,' says Archbishop Vaughan, 'in natural history ; he was a botanist, a chemist, a geographer, an architect, a geologist, and a mechanic, besides being an anatomist and an alchemist'

After modestly naming himself after his master—
'and I Thomas of Aquino'—Aquinas points out as the
third in the circle the spirit of Gratian, 'the father of
canon law,' as he has been called. 'The rules enacted
by the early church for its relations with the secular
power, its own internal administration, or the conduct
of its members, were called canons,' and were extended
in after times to include opinions of the Fathers and
Decretals of the Popes. Gratian, a Benedictine monk
of the Camaldolese Order, set himself about the middle
of the twelfth century to educe order out of the chaos
of canons and collections of canons which existed in
his day. Dante says that he 'gave such aid to the one
and the other forum that he gives pleasure in Paradise':
in other words, that he brought into harmony civil
and ecclesiastical law. Probably the severe verdict of
Gregorovius is much nearer the truth : ' This celebrated
law book of the Middle Ages remains, now that criticism
has long exposed the fictions contained within it, the
legal colossus of barbarism and darkness, under whose
spell mankind lay for so many centuries. It falsified
the legal conceptions of Church and State in order to
secure the dominion of the world to the Papacy.'[1] To
Dante, however, it was an effort, pleasing to Heaven,
to bring about that harmony between the temporal
and spiritual powers for which he himself wrought
and prayed.

The fourth light is Peter the Lombard, the famous
'Master of the Sentences,' as he was called from his
Sententiarum Libri Quatuor, a collection of sentences

(*Life of St. Thomas of Aquin*—abridged, p. 92). When in 1259 he accepted
the Bishopric of Ratisbon the General of his Order rated him almost as if
he were a renegade : 'Who would believe that you, in the very evening
of life, would set such a blot on your own glory and on that of the Order
which you have done so much to augment? Consider what has befallen
such as have suffered themselves to be drawn into such offices : what
their reputation now is, what fruits they have brought forth, how they
have ended their lives!' (Coulton's *From St. Francis to Dante*, p. 265).
In three years he resigned his see and resumed his life as a friar.

[1] *Rome in the Middle Ages*, iv. 643 (Engl. transl.). Though Dante thus
sets Gratian in this Heaven, he none the less denounces the way in which
the study of the Decretals had displaced that of the Gospels. See above,
p. 161.

from the writings of the Fathers, with objections and
replies, which became the great text-book of theology
in the Middle Ages. The reference in x. 107, 108 is to
the Preface in which Peter says he desires to offer, as
the poor widow did her mite, to the treasury of the
Lord. Aquinas himself wrote a commentary on the
Sentences. Peter had been a pupil of Hugh of St.
Victor, one of the souls in the second circle, but he
seems to have absorbed none of his mysticism. Milman
well calls him the Euclid of theology : within his short
cold authoritative statements, logic and reason could
disport themselves without fear of transgressing the
limits of orthodoxy laid down by the Church.[1]

It may be well to quote what is said of Solomon, the
fifth light, since a difficulty, which Aquinas afterwards
solves, arises from the last line :

> 'The fifth light, that among us is the fairest,
> Breathes forth from such a love that all the world
> Down there is greedy to learn tidings of him :
> Within there is the lofty mind, where wisdom
> So profound was put, that, if the true is true,
> To see so much there never rose a second.' [2]

The eagerness of the world below to hear news of
Solomon sprang from the uncertainty of his salvation.
'The theologians of the Greek Church, headed by
Chrysostom,' says Plumptre, ' were mostly for a
favourable judgment; Augustine and the Latin fathers
for an adverse.' In Pietro Lorenzetti's 'Last Judgment'
in the Campo Santo at Pisa, Solomon's final fate is left
hanging in suspense : he is just climbing out of a tomb
in the centre of the picture, and the only hint given is
that his face is turned towards Christ's right hand side.
In the great fresco of Aquinas in the Chapter House
of Santa Maria Novella in Florence, of all the Scriptural

---

[1] Peter was not the object of universal admiration even in his own
century. 'Walter of St. Victor, a monastic Prior,' says Ueberweg, 'gave,
in about the year 1180, to Abelard, Petrus Lombardus, Gilbert and Peter
of Poitiers, the name of the "four labyrinths of France," affirming that
all of them, "inspired with the Aristotelian spirit, had treated with
scholastic levity of the ineffable Trinity and the Incarnation"' (*History
of Philosophy*, i. 400).   [2] *Par.* x. 109-114.

writers ranged on each side of the Dominican, Solomon
is the only one who lacks the nimbus.[1] Plumptre thinks
that for Dante the scale was turned in his favour by
the mystical interpretation of the *Song of Songs* in St.
Bernard and Hugh of St. Victor, to which the 'love' of
line 110 refers. It was certainly the contrast between
this mystical love and sensual love which created the
uncertainty in men's minds. In the apocryphal book
of *Jesus the Son of Sirach* (xlvii. 19, 20), a passage in
praise of Solomon's wisdom ends with the great blot
upon his life: 'Thou didst stain thy honour, and
pollute thy seed: so that thou broughtest wrath upon
thy children, and wast grieved for thy folly.' In the
Purgatorio (xxx. 10 ff.) Dante had already virtually
decided Solomon's salvation by setting him in the
Procession of the Golden Candlestick, and putting in
his mouth the song of welcome to Beatrice: *Veni
sponsa de Libano*.

Of the sixth light, Dionysius the Areopagite, a
sufficient account has been given in the Introduction.
It is difficult to understand the extraordinary fascination the writings attributed to this 'mythical hero of
mysticism' had for the Middle Ages. 'In one sense he
may be called the father of scholasticism from the
influence he exercised on John of Damascus in the
Eastern, and on Aquinas in the Western, church.' It
has been declared that 'if the writings of Dionysius
were to be lost, they might be recovered piecemeal
from the various works of St. Thomas.'[2] He is the
great authority, as Dante says, on 'the Angelic nature
and ministry,' and we have seen that the entire structure of the *Paradiso* is based upon him. Dante seems,
however, to describe him as a little light—perhaps to
indicate that even this knowledge of the Angels is

---

[1] In the fresco of Christ's Descent into Hell in this Chapter House, our
Lord is represented as rescuing the Old Testament saints from Limbo,
but among them there is no figure that can be identified with Solomon.
On the other hand, in the Byzantine mosaic of the same subject in the
Cathedral of Torcello, two figures at Christ's right seem to be David and
Solomon. This would represent the more charitable judgment of the
Greek Church.

[2] Smith and Wace's *Dictionary of Christian Biography*, i. 847.

small compared with the knowledge of God, the proper subject of theology.

There is some dispute as to the identity of the seventh light, but the way in which it is described:

> ' That advocate of the Christian times
> Of whose Latin Augustine availed himself,'

seems to prove that Paulus Orosius is meant. In his *Historiae adversum Paganos* the phrase here used, 'Christiana tempora,' occurs frequently. 'Paulus Orosius, a native of Tarragona in Spain and a friend of Augustine, wrote his Seven Books of "Histories" about the year 417, while he was still a young man ('religiosus juvenis'), at the request of the Bishop of Hippo. They were to form a history of the world from the Deluge down to his own time (the last entry relates to the year 417), and the object of the book was to show that bloodshed, oppression, and misery had ever been the staple of human history, and that "Christian times" were unjustly blamed for the woes which the barbarians were then inflicting on the empire.'[1] The book was dedicated to St. Augustine, who used it in writing his *De Civitate Dei*. Dante was also indebted to it for many of his references to ancient history. He calls Orosius a little light, to distinguish him from the great schoolmen already named.

The eighth light has a greater number of lines devoted to it than any other member of the circle. It is Boethius, whose *De Consolatione Philosophiae* was one chief solace of Dante after the death of Beatrice.[2] His full name seems to have been Anicius Manlius

---

[1] Hodgkin, *Italy and her Invaders*, i. 245. The History of Orosius, says Toynbee, ' which attained a wide popularity under the title *Ormista* (supposed to represent *Or[osii] M[undi] ist[ori]a*), was translated into Anglo-Saxon (in a free and abridged version) by Alfred the Great.' For Dante's obligations to the *Ormista*, see Toynbee's *Dante Studies and Researches*, 121-136.

[2] *Conv.* ii. 13 ; 16. The 'Consolation' was also translated or paraphrased by King Alfred. Of the four works on the Trinity attributed to Boethius no trace is found till three centuries after his death, and critics declare that the style is not his. The suggestion is made that a second Boethius, or more probably a second Severinus, has been confused with the Roman senator (*Dicty. of Christian Biog.* i. 321).

Severinus Boethius (or Boetius). Born about A.D. 470, he rose to the highest honours under Theodoric, King of the Goths. In 510 he was Consul of Rome, and in 522 his two sons attained to the same honour. The very integrity of his character roused hatred in the Court and wrought his ruin. Under false accusations of treason, he was thrown into prison in Pavia, and finally executed with barbarous cruelty in 525. It was during his imprisonment that he wrote his *De Consolatione,*

> 'which the deceitful world
> Makes manifest to him who listeneth well '—

'a golden volume,' says Gibbon, 'not unworthy of the leisure of Plato or Tully, but which claims incomparable merit from the barbarism of the times and the situation of the author.'[1] In the course of a few centuries, Boethius came to be regarded as a martyr for the Christian faith—in particular for the orthodox doctrine of the Trinity, against the Arian heresy of Theodoric, and he was canonized under the name of St. Severinus. In 772 Luitprand, King of the Lombards, erected a tomb to his memory in the church named in line 128, San Pietro in Cieldauro in Pavia. Dante seems to have connected Boethius in his thoughts with his own ancestor Cacciaguida: in both cases he speaks of 'the fallacious world' and of their coming 'from martyrdom unto this peace.'[2]

The next three spirits are grouped together in a single *terzina*:

> ' See further onward flame the burning breath
> Of Isidore, of Beda, and of Richard
> Who was in contemplation more than man.'

St. Isidore, Bishop of Seville in the beginning of the seventh century, was the author of the *Origines*, an encyclopædia of the learning of the time, and one of the most famous books of study in the Middle Ages. The names of Bede and Richard bring us to our own land, the former being an Englishman and the latter a Scot. In his Epistle to the Italian Cardinals Dante

---

[1] *Decline and Fall*, chap. xxxix.　　　　[2] *Par.* xv. 145-148.

reproaches them for their neglect of Bede's works;[1] and in the Epistle to Can Grande he defends the mysticism of the *Paradiso* by referring his critics to the *De Contemplatione* of Richard of St. Victor, the Augustinian monastery at Paris. Like Peter the Lombard, he was a pupil of Hugh of St. Victor, whom he succeeded as Prior in 1162. He distinguished six stages of Contemplation, the highest transcending Imagination and Reason. When Dante says that Richard 'was in contemplation *more than man*,' he means that he passed out of the limits of human nature. There is in the highest stage of Contemplation, Richard held, a dividing asunder of soul and spirit. 'The spirit is joined to the Lord, and one with Him,—transcends itself and all the limitations of human thought. In such a moment it is conscious of no division, of no change; all contraries are absorbed, the part does not appear less than the whole, nor is the whole greater than a part; the universal is seen as particular, the particular as universal; we forget both all that is without and all that is within ourselves; all is one and one is all; and when the rapture is past the spirit returns from its trance with a dim and dizzy memory of unutterable glory.'[2] Richard is the most mystical spirit of this inner circle.

The twelfth light is that Siger of Brabant whom Aquinas, as we saw, opposed in the earthly life, now his nearest neighbour. The Street of Straw in which Dante says Siger lectured, is the *Rue du Fouarre* near the Place Maubert, itself called after Albertus Magnus (*du Maître Albert*), because for want of room the

---

[1] Plumptre says 'Bede, *Eccl. Hist.* v. 12, supplies another vision of a brighter Purgatory even than Dante's : "A vast and delightful field, full of fragrant flowers, in which were innumerable assemblies of men in white."' It must be remembered, however, that this is only that part of Purgatory, near the confines of Paradise, assigned to those who died in good works. For those who delayed repentance till the end of life, a very different Purgatory is allotted—a great valley with flames on one side and hail and snow on the other, and the deformed spirits tossed back and forward between the burning heat and the piercing cold. Dante has nothing so pitiless as this in his Purgatorio.

[2] Vaughan, *Hours with the Mystics*, i. 163.

Universal Doctor was forced to lecture in this square.
The Rue du Fouarre is said to have got its name from
the bundles of straw which the students of those days
used for seats; and the mention of it is thought by
some to be proof that Dante himself had attended
Siger's lectures. It is impossible to say what is meant
by the 'invidious truths' which Siger 'syllogized';
or why in his grave thoughts he felt death's advent
slow. Probably a somewhat melancholy man who
longed for a world of light to solve the weighty
problems under which his mind laboured.

It is at this point the comparison of this circle to
a horologe occurs. As the parts of a clock 'draw and
thrust' each other and thus sound forth the sweet
matin chime, so these various forms of theology act
and react on each other, producing by their very differences a heavenly harmony of movement and of music:

> Thus did I see the glorious wheel move round,
> And render voice to voice, in harmony
> And in sweetness that may not be known,
> Save there where joy doth make itself eternal.

The contrast to earth is so great that Dante marvels
at 'the insensate care of mortals,' entangled in 'the
cares of the world, and the deceitfulness of riches, and
the lusts of other things,' while he with Beatrice was
thus gloriously received in heaven.[1]

---

[1] *Par.* x. 142—xi. 12. We must regard as improbable the conjecture that
it was these first ten Cantos of the *Paradiso* which Dante sent, under
the pastoral figure of ten measures of ewe's milk, to his friend Giovanni
del Virgilio, professor of Latin in the University of Bologna. Giovanni
in an Eclogue had urged him to write in Latin, and Dante, as Tityrus,
sends a playful reply to his friend as Mopsus. The reference to the ewe
and the ten measures is in Dante's First Eclogue, ll. 58-64; and del Virgilio's Eclogue, to which this is a reply, contains a historical allusion (l. 29)
which fixes the date as not earlier than 1318-19:

> 'Dic Ligurum montes et classes Parthenopaeas'—
> 'Tell of the mountains of Liguria and the Parthenopæan fleets.'

'The mountains of Liguria' refers to Genoa, in which King Robert of
Naples was besieged from July 1318 to Feb. 1319; and his fleets are called
Parthenopæan, because the tomb of Parthenope, the Siren, was shown in
Naples. This, therefore, is the earliest date we can fix for Dante's reply;
and, since he died in 1321, it is almost incredible that the remaining
twenty-three Cantos of the *Paradiso* were written in those two or three
years. See note on p. 395 below. For a critical edition of the text of the
Eclogues, see Wicksteed and Gardner's *Dante and Giovanni del Virgilio.*

When the wheel had made full circle it stopped, and Aquinas explained the first of two difficulties which arose from his discourse. At the beginning of it he had said:

> 'I was of the lambs of the holy flock
> Which Dominic leadeth by a pathway
> Where well one fattens if he strayeth not.'[1]

The difficulty lies in the words '*where well one fattens*,' and Aquinas answers it, not by an exposition of St. Dominic's rule, as we might expect, but by a beautiful eulogy of St. Francis. The reason is that to praise the one is to praise the other. As we saw, Francis was 'all seraphical in ardour,' a burning heart of heavenly love; and Dominic 'a splendour of cherubic light,' a shining mirror of heavenly wisdom. Love and wisdom involve each other, and are the two great needs of the Church. Hence the unfathomable Providence of God gave these two Princes to guide the Church 'on this side and on that.' It follows that if Aquinas can worthily set forth the love of St. Francis guiding the Church on one side, he will thereby praise the wisdom of St. Dominic which God thought worthy to be her guide upon the other. There was undoubtedly, as we have already seen, the further reason that Dante wished thus to rebuke the unchristian jealousy and rivalry into which these two Orders had fallen.

Aquinas begins his eulogy by describing the situation of Assisi, the birthplace of St. Francis, as it hangs on 'a fertile slope' of Mount Subasio, overlooking the beautiful Umbrian valley.[2] He makes a play on the ancient form of the name, *Ascesi*—'I rose': to say Francis 'rose' is to say little—nothing short of *Orient* befits the place of his birth. He compares him to the sun as it rises from the Ganges, that is, at the summer

---

[1] *Par.* x. 94-96.

[2] *Par.* xi. 43-54. Dante after his manner describes Assisi by its relation to the neighbouring rivers: between Tupino and Chiascio, which rises in the hill near Gubbio where St. Ubaldo, afterwards Bishop of Gubbio, had his hermitage. Similarly La Verna is described as 'between Tiber and Arno' (l. 106).

solstice when its light and heat are at their fullest. The idea is probably taken from the Prologue of Bonaventura's *Life of St. Francis*, in which he says that 'he is thought to be not unmeetly set forth in the true prophecy of that other Friend of the Bridegroom, the Apostle and Evangelist John, under the similitude of the Angel ascending from the sunrising and bearing the seal of the Living God. For at the opening of the sixth seal, I saw, saith John in the Apocalypse, another Angel ascending from the sunrising and bearing the seal of the Living God.'[1] All the theologians here are but stars: Francis is the sun, rising out of the sacred East like a second Christ.

Thomas proceeds to narrate the story of the mystical marriage of St. Francis to Poverty,

> 'Such a Lady, that unto her, as unto death,
> The gate of pleasure no one doth unlock,'[2]

and for whose sake he braved his father's anger. Giotto has painted the scene of the great renunciation in the Upper Church of St. Francis at Assisi. Summoned by his father before the Bishop's Court, Francis without a moment's hesitation stripped off his garments and handed them to his father, renouncing not merely his inheritance, but his natural relationship: 'Hitherto have I called thee my father on earth, but henceforth

---

[1] Miss E. Gurney Salter's translation (Temple Classics). Dr. Moore traces the 'Oriente' of l. 54 to the Vulgate of Luke i. 78, 'visitavit nos *Oriens* ex alto,' with which he joins two prophecies of Zechariah iii. 8 and vi. 12, 'Servum meum Orientem,' 'Oriens nomen ejus'—in both which cases our version has 'the Branch' (*Studies in Dante*, 1st series, p. 64). Vellutello says that Thomas of Celano in the Prologue to his Life of St. Francis writes: 'Quasi sol oriens mundo, vita, doctrina, et miraculis claruit, vita inspirando spiritum lucis, doctrina seminando, miraculis fructificando.' Casini mentions another archaic form of Assisi—*Scesi*, 'I descended,' and says that if there were any certainty that Dante had used this form, it would be a sharp antithesis to *Oriente*, 'rising.' It is to be noted that in the above quotation Bonaventura identifies St. Francis with the Angel bearing the seal of the Living God (Rev. vii. 2), precisely as the Joachimite Franciscans did in the famous 'Introduction to the Eternal Gospel,' although, as we shall see, he persecuted them for holding the views contained in it. See below, pp. 231-233.

[2] *Par.* xi. 58-60. Comp. Guido Cavalcanti's *Song against Poverty* (Rossetti's transl.):

> Thou, hated worse than Death, by just accord,
> And with the loathing of all hearts abhorr'd.

I can confidently say " Our Father Which art in heaven,"
with Whom I have laid up my whole treasure, and on
Whom I have set my whole trust and hope.' In the
fresco the Bishop is seen casting an old cloak round
the naked saint,[1] while the father has to be restrained
from striking his renegade son. The allegory of the
Marriage with Poverty painted by Giotto over the
High Altar in the Lower Church is, as Mr. Gardner
says, 'a most precious artistic commentary on Dante's
lines,' though, of course, we must remember that the
fresco was painted long before the lines were written.[2]
Every detail of the picture has its significance. The
scene is the rocky summit of a steep mountain, such
as that on which Jesus endured His great fast and put
aside the temptation of the kingdoms of the world and
their glory. The Bride Poverty, a tall gaunt figure,
is clad in a tattered white garment, obviously her only
one, tied at the waist with 'the humble halter,' an old
cord broken and knotted again. Her naked feet are
standing, as Ruskin points out, among thorns of the
acacia, 'which, according to tradition, was used to

[1] Bonaventura says that when Francis stripped off his rich garments
he was seen to have a hair shirt next his skin. In Giotto's fresco the
upper part of the body is quite naked : the hair shirt is probably a later
embellishment of the legend.

[2] Painter and poet alike took their idea from the legend in Bonaventura
(*Life*, chap. vii.) that while on his way to Siena Francis was met by three
women, alike in height, age, and countenance, who greeted him with the
words, 'Welcome, Lady Poverty!' and then vanished. 'Verily, by those
three poor women, for such they seemed,' says Bonaventura, 'it was
fittingly shewn that the beauty of Gospel perfection,—touching chastity,
to wit, and obedience, and poverty,—shone forth perfectly in kindred form
in the man of God; howbeit, he had chosen to make his chief boast in the
privilege of Poverty, whom he was wont to name now his mother, now
his bride, now his lady.' It is to be noted that while Giotto did his best
as an artist for this doctrine of Poverty, as a man of common sense he
wrote a Canzone against it. It is an extreme which breeds vices; even
in those who profess to accept it voluntarily it is 'observed or unobserved
at will'; Christ's commendation of Poverty may have an inner sense,
not this literal one; and in point of fact, he asserts, those who profess
this Poverty are never at peace in their efforts to escape from it, and
become wolves in sheep's clothing:

'Hence, by their art, this doctrine plagues the world :
And hence, till they be hurl'd
From where they sit in high hypocrisy,
No corner of the world seems safe to me.'
(Rossetti's *Dante and his Circle*, 235).

weave Christ's crown.' In front, one boy is throwing
stones at her, another is thrusting the thorns against
her legs with a stick, a dog is barking furiously as at
a beggar. But she has her consolations. Christ Himself is holding her right arm, while St. Francis, already
bearing the stigmata, puts the ring on the fourth finger.
On her left stand her two bridesmaids—Hope clad
in green and pointing heavenward, Love clad in red,
crowned with white roses, and holding out the marriage
gift of a broken heart. Poverty herself is the third of
these virtues—Faith, with her white bridal veil upon
her head, and angel-wings already beginning to grow
from her ragged shoulders. Above her, these symbolic
colours are reproduced in the green leaves of the Tree
of Life, white lilies, and red roses—prophetic of the
reward of these virtues in the heavenly land. In other
parts of the fresco the critical moments in the renunciation of St. Francis are more directly indicated. In
the lowest corner to the right of Christ, Francis as
a youth is seen giving away his rich apparel to 'a
certain soldier, of noble birth, but poor and ill-clad';
and, this being one of his earliest acts of kindness, an
Angel is drawing him, while he performs it, upward to
his espousal of Poverty.[1] And finally, in the sky above
the lilies and roses, two Angels are ascending, one
bearing the purse and garments which he had laid
at his father's feet, the other the little Church of St.
Damian which he had repaired with his own hands,
while God Himself stoops out of Heaven to receive
them.[2]

'No human creature since Christ,' says a sober Pro-

---

[1] Bonaventura (*Life*, chap. i.) tells that the night following this act of
charity, Francis was rewarded with the vision of 'a great and fair palace.'
It is perhaps this vision which Giotto puts into the form of the Angel
drawing him with one hand and with the other pointing upward, at the
very moment when he is giving his garments to the old soldier.

[2] This part of the picture is, I think, generally misunderstood. E.g.
in *The Story of Assisi* (Mediæval Towns Series), p. 181, we read of 'two
angels who fly up carrying a temple with an enclosed garden, perhaps
symbolizing Charity, and a Franciscan habit, which may be the symbol of
Obedience.' There is no need of guessing, when there are critical incidents
which adequately explain the symbolism of the fresco. For an exposition
of the Marriage after Ruskin's manner, see *Fors Clavigera*, Letter xlv.

testant historian, 'has more fully incarnated the ideal
of Christianity than Francis';[1] and Dante's meaning
is the same when he represents Poverty as the widow
of Christ, unwooed, unsought for many centuries:

> 'She, reft of her first husband, scorned, obscure,
> One thousand and one hundred years and more,
> Waited without a suitor till he came.'

Neither her fearlessness, as in the heathen story of
Amyclas, nor her devotion to Christ in mounting with
Him to the Cross, while even Mary stayed below, availed
to gain her wooers; but the joy with which Francis
loved her swiftly won a household of followers, Bernard,
Giles, Sylvester, and others.[2] This ecstatic joy in
poverty, 'as having nothing, and yet possessing all
things,' is of the very essence of the spirit of St. Francis.
To us it carries the sad idea of renunciation of pleasures
and comforts, to him it was as the opening of prison
doors. As M. Sabatier says in his beautiful Life of the
Saint, 'Property is the cage with gilded wires, to which
the poor larks are sometimes so thoroughly accustomed
that they no longer even think of getting away to soar
up into the blue.' In justice to St. Francis also we
must remember that he never contemplated for his
friars a life of 'able beggary,' as Wyclif indignantly
called it. In his Will he strictly enjoins work: 'I
worked with my hands and would continue to do, and
I will also that all other friars work at some honour-

---

[1] Lea, *History of the Inquisition of the Middle Ages*, i. 260. Renan
says the same thing more poetically : ' Of all men, after Jesus, he possessed
the clearest conscience, the most perfect simplicity, the strongest sense
of his filial relation to the Heavenly Father. God was truly his beginning
and his end. In him, Adam seemed never to have sinned. His life
is a poetic madness, a perpetual intoxication of Divine Love' (*Studies in
Religious History*, Eng. transl., p. 306).

[2] *Par.* xi. 64-87. Amyclas is the Dalmatian fisherman who had no fear,
because he had nothing to lose, and was undismayed when Caesar himself
roused him at night to take him across the Adriatic (Lucan, *Phars.* v.
515 ff., quoted in *Conv.* iv. 13). In the *Fioretti* (chap. xiii.) we have the
idea of Poverty's mounting the cross with Christ : 'This it is that hung
with Christ upon the cross, with Christ was buried, with Christ rose up
again, with Christ ascended into heaven.' Bernard of Quintavalle, a
wealthy noble, was the first to join Francis (see *Fioretti*, chap. ii.). For
his devotion to his Master's ideal of poverty, he was 'hunted like a wild
beast,' says Sabatier, by the laxer members of the Order, and ' passed two
years in the forests of Monte-Sefro, hidden by a wood-cutter.'

able trade. Let those who have none learn one, not for the purpose of receiving the price of their toil, but for their good example and to flee idleness. And when they do not give us the price of the work, let us resort to the table of the Lord, begging our bread from door to door'—'the table of the Lord' being his name for the bread given by those to whom they had broken the bread of life.[1]

Aquinas proceeds to tell of the three 'seals' which Francis received on his Order. The first was its sanction in 1210 by Innocent III.—in reality, a mere verbal and qualified sanction.[2] 'The first Rule which he submitted to Rome has not come down to us; we only know that it was extremely simple, and composed especially of passages from the Gospels. It was doubtless only the repetition of those verses which Francis had read to his first companions, with a few precepts about manual labour and the occupations of the new brethren.'[3] The 'second crown' given by Honorius III.,

---

[1] Sabatier's *Life*, p. 338. 'He never dreamed of creating a *mendicant* order, he created a *labouring* order. It is true we shall often see him begging and urging his disciples to do as much, but these incidents ought not to mislead us; they are meant to teach that when a friar arrived in any locality and there spent his strength for long days in dispensing spiritual bread to famished souls, he ought not to blush to receive material bread in exchange. To work was the rule, to beg the exception; but this exception was in nowise dishonourable. Did not Jesus, the Virgin, the disciples live on bread bestowed?' (p. 121).

[2] Innocent simply gave them his blessing and permission to preach repentance, adding: 'But when God Almighty shall have multiplied you with a greater fellowship,'—they were but twelve in all, including Francis —'and grace, bring word unto us, and we will grant unto you more than this, and will commit unto you greater powers with more assurance.' Dante in l. 91 speaks of the royal manner (*regalmente*) in which Francis laid his 'stern intent' before the Pope. The reference is almost certainly to the curious parable in support of his petition, in which he compared himself to a poor woman in a wilderness whom a rich king married and who bore him sons—these followers of his. The King of kings will not allow His own lawful sons to starve (*Legend by the Three Companions*, Temple Classics, chap. xii). Sabatier rightly sees in this request for the Papal sanction the first unconscious step in the degrading of the movement to a mere clerical institution : 'the prophet had abdicated in favour of the priest.'

[3] Sabatier, p. 89. The verses referred to are those at which the Gospel opened thrice when Francis consulted it at the conversion of Bernard, his first follower : 'If thou wouldst be perfect go sell,' etc.; 'Take nothing with you on your journey'; 'He that will come after me,' etc. (See *Legend by the Three Companions*, chap. viii.)

in 1223, was very different. It contained, indeed, a clause commanding absolute poverty : 'The brothers shall appropriate nothing to themselves, neither a house, nor a place, nor anything; but as pilgrims and strangers in this world, in poverty and humility serving God, they shall confidently go seeking for alms. Nor need they be ashamed, for the Lord made Himself poor for us. This is that height of most lofty poverty, which has constituted you, my most beloved brothers, heirs and kings of the kingdom of Heaven, has made you poor in possessions, has exalted you in virtues.'[1] This seems explicit enough, but Francis promises in the Rule to be obedient to the Church, and this opened the way for Papal glosses which enabled the Order to hold as much property as it pleased. As we shall see, many a Franciscan paid with his life for daring to follow what was undoubtedly the will of the Founder.

Then follow the story of the preaching of Francis before the Soldan, 'in thirst of martyrdom,' his return to Italy, and his gaining of the stigmata at La Verna, the third and 'last seal':

> ' On the rugged rock 'twixt Tiber and the Arno
> From Christ did he receive the final seal,
> Which for two years his members bore.' [2]

The familiar story is that on the Feast of the Exaltation of Holy Cross, while Francis was meditating on the Passion of our Lord and yearning to enter into 'the fellowship of His sufferings' by martyrdom, there appeared to him a Seraph from heaven, having in the midst of his six wings of fire 'the Figure of a Man crucified, having his hands and feet stretched forth in the shape of a Cross, and fastened unto a Cross.' At first he was overwhelmed with joy, pity, wonder; but

---

[1] For the entire Rule, see Henderson's *Historical Documents of the Middle Ages*, p. 344. A year's probation is prescribed, and rules are laid down as to performing divine service, fasting, prayers, preaching, treatment of sick and of erring brothers, the duties of provincials, the election and, if necessary, the deposition of generals. Those who are able must labour for the necessaries of life, but in no case is any brother to receive money or coin, directly or indirectly, as either reward or alms.

[2] *Par.* xi. 100-108.

at length he understood, says Bonaventura, 'that he was to be wholly transformed into the likeness of Christ Crucified, not by martyrdom of body, but by enkindling of heart. Accordingly, as the vision disappeared, it left in his heart a wondrous glow, but on his flesh also it imprinted a no less wondrous likeness of its tokens. For forthwith there began to appear in his hands and feet the marks of the nails, even as he had just beheld them in that Figure of the Crucified. For his hands and feet seemed to be pierced through the midst with nails, the heads of the nails shewing in the palms of the hands, and upper side of the feet, and their points shewing on the other side; the heads of the nails were round and black in the hands and feet, while the points were long, bent, and as it were turned back, being formed of the flesh itself, and protruding therefrom. The right side, moreover, was—as if it had been pierced by a lance—seamed with a ruddy scar, wherefrom ofttimes welled the sacred blood, staining his habit and breeches.'[1]

It would serve no purpose to enquire into the genuineness of the Stigmata: it is enough to know that Dante shared in the general belief of his time, and saw in the gift of the five wounds the setting of Christ's own seal on the man most conformed to His image since He Himself hung upon the Cross.[2] In two years

[1] *Life* by Bonaventura, chap. xiii. (Temple Classics). The account in the *Fioretti* (Reflection iii.) is very similar, with the addition that during the vision the mount of La Verna shone with a bright light which illuminated all the surrounding country; that the Christ on the Cross promised Francis that every year on the day of his death he should descend to Purgatory and rescue any of his Order there, even as He had descended into hell and delivered His own: thus being conformed to Christ in death as in life.

[2] For a discussion of the historical evidence see Sabatier's *Life*, pp. 433-443, where the genuineness of the Stigmata is upheld—not as the result of a miracle, but as the reaction of an intensely religious soul upon the body. Renan, following Hase, holds a peculiarly repellent form of scepticism—that Elias, the evil genius of the Order, either invented the story, or himself inflicted the wounds during the night of the saint's death, when he was left alone with the body (*Studies of Religious History*, 324-327). We may be content, I think, to accept the conclusion of Archbishop Trench: 'Figure to yourselves a man with a temperament so impressible, of an organization so delicate, penetrated through and through with the anguish of his Lord's sufferings, passionately and continually dwelling on

Francis passed 'to the reward which he had merited by making himself lowly.' 'Brother Body,' to which he confesses he was somewhat stern, could bear no more, and he crept back to his beloved Little Portion, 'that he might yield up the breath of life there, where he had received the breath of grace.' Rejoicing that 'he had kept faith with the Lady Poverty even unto the end,' 'from her bosom' he resolved to make his departure. As at the beginning of his new life he had stood naked before the Bishop, so now he asked to be stripped and laid upon the naked earth. And thus, 'freed from burdens,' he entered into his reward, which, in the belief of his followers, was, after the Virgin's, the loftiest within the gift of Heaven. In the fourth of Giotto's frescoes over the High Altar in S. Francesco at Assisi, the Saint is seen seated on a throne in Paradise, surrounded by choirs of Angels. Above the throne hangs a banner with seven stars and a cross, and over the cross a Seraph with six wings. It is this Seraph which is the key to the interpretation. It tells us that Francis was exalted to the highest Order of Angels. It was the faith of his followers that he filled the throne left vacant by the fall of Lucifer, the Prince of the Seraphim. In the *Mirror of Perfection* a vision is narrated in which Brother Pacifico 'saw in Heaven many seats, whereof he saw one higher than the rest, and glorious beyond them all, shining and made fair with every precious stone. And marvelling at the beauty thereof, he began to think within himself whose seat it should be. And straightway he heard a voice saying unto him: "This seat was the seat of Lucifer, and in his stead shall the humble Francis sit herein."[1] Dante

all the circumstances of His crucifixion, yearning, so to speak, to be crucified with Him. For myself, when I so do, I can quite understand how all this found an utterance in these visible tokens; and I am as confident that there was no miracle as I am that there was no fraud' (*Mediæval Church History*, p. 243). Note that the acknowledgment of the stigmata by Aquinas is meant to rebuke the Dominican denial of their reality in Dante's day.

[1] See translation by Sebastian Evans of Sabatier's *Speculum Perfectionis*, p. 99. For Dante's belief that man was created to fill up the gaps in the celestial hierarchies caused by the fall of the Angels, see *Conv.* ii. 6. Comp. *Par. Lost*, vii. 139-161.

nowhere indicates his rank in the Angelic Hierarchies, but St. Bernard points him out in the White Rose of the Redeemed sitting immediately under John the Baptist, above Benedict and Augustine, in the second tier of the Eternal Flower.[1]

Thomas now returns to the difficulty of which this long eulogy was the explanation—how one 'fattens' if he stray not from the way of St. Dominic. If St. Francis was such as he has just described, what must 'our Patriarch' have been whom God thought worthy to be his colleague to hold 'the bark of Peter' on the high sea 'by the right sign,' the Cross? Few, alas, had kept close to the shepherd—a little cloth would furnish them with cowls. Most of his flock, in their greed for new food, are scattered abroad in diverse mountain-pastures, where the grass is poor, and from which they return to the fold 'empty of milk'—by which is probably meant 'the sincere milk of the word'—and therefore spiritually starved. The 'mountain-pastures' (xi. 126, *salti*) are usually understood as meaning the high offices in the Church which Dominic had forbidden his friars to accept. Once, the story runs, when Francis and Dominic were in Rome, the Bishop of Ostia, afterwards Gregory IX., asked them why their friars should not be made bishops and prelates, like the poor men who were the leaders of the primitive Church. Dominic's reply was: 'So far as in me lieth, never will I allow that they (his friars) should obtain any high place of dignity,' and the answer of Francis was still more emphatic in humility.[2] Neither Order obeyed the command of its founder. The Dominicans, says the *Catholic Dictionary*, evidently as proof of their greatness, have 'contributed three Popes to the roll of the Roman pontiffs, and can enumerate more than 60 cardinals, about 150 archbishops, and upwards of 800 bishops.'[3] Now, says Aquinas in conclusion,

[1] *Par.* xxxii. 35. Dominic's exact rank among the Redeemed is nowhere stated.

[2] *Mirror of Perfection* (Evans' translation), p. 68.

[3] Addis and Arnold's edition, 1893. The Dominicans were proud of the members of their Order who held high rank in the Church, as is seen in

'wilt thou see the plant that's torn away,
And thou wilt see the thong-wearer who reasons:
Where well one fattens if he strayeth not.'

The 'thong-wearer' (*coreggier*) is Aquinas himself—the leathern girdle being the sign of the Dominicans, as the cord was of the Franciscans. It is not without purpose that he uses the word. He himself had refused the archbishopric of Naples: just because he had obeyed the founder of his Order by remaining all his life a simple wearer of the thong, he knew by experience how well the soul prospers by refusing to wander to the 'mountain-pastures' of high office in the Church.[1]

the kind of predella painted by Fra Angelico at the base of his great fresco of the Crucifixion in the Chapter-house of S. Marco at Florence, consisting of St. Dominic and the great men of his Order, among the rest two Popes, a cardinal, an archbishop and a patriarch (see Mrs. Jameson's *History of our Lord*, ii. 192).

[1] *Par.* xi. 118-139. The reading *correger*, found in many MSS., gives the sense : ' thou wilt see the *rebuke* implied in the words,' etc.   I take the other reading, *coreggier*, because it gives far more point to what Aquinas says: ' Trust the word of one who has remained faithful to the *leathern girdle* of the Order, and who therefore knows how such faithfulness nourishes the soul.'   The MSS., it seems, are fairly divided, so that one has to fall back on internal evidence. The rapid degeneration of both Orders was due partly to the function they soon came to fulfil in relation to the Papacy.   'The wide employment of the friars by the popes as political emissaries necessarily diverted them from their spiritual functions, attracted ambitious and restless men into their ranks, and gave the institutions a worldly character thoroughly in opposition to their original design, Their members, moreover, were peculiarly subject to temptation. Wanderers by profession, they were relieved from supervision, and were subject only to the jurisdiction of their own superiors and to the laws of their own Orders, thus intensifying and rendering peculiarly dangerous the immunity common to all ecclesiastics' (Lea, *History of the Inquisition*, i. 294).

CHAPTER X

3. *The Franciscan Circle: Bonaventura*

AT the last word of Aquinas, 'the holy millstone,' as Dante calls his Circle, began to revolve, and before it completed the full round, a second Circle enclosed it, fitting ' motion to motion and song to song.' It is the Franciscan Circle, the relation of which to the Dominican has been discussed in Chapter viii. We need only remind ourselves here that it is the relation of Love to Knowledge, the Love being born of Knowledge, and being the wider circle : the heart embracing more than the head. The spokesman of this wider circle is St. Bonaventura, at the sound of whose voice Dante tells us he wheeled round as the needle to the pole[1] : the knowledge of Dominican theology is gained by the slow and laborious discourse of reason, but the heart flies by a swift spiritual instinct to the mystical seraphic love of the Franciscan.

The dance and song of the double circle being ended, Bonaventura returns 'the enkindled courtesy of Brother Thomas' to St. Francis by a corresponding eulogy of St. Dominic : as they had fought together, they should be praised together.[2] He begins by

---

[1] Scartazzini thinks Dante refers to the recent discovery of the use of the magnetic needle by Flavio Gioja, a pilot of Amalfi. According to Plumptre, the reference is to Marco Polo, who is said to have brought the knowledge from Cathay; and he thinks the fact that Roger Bacon dwells on it as a ' *miraculum in parte notum* ' indicates a possible source of Dante's knowledge.

[2] At the close of his eulogy (xii. 142-5) Bonaventura says the courtesy of Brother Thomas had moved him and his company to *envy*—for so I understand *inveggiar*—envy of the heavenly kind which moves him to rival the praise which Thomas had given to St. Francis : in obvious contrast to the unheavenly envy with which the two Orders regarded one another on earth.

describing the disorganized and dispirited state into which the Church Militant had fallen in the twelfth century:

> 'The soldiery of Christ, which it had cost
> So dear to arm again, behind the standard
> Moved slow and doubtful and in numbers few.'[1]

It is scarcely possible to exaggerate the demoralization of the Church. Monasticism meant the withdrawal of men from the world to save their own souls; but the world went with them, and we shall find St. Benedict lamenting that 'the walls which were wont to be an abbey are become dens of thieves.'[2] Simony and luxury were almost universal. Preaching was almost entirely neglected: the bishops alone were authorized to preach, and they were too much absorbed in worldly affairs to teach their flocks in faith and morals. It was a century too in which sprang up a wilderness of heresies, which had their roots for the most part in this scandalous condition of the Church. A pulse of intellectual life and enquiry began to beat throughout Christendom; the human mind left vacant by its professed teachers fell an easy prey to preachers of heresy, whose unanswerable argument was the state of the Church herself. It was in this crisis, says Bonaventura, that 'the Emperor who ever reigneth' sent forth these two champions to the succour of the broken straggling army, one by *deed*, the other by *word*. St. Francis restored the Christian life, St. Dominic, the Christian faith. As the former broke the worldliness of the Church, so the latter beat back the heresies which assailed her unity. 'Their reform consisted in a return to the ideal of self-denying poverty, but also in the rejection of a purely hermit-like form of life. The new monasticism took its stand in the cities amid the stir of life; it received laymen in the form of tertiaries. This active relation of the mendicant

---

[1] *Par.* xii. 37-39. 'To arm again' refers to the death of Christ which restored the armour of innocence lost by the Fall.
[2] *Par.* xxii. 76.

orders to all sides of life gave them an immeasurable
power.   The ancient orders had become aristocratic
and feudal.   Francis and Dominic made monasticism
democratic, and herein lay their power with the
people.   The doctrines of the heretics, the democratic
spirit in the towns, the upward pressure of the working classes and of all the vulgar elements, even in the
language, had prepared the soil for the appearance of
these saints.   Their doctrines were accepted like
popular manifestations, and were looked on as reforms
of the Church, by which the just accusations of the
heretics were reduced to silence.   The oppressed people
saw despised poverty exalted on an altar and placed in
the glory of heaven.' [1]

As Aquinas had connected Francis with the sun
rising in the Orient, so Bonaventura associates
Dominic with the 'sweet Zephyr,' the soft West wind,
whose breath clothes all Europe with ' the new leaves '
of Spring—symbolic, doubtless, of the wind of ,the
Spirit which, through him, wakened Christendom from
its wintry sleep.   He was born in 1170 in Calaroga
(now Calahorra) in Castille, not far from the beating
of the Atlantic waves.   The various legends which
gathered round his birth and early years are referred
to.   While still unborn, his mind was so full of living
power that it made his mother prophetic.   She
dreamed that she gave birth to a dog with a blazing
torch in his mouth with which he set the world on
fire : prophetic of the burning eloquence by which her
son was destined to become the watchdog of the
Church against heretics.   We have the echo of the
legend in the mediæval word-play which turned the
Dominicans into the *Domini Canes,* and, as we shall
see, the dog is their chosen symbol.   As Francis
wedded Poverty, so Dominic wedded Faith : the
former in manhood, the latter at the baptismal font.
Dominic's godmother, as she held him in her arms, saw

---

[1] Gregorovius, *Rome in the Mid. Ages,* v. 114 (Eng. trans.).   Comp.
Harnack, *Hist. of Dogma,* vi. 91-97 ; Lea, *Hist. of the Inquisition,* i. ;
Sabatier, *Life of St. Francis,* 28 ff.

a bright star descend and settle on his brow, and,
according to another form of the legend, a second on
the nape of his neck, in symbol of the heavenly light
he should shed on East and West. His very name
was given by heavenly inspiration : *Dominicus*, the
possessive adjective of *Dominus*, because, as the *Golden
Legend* says, he was to be 'keeper of the vineyard or
the flock of our Lord.' Well indeed was his father
named Felice, and his mother Giovanna or Johanna,
Grace of God.[1] The story of his nurse frequently
finding the child lying on the floor in penitence is
alluded to; and his first love is said to have been
to Christ's first counsel of perfection : 'If thou wilt
be perfect, go and sell that thou hast, and give to the
poor.' The allusion is probably to stories of his selling
his books while a student to feed the poor, and his
offering to sell himself to redeem a poor woman's
brother from captivity among the Saracens. It is
quite certain, however, that Poverty was never his
chosen bride as she was to St. Francis. Indeed, the
beginning of his Order was the donation of property
by a wealthy citizen of Toulouse.[2] He had no thought
of imposing a vow of poverty on his friars until he

---

[1] *Par.* xii. 79-81. 'It is curious that Bonaventura in heaven is still
dependent on Jerome for his Hebrew' (*Paradiso*, Temple Classics).
After times saw in Dominic's parents more than the appropriateness of
their names. 'His saintliness was so penetrating that it reflected back
upon his mother, who is reverenced as St. Juana de Aga, and at one time
there was danger that even his father might be drawn into the saintly
circle. Both parents were buried in the Convent of San Pedro de Gumiel,
until, about 1320, the Infante Juan Manuel of Castile obtained the body
of Juana to enrich the Dominican convent of San Pablo de Peñafiel which
he had founded; when Fray Geronymo Orozco, the Abbot of Gumiel,
prudently transferred the remains of Don Felix de Guzman to an
unknown spot in order to preserve it from an extension of acquisitive
veneration. Even the font of white stone, fashioned like a shell, in which
Dominic was baptized could not escape. In 1605 Philip III. transported it
with much pomp from Calaruega to Valladolid. Thence it was translated to the royal Convent of San Domingo in Madrid, where it has since
been used for the baptism of the royal children' (Lea, *History of the
Inquisition*, i. 248).
[2] 'In 1214 Pierre Cella, a rich citizen of Toulouse, moved by his
earnestness, resolved to join him in his mission-work, and gave for the
purpose a stately house near the Château Narbonnais, which for more
than a hundred years remained the home of the Inquisition' (Lea, *History
of the Inquisition*, i. 251).

saw the marvellous power it had in the Franciscan Order. Even then, at first he was startled and doubtful of its wisdom, though in the end he adopted it with enthusiasm. Nevertheless, it was no love-match, as in the case of Francis; rather we might call it a *mariage de convenance*. As Sabatier says, Dominic 'considered it only as a means; it was for him one more weapon in the arsenal of the host charged with the defence of the Church.'[1] Personally, indeed, he was from the first an entirely unworldly man. He sought no gain like the Cardinal of Ostia by the study of the Decretals, or like Taddeo by the study of medicine.[2] When, 'for love of the true manna,' he became a great teacher fit to tend the vineyard, he asked from the Head of the Church none of the evil privileges so eagerly sought for by others: to distribute only a third or a half of moneys left for charitable purposes, retaining the rest; to receive the first vacant benefice; or to use for himself the tithes which belong to God's poor. His one request was for leave to fight against an erring world for the seed of the Faith; and this he did with teaching and zeal and the apostolic office, smiting heresy where it was most obstinate, and watering 'the garden catholic' with the streams of his preaching friars sent forth into all parts of Christendom.[3]

This brings us to consider Dominic's relation to the Inquisition, with which his name is usually associated. In a few words Dante strikes his character sharply, as an image on a coin:

> 'The faithful lover
> Of the Christian Faith, the holy athlete,
> Benign to his own, and cruel to his foes.'[4]

---

[1] *Life of St. Francis*, 221 (Eng. trans.).

[2] *Par.* xii. 82-84. The Cardinal of Ostia was Enrico di Susa, author of a famous commentary on the Decretals used as a text-book in the law schools. He died in 1271. Taddeo is generally identified as Taddeo d'Alderotto of Bologna, a famous physician, who died in 1303. He is said to have accumulated great wealth by exorbitant fees. It is believed to be his translation of Aristotle's *Ethics* of which Dante speaks with contempt in *Conv.* i. 10. [3] *Par.* xii. 84-105.

[4] *Par.* xii. 55-57. I agree with Miss Hillard that to translate *l'amoroso drudo* 'the amorous paramour,' as Longfellow does, is to suggest an evil

We must guard against the error of taking this last line as a partial condemnation of the Saint. It is obvious from the entire eulogy that Dante's estimate of Dominic is substantially that of his age; and what this was may be seen on the walls of the Chapter House of the Dominican Convent of Santa Maria Novella in Florence. In the great fresco of the Church Militant and Triumphant, Dominic himself is represented in the act of urging on his friars, in the form of black and white dogs, the *Domini Canes*, against heretics, in the shape of foxes, who are destroying the flock of Christ. The legend grew up among his followers that he was one of the chief causes of the overthrow of the Albigensian heresies; that he bore a charmed life in the forefront of the crusading army; and that as a judge on the tribunals of the Inquisition, he handed over hundreds of heretics to the secular arm to be burned. Of by far the greater part of this, contemporary records know nothing; yet it is probably to it that Dante refers when he speaks of his 'apostolic office,' and says that he struck with greater impetus where the heretical resistances were strongest.[1] The

---

sense which was not in Dante's mind. 'The word *drudo* came originally from the Old German *trût, drût*, from *triuwi*, true or faithful, and meant first a true and faithful servant, St. Anthony being called "the *drudo* of our Lord Jesus Christ." Then it came to be used by the troubadours in the sense of *knight* or *cavalier*, the true and faithful servant of a lady; and finally, with the decay of chivalry, sank to its present debased sense of "a lover" in the lowest significance of the word. In Dante's day it was used in both ways. He himself employs it in the bad sense in *Inf.*, 18, 134, and *Purg.*, 32, 155' (*The Banquet of Dante Alighieri*, p. 121 n.). Indeed, the probability is that in calling Dominic *l'amoroso drudo* Dante is contrasting him with Philip the Fair, '*quel feroce drudo*' of *Purg.* 32, 155—'the faithful lover,' against the 'fierce paramour' of the Church.

[1] *Par.* xii. 97-102. For Dominic's part in the Albigensian Crusade, see Lea, *History of the Inquisition*, i. 249; Milman, *Latin Christianity*, Bk. IX. chap. ix. The latter thinks the words attributed to him on leaving Languedoc apocryphal: 'For many years I have spoken to you with tenderness, with prayers, and tears; but according to the proverb of my country, where the benediction has no effect, the rod may have much. Behold, now, we rouse up against you princes and prelates, nations and kingdoms!' Lea's estimate is very favourable: 'Divested of their supernatural adornments, the accounts which we have of him show him to us as a man of earnest, resolute purpose, deep and unalterable convictions, full of burning zeal for the propagation of the faith, yet kindly in heart, cheerful in temper, and winning in manner.'

truth seems to be that Dante shared in the practically universal belief of his age that the suppression of heretics was a sacred duty. A heretic was not a mere infidel as a pagan was. A heretic was one who had been a believer, had made profession of his faith, and therefore had come under promises and obligations of obedience to the Church. Such an one is no more at liberty to throw off his allegiance to the Church than a citizen is, to the State. Hence it is that Dante calls this rooting out of heretics by the Church *la sua civil briga,* 'her civil war'[1]: it is a revolt of her lawful subjects against her authority, and no more to be tolerated than a revolt in the State. The following quotation from Aquinas shows the distinction drawn between heretics proper and those outside the borders of the Church. He asks: 'Are unbelievers to be brought to the faith by compulsion?' and replies: 'Of unbelievers, some there are who have never received the faith, as Gentiles and Jews. Such persons are on no account to be brought to the faith by compulsion, that they themselves should become believers, because believing is of the will; they are however, if possible, to be compelled by the faithful not to stand in the way of the faith by blasphemies or evil persuasions, or open persecutions. And for this reason the faithful of Christ often make war on unbelievers, not to force them to believe, because, even though they had beaten them and got them prisoners, they would still leave them their choice whether they would believe or no, but for the purpose of compelling them not to put hindrances in the way of the faith of Christ. Other unbelievers there are who have at one time received the faith, and profess it, as heretics, and all manner of apostates. Such persons are to be compelled even by corporal means to fulfil what they have promised, and hold what they have once received.' He adds that extreme measures may be necessary to protect others from heretical infection. If, after due admonition, a heretic is found pertinacious, 'the Church, having no hope of his conversion, provides

---

[1] *Par.* xii. 108.

for the safety of others, cutting him off from the Church by the sentence of excommunication; and further, she leaves him to the secular tribunal to be exterminated from the world by death.'[1] There is no reason to think that either Dominic or Dante dissented from this theory of heresy and its suppression.

Following the example of Aquinas, Bonaventura proceeds to infer from this eulogy of Dominic the worthiness of his own master, Francis. If such was the one wheel of the war-chariot in which the Church won 'her civil war' in the field, what must the other wheel have been that was fit to be its fellow? And, once more following Aquinas, he reproves the degeneracy of his own Order in a variety of similitudes by no means easy to explain in detail. The Franciscan wheel has left the track followed by its highest part, Francis himself. The good wine which formed crust is now the bad wine which forms mould. The strife between the Spiritual and Conventual Franciscans seems to be next indicated:

> ' His family, that had moved straight forward
> With feet upon his footprints, is so turned
> That it throws him in front on him behind.'

And finally, Bonaventura foretells the fruit of this strife:

> ' And soon shall it be seen from the ingathering
> Of the evil culture, what time the tares
> Shall mourn that the ark is taken from them.'[2]

The word 'ark' (*arca*) seems to me to be left purposely ambiguous. It may mean the ark of the Church or the store-chest or granary; and events were happening in the Order during the years when Dante was writing the *Commedia*, which would justify either view. (1) As a result of the quarrel over the interpretation of the Rule, the Italian Spirituals, holding strictly to the poverty of the Founder, threw off their allegiance to the Order, seceded, and elected a general of their own. For this breach of their vow of obedience, they were

---

[1] *Summa*, ii-ii. q. x. a. 8 ; xi. a. 3 (Rickaby). [2] *Par.* xii. 106-120.

excommunicated—the ark of the Church was taken
from them. If this is the reference, 'the tares' are the
Spirituals, and their ultimate doom of perdition, as in
the parable, is clearly enough hinted. (2) The second
meaning of *l'arca*, however—the store-chest or granary
—might point as clearly to the rival party of the Conventuals, whose lax interpretation of the Rule per-
mitted them to hold what property they pleased. In
1317 John XXII. issued a decree which seriously curtailed
this liberty. 'It forbids,' says Lea in his summary of
it, 'the placing of coffers in churches for the collection
of money; it pronounces the friars incapable of enjoying inheritances; it deprecates the building of magnificent churches, and convents which are rather palaces;
it prohibits the acquisition of extensive gardens and
great vineyards, and even the storing up of granaries
of corn and cellars of wine where the brethren can live
from day to day by beggary; it declares that whatever
is given to the Order belongs to the Church of Rome,
and that the friars have only the use of it, for they can
hold nothing, either individually or in common.'[1] This
might well be described as the taking away of the
store-chest or granary, and in this case 'the tares'
would be the Conventuals. In view of the fact that in
the lines immediately after both extremes are condemned, I am not prepared to decide between these two
interpretations: it would be quite in the manner of
Dante to use a pregnant word like *arca* in order to
cover both kinds of tares. Bonaventura admits that a
strict search might discover a few who were still faithful to the Founder's rule, but declares that they are not
to be found in either party. The name of Matteo
d'Acquasparta, General of the Order from 1287 to 1289,
is singled out as representative of the Conventuals—an
easy-going, self-indulgent man who allowed things to
drift into laxity and disorder. The Spirituals are represented by Ubertino da Casale, whose advocacy of the
doctrine of strict poverty made it necessary to seek
safety by first joining the Benedictines and afterwards

---

[1] *Hist. of the Inquisition*, iii. 60.

taking refuge with Louis of Bavaria. According to
Bonaventura, both are extremes which have alike
departed from the Founder's ideal; although, when we
remember the absolute terms in which St. Francis for-
bade the holding of property, individually or as a
community, it is impossible to conceive any *via media*
between the two positions. In point of fact, the Order
was able to hold property only by a subterfuge which
Francis would have indignantly denounced : the property was vested in the Roman Church and Pontiff for
the use of the friars, and the actual receiving and
handling of money was to be done by third parties, who
were to be regarded as agents, not of the Order, but of
those who give the money or to whom it is paid. Even
the authority of Bonaventura in glory cannot make
this anything but what it is, a casuistical gloss upon the
Founder's plain words.[1] We shall see in next chapter
what share Bonaventura himself, who is generally
credited with a mild conciliatory policy, took in the
persecution of the Spiritual Franciscans.

The saint's discourse closes with the names of the
twelve souls that constitute the circle, beginning with
himself :

> ' I am the life of Bonaventura
> Of Bagnoregio, who in the great offices
> Always set last the left-hand care.' [2]

The reference is to Prov. iii. 16: 'Length of days is in
her right hand ; and in her left hand riches and honour'
—the meaning being that he made temporal affairs subordinate to his spiritual duty. 'The great offices' were
the Generalship of the Order and the Cardinalate of
Albano. The story is that when the Papal messengers
arrived with his cardinal's hat, they found him in the

---

[1] In 1279 Nicholas III. in the Bull *Exiit qui seminat* declared the pro-
prietorship of all that the Franciscans use to be ' vested, now and hereafter, in the Roman Church and pontiff, which concede to the friars the
usufruct thereof. The prohibition to receive and handle money is to be
enforced, and borrowing is especially deprecated ; but, when necessity
obliges, this may be effected through third parties, although the brethren
must abstain from handling the money or administering or expending it '
(Lea, *Hist. of the Inquisition*, iii. 30).

[2] *Par.* xii. 127-129.

garden of a little convent near Florence washing the
dish from which he had just dined, and that he asked
them to hang the hat on the branch of one of the trees
until he had finished his humble task. It is perhaps
this 'postponing' that Dante has specially in mind.[1]

The spirits immediately on Bonaventura's right hand
are two members of his Order, who were among the
earliest followers of St. Francis in his poverty.[2] Their
only claim to a place among these great theologians
is that their lives are their teaching. Illuminato, 'a
man verily of illumination and virtue,' is mentioned
twice in Bonaventura's life of St. Francis: once as his
companion when he preached before the Soldan, and
again as the disciple to whom he confided the secret of
the stigmata. Agostino, Minister of the Brethren in
Terra di Lavoro, had the blessedness of entering into
heaven in his Master's company. On the day Francis
died, Agostino, who was nearing his end, suddenly cried
out: ' Tarry for me, Father, tarry for me, lo, even now
I am coming with thee!' and passed with him into
Paradise.

In the next *terzina* three names are grouped together—Hugh of St. Victor, Petrus Comestor, and
Petrus Hispanus, ' who down below is shining in twelve
books.' Two of Hugh's pupils, Peter the Lombard and
Richard, are members of the first circle. He is, indeed,
the founder of mediæval mysticism in France. His
friend Bernard of Clairvaux was indebted to him for

---

[1] The meaning may have a more direct reference to the context. In
Summa, i-ii. q. cii. a. 4, Aquinas says, with special reference to Prov. iii.
16, that wisdom pertains to the right hand, but *temporal nutriment* to
the left. The reference, therefore, may be to the burning question of the
holding of property by the Franciscans. This 'left-hand care' Bonaventura made subordinate to the acquisition of wisdom.

[2] It is strange, as Dr. Liddon points out (*Essays and Addresses*, 200-
202), that, while Aquinas sets his master, Albertus Magnus, on his right,
Bonaventura's master, Alexander of Hales, is never once named. Born
in Gloucestershire, he studied and taught in Paris, joined the Franciscan
Order, wrote a *Summa* of Theology, and died in 1245. His pupils, among
whom was Bonaventura, named him *Doctor Irrefragibilis*. Dr. Liddon
suggests as a possible reason for his omission from the poem, 'his claim
to laurels which the poet may have thought the monopoly of his own
Dominicans.' A much likelier reason is that Alexander was an Aristotelian, while Bonaventura was by nature a Platonist. Alexander was

the essential features of his mysticism, and his numerous writings are often quoted by Aquinas.[1] Peter 'the Eater'—so called from his insatiable appetite for books —was dean of the Cathedral of Troyes, canon of St. Victor, and chancellor of the University of Paris. His chief work is the *Historia Scholastica*, or compilation of the historical parts of the Old and New Testaments. The third, Peter of Spain, has the distinction of being the only Pope, with the exception of 'the first Peter' himself, whom Dante sets in Paradise. Born in Lisbon, he became in succession Archbishop of Braga, Cardinal Bishop of Tusculum, and, in 1276, Pope under the name of John xxi. He did not long enjoy the dignity: some eight months after he was killed while asleep by the fall of a ceiling in his palace at Viterbo. The twelve books to which reference is made are his *Summulae Logicales*, a manual of Logic in which the well-known logical formula, *Barbara Celarent*, etc., occurs for the first time.

The three who follow—Nathan the Prophet, St. John Chrysostom, Patriarch of Constantinople, and Anselm, Archbishop of Canterbury—seem to be grouped to-gether because of their courage in rebuking the sins of those in high place, a courage in which Dante himself was by no means deficient. Nathan reproved David's sins. Chrysostom was banished for his public denun-ciations of the Empress Eudoxia and her court. And Anselm stubbornly resisted William Rufus and Henry I. in what he regarded as their encroachments on the rights of the Church. It is quite possible that Dante regarded this indignation against such sins as the noblest part of the theology of men like Chrysostom and Anselm: just as, in the Heaven of Saturn, the

---

the first to use the entire body of Aristotelian teaching for the exposition of Christian doctrine, and as such might have found a place in the inner circle beside Aquinas and Albertus, who perfected this system of ex-position. It was perhaps natural that a Platonist like Bonaventura should feel that an Aristotelian, even though he was his old master, would have been out of place in this semi-mystical circle.

[1] Hugo of St. Victor was born in Flanders in 1097, and died in 1141. A most interesting account of his mysticism will be found in F. D. Maurice's *Mediæval Philosophy*, 143-148.

rapture of the contemplative saints issues in a cry as
of thunder against the iniquities of modern prelates.[1]

It is with a feeling of surprise that we come on the
next name in this circle of theologians—'Donatus, who
to the first art deigned to set his hand.' Aelius Donatus,
the celebrated Roman grammarian of the fourth
century, wrote a Latin grammar which was used in all
mediæval schools, and known as a 'Donat.'[2] The
difficulty is to understand how a mere grammarian
is grouped with great theologians like Anselm and
Chrysostom. Plumptre traces the introduction of
Donatus at this particular point to 'the imperative
urgency of rhyme'; but a much more likely reason is
the mediæval conception of the dignity of Grammar
as the first of the seven liberal arts, and therefore the
gateway into a world of knowledge which rests only
in God Himself. There is a passage in the third
chapter of Bonaventura's *Itinerarium Mentis in Deum*
—a work to which undoubtedly the *Paradiso* is much
indebted—which shows the way in which these arts
were invested with the highest religious significance.
After arguing that in the threefold operation of the
human mind—memory, intellect, will—we have an
image of God in which, ' as through a mirror and in an
ænigma,' we see 'the mystery of the most blessed
Trinity,' Bonaventura proceeds to show that all philosophy is an aid to the same vision. He divides philosophy into natural, rational, and moral, corresponding
respectively to Father, Son, and Spirit. The second,
rational, is divided into Grammar, which gives the
power of expression—corresponding to the power of
the Father; Logic, which renders clear-sighted in argument—corresponding to the wisdom of the Son or
Word; and Rhetoric, which gives ability for persuasion
or warning—corresponding to the Love of the Holy
Spirit. However fanciful this may sound to us, it

---

[1] *Par.* xxi. 130-142. See p. 344.

[2] Donatus was Jerome's instructor in Rhetoric. The word *donat* or
donet became a synonym for the elements of any subject, as when Bishop
Pecock about 1440 called one of his books a *Donat into Christian Religion.*

explains why there seemed to Dante's mind no incongruity in setting a logician like Petrus Hispanus and a grammarian like Donatus in a circle of mystical theologians.

The circle completes itself in Rabanus Maurus and 'the Calabrian abbot Joachim.' Rabanus was born about 776 and became in succession abbot of Fulda and archbishop of Mainz. His principal works were commentaries on Scripture.[1] Concerning Joachim little need be said here, since he will form one of the chief subjects of the following chapter. As already indicated, his position in the circle is significant : Bonaventura during his earthly life strove to crush his theology in the form in which it appeared in the Franciscan Order; now he shines beside him, and his former opponent acknowledges that he was 'endowed with the prophetic spirit.'[2] The reference, as we shall see, is to the third circle of theology which Dante saw in this Heaven—the 'true sparkling of the Holy Ghost.'

[1] 'One of his works, *De Laudibus S. Crucis*,' says Butler, 'contains curious figures in which rows of letters are cut by outlines of stars, crosses, and the like, so as to mark out words and sentences'; and he suggests that Dante may have borrowed the idea in the Heaven of Jupiter, where the souls in the form of stars are arranged into words and the shape of an Eagle. See below, p. 282 f.

[2] Toynbee (*Dante Dictionary*, 275) says the words 'Di spirito profetico dotato' (l. 141) 'are said to be taken *verbatim* from the anthem still chanted on the festival of St. Joachim in the churches of Calabria.' Aquinas condemned Joachimite doctrine as severely as did Bonaventura. 'Guillaume de Tocco, his biographer, relates that, having found in a monastery the works of the Abbot of Flor, he read them through, underlined all that he considered erroneous, and imperiously ordered that all that his infallible authority had thus cancelled should be neither read nor believed' (Renan, *Studies in Religious History*, p. 279, Eng. trans.).

CHAPTER XI

FOURTH HEAVEN—THE SUN : THEOLOGIANS

4. *The Joachimite Circle* : *Era of the Spirit*

WHEN St. Bonaventura ended his discourse, the two circles, like four-and-twenty of the brightest stars of heaven in the form of a double Ariadne-crown,[1]

[1] It will probably be set down as a vice of the commentator, but I cannot think Dante had no purpose in the peculiar way in which he makes up the twenty-four stars : (1) *fifteen* from different regions of the sky (ll. 4-6) ; (2) *seven* of 'the Wain,' the constellation of the Great Bear, which circles round the N. pole-star, and never sets in 'our heaven'—i.e. in the latitude of Dante's country (ll. 7-9) ; (3) *two* from the Little Bear, the constellation to which the pole-star itself belongs. This constellation is here called a 'horn' : the pole-star (described as 'the point of the axle round which goes the first wheel,' the *Primum Mobile*) is at the end of the 'horn' which is applied to the lips ; and the two stars chosen by Dante are the two brightest at the *mouth* of the 'horn' (ll. 10-12). It is really difficult to believe that this complicated arrangement means nothing. I suggest two interpretations. *First* : Take Dante's statement in ll. 7-9 that 'the bosom of *our heaven* suffices night and day' for the revolution of the Wain round the pole-star, as meaning that *in Italy* these constellations never set, then the nine stars singled out from them might mean nine *Italian* theologians of the two Circles. Now, it happens that there are just nine of these, if we omit Anselm, who was born in Savoy, which lay between France and Italy : Aquinas, Bonaventura, Gratian, Peter Lombard, Boethius, Illuminato, Agostino, Donatus, Joachim. Of these, Aquinas and Bonaventura would naturally be the two stars that form the mouth of the horn—the Little Bear to which the pole-star belongs ; and the other seven would form the Wain or Great Bear. The fifteen from different parts of the sky would be the remaining theologians of the two Circles who were born in other lands. *Second* : Take 'the bosom of *our heaven*' in the wider sense of *Europe*, as Dante himself does in *Canz.* xv. 27-29 :

> Fled is every bird, that followeth the heat,
> From the region of *Europe, which loses not*
> *Ever the seven frozen stars.*

'The seven frozen stars' are those of the Great Bear, always visible, not to Italy merely, but to all Europe. On this view they would represent, with the two stars at the mouth of the horn (Aquinas and Bonaventura), nine theologians of European reputation, to use our modern phrase— stars that would never set. In this case they are not necessarily Italian, and the choice of them must be left to the reader according to his theological bent.

struck 'motion to motion and song to song,' hymning

> Three Persons in the Divine nature,
> And in one Person it and the human—

the mysteries of the Trinity and the Incarnation.
Song and dance being fulfilled, 'the holy lights' turned
their thoughts to the Pilgrims, 'making themselves
happy' by passing 'from care to care,' from the praise
of God to the service of man. St. Thomas proceeds
to solve a doubt which his own estimate of Solomon's
wisdom has raised in Dante's mind. In Canto x. 109-
114, he had called him ' the most beautiful' light of his
circle, and added:

> ' Within there is the lofty mind, where wisdom
> So profound was put, that, if the true is true,
> To see so much there never rose a second.'

The difficulty is that this seems to set the wisdom of
Solomon above that of Adam in his unfallen state and
of Christ, in both of whom it was believed that the
'Power that made the one and the other' had infused
whatever light human nature was capable of receiving.
Aquinas answers by showing, in the first place, that
Adam and Christ, by the very conditions of their
creation, stand by themselves and cannot be compared
with Solomon or any other. For perfect creation two
things are necessary : first, that the wax to be stamped
be perfectly disposed to receive the impress; and
second, that the seal of the whole Trinity be laid
directly, and without intermediate and secondary
causes, upon the wax. 'If the warm love (the Holy
Spirit) disposes and seals the clear Vision (the Son,
the Idea, the Word) of the Primal Power (the Father),
entire perfection is there acquired.' This happened
only twice: the immediate seal of the Trinity on the
perfect wax in Adam and Christ:

> ' Thus was the earth made worthy once
> Of the full animal perfection ;
> And thus the Virgin was made pregnant.' [1]

---

[1] *Par.* xiii. 79-84. Comp. *Summa*, i. q. xxvii. ; xxxiv. a. 3. For the use
of 'animal' applied to Adam, see below, p. 420. In the first instant of
His conception the human nature of Christ was perfect (*Summa*, iii.
q. xxxiv.). The knowledge of Christ is discussed in *Summa*, iii. q. ix-xii.

In the case of all other men, Solomon included, these two conditions do not exist. It is true, indeed, says Aquinas, that the whole Trinity is engaged in the work of creation. Everything that is, mortal or immortal, is simply the *splendor*, the reflected light, of that Idea (the Son) which our Lord (the Father) begets by the power of Love (the Holy Spirit). But this Trinity does not set its seal directly and immediately upon the wax; it works through a long series of secondary agencies. 'The living light' of the Divine Idea, remaining for ever united with the Father and the Spirit, gathers its rays into a unity, as in a mirror, in 'nine subsistences,' the nine Orders of Angels. These in turn distribute it through the nine Heavens of which they are the Movers; and as it descends from Heaven to Heaven, 'from act to act,' the creative energy, through the nature of the materials, sinks to 'the ultimate potentialities,' capable of producing nothing but 'brief contingencies'—things that may be or may not be, and pass from form to form. Aquinas explains that by 'contingencies' he means things generated, whether with seed or without, by the movement of the Heavens.[1] If the movement of the Heavens were uniform, and if the matter or wax were of one quality, 'the ideal signet' (that is, the imprint of the Divine Idea, the Son) would stamp all with the same light; but since they are both variable, it follows that trees of the same species differ in their fruit, and men in their genius. In short, Nature in the faultiness of her material is like an artist who has indeed the habit of his art, but his hand trembles. The argument then is that Solomon, who was formed of faulty material by faulty agencies, does not come into comparison with Adam and Christ, whose human nature is the direct impress of the seal of the Trinity upon wax that had no flaw.[2]

---

[1] *Summa*, i. q. lxxxvi. a. 3. For generation of plants without seed, see *Purg.* xxviii. 109-111.

[2] *Par.* xiii. 52-87. The editors of the Temple Classics *Paradiso* see in this passage 'the veiled dualism which may constantly be traced in

Aquinas proceeds to point out a second limitation in his estimate of Solomon's wisdom. He reminds Dante that he had said

'To see so much there never *rose* a second.'

The word *rose* shows that Aquinas was not comparing him with men in general, but with 'kings, the which are many, and the good are rare.' Solomon asked God for no mere speculative or scientific knowledge, but for wisdom to judge his people, 'that he might be sufficient as a king.' It is in this 'regal prudence,' then, that Solomon stands supreme.[1]

Now this may seem, as one writer thinks, a 'most lame and impotent conclusion' of the long and profound argument; and Plumptre says flatly that the reasoning seems to him 'almost a caricature of the method of Aquinas.' Probably Dante's reason for the whole passage was to emphasize his undoubted conviction that there is no Diviner wisdom than that of which it is written: 'By me kings reign, and princes decree justice.'[2] The real difficulty is that, history being the witness, all Solomon's wisdom did not make him 'sufficient as a king.' The outward brilliance of his reign was but a veil which hid for the moment the slow sapping of his people's strength and character through his luxury and licentiousness, his tyrannies, exactions, and idolatries. He sowed the wind, and his son reaped the whirlwind when the down-trodden people rent the greater part of the kingdom out of his hand. Whatever Dante may say, Solomon as a king was perhaps the wisest fool who ever lived.

In saying this, I am quite aware that I may be incur-

Dante's conception of the universe. . . . The *prima materia*, though explicitly declared in xxix. 22, 34; vii. 136, to be the direct creation of God, is here and elsewhere treated as something external, on which his power acts and which answers only imperfectly to it' (p. 166).

[1] *Par.* xiii. 88-111. 'Lo, I have given thee a wise and an understanding heart; so that there was none like thee before thee, neither after thee shall any *arise* like unto thee' (1 Kings iii. 12). In *Conv.* iv. 27 reference is made to the prudence of Solomon as the giver of good counsel; and the saying of Aristotle in the sixth of the *Ethics* is quoted: 'it is impossible for a man to be wise unless he is good.'

[2] Prov. viii. 15.

ring the censure on hasty judgments with which Canto
xiii. closes. Solomon's high place in Paradise, says
Aquinas, is to be a warning to Dante to be slow in
judging either doctrines or men. As to doctrines, 'he
is well down among the fools' who either affirms or
denies 'without distinction' of case from case.[1] Often
a hasty opinion leans to error, and, once formed,
prejudice, love of our own judgment, binds the intellect beyond the power of re-opening the question.
Moreover, the man 'who fishes for the truth and has
not the art,' not only catches no truth, but falls into
error: as witness, in philosophy, Parmenides, Melissos
and Bryson, and in theology, Sabellius and Arius, and
the fools who were as swords to the Scriptures, dis-
torting them as a man's face is distorted when he
views it in a sword-blade. The warning comes very
naturally from one who was himself a master of
the *distinguo*.[2]

The warning against rash judgments concerning
the ultimate fate of any man refers to the common
tendency to set Solomon among the lost. The last
moment of life may be critical for either salvation or
perdition, and may have power to reverse the apparent
character of a life-time:

> ' For I have seen all winter long the thorn
> First show itself intractable and fierce,
> And after bear the rose upon its top;
> And I have seen a ship direct and swift
> Run o'er the sea throughout its course entire,
> To perish at the harbour's mouth at last.' [3]

As an example of a soul lost almost at Heaven's gate,
we may remind ourselves of Guido da Montefeltro in

---

[1] Comp. *Conv.* iv. 8: 'The most beautiful branch that rises from the
root of reason is discrimination; for as says Thomas in Prologue to the
Ethics, "to know the relation of one thing to another is the proper act of
reason"; and this is discrimination.'

[2] In *De Mon.* iii. 4 Dante refers to Aristotle's condemnation of
Parmenides and Melissos: ' They accept what is false and they syllogize
wrongly,' i.e. they start from wrong premises and they draw wrong conclusions. Bryson is named by Aristotle as a dishonest reasoner. (For
the references in Aristotle's works, see Moore's *Studies in Dante*, i. 117-
118). Sabellius held a heresy concerning the Trinity, and Arius denied
that the Son is consubstantial with the Father. Aquinas refutes both in
his *Contra Gentiles*, Bk. iv. chaps. v-viii.   [3] *Par.* xiii. 130-142.

the Bolgia of the Evil Counsellors, whom Dante sets in intentional contrast to his son Buonconte, who put forth the flower of repentance in the article of death.[1] It is possible that he believed in a similar repentance on the part of Solomon; or his salvation may have been an inference from the words of Nehemiah (xiii. 26), ' Did not Solomon king of Israel sin by these things? Yet among many nations was there no king like him, who was beloved of his God.'

It is impossible to read this warning without remembering that no man needed it more than Dante himself. The whole poem is the passing of judgment on a vast multitude of men and women, whom he assigns omnisciently to their several places in Heaven, Purgatory, and Hell. We may take it then that the warning is the poet's declaration that his judgments are not the rash precipitate ones of ' Dame Bertha and Ser Martin '—the man in the street, as it were; but that they are pronounced after the utmost care and with a solemn sense of responsibility.[2]

This difficulty being disposed of, Beatrice asks the spirits to answer another question which she sees rising in Dante's mind, not merely before it is put in words, but even before it is formulated in thought. The question is twofold: first, will the light which enflowers the substance of these souls endure eternally as now? and second, if so, when the body is restored to them in the Resurrection, will not their eyes be hurt or injured by its brightness? The mere asking of the question threw the circles into an intensity of ' new joy,' evidently at the very thought of the restoration of their bodies: they quicken their dance, and raise their voices as they sing three times their hymn to the Trinity. The answer is then given by Solomon, ' the

---

[1] *Inf.* xxvii.; *Purg.* v. 85-129.

[2] Matt. vii. 1; 1 Cor. iv. 5. In *Summa*, ii-ii. q. lx. a. 3, 4, Aquinas discusses judgments of men upon suspicion, and decides that they involve moral flaws of varying degrees. To decide that our neighbour is wicked on slight grounds is contempt for him, and therefore mortal sin. Judgment of *things* must be according as things are ; judgment of *persons*, in doubtful circumstances, should lean to the most favourable construction.

divinest light in the lesser circle.'[1] Dante notes that
his voice is 'modest,' such perhaps as that of the Angel
to Mary, it being characteristic of the highest wisdom
in men and Angels that it is unassuming. It is sometimes supposed that Solomon is here retracting a
sceptical and materialistic view which he had expressed in the book of Ecclesiastes (iii. 18-22), that one
end comes to man and beast: 'That which befalleth
the sons of men befalleth beasts; even one thing
befalleth them: as the one dieth, so dieth the other;
yea, they have all one breath; so that a man hath
no preeminence above a beast: for all is vanity. All
go unto one place; all are of the dust, and all turn to
dust again. Who knoweth the spirit of man whether
it goeth upward, and the spirit of the beast whether it
goeth downward to the earth?' It is a mistake, however, to suppose that Dante regarded this as Solomon's
own view. Aquinas expressly denies this, and says
that Solomon is speaking 'in the character of the
foolish,' as is proved by Chap. ii. of the *Wisdom of
Solomon*, which opens with these words: 'For the
ungodly said, reasoning with themselves, but not
aright, Our life is short and tedious, and in the death
of a man there is no remedy.' The passage goes on
to refute this scepticism of the foolish: 'God created
man to be immortal, and made him to be an image
of His own eternity . . . and such as be faithful in
love shall abide with Him.' Solomon is certainly not
to be regarded as withdrawing in Heaven an error into
which he had fallen on earth: it is an error of others
which he states in his writings in order to refute.[2]

[1] Landino thinks the speaker is Peter the Lombard, who discusses the
question in the fourth Book of his *Sentences*. But *Par.* x. 109 seems
decisive for Solomon.

[2] *Summa*, i. q. lxxv. a. 6. The same view is taken by St. Gregory in his
Dialogues (Bk. IV. ch. iv.). Solomon, he says, is *Ecclesiastes*, the
Preacher. As such, he states this materialistic view of man as held by
others, and then confutes it in another passage (vi. 8) which runs thus in
the Vulgate: 'Quid habet amplius sapiens a stulto? et quid pauper, nisi
ut pergat illuc, ubi est vita?'—'What hath a wise man more than a fool,
and what a poor man, but that he may go thither where life is?'
Solomon's teaching, therefore, is 'that a wise man hath not only more
than a beast, but also more than a foolish man, to wit, that he goeth to
that place where life is'—i.e. to the immortal world.

Solomon's answer to the first half of Dante's question is that so long as Paradise endures, so long their love will ray round them this robe of light. The light varies according to a fixed spiritual law : its brightness is proportioned to the ardour of love in each soul ; the ardour, to the vision which the soul has of God; and the vision, to the amount of Divine grace bestowed upon it beyond its own worth or merit.[1] The meaning of this last clause seems to be that, while the Beatific Vision is the reward of the special merit of each individual soul, yet an illuminating grace over and above the merit is necessary for sight, and this grace is itself proportioned to the merit.[2] When, at the Resurrection, then, the holy and glorified body is restored, says Solomon, the happiness of the Redeemed will be increased, because man is neither body alone nor soul alone, but an essential union of the two. The completed nature will be able to receive more of the enlightening grace; and therefore the power of vision, the ardour of love, and the radiance which flows from these, will all increase. Although it is from the overflowing glory of the soul that the risen body gains its clarity,[3] yet the light of the body is not overpowered by that of the soul: it is like the white heat of a coal which shines through the flame which itself sends forth. Hence the body will be able to bear the brightness without weariness or pain :

'For the organs of the body will be strong
To all that hath the power to give delight.'[4]—

---

[1] I accept the common interpretation of *valore* in l. 42 as *merit*; but have hesitated as to whether Dante did not mean *natural ability*. Practically, however, it comes to the same thing. Even if Adam had remained in his integrity, says Aquinas, he could not without grace have attained to the Beatific Vision, because that vision lies beyond the measure of created nature. *A fortiori*, therefore, grace is necessary to lift the fallen nature above its own powers (*Summa*, i-ii. q. cxiv. a. 2).

[2] Comp. *Par.* xxix. 61, 62, for the union of *grace* and *merit* in the Angels:

'For the which their vision was exalted
With grace illuminating and with their merit.'

[3] *Summa*, Supp. q. lxxxv. a. i. 'This brightness will be caused by the overflow of the glory of the soul to the body. . . . As the soul will be of greater clearness according to its greater merit, so also there will be a difference of brightness in the body.'   [4] *Par.* xiv. 52-60.

the reference being to the words of St. Paul: 'It is sown in weakness; it is raised in power.'[1]

Scarcely had Solomon ceased speaking when an eager cry of *Amen* from the two 'choirs' revealed their longing for their dead bodies; and perhaps, adds Dante, not for their own merely,

> but for their mothers,
> For their fathers, and for the others who were dear,
> Or ever they became eternal flames.[2]

According to Aquinas, 'every imperfect thing seeks its own perfection, and therefore the separated soul naturally seeks conjunction with the body, and by reason of this desire proceeding from imperfection, its operation by which it is borne toward God is less intense.'[3] In other words, so long as this longing for the body exists the soul cannot lose itself wholly in God, as it will do after the Resurrection, when the longing is satisfied. As to the desire which perhaps these souls had for those near and dear to them here below, Dante is again following Aquinas who holds that, since the essential blessedness of the soul is in God, it is independent of friends: 'if there were only one soul enjoying God, it would be happy, without having any neighbour to love.' Nevertheless, since the love of our neighbour flows from the love of God,

---

[1] 1 Cor. xv. 43. This power, according to Aquinas, consists of *impassibilitas*, superiority to suffering; *subtilitas*, power to penetrate other bodies; *agilitas*, power to move at the spirit's will; *claritas*, the overflow of the soul's light on the body: whereby the glorified body becomes the perfect organ of the glorified soul. 'The glorious body will be entirely subjected to the glorified soul, not only in that there will be nothing in it which may resist the will of the spirit, for this was the case even in the body of Adam; but also in that there shall be in it a certain perfection flowing forth from the glorified soul into the body, by which it is rendered disposed to the aforesaid subjection, which perfection is called the marriage-portion of the glorified body' (*dos glorificati corporis*). (*Summa*, Supp. q. lxxxiv. a. 1.)

[2] *Par.* xiv. 64-67. 'The perverse ingenuity of commentators,' says Plumptre, 'has inferred from the absence of any relations except father and mother that he (Dante), for his part, did not desire to meet his wife in Paradise.' Dr. Moore (*Dante and his Early Biographers*, p. 18 n.) suggests that perhaps the commentators forgot that 'the spirits here are those of the great *Theologians*!' If jokes are to be made, we may remind ourselves that one of these Theologians—the last speaker—was a very much married man, to whom, possibly, the advent of wives might not have increased even the 'accidental' joy of Paradise.

[3] *Summa*, Supp. q. xciii. a. i.

'friendship is a sort of concomitant of perfect happiness,' an 'accidental' beatitude, such as the joy the spirits in Mercury felt when they saw Dante enter their Heaven:

> ' Lo, one who shall increase our loves!' [1]

We come now to the third circle, and as it requires careful examination, it will be well to quote the passage:

> And lo, all round about of equal clearness
> Rises a lustre over what was there,
> Like an horizon that again grows clear.
> And even as at the first rise of eve
> New appearances throughout the sky begin,
> So that the sight seems and not seems true ;
> It seemed to me that new subsistences
> Began there to be seen, and make a circle
> Outside the other two circumferences.
> O true sparkling of the Holy Spirit,
> How sudden and glowing did it make itself
> Unto mine eyes, which, conquered, bore it not. [2]

The interpretations given of this passage seem to me

---

[1] *Par.* v. 105: *Summa*, i-ii. q. iv. a. 8. Aristotle (*Ethics*, ix. 9) discusses the question, Does the happy man need friends? in relation, of course, to the present life. See above, p. 81.

The Resurrection of the body was regarded as a kind of justice for the service it renders to the soul. 'To the soul that loveth God,' says St. Bernard in his *De Diligendo Deo*, chap. xi., 'its body availeth in its infirmity, availeth in its death, availeth in its resurrection; first for the fruit of penitence, second for repose, third for consummation. And rightly doth the soul not will to be made perfect without that which it feeleth hath in every state served it in good things' (quoted in *Paradiso*, Temple Classics). Origen thinks it would be unjust to save the soul and let the body, the companion of its sufferings, perish : 'For how does it not seem absurd that this body which has endured scars for Christ, and, equally with the soul, has borne the savage torments of persecutions, and has also endured the suffering of chains and rods, and has been tortured with fire, beaten with the sword, and has further suffered the cruel teeth of wild beasts, the gallows of the cross, and divers kinds of punishments, —that this should be deprived of the prizes of such contests? If, forsooth, the soul alone, which not alone contended, should receive the crown, and its companion the body, which served it with much labour, should attain no recompense, for its agony and victory,—how does it not seem contrary to all reason that the flesh, resisting for Christ its natural vices, and its innate lust, and guarding its virginity with immense labour,—that one, when the time for rewards is come, should be rejected as unworthy and the other should receive its crown? Such a fact would undoubtedly argue on the part of God, either a lack of justice or a lack of power.' Parker, who quotes this in his translation of Dionysius the Areopagite, gives parallel passages from his works (*Eccles. Hier.* ch. vii. ; *Divine Names*, ch. vi.). [2] *Par.* xiv. 67-78.

singularly inadequate.   Some regard the vision as the
first dawning on the poet's eyes of the glory of the
next Heaven, Mars, which he is on the point of entering.   Others take it as a third circle of theologians of
whom Dante names none, either because, to quote
Landino, 'they have written subtly and with obscurity,
or because they were not known to him.'   A modern
commentator thinks the revelation of numerous other
spirits is 'intended to show that the twenty-four
saints who have hitherto appeared are only the more
conspicuous occupants of this Heaven'[1]—ignoring the
fact that this third circle flashes out into a brilliance
far surpassing that of the other two.   A third interpretation, relying on the word 'subsistences' in l. 73,
takes it to be a circle of Angels—according to Vellutello,
the Dominations, the Movers of the Sun, and the lowest
Order of the Second Hierarchy, which has its beginning here.   The word 'subsistences,' however, does not
necessarily mean Angels, though in Canto xiii. 59 it is
expressly applied to them.   The 'quality of being
separable from matter,' says Cornoldi, 'is called *subsistence*, and the forms endowed with it are called
subsistent.'[2]   'Subsistences,' therefore, can be used of
'separated souls' as well as of Angels.   One of the
most interesting suggestions is Mr. Gardner's, that
Dante is here the not altogether unconscious prophet
of modern science : 'It is, however, perfectly justifiable
to see in this episode a mystically expressed prophecy
of future discoveries and of scientists to come; an
acknowledgment that there were truths which the
mediæval schoolmen had not dreamed of, that a day
would come when the world would no longer say with
Dante himself in the *Convito*: *Assai basta alla gente per
la grande autorità di Aristotile a sapere che questa terra
è fissa e non si gira, e che essa col mare è centro del cielo*;[3]
and that Evolution would yet have its word to say

---

[1] Rev. H. F. Tozer, *English Commentary*, p. 503.
[2] *Physical System of St. Thomas*, p. 17.
[3] *Convito*, iii. 5.   'It is quite enough for people on the great authority
of Aristotle to know that this earth is fixed and does not revolve, and
that it with the sea is the centre of the heavens.'

upon creation and the origin of man. . . . It is not, perhaps, altogether fanciful to notice that Beatrice does not offer any explanation, but rather hurries him upward; and we may remember how the Ecclesiastic Authority was not exactly going to show itself favourable to the discoveries of Galileo, and that Theology has not always been prepared to accept the results of even more recent scientific investigations.'[1] Interesting as this is, it seems to me entirely out of harmony with this Heaven of the Sun. The great subject of study here is the Trinity, to which so many references are made; and it is not in the least likely that Dante regarded such things as theories of Evolution in relation to creation and the origin of man, could he have divined them, as the 'true sparkling of the Holy Spirit.' They would have belonged to what Aquinas calls the 'ascent through creatures to the knowledge of God by the natural light of *reason*':[2] a knowledge far beneath that of *faith*, as this, in turn, is beneath that of *sight*, the knowledge proper to Paradise. The 'true sparkling of the Holy Spirit' is obviously a climax of revelation, some direct and burning outflash of Divine light; whereas Mr. Gardner's theory throws us back to that knowledge by which the natural reason climbs its painful way toward God as far as creatures will carry it, and which Aquinas and Bonaventura alike regarded as the lowest stage. Dante dismissed it long ago in the Earthly Paradise with Virgil, its symbolic representative.

I have already indicated the view I hope to establish. It seems to me clear that Dante wishes to complete his symbolism of the Trinity, and that the 'true sparkling of the Holy Spirit' is suggested to him by the last named soul in the second circle, Joachim the Calabrian abbot, on Bonaventura's left hand.[3] This may seem an

---

[1] *Dante's Ten Heavens*, p. 109. On Mr. Gardner's idea that Beatrice stands for Ecclesiastical Authority, see above, p. 53. Even taking her in this character, she had, as we shall soon see, good reason for silence.

[2] *Contra Gentiles*, iv. 1.

[3] Joachimitism is virtually a recrudescence of Montanism. Comp. Tertullian's words in his Montanist days: 'Righteousness . . . was first

arbitrary suggestion unless we remember the extraordinary influence Joachim's theology had on the
Franciscan Order, an influence with which Dante was
perfectly familiar, as his reference to Casale and
Acquasparta shows.[1] Joachim was a Cistercian monk,
who in 1189 founded a community at Flora or Fiore
among the mountains of Calabria, and devoted himself
to the exposition of Scripture, especially the prophetic
and apocalyptic parts. He was believed to be, as Dante
says, 'endowed with the prophetic spirit,' and for
generations prophecies gathered round his name. His
three undoubted works are *Harmony of the Old and
New Testaments, Commentary on the Apocalypse,* and
Psalter of Ten Chords.[2] A man of glowing imagination,
of deep mystical spirit, and of ardent enthusiasm for
perfect conformity to Christ, it was impossible for
Joachim to believe that Christianity as he saw it
around him, was the final flower and fruit of the kingdom of God. His longing for a perfect world wrought
out a philosophy of history in which Christianity itself
is but a passing phase. All history he divided into
three great eras, corresponding to the three Persons of
the Trinity. The first—that of the Father—is that 'in
which men live under the rigour of law; the second—
that of the Son—under the favour of grace; the third—
that of the Spirit—in the fulness of the same grace. In
the first slavish servitude has place, in the second filial,
in the third liberty. In the first men live in fear, in
the second they rest in faith, in the third they burn
with charity. The first period belongs to the old, the
second to youths, the third to children. The first to

in a rudimentary state, having a natural fear of God : from this stage it
advanced, through the Law and the Prophets, to infancy; from that
stage it passed, through the Gospel, to the fervour of youth : now, through
the Paraclete, it is settling into maturity. He will be, after Christ, the
only one to be called and revered as Master. . . . He is the only prelate,
because He alone succeeds Christ' (*On the Veiling of Virgins,* ch. i.,
Ante-Nicene Library, vol. iii. p. 155).

[1] *Par.* xii. 124. See above, p. 212.

[2] Renan (*Studies of Relig. Hist.,* 222) says that in editions of the *Psalter*
are found two hymns on Paradise. 'The second of these compositions,
purporting to be the relation of a journey through the supernatural world
of spirits, is curious as having preceded the Divine Comedy.'

slaves, the second to freemen, the third to friends. In the first the stars shone, in the second the dawn whitens, in the third is full day. In the first winter reigns, in the second spring, in the third summer. The first produced nettles, the second roses, the third lilies. The first grass, the second ears, the third grain.'[1] The idea that the second era was rapidly drawing to its close and the third about to open fired the hearts of all who were sick of the sins of the Church; and none caught the flame faster than the Spiritual Franciscans. In the year 1254,—fifty-two years after Joachim's death —the Church was thrown into consternation by a book which struck at its very existence. It drew its title, *The Everlasting Gospel*, from Rev. xiv. 6 : 'And I saw another angel fly in the midst of heaven having the everlasting gospel to preach unto them that dwell on the earth, and to every nation, and kindred, and tongue, and people.' It consisted of the three works of Joachim named above, and an Introduction in which the abbot's doctrines were boldly developed. The New Era was dated to begin in 1260. The writings of Joachim, as the Scriptures of the Eternal Gospel, would displace the Old and New Testaments.   'The preaching and dissemination of this supreme and eternal law of God is committed to the barefooted Order (the Franciscans). At the threshold of the Old Law were three men, Abraham, Isaac, and Jacob; at that of the New Law were three others, Zachariah, John the Baptist, and Christ; and at that of the coming age are three, the man in linen (Joachim), the Angel with the sharp sickle [? St. Dominic], and the Angel with the sign of the living God (Francis).'[2] The sacraments and observances of the Second Era would pass away in the final reign of the Love of the Spirit.

It is unnecessary for our present purpose to enter

---

[1] Felice Tocco, *L'Eresia nel Medio Evo*, p. 374.

[2] Lea, *Hist. of the Inquisition*, iii. 21.   Renan in suggesting that Dominic was 'the Angel with the sharp sickle' says 'this interpretation is not given in the manuscripts, no doubt because the Dominican censors would not have been pleased to see the name of their patriarch mixed up with these dangerous doctrines.'

into the storm the book produced.[1] It was finally
condemned by a commission of Cardinals at Anagni
in 1355. We have yet to see, however, the attitude of
Bonaventura to this movement of the Spirituals of his
Order. At the time of the publication of the book, the
General of the Order was John of Parma, a strong
supporter of the Spirituals. At first suspicion fell on
him, but there is little doubt that the author was
another of the Spiritual Franciscans, Gherardo da
Borgo San Donnino, a man of learning and purity.
John of Parma was forced to resign; an intermediate
party was formed ; and, as Renan says, 'orthodoxy and
a decorous mysticism carried the day in the person of
St. Bonaventura,' his successor. We may agree with
Tocco that 'the new General bore himself with much
humanity to the Joachimite party' as a whole; but his
treatment of John and Gherardo was not remarkable
for leniency. John was tried by a special court, and
would have been condemned with Bonaventura's
consent but for the strong intercession of Cardinal
Ottoboni, afterwards Pope Adrian V. He was allowed
to choose his place of retirement. Gherardo was
thrown into an underground dungeon, put in chains,
and fed with bread and water for eighteen years; and
when death gave him release, the rites of the Church
were refused, and his body was buried in the ashpit of
the garden of the convent where he died. Two of his
comrades had a similar fate. If we wish to learn how
the Spirituals regarded the clemency of St. Bonaventura
we have only to read the vision of Brother Jacopo della
Massa in Chap. xlviii. of the *Fioretti*. In his vision

---

[1] An echo of the storm is heard in Jean de Meun's *Romance of the Rose*,
which identifies the Franciscans with Antichrist, and denounces the new
Gospel :

> 'The prime exemplar of a book
> So vile that by the devil's crook
> It well were written, and about
> 'Twas set for clerks to copy out
> And circulate when duly dight;
> The Everlasting Gospel hight
> This trash and friars avouched its merit,
> As writ by God's most Holy Spirit.'

(From Temple Classics translation by F. S. Ellis, ll. 12443 ff.).

Jacopo saw John of Parma on the highest point of the
Tree of the Order. St. Francis at Christ's command
offered to all the brethren on the Tree 'a chalice full
of the spirit of life.' Those who devoutly drank it all
shone as the sun. Those who spilled it all became
black and deformed. Those who spilled some and
drank some became dark and shining in proportion to
each. John, who shone brightest of all, foreseeing the
storm about to shake the Tree, came down from the
topmost branch and 'hid himself in the solid root, and
was all rapt in thought'—an obvious reference to his
resignation and retirement. Then 'one of the brothers
that had taken part of the chalice and part had spilt'—
an allusion to Bonaventura's intermediate position in
the controversy—'climbed up on that branch and to
that place, whence Brother John had come down. And
when he was come to that place, the nails of his hands
became iron, sharp and keen as razors: whereat he left
the place to which he had climbed, and with rage and
fury sought to hurl himself upon the said Brother John
for to do him hurt.' John was saved only by St. Francis,
at Christ's word, cutting off the nails of that brother
with a sharp flint stone.[1]

Now, it seems to me clear that Dante in this third
circle wished to show how far his sympathy with these
Joachimite views went. In general, he accepts the
doctrine of a third era of the Holy Spirit. If we take
the three circles to correspond to the Trinity, we may
say that the first, the Dominican, represents the
Father, the reign of law and fear; and the second, the
Franciscan, the Son, the favour of the grace of Christ,
whose image St. Francis bore. But Dante believes
that these two types do not exhaust the possibilities
of Theology. Joachim and his followers were not mistaken in their hope of a third era worthy to be called,
in comparison with the others, the 'true sparkling of the
Holy Spirit,' far wider in its range, far more brilliant
in its shining. Dante cannot describe it definitely; it
lies far off on the dim horizon of the future. It has the

---

[1] *The Little Flowers of St. Francis* (Temple Classics).

mystery of the evening when the stars are scarcely
seen, for it is the passing away of one era. It has the
mystery of the morning when the dawn whitens, for it
is the beginning of a new day of the Spirit,—perhaps
the eternal day itself:

> Earth breaks up, time drops away,
> In flows heaven, with its new day
> Of endless life.[1]

In this sense, then, and to this extent, Dante proclaims himself a Joachimite in his hope of the great
Era of the Spirit. The details and implications of the
doctrine as held by the Spiritual Franciscans made it
impossible for him to bind himself more definitely. It
identified the new era with the Franciscan Order. It
declared monasticism to be the final and perfect form
of human society.[2] It substituted the writings of
Joachim for the Old and New Testaments. It abolished
the Church as an institution, with all its sacraments
and rites. Dante did not wish to commit himself to
any of these implications of the doctrine; but he has
no hesitation in declaring his conviction that the
highest types of Theology known to him fall far short
of the vast circle of light which the Divine Spirit will
yet flash into the souls of men in some great day of
'the revealing of the sons of God.'

[1] Browning's *Christmas Eve*. The reference to morning and evening
in C. xiv. 67-75 reminds us of St. Augustine's mystical interpretation of
Genesis i. The Angels have a *morning* knowledge (*cognitio matutina*),
when they know things in the Word; and an *evening* (*vespertina*) knowledge, when they know things in their own nature. See *City of God*,
xi. 29; *Summa*, i. q. lviii. a. 6.

[2] The three eras correspond to three orders (1) the married (Father);
(2) the priesthood (Son); (3) monks (Spirit). As Tocco says, Joachim
seems never to have asked how the human race is to continue in an era
of universal monachism (*L'Eresia nel Medio Evo*, Bk. ii. ch. i. v).

CHAPTER XII

1. *Cacciaguida :* '*O sanguis meus !*'

THE outline of the story of Mars, the Fifth Heaven, on which we now enter, is as follows. Dante's eyes, dazzled by the 'true sparkling of the Holy Spirit' in the third circle of the Sun, are restored by the beauty and smile of Beatrice, as he rises to 'a loftier salvation.'[1] He found himself in Mars, which seemed ruddier than its wont. Across its glowing surface a great white Cross[2] shone like the Milky Way, and through its light Christ Himself flashed forth mysteriously. Souls of martyrs and crusaders in the form of 'ruby splendours' moved up and down and from side to side along the white pathway of the Cross, singing as they moved a song of praise of which he understood only the words, 'Arise and conquer.' When the song ceased, the soul of his ancestor Cacciaguida flashed down from the right arm of the Cross to welcome him. He tells how simple was the life of the ancient Florence into which he was born; how he was baptized and married; how he joined the Crusades, was knighted by the Emperor Conrad, died for Holy Land, and 'came from martyrdom unto this peace.' He explains how Florence has

---

[1] The idea is probably that Dante's eyes were dazzled with the vision of future revelations of the Spirit, and restored by Beatrice leading him up from this matter of speculation to the lives of soldiers and martyrs of Christ—the 'loftier salvation' of sharing in 'the fellowship of His sufferings.'

[2] Plumptre notes that the Cross is 'after the Greek pattern, such as that with which early Byzantine and Italian art was familiar in the aureole of our Lord, as distinguishing Him from the saints.' Dante describes it as

the venerable sign

Which junctures of quadrants in a circle make (xiv. 101).

fallen from its ancient peace and simplicity to its
present state of luxury, the decay of its old families,
and the baleful influence over it of its former patron,
the god Mars. He then foretells how Florence will
make a martyr of Dante himself by banishment, and
what will be his lot in exile. He exhorts him to bear
all in the true martyr spirit, speaking out the truth
even about the loftiest names in scorn of consequence.
Finally, he points out some of the warrior-souls who
have now the Cross for which they fought and suffered
as their eternal home and joy.

Dante's leading idea in this Heaven is to draw a
contrast between war in its celestial nobility and war
in its earthly baseness; or, to put it otherwise, between
this Heaven of Mars with its soldiers of the Cross, and
the city of Florence under the influence of the god
Mars, whose statue stood at the Ponte Vecchio. For
instance, Cacciaguida speaks of the Florentines of his
day,

> 'All those who at that time were there between
> Mars and the Baptist, fit for bearing arms.'[1]

'Mars and the Baptist' — in these words was com-
pressed, for Dante's mind, much of the entire history
of Florence. They indicate the boundaries of the city
in his forefather's day : on the south, the statue of Mars
standing at the entrance of the Old Bridge, and, on the
north, the Baptistery of St. John where it is to-day.
But to a Florentine the names meant much more than
boundaries. According to Villani, the Baptistery was
originally the Temple of Mars, built before the Christian
era, to commemorate a great victory of the Romans
over the Fiesolans.[2] On the conversion of Florence to
Christianity, the Temple was dedicated to John the
Baptist, and the statue of Mars was carefully set in a
high tower on the Arno, an ancient prophecy having
declared that its destruction would cause great damage
to the city.[3] This tower was believed to have been
overthrown and the statue cast into the Arno in the

---

[1] *Par.* xvi. 46.   [2] *Chron.* i. 42.   [3] Villani, *Chron.* i. 60.

mythical destruction of Florence by the Goths; and
when the city was rebuilt, it was drawn from the river
and set on a pillar at what is now the head of the
Ponte Vecchio, under the conviction that only thus
was the rebuilding possible.[1] To our minds all this is
proof that the Florentines were as much devoted to
war after their conversion to Christianity as before it;
but to the citizens it meant that the perpetual fighting
within the walls was due to the anger of the offended
deity. In the *Inferno* (xiii. 143-145) a Florentine suicide
is made to say :

> 'I of that city was which for the Baptist
> Changed its first patron, wherefore he for this
> For ever with his art will make it sad.'

And, in the Cantos before us, Cacciaguida connects the
strife of Guelphs and Ghibellines in the city with the
statue of the god. He is speaking of ancient Florentine
families, and the last he names are the Amidei:

> 'The house from which your wailing sprang,
> Through the just wrath which has brought death to you,
> And put an end unto your joyous living,
> Was honoured in itself and in its allies.
> O Buondelmonte, how evil was the hour
> Thou fled'st the bridal at another's promptings !
> Many would be rejoicing who are sad
> If God had thee surrendered to the Ema
> The first time that thou camest to the city.
> But it was meet that to that mutilated stone
> Which guards the bridge, Florence should give
> A victim in her last hour of peace.'[2]

The reference is to the well-known story of the murder
of Buondelmonte de' Buondelmonti in 1215. This young
nobleman was betrothed to a lady of the Amidei
family, but forsook her for a daughter of the house of
the Donati. The kinsmen of the insulted lady waylaid
and slew him at the foot of the statue of Mars, 'that
mutilated stone,' as he rode into the city on Easter
Day.[3] Well for the city, says Cacciaguida, if the first
time he came to it he had been drowned in the little

---

[1] Villani, *Chron.* iii. 1; *Inf.* xiii. 146-150.   [2] *Par.* xvi. 136-147.
[3] Villani, *Chron.* v. 38; Dino Compagni, i. 2.

stream of the Ema which flows through the Valdi-
greve, a little south of Florence, where his castle lay.
The murder was generally regarded as the beginning
of the feuds of Guelphs and Ghibellines of which
Dante himself was a victim; although, as Villani
admits, 'long before there were factions among the
noble citizens, and the said parties existed by reason
of the strifes and questions between the Church and
the Empire.'[1] From all this it is obvious that Dante's
aim is to draw a contrast between the two influences
of Mars: the Christian, as seen in these soldiers of the
Cross who fought for some noble cause, such as the
recovery of Holy Land; and the heathen, as seen in
the deadly feuds of Florence, rooted in luxury and the
breaking of faith, and producing as fruit the decay of
ancient families and the banishment of its citizens. It
is scarcely possible that Dante could write these Cantos
without remembering the portent which he mentions
in the *Convito* (ii. 14): 'And in Florence, in the beginning
of her destruction, was seen in the air, in the figure of
a cross, a great quantity of those vapours which are
followers of the star of Mars,'—a sign said to have been
seen on the evening of November 6, 1301, a few days
after the entry of Charles of Valois.[2]

And now, having the general idea before us, let us

---

[1] *Chronicle*, v. 38. 'By reason of the death of the said M. Bondel-
monte,' says Villani, 'all the families of the nobles and the other citizens
of Florence were divided, and some held with the Bondelmonti, who took
the side of the Guelfs, and were its leaders, and some with the Uberti,
who were the leaders of the Ghibellines, whence followed much evil and
disaster to our city, as hereafter shall be told; and it is believed that it
will never have an end, if God do not cut it short. And surely it shows
that the enemy of the human race, for the sins of the Florentines, had
power in that idol of Mars, which the pagan Florentines of old were wont
to worship, that at the foot of his statue such a murder was committed,
whence so much evil followed to the city of Florence.'

[2] Dino Compagni in his *Chronicle* (ii. 19) says he saw it: 'In the evening
a marvellous sign appeared in the sky, namely, a bright red cross above
the Priors' Palace. Its beams were more than a span and a half in width,
the length of the one line appeared to be 20 cubits, that of the transverse
a little less. This appearance lasted during such time as a horse would
take to run twice in the tilt. Wherefore the people who saw it, and I
who clearly saw it, might understand that God was greatly angered
against our city' (Temple Classics transl.). In Mars, it is the star that is
red, while the cross is white.

look at the details. The colours of this Heaven are probably symbolic. Dante speaks of the burning smile and redness of the planet, both, doubtless, representing the love which made it possible to lay down life itself: hence the souls themselves are in the form of ruby lights. As white is the symbolic colour of faith, the white pathway in which they move may be taken to represent that faith of the Cross in which they fought and conquered.

Dante finds it impossible by any 'worthy example' to tell in what fashion Christ flashed forth in that white dawn of the Cross. The only interpreter is experience: the man who takes his cross and follows Christ will excuse his silence when he sees the same mysterious lightning. For it is to be noted that it is the flash of lightning (*balenar*, l. 108): 'as the lightning cometh out of the east, and shineth even unto the west; so shall also the coming of the Son of Man be,'[1] and in every warfare of His saints against the world He flashes forth in the lightning of judgment. We may also note here that this is the first of three visions of Christ vouchsafed to Dante in the *Paradiso*. Here He flashes forth from the Cross through those who shared 'the fellowship of His sufferings.' In the Heaven of the Fixed Stars He appears in His Triumph as the central Sun of the starry hosts of His saints in their victory over death and hell. The final vision is the mystery of the Incarnation, the union of the Divine and human, which came to Dante as by a flash of lightning, beyond his natural powers.[2]

The 'ruby splendours' of these warrior-souls move in the white arms of the Cross like motes in a sunbeam that comes through a chink into a darkened room, or like fire behind alabaster—the glow of their love shining through the white light of their faith; and as they meet and pass each other they sparkle brightly in their mutual joy and love. All their movements are in music: their song is to Dante like a lute or harp of many strings—he hears the notes but cannot

---

[1] Matt. xxiv. 27.
[2] *Par.* xiv. 103-108; xxiii. 28-39; xxxiii. 127-145.

understand the words. One phrase alone comes to him : 'Rise thou and conquer,'—perhaps a hymn of praise for the victory of their Lord over sin and death.[1] The meaning seems to be that Dante is as yet unable to enter into 'the high praises' of those who have 'fought the good fight' and won their 'crown of life': the bitterness of the struggle is still upon him, and he is not yet able to glory in sufferings. But the melody of those who can thus glory in the cross is the sweetest thing he has yet known in Paradise; though he is careful to tell us that when he said this he had not looked at the eyes of Beatrice since he entered this Heaven.[2]

In this connection it is interesting to mark the completeness of Dante's thanksgiving for being raised to this loftier salvation of suffering with his Lord:

> With all the heart, and in that speech
> Which is the same in all, such holocaust
> To God I made as the new grace beseemed.[3]

The important word here is 'holocaust' or 'whole burnt offering,' a word which Dante cannot have used without having in mind the significance it had in the theology and practice of his Church. It is almost a technical word for the absolute and complete surrender of the entire self to God in the 'religious' life. As Aquinas says : 'They are called eminently *religious*, who hand over the dominion of themselves to the divine service, offering as it were a holocaust to God'; and he quotes Gregory: 'When a man has vowed to Almighty God his whole having, his whole living, and

---

[1] Landino's note is : 'These two words from the holy Scripture are spoken to Christ : Rise from death and conquer the devil. The author feigns that of the whole hymn which the souls sang to Christ he understood only Arise and conquer, to show that it is easy for every one to understand that the passion and death of Christ was the victory by which He delivered us from bondage to the devil, but that many other wonderful things which are involved in that victory are not understood save by the most learned men.' It is much likelier that Dante meant to say that it is only souls in Paradise, who themselves have fought and overcome, who know all the reasons for praising Christ for his great victory over sin and death.

[2] *Par.* xiv. 130-139. It is only in xv. 34 that he sees her eyes. See p. 243.   [3] *Par.* xiv. 88-90.

his whole liking, that is a holocaust.'[1] This is quoted
to prove that this holocaust is made by the three vows
of religion, poverty, chastity, obedience—vows which
Dante certainly had not taken. In using the word
here, therefore, the implication is that holocaust can
be made in other ways, such as martyrdom, to which,
plainly, Dante here devotes himself.[2]

The warm glow of his holocaust had not yet left his
breast when Dante received assurance of its acceptance
by the appearance of the souls of the star—splendours
so radiant and ruby-coloured that he broke into the
exclamation: 'O Elios, who dost so adorn them!'
'Elios' is probably a mingling of the Hebrew name of
God *El* (see Canto xxvi. 136) and the Greek *Helios*, the
Sun, God being the Sun of all heavenly spirits: in the
next Canto, for example, He is spoken of as 'the Sun
who illumed and tired you with heat and light' (l. 76).
One is tempted, however, to hear in the word an echo
of the 'Eli, Eli' of Calvary. Dante seems to have in
his mind the contrast between the Cross on earth and
the Cross in Heaven. On Calvary the sun withdrew its
light, and in the darkness Christ felt as if He were
forsaken of God: 'Eli, Eli, lama sabachthani?' Here
in Paradise Elios, the Sun, shines upon the Cross and
kindles into joy and beauty the souls of the noble army
of martyrs who entered into the fellowship of His
sufferings.[3]

[1] *Summa*, ii-ii. q. clxxxvi. a. 1, 6.

[2] This, of course, is entirely in harmony with Aquinas who teaches that
'of human acts, martyrdom is the most perfect of its kind, as being the
sign of the greatest charity'—since the martyr gives up life, the thing
most loved, and faces a painful death, the thing most hated. It is
doubtful, however, whether Dante's claim of martyrdom would have
been allowed, Aquinas holding that 'the essence of martyrdom, full and
perfect, requires the suffering of death for Christ' (*Summa*, ii-ii. q. cxxiv.
a. 3, 4).

[3] Matt. xxvii. 46. Toynbee in his *Dante Dictionary* quotes the *Magnae
Derivationes* of Uguccione da Pisa: 'Ab *ely*, quod est deus, dictus est sol
elyos, quod pro deo olim reputabatur'; and Longfellow refers to St.
Hildebert's hymn *Ad Patrem*:

> 'Alpha et Omega, magne Deus,
>   Heli, Heli, Deus meus.'

For the secret joy with which Christ said 'Eli' on the cross—enduring
even that final desolation gladly for our sakes—see *Purg.* xxiii.
70-75.

Then followed silence in Heaven—the hymn of lofty praise was stilled in order to give Dante the opportunity of making his request known to these martyr-saints, a proof to his mind that they would never be deaf to 'righteous prayers.' Suddenly in the silence, out of a constellation in the right hand cross-beam, there darted like a falling star one of the splendours to the foot of the Cross. It is the soul of Cacciaguida, one of the poet's forefathers, who greets him as eagerly as Anchises did his son Aeneas in the Elysian Fields.[1] There are several points worthy of notice here. Dante sets his ancestor in the place of honour, Christ's right hand: even among martyrs and soldiers of the cross he ranks him high. The constellation out of which he flashes is probably a group of crusaders who died for Holy Land. Further, his eager haste to welcome his descendant did not carry him beyond the shining pathway of the Cross :

> Nor was the gem dissevered from its ribbon,
> But down the radiant fillet ran along,
> So that fire seemed it behind alabaster.[2]

The idea of some that the souls were moving in a circle 'from horn to horn' of the Cross, and from summit to base (xiv. 109), must be set aside. Dante's idea is that they never left the outline of the Cross : as they had lived and died for it, it has now become their eternal home. It forms their bond of union with one another: to use the poet's figure, the Cross is a ribbon on which they are strung as jewels. This unity is an essential part of the allegory, as will be seen if we bear in mind the contrast, which Dante never forgets, of the influence of Mars in Florence, where man from man, family from family, party from party, were severed by every form of faction and hatred.

Cacciaguida's greeting is in Latin, either because, as Plumptre thinks, in his day 'the "vulgar tongue" of modern Italian had not yet been formed,' or, as others

---

[1] *Aen.* vi. 684 ff.   [2] *Par.* xv. 22-24.

suggest, because it is regarded as the more dignified language:

> *'O sanguis meus, O superinfusa*
> *Gratia Dei! sicut tibi, cui*
> *Bis unquam coeli ianua reclusa ?'* [1]

The 'sanguis meus' is taken from the rebuke given by Anchises to the shade of Julius Caesar for his declaration of civil war.[2] In Cacciaguida's lips it indicates the continuance even in Paradise of the ties of flesh and blood—the desire, referred to in the preceding Canto, for the very bodies of those dear to them in the earthly life. The opening of the gate of heaven to Dante twice means now and at his death.[3]

At this point Dante for the first time since he entered this Heaven turned to look at Beatrice, and, between his forefather and her, was struck with amazement:

> For in her eyes was burning such a smile
> That with mine own methought I touched the bottom
> Both of my grace and of my Paradise.[4]

The smile within the eyes is the source of this fulness of joy. We must recall the symbolism of Beatrice, the Heavenly Wisdom. 'The *eyes* of Wisdom,' says the *Convito* (iii. 15), 'are her *demonstrations*, in which the Truth is seen with the greatest certainty; and her *smile* is her *persuasions*, in which is revealed the inner light of Wisdom underneath any veil; and in these two is felt that highest pleasure of beatitude which is the greatest good in Paradise.' It is this union of eyes and smile—the persuasion within the demonstration, which so enraptures Dante's soul that he can think of no higher bliss than to be re-united with his ancestor and

---

[1] *Par.* xv. 28-30.
[2] *Aen.* vi. 834-5.
> 'Tuque prior, tu parce, genus qui ducis Olympo;
> Projice tela manu, sanguis meus.'
On Cacciaguida's use of Latin, see note, p. 251.
[3] Cacciaguida's question seems to imply that no one had ever ascended to Paradise before during his lifetime, whereas St. Paul was caught up to the third heaven. Casini thinks the cases are different: Dante ascended to prepare himself for salvation after death; Paul, because he already merited beatitude. [4] *Par.* xv. 34-36.

share his Heaven of the Cross. It is perhaps for this reason that much of what followed in Cacciaguida's speech lay beyond the bounds of mortal thought: the joy of souls when their own blood gains the blessed world passeth all understanding of men still in the flesh.

When the speech returned to the level of Dante's intellect, the first thing he understood was his forefather's praise to God, the Three and One, for His 'courtesy' to him in his seed. Cacciaguida then tells him that he has assuaged in him a long sweet hunger, created by reading of his coming in the volume of the mind of God. He knows that Dante's silence is due to this same cause—he asks no question because the saints see his every thought in the Divine Mirror even before it rises. Nevertheless, Cacciaguida begs him, although he already knows his wish, to give it utterance, the better to fulfil, by the very sound of his voice, the sacred love which had made him watch and wait for his coming. In reply, Dante begs the 'living topaz' to satisfy him with his name, prefacing the question with an apology for the ignorance which made it necessary to ask. 'God,' he says, 'is the Prime Equality—in Him, and therefore in you who are illumined and fired by Him, love and knowledge are equal. But in me, a mortal, love and knowledge have unequal wings. With the love of the heart only can I thank thee for thy paternal welcome; my lack of knowledge corresponding to the love compels me to ask thy name.'[1]

Cacciaguida then tells Dante that the Alighiero from whom his surname came was his son and the poet's great-grandfather: for more than a hundred years[2] he had been circling the Terrace of Pride on Mount Purgatory, and he begs him to shorten his toil there by his works. He then gives a picture of the Florence of his day—the Florence of the beginning of the twelfth

---

[1] *Par.* xv. 43-87.
[2] Toynbee tells us that there is documentary proof that this Alighiero was alive on Aug. 14, 1201, and therefore cannot have been in Purgatory 'a hundred years and more' in the year 1300, when Cacciaguida spoke. Probably Dante did not know the precise date of his death.

century, in contrast with that of Dante's time. Then
the city was worthy of its patron saint, the Baptist, in
the austere simplicity of its life and manners. In
modesty of dress, in the marriages of their daughters,
in their morality, their architecture, their family life,
the ancient citizens far surpassed their descendants.[1]
A passage in Villani (vi. 69) draws a similar picture of
the Florence of about the time of Dante's own birth:
'The citizens of Florence lived soberly, and on coarse
food, and with little spending, and in manners and
graces were in many respects coarse and rude; and
both they and their wives were clad in coarse garments,
and many wore skins without lining, and caps on
their heads, and all wore leather boots on their feet,
and the Florentine ladies wore boots without ornaments, and the greatest were contented with one
close-fitting gown of scarlet serge or camlet, girt with
a leathern girdle after the ancient fashion, with a
hooded cloak lined with miniver, which hood they wore
on their head; and the common women were clad in

---

[1] *Par.* xv. 97-129. The details of this golden age are interesting. The
time is marked by 'the ancient circuit' of the walls begun in 1078 (Vill.
iv. 8): the Benedictine monastery of the Badia, from which the city took
its time ('tierce and nones') was just inside it (ll. 97-99). The women wore
no chains, or coronets, or embroidered shoes, or girdles so rich that they
withdrew the eye from the wearer (100-102). The birth of a daughter was
not then a terror to the father as it is now, when the daughters marry too
early and must have a dowry too great (103-105). No house was empty of
its household—perhaps through war or exile, though the reference to
Sardanapalus and to what can be done 'in camera' seems rather to imply
the childlessness which is the issue of unnatural luxury (106-108). In the
splendour of its buildings, the Florence of Dante's day surpassed Rome:
Montemalo (now Monte Mario) is the hill on the way from Viterbo from
which the splendour of the Eternal City is first seen; and Uccellatoio is
the point on the road from Bologna from which the first flash of the
greater splendour of Florence breaks on the traveller's view (109-111).
Bellincion Berti, Dante's beau-ideal of a Florentine citizen, was content
with a leather belt with a bone clasp, while his wife left her mirror with
unpainted face. The heads of the noble families of the Nerli and the
Vecchietti dressed in unlined leathern jerkins, and their dames handled
the spindle and the flax (112-117). One tended the cradle; another at her
wheel told her household tales of the Trojans, and Fiesole, and Rome—
patriotic legends of the city (121-126). In those golden days a Cianghella,
a profligate lady of Dante's day, would have been as great a wonder as a
Cornelia, 'the mother of the Gracchi,' would be now; and a Lapo Salterello,
a notoriously unjust judge, as a Cincinnatus, the Roman farmer who saved
the Republic (127-129).

coarse green cambric after the same fashion; and 100
lire was the common dowry for wives, and 200 or 300
lire was, in those times, held to be excessive; and the
most of the maidens were twenty or more years old
before they were wedded. After such habits and plain
customs then lived the Florentines, but they were true
and trustworthy to one another and to their common-
wealth, and with their simple life and poverty they did
greater and more virtuous things than are done in our
times with more luxury and more riches.'[1] This golden
age of simple virtue was also a golden age of peace:
wives and mothers were secure of their place of burial;
none was deserted in her couch because of France;[2]
the cradle and the distaff and ancient tales of patriotism
filled their days. And then in a few lines Cacciaguida
sums up the story of his life:

> ' To such a restful, such a beautiful
> Life of citizens, to such a loyal
> Commonwealth, to so sweet a home,
> Did Mary give me, with loud cries invoked,
> And in your ancient Baptistery at once
> Christian and Cacciaguida I became.
> Moronto was my brother, and Eliseo;
> From Val di Pado came to me my wife,
> And 'twas from her thy surname was derived.
> I followed afterward the Emperor Conrad,
> And he begirt me knight among his chivalry,
> So by good deeds I came into his grace.
> In his train I went against th' iniquity
> Of that Law, whose people doth usurp
> Your just possession, thro' the Pastors' fault.
> There was I by that race of shame
> Freed from the coil of the deceitful world,
> The love of which full many a soul befouls,
> And came from martyrdom unto this peace.'[3]

This is virtually all we know of Dante's ancestors.

---

[1] Miss Selfe's translation. For a picture of the luxury of after times
see the account of Frate Francesco Pippino who wrote in 1313, quoted in
Napier's *Florentine History*, ii. 542.

[2] This is frequently taken as a reference to the absence of husbands
in France for purposes of trade, but it is difficult to suppose that Dante
was not thinking of his own wife among others, deserted because he had
been driven into exile by the French adventurer, Charles of Valois.

[3] *Par.* xv. 130-148.

The brothers of Cacciaguida, Moronto and Eliseo, are mere names. The latter has given rise to the conjecture that the poet sprang from the Elisei, whom Boccaccio traces to the ancient Roman family of the Frangipani. There seems to be no proof of this whatever, though it is to be noted that Dante prides himself on his descent from the ancient Roman stock.[1] Cacciaguida's wife is generally believed to have been one of the Aldighieri or Alighieri of Ferrara,[2] and an attempt has been made to derive the name from *alga*, the seaweed which abounds in the swampy valley of the Po. Federn has no doubt it is a German name, 'most probably derived from "Aldiger," which has about the same significance as the word "Shakespeare," meaning "the ruler of the spear."' All this is conjecture; but it is well to remember, as this author points out, that the omission of the Alighieri by Villani and Machiavelli from their catalogues of noble families does not necessarily exclude them. 'Alighieri was not then a family name—it was the time when family names were first introduced, but were still unusual except those derived from castles and feudal estates—Alighiero was but the name of Dante's father and of his great-grandfather. Perhaps they belonged to another of the great Florentine families.'[3]

Some doubt has been thrown on the commonly accepted view that the Emperor whom Cacciaguida followed to the Crusades was Conrad iii. of Suabia, but without reason. Founding on a passage in Villani (iv. 9), Casini suggests Conrad ii., the Salic, who was Emperor from 1024 to 1039. According to Villani, this Emperor (whom he calls Conrad i. and misdates) visited Florence frequently and knighted many of its citizens. The only crusade he undertook was against the Saracens in Calabria, so that on this view Cacciaguida never was in Holy Land, and his birth

---

[1] *Inf.* xv. 70-78. It is to be remembered, however, that our inability to prove Dante's descent from the Elisei and Frangipani is no proof that he himself did not believe in it.

[2] Parma and Verona also claim her.

[3] Karl Federn, *Dante and his Time*, 196, 197.

must be pushed back at least a century before the generally received time. It is obviously impossible that he could in that case be the father of the Alighiero whom he calls his son, who died more than a hundred and sixty years later. There is no reason for giving up the ordinary view that the Emperor referred to is Conrad III., who in 1147, with Louis VII. of France, undertook the disastrous Second Crusade, so enthusiastically preached by St. Bernard of Clairvaux.[1]

---

[1] Bernard's defence for the failure of this Crusade which roused all Europe against him is that it was due to the sins of the Crusaders themselves. They fell as the Israelites fell in the wilderness, and from the same cause. His remedy is—faith and a third Crusade (*De Consideratione*, ii. 1).

CHAPTER XIII

2. *Cacciaguida and Ancient Florence*

THE opening line of Canto xvi. strikes the keynote
of the thought which runs all through it:

> O thou our poor nobility of blood!

Blood is not everything; yet on earth it counts for
much: the degeneration of Florence flowed from a mixture of inferior blood. In Paradise itself the poet was
unable to restrain a thrill of pride as he thought
of the nobility of the blood from which he sprang.
We must, however, remember what Dante meant by
nobility. In the Fourth Book of the *Convito* the
question is discussed at length, and several theories
are set aside. Nobility is not created by wealth, or
passage of time, or even descent from a family that
once was noble. A base man who is descended from a
noble stock is doubly base in that he has wilfully
departed from the path marked out by the footsteps
of his ancestors, and he is 'as a dead man who walks
the earth.' The mere passage of time may only wear
nobility away unless the nobility is renewed generation after generation:

> Truly thou art a cloak that quickly shortens,
> So that, unless we piece thee day by day,
> Time goeth round about thee with his shears!

The decay of the ancient families of Florence in this

---

[1] *Par.* xvi. 7-9.

Canto is an example of this gradual clipping of the shears of Time. Dante's conclusion in the *Convito* is :

> Gentlehood is wherever virtue is.

Biographers of Dante discuss whether he was of noble stock in the popular sense. He himself cared nothing about it. His pride here in his forefather was not that he was a knight, but that his knighthood had been earned by noble deeds wrought for Holy Land, deeds which ended in his martyrdom.[1]

This pride in such nobility of blood, therefore, is not sinful in itself ; nevertheless it is not proper to Paradise. The good and the less good in it are indicated by the attitude of Beatrice. When Dante next speaks he addresses his knightly ancestor with the reverential *you* (*voi*), instead of the more familiar *thou* (*tu*) which he had hitherto used :

> With the *you* which Rome was first to suffer,
> Wherein her family less doth persevere,
> Yet once again my words beginning made.[2]

The belief was that when Caesar became Dictator and all offices were united in him, the Romans addressed him as *you*, as if he were many persons in one,—a reverence to the Emperor, Dante hints sarcastically, in which the family of Rome no longer persevered.[3] Now, when Beatrice heard the *voi* she gave a warning smile :

> Whence Beatrice, who was a little sundered,
> Smiling, appeared like unto her who coughed
> At the first failing writ of Guinevere.

The allusion is to the Lady of Malehaut who was in love with Sir Lancelot. When she saw the Queen give

---

[1] Contrast this pride in nobility of blood with that of Omberto Aldobrandeschi in *Purg.* xi. 58-72. 'The gallant deeds' of the Aldobrandeschi were lawlessness and outrage which turned their territory of Santafiora in the Sienese Maremma into a den of robbers. See *Purg.* vi. 111.

[2] *Par.* xvi. 10-12.

[3] Other examples of the *voi* are : to Brunetto Latini (*Inf.* xv. 30, 35, etc.); Farinata degli Uberti (*Inf.* x. 51, 94, etc.) ; Cavalcante Cavalcanti (*Inf.* x. 63); Beatrice (*Purg.* xxxi. 36 ; xxxiii. 30, 81, etc. ; *Par.* ii. 49, etc.). Mr. Gardner points out that Dante uses *tu* when he addresses the Emperor Henry VII. in the letter in which he rebukes his delay in attacking Florence : 'Tu, Caesaris et Augusti successor.'

him the first kiss which led to the after sin, she coughed
to let them know she was aware. The idea is that well
had it been for the Queen if she had taken the warning and let the first slight failing have been the last.
And this is the point of the comparison. Dante's *voi*
is but the first slight failing, and therefore Beatrice
smiles; but also she stands aloof, as withholding full
approval.[1]

After an address in which the *voi* occurs again and
again, Dante begs Cacciaguida for further information :

> 'Tell me then, my dear ancestral root,
> Who were your ancestors, and what the years
> That in your boyhood chronicled themselves.
> Tell me of the sheepfold of Saint John,
> How large it was, and who the people were
> Within it worthy of the highest seats.' [2]

At this fourfold question Cacciguida's soul glowed like
a coal fanned by the wind, and his voice grew sweet
and soft, as he answered in the ancient dialect of the
city he loved.[3] He begins with the second question,
the date of his birth, calculating it by the revolutions
of his star, Mars. From the Incarnation—'that day
when *Ave* was said '—to the day of his birth, Mars had
returned to the sign of the Lion 'five hundred and
fifty and thirty times.' Taking the sidereal period of
Mars, according to Ptolomy, at 687 days approxi-

---

[1] *Par.* xvi. 13-15. The passage in the Lancelot Romance containing
the above incident is translated from a thirteenth-century MS. by Dr.
Toynbee in his *Dante Studies and Researches*, 9-37, though it contains no
reference to the cough of the Lady of Malehaut. See *Inf.* v. 137 for Francesca's pathetic reference to the Romance of Lancelot as having been
Galeotto to her and Paolo. Galeotto was the knight who acted as inter-
mediary between Lancelot and the Queen. Mr. Gardner's view of the
attitude of Beatrice is that 'Theology in the person of Beatrice stands
apart, since matters are to be discussed which do not come within her
province, and smiles in kindly superiority at this little exhibition of
human weakness' (*Dante's Ten Heavens*, 118).

[2] *Par.* xvi. 22-27.

[3] 'Not with this modern dialect' (xvi. 33). Since Cacciaguida addressed
Dante at first in Latin ('O sanguis meus,' xv. 28), some think the ancient
language is referred to here. It seems more natural to suppose, however, that in speaking of his beloved city, he would use its own Tuscan
tongue, but with certain archaic forms of language and pronunciation.
But comp. xvii. 35, which *may* mean that the Latin tongue was used.

mately, this brings Cacciaguida's birth down to the
year 1091.[1]

The answer to the question about Cacciaguida's
ancestors has given rise to much dispute :

> 'My ancestors and I were born in the place
> Where the last *sesto* first is found
> By him who runneth in your annual game.
> Suffice it of my elders to hear this ;
> Who they were, and whence they thither came,
> To keep silence is more seemly than to speak.'[2]

The use of the word *sesto* by Cacciaguida is, strictly
speaking, an anachronism. It is proper to a later
time when the city was much larger, was enclosed in a
second line of walls, and was divided into *six* wards or
sestieri. The smaller city of Cacciaguida's day lay within the first wall, and was divided into *four* wards—
quartieri, formed by a line of streets running from the
ancient Porta del Duomo on the north to the Ponte
Vecchio on the south, and crossed by another line from
east to west, running through the Mercato Vecchio,
now demolished to make way for the hideous Piazza
Vittorio Emanuele. The *quartiere* in which the house
of his ancestors stood was that named after the eastern

---

[1] This date is rendered uncertain by two things: (1) a various reading
in l. 38 of *tre* instead of *trenta*, thus reducing the revolutions of Mars to
553 ; (2) the fact that in the *Convito* (ii. 15) Dante speaks of the period
of Mars as about two years.   Multiplying 553 by 2 gives us 1106 as the
date of Cacciaguida's birth.   Against this there are two objections.
First, the reading *tre* instead of *trenta*, Dr. Moore tells us, is 'almost
entirely devoid of manuscript support,' so that we must take the number
of revolutions to be 580 as above.   Second, in the *Convito* Dante is speaking approximately when he regards the period as about two years ;
whereas in this Canto he is obviously aiming at great exactness.   The
question is not one of first importance, though some of the calculations
make Cacciaguida join the Crusade at the age of 100, or even be born
thirteen years after his death ! (Toynbee's *Dictionary*, p. 107).   I follow
Dr. Moore's view : 'The sidereal period of Mars, according to Ptolemy,
and as Dante might have seen it in Alfraganus, c. xvii., was 1 year, 10
months, and 22 days, nearly (*ferme*), i.e. c. 687 days : and 687 × 580 = 398,460
days, which would give the date 1091 for Cacciaguida's birth, making
him 56 at the time of his death in the 2nd Crusade in 1147.'   Dr. Moore
adds in a note, 'Observe how appropriately the brave crusader is represented as being born under the sign of Leo' (*Studies in Dante*, 3rd series,
60).   For the relation of Mars to 'its own Lion' in mediæval astronomy
(or astrology), see 'Leone' in Toynbee's *Dictionary*.
[2] *Par.* xvi. 40-45.

gate, Porta San Piero. An annual game was run on
June 24, the day of the patron saint of the city, and,
as its course was from west to east, this quarter was
the last the competitors reached. And what Cacciaguida says is that the house in which he and his forefathers were born stood just at the point where the
runners entered this last quarter of the city. This
would localize it in the Via degli Speziali which runs
off the Piazza Vittorio Emanuele towards the Corso,
and here a marble tablet, bearing lines 40-42, has been
recently set up to mark the spot, on the authority,
probably, of Villani (iv. 11), who says the Elisei had
their dwellings near the Mercato Vecchio. As already
said, however, there is no certainty that Boccaccio is
right in tracing Dante's descent to the Elisei, a branch
of the Frangipani of Rome.[1]

Cacciaguida's refusal to say another word of his
ancestors, who they were and whence they came, is
one of the standing problems of the commentators.
As to why silence should be seemlier than speech, we
have little but conjecture. Yet even conjecture should
follow the lines of probability. If, as some think, this
is only a device to cover his ignorance, there is nothing
'seemly' in it, unless it be seemly not to invent a pedi-
gree. On the other hand, if his silence conceals
something dishonourable in his ancestry, as some will
have it, why should he put a question which thus leads
up to the very verge of what he wishes to remain
unknown'? To my mind it is plain that Cacciaguida is
simply acting in harmony with the warning smile of
Beatrice. He might tell much more of the nobility of

---

[1] Casini thinks that Cacciaguida refers to the present Casa di Dante,
or rather the house that it represents. This was certainly in possession
of Cacciaguida's sons. A document of 1189 exists in which two of them
(Preitenitto and the Alighiero of Canto xv. 91-96) promise the rector of
S. Martino, the little church almost directly opposite the Casa di Dante,
to remove a fig-tree growing in their garden near the Church. This
house, however, does not stand at the entrance of this ward of the city
on the west, as Cacciaguida says the house of his ancestors did. Besides,
if he had meant that he and his forefathers were born in precisely the
same house as Dante was born in, it is almost impossible to think that
the poet would have given no hint of it. He seems to me to be describing a house in a quite different situation.

his blood, but such pride is unseemly in Paradise,
where this and all other gifts are seen to come from
the sovereign grace of God. Besides, we are apt to
forget how much he has already implied in the mere
fact that his ancestors belonged to 'the last *sesto*' of
the city. As it stands in the passage, this means the
last ward reached by the runner in the annual game;
but I have no doubt whatever that Dante wished to
hint at another significance which no Florentine would
miss. Villani tells us how Florence was rebuilt by
Charlemagne and enclosed within the first walls, of
which Dante is here thinking, and divided into four
quarters. Later, the increase of the city made a second
and much larger line necessary, the division now being
into six wards. These six wards went forth to battle
in a certain fixed order, and Dante's was 'the last *sesto*,'
for a reason of which he was certainly not ashamed.
Villani's words are: 'Porta San Piero went forth last,
with the ensign of the keys, and seeing it was the first
sesto inhabited in Florence, in the going forth of the
host it was placed in the rear-guard, forasmuch as in
olden time there were always the best knights and
men-at-arms of the city in that sesto.' It is impossible
that Dante could have used the words 'l'ultimo sesto'
without having all this vividly in mind. 'The last sesto'
meant the most ancient blood in Florence, unpolluted
by the 'confusion of persons' of later times, and the
bravest men and best fighters the little republic could
send into the field.[1]

In answer to Dante's third question as to the size
of 'the sheepfold of St. John,' Cacciaguida laments

---

[1] *Chronicle*, iii. 2. In support of the above view, we must bear in mind
other passages in which the silence of Dante conceals things that were to
his honour. In *Inf.* iv. 103-105 he refuses to record the high discourse he
held with the great poets in Limbo:

> Thus went we on as far as to the light,
> Speaking things of which silence is becoming,
> Even as speech befitted where I was.

Similarly, in the *Vita Nuova* (xxix.), he preserves silence concerning the
death of Beatrice for this among other reasons: 'It would be unseemly
for me to speak thereof, seeing that thereby it must behove me to speak
also mine own praises: a thing that in whosoever doeth it is worthy of
blame' (Rossetti's transl.) Comp. a similar passage in *Conv.* i. 2.

bitterly the great increase of the city and the means by
which it came about. In his day the number capable
of bearing arms 'between Mars and the Baptist,' the
ancient boundaries of the city, were only one-fifth of
those of Dante's time: 6000 against 30,000.[1] This, however, was not necessarily an advantage since 'often
times one sword cuts more and better than five,' and
the very size of Florence might but ensure a heavier
crash of ruin: 'a blind bull more headlong falls than a
blind lamb.' Far better had she been content to fix
her boundaries at Galluzzo on the south and Trespiano
on the north, instead of polluting the blood of her
citizens which, Cacciaguida declares, was pure in his
day down to 'the last artisan,' by admitting the
inhabitants of such places as Campi, Certaldo and
Fighine.[2] Dante singles out two of these incomers for
special infamy: better had Florence been content with
smaller territory than

> 'to endure the stench
> Of the boor of Aguglion and him of Signa,
> Who already hath the eye for barratry sharp-set.'[3]

Aguglione was a castle in the Val di Pesa, south of
Florence. 'The boor' is generally identified with Baldo
d'Aguglione, the lawyer who in 1311 drew up the decree
in which Dante was expressly named among others as
excluded from the amnesty granted to certain of the

---

[1] 'It has been reckoned that in 1300 the population of Florence was
about 70,000, of whom 30,000 were fit to bear arms; consequently in Cacciaguida's day (circ. 1090-1147) the number of those fit to bear arms would
have been about 6,000, and the total population about 14,000' (Toynbee's
Dante Dictionary, p. 241). Villani (iv. 7) says that after the destruction
of Fiesole in 1010 the population was greatly increased, many of the
Fiesolans coming to reside in the city; yet even then the inhabitants
were not the half of those in his time.

[2] Galluzzo is a village south of Florence, about two miles from the
Porta Romana, and Trespiano is another village to the north, about three
miles from the Porta San Gallo. Campi in the Val di Bisenzio, Certaldo
in the Val d'Elsa, and Fighine in the Valdarno are singled out, Casini
thinks, because from Fighine came the brothers Franzesi, usurers and
evil counsellors of the King of France, who returned to Florence with
Charles of Valois, and that Baldo Fini, doctor of laws, whom the Blacks
sent in 1311 to stir up the King of France against Emperor Henry VII.;
while from Certaldo came that judge Jacopo d'Ildebrandino who was one
of the Priors in 1289, and afterwards one of the intriguers of the Black
Party.   [3] *Par.* xvi. 46-57.

Florentine exiles. It must have been most galling to
Dante, a Florentine of the purest blood, to be thus shut
out from his native city by a 'boor' from a neighbouring village,—a man too who had himself been banished
for defacing the public records to defeat the ends of
justice, and who had escaped sharing in the poet's
exile only by a timely desertion to the Black Guelphs
in 1302. He of Signa, with the sharp eye for barratry,
is believed to be Baldo's fellow-renegade from the
White Party, Fazio or Bonifazio da Signa, another
lawyer. Dino Compagni names them together as
having assisted in driving their former allies into
exile. It would put an edge on Dante's anger that
this Fazio was sent, as Toynbee says, 'as ambassador
to Clement v. in 1310 for the purpose of organizing the
opposition to the Emperor Henry VII. when he came
into Italy'; and we can understand how bitter it must
have been to think that while he, an innocent man,
was banished on a charge of barratry, this man who
was really guilty of it had power to make his exile
perpetual.[1]

It is to this 'confusion of persons'—this contamina-
tion of a pure citizenship by the introduction of
inferior blood from the surrounding country,[2] that
Cacciaguida traces the evil that had befallen the city,
and the blame of this he lays upon the Church, 'the
people that on earth degenerates most.' Had the
Church acted the part of a mother instead of a stepmother to Caesar, there had been no need for the

---

[1] In his *Chronicle* (ii. 23) Dino Compagni says: 'Many of the White
Party, and ancient Ghibellines of long standing, were received by the
Blacks as associates, solely by reason of their evil doing. Among these
were M. Betto Brunelleschi, M. Giovanni Rustichelli, M. Baldo
d'Aguglione, and M. Fazio da Signa, and several others, who gave
themselves up to destroy the Whites'—their former allies. Baldo's
falsification of the public records to destroy evidence against his client,
Niccola Acciaiuoli, is referred to in *Purg.* xii. 105. The story will be
found at length in Dino Compagni's *Chronicle*, i. 19: 'M. Niccola was
taken and condemned to a fine of 3000 lire; and M. Baldo fled, but was
condemned to a fine of 2000 lire and banishment for a year.'

[2] Hosea (vii. 8, 9) traces Israel's decay to a like cause: 'Ephraim, he
mixeth himself among the peoples; Ephraim is a cake not turned.
Strangers have devoured his strength, and he knoweth it not: yea, gray
hairs are here and there upon him, and he knoweth it not' (R.V.).

Cerchi, the Buondelmonti, and others to have been
brought within the city walls.[1] To understand this,
we must remember that the strife in Florence sprang
from the existence within her of two races. Villani
and Dante alike trace the origin of this difference to
the conquest of Fiesole by Florence, and the consequent
mingling of the two peoples. According to Villani,
'the Florentines are to-day descended from two
peoples so diverse in manners, and who ever of old
had been enemies, as the Roman people and the people
of Fiesole; and this we can see by true experience, and
by the divers changes and parties and factions which,
after the said two peoples had been united into one,
came to pass in Florence from time to time.'[2] In the
denunciation of the Florentines which Dante puts into
the mouth of Brunetto Latini, the same view is taken
of the contrast between

> 'That ungrateful and malignant people
> Which of old time from Fiesole descended,
> And smacks still of the mountain and the granite,'[3]

and 'the holy seed of the Romans,' from which the
poet undoubtedly believed himself descended. Even if
we put aside much of this as legendary, it remains true,
as Prof. Villari says, that 'the diversity between the
Germanic strain in the nobility and the Latin blood
of the people, really constituted a strong element of
discord. . . . Its whole territory bristled with the
castles of feudal barons of Germanic descent, all hostile

---

[1] *Par.* xvi. 58-66. It is not known who was the incomer from Simifonti, now a Florentine banker and merchant, but whose grandfather
went round begging in his native village. Simifonti is in the Val d'Elsa.
For the taking and destruction by the Florentines in 1202, see Villani,
Chron. v. 30; Villari, *Flor. History,* 163-166. The Cerchi came from
Acone, a village near Florence whose exact situation is uncertain. They
rapidly became one of the richest families, lived in grand style, yet remained rustic and uncultured in manners : Villani calls them 'luxurious,
inoffensive, uncultured and ungracious, like folk come in a short time to
great estate and power' (viii. 39). As the leaders of the White Guelphs,
Dante calls that party *la parte selvaggia* (*Inf.* vi. 65), the savage, rustic,
boorish party. For the further reference to them in the present Canto
(94-99) see note on p. 259. The Montemurlo of l. 64 was a castle near Pistoja,
which the Conti Guidi were forced to sell to Florence because they were
not able to hold it against the Pistojans. See Villani, v. 31.

[2] *Chronicle,* iv. 7. See also i. 38.   [3] *Inf.* xv. 61-78.

to Florence, and many of whom, safely ensconced on
the neighbouring hill of Fiesole, were always ready to
swoop down on Florentine soil.'[1]   As the commerce of
the city grew, it became necessary to make the roads
safe for traffic, and the only way of doing this seemed
to be by compelling the robber-barons to come inside
the city-walls.   But, as Green says, 'it was equally
perilous for an Italian town to leave its nobles without
the walls or to force them to reside within.   In their
own robber-holds or their own country estates they
were a scourge to the trader whose wains rolled
temptingly past their walls.   Florence, like its fellow
Italian States, was driven to the demolition of the
feudal castles, and to enforcing the residence of their
lords within its own civic bounds.   But the danger was
only brought nearer home.   Excluded by civic jealousy,
wise or unwise, from all share in municipal government, their huge palazzi rose like fortresses in every
quarter of the city.   Within them lay the noble, a
wild beast all the fiercer for his confinement in so
narrow a den, with the old tastes, hatreds, preferences
utterly unchanged, at feud as of old with his fellow-
nobles, knit to them only by a common scorn of the
burghers and the burgher life around them, stung to
madness by his exclusion from all rule in the common-
wealth, bitter, revengeful, with the wilfulness of a
child, shameless, false, unprincipled.'[2]   And this terrible
state of things Dante traced to the Papacy.   Had the
Church given the temporal power to Caesar as it ought
to have done, the Emperor, in Dante's belief, would
have proved strong enough to have brought the terri-
torial nobles under the restraint of law, and thus
have obviated the necessity to which the cities were
reduced of adding a new and dangerous element of
discord to those already existing within their walls.

This brings us to Dante's last question, as to the

[1] *The First Two Centuries of Florentine History*, p. 73 (Eng. transl.)—
an invaluable book for the understanding of the ever-changing factions
of early Florence.

[2] John Richard Green, *Stray Studies from England and Italy*, p. 162.

great Florentines of his forefather's day. It would
serve no purpose to go through the long catalogue of
ancient families named by Cacciaguida, most of them
in decay, or even extinct, in the poet's time: those
curious in these matters may read the account of them
given by Villani.[1] Their rise and fall, says Cacciaguida,

---

[1] *Chronicle*, iv. 10-13. It may, however, be well to explain some of the
more obscure allusions.

(1) ll. 94-99 refer to the Cerchi (see note, p. 257). Their houses were above
the Porta San Piero, and had been acquired by this wealthy family from
the Conti Guidi, who sprang from the ancient house of the Ravignani,
the head of which was the Bellincion Berti of *Par.* xv. 112. The *fellonia*
or treason charged against the Cerchi seems to be their failure as leaders
of the Whites to defend the city against the Blacks in Nov. 1301. Dino
Compagni says 'their hearts failed them through cowardice': the Priors
gave them orders to prepare for defence and urged them 'to play the
man.' But 'from avarice' they refused to pay the hired troops, made
practically no preparations, and so handed over the city to six terrible
days of outrage and pillage. The exile of the Whites which followed is
the 'lightening of the barque' to which Dante refers in l. 96. For a full
account of this disastrous struggle between the Bianchi and the Neri, see
Dino Compagni's *Chronicle*, Bk. II. and Villani's, viii. 38-40.

(2) ll. 109-111. Those 'undone by their pride' are the Uberti, the great
Ghibelline family, banished in 1258, and never allowed to return. Farinata
who saved Florence after Montaperti (1260) belonged to it (*Inf.* x. 22 ff.).
The other family, referred to by its coat of arms, the 'balls of gold,' is the
Lamberti. To it belonged Mosca, whose famous phrase, *Cosa fatta capo
ha*, sealed Buondelmonte's fate—and his own (*Inf.* xxviii. 103 ff.).

(3) ll. 112-114. The reference is to the Tosinghi and the Visdomini,
whom Villani (iv. 10) calls 'patrons and defenders of the Bishopric.'
During a vacancy, they enjoyed the use of the Bishop's palace until a
successor was appointed, and apparently did not spare the larder.

(4) ll. 115-120. A bitter stroke at the Adimari,—dragons to the timid,
but to men with teeth or purse, lambs. Dante's bitterness is not un
natural when we remember that, according to early commentators, one
of this family, Boccaccino, gained possession of the poet's property, and
therefore opposed strenuously his recall from exile. This might account
also for his scorn of Filippo Argenti (*Inf.* viii. 31-64), who belonged to a
branch of the Adimari.

(5) ll. 124-126. That one of the gates of 'the small circuit'—the first
city-wall—viz., the Porta Peruzza, was named after the Della Pera family
might seem incredible for various reasons that have been suggested : (a)
how small the circuit must have been when this was one of the city-
gates ; or (b) how free of jealousy ancient Florence must have been when
one of its gates was named after a private family ; or (c) how hard to
believe that a family so forgotten now was so ancient that a gate in the
earliest circuit of walls was named after it. The drift of the comments
on the other families favours the last interpretation.

(6) ll. 127-132. 'The great baron' was the Marquis Hugh of Branden-
burg, viceroy in Tuscany of Otho III. Villani says he knighted five
Florentine families, who for love of him bore his arms. One of these, the
Della Bella, is here referred to as having surrounded the arms with a
border of gold. It was a member of this family, the famous Giano della
Bella, who in 1293 proposed the *Ordinances of Justice*, in order to curb

shows the tide-like ebb and flow of Fortune in the city;
and he closes with the most disastrous stroke of all, the
murder of Buondelmonte, already spoken of, which let
loose all the elements of discord and ruin. And then
over against all this he sets what is no doubt an
idealized picture of the ancient Florence of his day,
in a state of idyllic peace under the great families he
has named :

> ‘ With these houses, and with others with them,
> Saw I Florence in so great repose,
> That she had no cause for which to weep ;
> With these houses saw I so glorious
> And just her people, that the lily
> Never on the lance was set reversed,
> Nor by division changed into vermilion,’— [1]

that is, the banner of Florence was never dishonoured
by foes without or citizens within. The reference to
the reversal of the lily is an allusion to the custom of
the time to trail the banner of a conquered foe in the
dust: after the battle of Montaperti, the victor dragged
the standard of Florence into Siena at the tail of an
ass. This indignity was never suffered by the ancient
city. Nor was the lily ever changed for party purposes
or dyed with the blood of the citizens in civil war, for
the words cover both meanings. Probably there is a
hint in the word *popolo* in l. 152 of the special circumstances under which the lily was ‘changed into vermilion.’ In 1250 the citizens, goaded past endurance
by the outrage and violence of the Ghibelline nobles,
and especially the Uberti, formed the constitution
known as the *Primo Popolo*, the First Popular Government. In the following year the Popolo drove out the
Ghibellines, and the Guelphs changed the ensign of the
city from a white lily on a red field to a red lily on a
white field. The *Popolo* of his day, Cacciaguida seems

the lawlessness of his own order, the nobles, and it is probably he who is
referred to as having ‘ joined himself with the people.’ How the Marquis
Hugh was converted, built the Badia, died on S. Thomas’ Day, and was
buried in the monastery, will be found in Villani, iv. 2.

(7) ll. 136-139 refer to the Amidei. For Buondelmonte’s desertion of a
lady of this family to whom he was betrothed and its results, see p. 237.

[1] *Par.* xvi. 148-154.

to mean, was too 'just' thus to split up into parties and change the very arms of the Republic to gratify the spirit of faction.[1]

[1] See Villani's *Chronicle*, vi. 39, for the *Primo Popolo*, and 43, for the change of flag. Ruskin found in this change a very different meaning—the emancipation of Florentine commerce. In a lecture to his students he says : 'It (the Lily) is red, not as ecclesiastical, but as free. Not of Guelph against Ghibelline, but of Labourer against Knight. No more his serf, but his minister. His duty no more " servitium," but "ministerium," "mestier". . . . Draw that red lily then, and fix it in your minds as the sign of the great change in the temper of Florence, and in her laws, in mid-thirteenth century ; and remember also, when you go to Florence and see that mighty tower of the Palazzo Vecchio . . . that, as the tower of Giotto is the notablest monument in the world of the Religion of Europe, so, on this tower of the Palazzo Vecchio, first shook itself to the winds the Lily standard of her liberal,—because honest,—commerce' (*Val D'Arno*, iv. 110-111). Unfortunately for Ruskin's exhortation, the Palazzo Vecchio was not begun till nearly fifty years after this change of the Lily.

CHAPTER XIV

3. *Cacciaguida's Prophecy of Dante's Exile*

THE idea underlying the whole of this Seventeenth Canto is that Dante is here claiming his share in the martyrdom through which the souls in this planet had passed. True, for full and perfect martyrdom, as Aquinas says, the actual suffering of death for Christ may be necessary.[1] To Dante his exile was a living death. True also, he had not fought like his ancestor against the heathen; but was it an easier warfare to struggle against his fellow-citizens?

> Life may be given in many ways,
> And loyalty to Truth be sealed
> As bravely in the closet as the field,
> So bountiful is Fate.[2]

Hence the old crusader foretells his exile and sufferings with joy, and commands 'his blood' to be utterly faithful to the truth in scorn of consequence, not indeed in order to wound, for martyrdom must flow from charity, not revenge, but to give men the very nutriment of life.

Beatrice, seeing a desire rise in Dante's mind, asks him to give it utterance, not because it was not already known to her and to his forefather, but because only through his utterance could they satisfy his thirst. Whereupon he begs Cacciaguida to tell him certain 'contingent' things concerning his own

---

[1] *Summa*, ii-ii. q. cxxiv. a. 4.
[2] James Russell Lowell's Harvard Commemoration Ode.

future. For present purposes, and apart from
scholastic subtleties, contingent things are things
which are dependent on the movements of human
wills, and which therefore may or may not happen.
These, Dante believed, were seen by the blessed souls
with the certainty with which mathematical truths
are seen by us ; seen, before they come into actuality,
in the mind of God to which the future is as the
present. While he was with Virgil climbing the
Mountain and descending into 'the dead world,' Dante
had heard ' heavy words' about his own future; and
although he was no coward, although he felt that
he stood 'foursquare to the blows of chance,' yet he
wished to know the worst, since 'an arrow foreseen
comes more slowly,' and therefore less violently.[1]

With a smile which at once revealed and concealed
the soul within, the 'love paternal' answered 'in clear
words and with precise discourse.'[2] The smile is
significant in view of the ruin of Dante's earthly
fortunes, about to be foretold : to 'glory in tribulations' is natural from the standpoint of that Heaven
which is their reward. Cacciaguida begins with the

---

[1] *Par.* xvii. 7 27. The mathematical illustration is taken from Geometry
—' two obtuse angles cannot be contained in a triangle'—to indicate the
most absolute form of certainty : Geometry is ' without spot or error and
most certain in itself' (*Conv.* ii. 14). The 'foursquare to the blows of
chance' comes from Aristotle's *Ethics*, i. 11 : ' nor is there any who will
bear the chances of life so nobly, with such a perfect and complete
harmony, as he who is truly good and "foursquare without a flaw."'
Welldon, whose translation I quote, reminds us that the phrase is from
Simonides, and is quoted by Plato in his *Protagoras*, 339 : ' Hardly on
the one hand can a man become truly good ; built foursquare in hands
and feet and mind, a work without a flaw.' He also reminds us that
Tennyson speaks of the great Duke of Wellington as

' that tower of strength
Which stood foursquare to all the winds that blew.'

The 'heavy words' about Dante's future were spoken by Farinata (*Inf.*
x. 76 ff.); Brunetto Latini (*Inf.* xv. 61 ff.); Currado Malaspina (*Purg.*
viii. 133 ff.) ; Oderisi (*Purg.* xi. 139-141) ; Bonagiunta (*Purg.* xxiv. 43-
48).

[2] *Par.* xvii. 34-36 : 'con preciso Latin,' which some take to mean that
he spoke in the Latin tongue ; but see note on p. 251. ' Latino' is used in
the sense of 'language,' 'speech,' 'discourse,' in *Par.* xii. 144; and in
Conv. ii. 3, 'latinamente' is used to indicate 'clearly,' 'in plain speech.'

contingent things of which Dante had spoken. Contingency, he says, does not exist beyond the little volume [1] of this material world. All contingent things are depicted in 'the eternal vision.' To us in this world of Time, things are of necessity past, present, or future; but Eternity, being beyond this world of motion, is that which, to quote Boethius, 'grasps and possesses wholly and simultaneously the fulness of unending life, which lacks naught of the future and has lost naught of the fleeting past'; and therefore what we call the foreknowledge of God is more rightly held to be 'a knowledge of a never-failing constancy in the present, than a foreknowledge of the future,' and Providence 'a looking forth rather than a looking forward.'

The question rises instinctively in the human mind: Is this Divine knowledge of future contingent events consistent with the existence of human freedom? If God foreknows all things, does not this imply that they must take place: in other words, that they are not contingent at all, but subject to a law of necessity? Cacciaguida denies this conclusion: God's knowledge of future events no more necessitates their coming to pass than my sight, in which a ship is mirrored as she drops down stream, is the compelling cause of her motion. Hence Dante's misfortunes, about to be foretold, are no necessity due to the knowledge or foreknowledge of God: they spring from contingencies of the human will, which, like all contingencies, mirror them-

---

[1] *Par.* xvii. 37. The word used, *quaderno*, is literally a sheet of paper folded into four, and therefore constituting a very small book. The idea is that this material world, in which alone contingency has place, is a very small space in comparison with the ten Heavens which surround it, and which lie beyond the action of contingency. In this contrast between the earth and the heavens, Dante follows Aquinas, and Aquinas is, as Father Rickaby says, 'like an observer at work with a telescope out of focus. The thought of the Angelic Doctor is blurred by that fatal misconception which it was reserved for Newton to dissipate, that, in the heavens above, physical nature works necessarily and uniformly, but, on the earth beneath, contingently (so that the effect might be otherwise) and with some anomaly and irregularity. We must say boldly that the case is not so; that throughout all time and all space physical nature works necessarily' (Transl. of *Summa Contra Gentiles*, p. 254 n.).

selves in the Divine Mind, and are thence reflected to the souls of the Redeemed.[1]

Cacciaguida proceeds to prophesy to Dante the disasters about to overwhelm his earthly happiness. We must bear in mind, of course, that Dante is speaking from the standpoint of the year 1300, and that the doom of exile did not fall till 1302. While, therefore, the form is prophetic, the substance is the plain history of the poet's life and sufferings since the day when he began to eat 'the bitter bread of banishment.'[2] He indicates by a beautiful touch the change which was coming over his feelings concerning it. In one of his finest Canzoni, that of the three exiled Ladies, he says that in his own exile 'Death had laid the key upon his breast.'[3] Now, however, that bitterness of death is past, or passing. To his forefather, at least, even this disaster comes 'as sweet harmony from an organ,' partly because he sees it all clearly in God; and partly because he knows Dante to be an innocent man, suffering an unjust sentence. This is implied in the parallel drawn between Dante and Hippolytus, the son of Theseus :

> 'As from Athens Hippolytus was sundered,
> Through his stepmother, treacherous and cruel,
> So thou from Florence must perforce depart.'

---

[1] Compare Newman's beautiful figure in ' A Voice from afar' :

> A sea before
> The Throne is spread ;—its pure still glass
> Pictures all earth-scenes as they pass.
> We, on its shore,
> Share, in the bosom of our rest,
> God's knowledge, and are blest.

The subject of the relation of God's knowledge to things contingent is discussed by Aquinas, *Summa*, i. q. xiv. a. 13, and Boethius, *De Consolatione*, Bk. v. The latter says God's knowledge of *future* events 'does not change the nature or individual qualities of things,' any more than our knowledge of *present* things changes their nature or qualities. A thing contingent in its nature, He sees as contingent; a thing necessary, as necessary. ' For instance, when you see at the same time a man walking on the earth and the sun rising in the heavens, you see each sight simultaneously, yet you distinguish between them, and decide that one is moving voluntarily, the other of necessity.' God's vision of future events, in similar fashion, makes no change on the contingent or necessary nature of this thing or that (Temple Classics Transl. p. 164).

[2] *King Richard* II. Act III. Scene 1.

[3] *Canzone* XX. It seems impossible to identify the three exiled Ladies. The first, indeed, names herself Righteousness (*Drittura*, l. 35); the

Such a stepmother would Florence prove to Dante. Phaedra made dishonourable proposals to her stepson, and on his rejection of them secured his banishment on the charge of sinning the sin of which she herself was guilty. Similarly Dante was banished on a false charge of barratry by men who were themselves barrators. Some think the parallel may be carried further—that his exile was due to his rejection of some dishonourable proposal made to him by the Black Guelphs, though of this there is no evidence.[1] The plot for his ruin was hatched at Rome, in the Papal Court itself:

> 'This is willed, and already this is sought,
> And soon it shall be done by him who thinks it,
> There where Christ all day is bought and sold.'

The sting is in the last line: the charge of barratry, that is, the buying and selling of the State, was forged against him by a corrupt Church in which simony, the buying and selling of Christ Himself, went on all day long.[2] It was Phaedra and Hippolytus once more. In this very year, 1300, Boniface VIII. was intriguing with Germany to have the Emperor's rights in Tuscany renounced in his favour. To secure the success of his policy he summoned Charles of Valois from France, and appointed him 'Peacemaker' to Florence, his real mission being, as Villani says, 'to abase the Popolo and the Whites,'[3] the party to which Dante at that time belonged. To this policy the poet was bitterly opposed.

second, she says, is her child, born near the sources of the Nile (ll. 45-51); the third is the child of this second. The last two are sometimes identified with Generosity and Temperance (*Larghezza e Temperanza*) named in l. 63. Dante seeks comfort in the thought that such noble Ladies are his companions in exile; but the thought that his beloved Florence is so far away that he cannot see it sets him in a fire, which 'has already so consumed my bone and flesh that Death upon my breast hath laid the key' (ll. 81-87). Dr. Wicksteed takes the daughter and grand-daughter of Righteousness to be civil and canon law. Gabriele Rossetti, pursuing his fantastic political interpretation, regards them as the three sects, Templars, Albigenses, and Ghibellines (*The Antipapal Spirit*, Eng. transl., i. 232-235).

[1] *Par.* xvii. 46-48.

[2] *Par.* xvii. 49-51. Compare the retort of the charge of barratry on his accusers in Florence, in the Bolgia of the Barrators (*Inf.* xxi-xxii.). I may refer to my *Exiles of Eternity*, 326-329.

[3] Villani's *Chronicle*, viii. 42.

In October 1301, an embassy, consisting of Dante and
two others, was sent to Rome to protest against it.
Dino Campagni gives us a vivid glimpse into the
negotiations. 'When the ambassadors arrived in
Rome, the Pope received them alone in his chamber,
and said to them secretly, "Wherefore are ye thus
obstinate? Humble yourselves before me. And I
declare to you in truth, that I have no other intention
but to promote your peace. Let two of you go back,
and let them have my blessing if they can cause my
will to be obeyed."' The one retained by the Pope was
the man who had already opposed him in Florence,
Dante himself. He never set foot again in his native
city. On November 1st Charles of Valois made his
entrance into Florence; on January 27th a decree of
banishment for two years was launched against Dante
and others of his party; on March 10th the decree
was made perpetual. Is it to be wondered at that
Dante should feel that he was the victim of a Papal
plot, and that he had been retained in Rome until it
should be a *fait accompli*?[1]

Cacciaguida warns Dante that while the vengeance
of God will reveal the truth, yet in the meantime

[1] The above statements assume the genuineness of Dino Compagni's
Chronicle, now accepted by such authorities as Bartoli, Del Lungo, and
Villari. It is true, Villani has no mention of the embassy to Rome; but
Dino is clear and circumstantial. In Bk. II. 4, he gives the above-quoted
interview with the Pope. In II. 25, among those exiled by Charles of
Valois and the Blacks, he gives the name of 'Dante Alighieri who was
ambassador at Rome.' In II. 11, he narrates how the two ambassadors
who were sent home reported the Pope's answer to the Signory. Their
names were Maso di Ruggierino Minerbetti, and Corazza of Signa, an
ardent Guelph. The former, whom Dino calls 'a false *popolano*,'
treacherously revealed the Pope's answer to the Blacks, who thereupon
broke into insurrection against the Government, and for six days ravaged
the city with fire and sword (see Dino Compagni, ii. 15; Villani, viii. 49).
Even if no such embassy existed, it does not alter the truth of Dante's
charge against Rome. The storm in which his earthly fortunes sank for
ever was undoubtedly the result of a plot between Boniface, Charles of
Valois, and the Black Guelphs. (See Villari, *The Two First Centuries
of Florentine History*, chap. ix.) That Dante believed himself personally to be the object of the hostility of Boniface is obvious from *Purg.*
xxxii. 154-155, where he says of the harlot-church, 'her lustful and roving
eye on me she turned.' Did Boniface, during Dante's compulsory stay in
Rome, make dishonourable proposals to him, seeking to buy him over to
his interests?

report, as its custom is, will lay the blame on the side that has suffered the wrong. We are reminded of the pathetic passage in the *Convito*, which is the most fitting introduction to the prophecy of his exile : 'Since it pleased the citizens of the fairest and most famous daughter of Rome, Florence, to cast me forth from her most sweet bosom (wherein I was born and nourished up to the climax of my life, and wherein, by their good leave, I long with all my heart to rest my weary soul, and to end the days allotted to me), through almost every part where her language is spoken I have wandered, a pilgrim, almost a beggar, displaying against my will the wounds of fortune, which are often wont to be imputed unjustly to the wounded one himself. Truly have I been a vessel without sail or rudder, borne to divers ports and straits and shores by the dry wind which blows from dolorous poverty; and have appeared vile in the eyes of many who, perhaps, through some fame of me, had imagined me in other guise; in whose consideration not only did I in person suffer abasement, but all my work became of less account, that already done as well as that yet to do.'[1] It may be well to have before us the entire passage in which Cacciaguida foretells the martyrdom of suffering which awaits him in the coming years :

> 'Thou shalt abandon everything beloved
> Most tenderly, and this that arrow is
> Which first the bow of banishment shoots forth.[2]
> Thou shalt have proof how savoureth of salt
> The bread of others, and how hard a road

---

[1] *Conv.* i. 3 (Miss Hillard's transl. slightly altered).

[2] It is absurd to say, as some do, that Dante's wife, Gemma Donati, was not included in the 'ogni cosa diletta più caramente.' Even Boccaccio, who started the fiction of his indifference to her, gives a good reason for her not joining her husband in his exile—the tender age of their children, and the necessity she was under of providing for them by rescuing, under the title of her dowry, some small remnant of their father's possessions in the city. If, as Leonardo Bruni says, Dante was in Rome as ambassador at the time when sentence was pronounced against him, and only heard the particulars on reaching Siena, it must have added bitterness to his anguish that he had no opportunity of saying farewell to wife or child or native city. 'Weep ye not for the dead, neither bemoan him : but weep sore for him that goeth away : for he shall return no more, nor see his native country' (Jer. xxii. 10).

The going down and up another's stairs.[1]
And that which most shall weigh upon thy shoulders
Will be the bad and foolish company
With which into this valley thou shalt fall;
For all ingrate, all mad and impious
Will they become against thee; but, soon after,
They, and not thou, shall have the forehead red.
Of their bestiality their own proceedings
Shall furnish proof; so 'twill be well for thee
A party to have made thee by thyself.'[2]

It is almost impossible now to discover what precisely underlies this reference to the party with which
Dante fell into the valley of exile; but we may attempt
an ideal reconstruction of the crisis of political conversion through which he passed in those years of convul-
sion. Before his exile Dante belonged to the party of
the White Guelphs; and if we take Guelphism to be
virtually the cause of Italian freedom and independence,
to be secured under the protection of the Papal power,
obviously the events of 1301 made it impossible to hold
to it any longer. He saw his native city betrayed by
the Pope to a French prince, its freedom and independence destroyed, himself and others driven into exile
by the very power they had sought to serve. In the
natural reaction against the Papacy, Dante at first
attached himself to the Ghibellines, the party that
supported the Emperor in the great struggle against
the usurpations of the spiritual power. How long he
remained with them, and how far he took part in their
various attempts to fight their way back into Florence,
we do not know;[3] but he must quickly have discovered
that their aims and ideals were not less false and sel-

---

[1] There would rise to Dante's mind the words of the Son of Sirach: 'It
is a miserable life to go from house to house: for where thou art a stranger, thou darest not open thy mouth . . . Thou shalt hear bitter words . . .
Give place, thou stranger, to an honourable man; my brother cometh to
be lodged, and I have need of mine house: These things are grievous to
a man of understanding; the upbraiding of house-room, and reproaching
of the lender.' 'My son, lead not a beggar's life; for better it is to die
than to beg. The life of him that dependeth on another man's table is
not to be counted for a life; for he polluteth himself with other men's
meat; but a wise man well nurtured will beware thereof' (Ecclesiasticus,
xxix. 24-28; xl. 28, 29).　　　　　　[2] *Par.* xvii. 55-69 (Longfellow).
[3] See Toynbee, *Life of Dante*, 118.

fish than those of their opponents. His conception of
the Emperor was that of an incarnate Righteousness,
who would create a condition of universal justice, and
therefore of universal peace, holding the lawless nobles
in check. Those nobles themselves, naturally, had
another use for the Emperor: they turned the imperial Eagle, as Dante says, into the standard of their
faction, to serve their own lawless ends. Imagine a
passionate lover of righteousness and peace flung into
the company of men like this, to whom injustice and
violence were as the breath of their nostrils, and it is
inevitable that they will soon be as eager to get rid of
him as he of them. The *De Monarchia*, with its sharp
separation of the spheres of the temporal and spiritual
powers, shows us what Dante meant by making a
party by himself. Gregorovius calls him, during his
exile, 'the prophet of the Ghibelline ideal.' Nothing
could be more mistaken, if by this is meant the ideal of
the Ghibelline party. He found in those early years
of his exile that his ideal and theirs had absolutely
nothing in common, and he resolved to stand alone.[1]

Dante proceeds to make grateful acknowledgment
of the generous welcome he had received from the
head of the great house of the Scaligers at Verona: it
is, of course, Cacciaguida who speaks:

[1] Dr. Wicksteed is right when he says that we cannot define Dante's
position 'by calling him a Guelf or a Ghibelline, or both. His political
ideals were his own. They were the outcome of his life and thought,
intensely personal, as was all else about him. They cannot be labelled,
but must be studied in his life and in his works.' But he seems to me to
unsay much of this when he adds that 'if we are to use the current terms
at all, we shall perhaps come nearest to the truth by saying that Dante
was a Guelf in his aims, but that he approximated to the traditions if not
to the practices of the Ghibellines in the means by which he hoped to see
them realized' (Introduction to Miss Selfe's *Selections from Villani*, p.
xlvi). The *De Monarchia* shows that his political ideal was not this
patchwork of the two parties. Compare his repudiation of both in *Par.*
vi. 97-108, a repudiation in which Henry VII. shared (see note, p. 112). Of
course, it is not to be supposed that the party from which Dante here
breaks away had no cause of complaint against him. His haughty
idealism must have seemed to them a thing in the sky, beyond the bounds
of practical politics, and probably his temper did not commend it to them.
The epithets flung at them in this passage, however they may have earned
them, show that they on their side may also have had something to put
up with.

> 'Thy first refuge and thy first resting-place
> Shall be the courtesy of the great Lombard,
> Who on the ladder bears the holy bird,
> Who such benign regard shall have for thee
> That 'twixt you twain, in doing and in asking,
> That shall be first which is with others last.'[1]

The common order is that the patron waits until the client asks, but 'the courtesy of the great Lombard' anticipates the poor exile's prayer and spares him the shame of becoming a beggar. Dante, who knew what it was to 'tremble through every vein'[2] in the asking of a favour, could think of no higher praise. It is the prevenient grace of the Angel of Meekness on the Terrace of Anger,[3] nay, of her whose face is likest Christ's:

> 'Not only thy benignity gives succour
> To him who asketh it, but oftentimes
> Forerunneth of its own accord the asking.'[4]

There can be little doubt that 'the great Lombard' is Bartolommeo della Scala, though other members of the family have their advocates. A simple process of elimination, however, leaves little uncertainty. Alberto della Scala had three sons, all of whom in turn succeeded him in the lordship of Verona. Alberto himself is out of the question here, since he died on Sept. 10, 1301,[5] and Dante was not banished till the following January. His second son, Albuino, who came to the lordship in 1304, on the death of his brother Bartolommeo, is ruled out by the half-contemptuous way in which Dante

---

[1] *Par.* xvii. 70-75.

[2] *Purg.* xi. 133-141.

[3] *Purg.* xvii. 55-60.

[4] *Par.* xxxiii. 16-18. In *Conv.* i. 8 Dante holds that it is an essential of perfect liberality to give without asking. To compel a man to beg reduces the whole transaction to a traffic, in which the prayers are the price—the dearest a man can pay. Boccaccio in his *Life of Dante* says of Guido Novello da Polenta of Ravenna what is here said of 'il gran Lombardo'—that he did not wait to be asked for hospitality by the poet, but offered it freely, 'requesting from Dante of special grace that which he knew Dante must needs have begged of him.' Thus the exile's first refuge and his last were rendered as little bitter as might be by the gracious courtesy of his hosts.

[5] In *Purg.* xviii. 121 Alberto is spoken of, from the ideal standpoint of 1300, as having 'already one foot in the grave,'

refers to him in the *Convito*:[1] it would be impossible
to retain any respect for the poet if he could thus
speak with double tongue. The youngest son, Can
Grande, succeeded his brother Albuino in 1311, but he
is set aside by the fact that, in the lines immediately
following, he is named along with 'the great Lombard'
as a separate person. There remains, therefore, only
the eldest son, Bartolommeo,[2] who succeeded his father
in 1301 and died in March 1304. Against this an objection
is raised from l. 72: 'who on the ladder bears the holy
bird.' The eagle, it is said, was not added to the ladder
of the Scaligers until the year 1311, when Albuino was
made Imperial Vicar. There seems, however, to be
no proof of this assertion; and, as Casini says, Bartolommeo's marriage in 1291 to Constance of Suabia,
daughter of Conrad of Antioch and grand-daughter of
Frederick II., would entitle him to add the imperial
eagle to his coat of arms. Since Bartolommeo died in
March, 1304, Dante must, of course, have taken refuge
with him sometime before that date. Probably he
severed his connection with the exiled Whites and
Ghibellines after the series of disasters which befell
them in the preceding year in their attempts to regain
an entrance to the city.[3]

There is, however, a greater than 'the great Lombard'
—Bartolommeo's youngest brother, Can Francesco,
known as Can Grande della Scala, at this time a boy

[1] *Conv.* iv. 16. If the word 'noble' is derived, as some say, from *nosco*,
to know, and therefore means 'named and known by many,' it would
follow, says Dante, that 'Albuino della Scala would be more noble than
Guido da Castello of Reggio,' which, he says, is false. Guido is 'il semplice
Lombardo' of *Purg.* xvi. 125, 126.

[2] I omit as entirely out of the question Alberto's illegitimate son,
Giuseppo, whom he made Abbot of San Zeno in Verona. In *Purg.* xviii.
124, he is spoken of contemptuously as 'deformed in his whole body, and
worse in mind, and basely born.'

[3] For these mismanaged attempts, see Dino Compagni's *Chronicle*, Bk.
II. chaps. xxix-xxxvi. The whole subject of the date of Dante's leaving
the exiles is fully discussed in Latham's *Dante's Eleven Letters*, 243-267.
The author's conclusion is that the poet was with the Whites until
immediately before the battle of Lastra in July, 1304; and that since Bartolommeo died the preceding March, 'the great Lombard' must have been
his successor Albuino. The arguments, however, do not seem to me very
convincing.

of nine.　His 'magnificence' and career as a soldier are foretold by Cacciaguida :

> ' With him thou 'lt see that one who, at his birth,
> Was so impressed by this strong star
> That worthy of note shall be his deeds.
> Not yet the people are aware of him,
> Through his young age, since only nine years yet
> Around him have these wheels revolved.
> But ere the Gascon cheat the lofty Henry,[1]
> Some sparkles of his virtue shall appear
> In caring not for silver nor for toils.
> His magnificences[2] shall yet be known
> In such sort that his very enemies
> Shall not be able to keep silent tongues.
> On him wait thou, and on his benefits ;
> By him shall many people be transformed,
> Rich men and paupers changing their condition.
> And thou shalt bear it written in thy mind
> Of him, but shalt not tell it '—and things he said
> Incredible to those who shall be present at them.[3]

This passage was written doubtless in gratitude for the hospitality and kindness which the exiled poet received from Can Grande.　The time of his sojourn in Verona is unknown, but the probability seems to be that it was in the year 1316.　The hospitality of 'the magnificent and victorious lord,' as Dante elsewhere calls Can Grande, is thus described in a passage quoted by Sismondi : 'Different apartments were assigned to

---

[1] 'The Gascon' is Pope Clement v., under whom the Papal Court was transferred to Avignon.　As a tool of Philip the Fair he was compelled to favour the election of Charles of Valois as Emperor, but in secret he wrought for the election of Henry of Luxemburg.　Yet when Henry in 1312 sought coronation in Rome, Clement strove to impose conditions which the Emperor indignantly rejected as a humiliation.　This seems to be the 'cheating' here referred to.　For further particulars, see xxx. 139-148, p. 477 f.　The 'sparkles' of Can Grande's virtue refer apparently to the aid he gave to Henry's cause prior to 1312, when the Pope's treachery became manifest.

[2] 'Magnificence' in the Aristotelian sense (*Ethics*, iv. 4, 5) means expenditure on a large scale, in an ungrudging spirit, on a worthy object, by one who can afford it.　Aquinas (*Summa*, ii-ii. q. cxxxiv. a. 4) regards magnificence as a potential part of the cardinal virtue of Fortitude, since a man, in order to be magnificent, must curb the love of money.　Another part of Fortitude is the power to endure toils and hardships without giving way.　These two forms of Fortitude are referred to when it is said that Can Grande cares not 'for silver or for toils' (l. 84).

[3] *Par.* xvii. 76-93.

each guest with servants, and each took his meals, daintily served, in his own room.   The different rooms were indicated by diverse symbols and devices; frescoes of Triumphs for warriors; of Hope for exiles; of the Muses for poets; of Mercury for players; of Paradise for preachers.   During the repast musicians, buffoons, and jugglers perambulated the chambers; the halls were adorned with paintings which suggested the vicissitudes of Fortune; and Cane sometimes invited certain of his guests to his own table, notably Guido di Castello of Reggio, who, on account of his sincerity, was called the simple Lombard, and the poet Dante Alighieri.'[1]   Even this magnificence of hospitality would not have kept the bread from savouring of salt to the homeless exile if the old stories of Can Grande's discourtesy to him were true; but fortunately there is no foundation for them, and they are utterly inconsistent with every reference to him in the poet's works.[2] Even if we do not identify Can Grande with the Veltro of the *Inferno* (i. 100-111) or the DXV of the *Purgatorio* (xxxiii. 37-45), there remains the Epistle in which Dante dedicates to him the crowning Cantica of his great poem.[3]   The opening sentences of the Epistle have much that is reminiscent of the present passage: 'The glorious renown of your magnificence, which Fame

---

[1] Sagacius Mucius Gazata, a historian of Reggio, himself an exile at Verona, quoted in *History of the Italian Republics*, Bk. iv.   Sismondi's estimate of Can Grande is very favourable: 'A man of unflinching character, he was frank of speech, faithful to his principles, and scrupulously observant of his word.   He secured not only the love of his soldiery, but of his people, and even of his foes.'

[2] Rossetti's version of one of these stories may be quoted from his *Dante at Verona*.   Can Grande, amused with his jester one day, turned to the poet who sat silent :

> Then, facing on his guest, he cried,—
> 'Say, Messer Dante, how it is
> I get out of a clown like this
> More than your wisdom can provide.'
> And Dante : ''Tis man's ancient whim
> That still his like seems good to him.'

[3] As I have said elsewhere, I regard the authenticity of this Epistle as established.   For a full discussion of the arguments for and against, see Dr. Moore's *Studies in Dante*, 3rd series, 284 ff.

proclaimeth abroad on never resting wing, leadeth different men to such opposite conclusions, that it emboldeneth some to hope for good fortune and driveth others to fear for their very existence. Indeed, I once thought such a renown, too lofty for modern deeds, somewhat beyond the truth and excessive. But that a long uncertainty might not keep me in too great suspense, as the Queen of the East sought Jerusalem, as Pallas sought Helicon, so sought I Verona to examine with faithful eyes the things that I had heard. And there I beheld your splendour; and likewise I beheld and enjoyed your bounty. And even as at first I had suspected an excess in the reports, so afterward I recognized that the excess was in the deeds themselves. And thus it came to pass, that as before from hearsay alone I had been, with a certain subjugation of spirit, your well wisher, so on first seeing you I became both your most devoted servant and your friend.'[1]

Cacciaguida winds up his 'glosses' of the mysterious warnings which Dante had received in the course of his

---

[1] *Epis.* x. (Latham's translation). Boccaccio in his *Life of Dante*, § 14, says that when the poet had settled in Ravenna, his last refuge as Verona was his first, 'it was his wont, whenever he had done six or eight cantos [of the *Paradiso*], more or less, to send them from whatever place he was in, before any other had seen them, to Messer Cane della Scala, whom he held in reverence above all other men; and when he had seen them, Dante gave access to them to whoso desired' ('Wicksteed's transl.). A sonnet in which the Venetian poet, Giovanni Quirini, begs Can Grande to publish some cantos of the *Paradiso*, and thus fulfil the poet's intention, seems to support the statement of Boccaccio. See Vernon's *Paradiso*, i. Preliminary Chapter, p. xxx.; and Wicksteed and Gardner's *Dante and del Virgilio*, Prolegomena, pp. 91, 92. The latter work (Prolegomena, Albertino Mussato) may be consulted for an account of Can Grande's career as a soldier. Ruskin's short summary of his life is interesting: 'First he won his wife, Joanna, by a *coup de main*; he fell in love with her when she was a girl, in Rome; then, she was going to be sent into Scotland to be married; but she had to go through Verona, to the Adige gate. So Can Grande pounced upon her; declared she was much too precious a gem—*preziosa gemma*—to be sent to Scotland, and—she went no farther. Then he fortified Verona against the Germans; dug the great moat out of its rocks; built its wall and towers; established his court of royal and thoughtful hospitality; became the chief Ghibelline captain of Lombardy, and the receiver of noble exiles from all other states; possessed himself by hard fighting of Vicenza also; then of Padua; then, either by strength or subtlety, of Feltre,—Belluno,—Bassano; and died at 37,—of eating apples when he was too hot,—in the year 1329' (*Verona and its Rivers*, § 22). For some notice of his wars, see p. 147 f. above.

pilgrimage by an injunction to avoid envy of those
who should inflict on him the miseries just foretold :

> 'Yet would I not thy neighbours thou shouldst envy,
> Because thy life itself infutures far
> Beyond the punishment of their perfidies.'[1]

It is surely an error to think that Dante means simply
that he will long outlive the punishment of his enemies.
The word he coins—'infutures itself'—demands some
larger interpretation. He is thinking of his 'life among
those who shall call this time ancient,' as is obvious
from lines 119, 120. What was the life of his enemies,
soon to vanish away in the righteous judgment of God,
in comparison with the immortality of fame which the
poet felt was now his? This is perhaps the reason
why, on the Terrace of Envy, he says he would not
there lose his eyes for long : they had never been
greatly guilty of that sin.[2]

At this point Dante gives expression to a fear which
must have haunted his mind during his exile. In the
course of his pilgrimage through the three worlds
of the unseen, he had learnt things of great men and
families, of cities, of nations, which, if published abroad,
would have 'a savour of strong bitterness to many.'
Would it not be a matter of common prudence to sup-
press the dreadful news lest he should create so many
enemies that every refuge would be closed against him?
It was certainly no imaginary danger. To many a
great family the poet's words must have seemed a
wanton outrage upon their dead. His denunciation of
the corruption of the Dominicans and Franciscans
might well have shut in his face the door of every
cloister belonging to them. And his plain condemnation of almost every Christian king was enough to
have closed all Europe against him. In those days of
the vendetta it is a marvel that a sudden knife in the
heart did not send Dante to make actual acquaintance
with that invisible world whose secrets he feigned to
know. On the other hand, if he shrank from proclaim-

---

[1] *Par.* xvii. 97-99.   [2] *Purg.* xiii. 133-135

ing the truth, his fame with future generations, which
Cacciaguida had just foretold, would be lost:

> ' And if to truth I am a timid friend,
> I fear to lose my life 'mong those
> Who yet shall call this time the ancient.' [1]

In reply to this dilemma, Cacciaguida flashed forth
like a golden mirror smitten by a sunbeam, to indicate
that his words are a pure reflection of the Divine light:
' Lay all falsehood aside, and speak thy vision utterly.
True, a conscience darkened by its own sin or another's
will find thy words bitter; yet afterwards, when well
digested, they will leave the nutriment of life.' [2] Unless
we are to regard Dante as a consummate hypocrite,
these words refute the too common idea that he used
the poem as a means of avenging himself on his personal
enemies. His purpose is to impart the nutriment of
life; or, as he puts it in the Epistle to Can Grande, 'the
end of the whole and of the part is to remove those
living in this life from a state of misery, and to guide
them to a state of happiness,'—the only happiness for
man being the vision of God's Face.

Cacciaguida proceeds to set Dante's task in its most
perilous form. It is not the poor unknown crowd he
is to judge, but the great ones of the world; as the
Irish proverb has it, 'The high wind is for the high

---

[1] *Par.* xvii. 118-120. 'If to truth I am a timid friend' refers probably
to Aristotle's *Ethics*, i. 4: ' It will perhaps seem the best, and indeed the
right course, at least when the truth is at stake, to go so far as to sacrifice
what is near and dear to us, especially as we are philosophers. For
friends and truth are both dear to us, but it is a sacred duty to prefer the
truth.' This choice between friendship and truth was a very frequent
one with Dante if we are to judge by the number of times he refers to
this passage: *Conv.* iv. 8; *De Mon.* iii. 1; *Epis.* viii. 5. He seems to rely
for immortality on the truth of his moral judgments rather than on
the beauty of his poetry.

[2] *Par.* xvii. 121-132. Of line 129, ' And let them just scratch, where is
the itch,' Butler says: ' This is perhaps the most remarkable instance of
a characteristic feature of the Paradise; namely, the introduction of
vulgar and even coarse images in the midst of the most elevated passages.
Cf. xii. 114; xiii. 139; and xxxii. 140 (where St. Bernard, in the very
highest Heaven, talks of cutting the coat according to the cloth). It is
as if the writer's mind, overwrought by the fervour of his own imagination, sought a certain relief in these trivialities. Hamlet's "let the
galled jade wince" conveys the same idea in a somewhat more dignified
image.'

hill.' Thus to strike the loftiest summits will be, he declares, 'no little argument of honour': will prove his courage in not fearing to proclaim the vices of the great and powerful, and his wisdom, because only by great and conspicuous examples can the evil of sin be driven home to the conscience. According to Mr. Vernon this is simply an instance of Dante's 'contempt for mediocrity or lukewarmness,' such as is expressed in the doom of the Neutrals.[1] This seems to me a misconception of the present passage: Dante's own express statement is that throughout his pilgrimage 'only the souls that unto fame are known' have been shown to him, because these alone arrest the mind and fix the faith of the hearer. There is no hint whatever of contempt for the obscure; the great are chosen for the simple reason that they form, by their very greatness, a more striking and effective object lesson.[2]

The word which he had just spoken[3] filled Caccia-guida with pure delight; but in Dante the bitter was tempered with the sweet, he was not yet able to glory in the cross. Whereupon Beatrice gave him a gentle rebuke:

> 'Change thy thought, think that I am
> Near unto Him who every wrong disburdens.'

It is an echo of a passage in the *Vita Nuova* in which Dante tells of the surpassing virtue of the salutation of Beatrice: 'When she appeared in any place, it

---

[1] *Inf.* iii. 22-69.   [2] *Par.* xvii. 133-142.

[3] I find it difficult to take *il suo verbo* of xviii. 1, in the sense of *his thought*, that is, that Cacciaguida, as a 'blessed mirror' (l. 2) of Divine truth was at this point re-absorbed in his thought of God. What he rejoices in is just what to Dante is bitter tempered with sweet—his own word and thought concerning the poet's coming misfortunes. Mr. Tozer thinks 'it is harsh to represent the Poet's ancestor as rejoicing in his predictions of impending sorrow'; but this is to confuse the standpoint of Paradise with that of earth. From the latter standpoint, which was Dante's, it was bitter-sweet; but from the standpoint of 'the blessed mirror,' who saw the issue of the sufferings in God, there was no cause for anything but pure joy—joy that his descendant could suffer martyr-dom for truth's sake. Compare his words when he begins to foretell Dante's sorrows:

> 'as cometh to the ear
> Sweet harmony from an organ, to me there comes
> In sight the time that is preparing for thee' (xvii. 43-45).

seemed to me, by the hope of her excellent salutation, that there was no man mine enemy any longer; and such warmth of charity came upon me that most certainly in that moment I would have pardoned whosoever had done me an injury; and if one should then have questioned me concerning any matter, I could only have said unto him "Love," with a countenance clothed in humbleness.'[1]   So here, 'the love within her holy eyes,' beyond both words and memory, and the radiance of her smile, a reflection of 'the eternal pleasure,' banished every bitter thought against his enemies.   So intent was his gaze upon her, that once she had to rebuke him with a smile:

> 'Turn thee and hear,
> For not in my eyes alone is Paradise.'[2]

There is a similar rebuke in Canto xxiii. 70-72, when her face so enamoured him that he forgot to look at 'the fair garden' of the Virgin and the Apostles.   Both passages are the confession of a weakness of which Dante was conscious,—that of becoming too much absorbed in Theology as a scheme of thought, as contemplation without action.   Hence Beatrice, in her symbolic character of Theology or Divine Wisdom,[3] turns him away from her eyes to the heroic soldier-spirits who fought and died for Christ: if he was to share their Paradise, he must enter into the fellowship of their sufferings.   When, in obedience to his Lady, he turned away from her, Cacciaguida pointed out to him eight of his fellow-warriors.   That they are among the most illustrious is implied in the fact that they are all in the 'horns' of the Cross,—the crossbar; and each, as his name is called, flashes along the Cross like lightning, with the eager obedience of the good soldier.

---

[1] *Vita Nuova*, § 11 (Rossetti's transl.).

[2] *Par.* xviii. 19-21.

[3] It is, of course, possible, as Plumptre suggests, that the reference is to Beatrice as the woman Dante loved, and that her warning is that 'Paradise is not found in the contemplation of any human holiness, however perfect, but in the beatific vision with which the *Paradiso* ends.' All the same, it *is* to human holiness, in the person of these soldier-saints, that she immediately points the poet.

They were all men who had fought for Holy Land or
for the Church against the infidel : Joshua and Judas
Maccabæus, Charlemagne and his nephew Roland,
William of Orange and his brother-in-law Renouard,
Duke Godfrey of Bouillon and Robert Guiscard.[1] And
then Cacciaguida joins them, and, by the skill of his
song in the heavenly choir, shows that, simple knight
as he was, he was worthy to take place and rank
even in that great and glorious company of soldiers
of the Cross.[2]

[1] *Par.* xviii. 22-48. Joshua wrested the Land of Promise from the
Canaanites. Judas Maccabæus fought against the Syrians in defence of
the Hebrew faith. Charlemagne gained the title of Champion of the
Faith and Defender of the Holy See for his wars against the Saracens of
Spain and the Arians of Lombardy. The rear-guard of his army under
his nephew Roland, according to the *Chanson de Roland*, was destroyed
by the Saracens in the famous pass of Roncesvalles, Roland himself being
among the slain. The exploits of William of Orange against the Saracens
in the South of France, and of his brother-in-law Renouard, a converted
Saracen, his companion in arms, are told in the *Chanson*, the *Geste de
Guillaume*. Godfrey of Bouillon in the Ardennes was one of the leaders
of the First Crusade. On the capture of Jerusalem in 1099, he was
unanimously chosen king, but where his Saviour had worn a crown of
thorns he would not wear one of gold. Robert Guiscard (i.e. the Cunning)
was a son of Tancred de Hautville in Normandy. Gregorovius calls him
faithless and unscrupulous, a blood-stained condottiere, a mighty robber.
He was twice excommunicated by the Pope, yet became his vassal and
fought against the Greeks and Saracens in the South of Italy. He died
in 1085, and on his tomb he is called ' terror mundi.' His great slaughter
of the heretics is referred to in *Inf.* xxviii. 14.

[2] This I take to be the meaning of xviii. 49-51. I do not understand
Dante to mean that his ancestor rejoined the souls in general, but this
great company just named. He also belonged to the highest part of the
Cross,—the right crossbar (xv. 19)—as they do ; and the artist-quality of
his song among the other singers is proof that he is worthy to rank with
them.

CHAPTER XV

1. *The Eagle of the Celestial Empire*

IT is impossible to understand this Heaven of Just
Rulers without bearing clearly in mind the poet's
political convictions as set forth in the *De Monarchia*.
We saw in Chapter v. that he takes Monarchia in an
absolute sense,—the government of one man, not as
with us over one country, but over the world. This
one man could be to Dante no other than the Roman
Emperor; and now that his political hopes on earth
were buried in the tomb of Henry VII., he transfers
them to the eternal world in a magnificent apotheosis
of the Empire. The Roman standard, the Eagle, however it might seem for the moment to suffer defeat, is
still 'the Holy Bird,' 'the Bird of God,' and must have
its victory and kingdom elsewhere. In the Heaven of
Mercury, the Emperor Justinian narrated the story of
its glorious flight on earth from the days of Troy down
to the unworthy times when the Guelphs fought against
it and the Ghibellines degraded it into the standard of
a party.[1] Now, in the Heaven of 'the temperate star,'
we are to see it as the ensign of the Eternal Emperor,
the fulfilment of His righteousness, dependent upon
His authority, and upon His alone.[2]

The knowledge that he had risen to a wider orbit
came to the poet partly by an increased delight in doing
well, and partly by the changes which he saw in his

---

[1] *Par.* vi. 97-111.

[2] It is to be noted that even here the mythological reference is not
forgotten, the Eagle being the bird of Jupiter. Comp. *Purg.* xxxii. 109-
117.

Lady. Her eyes had a purer light and joyance, and her face, which had glowed with the red light of Mars, had faded into a paleness, caused by 'the whiteness of the temperate sixth star.'[1] In the *Convito* (ii. 14) a quotation from Ptolemy is given to the effect that 'Jupiter is a star of temperate complexion, midway between the coldness of Saturn and the heat of Mars.' This is echoed in *Par.* xxii. 145, where Dante speaks of 'the tempering of Jove between the father (Saturn) and the son (Mars).' This temperateness of the planet is symbolic of one attribute of the just rulers who are revealed in it,—namely clemency. Temperance as a general virtue is described by Aquinas as 'a certain *attempering*, or moderation, which is the work of reason upon human actions and passions'; and clemency is a 'potential' part of Temperance, inasmuch as it is 'a moderation of temper withholding a man from using his full power to inflict penalties.' In short, 'the temperate star' represents that balance and equipoise of justice and clemency which constitute the spirit of equity, essential to a righteous ruler of men.[2]

'The *whiteness* of the temperate star' has also its symbolic significance, for which we must again turn to the *Convito*. In the passage above referred to, Jupiter, it is said, 'among all the stars shows white, almost as if silvered.'[3] In this it represents Geometry, which is 'most white, inasmuch as it is without spot of error, and most certain in itself.' We may take it, then, that the whiteness of the star represents to the poet's mind the righteousness of the rulers whom he meets in it,— a certain clearness of justice, 'without spot of error,' and measured out with geometrical exactness.

We turn now to the souls in Jupiter. They appear at first in the form of lights flying through the air like birds. It is to be noted that in this Heaven of the

---

[1] *Par.* xviii. 52-69.
[2] Comp. *Summa*, ii-ii. q. cxli. a. 2; q. cxliii. a. 1; q. clvii. a. 1-4. 'Clemency,' says Aquinas, 'in abating penalties seems to come very near to charity, which is the chief of virtues, prompting us to do good to our neighbours and prevent evil to them.'
[3] Comp. *Par.* xviii. 95, 96.

Eagle nearly all the similes are taken from bird-life.[1]
The special point in the present comparison is that these
spirits are like birds, wheeling and singing with joy
over their food : righteous government is their meat
and drink.[2] The flying lights proceed to arrange themselves in letters which spell out slowly the opening
words of *The Wisdom of Solomon*: *Diligite iustitiam, qui
iudicatis terram.* The general idea seems to be that
the complete sentence, the perfect kingdom of righteousness, cannot be spelt out by one man or one
generation. It is spelt out letter by letter, each
righteous ruler in every land and age contributing his
share. We may notice too that when one letter is
formed, the souls that compose it pause awhile and
are silent from their singing.[3] This cannot be simply
in order to give Dante time to read it; rather it means
that one letter—one fragmentary form of just government—comes into existence, has its day, and passes on
into another form, a new letter, thus spelling out
through the slow ages the complete righteousness of
God.

> 'The old order changeth, yielding place to new,
> And God fulfils himself in many ways,
> Lest one good custom should corrupt the world.'[4]

Throughout these Cantos one of Dante's leading
ideas is to show the unity of the celestial Empire, all
rulers and governments finding their life and freedom
in their due subordination to the Imperial Eagle of
which they form a part. The idea is carried out in
many ingenious ways which reveal the love with
which the poet's mind kept working round it.

1. The first has been sufficiently noted: the individual
letters, the 'five times seven vowels and consonants,'

---

[1] E.g., in addition to the Eagle and the present passage: xviii. 111, the
mysterious reference to *nests*; xix. 34, the *falcon* issuing from its hood;
xix. 91, the comparison of the Eagle to the *stork* hovering over its young;
xx. 73, the *lark* pausing content with 'the last sweetness' of its song.
See the chap. on 'The Birds of Dante' in Christopher Hare's *Dante the
Wayfarer.*

[2] Matt. v. 6 (Vulg.) 'Beati qui esuriunt et sitiunt iustitiam.'

[3] *Par.* xviii. 79-81.

[4] Tennyson's *The Passing of Arthur.*

the 'verb and noun,' all making up the one complete sentence of justice.

2. The second is by no means so simple. At a certain point the lights pass through a series of transformations, described so carefully that it is obvious Dante had, in each change, some very exact symbolic purpose. This series we must get clearly before both mind and eye.

(1) When the starry souls formed themselves into the last letter (M) of the last word of the sentence (*terram*), they remained in that shape, the planet appearing like silver inlaid with gold. Now, there can be little doubt that the M stands in Dante's mind for *Monarchia*, all the previous transformations working towards this unity of government. Also, it is necessary for our understanding of further changes to remember that

FIG. 1.

the shape of the mediæval M was very different from ours. I give it in Fig. 1.

(2) As Dante looked at this M, he saw descending from above other lights which settled on the summit of the M, singing

FIG. 2.

the Justice which drew them to itself. These appear to be the rulers who were distinguished on earth for the highest and purest righteousness, and who therefore had the right to form the head and crown of the M. They probably shaped themselves as in Fig. 2; for, as we shall see, Dante seems to have had the Lily of Florence all the time before his eyes. See Fig. 4.

(3) Then, like sparks struck from a burning log,

FIG. 3.

there rose from the top of the M more than a thousand lights, and formed themselves into the head and neck of an Eagle, each light taking its place higher or lower, according to the rank allotted it by God, that is, according to the proportion of its righteousness. The shape would then be as in

Fig. 3,—not yet the perfect Eagle, the wings being defective.

(4) The remedying of this defect forms the final change; and as the passage is, I think, generally misunderstood, I shall translate it as literally as possible:

> The other blessedness which at first did seem
> Content to make itself the lily to the M,
> By a slight motion followed the imprint,

that is, carried out the image of the Eagle. Now, as I said, Dante had in mind the Lily of Florence, as in Fig. 4. Compare this with the M of Fig. 1, and it will be seen that the stem and rounded petals of the lily correspond almost exactly with the stem and rounded wings of the M. As Dante puts it, they 'make themselves the *lily* to the M,' and only a slight movement is necessary in order to change them into the body and wings, and so fulfil the image of the Eagle, as in Fig. 5. The reference in the poet's mind, I have no doubt, is to the Lily of his native city, the symbol of the Guelph party. In his opinion it required no very revolutionary change to bring even Guelph Florence into harmony with the Empire. At all events, he saw the change take place with perfect ease in Heaven: 'the other blessedness'—that is, the company of souls that had hitherto been content to form the lily-part of the M, — by a slight movement became the body and wings of the Celestial Eagle.[1]

FIG. 4.

FIG. 5.

---

[1] I follow here, as all recent commentators do, the suggestions of the late Duke of Sermoneta: see the figures in Vernon's *Paradiso*, ii. 51, 52, and Toynbee's *Dante Dictionary*, 'Aquila.²' But I am unable to accept some of the details of his explanation. The chief point of difference is that, according to the Duke, the lily-part of the M is simply the little top on the letter as in Fig. 2 above; whereas a glance at the Lily in Fig. 4 will show that the chief portion of the flower consists of the stem and the curving petals. Further, he thinks it was this little top, which he calls the Lily, that by a slight movement adapted itself to the head and neck of the Eagle, whereas it seems to me far more natural to suppose that the lily-like stem and petals of the Gothic M made this movement, and thus carried out the form of the Eagle's body and wings. Of course,

3. In the beginning of Canto xix. Dante returns in a
very emphatic way to this unity of the Eagle. It
appeared to him with wings outspread, every soul
composing it shining like a ruby smitten by the sun,
with joy of the beauty of the completed image. And
then he tells what he regards as a thing absolutely
unknown, undreamt of, upon earth:

> And what it now behoves me to retrace
> Nor voice has e'er reported, nor ink written,
> Nor was by fantasy e'er comprehended;
> For speak I saw, and likewise heard, the beak,
> And utter with its voice both *I* and *My*,
> When in conception it was *We* and *Our*.[1]

This mysterious unity—all kings, governors and nations
of all ages uttering their thought with one voice—is
compared in the same passage to one heat issuing from
many embers, one perfume breathing from many
flowers.

4. We may set alongside this the converse phenomenon recorded in the opening lines of Canto xx.—the
mysterious ebb and flow, action and reaction, between
the one voice and the many, between the Empire and
the individual states of which it is composed: for there
can be no doubt that this is the underlying conception.
Just as at sunset, when the one great light sinks, a
multitude of lesser lights appear, so, when the beak of
the Eagle became silent, all the living lights composing it broke forth into songs too high for the poet's
memory. And then, when these in turn were silent,
there came to his ear as it were

> a murmuring of a river
> That clear descendeth down from rock to rock,
> Showing the affluence of its mountain-top.[2]

Then the murmuring rose up through the neck, as if it

whichever view we take, the political idea remains substantially the
same. The Roman Emperor has the right of universal monarchy, and all
lower kings, princes and rulers are in duty bound to submit to his
authority and follow out the imprint of the Eagle. This may meantime
be denied on earth, but the kingdom of eternal righteousness in Paradise
is the Divine 'form' or idea of it.

[1] *Par.* xix. 7-12.   [2] *Par.* xx. 19-21.

had been hollow,[1] became a voice, and the beak turned
the murmur into articulate speech. 'Which things are
an allegory.' The unity of the Empire and the supreme
authority of the Emperor did not mean for Dante a
central tyranny, which denied to individual states a
reasonable freedom of self-government. When the
beak of the Eagle is silent, the separate lights are at
liberty to begin their songs. When the songs cease,
the echo and murmur of them passes through the entire
community, ascends through the neck and becomes
articulate. The meaning certainly seems to be that
the individual princes and states have their voice in
the affairs of the entire Empire. It is the murmur of
their songs which becomes the voice of the supreme
authority in the end: of their *songs*, it must be noted,
—of their joyous and peaceful life, not their angry and
warlike rebellions. All this, as Mr. Gardner well points
out, is stated in the *De Monarchia* (i. 14) without any
veil of allegory: 'It must be carefully observed that
when we say that mankind may be ruled by one
supreme prince, we do not mean that the most trifling
judgments for each particular town are to proceed
immediately from him. . . . For nations and kingdoms
and states have, each of them, certain peculiarities
which must be regulated by different laws. . . . But our
meaning is that it is in those matters which are common
to all men, that men should be ruled by one Monarch,
and be governed by a rule common to them all, with a
view to their peace.'[2] It is obvious, then, that Dante
had some conception of the modern national state;
but it is probable, as Professor Villari says, that the
universal Empire for which he longed so passionately
was what rendered the rise of such a state impossible.

[1] Which it was not. Dante is remembering that it is not an actual
eagle with an actual neck, but only the image of one traced out with
stars.

[2] In this section Dante gives as an example the relation of Moses to
the elders: 'He took the elders of the tribes of the children of Israel, and
left to them the lesser judgments, reserving to himself such as were more
important, and wider in their scope; and the elders carried these wider
ones to their tribes, according as they were applicable to each separate
tribe.'

'It was precisely the emperor's yearning to be lord of all men and all things that was so opposed to the national spirit that was already beginning to stir many minds, and that—if almost unawares—Alighieri was so earnestly lauding, while practically denying it by imploring the resurrection of the Empire.'[1] This criticism, however, it must be remembered, scarcely applies to the present passage, in which the whole subject is viewed *sub specie aeternitatis*.

In these Cantos Dante takes the opportunity of expressing another of his strongest political convictions, namely, that the Empire derives its being and authority directly from God, and not from the Pope. When he saw the M gradually shape itself into the form of an Eagle, he knew that the mysterious power which wrought the change was Divine :

> He who there paints has none to be His guide,
> But Himself guides ; and from Him is brought to mind
> That virtue which is form for the nests.[2]

The thought is obscure and difficult, and depends on a right understanding of the word 'form.' It is not to be taken in its modern popular sense of *shape*, as if Dante was thinking only of the shape or pattern of a bird's nest. 'Form' in its scholastic sense is the Divine idea of all that the nest implies—the nest itself, the egg, the formation of the bird within the egg. The power or 'virtue' which, in every bird's nest brings this 'form' or Divine idea to fulfilment, is the same power which brings this celestial Eagle—this Empire of Righteousness—into existence, as Dante sees it here depicted. The difference is that in the case of 'the nests,' the Divine virtue works by a mere instinct in the birds ; whereas in the Eagle, it works through mind (*si rammenta*), through conscious human reason, since law, as Aquinas says, 'must be some function of reason.'[3] Nevertheless, one cannot help feeling that

---

[1] *Florentine History*, chap. x. § ix.   [2] *Par.* xviii. 109-111.

[3] *Summa*, i-ii. q. xc. a. 1.   I am aware that in thus interpreting 'si rammenta' I am departing from the generally received view. The words are variously rendered 'is remembered,' 'is recognized,' 'is had in mind,' 'comes to the mind,' etc. ; but none of these renderings carries any definite sense to my mind. My own version 'is brought to mind' has in

Dante wishes to suggest that even in the human reason
by which this kingdom of righteousness is evolved,
there is an element of instinct, what Ruskin calls the
'heavenly involuntariness in which a bird builds her
nest.'[1] Each of these spirits wrought his own fragment of righteous rule on earth according to his reason;
and now he finds that the Eternal Reason has all the
time been working his fragment, beyond his intention,
into the body and substance of the Eternal Righteousness. Hence it follows that all human righteousness is
an issue of this planet:

> O sweet star! of gems what kind and number
> Did demonstrate to me that all our justice
> Effect is of the Heaven that thou engemmest.[2]

This is an obvious repudiation of the Papal claim to be
the fountain of imperial authority and civil righteousness. Almost the last words of the *De Monarchia* are:
'It is therefore clear that the authority of temporal
Monarchy comes down, with no intermediate will, from
the fountain of universal authority; and this fountain,
one in its unity, flows through many channels out of
the abundance of the goodness of God.' Nay, so far
from being the source of human justice, the Papacy is
the smoke which so vitiates this planet's ray that once
more Christ's wrath is kindled against buying and selling in the Temple—a Temple more precious than that
of old in that 'its walls were built of blood and martyr-

itself no superiority, save that it is capable of a definite meaning. Dante,
in short, is thinking of the various ways in which the creatures share,
according to their nature, in the mind of the Creator. The bird shares
by *instinct*, instinct in the making of the nest and in the whole process
which the nest implies. Man shares by *reason*—what is instinct in the
bird is 'brought to *mind*' in the man, raised to conscious thought. It is
by this process, then, of a reasonable mind in men that God brings into
existence the Eagle, the kingdom of His righteousness; but the reasonable mind itself is a participation of the Divine mind. To quote Aquinas:
'Even irrational animals share in the Eternal Law in their own way, as
also does the rational creature. But because the rational creature shares
in it intellectually and rationally, therefore the participation of the
Eternal Law in the rational creature is properly called a *law*; for law is
a function of reason: but in the irrational creature it is not shared
rationally; hence it cannot be called a *law* except by a similitude'
(*Summa*, i-ii. q. xci. a. 3).

[1] *Fors Clavigera*, Letter lxxxiii. 7.   [2] *Par.* xviii. 109-111; 115-117.

doms.'¹ Dante begs the prayers of the 'soldiery of Heaven,' these just princes, for earthly rulers, who are all led astray by this evil example. The special form of this wicked merchandise singled out is excommunication—the taking away arbitrarily ('now here, now there,' xviii. 128) of 'the bread the pitying Father locks up from none.' And this excommunication is used as a weapon of war, instead of the old frank use of the sword. It was, indeed, no mean weapon, and, from the ninth century onward, was used unscrupulously to build up the temporal power of the Church. When a Pope quarrelled with an Emperor or King, he had only to launch against him a decree of excommunication, in order to ruin him in both worlds. The sacraments were withdrawn; all civil rights were forfeited, and he became an outlaw in his own territory; his subjects were solemnly released from all oaths of allegiance; to aid him was to subject themselves to the ban laid on him, and rebellion became a positive duty. It was a weapon which smote the spirit not less than the flesh. As Milman says, 'the Interdict, the special prerogative of the Pope, as the antagonist, the controller of Sovereigns, smote a kingdom with spiritual desolation, during which the niggardly and imperfect rites, the baptism sparingly administered, the rest of the life without any religious ceremony, the extreme unction or the last sacrament coldly vouchsafed to the chosen few, the churchyard closed against the dead, seemed to consign a whole nation, a whole generation, to irrevocable perdition.'²

There remained one further step of degradation for this terrible power—to use it as an instrument of blackmail for the extortion of money. In the closing lines of Canto xviii., the poet does not hesitate to bring this shameful charge against some individual, whom

---

¹ I follow the Oxford *Dante* in reading *sangue*, instead of *segni* in xviii. 123. The latter has large MS. authority, but the building of the Church by blood seems much more appropriate to the thought than by miracles. Comp. *Par.* xxvii. 40-45. Dante is contrasting the building of the Temple walls with the blood of martyrs, with another form of building with blood. The words of Micah iii. 10: 'They build up Zion with blood,' formed a common ironical description of nepotism.

² Milman's *Latin Christianity*, Bk. xiv. ch. i.; *Par.* xviii. 118-129.

he addresses as 'thou,'—the charge, namely, of issuing
decrees of excommunication in order to extort money
for their cancelment. Much controversy has arisen as
to the identity of this individual.[1] If we adopt the
standpoint of the year 1300, the ideal date of the poem,
he must be identified with Boniface VIII. If, however,
we assume that Dante was influenced by later events,
no occupant of the Papal Chair would better correspond to his words in this passage than John XXII.,
whose Pontificate, as Vernon says, was 'a never-ending
sequence of excommunications and re-communications
for the object of extorting money, so that it might well
be said of him that he wrote his edicts for the sole
object of being paid for revoking them.' The passage
is remarkable for its biting Dantesque irony:

> Yet thou, who writest but to cancel, think
> That Peter and that Paul, who for the vineyard
> Which thou art wasting died, are still alive!
> Well canst thou say : 'So steadfast my desire
> Is unto him who willed to live alone,
> And for a dance was led to martyrdom,
> That I know not the Fisherman nor Paul.'

It is worth while examining this with a little care to
see how almost every word is steeped in irony. The
reason why Peter and Paul are mentioned is that
it was by authority of these Apostles excommunications were launched, as in Gregory's second decree
against Henry IV. which begins : 'St. Peter, chief of the
Apostles, and thou St. Paul, teacher of the nations,
deign, I beg, to incline your ears to me and mercifully
to hear me.' 'Remember,' says Dante, 'they still live
and have power to punish this unholy abuse of their
authority—Peter holds the keys, and Paul has not lost
his power to deliver to Satan.' Then there is a significant variation in the naming of them which ought not

---

[1] Also whether it is an individual at all, and not the Church or the
Papacy in general. Even if this were so, it is probable that some one
Pope stood out in Dante's mind as the supreme and typical sinner, and
John XXII. deserves that evil distinction. Against this, however, is the
fact that the passage is in the present tense, whereas Dante's custom is
to refer to future persons and events in the form of prophecies. If the
reference is to John, this passage must have been written sometime later
than 1316, the year of his election.

to escape notice. When Dante himself speaks in line 131, their proper names are given, *Pietro e Paolo* ; but when the Pope speaks, Pietro becomes 'the Fisherman,' and *Paolo* the colloquial *Polo*, to indicate a certain contemptuous tone which he assumed toward the chief Apostles. No doubt, says Dante with still deeper irony, the Pope may well excuse his ignorance of 'the Fisher' and 'Polo' by his fixed devotion to another saint, John the Baptist, who 'lived alone' in the wilderness, and was 'led to martyrdom' by the dancing of the daughter of Herodias. The reference is to the image of the Baptist stamped on the gold florin of Florence:[1] he whose devotion was fixed on this golden saint was not likely to know Peter or Paul, who cared little for florins. The way in which the Baptist is named—

'who willed to live alone,
And for a dance was led to martyrdom '—

is probably, as Plumptre suggests, a sarcastic stroke at the life of the Papal Court at Avignon. In that gay throng there was no 'willing to live alone,' no retiral to desert solitudes. Dances there were, indeed, but they led to no martyrdom. The devotion to the Baptist was strictly and severely limited to the florin. No wonder Dante refused to regard men whose avarice, like a smoke, darkened the ray of this Heaven of Justice, as the fountain-head of imperial authority, or as the guide of God in the shaping of the Eagle of righteous government.[2]

[1] For a similar use of the Lily, 'the accursed flower' stamped on the other side of the florin, see p. 161 on Canto ix. 127 ff.

[2] Mr. Gardner, who thinks Dante here addresses John XXII., reminds us that this Pontiff coined florins like those of Florence with his own name on one side instead of the Baptist, though he excommunicated some Italian noblemen for following his example. This, however, was in 1322, the year after Dante's death, and therefore cannot be here referred to. Mr. Gardner adds : 'However, Dr Pastor well points out the injustice of condemning these Avignon pontiffs merely upon the grounds of their financial and political policy, and leaving out of sight their grand efforts for the propagation of Christianity in the East.' Let any one read Milman's or Lea's account of this Pope's utterly unscrupulous ways of amassing the vast fortune which he left, and Petrarch's denunciations of the unspeakable immorality of the Avignon court, and then let him judge the value of efforts to propagate such Christianity either East or West. One remembers that the Lord of the Church spoke of men who 'compassed sea and land to make one proselyte'—but not with admiration of their 'grand efforts.'

CHAPTER XVI

SIXTH HEAVEN—JUPITER: RIGHTEOUS RULERS

2. *Divine Justice and the Heathen World*

WHEN the Eagle, with outspread wings, uttered the thought of many with the voice of one, its object was to tell how it had reached the glory of this Heaven:— not as kings too often strive to reach glory on earth, by mere desire, but by the practice of justice and mercy:

> 'By being just and merciful
> I am exalted here unto that glory
> Which does not let itself be conquered by desire,'

or ambition.[1] The union of justice and mercy, in due proportion, is what constitutes righteous government in man even as in God, and therefore it raises these rulers to the glory of this Heaven. Even on earth the Eagle is not without a certain glory: the memory of its justice and mercy extorts the praise even of wicked governors who refuse to follow it.[2]

This utterance of the Eagle quickens in Dante the hope that these 'perpetual flowers of the eternal joy,'

---

[1] *Par.* xix. 13-15. To translate *giusto e pio* (l. 13) 'just and *good*,' as is often done, is, I think, to miss the very point of the utterance. 'Good' is far too vague for *pio*. Dante is thinking of *pietà*, pity the mercy without which justice often becomes injustice. The meaning of ll. 14, 15,

> 'Son io qui esaltato a quella gloria,
> Che non si lascia vincere a disio,'

is much disputed. Two interpretations are suggested: (1) that this glory of Jupiter is superior to all human desire; (2) that it does not allow itself to be won by mere desire—it must be worked for (Matt. vii. 21). I venture to suggest a third: the common way in which kings aim at glory is at their own 'desire' or ambition, and earthly glory may be so won. But not so the glory of this Heaven: it can be 'conquered' only 'by being just and merciful.'

[2] *Par.* xix. 16-18.

as he calls the spirits that compose it, would be able to break within him, to use his own words,

> 'the great fast
> Which a long season has in hunger held me,
> Not finding for it any food on earth.'

He does not tell them what the fast is, knowing that they see it in God. It is the great problem of the Divine justice in the condemnation of the heathen world. Not unnaturally Dante thinks that here if anywhere, in this Heaven of just rulers there must be perfect insight into the mysteries of the righteous government of God. It is true, as he says, that another realm of Paradise,—namely Saturn, the Heaven immediately above, — is the mirror of the Divine justice, since it is presided over by the Third Order of Angels, the Thrones of Judgment; but the reflection from that mirror is seen without a veil by these 'spirits of just men made perfect.'[1] The Eagle now states the problem which Dante had left unspoken. His eagerness to discourse of the Eternal Justice is like that of a falcon issuing from its hood, clapping its wings for flight; and his joy is such that he is 'woven of the praises of Divine grace.' Not of Divine *justice*, as the connection of thought might lead us to expect: grace, as we shall see, being the wider thought with which this Heaven closes.

> 'A man is born upon the bank
> Of the Indus, and there is no one there to speak
> Of Christ, nor none to read, nor none to write;
> And all his volitions and his actions
> Are good, as far as human reason sees,
> Without a sin in life or in discourse:
> He dieth unbaptized and without faith;
> Where is this justice that condemneth him?
> Where is his fault, if he do not believe?'[2]

The only answer is virtually that of St. Paul: 'Nay but, O man, who art thou that repliest against God?'[3] The human intellect is absolutely incapable

---

[1] *Par.* xix. 22-30; ix. 61-63.
[2] *Par.* xix. 70-78.   [3] Rom. ix. 20.

of judging; nay, it lies beyond the range of the highest created Intelligence. The reason is that 'He who rolled the compass round the limit of the world,' could not express His entire being by means of the whole universe. Nothing but His own Word, whom He generates, and who has the same nature, can utter His whole being. Hence 'the Word remains in infinite excess' of all created things. In the words of Aquinas, 'the Divine goodness is an end which exceeds beyond proportion created things.'[1] Hence the only wisdom of the creature is a profound humility of intellect, which awaits patiently the unfolding of that Divine goodness which is the end of creation. It was by his refusal thus to wait for light that Lucifer, 'the first proud being, who was the sum of every creature,' 'fell unripe,'—failed to reach the full maturity of his powers. According to Aquinas, following Augustine, there were two moments in the knowledge of the Angels immediately on their creation. In the words, 'And the evening and the morning were the first day,' Augustine distinguishes *cognitio vespertina* and *cognitio matutina*. The knowledge *of the evening* is knowledge of created things in their own proper nature; and this knowledge was common to all the Angels. But some, remaining in this lower knowledge, had their intellects turned only to themselves, and their pride caused the evening to pass into the darkness of night. The knowledge *of the morning* is knowledge of created things as they exist in the Word; and the good Angels, accepting by one decisive act of free will the Divine grace, turned their intellects away from themselves to the Word, and thus entered into the vision of God which constitutes beatitude. The pride of Lucifer was not that he aimed at *equality*

[1] *Summa*, i. q. xxv. a. 5. In this Article: *Utrum Deus possit facere quae non facit*, Aquinas refutes Abelard's contention that God could not have made another world than this. The argument is that the Divine Goodness, which is the end of creation, so far exceeds all created things that it might be wrought out in other ways. Hence the Divine Wisdom is not so limited to the present order of creation that no other order was possible. The present order, however, is the best possible for the display of His goodness which God desired to make.

with God—every Angelic Intelligence knows this to be
impossible in its nature. What he aimed at was *inde-*
pendence—rising to the *cognitio matutina* by the power
of his own intellect, without the aid of Divine grace.
But since grace is as necessary for the highest Angel
as for man, the result of this refusal to ' wait for light '
upon God was that he 'fell unripe,'—his intellect never
reached the vision of God for which it was created.[1]
If this is true of the highest created intellect, it follows
that lesser natures like our own cannot contain the
infinite Goodness. Our sight is but a ray of the Mind
that fills all things, and its limitations must make it
aware that its Source discerns far beyond what it can
see. The eternal justice is like the ocean : near the
shore the eye discerns the bottom ; far out in the open
sea the bottom is invisible, yet none the less it exists.
It is vain to search for light save in ' the serene which
never is disturbed,' in some revelation from God
Himself ; anything else that professes to offer a
solution of the mystery is

> ' darkness,
> Either shadow of the flesh or else its poison,'

that is, ignorance, due to one of two causes,—the
natural dimness of the senses, or the poison of them,
which we call sin.[2] And then the doubter is crushed
with the rebuke :

---

[1] *Summa*, i. q. lviii. a. 6, 7 ; q. lxii. a. 2 ; q. lxiii. a. 3. Of the morning
and evening knowledge Augustine says : 'The knowledge of the creature
is, in comparison of the knowledge of the Creator, but a twilight ; and
so it dawns and breaks into morning when the creature is drawn into
the praise and love of the Creator ; and night never falls when the
Creator is not forsaken through love of the creature' (*De Civ. Dei*, xi. 7).
In chap. 29 of the same Book, he says that all things 'are known in one
way by the angels in the Word of God, in which they see the eternally
abiding causes and reasons according to which they were made, and in
another way in themselves : in the former, with a clearer knowledge ; in
the latter, with a knowledge dimmer, and rather of the bare works than
of the design. Yet, when these works are referred to the praise and
adoration of the Creator Himself, it is as if morning dawned in the minds
of those who contemplate them' (Dr. Dods' transl.).

[2] *Par.* xix. 40-66. The 'poison' in l. 66 is often taken to be sensuality,
but many other sins as well as this produce the 'darkness' of which
Dante speaks. I take the poison to be sin in general.

> 'Now who art thou wouldst sit upon the bench
> To judge at distance of a thousand miles
> With the short sight that carries but a span?'[1]

The Eagle admits that were it not for the authority and revelation of Scripture, one who entered into subtle arguments concerning justice might find ample room for doubt.[2] Scripture reveals what the will of God is, and this is absolutely decisive of the question of justice. For the Primal Will never departs from itself, which is the highest good; as Aquinas puts it, 'God is His own goodness.' Hence justice is simply whatever is in conformity with that will.[3] Nor are we to think that the will of God in saving any man is moved thereto by the man's goodness—as seems implied in the case of the virtuous Pagan born on the banks of Indus; on the contrary, such goodness is itself a ray of the Divine will shining into the man.[4] This is the clearest light Dante can reach—the best food which even this Heaven of Justice can offer to his

---

[1] *Par.* xix. 79-81. This is, as said above, Paul's question, 'Nay but, O man, who art thou that repliest against God?' (Rom. ix. 20). The comparison of Divine justice to the sea comes probably from Ps. xxxvi. 6, 'Thy judgments are a great deep,' and Rom. xi. 33-34.

[2] *Par.* xix. 82-84. I take the difficult words in l. 82, 'colui che meco s'assottiglia,' literally 'he who makes himself subtle with me,' to mean one who will argue out the problem of Divine justice by every device of reason. There is a suggestion of over-subtlety, almost hair-splitting, as the word *sottigliezza* implies. Indeed, *assottigliatore* means a caviller, a trifler or hair-splitter. The *meco*, 'with me,' means that the Eagle regarded itself as the representative of the Divine justice thus brought under the scrutiny of the human reason.

[3] Comp. *De Mon.* ii. 2: 'Since all Right (*Jus*) is good, and since all that is in the mind of God is God, according to the saying, "What was made, in Him was life"; and as God chiefly wishes for what is Himself, it follows that Right is the wish of God, so far as it is in Him. And since in God the will and the wish are the same, it further follows that this Right is the will of God. Again it follows that Right in the world is nothing else than the likeness of the will of God, and therefore whatever does not agree with the divine will cannot be Right, and whatever does agree with the divine will is Right itself. Therefore to ask if a thing be Right is only to ask in other words if it is what God wills. It may therefore be assumed that what God wills to see in mankind is to be held as real and true Right' (Church).

[4] In *Summa* i-ii. q. cxii. a. 1, Aquinas shows that God alone is the cause of grace; and in q. cxiv. a. 5, that man cannot merit the first grace (1) because grace is free; (2) because it exceeds the measure of nature; (3) because sin is an impediment to earning grace.

long fast. It is the will of God revealed in Scripture that even virtuous heathen without faith and baptism cannot be saved, and the will of God is the goodness of God in action. The discussion here may be compared with a similar passage in the *De Monarchia* (ii. 8): 'There are some judgments of God to which, though human reason cannot reach them by its own powers, yet by the aid of faith in those things which are told us in Holy Scripture it can be lifted up: as, for instance, that no one, however perfect he may be in moral and intellectual virtues, both in habit and in action, can be saved without faith; it being supposed that he never heard aught of Christ. For human reason cannot of itself see this to be just, yet by faith it can. For in the Epistle to the Hebrews it is written, "without faith it is impossible to please God."'[1] It is pathetic to watch the struggle of the poet's heart against the trammels of his Church's creed; for in all this he is simply following his Master in theology. It is the teaching of Aquinas that faith in Christ is absolutely necessary, faith explicit or implicit; and that since there can be no faith without a revelation, the knowledge of Christ is given by God even to heathen souls, if they truly long for salvation. 'God,' he says, 'never suffers any one to want what is necessary to his salvation, if he only desires it. No one loses his soul save through his own fault; since God makes known to him truths which are essential to his salvation, either through interior revelation, or, as in the case of Cornelius, by the voice of a preacher.'[2]

---

[1] Church's translation. Dante follows with another proof-text so curious that it may be quoted, its object being to show that not faith in general, but faith *in Christ*, is necessary for salvation: It is written 'in Leviticus, "what man soever there be of the House of Israel that killeth an ox, or lamb, or goat in the camp, or that killeth it out of the camp, and bringeth it not to the door of the tabernacle to offer an offering unto the Lord, blood shall be imputed to that man." The door of the tabernacle stands for Christ, who is the door of the kingdom of heaven, as may be proved from the Gospel: the killing of animals represents men's actions.' The idea seems to be that the actions of men, no matter how right in themselves, are not accepted unless done in faith in Christ.

[2] Quoted by Hettinger, *Dante's Divina Commedia* (p. 211 n.).

The following curious passage tells us what Aquinas meant by implicit faith: 'To many of the Gentiles a revelation concerning Christ was made, as is plain from the things which they foretold. For (Job xix. 25) it is said: *I know that my Redeemer liveth.*[1] A Sibyl also prophesied certain things concerning Christ, as Augustine relates (*Cont. Faust.*, xiii. 15).[2] Also it is found in histories of the Romans, that in the time of Constantine Augustus and Helena his mother a certain sepulchre was found, in which was lying a man having on his breast a golden plate on which was written: "Christ shall be born of a Virgin, and I believe in him. O Sun, under the times of Helena and Constantine thou shalt see me again." If, nevertheless, any have been saved to whom no revelation was made, they were not saved without faith of a Mediator; for though they had not explicit faith, they yet had implicit faith in Divine providence, believing God to be the deliverer of men according to the means that are pleasing to Him, and according as the Spirit revealed to those who know the truth, according to that saying (Job xxxv. 11): *Who teacheth us more than the beasts of the earth.*'[3] The point to note is the universal necessity of faith in Christ as Mediator: in the words of the Eagle:

---

[1] The point is that Job was a Gentile. Augustine, discussing this very matter, adduces 'the case of the holy and wonderful man Job, who was neither a native (i.e. an Israelite) nor a proselyte, that is, a stranger joining the people of Israel, but, being bred of the Idumean race, arose there and died there too, and who is so praised by the divine oracle, that no man of his times is put on a level with him as regards justice and piety. . . . And I doubt not it was divinely provided, that from this one case we might know that among other nations also there might be men pertaining to the spiritual Jerusalem who have lived according to God and have pleased Him. And it is not to be supposed that this was granted to any one, unless the one Mediator between God and men, the Man Christ Jesus, was divinely revealed to him' (*The City of God*, xviii. 47, Dr. Dods' transl.).

[2] According to Augustine, the Erythræan Sibyl. For a translation of a Greek poem attributed to her, see his *City of God*, xviii. 23. The initial letters of the lines when put together made up the Greek words: Ἰησοῦς Χριστὸς Θεοῦ υἱὸς σωτήρ, 'Jesus Christ the Son of God, the Saviour.' The initials of the Greek words make the word Ἰχθύς, 'that is, "fish," in which word Christ is mystically understood,' says Augustine, 'because He was able to live, that is, to exist, without sin in the abyss of this mortality as in the depth of waters.'   [3] *Summa*, ii-ii. q. ii. a. 7.

'Unto this kingdom
Never rose one who had not faith in Christ,
Neither before nor since He to the tree was nailed.' [1]

Even when, in this Heaven, two heathen souls, Rhipeus
and Trajan, are saved, Dante has to exert his utmost
ingenuity to invest them with a faith of some kind,
implicit or explicit, which may gain them an entrance
into the kingdom. The wonder is that he stopped with
two. If, as he plainly means us to understand, the
justice of Trajan and Rhipeus led up to faith, there
seems no reason why the justice and prudence, temperance and fortitude which he freely attributes to Virgil
and his companions in the Limbo of the Unbaptized,
should not have the same saving power in their case.[2]
For some reason the poet's courage seems to have
failed. All that he dares is to make the place of the
virtuous heathen as tolerable as lies within his power.
In their Limbo there is no torment beyond that of unsatisfied longing,—a sigh of the soul for God that
'makes tremulous the eternal air.' The 'noble castle'
of their wisdom, with its seven walls and seven gates,
remains to them, and the green meadow of their fame ;
while round all glows a hemisphere of light, the illumination of the natural reason.[3] The other hemisphere
of faith will never shine for them. There is really no
logic in the moral situation, and we cannot but wish
that Dante had had the courage of his own heart's
desire. It is difficult to believe that the Eagle's answer
contented him. It might ' break his long fast,' but it

[1] *Par.* xix. 103-105.

[2] E.g. Virgil's words to Sordello about his abode in Limbo (*Purg.* vii.
34-36) :

'There dwell I among those who the three saintly
Virtues did not put on, and without vice
The others knew, and followed all of them.'

'The three saintly virtues' are, of course, Faith, Hope, and Love ; 'the
others' are the four cardinal virtues, Prudence, Justice, Temperance,
Fortitude. There seems to be no reason why these four should not have
brought Virgil to Faith, when one of them, Justice, was able to bring
Rhipeus—though, of course, we must remember that Justice implies the
other three.

[3] *Inf.* iv. For the exposition I may refer to my *Exiles of Eternity*,
chap. iv.

could scarcely satisfy his hunger. Indeed, he seems
unconsciously to confess as much. He compares himself to the young stork, the emblem of filial piety, that
lifts its head gratefully to the mother that has fed it:
so did he lift his eyes to the Eagle in filial thankfulness for the food just given. But the kind of food is
indicated by the Eagle's song as it wheeled above him:

> ' As are
> My notes to thee, who dost not comprehend them,
> Such is the eternal judgment to you mortals.' [1]

We cannot suppose that Dante's hunger was satisfied
with the assurance that it could *not* be satisfied.

The Nineteenth Canto closes with a great arraign-
ment in which Dante amply fulfils the command of his
forefather to strike the highest summits. He sets all
the Princes of Christendom, from the Emperor downward, at the bar of final judgment, and foretells their
doom. While indeed it is true, says the Eagle, that
only believers in Christ can be saved, yet many an
Ethiopian who never knew Him will be far nearer
Him than many who cried 'Christ, Christ!' Persian
heathens will condemn Christian kings, when the
volume in which their deeds are recorded is opened.
There shall be seen [2] the destruction of Bohemia soon
to be wrought by the Emperor, Albert I.; [3] the woe
inflicted on Paris by the falsification of the coinage

---

[1] *Par.* xix. 85-99.

[2] We may note here the symmetrical arrangement of ll. 115-141. The
first three *terzine* begin with *Lì si vedrà*, 'There shall be seen'; the
second three with *Vedrassi*, 'Shall be seen'; the third three with the
conjunction *e*. Compare with this the repetition, like a refrain, of *Ora
conosce*, ' Now knoweth he,' in the next Canto, ll. 37-72. The most
striking instance is *Purg.* xii. 25-63, in which four *terzine* begin with
Vedea, four with *O*, and four with *Mostrava*; while a closing terzina
begins each line with one of the three words:

> *Vedea* Troia in cenere e in caverne:
> *O* Ilion, come te basso e vile
> *Mostrava* il segno che lì si discerne !

[3] *Par.* xix. 115-117. It must be taken as a principle of identification
that all the kings referred to were alive and reigning in the year 1300,
the ideal date of the poem. The reference here is to Albert's ruthless
invasion of Bohemia to force his brother-in-law, Wenceslaus IV. ('him of
Bohemia,' l. 125), to exclude his son from the succession in favour of
Charles Martel's son, Charles Robert. For other references to Albert,
see *Purg.* vi. 91-117; *Conv.* iv. 3.

by Philip the Fair;[1] the pride which brought about the
incessant border wars between Scotland and England.[2]
The sensuality and effeminacy of Ferdinand IV. of
Castile, and of Wenceslaus IV. of Bohemia;[3] the
character of Charles II. of Naples, 'the cripple of
Jerusalem'—his goodness represented by an I, his vices
by an M; the avarice and cowardice of Frederick II.
of Sicily: all will be found written in that volume,—
the last in small space crowded with contracted
letters.[4] There too will be recorded the foul doings

---

[1] *Par.* xix. 118-120. Villani (viii. 58) tells us that Philip, to meet the
expenses of his wars in Flanders in 1302, debased the coinage to a third
of its value. Allusion is made prophetically to Philip's death in 1314 by
accident while hunting. The references to Philip are very numerous:
he is 'the evil of France' (*Purg.* vii. 109); 'the new Pilate' (*Purg.* xx.
91); the Giant-lover of the Harlot-Church (*Purg.* xxxii. 152, 155; xxxiii.
45). His outrage on Boniface VIII. at Anagni is mentioned, *Purg.* xx. 91;
his destruction of the Templars, *Purg.* xx. 92, 93.

[2] *Par.* xix. 121-123. The *Inghilese* is Edward I. By *lo Scotto* Dante
probably meant Robert the Bruce, though it was 1306 before he was
crowned. Edward I. is better spoken of in *Purg.* vii. 132, hence Casini
thinks Edward II. must be meant. There is an interesting reference in
Villani (viii. 67) to these border wars: 'In this same year (1303), the said
King Edward being ill, the Scots marched ínto England, for which cause
the king had himself borne in a litter, and went out with the host
against the Scots, and defeated them, and became lord over all the lands
of Scotland, save only the marshes and rugged mountains, wherein the
rebel Scots had taken refuge with their king, which was named Robert
Bruce, which, from lowly birth, had risen to be king.'

[3] *Par.* xix. 124-126. Ferdinand died suddenly in 1312 in his twenty-sixth
year. He bore the strange surname of *El Emplazado*, 'the Summoned.'
Two brothers whom he unjustly put to death for murder summoned him
to appear before the bar of heaven's justice within thirty days. Precisely
at the end of this time he was found dead after dinner, some said of a
surfeit, others by judgment of God. Wenceslaus IV. of Bohemia is again
referred to in similar terms in *Purg.* vii. 100-102.

[4] *Par.* xix. 127-135. Charles II. of Naples was the object of Dante's
deepest contempt. The one good quality he allows him is liberality
(*Par.* viii. 82); Justinian warns him not to oppose the Eagle (*Par.* vi.
106); his wars with Frederick of Aragon make Sicily weep (*Par.* xx. 62);
his inferiority to his father is referred to in *Purg.* vii. 127, and his sale of
his youngest daughter Beatrice to the old marquis of Este, Azzo VIII., in
Purg. xx. 79. In a general denunciation of kings in *Conv.* iv. 6, Charles
and Frederick are singled out for special mention. For Frederick's
relation to Sicily, see Moore's *Studies in Dante*, 2nd series, pp. 296-298.
The meaning of ll. 133-135 seems to be (1) that Frederick is not of sufficient
importance to occupy a large space in the volume of judgment (l. 113);
and (2) that his small allotted space will be so crowded with his vices that
the recording angel will need to write them in contracted forms of the
words and letters. Yet, as Toynbee says, Frederick's reign was 'most
beneficial to Sicily, and he appears to have been greatly beloved by his
subjects.'

of Frederick's uncle and brother,—James of Majorca
and James of Aragon, who dishonoured a noble family
and two crowns;[1] of Dionysius of Portugal, Hakon
Longshanks of Norway, and Stephen Ouros of Rascia,
who counterfeited the coinage of Venice.[2] A word
of warning is then addressed to Hungary to resist
further ill-usage, and to Navarre to hold the shield
of the Pyrenees between her and France,[3] lest her
fate be that of Cyprus, whose cities, Nicosia and
Famagosta, wail 'because of their beast,' Henry ii.
de Lusignan, a French prince who kept pace with 'the
other beasts' in their misgovernment.[4] We may

[1] *Par.* xix. 136-138. Frederick's uncle, James of Majorca, joined
Philip iii. of France in the campaign of 1284 against his own brother,
Pedro iii. of Aragon. For this he lost his kingdom for ten years.
Frederick's brother James ii. of Aragon treacherously yielded up Sicily
to Charles the Lame, but Frederick held the island and was crowned as
'King of Trinacria.' See the passage from Dr. Moore referred to in the
preceding note.

[2] *Par.* xix. 139-141. Dante seems unjust to Dionysius or Diniz of
Portugal, who, on the whole, was a good king. 'He was himself a poet
and loved letters; he was a great administrator and loved justice; above
all he saw the need of agriculture and the arts of peace to take the place
of incessant wars, and nobly earned the title of the *Ré Lavrador*, or
Diniz the Labourer' (*Historians' History*, x. 441). Butler suggests that
leniency to the Moorish population may have been the real ground of the
condemnation: 'It is remarkable that all the sovereigns of the Spanish
peninsula come in for a share in this invective, that about this time there
was a pause in the process of expelling the Mussulmans from that
country, and that nearly all the others named are rulers of territories on
the outskirts of Christendom. It looks almost as if Dante intended this
list as a kind of counterpart to the roll of champions of the faith given in
the last Canto.' Hakon of Norway may be condemned partly for the
incessant wars with Denmark which impoverished the country and
thinned the population, and partly for the extravagant expenditure of
his court. From his time to the union with Sweden and Denmark in
1397, the prosperity of Norway steadily declined. Rascia is the mediæval
name for Servia, which included parts of modern Servia, Bosnia, Croatia,
and Dalmatia. Toynbee (*Dante Dictionary*, p. 460) quotes a Venetian
decree against the counterfeit coinage.

[3] *Par.* xix. 142-144. In 1300 the King of Hungary was Andrew iii.
The crown passed in 1308 to Charles Robert, son of Dante's friend Charles
Martel (Canto viii.). Some think Dante's hope of better days for Hungary
has a touch of sarcasm at the idea of any member of the house of Anjou
governing well. Navarre in the poet's day was an independent kingdom
between France and Spain. The marriage of its Queen, Joan, with
Philip the Fair threatened its absorption in the kingdom of France,
which indeed took place in 1314 under Louis x. Dante's profound distrust
of all French princes makes him warn Navarre to maintain its independence if it do not wish to share the fate of Cyprus.

[4] Dante's contempt for Henry ii. de Lusignan for his misgovernment

suppose that Dante had in mind the warning to princes in *The Wisdom of Solomon*, the opening words of which, 'Love righteousness, ye that be judges of the earth,' were spelt out letter by letter by the righteous rulers of this Heaven: 'Hear therefore, O ye kings, and understand; learn, ye that be judges of the ends of the earth. Give ear, ye that rule the people, and glory in the multitude of nations. For power is given you of the Lord, and sovereignty from the Highest, Who shall try your works, and search out your counsels. Because, being ministers of His kingdom, ye have not judged aright, nor kept the law, nor walked after the counsel of God; horribly and speedily shall He come upon you: for a sharp judgment shall be to them that be in high places. For mercy will soon pardon the meanest: but mighty men shall be mightily tormented.'[1]

of Cyprus is probably intensified by Henry's cowardice at the siege of Acre in 1291. He went to the relief of the city with a few hundred men, but the successful assaults of the Saracens so frightened him that he seized a few ships and fled to Cyprus. Acre fell, and the Holy Land was for ever lost to Christendom.

[1] *Wisdom of Solomon*, vi. 1-6.

CHAPTER XVII

3. *The Eagle's Eye and Eyebrow*

WHEN the Eagle's denunciation of the kings of Christendom ceased, the individual lights, flashing into greater brilliance, broke into song,—both song and brilliance indicating, apparently, their approval of the doom pronounced on unrighteous rulers. At the close of the song Dante seemed to hear that strange inward murmur of the music already referred to, as of the clear waters of a river falling from rock to rock.[1] Then the murmur, gathering itself together, rose through the Eagle's neck and issued in a voice from the beak which spoke forth the praises of the souls that composed the eye and eyebrow. It is, obviously, the utterance of that inward murmur of joy which the whole company of just rulers take in those who are supreme in justice, or, to use the poet's figure, who form the eye which sees and endures the Sun of Righteousness. Of these supreme spirits there are six: one forming the very pupil of the eye, the remaining five

---

[1] This 'murmur of a river which falls clear from rock to rock' is surely meant to be a contrast to the river of tears—the tears of the sinful suffering human race—that fell down through the broken body of the Great Old Man of Crete in *Inf.* xiv. 94-120, to form the Rivers of Hell:

> ' Each part, except the gold, is by a fissure
> Asunder cleft, that dripping is with tears,
> Which gathered together perforate that cavern.
> From rock to rock they fall into this valley ;
> Acheron, Styx, and Phlegethon they form ;
> Then downward go along this narrow sluice
> Unto that point where is no more descending.
> They form Cocytus' (Longfellow).

the circle of the eyelid.[1]   It may be noted that no mention is made of the other eye.   Dante is thinking of the Eagle with its head turned to one side as in the standard of the Roman Empire ; and the one eye which is visible to him is sufficient for his symbolic purpose. Also, the metrical arrangement of the passage may be pointed out.   In each case, after naming the soul in one *terzina*, he adds another beginning, ' Now knoweth he,'—the knowledge being what each has learnt in the new heavenly life.

1. The pupil of the eye, that which has power to gaze directly at the sun, is David, who is described as

> ' the singer of the Holy Spirit
> Who transferred the ark from city unto city.' [2]

It is interesting to ask why David, who had nothing to do with the Roman Empire, is thus set as the very pupil of the eye of the Roman Eagle.   The answer is found in the *De Monarchia* and the *Convito*.   Rome and Israel were to Dante elect nations : the former to establish a temporal empire, the latter a spiritual.   Hence there must be some essential connection between the two,— a connection which Dante finds in the birth of David being nearly contemporary with the founding of Rome : ' It was at one and the same time that David was born and that Rome was born; that is, that Aeneas came from Troy into Italy, which was the origin of the most noble city of Rome, as our books witness.   Thus the divine election of the Roman Empire is made very evident by the birth of the holy city, which was contemporaneous with that of the root from which sprang

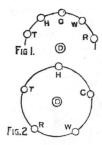

[1] The usual understanding of this is that these five form the semi-circle of the eyebrow, as in Fig. 1.   But the statement in l. 43 that they 'make a *circle* for the eyelid' seems to imply the complete round of the eyelid, as in Fig. 2.   I cannot quite make up my mind between the two arrangements, though I incline to the latter.   Nothing important depends on the question; but it is certain that the arrangement indicates the relative importance of each spirit in Dante's judgment.   E.g. in Fig. 1 Constantine is the central and highest spirit of the upper arch ; in Fig. 2, Hezekiah.   [2] *Par.* xx. 37-39.

the race of Mary.'[1] The connection here indicated is, to our minds, an artificial one; but in the passage before us spiritual reasons are given for making David the pupil of the Eagle's eye. In the first place, he was 'the singer of the Holy Spirit.' His righteousness as a king was by direct inspiration of the Spirit of God, and by the same inspiration he was able to turn the Divine laws into music: 'Thy statutes have been my songs in the house of my pilgrimage.'[2] Further, David 'bore the ark from city unto city.' The reference is to 2 Samuel vi., where it is told how David brought the ark from Kirjath-jearim to Mount Zion. On the Terrace of Pride one of the sculptured scenes of Humility is David dancing before the ark;[3] but in the present passage the ark is looked at in its relation to righteous government. The idea is that David founded his new capital, Jerusalem, which he had just taken from the Jebusites, in religion,—in the ark, which represented the presence and worship of God in the city. In short, David is the pupil of the eye, the very power of vision for the whole Eagle, because through him the revelation is given to all rulers that there is no civil righteousness save by inspiration of the Holy Spirit, and no stability of cities that is not founded on the presence and public recognition and worship of God.

The knowledge which the heavenly life has brought to David is specially connected with his inspiration:

> 'Now knoweth he the merit of his song,
> So far as 'twas effect of his own counsel,
> By the reward which is of equal measure.'[4]

It is obvious that Dante recognizes a human element in the inspiration of Scripture. According to the teaching of the Church, the higher truths cannot be known by the human intellect, 'unless it is fortified by a stronger light, as by the light of faith or prophecy, which is called the light of grace, forasmuch as it is

---

[1] *Conv.* iv. 5 (Miss Hillard's trans.). [2] Ps. cxix. 54.
[3] *Purg.* x. 55-69. [4] *Par.* xx. 40-42.

superadded to nature.'[1] David's merit consisted in his
freely turning his intellect to this *lumen gratiae* and
receiving its illumination; and it is the reward of this
free acceptance which he now enjoys in this Heaven.
A passage in the *De Monarchia* (iii. 4) shows that Dante
regarded the human element in inspiration as entirely
subordinate to the Divine. Discussing the question of
the interpretation of Scripture, he exclaims : 'Oh worst
of crimes, even though a man commit it in his dreams,
to turn to ill use the purpose of the Eternal Spirit.
Such an one does not sin against Moses, or David, or
Job, or Matthew, or Paul, but against the Eternal
Spirit that speaketh in them. For though the reporters
of the words of God are many, yet there is one only
that tells them what to write, even God, who has
deigned to unfold to us His will through the pens of
many writers.'[2]

2. Turning now to the circle of the eyelid, the spirit
nearest the beak is the Emperor Trajan, he who 'consoled the poor widow for her son.'[3] The story as told
in the *Legenda Aurea* is as follows. 'In the time that
Trajan the Emperor reigned, and on a time as he
went toward a battle out of Rome, it happed that in
his way as he should ride, a woman, a widow, came to
him weeping and said: I pray thee, sire, that thou
avenge the death of one my son which innocently and
without cause hath been slain. The Emperor answered:
If I come again from the battle whole and sound then
I shall do justice for the death of thy son. Then said
the widow: Sire, and if thou die in the battle who
shall then avenge his death? And the Emperor said:
He that shall come after me. And the widow said:
Is it not better that thou do to me justice and have the
merit thereof of God than another have it for thee?
Then had Trajan pity and descended from his horse
and did justice in avenging the death of her son.'[4]
The scene is sculptured on the Terrace of Pride on

---

[1] *Summa*, i-ii. q. 109, a. 1.   [2] Church's transl.   [3] *Par.* xx. 43-45.
[4] *The Golden Legend*, Life of St. Gregory (Caxton's trans.).

Mount Purgatory as an example of Humility;[1] and it
is set next to the *bas relief* of David dancing before the
ark, so that there as here Hebrew king and Pagan
emperor are united in the same virtue. Dante's idea
seems to be that justice is rooted in humility: a proud
and overbearing man would have swept a poor widow
out of his path as he marched to battle.

The knowledge which the other world had taught
Trajan is connected with a very curious legend:

> 'Now knoweth he how dear it costs
> Christ not to follow, by the experience
> Of this sweet life and of the opposite.'[2]

The mediæval legend was that St. Gregory, meditating
on the humility and justice of Trajan, prayed God to
pardon him; whereupon a voice from God answered
him: 'I have now heard thy prayer, and have
spared Trajan from the pain perpetual.'[3] The soul
of Trajan then 'returned to its bones,'[4] believed in
Christ, was baptized, and, dying a second time, passed
to this Heaven of Righteous Kings. The experience of
both Hell and Heaven taught him the cost of not
following Christ: for nearly five hundred years[5] he

---

[1] On a capital of the Ducal Palace in Venice is a similar sculpture:
'Trajan on horseback, armed and holding weapons in his right hand,
while the widow is seen on her knees before him, and below is the inscription: TRAIANO IPERADORE CHE FE JUSTITIA A LA VEDOVA' (Didron's
Christian Iconography, ii. 251).

[2] *Par.* xx. 46-48.

[3] *The Golden Legend*, Life of St. Gregory.

[4] *Par.* xx. 107. See below, p. 317.

[5] Trajan died in 117 A.D., and Gregory was Pope 590-604. Even if
Gregory offered up his prayer for him at the very beginning of his
Pontificate, Trajan had been at that time 473 years in the Inferno, a
sufficient time certainly to teach him 'the cost of not following Christ.'
The 'not following Christ,' indeed, sets Trajan's attitude to Christianity
in the most favourable light possible. Dante seems to ignore deliberately
Trajan's reputation as a persecutor of the early Christians. Perhaps he
was influenced by a certain humanity and justice which breathe through
the Emperor's instructions to Pliny the Younger, Proconsul of Pontus
and Bithynia: 'The Christians are not to be sought out: but if they are
brought up and convicted, they must be punished: yet in such a way
that, if any one denies he is a Christian, and proves what he says by
some deed, such as making offerings to our deities, though he may be
open to suspicion about the past, yet he should be pardoned in consequence of his repentance. But indictments put forth anonymously
cannot be admitted in the case of any crime. For this would be a most

had not merely suffered the pains of Hell, but lost the joy of 'this sweet life.'

3. The next spirit on 'the upper arch' of the eyelid is Hezekiah, king of Judah, of whom it is written that 'he did that which was right in the sight of the Lord, according to all that his father David did.' His removal of the high places, breaking of the images, cutting down of the groves, and restoration of the Temple worship, doubtless secured him his place of honour in the eye-brow.[1] It is not this, however, but his penitence which is chosen for special mention: he is described as he who

> 'Postponed death by a true penitence.'

It certainly appears, as many commentators point out, that Dante has here fallen into some confusion concerning two separate moments in Hezekiah's life. No penitence is mentioned in connection with the addition of fifteen years to his life. It is rather the opposite of repentance: he wept sore, and reminded God that he had walked before him 'in truth and with a perfect heart.'[2] It was in consequence of this that his death was post-poned. On his recovery, 'his heart was lifted up'; and when he 'humbled himself for the pride of his heart,' the wrath of the Lord was stayed during his day. This was the occasion of his penitence and its consequence— not postponement of the king's own death, but of the execution of judgment on his country.[3]

The special knowledge which Hezekiah has gained in the heavenly world is the relation of prayer to the Divine providence:

> ' Now knoweth he that the eternal judgment
> Is not transmuted because a worthy prayer
> Makes down below to-morrow of to-day,'—[4]

that is, postpones to the future what otherwise would

---

dangerous precedent and incompatible with the age in which we live.' Tertullian (*Apology*, 2) ridicules this as Justice 'playing a game of evasion on itself'; but perhaps it is as much as could be expected from a heathen ruler who was just and humane at heart.

[1] 2 Kings xviii. 3-7; 2 Chron. xxix. 2 ff., etc.　　　[2] 2 Kings xx. 3.
[3] 2 Chron. xxxii. 24-26.　See Moore's *Studies in Dante*, 1st series, 72.
[4] *Par.* xx. 52-54.

happen in the present. It is strange to find Mr. Vernon
interpreting this as meaning nothing more than that
Hezekiah died eventually, and thus discovered that
'his prayer did not alter God's decree that he must
die.'[1] Hezekiah was never so far deluded as to think
that his prayer had made him immortal upon earth:
the promise was for fifteen years. The reference is, as
already said, to the relation of prayer to the Divine
decrees: if prayers are answered, does not this imply
that they have power to change what has been
ordained by God? Gregory discusses the problem
in a case the exact opposite of that of Hezekiah—the
shortening of life by prayer. A certain monk, when
his Abbot was dying, prayed that he might follow him
within seven days, and, by the Abbot's intercession, his
prayer was granted. Was not this a case of altering
by prayer things predestinate of God? Gregory's reply
is, No: 'those things which holy men do by their
prayers effect, were from all eternity predestinate
to be obtained by prayers.'[2] Aquinas, referring to
this passage, takes the same view: 'We do not pray to
alter the divine plan, but to obtain what God has
arranged to be fulfilled by prayers, "to the end that
men by asking may deserve to obtain what God
Almighty before all ages has arranged to give them,"
as Gregory says.'[3] In short, what Hezekiah now

---

[1] *Readings on the Paradiso*, ii. 104. Yet the author in a footnote
refers to the passage in the *Summa* (ii-ii. q. lxxxiii. a. 2) quoted below in
this paragraph, which gives the true idea.

[2] *The Dialogues of St. Gregory*: an Old English Version, Bk. I.
chap. viii.

[3] *Summa*, ii-ii. q. lxxxiii. a. 2. Comp. the discussion of the same question in the *Contra Gentiles*, Bk. III. 95, 96. The argument is that prayers,
being included as causes in the universal system of things, will produce
effects as other causes do, and are not, any more than those other causes,
to be regarded as an interference with the universal system. 'To say
that we should not pray to gain anything of God, because the order of His
providence is unchangeable, is like saying we should not walk to get to a
place, nor éat to support life. . . . One might as well exclude the effects of
other every-day causes as exclude the effect of prayer. . . . Prayers avail,
not as changing a system arranged from eternity, but as being themselves
part of that system. . . . Hence Gregory says that God does not change
His counsel, though He sometimes changes His sentence, not the sentence
which declares His eternal arrangements, but the sentence which declares
the order of inferior causes, according to which Ezechias was to die'
(Father Rickaby, *Of God and His Creatures*).

knows in Heaven is the mystery of how prayer harmonizes with and fulfils 'the eternal judgment,' instead of being, as it seems, an alteration of it.

4. The fourth of these supreme spirits is Constantine the Great:

> 'The next who follows, with the laws and me,
> Under the good intent which bore bad fruit,
> To give place to the Pastor, made himself a Greek.
> Now knoweth he how the ill deduced
> From his good work not to himself is harmful,
> Although the world may thereby be destroyed.'[1]

The reference is to the 'Donation of Constantine,' 'the most stupendous of all the mediæval forgeries,' as Bryce calls it. In this document, Constantine, after narrating the cure of his leprosy by Pope Sylvester, bestows on him and his successors for ever his 'palace, as also the city of Rome and all the provinces, districts and cities of Italy or of the western regions,'—he himself withdrawing to 'the regions of the East,' to found there a new capital, because 'where the supremacy of priests and the head of the Christian religion has been established by a heavenly Emperor, it is not just that an earthly emperor should hold power.' Dante, of course, accepted the document as genuine, but argued in the *De Monarchia* that it was beyond the power of Constantine to alienate any part of the Empire, and equally beyond the power of the Church to receive it, since her Lord had forbidden her to possess gold or silver. The only thing the Emperor had a right to give, or the Church to receive, was a patrimony to be held by the Vicar of Christ as steward for the poor of

---

[1] *Par.* xx. 55-60. The words 'made himself a Greek' (l. 57) must mean in Dante's lips something more than that Constantine transferred his capital to Byzantium. The Greeks were the ancient enemies of the Trojans, the forefathers of the Roman people. To abandon Rome in order to become a Greek must have seemed to the poet's passionate patriotism almost the act of a renegade. In *Par.* vi. 1-3 we have a parallel condemnation of Constantine for having 'turned the Eagle against the course of heaven'—that is, back to the East (see p. 105, n. 2). The 'Great Old Man' of Crete (*Inf.* xiv. 103 ff.) stands with his back to the East, and 'gazes at Rome as if it were his mirror'—the Divinely ordained seat of Empire. See my *Exiles of Eternity*, pp. 220-224.

Christ.[1] In passage after passage Dante admits Constantine's good intention, while holding firmly that the gift was the destruction of the world. It was the beginning of the lust for wealth and temporal power in the Popes which led to luxury and simony, arrayed Church and Empire as deadly enemies, destroyed civil government in Italy, and provoked the feuds of Guelphs and Ghibellines. So bitterly did Dante feel this that he regarded the birth of Constantine as a calamity to the Roman Empire: 'Oh happy people,' he exclaims, 'oh Ausonia, how glorious hadst thou been, if either he, that weakener of thine empire, had never been born, or if his own pious intention had never deceived him!'[2]

It is this 'pious intention,' however, which helps to form his paradise. One might naturally think that the knowledge of the disastrous consequences of his gift would cast some shadow on his eternal joy; but it is not so. Constantine has now learnt that Divine justice regards nothing but the purity of the motive, 'the interior act of the will.' In the words of Aquinas, 'an event following does not make an act bad which was good, nor good which was bad; for instance, if one give alms to a pauper, which he abuses for sin, nothing is lost to him who did the alms.'[3] 'It is the will,' says Chrysostom, 'which is either rewarded for good or condemned for evil.'

5. The fourth spirit of the eyelid—'on the declining arch'—is William II., surnamed the Good, King of Sicily and Naples. He died in 1189 at the age of

---

[1] *De Mon.* iii. 10.

[2] *De Mon.* ii. 13. The following are the chief references in the *Commedia*. The cure of his leprosy by Sylvester (*Inf.* xxvii. 94: cf. *De Mon.* iii. 10): a lament for the evil wrought by the 'marriage-dower' which he gave to 'the first rich Father'—Sylvester (*Inf.* xix. 115-117), the covering of the Chariot of the Church with the Eagle's feathers, the possessions of the Empire (*Purg.* xxxii. 124-129. Cf. the same imagery for the later Donations of Pepin and Charles, and the monstrous heads which grew on the Chariot in consequence, ll. 130-147 of same Canto). Dante's view was substantially that of the Catharist heretics who called Sylvester the Antichrist, the Man of Sin, the Son of Perdition, and traced the ruin of the Church and its downfall from primitive Christianity to his acceptance of Constantine's Donation (Tocco's *L'Eresia nel Medio Evo*, p. 84).

[3] *Summa*, i.-ii. q. xx. a. 5.

thirty-five—deplored, says the Eagle, by 'the land that weeps for Charles and Frederick yet alive.'[1] According to Villani (iv. 20), 'this William honourably and magnificently ruled the kingdom of Sicily,' and it is said that in his time 'there was more security in the thickets of Sicily than in the cities of other kingdoms.' The body of the good king lies in the magnificent cathedral of Monreale which he built, and the original inscription on his tomb was the simple sentence: *Hic situs est bonus rex Gulielmus.* It is possible that Dante had a special favour for him because he claimed to hold his kingship direct from Christ, instead of His Vicar. In the choir of the Cathedral of Monreale a mosaic above the royal throne shows Christ in the act of placing the crown on William's head; and Dante would have a natural liking for a king who put in practice the thesis of his *De Monarchia.*[2]

The greatness of the love of God for a just king is the special knowledge which Paradise has taught this soul:

> 'Now knoweth he how heaven enamoured is
> With the just king, and in the outward show
> Of his effulgence he still makes it seen.'[3]

The emphasis is on the word 'king,'—justice in a king involving more virtue than in a private citizen. 'As a higher virtue is required to rule a family than simply to rule oneself,' says Aquinas in his *De Regimine Principum,* 'much higher is it to rule a city or kingdom. It

---

[1] *Par.* xx. 61-63. Another stroke at Charles the Lame of Naples and Frederick II. of Sicily. See *Par.* xix. 127-135, and notes on p. 302 above.

[2] In the church *La Martorana* in Palermo is a similar mosaic of William's grandfather, the great Roger I., receiving his crown from the hand of Christ. At the same time, it is to be remembered that these Norman Kings held their kingdom in fief of the Holy See, and William the Good, like his father William the Bad, was an upholder of the Papacy against the Empire. One indelible stain rests on his arms—the frightful atrocities committed by his soldiers in the sack of Thessalonica in 1185. Yet so far as Sicily is concerned, its best days died with him. Richard de St. Germano says: 'In his time the cultivation of law and justice flourished in the realm; every one was contented with his lot; everywhere peace, everywhere security, the traveller feared not the ambushes of robbers, nor the sailer of the sea the attacks of pirates' (quoted by Gibbon in a note to chap. lvi. of the *Decline and Fall*).

[3] *Par.* xx. 64-66.

belongs therefore to surpassing virtue to exercise the office of a king well. And hence in bliss he ought to receive a surpassing reward. . . . For a private person is praised by men, and God reckons it to him for reward, if he succours the needy, brings peace to them at variance, delivers the oppressed, and, finally, if he confers on any one any sort of help or counsel for his welfare. How much more therefore ought he to be praised by men and rewarded by God who establishes a whole province in peace, restrains violence, administers justice, and by his laws and precepts directs what is to be done by men? For in this way also the greatness of a king's virtue appears in that he specially bears the likeness of God, for he performs in his kingdom what God does in the world, whence in Exodus (xxii.) the judges of a multitude are called gods. But so much the more acceptable is any one to God in the degree that he approximates to His likeness, and hence the Apostle warns in Ephesians (v. 1): "*Be ye imitators of God as most dear sons.*" . . . So it may be taken as true that the king's reward is an eternal honour and glory. For what worldly and perishable honour can be compared to this honour, that a man may be a citizen and friend of God, and reckoned among his sons, and may attain with Christ to the heirship of the heavenly kingdom?"[1] It is the burning joy of this reward of a just king that Dante sees flashing from this fourth spirit of the eyebrow.

6. The quotation just given throws into relief the fifth and last spirit of the circle of the eyelid, for if heaven is thus enamoured of a just king, how great must have been the justice of a private citizen when it was counted worthy to rank with emperors and kings in the eternal bliss! It is the soul of the Trojan Rhipeus, of whom we know nothing beyond what an incidental allusion in the Aeneid suggests. Aeneas tells Dido that he was among the fallen in the terrible night of the sack of Troy:

---

[1] *De Reg. Prin.* Bk. i. chaps. viii. ix. (O'Neill's transl.).

> ' Cadit et Rhipeus, iustissimus unus
> Qui fuit in Teucris, et servantissimus aequi :
> Dis aliter visum.' [1]

It is undoubtedly to these lines that Rhipeus owes his place in Paradise—a place inconceivable to earthly minds :

> ' Who would believe, down in the errant world,
> That e'er the Trojan Rhipeus in this round
> Could be the fifth one of the holy lights?
> Now knoweth he enough of what the world
> Has not the power to see of grace divine,
> Although his sight may not discern the bottom.' [2]

Dante is here satisfying his own hunger for the salvation of the heathen; but it is not without meaning that it is a Trojan that is chosen. Mr. Gardner is undoubtedly right in saying that ' Dante's main object is clearly to indicate that the race whom he regards as the ancestors of the Roman People were not without divine light.' [3] The justest citizen among the ancient race, and the justest Emperor among their descendants, are chosen out of the heathen world as examples of a Divine grace which overflows the bounds of the ordinary means of salvation, according to the astonished words of St. Peter : ' Of a truth I perceive that God is no respecter of persons : but in every nation he that feareth him, and worketh righteousness, is accepted with him.' [4]

The most important point in all this may be easily overlooked. It is, I think, the transference of the mystery from the *justice* of God to His *grace* in the salvation of the heathen. We saw how Dante ques-

---

[1] *Aen.* ii. 426-428 : ' Rhipeus too falls, the most just man among the Trojans, and the strictest keeper of equity : to the gods it seemed otherwise.' ' Dis aliter visum ' can scarcely mean that the gods mistook his character, and, thinking him unjust, slew him in the fight. Virgil has the natural feeling that a truly just man ought to be under the special protection of the gods, but that often, for some mysterious reason, it seems otherwise to their larger vision, and the justest of men appears to perish. It is at this point the Christian poet takes up the problem of the heathen poet, and solves it by showing the glory to which Rhipeus passed when he fell in the horrors of that night. This, in short, is the ' otherwise ' as it ' seemed ' to the Eternal Justice.

[2] *Par.* xx. 67-72.   [3] *Dante's Ten Heavens*, p. 149.

[4] Acts x. 34, 35.

tioned the justice of God in the condemnation of
virtuous heathen who never heard of Christ, and was
silenced by the statement that the Divine judgments
are a great deep, too profound for human eyes. And
now he states the other side, and draws great comfort
from it: God's grace is as unfathomable as His justice.
If His justice holds in it strange condemnations of the
heathen, His grace contains equally mysterious salvations of them. This seems plainly to be the idea.
Rhipeus, for all that Paradise has taught him of the
Divine grace by which he was saved, cannot discern
the bottom of it; and to this unfathomableness Dante
returns in ll. 118-120:

> ' That grace which from so deep
> A fountain wells that never creature thrust
> The eye as far as to its primal wave.'

Further, when the Eagle has finished its description of
the souls that form the eye, Dante compares it to a
lark that sings and then is silent in contentment with
' the last sweetness' of its song.[1] Now, 'the last sweetness' is just this closing statement of the unfathomableness of the Divine grace. The thought that the grace
of God was as profound a deep as His justice, and that
out of it might flow marvellous salvations of heathen
souls like Trajan and Rhipeus, was to Dante so surpris
ing and overpowering that an involuntary cry broke
from his lips: 'What things are these?' Whereupon
the Eagle proceeds to explain the cause of his astonishment.[2]

In the first place, it tells Dante he was mistaken in
thinking that Trajan and Rhipeus 'issued from their
bodies' as Gentiles; they were both Christians firmly
believing, one in the future, the other in the past, sufferings of Christ. In the case of Trajan 'the kingdom
of heaven suffered violence'[3]—the violence of 'warm
love and living hope' which conquers the Divine will,

> ' because it willeth to be conquered,
> And, conquered, conquers with its own benignity.'

---

[1] *Par.* xx. 73-78. [2] *Par.* xx. 79-129. [3] Matt. xi. 12.

The 'living hope' is that of Pope Gregory. We must
remember, of course, that hope in the Catholic faith
means specifically 'the hope of glory' in the eternal
world. What Gregory hoped for was the everlasting
blessedness of a soul in Hell. So long as it remained
there it could 'never return to a good will' (ll. 106, 107),
and therefore never could be saved. There must be a
stupendous miracle of resurrection: the soul of Trajan
must 'return to its bones' (l. 107), the bones must be
clothed with flesh (l. 113), and a sufficient space of time
given for the gaining of faith in Christ. All this
happened, according to the story already told. Trajan's
soul remained a short space in the flesh, believed in
Christ,

> ' And in believing was kindled into such a fire
> Of true love, that at the second death
> Worthy it was to come unto this mirth.'

This is the violence of 'warm love' referred to in line
95,—violence which passes unhurt through 'the second
death,' takes the kingdom of heaven by force, and
enters in as 'one born out of due time.' The obvious
meaning is that God's grace is not bound to flow only.
in ordinary and conventional channels. It requires
nothing but faith and a burning love and a living hope
to work miracles, and break the bars of doom, and
storm the kingdom.[1]

---

[1] *Par.* xx. 94-117. The *viva speranza* (l. 95), *viva speme* (l. 109) of St.
Gregory comes from 1 Pet. i. 3 : 'Benedictus Deus et Pater Domini nostri
Jesu Christi, qui secundum magnam misericordiam suam regeneravit nos
in spem vivam per resurrectionem Jesu Christi ex mortuis.' The 'living
hope' might avail to raise the dead by the force of its prayers,—to bring
a soul even from Hell, 'that its will might have power to be moved' (l.
111.). Aquinas found great difficulty in reconciling this story of Trajan
with the orthodox doctrine that prayers are of no avail for those in Hell
because 'they are beyond the bond of charity (*extra vinculum charitatis*)
by means of which the works of the living are connected with the dead.'
Either Trajan was not *finally* consigned to Hell, but punished only for
what he deserved at the moment, to be recalled to life for higher reasons
and otherwise disposed of; or Gregory's prayer only suspended his
punishment till the day of the final judgment (*Summa*, Suppl. q. lxxi. a.
5). Dante does not accept either suggestion. In *Summa*, i-ii. q. cxiv. a.
6, Aquinas asks whether one man can merit for another the first grace, as
Gregory seems to have done for Trajan ; and answers that a man who is
himself in grace may win the first grace for another, not as a matter of

The Eagle turns now to the case of Rhipeus, and traces his salvation to the same unfathomable grace of God, working in him the same supernatural virtues of Faith, Hope, and Love. Rhipeus, however, began with the natural virtue of justice:

'All his love below he set on righteousness.'[1]

Even this natural virtue, however, was possible to him only through that grace whose 'first wave' no created eye has ever seen: man's natural powers, impaired by the Fall, are no longer of themselves able to fulfil the virtues natural to them.[2] Through this love of righteousness, itself inspired by grace, God led this heathen soul on from 'grace to grace' until He 'opened

His eye to our redemption yet to be.'

Accepting the coming salvation by faith, Rhipeus testified against 'the stench of Paganism' by which he was surrounded, and received the inward baptism of the supernatural virtues without which the supernatural life is impossible to man:

'Those Ladies three, whom at the right-hand wheel
Thou didst behold, were unto him for baptism
More than a thousand years before baptizing.'

The teaching of Aquinas is that baptism is absolutely necessary for salvation, since only through it are we united with Christ.[3] But he distinguishes three baptisms—of water, of blood, and of desire. Either of the last two may stand for the baptism of water.

merit, but of friendship with God : 'since a man in a state of grace fulfils the will of God, it is fitting according to the analogy of friendship (*secundum amicitiae proportionem*) that God should fulfil the will of man in the salvation of another, although sometimes it may have an impediment on the part of him whose justification the saint desires.'

[1] *Par.* xx. 121.

[2] *Summa*, i-ii. q. cix. a. 2.

[3] *Summa*, iii. q. lxviii. 2. In this Art. Aquinas teaches that baptism is necessary to salvation—meaning baptism of water ; but that 'when one desires to be baptized, but is by some accident prevented by death, before he receives baptism, he can gain salvation without actual baptism, on account of the desire of baptism, which proceeds from faith which worketh by love, through which God, whose power is not bound to the visible sacraments, sanctifies man inwardly.' Aquinas is speaking of Christians, but the principle would cover the heathen world.

The baptism of blood is martyrdom, fellowship in the passion of Christ. The baptism of desire is when the heart within is moved by the Holy Spirit to faith and love and penitence ; and by this the effect of baptism is communicated to the soul apart from either water or blood.[1] This is obviously the baptism received by Rhipeus. The Spirit of God wrought within his heart the supernatural virtues of Faith, Hope, and Love, and these formed the baptism of desire. Dante indicates that the ordinary place of these 'three Ladies' is where he saw them in the Earthly Paradise—at the right wheel of the Chariot of the Church.[2] But they are not bound to the Chariot. Divine grace is not the slave of the ordinary means by which it works.

The Eagle closes its discourse with a warning to mortals to refrain from passing judgment upon God.

> 'O predestination, how far removed
> Thy root is from the vision of all those
> Who see not the First Cause in its entirety.'[3]

That is, of course, from all created vision, for no creature can know the entire being of God. 'We who see God,' says the Eagle, 'know not yet all the elect.'[4] This deficiency of knowledge, far from troubling them, was a joy: it refined their good with the still higher good of willing what God willed, certain, even in their ignorance, that His will was right and loving. In this, Dante is thinking of the teaching of Aquinas on Predestination. Predestination is part of the universal providence of God which orders everything to its

---

[1] *Summa*, iii. q. lxvi. a. 11. The principle laid down in this Art. is that baptism of water, having its efficacy from the passion of Christ, the baptism of blood, being a direct participation in that passion, will have the same efficacy ; and since both these baptisms have their efficacy from the Holy Spirit as first cause, the baptism of desire, being the inspiration of the heart by the Spirit with faith, love, and penitence, must have the effect of baptism in the ordinary sense.

[2] *Purg.* xxix. 121-129.   [3] *Par.* xx. 130-133.

[4] In *Summa*, i. q. xxiii. a. 7, Aquinas says : 'Some say that out of mankind as many will be saved as angels fell ; some, as many as angels remained ; some, as many as angels fell, and over and above, as many as the number of angels created. But it is better to say that "to God alone is known the number of the elect who are to be set in supernal bliss" (as the *Collecta pro vivis ac defunctis* has it).'

proper end. The end of the elect is eternal life, which consists in the Divine vision; and since this is an end beyond the power of human nature, it is necessary that God should direct us to it, as an archer sends an arrow to the mark. For this, two things are needed—grace in the present and glory in the future; and of both Predestination is the cause. The *ratio* or ground of this Predestination is absolutely unknown to us : it must be referred simply to the will of God, and God of necessity wills His own goodness. Hence Predestination is defined as 'Divine Providence leading rational creatures to their supernatural end, the Beatific Vision,' the entire process, from beginning to end, having its reason in the Divine will alone. It is not dependent on the foreseen merits of the elect; and the prayers of saints (such as Gregory's for Trajan) are only part of the second causes by means of which the decree of Predestination is worked out.[1]

It is not easy to decide Dante's precise meaning when he says that the Eagle's discourse was as 'sweet medicine' 'to make clear his short sight.' Taking the whole context into account, the idea seems to be that the very mystery of Predestination gave room for a larger hope of the salvation of the heathen. The problem of Divine justice, with which Dante's perplexity began, was absorbed and lost in the mysterious movement of the Divine grace—grace which loved to suffer violence, and overflowed the bounds of Revelation and the ordinary means of salvation. This cleared the shortness of his sight, and gave him a 'living hope' that many more than Trajan and Rhipeus might be rescued from the heathen world. And the same hope, apparently, filled these two spirits themselves; for Dante says that, while the Eagle spoke, Trajan and Rhipeus moved their flames like two eyes that wink together, keeping time to its words and increasing his pleasure, as a good harpist makes the strings quiver to the song of a good singer. It is the joy kindled by the hope that, in the

---

[1] *Summa*, i. q. xxiii. a. 1-8. That 'God of necessity wills His own goodness,' is taught in q. xix. a. 3.

Predestination of the mysterious grace of God, many who, like themselves, had 'sat in the region and shadow of death' might yet stand 'before the throne, and before the Lamb,' among the 'great multitude which no man can number, of all nations, and kindreds, and peoples, and tongues.'[1]

[1] Rev. vii. 9. The idea that the quivering of their flames means their joy that the Divine grace had saved themselves, seems to me to fall far short of the entire spirit of the context. The problem is the salvation or non-salvation of the heathen, and the joy is that God's Predestination is so unfathomable that no one knows the number of the elect (ll. 134, 135), and that among them may be many from the world of Paganism of whose salvation 'the erring world' cannot conceive (ll. 67-69). The marvel is, as already said, that Dante used the hope so sparingly to satisfy his long fast.

CHAPTER XVIII[1]

1. *The Golden Stair*

IT is difficult to put ourselves back, even in imagination, into the conceptions which underlie the contrast drawn by the mediæval mind between the Active Life and the Contemplative,—conceptions which run through all Dante's works, and constitute the very 'form' of the *Commedia*. The contrast comes to the poet first on Mount Purgatory in a dream in which he sees Leah,

[1] If we are to believe the strange story told by Boccaccio (*Life of Dante*, xiv.), these last thirteen Cantos were rescued from destruction only by the return of Dante himself from the other world. After his death, the most careful search failed to discover them, and 'every admirer of his in general was enraged that God had not at least lent him to the world so long that he might have had opportunity to finish what little remained of his work.' One of his friends in Ravenna, Piero Giardino, related that after a fruitless search of eight months, the poet's son Jacopo 'came to him one night, near to the hour that we call mattins, and told him that that same night, a little before that hour he, in his sleep, had seen his father, Dante, approach him, clad in whitest garments, and his face shining with an unwonted light; whom he seemed to ask if he were yet living, and to hear in reply that he was, but in the true life, not in ours. Whereon he seemed further to ask him if he had finished his work or ever he passed to that true life ; and, if he had finished it, where was the missing part which they had never been able to find. To this he seemed to hear again in answer, "Yea! I finished it." Whereon it seemed that he took him by the hand and led him to that chamber where he was wont to sleep when he was living in this life; and touching a certain spot, he said, "Here is that which ye so long have sought." And no sooner was uttered that word than it seemed that both Dante and sleep departed from him at the same moment.' The two friends went together 'to the place indicated, and there found a mat fixed to the wall, which they lightly raised, and found a recess in the wall which neither of them had ever seen, and there they found certain writings, all mouldy with the damp of the wall, and ready to rot had they stayed there much longer ; and when they had carefully removed the mould and read, they saw that they contained the thirteen cantos so long sought by them.' The discovery saved us from an attempt on the part of Dante's sons, Jacopo and Piero, to complete their father's work, to which they were being urged by their friends.

the symbol of the Active Life, gathering flowers for
her own adornment, while her sister Rachel, the Life
Contemplative, sits at the mirror gazing ever at her
own beauteous eyes.[1] The dream finds its correction
and its fulfilment in the Earthly Paradise on the
mountain top: Matelda, the true Active Life, gathers
the flowers, *not* for her own adornment, but in pure
joy in God's works[2]; and Beatrice, as the symbol of
Heavenly Contemplation, instead of gazing at her own
eyes in a mirror turns them to Christ, until they
become mirrors of His twofold nature.[3] Then in the
De Monarchia (iii. 16), the contrast between the two
Lives is made to serve the purposes of Dante's political
and ecclesiastical theory: 'Two ends have been laid
down by the ineffable Providence of God for man to
aim at: the blessedness of this life, which consists in
the exercise of his natural powers, and which is pre-
figured in the earthly Paradise; and next, the blessedness of the life eternal, which consists in the fruition
of the sight of God's countenance, and to which man
by his own natural powers cannot rise, if he be not
aided by the divine light; and this blessedness is understood by the heavenly Paradise. . . . Therefore man
had need of two guides for his life, as he had a twofold
end in life; whereof one is the Supreme Pontiff, to
lead mankind to eternal life, according to the things
revealed to us; and the other is the Emperor, to guide
mankind to happiness in this world, in accordance
with the teaching of philosophy.'[4] The contrast
underlies very plainly the Cantos through which we
have just gone and the passage before us. The three
Heavens immediately below are Heavens of the Active
Life: in the Sun, the activity of the intellect engaged
on the problems of Theology; in Mars, of soldiers of
the Cross warring for the Faith; in Jupiter, of rulers
governing the State in justice. These three forms of the

---

[1] *Purg.* xxvii. 91-108.   [2] *Purg.* xxviii. 37-81.
[3] *Purg.* xxxi. 115-123. For expositions of these three references, I may
refer to my *Prisoners of Hope*, pp. 361-365 (Rachel and Leah); 376-382
(Matelda); 421; 459-461 (Christ reflected in the eyes of Beatrice).
[4] Church's version.

Active Life lead up to the Contemplative, and in Dante's regard constitute the necessary foundation of it.[1]

The origin of this all-pervading contrast was the peculiar cleavage made by Aristotle between the practical Reason and the theoretical.[2] According to his philosophy, Reason is the distinguishing peculiarity of man. But Reason is partly passive, and partly active. As passive, it is dependent on the material world for sense-impressions capable of being converted into thought, and on the world of men for relations of practical life, out of which Ethics can be evolved. This aspect of Reason, dependent on a world of things beyond itself, cannot be its highest, purest form. There must be another which is active, self-determining, immortal, dealing directly and immediately with universal ideas within itself. This contemplation, this emancipation of the Reason from all dependence on the ever-moving world of time and sense by its own essential power of vision of ideas, constitutes, says Aristotle, the true happiness of man, as it constitutes the happiness of God. He is positively contemptuous of the idea that a Divine being could stoop to any kind of practical activity. 'Our conception of the Gods is that they are pre-eminently happy and fortunate. But what kind of actions do we properly attribute to them? Are they just actions? But it would make the Gods ridiculous to suppose that they form contracts, restore deposits, and so on. Are they then

---

[1] *De Mon.* i. 3. Aquinas expresses the connection by saying that the active virtues are related to the contemplative not *essentialiter* but *dispositive*. By *dispositive* he means that the active virtues create a certain disposition of soul and of circumstances favourable to contemplation. 'The act of contemplation, in which essentially consists the contemplative life, is hindered, both by the vehemence of the passions, by which the "intention" of the soul is withdrawn from objects of intellect to objects of sense, and by tumults of the outward life. But moral virtues check the vehemence of the passions and allay the tumults of outward occupations. And therefore the moral virtues pertain to the contemplative life *dispositive*' (Summa, ii-ii. q. clxxx. a. 2). See also p. 330 below for the function of civil government in producing a state of peace in which the contemplative life will become possible.

[2] For a statement and criticism of Aristotle's view of the Practical and Theoretical Reason, see Prof. Edward Caird's *Evolution of Theology in the Greek Philosophers*, Lects. xi-xiv.

courageous actions? Do the Gods endure dangers and alarms for the sake of honour? Or liberal actions? But to whom should they give money? It would be absurd to suppose that they have a currency or anything of the kind. Again, what will be the nature of their temperate actions? Surely to praise the Gods for temperance is to degrade them; they are exempt from low desires. We may go through the whole category of virtues, and it will appear that whatever relates to moral action is petty and unworthy of the Gods. Yet the Gods are universally conceived as living and therefore as displaying activity; they are certainly not conceived as sleeping like Endymion. If then action and still more production is denied to one who is alive, what is left but speculation? It follows that the activity of God being pre-eminently blissful will be speculative, and if so then the human activity which is most nearly related to it will be most capable of happiness.'[1]

Further, this activity of contemplation, being the true life of God, lies beyond the power of man as man; it becomes possible only in virtue of a Divine something in him, which Aristotle inconsistently regards as at once our true nature and a transcendence of it. 'But such a life will be too good for Man. He will enjoy such a life not in virtue of his humanity but in virtue of some divine element within him, and the superiority of this activity [i.e. contemplation] to the activity of any other virtue will be proportionate to the superiority of this divine element in man to his composite or material nature. If then the reason is divine in comparison with the rest of Man's nature, the life which accords with reason will be divine in comparison with human life in general. Nor is it right to follow the advice of people who say that the thoughts of men should not be too high for humanity, or the thoughts of mortals too high for mortality; for a man, as far as in him lies, should seek immortality and do all that is in his power to live in accordance

[1] *Ethics*, x. 8 (Welldon's transl.).

with the highest part of his nature, as, although that part is insignificant in size, yet in power and honour it is far superior to all the rest. It would seem too that this is the true self of every one, if a man's true self is his supreme or better part.'[1]

It requires no deep acquaintance with mediæval theology to see that the whole system of Aquinas is based on this Aristotelian disruption of human nature into a natural and a supernatural element, corresponding to the Active and Contemplative Lives. By the natural virtues of Prudence, Justice, Temperance, Fortitude, man is equal to the demands of the Active Life; but the Contemplative Life, being supernatural, is possible only when man is lifted beyond himself and becomes 'partaker of the divine nature,'[2] by the power of the supernatural virtues of Faith, Hope, and Love. In the following passage Aquinas expressly bases the superiority of the Contemplative Life on the reasons given by Aristotle. 'We must say then the contemplative life is, absolutely speaking, better than the active. Which the Philosopher proves by eight reasons: of which the first is, because the contemplative life becomes a man in respect of the most excellent element in his nature, namely, his understanding. The second is, because the contemplative life can be more continuous, though not in its highest act. The third is, because the delight of the contemplative life is greater than that of the active. The fourth is, because in the contemplative life man is more self-sufficient and needs fewer things. The fifth is, because the contemplative life is loved for its own sake, while the active life is directed to something ulterior to itself. The sixth is, because the contemplative life consists in a certain stillness and rest, according to the text: "Be still and see that I am God." The seventh is, because the contemplative life is formed upon divine things, but the active life upon human things. The eighth is, because the contemplative life is life according to that which is proper to man, namely, the intellect, whereas in the

---

[1] *Ethics*, x. 7 (Welldon).   [2] 2 Peter i. 4.

operations of the active life the lower powers concur,
which are common to us with dumb animals. A ninth
reason is added by our Lord when He says: "Mary
hath chosen the good part, which shall not be taken
away from her" (Luke x. 42), which is explained by
Augustine: "From thee shall one day be taken away
the burden of necessity, but the sweetness of truth is
eternal."[1] In another passage, discussing the question
whether happiness is an activity of the speculative or
of the practical understanding, Aquinas says: 'In the
contemplative life man is partaker with his betters,
namely, with God and the angels, to whom he is
assimilated by happiness: but in what concerns the
active life other animals also after a fashion are
partakers with men, albeit imperfectly. And therefore
the last and perfect happiness which is expected in the
world to come, must consist mainly in contemplation.
But imperfect happiness, such as can be had here,
consists primarily and principally in contemplation,
but secondarily in the activity of the practical understanding directing human actions and passions.'[2] The
lost are described by Dante as those 'who have fore-
gone the good of the intellect'—that good being the
vision of truth, the substance or essence of God
Himself.[3]

I have thought it well to give this perhaps too
lengthy explanation in order that we may have before
us the ideas which were certainly in Dante's mind
when he set the contemplative saints in a higher bliss
than the three forms of the active life in the Heavens
immediately preceding. We must not, however, press
the contrast beyond the poet's intention, as if the

---

[1] *Summa*, ii-ii. q. clxxxii. a. 1 (Rickaby).

[2] *Summa*, i-ii. q. iii. a. 5 (Rickaby). Comp. Father Rickaby's discussion
of Happiness in his *Moral Philosophy*, pp. 3-27.

[3] *Inf.* iii. 17-18. 'The good and evil of the speculative intellect, which
is neither practical nor productive, are truth and falsehood. For the
function of the intellect generally is the apprehension of truth' (*Ethics*,
vi. 2). It is perhaps to this passage Dante refers in the *Convito* (ii. 14)
when he says that our power to see the truth by speculation is 'our final
perfection, as saith the Philosopher in the sixth of the *Ethics*, when he
says that the truth is the good of the intellect.'

spirits of the active life had no share in the contemplative. The eternal blessedness of the Theologians, Warriors, and Rulers consists also in contemplation, the vision of God 'face to face.' But their vision is conceived of as conditioned by the active life in which they spent their earthly years, their very mingling with practical affairs shutting them out from the depth of vision enjoyed by souls that had withdrawn themselves from the distractions of the world. It is possible that Dante divined some higher unity which transcended the contrast, and that, for example, in choosing St. Bernard to take the place of Beatrice as his guide in the White Rose, his meaning is that the final vision is given in its fulness to one in whom Action and Contemplation had dwelt in perfect balance and harmony.[1]

We are now ready to examine the symbolic correspondences between Saturn, 'the seventh splendour,' and the souls whom Dante sees in it. To begin with, it is the cold planet,—Jupiter is called 'the temperate sixth star,' because it is midway 'between the cold of Saturn and the heat of Mars.'[2] At the same time, this cold is mingled with heat, as Beatrice tells her companion when they rise into it:

> 'We are uplifted to the seventh splendour,
> That underneath the burning Lion's breast
> Now radiates downward mingled with its power.'[3]

The Lion is the sign of the Zodiac in which Saturn was at Easter 1300. The mingling of cold and heat may signify, no doubt, as Plumptre says, that 'extremes meet in the experience of the mystic,' as the volcano burns beneath the snow. The meaning, however, is probably more specific. Dante is not thinking merely of alternations between fiery ecstasy and cold reaction. The coldness must refer to that deadness to the world, and the heat to the burning desire for the vision of

---

[1] *Par.* xxxi. 58 ff.   See below, pp. 490-494, and Introduction, p. 31.
[2] *Par.* xviii. 68; xxii. 145, 146; *Purg.* xix. 1-3; *Conv.* ii. 14; *Canz.* xv. 7. Comp. *Georgics*, i. 336, 'Frigida Saturni sese quo stella receptet.'
[3] *Par.* xxi. 13-15.

God, without which contemplation is impossible. We may add to this the Lion's courage with which men, thus cold and dead to the world, are able to confront the world's sins, as in the thunder-peal of judgment which follows St. Peter Damian's denunciation of Cardinals at the end of this Canto.

In the next place, the planet is described as

> the crystal which doth bear the name,
> Circling the world, of its illustrious leader,
> Beneath whom all wickedness lay dead.[1]

The reference is, of course, to the Golden Age of heathen mythology under Saturn, King of Crete. Dethroned by his son Jupiter, he established a kingdom in Italy of pastoral and idyllic peace, founded upon law, order, and justice. What underlies the reference is the twofold condition of contemplation,—internal and external peace. Two requisites are specially named by Aquinas: 'rest from the disturbing forces of passion: that is attained by the moral virtues and prudence. Likewise rest from exterior troubles, which is the whole aim of civil life and government.'[2] The Golden Age of Saturn fulfilled both conditions. It was an age of 'crystal' purity, when 'every wickedness lay dead'; and it was an age when justice secured that state of heavenly peace in which the contemplative life becomes possible.

Within this crystal sphere of purity and peace Dante sees, as in a mirror, a great stairway stretching up, and on its shining steps so many 'splendours' descending that heaven seemed to be pouring down all its stars:

---

[1] *Par.* xxi. 25-27. Comp. *Inf.* xiv. 95, 96: 'Crete, under whose king the world once was chaste'; *Purg.* xxviii. 139 (poets who sang of the Golden Age were dreaming of the Earthly Paradise, symbolic of civil justice and peace); *De Mon.* i. 11.: 'The world is ordered best when justice is most paramount therein: whence Virgil, wishing to celebrate that age, which in his own time seemed to be arising, sang in his *Bucolics* (*Ecl.* iv. 6): "Now doth the Virgin return, and the kingdom of Saturn." For Justice was named "the Virgin," and also Astraea. The kingdom of Saturn was the good time, which they also called the Golden Age.' Cf. *Aen.* viii. 319-325.

[2] *Cont. Gent.* iii. 37; *Summa*, ii-ii. q. clxxxii. a. 3.

> Of colour of gold, in which a ray shines through,
> I saw a ladder to so great a height
> Uplifted that my eye pursued it not.[1]

This stairway is identified in the next Canto (ll. 70-72) with Jacob's ladder,—the patriarch being able to see what is as yet hidden from Dante, the upper part thronged with angels.[2] The comparison to gold implies that contemplation is the most precious form of life, and the ray shining through is probably the *lumen gratiae* by which the natural powers are raised, as it were, above themselves, or perhaps the *lumen gloriae*, without which God in His essence cannot be seen by man.

Concerning this 'scala santa' there are several important points which it may be helpful to gather out of the narrative. The first is the height of the ladder—it ascends beyond Dante's power of vision. As St. Benedict afterwards explains, it goes up to 'the last sphere,' the Empyrean, which 'is not in place,' since it is only in the Divine Mind, 'and is not on poles,' that is, has no movement, because it has no unrest of desire unsatisfied.[3] Dante being unable yet to rise to this last height of contemplation, the contemplative saints in accommodation to his weakness descend to 'a

---

[1] *Par.* xxi. 28-30. The 'colour of gold, in which a ray shines through' (*traluce*) is from Rev. xxi. 21 : 'Et platea civitatis aurum mundum tamquam vitrum perlucidum' (Vulg.).

[2] Gen. xxviii. 12. Butler says 'it is hard to believe that there was not a secondary intention of paying a magnificent compliment to Can Grande, whose ladder is made to play a similar part in Saturn to the imperial eagle in Jupiter.' This seems to me utterly unlikely : Dante would never thus set the ladder of the Vicar of the Emperor a whole heaven above the Eagle of the Emperor himself. Compare the relative positions of the two in *Par.* xvii. 72—'who *above* the ladder bears the holy bird.' The imagination of the mystics, like the angels, was always ascending and descending on Jacob's Ladder. The figure lent itself pliantly to every play of pious fancy, and the Ladder could be fitted with any number of steps desired. To Bonaventura, it is now 'nostra scala,' Christ, whose threefold substance—corporeal, spiritual, divine—form the steps; and again the Virgin, the 'scala coelica,' by which the ascent to the eternal is opened. To Bernard, it is Humility and Obedience, the ascending and descending of the angels implying that Obedience is the angelic life.

[3] *Par.* xxii. 61-69 ; *Conv.* ii. 4. See below, p. 462 ff.

certain step' to meet him. What this step is must be carefully examined later on.

Notice, in the next place, a certain union of action and contemplation in these saints. According to the teaching of Aquinas, 'after the state of the present life there will be no active life; for then either external actions will wholly cease, or they will be referred to contemplation.' This last clause, however, seems to allow a good deal of action to enter into the contemplation of the saints *in patria*. For example, the traditional interpretation of Jacob's ladder was that the ascending of the Angels was for contemplation, and their descending for action; and the subordination of action to contemplation is asserted by Gregory when he says that the Angels 'do not so go forth from the divine vision, that they are deprived of the joys of internal contemplation.'[1] And although Aquinas denies to the souls of the blessed what he grants freely to Angels, namely, the active life of teaching inferiors the mysteries of God, just this is what Dante here represents these spirits as doing. St. Peter Damian tells him that he came so far down the steps of 'the holy ladder' 'to do him joyance' with his speech and light;[2] and both he and St. Benedict act as his teachers. Indeed, all through the *Paradiso* the souls suspend their absorption in the Beatific Vision to instruct the Pilgrim in the Divine mysteries. Beatrice herself left the place where she was 'sitting with the ancient Rachel,' symbol of Contemplation, in order to visit Limbo and secure Virgil as his guide;[3] and afterwards to be herself his guide to the final vision. It is difficult to see any basis for the doctrine of the Intercession of the Saints if they are debarred from all action, prayer itself being a certain action of the soul.

We come now to the difficult question of the steps of the Ladder. The following curious passage describing

[1] *Summa*, ii-ii. q. clxxxi. a. 4.
[2] *Par.* xxi. 64-66.
[3] *Inf.* ii. 52-126. Beatrice came at the request of Lucia, Lucia was sent by the Virgin. All three were thus engaged in the active life on his behalf.

the descending saints demands some answer to the question:

> And as, according to their natural custom,
> The daws together at the break of day
> Do move themselves to warm their feathers cold;
> Then some do go away without return,
> Others round back to where they started from,
> And others wheeling make a sojourn;
> Such fashion it appeared to me was there
> Within that sparkling which together came,
> Soon as upon a certain step it struck.[1]

The meaning turns, obviously, on the words 'a certain step,' and one cannot but be surprised at the unanimity with which commentators ignore them. They act on Virgil's advice to Dante about the Neutrals.

> 'Non ragioniam di lor, ma guarda e passa.'[2]

To Dante's own mind, 'a certain step' must have had some quite definite meaning. In its most general sense, it is the step at which communication became possible between him and these great contemplative spirits. The top of the ladder stretched far beyond his sight into the Divine mysteries of the highest Heavens. Out of the vision of those mysteries, these spirits must come down in condescension to the weakness of his intellect. The question is, how far?—to what step of the ladder? There is a passage in Aquinas which, I think, gives the answer. 'Although the contemplative life,' he says, 'is perfected in one single act of contemplation, yet men ascend to it by various operations of the mind, as hearing, reading, prayer, meditation, consideration, thought, etc.' He then takes Richard of St. Victor's six steps of Contemplation, reduced by Richard himself under three heads, *Cogitatio* (*Thought*), *Meditatio* (Investigation or Consideration), and *Contemplatio* (Contemplation proper). The organ of Thought is Imagination, the faculty by which images received through the senses are converted into mental forms. The organ of Meditation is Reason, the faculty by which we search out the principles of certain truths. The organ of

---

[1] *Par.* xxi. 34-42. [2] *Inf.* iii. 51.

Contemplation is the Intellect, the faculty which, by one single intuitive gaze, sees the invisible truth which lies above both Imagination and Reason.[1]

Now, the 'certain step' to which these contemplative spirits descend on the ladder seems to me to correspond to the second of these grades, Meditation, defined by Richard as 'consideration of the mind engaged in the search for truth.' Aquinas identifies it with 'speculation,' and after quoting Augustine to the effect that this word is derived from *speculum*, a mirror, not *specula*, a watch-tower, adds: 'To see anything through a mirror is to see the cause by the effect, in which its likeness shines back; from which it is seen that speculation is reduced to meditation.'[2] Now, it so happens that Dante in a very pointed way draws attention to this 'speculation' as the seeing of things in a mirror, by the use of *specchio*, the Italian form of *speculum*, twice in one *terzina*. Beatrice, after telling him that they have entered 'the seventh splendour,' says:

> 'Ficca diretro agli occhi tuoi la mente,
> E fa di quegli *specchi* alla figura,
> Che in questo *specchio* ti sarà parvente.'[3]

'Fix behind thine eyes thy mind, and make of those *mirrors* to the figure which in this *mirror* (i.e. Saturn) shall be to thee apparent.' In plain words, Dante is conscious that even yet he sees nothing 'face to face,' but only—to quote the passage from the Vulgate which was in his mind—*per speculum in aenigmate*.[4] What he has power to see is the reflection of a reflection from one mirror to another. Nay, even this is an understatement. We must remember that this sphere of

---

[1] *Summa*, ii-ii. q. clxxx. a. 3.   Richard of St. Victor's distinction of the three, as quoted by Aquinas, is as follows: 'Contemplatio est perspicax, et liber contuitus animi in res perspiciendas; meditatio autem est intuitus animi in veritatis inquisitione occupatus; cogitatio autem est animi respectus ad evagationem pronus.' For some account of Richard and his theology, see Vaughan's *Hours with the Mystics*, i. 159 ff. His six steps of Contemplation, by which we ascend through creatures to the vision of God, are given in *Summa*, ii-ii. q. clxxx. a. 4.

[2] *Summa*, ii-ii. q. clxxx. a. 3.

[3] *Par.* xxi. 16-18.

[4] 1 Cor. xiii. 12: 'Videmus nunc per speculum in aenigmate, tunc autem facie ad faciem.'

Saturn is presided over by the Thrones, the third Order of Angels, and that Dante expressly calls them 'mirrors,' reflecting the Divine judgments to all spheres from this downward.[1] Hence we have a succession of mirrors: the mirror of the Thrones sends an image of the Divine truth into the mirror of Saturn ; the mirror of Saturn reflects it to the mirror of the poet's eyes; and finally, the mirror of the eyes reflects it to the mind behind the eyes. No wonder Dante says these spirits who see 'face to face' had to descend to this step of speculation, before they could hold any communication with one so dependent on the *specula* or mirrors of Divine truth.

And now we are in a position to understand better the curious comparison of the Contemplatives to a flock of daws flying in the morning air. It is possible that daws are taken because, as Benvenuto suggests, they love solitude and choose the desert for their habitation. But what we specially wish to know is why the contemplative saints, when they reach this step of speculation, should fly off in the threefold fashion so carefully described by Dante. It is easy to smile at the question as an over-subtlety of the commentator; but long experience of Dante's similes teaches one that they are never without a central core of significance. It might seem a mere expository conceit to say that the three movements of the daws represent three movements of the contemplative mind, were it not the fact that Aquinas gravely discusses this very question: 'Whether the operation of contemplation is rightly distinguished by three motions, circular, straight and oblique.' In this article he quotes Richard of St. Victor to the effect that in contemplation there are many motions after 'the similitude of the flying things of the heaven,' and proceeds to reduce these many motions to the three just named : 'the circular, by which all operations of the soul are reduced to simple contemplation of the divine truth; the straight, by which it is raised from exterior objects of sense to ideas of the

[1] *Par.* ix. 61-63.

intellect; the oblique, by which it uses divine illuminations for purposes of reasoning.'[1] It may be admitted
that it is not easy to identify these three motions of
the soul with the comparison to the three motions of
the daws; but it is still less easy to suppose that this
discussion by Aquinas was not before Dante's mind.
What I understand him to mean is to this general
effect. These spirits, in condescension to the weakness
of his intellect, came down from those heights of contemplation to which he had as yet no power to follow
them. They paused at 'a certain step'—that, namely,
at which meditation or speculation meets contemplation proper, and from which they could hold communication with Dante, who, as we saw, had risen only
to this stage of speculation. It is the step at which
the soul returns from the ecstasy of contemplation to
'discourse of reason': that is, from the rapt gaze of the
soul which, at one single glance, sees all things in God,
to the division of the intellect on the multiplicity of
objects. It is the various forms of this *discursus
rationis* that are represented by the three motions of the
birds.[2] Some of the souls 'go away without return,' that
is, without doubling back: they represent the *straight*
motion which goes direct from things of sense to things
of intellect. Some 'turn back to where they started
from'—to the certain step from which their flight began:

---

[1] *Summa*, ii-ii. q. clxxx. a. 6. The discussion in Aquinas has its origin
in Dionysius the Areopagite's treatise *On the Divine Names* (ch. iv. part. i.
lect. 7), where a distinction is drawn between these three motions of
the soul in contemplation. It is to be remembered that with the scholastics
the word *motion* covered any succession of changes in the mind. Dante
is only throwing these intellectual movements into a visible form when
he compares the motions of these saints to the flight of birds. See note
on p. 91, above.

[2] *Discursus* is, of course, to be taken in its proper sense, as a certain
running hither and thither, comparing, discriminating, drawing infer-
ences: a process which would have been unnecessary to these spirits had
Dante been able to see, as they did, the whole in one intuitive glance.
Comp. Raphael's distinction between Reason in its human and angelic
forms:

'whence the Soul
Reason receives, and Reason is her being,
Discursive or Intuitive: Discourse
Is oftenest yours, the latter most is ours'
(*Par. Lost*, v. 486-489).

they represent the *oblique* motion, which is composed, says Aquinas, of a mixture of straight and circular, of reason and divine illumination.   And some, 'wheeling, make a sojourn': they represent the *circular* motion,— that perfect movement by which the intellect turns uniformly round one centre of Divine truth, the 'sojourn' signifying the immobility of this motion, as of a revolving wheel that sleeps upon the axle.

CHAPTER XIX

2. *St. Peter Damian and St. Benedict*

WE come now to the narrative. Just as 'the spirits contemplative' had to come down to 'a certain step' of the Ladder in condescension to the weakness of Dante's intellect, so this Heaven mercifully accommodated itself to the corresponding weakness of his senses. On entering this 'seventh splendour' the poet, in the effort to rise into the contemplative spirit, fixed his eyes on his Lady's face, and with his eyes his mind, 'withdrawn from every other intent'; yet the intensity of his gaze could not draw from her one smile. She explains that her beauty, which had increased with every Heaven, has now become so great that a smile would burn him up like Semele, and shatter his 'mortal power' as with a lightning flash. We must remember the symbolic sense which the smile bears in the *Convito* (iii. 15): 'The *eyes* of Wisdom are her demonstrations, whereby the truth is seen with the greatest certainty; and her *smile* is her persuasions, whereby the inner light of Wisdom is shown beneath any veil.'[1] In the lower Heavens Dante was able to bear the persuasion of the smile, but the full beauty of contemplation would have been too great for his mere mortal power. The capacity comes in the next Heaven when 'the shining substance'

---

[1] This is in exposition of the following lines in Canzone ii. :
> Things are revealed within her countenance
> Which show us of the joys of Paradise;
> Within her eyes, I say, and her sweet smile,
> Which bringeth Love to her as to his place.
> They overpower our intellect
> As the sun's ray doth a feeble sight.

of Christ blinds his eyes and so dilates his mind that it
'issues forth from itself.'[1]

A similar compassion is shown to the infirmity of
his hearing. The spirit that came nearest him on the
Ladder was that of St. Peter Damiani, and Dante,
receiving liberty from Beatrice, puts to him two
questions : why he has placed himself so near him, and
why 'the sweet symphony of Paradise,' which through
all the lower Heavens sounds so devoutly, is silent
here. Replying to the last question first, Damiani says

> ' there is no singing here
> For the same cause that Beatrice hath not smiled,'—

sight and hearing are alike mortal. As to why he had
descended so far, it was simply to give joy to the Pilgrim
by his word and light. It was not because he had more
love than others, for, as Dante may see from their
shining, many higher up the Ladder have as great or
greater love than he; but the high Love allots to each
his task.[2] This, however, is not precisely what Dante
wishes to know,—why this spirit alone among all his
companions was predestinated to this office.

Scarcely was the last word spoken when the light
began to revolve like a swift millstone on its own
centre,[3]—the motion representing, apparently, the joy
of obeying the decree of God in 'free love,' asking no
question why. No power of contemplation, however
lofty, says Damiani, can answer this question. The
Divine light, for example, was focussed upon himself,
piercing through the light in which he was enveloped;
its power, conjoined with his own sight, uplifted him
so far above himself that he was able to see the Divine
Essence from which it flowed; and from this vision
came the joy with which he flamed. Yet all this gave
him no power to pierce 'the abyss of the eternal statute.'
Nay more, he says,

> 'That soul in Heaven that shineth clearest,
> That Seraph who hath his eye most fixed on God,
> Will this demand of thine not satisfy.'

---

[1] *Par.* xxiii. 19-48. See below, p. 371.
[2] *Par.* xxi. 43-72.   [3] Comp. *Par.* xii. 1-3.

Hence Dante is enjoined to warn men down below against the presumption of asking such a question: if minds that shine in Heaven cannot answer it, how should minds on earth that are darkened with their own smoke?[1]   Dante is sometimes censured for again raising the question of Predestination, after the assurance of the Eagle in the preceding Heaven that it lay entirely beyond man's sight; but the problem here is not quite the same.   The one is Predestination to salvation to be wrought out *in time*;[2] the other is Predestination to service *in eternity*; and it was not unnatural for Dante to think that contemplative spirits *in patria* might know the ground or principle of the Divine decree which allotted to each his task.

At this rebuke Dante abandons the question, and confines himself to asking humbly who this spirit is; and perhaps, in the answer, we may find at least Dante's own reason for electing him to this service, as the soul that could come nearest to himself.   His name, as we have seen, was Peter Damiani.   He was born at Ravenna in 1007, and died at Faenza in 1072.   The family was poor, and one of his brothers made a swineherd of the child.   From this he was rescued by Damian, another brother, who took care to have him well educated; and it was in gratitude for this fatherly care that he called himself Petrus Damiani—Peter son of Damian.   In the midst of a most successful career as a teacher, he suddenly withdrew to the Benedictine monastery of Fonte Avellana under the shadow of the great ridge of the Apennines called Monte Catria, near Gubbio. His learning and austerity of life soon raised him to the office of Abbot.   He describes himself as so satisfied with his own contemplative thoughts that he subsisted on food of olive juice.[3]   The commentators explain this to mean food seasoned with olive oil instead of rich condiments, but this is doubtful.   Butler in his *Lives*

---

[1] *Par.* xxi. 73-102.
[2] *Summa*, iii. q. xxiv. a. 1: 'Predestination is properly understood as a divine pre-ordination from eternity of those things which through the grace of God are to be done in time.'   [3] *Par.* xxi. 115-117.

of the Saints (Feb. 23) says of him : 'He lived shut up in his cell as in a prison, fasted every day except festivals, and allowed himself no other subsistence than coarse bread, bran, herbs, and water, and this he never drank fresh, but what he had kept from the day before.' For the reformation of monasticism Damiani trusted almost entirely to a penitential discipline which cleared off the debt of sin according to a fixed scale of rates, by flogging, repetition of Psalms, or an equivalent in money; and the pains he laid on others he certainly did not shrink from himself. He describes himself in this passage in words which have given rise to much dispute. Accepting the reading in the Oxford text,[1] the translation is as follows : 'In that place (the monastery of Fonte Avellana) I was Pier Damiano; and Peter the Sinner was I in the house of Our Lady upon the Adriatic shore,' some other monastery not named. The difficulty is discussed in the note below,

---

[1] *Par.* xxi. 121-123 :

> 'In quel loco fu' io Pier Damiano ;
> E Pietro peccator fui nella casa
> Di Nostra Donna in sul lito Adriano.'

The different interpretations may be reduced to the following :

(1) For *fui* in l. 122 there is a various reading *fu*; and if this is adopted, 'Pier Damiano' and 'Pietro peccator' are two different persons, and Dante's purpose is to clear up some confusion between them : 'I, Peter Damiani, was in Fonte Avellana; but Peter the sinner was in another monastery on the Adriatic.' This second Peter is generally identified with Pietro degli Onesti, who is said to have called himself 'Petrus peccator,' and whose monastery was Santa Maria in Porto fuori at Ravenna. It is doubtful whether this Peter ever gave himself this name; it was applied to him some centuries later.

(2) Retaining *fui* in l. 122, 'Pier Damiano' and 'Pietro peccator' become, of course, one and the same person; but the meaning varies according to the punctuation adopted. (a) The pointing given above implies that Peter was known by two separate names at the two monasteries referred to—as 'Pier Damiano' at Fonte Avellana, and as 'Pietro peccator' at the house of Our Lady. (b) If we put a comma after Damiano (l. 121) and a semicolon or period after 'peccator' (l. 122), the meaning would be that in Fonte Avellana he was called by both names ; but that he had visited the monastery on the Adriatic coast,—a statement without meaning or purpose apparently. In any case, the monastery on the Adriatic could not be that of Santa Maria in Porto fuori, as many commentators say, since it was not built till 1096, nearly twenty-five years after Damiani's death. The researches of Mercati have shown that, as stated above, Damiani lived for two years in another monastery, Santa Maria in Pomposa, at the mouths of the Po, and doubtless the reference is to it (see Toynbee's *Dante Dictionary*, 187, 188).

but the general meaning I take to be to this effect. It appears to be now proved that in his early life Peter lived for two years in the monastery of Santa Maria in Pomposa, on a small island at the mouths of the Po, near Comacchio. Here he took, or received, the name by which ever after he described himself in his letters and writings, *Petrus peccator monachus.*

Peter Damiani then proceeds to tell how in the eve of his days the dignity of Cardinal was thrust upon him:

> ' Little of mortal life remained to me
> When I was called and dragged forth to the hat
> Which shifteth evermore from bad to worse.' [1]

In 1058, fourteen years before his death, he was compelled to accept, under threat, it is said, of excommunication, the office of Cardinal and Bishop of Ostia. There is no doubt that in this the moving mind was Hildebrand, who found the biting tongue of the simple, honest, bigoted monk a ready tool for his schemes of reform.[2] For Peter Damiani, however great he may have been as a contemplative saint, had an undoubted genius for abusive language, and it is difficult to believe that he did not enjoy the use of his gift. He constituted himself a kind of universal censor: Popes, prelates, clergy, monks, all fell under the lash of his tongue. He himself was quite aware of the danger of the gift, and lamented that he could not control his ' scurrilitas.' Even here in this seventh Heaven some-

---

[1] *Par.* xxi. 124-126.

[2] ' One and the same age gave birth to Dominicus of Sora, Bruno of Segni, Gualbert of Vallombrosa, Guido of Pomposa, and Peter Damiani, a mighty power of monasticism, not in the old sense creative or practical, but an enthusiastic and mystical force, a force which Hildebrand adroitly employed to kindle the world into ecstasy, while he himself, a man of cold and calculating foresight, framed his hierarchical system' (Gregorovius, *Rome in the Mid. Ages*, iv. 102 (Eng. trans.). See pp. 102-109; Milman's *Lat. Christ.* Bk. VI. ch. i. iii.; Bk. VII. ch. i.). Peter Damiani chafed against his being made a tool of by Hildebrand, whom he called his ' hostile friend,' his ' saintly Satan.' Finally, he broke away and returned to his monastery, where we catch a glimpse of the old man relieving the strain of the contemplative life by carving wooden spoons and sending them with epigrammatic couplets to the Pope!

thing of the old power remains in his denunciation of Cardinals :

> ' Came Çephas, and the mighty Vessel came
> Of the Holy Spirit, meagre and barefooted,
> Taking the food of any hostelry.
> Now some one to support them on each side
> The modern shepherds need, and some to lead them,
> So heavy are they, and to hold their trains.
> They cover up their palfreys with their cloaks,
> So that two beasts go underneath one skin ;
> O Patience, that dost tolerate so much !' [1]

It would certainly add greatly to the interest of this passage if we could believe with Mr. Gardner that Dante's famous Epistle to the Italian Cardinals met in conclave at Carpentras in 1314 to elect a successor to Clement V., was possibly written in the monastery of Fonte Avellana, to which he may have retired after the death of Henry VII. the previous year.[2] At all events, we cannot be far wrong in believing that one main reason for Dante's choice of Peter Damiani as the soul who could come nearest him upon the Ladder, was their common indignation against prelates whose unbridled avarice and luxury were the ruin of the Church.   There was probably another bond of sympathy, though it does not appear in this Canto, the sharp line drawn by both between the Empire and the Church. When, for example, in 1053 Pope Leo IX. drew the sword in defence of the Papal States against the Normans of Southern Italy and was defeated, Damiani sharply rebuked him for murdering Christians 'for temporal and transitory possessions.' ' Has a holy Pope ever risen in arms?' he asks indignantly. 'The laws of the forum or the edicts of the council may settle the disputes of the Church, but matters belonging to the judicial tribunals or to the

---

[1] *Par.* xxi. 127-135 (Longfellow).

[2] *Dante's Ten Heavens*, pp. 157, 267-273.   The only proof of Dante's having lived in this monastery is a tradition to that effect preserved among its monks.   If he did, his estimate of its occupants was far from high.   He makes St. Peter Damiani say that it no longer bears the ample fruit it once yielded to these Heavens.   The very Cardinals are worse than in Peter's day, though his wealth of denunciation makes it difficult to think worse possible.

papal sentences should not be decided to the disgrace
of the Church by force of arms.'[1] Dante could not
fail to be drawn to a contemplative whose views of
Church and State so completely supported his own.

At Damiani's exclamation : ' O Patience, that dost
tolerate so much!' Dante saw a multitude of flames
come crowding down the steps, whirling as they came,
and with every revolution growing more beautiful.
Gathering round Peter Damiani, they uttered a loud
cry like thunder, which so stunned Dante that he understood nothing of its meaning, and turned to Beatrice
as a terrified child to its mother.   Mr. Gardner, following Benvenuto, takes this to represent the shock which
Dante's faith received from contemplation of the
wickedness of the Church.   'Taking Beatrice as representing both Theology and the ideal spiritual guide
of the *De Monarchia*, the allegorical meaning apparently is that, himself seeing the wickedness and corruption of the Popes and prelates, reading too in the
writings of Peter Damian of even worse things in his
time, and finding these scandals confirmed in the books
of so many other holy writers, Dante was assailed with
doubts as to the truth of the faith that he held, but
yielded his own judgment to the authority and theological teaching of the Church.'[2]   This, I think, is
entirely in error, for the simple reason that the reas-
surance given by Beatrice shows it was the cry of the
contemplative saints that shocked Dante, not the sins
against which it was directed.   Her reply begins :

> ' Knowest thou not thou art in heaven?
> And knowest thou not that heaven is holy all,
> And what is done here *cometh from good zeal*?'

and she proceeds to say that the cry consisted of
prayers for vengeance, which he should see before his
death.[3]   The meaning obviously is that what shocks
Dante is the apparently merciless and implacable zeal

---

[1] For an account of this battle of Civita in the Capitanata, which he calls
' perhaps the most memorable in the annals of the temporal Papacy,' see
Gregorovius, *Rome in the Mid. Ages*, iv. pp. 79-91 (Eng. trans.).

[2] *Dante's Ten Heavens*, p. 272.   [3] *Par.* xxii. 1-18.

for vengeance which broke like thunder from these
gentle spirits of the contemplative life. He has yet to
learn that it is the very power of contemplation—the
very intensity of their absorption in God—which
generates this passionate zeal.   For, says Aquinas,
'zeal, whichever way we look at it, comes of intensity
of love.   For clearly, the greater the intensity wherewith any power tends to an end, the more vigorously
does it bear down all opposition or resistance.' [1]   And in
another place, discussing the lawfulness of vengeance,
he says : ' The good bear with the wicked to this extent, that, so far as it is proper to do so, they patiently
endure at their hands the injuries done to themselves ;
but they do not bear with them to the extent of enduring the injuries done to God and their neighbours.' [2]
It is for such reasons as these that Beatrice assures
Dante that even the cry of thunder for vengeance
' comes from good zeal,' from the intensity of the love
of these souls for Divine righteousness.   A passage in
St. Bernard's *De Consideratione* (Bk. v. chap. xiv.)
regards the Divine judgments as one of the great
subjects of contemplation.   In a mystical exposition
of the words ' comprehend with all saints what is the
breadth, and length, and depth, and height,' he says
that these four represent four kinds of contemplation,[3]
the second of which beholds the ' depth,' that is to say,
the judgments of God.   This kind of contemplation
'may violently shock the beholder with the fearful
vision, but it puts vice to flight, firmly bases virtue,
initiates in wisdom, preserves humility.'   It is plainly
the shock of this contemplation of the ' depth' which
here stuns the Pilgrim.   The cry is an echo from the
Thrones of the Divine judgments who preside over
this Heaven, and the very echo shakes Dante to the

---

[1] *Summa*, i.-ii. q. xxviii. a. 4.   [2] *Summa*, ii.-ii. q. cviii. a. 1.
[3] St. Bernard distinguishes the four kinds thus : meditation on the
promises coincides with the '*length*,' for length is eternity, and the
promises are eternal ; the remembrance of benefits with the '*breadth*,'
for breadth is love, out of which all benefits flow ; the contemplation of
God's Majesty with the '*height*,' for height is the infinite power of God ;
and consideration of His judgments with the '*depth*,' for ' His judgments
are a great deep' (Ps. xxxvi. 6 ; Rom. xi. 33).

soul; and Beatrice asks how, if the 'depth' so shook him, he could have borne the 'height'—the lofty ecstatic joy of contemplation represented by her smile.

After assuring the poet that the sword of Divine judgment strikes in its own time, and not according to the hopes or fears of men, Beatrice bids him turn his eyes to other 'illustrious spirits' of this Heaven. Turning at her word, he saw a company of 'a hundred spherules,' beautifying one another 'with their mutual rays.' In the true spirit of a contemplative, Dante represses his desire to speak; and seeing this, 'the greatest and brightest of these pearls,' St. Benedict, himself a lover of silence,[1] advanced to satisfy his unspoken wish. The comparison of these souls to pearls carries the mind back to the use of the same comparison in the Heaven of the Moon. The pearl seems to represent in the poet's mind a certain calm, pure, unearthly loveliness of cloistered souls, to whom the world is dead. But if, for any reason, they allow themselves to be thrust back into the world, this pearl-like beauty fades into a dimness scarcely visible. Hence Dante compares the souls in the Moon, who broke their vows, to a white pearl on a white forehead, hardly noted by the eye;[2] whereas these pearls of 'the seventh splendour' shine luminous and clear, because, to use Benedict's words, they 'within the cloisters

Stayed the feet and kept the steadfast heart'[3]—

words which undoubtedly refer to the *votum stabilitatis*, the irrevocable vow of steadfastness, which Benedict imposed on his monks after a year's probation.[4]

---

[1] *Par.* xxii. 19-30. Dante's attitude in ll. 25-27 is an exact fulfilment of the words in the Rule of St. Benedict (ch. 7): 'The ninth degree of humility is that a monk restrain his tongue from speaking; and, keeping silence, do not speak until he is spoken to.'

[2] *Par.* iii. 14, 15. [3] *Par.* xxii. 50, 51.

[4] During the year of probation the Rule was read over to the candidate three times. If he adheres to it at every reading he is 'received in the congregation, knowing that it is decreed, by the law of the Rule, that from that day he shall not be allowed to depart from the monastery, nor to shake free his neck from the yoke of the Rule, which, after such tardy deliberation, he was at liberty either to refuse or receive.' He is then to lay on the altar of the oratory in presence of all, and in name of the saints

Benedict proceeds to tell Dante who he is by giving an account of the great work of his life—the founding in 529 of the famous monastery of Monte Cassino, where, in the words of Urban II., monastic religion ' flowed from the heart of Benedict as from a fountain-head of Paradise ':[1]

> ' That mountain on whose side Cassino lies
> Frequented was of old upon its summit
> By the deluded folk and ill-disposed ;
> And I am he who first up thither bore
> The name of Him who brought upon the earth
> The truth which lifteth us so high ;
> And such abundant grace did o'er me shine
> That I drew back the towns that lay around
> From the impious worship that seduced the world.'[2]

This is taken from the *Dialogues of St. Gregory*, virtually our only source for the life of Benedict. ' For the town, which is called Cassino,' says Gregory, himself a Benedictine, ' standeth upon the side of an high mountain, which containeth, as it were, in the lap thereof, the aforesaid town, and afterwards so riseth in height the space of three miles, that the top thereof seemeth to touch the very heavens : in this place there was an ancient chapel in which the foolish and simple country people, according to the custom of the old Gentiles, worshipped the god Apollo. Round about it likewise upon all sides there were woods for the service of the devils, in which, even to that very time, the mad multitude of infidels did offer most wicked sacrifice. The man of God coming thither, beat in pieces the idol, overthrew the altar, set fire on the woods, and in the temple of Apollo built the oratory of St. Martin : and where the altar of the same Apollo was he made an oratory of St. John : and by his continual preaching he brought the people dwelling in those parts to embrace

whose relics were there, a vow promising steadfastness, amendment of life, and obedience to God and His saints. He shall then change his garments for those of the monastery ; but the old garments are to be laid up in the vestiary, so that if, by the temptation of the devil, he return to the world, he may put them on again, and 'may be cast out' (ch. 58). After a third departure all return was denied (ch. 29). The quotations are from Henderson's *Historical Documents of the Mid. Ages*, 274-314.

[1] Montalembert, *Monks of the West*, ii. 20.
[2] *Par.* xxii. 37-45.

the faith of Christ.'[1] Benedict was almost fifty years
of age when he founded the great monastery, but
Dante gives no hint of how he was prepared for the
labour: his flight at fourteen from the learning and
corruption of Rome to his cave at Subiaco; his thirty-
five years of work in the wild valley of the Anio;
the twelve monasteries which he founded there; the
jealousy and hatred roused by the sternness of his discipline, which drove him forth to seek a new retreat.
Yet in the cave of Subiaco the enthusiastic veneration
of Montalembert saw 'the sanctuary from which issued,
with the rule and institution of St. Benedict, the flower
of Christian civilization, the permanent victory of the
soul over the flesh, the intellectual enfranchisement of
Europe, and all that charm and grandeur which the
spirit of sacrifice, regulated by faith, adds to knowledge, labour, and virtue.'[2]

Benedict proceeds to point out two contemplatives
in the company to which he belongs, Macarius and
Romoaldo,[3] whose very names warn us against an
error into which we are apt to fall. Modern defenders
of Monasticism dwell on the great services which the
monks undoubtedly rendered to the cause of learning
and agriculture. In the devotion of the Benedictine
Order to letters we may find, as one has said, 'a breath
of the Muses from the ruined Temple of Apollo'; and
Ruskin sees in the legend of the mending of the sieve
by Benedict when a child, the omen and prophecy of
that manual labour which he laid upon his monks, by
which the waste places were redeemed and the peasants
taught the art of agriculture.[4] But we must remember
that this intellectual and practical activity of the

---

[1] *The Dialogues of St. Gregory*, ii. 8 (Old Eng. Version).
[2] *The Monks of the West*, ii. 12.   [3] *Par.* xxii. 46-51.
[4] Ruskin's *Valle Crucis*, ii. Mending the Sieve. The legend is told in
The Dialogues of St. Gregory, Bk. ii. ch. i. I am tempted to quote the
passage which Ruskin translates from Viollet-le-Duc concerning the great
social services rendered to all Europe by the Benedictine Order: 'We who
live under regular governments, and in legally protected society, can only
with difficulty conceive the disorder which followed the fall of the Roman
Empire in the West. Everywhere ruin and distraction,—the triumph of
brutal force, the loss of all respect for human dignity, the cultivated

monks was purely incidental, a mere accessory to their
primary and essential purpose of contemplation.[1] To
that essential purpose the mention of Macarius and
Romoaldo recalls us. The former—whichever of the
two who bore the name Dante may have meant[2]—was

lands trampled by famished multitudes, the cities devastated, entire
populations driven out or massacred, and over all this chaos of society in
agony, wave upon wave the inundations of barbarians as tides upon the
sea-sand. The monks descending from Monte Cassino spread themselves
through Germany and Gaul even to the northern limits of Europe, opening out the forests, directing the watercourses, and founding monasteries
surrounded by workshops, which became centres, to the peasantry, of
moral force and protected industry ; to whom the new apostles, after
providing for their safety and support, taught letters, sciences, and arts ;
fortified their souls, gave them the example of self-denial, taught them
to love and to protect the weak, to succour the poor ; to expiate faults,
and to exercise themselves in virtue. They sowed among servile and
degraded races the first seeds of independence and liberty, and they
opened to them, as the last asylum against distress of body and soul,
inviolable and sacred houses of prayer.'

[1] See Montalembert's *The Monks of the West*, i. 11, 12 (Eng. trans.):
'Among so many founders and legislators of the religious life, not one
has dreamt of assigning the cultivation of the soil, the copying of manuscripts, the progress of arts and letters, the preservation of historical
monuments, as a special aim of his disciples. These offices have been
only accessory—the consequence, often indirect and involuntary, of an
institution which had in view nothing but the education of the human
soul, its conformity to the law of Christ, and the expiation of its native
guilt by a life of sacrifice and mortification. This was for all of them the
end and the beginning, the supreme object of existence, the unique ambition, the sole merit, and the sovereign victory.' So also Milman (*Latin
Christianity*, Bk. III. ch. vi.): 'The adventitious advantages, and great
they were, of these industrious agricultural settlements, were not contemplated by the founder.'

[2] 'There were two Macarii ; one called the *Egyptian*, or the elder, who
was the first to establish himself in the vast desert of Scete, between
Mount Nitria and the Nile ; the other, called the *Alexandrine*, who,
among so many penitents, distinguished himself by the incredible rigour
of his austerities' (Montalembert, *The Monks of the West*, I. 312). Probably Dante did not distinguish between the two. In the famous fresco
of the Triumph of Death in the Campo Santo of Pisa, St. Macarius in his
hermit's garb meets a gay hunting party and points them to three corpses
in their coffins. For the connection of this fresco with the French
'Morality,' *Les Trois Morts et les Trois Vifs*, and with the Danse Macabre
or Dance of Death, see F. Douce, *Holbein's Dance of Death*, chap. iii.,
where *Macabre* is derived from Macarius. In the fresco the hermit is
holding a scroll with the words, according to Didron (*Christian Iconography*, ii. 166):

> Se nostra mente fia ben accorta,
> Tenendo fisa qui la vista afflitta,
> La vana gloria ci sarà sconfitta
> E la superbia ci sarà ben morta.

In the next fresco—that of the Hermits of the Thebaid—Macarius appears again, conversing with a skull on the ground.

a monk in the strict sense of the word, a hermit or solitary of the East; and Romoaldo's reform of the Benedictine Order was virtually a reversion to this oriental type. In the Hermitage of Camaldoli which he founded in 1012, his monks lived under the severest rule of devotion, silence, and diet. Each had his separate cell, and held no intercourse with his brethren save for purposes of worship. One class, the recluses, had attained so great a height of contemplation that even this association was no longer necessary.[1]

Under the rays of love which shone from Benedict and his company, Dante's confidence so expanded, like a rose in sunlight, that he ventured to ask the saint if he could receive grace to see him 'with uncovered image,' that is, without the sphere of light which now concealed his soul.[2] Various reasons for this desire have been suggested. If I do not misunderstand Mr. Gardner, he traces it to a certain analogy which Dante felt between Benedict and himself: 'The envy and treachery of Florentius drove Benedict from his abbey to found his new convent of Monte Cassino; the envy and treachery of the Florentines drove Dante into exile to write his mighty poem. Nor is it in the least too fanciful to assign to Monte Cassino in the history of monasticism a place analogous to that of the Divine Comedy in poetry, and to compare the founder of western monasticism with the creator of modern European poetry.'[3] We may admit the analogy to some extent, but that it was consciously before Dante's mind seems extremely improbable. Much more likely is the view of the older commentators that, since contemplation rises through creatures to the vision of

---

[1] For an account of Camaldoli in its present state, see Montgomery Carmichael's *In Tuscany*, 247 ff. The Monastery is now an hotel, and the Hermitage is about a thousand feet higher up the mountain. 'There are two distinct religious states in the Camaldolese Order—the Eremitic and the Monastic—as is typified in the arms of the Order: on a field celestial, two silver doves drinking out of the same golden chalice.' Benedict draws the distinction in his Rule (ch. i.)—the hermit being the man who, by a long probation in a monastery under an abbot, has now learnt to fight against the devil and the flesh 'with his own hand,' and therefore can with safety face the solitary life.

[2] *Par.* xxii. 52-60.   [3] *Dante's Ten Heavens*, p. 161.

God, and since the human soul is made in the image of
God, it is natural that in this Heaven of contemplation
Dante should desire to see the essence of the soul.[1]
But perhaps we may trace it to the simple human
longing with which we are all familiar to see the very
face and features of one we deeply love and reverence.
Dante knew the longing well. When at last, in the
highest Heaven, the soul of St. Bernard is revealed
to him, he compares the eagerness of his gaze to that
of the pilgrim who, seeing the Veronica for the first
time, keeps saying in his thoughts:

> 'My Lord Jesus Christ, God of very God,
> Now was Thy semblance fashioned like to this?'[2]

If we wish a further reason, it is possible that the
desire was suggested by the legend told in the *Dialogues
of St. Gregory* that Benedict himself received a vision
of the soul of his sister, St. Scholastica, and of
Germanus, Bishop of Capua, ascending to Paradise.[3]

For such a vision, however, Dante is not yet able to
receive sufficient grace, but Benedict promises it when
he has climbed to the top of the Ladder:

> 'Brother, thy high desire
> Shall be fulfilled up in the last sphere,
> Where all the others are fulfilled, and mine,'[4]—

---

[1] In *Contra Gentiles*, Bk. III. chap. xii., Aquinas discusses the question
whether it is possible for any one in this life to understand 'a separately
subsistent intelligence'—that is, an angel—in its essence, and decides
that it is impossible. Were it possible, then since these higher intelligences by some mode of vision see God Himself, in knowing them in their
essence we would know Him with a higher knowledge than is attainable
by speculations of science or philosophy. Father Rickaby calls this
'picking the brains of angels'—a thing of course impossible to man in
this present state. There is a long and intricate discussion on the subject
in *Summa*, i. q. lxxxviii. a. 1. The same argument would apply in some
degree to 'separated souls,' like that of Benedict.

[2] *Par.* xxxi. 103-111. Compare the way in which in ll. 61-63 of the
same Canto Dante describes the face and gesture of St. Bernard. See
p. 488 f.

[3] Bk. II. chaps. xxxiv., xxxv. It is true, it is not said that the souls
were seen in their proper form or essence. His sister's appeared in the
likeness of a dove; and of the Bishop it is said, 'he saw the soul of
Germanus, Bishop of Capua, in a fiery globe to be carried up by Angels
into Heaven.' Still, Dante's familiarity with these stories in the life of
Benedict may have suggested his request here.

[4] *Par.* xxii. 61-63. The *frate* of Benedict is, apparently, in reply to
Dante's *padre* in l. 58, as if the saint disclaimed all the old superiority

Benedict's own desire being, apparently, to satisfy Dante's longing to see him. He recognizes the poet as a kindred spirit, and by addressing him as '*Frate*' admits him as a brother of his celestial Order. The reason why every 'high desire' is satisfied in the last sphere is that 'it is not in space, nor hath it poles.' It is not in space, it exists only in 'the Primal Mind.'[1] It has no poles on which it revolves, like the other spheres, with the movement of unsatisfied desire, which cannot but wheel until it reach its final end. It is the Empyrean of perfect peace, because, when the soul reaches it, all its desires are 'perfect, ripe, and whole,' and it finds there 'every part where it always was'— the eternal unity for which it sought. To this last sphere the Ladder of Contemplation stretches, far beyond Dante's present power of vision,—that upper part which Jacob once saw, laden with angels. The mention of Jacob's vision reminds Benedict of the violation of his Rule of which his own monks were now guilty. In the Rule he had compared our life in this world to Jacob's ladder, set up by the Lord in a humbled heart. The two sides of the ladder are body and soul, and the steps are distinct acts of humility and discipline.[2] None now lifts his feet to climb it; his Rule only wastes the parchment it is written on; houses once of prayer have become dens of thieves; and the gowns of the monks are now sacks full of corrupt meal. The special sin is avarice, more hateful to God in a monk than usury: avarice which squandered the patrimony of the poor on kindred and on worse.[3]

of earth. Piccarda, another spirit of the cloister, calls Dante *frate* (*Par.* iii. 70); and twice in Canto vii. (58, 130) Beatrice addresses him as 'brother.'

[1] *Conv.* ii. 4; Epis. x. 24-26. See Introduction, p. 11.

[2] *Rule of St. Benedict*, ch. 7.

[3] *Par.* xxii. 64-84. Benvenuto narrates how Boccaccio, when he visited Monte Cassino, found the door of the great library without a fastening, grass growing in the windows, the books and shelves covered with dust. Many books were mutilated — pages cut out to make psalters and breviaries which the greedy monks sold to boys and women. Hettinger thinks Dante exaggerates the degeneracy of the Benedictines: 'Dante, we must remember, demands from Religious the primitive observance of

Benedict proceeds to lament that so seductive is the flesh that on earth 'a good beginning' endures a shorter space than from the birth of an oak to the bearing of acorns—less than a generation of human life. The 'good beginning' seems to refer to the words with which St. Benedict closed his Rule: 'Thou, therefore, whoever doth hasten to the celestial fatherland, perform with Christ's aid this Rule written out as the least of beginnings: and then at length, under God's protection, thou wilt come to the greater things that we have mentioned; to the summits of learning and virtue.' He gives three instances of the swift failure of good beginnings:

> 'Peter began with neither gold nor silver,
> And I with praying and with fasting,
> And Francis with humility his convent.'

In all three, the white had turned brown. Nevertheless Benedict does not despair: the God who wrought the greater marvels of turning back the waters of the Jordan and the Red Sea, could once more send deliverance. At these words of hope in God, St. Benedict drew back to his company, the company closed in, and, 'like a whirlwind, all gathered itself on high.' Dante himself is caught up by the same wind of the Spirit:

> The sweet Lady urged me on behind them
> With a single sign, up by that ladder,
> So did her virtue my nature overcome,—

the ecstasy of contemplation being an experience which lifts the soul above the bounds of the natural life. One moment, and he is rapt into the next sphere; the

their rule in all its strictness, while the Church, on the other hand, had sanctioned mitigations in it. Nor was laxity ever universal at any one period, either in one or all the Orders. The discipline of Clugny, which had decayed under Abbot Pontus, was restored by Peter the Venerable, who died in 1156. St. Bernard and his Order were fruitful labourers in the vineyard, in the thirteenth century; equally so St. Romuald and his new Congregation in the eleventh; St. Norbert and the Premonstratensians in the twelfth. The vigorous Benedictine stock never ceased to put forth new and healthy branches, and John of Salisbury says even of the unreformed Orders: "that great saints were to be found in all"' (*Dante's Divina Commedia*, 350 n.).

last of the Seven Planets is left behind, and he enters
into the glorious Heaven of the Fixed Stars.[1]

[1] *Par.* xxii. 85-111. It is probably not without significance that the
ecstasy of Benedict and his company, in which Dante shares, follows
immediately on the expression of hope in the Divine power to reform
the Benedictine Order.   We have heard so many denunciations — of
Dominicans, Franciscans, Florentines, Kings, Cardinals, Monks, Popes,
and others—that we are apt to think Dante despaired of the Church and
world.   The present passage shows him as a man of hope—hope in God ;
and we should perhaps connect it with what Beatrice says of him when
she presents him to St. James in the next Heaven for his examination in
Hope :

> ' The Church Militant hath not any son
> With greater hope ' (*Par.* xxv. 52)—

though, of course, it is to be remembered that hope here means the hope
of glory.

UP THE GOLDEN STAIR
Cantos XXII-XXXIII

Viditque in somnis scalam stantem super terram, et cacumen illius tangens coelum : angelos quoque Dei ascendentes et descendentes per eam, et Dominum innixum scalae.

Gen. xxviii. 12, 13.

Beati mundo corde, quoniam ipsi Deum videbunt.

Matt. v. 8.

Inebriabuntur ab ubertate domus tuae : et torrente voluptatis tuae potabis eos. Quoniam apud te est fons vitae: et in lumine tuo videbimus lumen.
Psalm xxxvi. 8, 9.

Videmus nunc per speculum in aenigmate, tunc autem facie ad faciem : nunc cognosco ex parte, tunc autem cognoscam sicut et cognitus sum. Nunc autem manet fides, spes, caritas, tria haec : maior autem his est caritas.
1 Cor. xiii. 12, 13.

> Io, che al divino dall' umano,
> All' eterno dal tempo era venuto,
> E di Fiorenza in popol giusto e sano,
> Di che stupor dovea esser compiuto!

Par. xxxi. 37-40.

> Noi semo usciti fuore
> Del maggior corpo al ciel ch' è pura luce ;
> Luce intellettual piena d'amore,
> Amor di vero ben pien di letizia,
> Letizia che trascende ogni dolzore.

Par. xxx. 38-42.

> Lume è lassù, che visibile face
> Lo Creatore a quella creatura,
> Che solo in lui vedere ha la sua pace.

Par. xxx. 100-102.

Introduxit me in cellam vinariam, ordinavit in me caritatem.

Cant. ii. 4.

CHAPTER XX

1. *The Vision of the Threshing-floor*

WE enter now the final great division of Paradise. Since the three Heavens of which it is composed are the upper part of the Golden Ladder, the revelations here given to the Pilgrim form an ascending stairway of the mysteries which contemplation alone has power to see: the Triumph of Christ in the hosts of the Redeemed; the Nine Orders of Angels; the final blessedness of the saints in the Beatific Vision of God. Dante indicates the gradual nature of the ascent by clothing the revelations of the Eighth and Ninth Heavens in the form of figures and similitudes; it is only in the Empyrean that these 'shadowy prefaces of their truth,'[1] as he calls them, give way to the realities, and the *lumen gloriae* changes faith to sight.

It may be well to remind ourselves of the place this Starry Heaven, or Heaven of the Fixed Stars, holds in Dante's system of the universe. All power and virtue necessary for the whole creation flow from the Empyrean, the Tenth Heaven, the Mind of God. They pass through the highest Order of Angels, the Seraphim, who govern the Primum Mobile, to the Cherubim, the movers of this Heaven of the Fixed Stars. It is the function of these stars to break up and divide this Divine power and virtue among the lower spheres, impressing upon each some special quality. The reason for this breaking up of the Divine influence is the

---

[1] *Par.* xxx. 78. 'Son di lor vero ombriferi prefazii.' For the emphatic threefold repetition of 'io vidi' which follows almost immediately (ll. 94-99), see p. 468 f.

necessity to secure the varied powers and virtues required to create human society—each man being impressed by the special quality of the star under which he is born. And this variety persists even in the eternal world. As ' one star differeth from another star in glory,' so do these souls who form the hosts of Christ's Triumph. Their brightness varies according to their joy and vision; and the difference in their rates of motion is compared to a horologe in which the first wheel ' seems still and the last to fly.' [1] In short, they bear within them all the differences of character, and therefore of blessedness, which we have seen in the Heavens of the lower stars, for the simple reason that many of them are the very souls we have already met there, now gathered together for the Triumph of their Redeemer and Lord. In one of the most beautiful similes in the poem, Beatrice on entering this Heaven is compared to a bird above the nest watching for the dawn that she may find food for her young. The dawn is the starry host of the Redeemed, and when the heaven brightens with their coming, she says to her companion:

> ' Behold the hosts
> Of the Triumph of Christ, and all the fruit
> Ingathered by the circling of these spheres!' [2]

By 'the Triumph of Christ' may be meant specially His ' descent into Hell' and victorious deliverance from Limbo of the Old Testament saints; [3] while those 'ingathered by the circling of these spheres,' may refer to the souls saved after Christ's Advent. Many of the latter Dante has already seen in the lower Heavens; but some of the greatest of them, such as the Virgin and the Apostles, have remained above in the immediate presence of their Lord.

The moment the poet entered this Starry Heaven he saw with joy that he was in the constellation under which he was born—Gemini, ' the sign that follows Taurus':

---

[1] *Par.* xxiv. 13-18.   [2] *Par.* xxiii. 19-21.   [3] *Inf.* iv. 52-63.

O glorious stars, O light impregnated
With mighty virtue, from which I recognize
All of my genius, whatsoe'er it be,
With you was born, and hid himself with you,
He who is father of all mortal life,
When first I tasted of the Tuscan air;
And then, when grace was freely given to me
To enter the high wheel which turns you round,
Your region was allotted unto me.
To you devoutly at this hour my soul
Is sighing, that it virtue may acquire
For the stern pass that draws it to itself.[1]

'In the astrology of the Middle Ages,' says Plumptre,
'the sign Gemini is.in the house of Mercury, and is, therefore, the source, in the theory of stellar influences, of
the gifts of genius and skill of speech';[2] and when the
sun is in this sign, as it was at the poet's birth,[3] this
intellectual influence is greatly intensified. Dante
regards it as a most happy omen that in his case the
natural life and the spiritual were in perfect harmony.
When by grace he rose to this 'high wheel' of the
Starry Heaven, he found that the part of it allotted to
him was the very constellation which had set its seal
upon him at his natural birth. It is this conjunction
of nature and grace which encourages him to pray to
the 'glorious stars' for virtue for the hard pass to
which his soul was drawing near. As Mr. Gardner
says, this is virtually a prayer to the Cherubim who
are the governors of this sphere. 'The hard pass' is
not, as some think, the end of his mortal life, now not
far off, but 'the last passage from the things of sense
to the suprasensible,' the vision of these final Heavens.
For this he needed the aid of the Cherubim, the Order
of Angels that sees most profoundly into 'the depth of

[1] *Par.* xxii. 112-123 (Longfellow, slightly altered).
[2] In *Par.* v. 97-99, in Mercury, Dante represents himself as mercurial :

If the star itself was changed and smiled,
What then did I, who by my very nature am
Susceptible to change through every guise !

See above, p. 99.
[3] This passage, says Toynbee, 'is important as fixing approximately
the date of Dante's birthday. It has been calculated that in 1265 the Sun
entered Gemini on May 18 and left it on June 17, so that the day was
between.those two dates' (*Dante Dictionary*, p. 263).

the riches both of the wisdom and knowledge of
God.'[1]

It is probably in response to this prayer that Beatrice
bids him look down and see 'how great a world she
had put beneath his feet.' And this for two reasons.
First, to make his eyes 'clear and keen' for 'the last
salvation,' the vision of God, to which he was so near.
In the Heaven below this, we saw 'speculation' in one
sense—the seeing of the things above, as in a *speculum*
or mirror.[2] Now we come to another form of 'speculation'—the seeing of things below, as from a *specula*
or watch-tower. From this watch-tower of the supernatural, Dante looks down on the entire system of
the natural life and world to which he once belonged,
and values it at its true worth. We must not assume,
as is generally done, that the entire world beneath is
dismissed with one glance of scorn. The earth is the
only portion of it that is condemned. It is called 'the
threshing-floor that makes us so fierce,' and Dante
smiled at its 'mean semblance.' But there is no hint
of contempt for the Seven Planets. We must not
forget that they still bear their symbolic meaning.
They represent Heavens,—steps of the great stairway
by which he has climbed thus far. But in so far as
they belong to the natural life and its virtues, he now
stands above them, not as despising them, but as being
independent of them, and therefore able to judge them
truly. He sees the better side of the Moon, the side
that has no perplexing shadow. His eyes are strong
to bear the light of the Sun. He sees the relations of
the various Heavens to each other, their movements,
'how great they are, how swift, how distant in their
habitations.' In short, while the earth is, indeed, a
small threshing-floor, the Heavens of the Seven Planets
constitute a world whose greatness he now sees for the
first time, just because he is raised above it by the
power, if not yet of contemplation, of 'consideration'

---

[1] Rom. xi. 33. Of course, Dante's prayer is not to Angels as such, but
as the channels through which the Divine virtue flows to mankind.

[2] See above, p. 334.

in its literal sense, the pondering of the stars.[1] This
consideration of the 'mean semblance' of earth, and of
the great world of natural virtue represented by the
planets, clears the eyes for 'the last salvation,' the
supernatural vision of God by contemplation. And
with this is closely bound up a second reason. This
downward glance would widen the Pilgrim's heart to
its utmost capacity of joy, and thus prepare it to meet
the triumphant throng of blessed spirits now drawing
near through 'this round ether.' If he has any
lingering regret for the things beneath, it will lessen
his power of communion with their bliss.[2]

It may be well at this point to face one of the most
difficult problems in the poem, though in doing so it is
necessary to anticipate many things awaiting exposition. This downward look on entering the Eighth
Heaven (xxii. 124-154) is repeated immediately before
leaving it (xxvii. 76-87), and this in such a way as to
make it necessary to consider them together. The
passages are as follows :

> The threshing-floor that maketh us so fierce,'
> While I rolled round with the eternal Twins,
> To me did all appear from hills to river-mouths :
> Then back I turned my eyes to the eyes beautiful (xxii. 151-154).

>   ' Cast down
> Thy sight, and see how far thou art rolled round.'
> From the hour when I had looked at first,
> I saw that I had moved through the whole arc
> Which from the middle to the end the first Clime makes.
> So that I saw the mad course of Ulysses
> Past Gades, and this side, well nigh the shore
> Whereon became Europa a sweet burden.
> And more to me had been disclosed the site
> Of this threshing-floor ; but the sun was in advance,
> Beneath my feet, a sign and more removed (xxvii. 77-87).

---

[1] St. Bernard (*De Consideratione*, Bk. II. ch. ii.) thus distinguishes :
'*Contemplation* may be defined as the soul's true unerring intuition, or
as the unhesitating apprehension of truth. But *consideration* is thought
(cogitatio) earnestly directed to research, or the application of the mind
to the search for truth ; though in practice the two terms are indifferently
used for one another' (Lewis' transl.). Both words are believed to come
from augurial rites : Contemplation, from *com* and *templum*, the marking
out of a *templum*, or sacred space open to the sky ; and consideration,
from *com* and *sidus* (*sideris*) a star, or constellation, observation of the
stars.   [2] *Par.* xxii. 124-132.

I may say at once that no explanation of these two passages that I have seen clears up all the geographical and astronomical questions involved, and it is doubtful whether any perfectly satisfactory solution is possible. I confess too that my own interest in these questions is subordinate to the moral and spiritual significance, to which they form, so to speak, a kind of starry veil. The geographical and astronomical aspect will be discussed only so far as is necessary to bring out what I conceive to be this inner significance.

1. Dante's geography was, of course, very different from ours. His interest was virtually confined to the habitable part of the globe. The centre of this part was Jerusalem, according to the words of Ezekiel (v. 5): 'Thus saith the Lord God: This is Jerusalem: I have set it in the midst of the nations, and countries that are round about her.'[1] The habitable globe stretched from this centre 90° east to the Ganges, and 90° west to Gades or Cadiz. Rome, the other Holy City, was in the exact centre of this western half, 45° to the west of Jerusalem. The limits north and south were less symmetrically defined. Southward the habitable world stretched to the land of the savage Garamantes along the line of the Equator, beyond which lay nothing but the great Southern Ocean; and Northward it shaded off into the icy country of the Scythians, 'who live outside the Seventh Clima.'[2] When Dante says he saw the whole of 'the threshing-floor' 'from the hills to the river-mouths,' it is this habitable part of the earth he is thinking of; and that is perhaps one of his reasons for introducing Adam, the First Father of the entire population of the world he has just seen from the constellation of his own birth.

2. The problem is to discover from the two passages quoted above what part of this habitable globe Dante wishes us to understand he has travelled over, between

---

[1] In *Summa*, iii. q. xlvi. a. 10, Aquinas calls Jerusalem 'umbilicus terrae,' and gives its centrality as a good reason for its being chosen as the scene of the Crucifixion, the virtue of which was to radiate to the confines of the world.

[2] *De Mon.* i. 14; *Conv.* iii. 5.

his first look downward and his second.   In the earlier
passage, he says the whole of the threshing-floor was
visible to him; and from this it has been inferred that
he was in the meridian of Jerusalem, since only from
that central point could the entire area of the habitable earth be seen, from Cadiz to the Ganges.   Against
this, however, is the statement in the second passage
that the sun was in front of him 'a sign and more':
that is, Dante was in Gemini, the sun was in Aries, and
the sign of Taurus lay between.   Since a sign is 30°, if
Dante was in the meridian of Jerusalem, the sun must
have been to the west of Jerusalem more than 30°—
perhaps 40° or 45°—and therefore the same space eastward to the Ganges would lie in darkness and be
invisible to the poet.   To escape this difficulty, Dr.
Moore in his essay on the Astronomy of Dante thinks
it was the *sun*, not Dante, that was over Jerusalem at
the first look downward; that Dante's position was 'a
sign and more' to the east of it, say, 45°; and that he
saw the whole of the threshing-floor or habitable part,
not in the one first downward glance, but during the
course of the entire journey—'*while I rolled round* with
the eternal Twins.'   The difficulty of this view is that
Dante says expressly that he had travelled 'through
the whole arc which the first Clime makes *from the
middle* to the end.'   Assuming 'the middle' to be the
meridian of Jerusalem, that must be taken as Dante's
starting-point, whereas Dr. Moore's theory compels
him to make the starting-point about 45° east of that
meridian.

3. It is necessary at this point to understand the
reference to 'the first Clime' (*il primo clima*).   The
word is the Greek κλίμα, a slope or incline, and was
applied especially to the apparent slope or inclination
of the earth toward the pole.   In the Middle Ages the
known habitable part of the globe was divided into
seven of these *climata* or zones, running east and west
parallel to the Equator, the breadth of each being determined by the varying length of day.   'Each "clima,"
going northwards, included such a space that the mean

length of the longest day was half-an-hour longer
than that of the longest day in the previous "clima"
to the south.'[1] Now, 'the first Clima,' according to one
of Dante's authorities, Alfraganus, began at a little
more than $12\frac{1}{2}$ degrees north of the equator and ended
at $20\frac{1}{2}$ degrees north, the middle point of its breadth
being Meroë, the ancient capital of Ethiopia. As I
understand Dante, his meaning is that in Gemini he
moved *from east to west* through the whole arc made
by ' this first Clime' or equatorial zone, as we might
call it, from the middle of it, measuring east and west
(that is, from the meridian of Jerusalem, but, of course,
far to the south of the city), to about the meridian of
Gades on the Atlantic (though again far to the south
of this); and that, in the course of this journey of 90°,
he saw the whole of ' the threshing-floor that maketh
us so fierce,' that is, the entire circle of countries that
surround the Mediterranean Sea, ' from the hills to the
river-mouths.'

4. Now, in this statement there are several things
that require explanation in order to bring out the
moral and spiritual significance of this vision. The
first is that Dante is travelling all the time in 'the arc
made by the first Clime,' that is, *the zone nearest to the
Equator*. Many commentators leave the impression,
perhaps unintentionally, that this first Clime is the
zone that covers the Mediterranean, and that therefore
this sea lay directly beneath Dante's feet. This is
certainly not so. His whole course lay in the first
Clime, the zone nearest the Equator, and therefore far
south of the great inland sea. And the reason for this
seems plain. In *Convito* ii. 4 Dante says that the
nearer any Heaven is to its equator the nobler it is
in comparison with its poles: ' because it has more
motion, and more actuality, and more life, and more
form, and has more touch of the one that is above it,
and by consequence has more of virtue. Hence the
stars of the Starry Heaven are more full of virtue, as
between themselves, according as they are nearer to

[1] Moore, *Studies in Dante*, 3rd series, 131.

this circle.' What Dante wishes to tell us is obviously this: that he travelled *the noblest part* of the Starry Heaven, its first Clima, which corresponds to the first Clima of earth,[1] is nearest to its equatorial circle, and therefore has most of motion, actuality, life, and form. Symbolically, the meaning is that he passed through the noblest stars of this Heaven, the souls shining with the greatest virtue, such as the Virgin and the Apostles. Apart from some such symbolic meaning, it is difficult to see any purpose to be served by the mention of 'il primo clima' at all.

5. The next point that needs justification is the limiting of 'the threshing-floor' to the countries that surround the Mediterranean. It is generally taken to mean the entire area of the habitable globe, from Gades to Ganges: but it is questionable whether Dante's interest went much farther east than the neighbourhood of Jerusalem.[2] I lay emphasis on the words descriptive of the threshing-floor: 'which maketh *us* so fierce,' as limiting the reference to that part of the world in which he was specially interested, and whose history, he knew, was that of one perpetual battlefield.

There is, however, another reason for this limitation of the area to Europe and the western region of Asia, namely, the contrast between the scene above and the scene below, between the faith, hope and love of Peter, James and John, and the fading away of these virtues from that very world which they had evangelized, until it had now become the threshing-floor on which nations fought out their passions. The part of the habitable globe over which Dante journeyed in converse with the Apostles, was precisely that in which they had once sowed the seed of the supernatural virtues; and the

---

[1] 'The zones of the climata, though terrestrial in origin and purpose, may be supposed to be "projected" on the heavens, like the equator or the poles of the earth' (Moore, *Studies in Dante*, 3rd series, 70 n.).

[2] 'I prefer to understand it,' says Butler, 'as the region around the Mediterranean, or Western Asia and Europe. It could hardly be said that any regions farther east affected the men of that time in any way.' On the other hand, Dante's theological interest extended as far east as the Indus (*Par.* xix. 70 ff.).

places he hints at or names seem to show that this was in his mind. The meridian of Jerusalem indicates the starting-point of the Gospel. Travelling westward, the reference to Dante's seeing almost to the coast of Phœnicia, might be taken as carrying the mind back to Asia Minor, the scene of John's labours, now, indeed, sinking into darkness. Still farther to the west, we come to Rome, the scene of Peter's labours, worthy now only of his bitterest denunciations. And at the extreme western limit was the tomb of him 'for whose sake down on earth Galicia is visited'[1]—St. James, to whose shrine at Compostella the Milky Way that runs through this Starry Heaven was regarded as a sign for the guidance of pilgrims.[2] Thus, from Jerusalem to Spain, Dante surveys the whole field of the labours of the three Apostles with whom he holds converse, and sees that the world into which they went forth, 'poor and fasting,'[3] as the messengers of faith, hope and love, is now a threshing-floor which makes men fierce with lust of conquest and possession.

6. One last point claims attention, though it may be regarded as fanciful. The commentators tell us that Dante applies the word '*aiuola*,' 'threshing-floor,' to the earth in contempt of its littleness—a threshing-floor being a little round flat area, such as this world seemed when seen from the height of a supernatural life. And doubtless this is part of the thought. *Aiuola* is the Italian form of *areola*, a diminutive of *area*;[4] and the smallness of the petty plot of ground for which men fight so fiercely was certainly in Dante's mind. But another thought seems to pervade, in an elusive way, the entire passage that treats of this Heaven. Twice in the course of it—at the beginning and at the end—Dante uses this word 'threshing-floor'; and it is difficult to think that in doing so he did not remember, and wish us to remember, the dark and threatening

[1] *Par.* xxv. 18.   [2] *Conv.* ii. 15.   [3] *Par.* xxiv. 109.
[4] Comp. *De Mon.* iii. 16 : 'This is that mark at which the guardian of the world, who is called the Roman Prince, should chiefly aim : to wit, that on this little threshing-floor (*areola* : Church translates *little plot of earth*) of mortals, life may be freely lived with peace.'

application of it to Babylon by a prophet with whose spirit he often shows a striking affinity. In the long and terrible judgment which Jeremiah in the closing chapters of his Book pronounces upon Babylon, occur these words: 'The daughter of Babylon is like *a thresh-ing-floor*, it is time to thresh her: yet a little while, and the time of her harvest shall come'; or in the form in which Dante would read it in the Vulgate: 'Filia Babylonis quasi *area*, tempus triturae eius: adhuc modicum, et veniet tempus messionis eius.' When we remember the application in the Apocalypse of the name Babylon to Rome, there seems no improbability in supposing that in using the word 'threshing-floor' at the beginning and at the close of his journey through this Heaven, Dante means to warn the Church that her doom will be that of Babylon: her iniquities are ripe almost to the harvest, and soon the voice of the Divine judgment will sound: 'It is time to thresh her.' This would fit in, not only with St. Peter's denunciation of the Papacy, but also with what must have been vividly present to the poet's mind when he wrote these Cantos —the 'Babylonish captivity' of the Church at Avignon. This, it is true, had not taken place in 1300, the ideal date of the poem, but there are prophetic allusions to it.[1] One hint in particular seems plain, though I have not seen it noticed. In the closing lines of Canto xxiii., the Apostles are compared to chests that overflow with another harvest than that of Babylon in the Prophet's message; and then Dante adds:

> Here have they life and joyance in the treasure
> Which was acquired by weeping in the exile
> Of Babylon, where the gold was left behind.[2]

I find it difficult to think that Dante did not mean to contrast here the two exiles of Babylon—that of the Apostles during the earthly life, when they scorned gold for the treasure in heaven; and that of the Church

---

[1] The principal one, of course, is Dante's seventh vision in *Purg.* xxxii. 148-160, in which he sees the Giant, Philip the Fair, dragging the Chariot of the Church through the forest—i.e. to Avignon.

[2] *Par.* xxiii. 130-135.

in Avignon, in which certainly the gold was not left
behind. In short, in these Cantos it is as if the poet
saw once more the Angel of the Lord that stood with
the drawn sword ' by the threshing-floor of Ornan,'
not now to stay his hand, but to 'execute judgment
and justice in the earth,' and to do 'terrible things in
righteousness.' [1]

[1] 1 Chron. xxi. 15; Jer. xxiii. 5; Ps. lxv. 5. For other Scriptural references to the *area* or threshing-floor which may have been in Dante's
mind, see Isaiah xxi. 9, 10, and Matt. iii. 12.

CHAPTER XXI

EIGHTH HEAVEN—THE FIXED STARS: THE REDEEMED

2. *The Triumph of Christ*

AFTER his first downward look at the Earth and the
Seven Planets, Dante 'turned back his eyes to the eyes
beautiful': if Beatrice, the Divine Wisdom, had 'set so
great a world beneath his feet,' what must that world
be to which this was but the prelude? He compares
her to a mother-bird poised on an open spray above her
nest, in eager outlook for the dawn which will give her
light to find food for her young: with the same intent-
ness are the eyes of Beatrice turned to the meridian,
'the region under which the sun shows least haste,'[1]
waiting 'until the day breathe, and the shadows flee
away.'[2] Allegorically, the meaning seems to be that all
Dante has yet seen of Paradise—the light and glory of
the Seven Heavens below—is but the darkness of the
night in comparison with the dawn about to brighten.
That this contrast is no exaggeration will be apparent
if we remember that the Sun for whom they look is
Christ Himself, kindling into light and glory the
triumphant hosts of His Redeemed. They had not long
to wait. Suddenly the Heaven grew radiant and ever
more radiant; and Beatrice, her face burning with love
and her eyes with joy, exclaimed:

> 'Behold the hosts
> Of the Triumph of Christ, and all the fruit
> Ingathered by the circling of these spheres!'—

---

[1] *Par.* xxiii. 10-12. This is the usual interpretation; but Antonelli,
says Casini, 'thinks that from the constellation of the Twins Beatrice
would look into that of Cancer, that is, toward the East, from which it
was fitting that Christ should appear in triumph.' But is there any East
or West in Paradise ?

[2] Cant. ii. 17: 'Donec aspiret dies, et inclinentur umbrae' (Vulg.).

that is, by the power and grace of God flowing out
through Christ to the Nine Orders of Angels, and
through them to the spheres of which they are the
movers, and thus down to men on earth.[1]

> As when in nights serene of the full moon
> Smiles Trivia among the nymphs eternal
> Who paint the firmament thro' all its gulfs,
> Saw I, above the myriads of lamps,
> A Sun that one and all of them enkindled,
> Even as our own doth the supernal sights.
> And thro' the living light transparent shone
> The lucent substance so intensely clear
> Into my sight that I sustained it not.
> O Beatrice, thou gentle guide and dear !
> To me she said : ' What overmasters thee
> A virtue is from which naught shields itself.
> Therein is the Wisdom and the Power
> That opened the pathways between heaven and earth,
> For which there erst had been so long a yearning.'[2]

The chief difficulty of this passage is in ll. 31-33 :
Dante's eyes cannot endure 'the lucent substance'
which shone through 'the living light' of Christ, the
Sun that kindles the starry hosts of His Triumph. The
usual interpretation is that 'the lucent substance' is
the glorified Humanity of our Lord, 'the body of His
glory,' to use St. Paul's phrase ; and that 'the living
light' through which it shines is the glory of His soul,
from which the glory of His body flows. According to
Aquinas, the soul of Christ from the instant of His
conception was glorious by its perfect fruition of
Divinity. In the ordinary course of the spiritual life,
this glory of His soul would have 'redounded' to His

---

[1] *Par.* xxiii. 1-24. For the way in which Christ is conceived as ' the
Living Light' which ' unites its rays in nine subsistences,' the nine
Angelic Orders, and flows down to the ' brief contingencies' of earth, see
Par. xiii. 52-66, and p. 220 above.

[2] *Par.* xxiii. 25-39. In 1 Cor. i. 24, Christ is called ' the power of God,
and the wisdom of God.' The opening of the pathways refers to *Par.* vii.
109-111 :

> ' The Divine Goodness, which imprints the world,
> Was well contented to proceed by *all*
> *Its ways*, to lift you up again.'

See p. 124. *Trivia* is the Moon, so called from the temple of Diana, the
Moon-goddess, which was frequently built at the meeting of three roads
(*Aen.* vi. 13, 35, etc.). The nymphs are the stars (*Purg.* xxxi. 106).

body and made it glorious; but there was a dispensation from this natural law 'in order that He might fulfil the mystery of our redemption by His Passion.' This being done, the soul imparted its glory to the body, which it resumed in the Resurrection. In this Heaven, then, where the fruits of that Passion are gathered in, ' the lucent substance' of Christ's body, once veiled for our salvation in the humiliation of earth, shines through the glory of His soul, to be the eternal sunlight of His Redeemed. That 'body of His glory' is the earnest of the glory of their own bodies in the Resurrection; for, as Aquinas says in the passage just referred to, 'the Resurrection of Christ was the exemplar and the cause of ours.'[1]

This flash of the glory of the Risen Christ, shining on the blessed souls who yet await the Resurrection, is Dante's first vision of the Contemplative Life; and, brief and blinding as it was, it broke down the limits of nature, and his mind 'issued forth from itself,' he knew not how, as lightning bursts from a cloud. From this ecstatic trance he is recalled by the voice of Beatrice:

> ' Open thine eyes, and look at what I am ;
> Thou hast beheld things such that mighty
> Hast thou been made to bear my smile.'[2]

Since entering the Heaven of Saturn Beatrice, for Dante's sake, has not dared to smile.[3] Now he is able to bear the ' joy unspeakable and full of glory.' The

---

[1] *Summa*, iii. q. liv. a. 3. This interpretation harmonizes with what Solomon says of the human body in the Resurrection (*Par.* xiv. 52-57). The risen body is compared to a live coal which conquers the glow of its own flame and 'maintains its own appearance' in the very midst of it. This would correspond exactly to 'the lucent substance' of Christ's body shining through ' the living light' of the soul.

A quite different view is given by Vellutello : '*E per la viva luce*, that is, through the splendour of the Humanity of Christ shone forth *la lucente sustanzia*, that is, the splendour of His Divinity, which was contained in such a Humanity.' The use of the word *substance* seems in favour of this interpretation. The meaning would then be that what blinded Dante was not the glory of the body and soul of Christ, but of His Humanity and Divinity. Perhaps, taking into account the Heaven we are in, the former is likelier to be the stage of vision Dante has reached : the union of Humanity and Divinity in Christ is reserved for the Empyrean (xxxiii. 127-141). This is the second of three visions of Christ in the *Paradiso* : see p. 239.

[2] *Par.* xxiii. 46-48.   [3] *Par.* xxi. 4 f.

meaning appears to be to this effect. The mind of
mortal man cannot remain at the ecstatic height of
contemplation for ever; Dante must return to Beatrice
in her symbolic character of Theology—meditation on
what he has seen in vision. But Theology is now
transfigured and glorified. The things he has seen—
the glory of Christ and His saints—have invested her
with a sweetness and beauty he never saw before, a
smile which made the holy face so pure that all the
poets most nourished by the Muses had been powerless
to enable him to sing it. Hence he is forced to pass it
by in silence. The voyage is not one for a little ship,
or for 'a helmsman who spares himself'; no wonder if
the mortal shoulder tremble under the weighty theme.

So long and eagerly did Dante gaze at his Lady's
smile that at last she had to turn away his eyes to the
souls of the Redeemed :

> 'Why doth my face so much enamour thee,
> That to the garden fair thou turnest not,
> Which 'neath the rays of Christ enflowers itself?
> There is the Rose in which the Word Divine
> Made itself flesh ; there are the Lilies
> At whose odour the good way was taken.'[1]

From several similar passages, it is plain that Dante
regarded as a failing his habit of absorption in
Theology, to the neglect of the lives of the saints.
Again and again, in the course of the poem, he has to be
roused from some abstract meditation, and his attention turned to good men as a source of knowledge of
things Divine.[2] At this point, when his eyes cannot
bear the direct vision of Christ, he must train himself
to see His light reflected in the Redeemed, that he
'may be able to comprehend *with all saints* what is the
breadth, and length, and depth, and height; and to know
the love of Christ, which passeth knowledge.'[3] The

---

[1] *Par*. xxiii. 70-75.

[2] For example : in *Purg*. xxix. 61, Matelda reproves him for gazing at
the sevenfold light of the Spirit, to the neglect of the Procession of Scripture writers inspired by that Spirit ; in *Purg*. xxxii. 1-9, the Theological
Virtues say 'Too fixed,' when they see him forget all else in looking at
'the second beauty' of Beatrice ; and in *Par*. xviii. 20, Beatrice reminds
him that all Paradise is not in her eyes, and turns him to the warrior-
saints of Mars (see p. 279).

[3] *Eph*. iii. 18, 19.

comparison of the Redeemed to a garden comes, of course, from the garden which man lost: this is the Celestial Eden or Paradise, won by Christ's Passion, in which every soul is a fair flower lifting its shining head to the Sun of its salvation. It is for this reason, as Mr. Gardner points out, that there are so many correspondences between this Heaven and the Earthly Paradise on the top of Mount Purgatory. The Procession of the Church down below answers to the Triumph of Christ here. 'It was in the Earthly Paradise, the highest region of the terrestrial world, that Dante beheld the despoiled Tree from which the forbidden fruit had been taken, and heard the reproachful murmur of "Adamo" (*Purg.* xxxii. 37-39); so now in the Firmament, the highest visible region of the celestial world, the poet sees the fruit of the redemption and atonement by Christ. Each again is but a prelude to the ascent to *più alta salute.* The passage of Lethe in the Earthly Paradise corresponds to the examination upon the theological virtues in the Firmament; at the intercession of the three maidens, presenting Faith, Hope and Charity, Beatrice had unveiled her countenance to Dante's gaze, and similarly it is his examination as to his knowledge of these three virtues which will permit him to make the further ascent into the hidden things of God. Also it is in this heaven that Adam himself appears to instruct Dante upon the fall, now that he has seen the mystery of Redemption; and to speak to him of the nature of his life in the Earthly Paradise, now that the poet has had a vision of the triumph of the new Adam in its celestial counterpart, the Firmament.' And finally, the contrast between Eve and Mary is striking and obvious; 'for Mary had healed the wound that Eve dealt the human race (*Par.* xxxiii. 4-6); or as St. Bernard puts it: Eve was the thorn, Mary came forth as the Rose; Eve was the thorn whose pride brought death to all, but Mary was the Rose diffusing the sweet odour of eternal salvation to all.'[1]

In naming the Virgin-Mother the Rose, Dante was

[1] *Dante's Ten Heavens,* 170, 171.

doubtless influenced by many associations. The direct origin was probably the Litany of the Blessed Virgin, in which she is called the *Rosa Mystica*,[1] on account of the place which the rose occupies among the flowers. The Virgin, says Landino, is 'deservedly compared to the rose, which by usefulness in divers diseases, by beauty, and by fragrance, holds the supremacy among the flowers.' It is quite possible, as Butler suggests, that Dante had in mind the name of the Cathedral of his native city, Santa Maria *del Fiore*.[2] According to Lana, the Apostles are called Lilies for three reasons. The whiteness of the outside of the flower signifies purity and faith; the red heart, incorruptibility and charity; the odour, their preaching and hope.[3]

At the word of Beatrice, Dante betook himself to 'the battle of the feeble brows,' that is, the effort to look with his weak eyes upon the splendour of the shining hosts of saints. In pity for the frailty of his sight, Christ had risen with His blinding glory to the upper Heavens, though His rays still lighted up the garden of souls. The poet compares what he saw to a meadow of flowers on which a ray of sunlight streams through a broken cloud, while his own eyes are in the shadow. 'The name of the beautiful Flower which he invoked morning and evening' drew all his mind to the greatest star,

---

[1] In his *Laus B.V.M.*, Bonaventura calls her 'Rosa decens, rosa munda'; and in his *Psalterium Minus B. Mariae Virginis* occurs the verse:

> Ave Virgo speciosa,
> Cuius quasi recens rosa,
> Spirat caro, cor laetatur,
> Mens in bonis demoratur.

[2] Compare *Par.* xxiii. 88: 'Il nome del bel fior,' i.e. of Mary.

[3] 'I am the Rose of Sharon and the Lily of the Valleys' (Cant. ii. 1, 2) was applied mystically to the Virgin. The Angel of the Annunciation is represented as bearing a lily in token of her purity, and for this reason both Florence and France chose the lily as their device. In pictures of the Coronation of the Virgin roses and lilies are usually introduced. A plantation of roses is often set in the background of pictures of the Madonna ('Quasi plantatio rosae in Hiericho'—*Ecclus.* xxiv. 14); and in some paintings of the Coronation the apostles down on earth stand round an open tomb, filled with roses and lilies, from which her body has just risen. See *Legends of the Madonna*, Introduction, for this and the following note.

> the sapphire beautiful
> With which the most clear heaven itself ensapphires, —

perhaps in allusion to the blue mantle with the star on the right shoulder, in which Christian art often clothes her.   Or, possibly, there is a reference to the '*Ave Maris Stella*' of the hymn, one mediæval interpretation of the Virgin's Hebrew name, Miriam, being *Star of the Sea*.[1]   In the colour Dante appears to be thinking of the vision of God in Exodus xxiv. 10: 'and there was under his feet as it were a paved work of a sapphire stone, and as it were the body of heaven in his clearness.'   We miss much of Dante's meaning if we think of the blue colour as confined to the Virgin; her sapphire star is so great that it 'ensapphires' the entire Heaven.   It is, indeed, the symbolic colour of this Eighth Heaven.   The Cherubim who preside over it, as we have seen more than once, are the Angels who excel in the wisdom and knowledge of God; and, in token of this, the proper colour of their wings in Christian art is blue, the clear sapphire blue of the sky, which represents unclouded Truth.[2]   In short, the

---

[1] 'When, instead of the single star on her veil or mantle, she has the crown of twelve stars, the allusion is to the text of the Apocalypse (xii. 1): "And there appeared a great sign in heaven : a woman clothed with the sun, and the moon under her feet, and upon her head a crown of twelve stars," and the number of the stars is in allusion to the number of the Apostles.'   The *Catholic Dictionary* in a note on the name Miriam (Art. 'Mary') says : 'The mediæval notion that the word "Mary" was connected with the Latin "mare" is curious.   The last syllable "yam," סָם, does mean the sea.   But how St. Bernard came to think "Mary" meant "star of the sea," we cannot say (מָאוֹר יָם, "light of the sea"?).   No part of the word resembles any word for star in Hebrew, Syriac, Chaldee, or, so far as we are aware, in any language.'   The interpretation gave scope for the play of pious fancy.   In the *Speculum* of the Virgin (Lectio iii.) Bonaventura writes : ' Well does Innocent say : By what aids can ships pass through so many perils to the shore of the Fatherland?   Assuredly, he says, by two, namely, by wood and star, that is, by the faith of the cross, and by the virtue of the light, which Mary, the star of the sea, brought forth for us.   Well, indeed, is Mary likened to a star of the sea, for purity, for radiancy, and for utility.   For Mary is a star most pure, a star most radiant, and a star most useful.   Mary is a star most pure, by living most purely ; and Mary is a star most radiant, by bringing forth the Eternal Ray ; Mary is a star most useful, by directing to the shore of the Fatherland.'

[2] For the symbolism of angelic colours, see Mrs. Jameson's *Sacred and Legendary Art*, 47-49.   As blue was the colour of the Cherubim, red was

colour with which the sapphire star of Mary ensapphires this Heaven represents the knowledge of
God shed forth through her, who, in Bonaventura's
words, 'gave birth to the Eternal Ray.'

Then follows what we may call the celestial Assumption of the Virgin,—not, as some call it, her Apotheosis.
Dante is obviously thinking of the heavenly counterpart of the Assumption of the body of Mary, which,
according to the belief of the Church, God did not
suffer to see corruption.   Like her Son, she rose from
the dead on the third day, and was received by Him
and the Angels into the joy of Paradise.   Speaking of
the Feast of the Assumption, St. Jerome says, as quoted
in the *Golden Legend*: 'It is on this day that the
chivalry of heaven came hastily for to meet with the
mother of God, and environed her with great light,
and brought her to her seat with praisings and songs
spiritual.   And then enjoyed them the celestial company
of Jerusalem with so great gladness that no man may
recount ne tell, and made joy and song.'[1]   It is this joy
of Paradise which begins here in the hymn of the
Archangel Gabriel.   'This great Ambassador of the
Holy King celestial'[2] descends once more on an errand
to the Virgin.   In the form of a crown of fire he
encircles the sapphire star, and revolves around her
with melody so heavenly sweet that the sweetest
music of earth had seemed the rending of a cloud in
thunder:

> 'I am Angelic Love, that circle round
> The joy sublime which breathes from out the womb
> That was the hostelry of our Desire;

---

that of the Seraphim, who burned with Divine love.   By the end of the
fifteenth century the distinction was disregarded.   For example, 'in
Raphael's Madonna di San Sisto, the whole background is formed of
Cherubim and Seraphim of a uniform delicate bluish tinge, as if composed
of air, and melting away into an abyss of golden glory, the principal
figures standing relieved against this flood of living love and light—
beautiful!'

[1] The Assumption of our Lady, Caxton's translation.   The bodily assumption is not an article of faith, but it is so commonly believed in the
Church that to deny it would be 'a mark of insolent temerity.'   Dante
accepted it without any doubt (*Par.* xxv. 127-129).

[2] *Conv.* ii. 6.

> And I shall circle, Lady of Heaven, while
> Thou followest thy Son, and mak'st diviner
> The sphere supreme, because thou enterest there.'[1]

I cannot but think that this has more meaning than is
usually found in it. Aquinas distinguishes between
the *essential bliss* of heaven and the *accidental reward*.
The essential bliss he calls the *corona aurea*, or simply
aurea; and the accidental reward, *aureola*, a diminutive
of *aurea*. All saints in the Fatherland receive the
aurea, the essential bliss of perfect union of the soul
with God; but the *aureola*, or accidental reward, is
given only to those who, in the earthly warfare, have
won an excellent victory over some special foe: virgins,
martyrs, and doctors and preachers.[2] Now, according
to another passage in Aquinas, it was fitting that the
Annunciation should be made by an Angel because of
the virginity of the Mother of God, since virginity is
'cognate to the Angels.'[3] I suggest, then, that the
meaning is to this effect: The Archangel Gabriel forms
himself into the *aureola*, the accidental reward of
Mary's virginity;[4] and it is to this he refers when he
says, 'I am Angelic Love,' the Love cognate to that
virginity. We must remember, of course, that the
word 'accidental' does not imply a lowering, but a
heightening of the essential bliss, 'as political felicity
is adorned by nobility, and bodily felicity by beauty.'[5]
Further, all this has its bearing on the blessedness of
Gabriel himself and all the hosts of Angels. Aquinas

---

[1] *Par.* xxiii. 91-108 (Longfellow). 'Our Desire' is probably a reference
to 1 Peter i. 12: 'which things the angels desire to look into.'

[2] *Summa*, Supp. q. xcvi. a. 1, 11. See above, p. 135 note.

[3] *Summa*, iii. q. xxx. a. 2. What Aquinas means by 'cognate' is seen
from *Summa*, Supp. q. xcvi. a. 9: 'Virginity is said to be the angelic life,
inasmuch as by grace virgins imitate that which angels have by nature.'

[4] In *Summa*, Supp. q. xcvi. a. 5, Aquinas discusses whether the *aureola*
can be rightly said to be given to the Virgin since she had no struggle to
maintain her purity, and therefore cannot be said to have gained an
excellent victory. His decision is that 'she rightly has the *aureola*, that
she may be conformed to the other members of the Church in whom is
found virginity'; and that the struggle came to her, as to her Son,
through other temptations of the enemy.

[5] *Summa*, Supp. q. xcvi. a. 10: The *aureola* is properly in the mind, but
from its joy 'there redounds a certain comeliness to the body.'

denies that the *aureola* can be earned by Angels,[1] yet
admits that they can win an accidental reward in the
joy they have in the salvation of those to whom they
minister.[2]   This is Gabriel's joy here, as he circles round
'the hostelry of our Desire': these hosts of souls
redeemed were the fruit of his Annunciation to the
Virgin, when he 'opened his wings' in Nazareth
centuries ago.   I do not press this interpretation, but
all these things were familiar to Dante's mind, and it
would certainly give a much more definite significance
to the whole passage.

The Assumption follows.   Joining in the Archangel's
song, the other lights fill Heaven with the sound of
Mary's name; and, surrounded thus by the praises of
the souls redeemed by her Son, 'the crowned flame'
passes up beyond the poet's sight into the Primum
Mobile, 'the royal mantle' that folds in all the spheres
with love and life.   Yearningly the white souls reach
up after her with their flames, as in pictures of her
Coronation we see Apostles and saints stretching up
their hands.   Meantime they remain behind, as waiting
for 'the redemption of their bodies,' and sing the
Regina coeli, the Easter Antiphon at lauds and compline,
in hope of their own rising from the dead.   And the
sweet music of that hope never faded from the Pilgrim's
heart.[3]

---

[1] *Summa*, Supp. q. xcvi. a. 9.

[2] *Summa*, i. q. lxii. a. 9; Luke xv. 10.   This 'accidental' joy of the
Angels may increase until the day of judgment, that is, until the number
of the 'heirs of salvation' is fulfilled.

[3] *Par.* xxiii. 109-129.   The Antiphon is:

> Regina coeli, laetare! alleluia,
> Quia quem meruisti portare, alleluia,
> Resurrexit, sicut dixit, alleluia.
> Ora pro nobis Deum; alleluia.

CHAPTER XXII

3. *St. Peter examines Dante on Faith*

WHEN Mary passed out of his sight into the Crystalline Heaven, Dante broke into an exclamation of wonder and praise as he turned his eyes to contemplate the heavenly treasures stored up in the Apostles. The metaphors, it must be confessed, are somewhat mixed. The Apostles are at once the sowers or the soil (according as we understand *bobolce* of xxiii. 132), and the chests in which the abundant harvest is stored. The harvest is not simply their own personal bliss, but the life and joy they have in the treasure of redeemed souls all around them in this Heaven, won in weeping in the Babylonian exile of earth, where, for this wealth, they abandoned gold. Next to the Son of God and Mary triumphs St. Peter, 'who holds the keys of such a glory.'[1]

Beatrice now appeals to 'the fellowship elect to the great supper of the blessed Lamb' to share the feast

[1] *Par.* xxiii. 130-139. The meaning is that Peter is the third in this Triumph of Christ's Church: in the White Rose his place is at Mary's right hand (xxxii. 124-126). The older commentators take *bobolce* of l. 132 as equivalent to the Latin *bubulcus*, a ploughman (comp. *bifolco* in ii. 18), though the form is feminine to correspond with *arche* of the previous line. Others derive it from *bubulca* or *bubulcata*, the quantity of land a yoke of oxen can plough in a day. Dante seems to have had a number of passages of Scripture in his mind: the parable of the sower, where soil and seed are identified (Matt. xiii. 23: 'He that was sown in the good soil,' R.V. and Vulgate); Gal. vi. 8: 'He that soweth to the Spirit shall of the Spirit reap eternal life'; 2 Cor. ix. 6: 'He that soweth bountifully shall reap also bountifully'; and the references to Babylon and weeping are from the Psalms : cxxxvii. 1: 'By the rivers of Babylon, there we sat down, yea, we wept, when we remembered Zion'; and cxxvi. 5, 6: 'They that sow in tears shall reap in joy. Though he goeth on his way weeping, bearing forth the seed, he shall come again with joy, bringing his sheaves with him' (R.V.).

with the Pilgrim.[1] Already he has a foretaste of the
crumbs that fall from their table ;[2] and she prays them
to satisfy his boundless yearning by sprinkling him, as
with drops of dew, from that Fountain of which they
ever drink. Whereupon the souls, in joyous response
to this prayer, made themselves into 'spheres on fixed
poles,' outflashed like comets, and, in fashion of the
wheels of a clock, revolved swift or slow, according to
the measure of the riches of their love. This is often
taken to mean that groups of saints formed themselves
into *crowns* and encircled Beatrice and Dante in
'carols' (*carole*, 1. 16) or dance-rings. This, I think,
is a mistake. Dante says nothing about crowns ; the
word he uses is *spere*, spheres, a quite different thing.
Crowns do not revolve ' on fixed poles.' What Dante
sees is the various groups of souls forming themselves
into globes or orbs of fire, according to natural, or, if
we prefer it, supernatural, spiritual affinity, and thus
separating themselves into the various 'carols' or choirs
that constitute the harmony of that world of love.
Each carol is a full orb, perfect and complete in itself,
yet, like the wheels of the horologe, only part of the
entire harmony of the celestial dance. The poet is
thinking of the way in which the saints were believed
to be divided into different ' choirs' according to the
degree and quality of their holiness, corresponding
to the nine choirs of Angels.[3] The highest of these
is 'the glorious company of the Apostles,' and to it
Dante's eye is now drawn as the sphere of greatest
beauty. From this glowing orb there issue forth in

---

[1] Rev. xix. 7-9.   [2] *Conv.* i. 1.
[3] For example, in the 'Byzantine Guide to Painting,' a manual for the
decoration of churches with scenes from Scripture, in the instructions
for the representation of the Second Advent the various choirs of the
saints rise to meet their Lord in the air, in the order of the measure of
grace they have received : 1st, the choir of apostles ; 2nd, of our first
parents ; 3rd, of patriarchs ; 4th, of prophets ; 5th, of bishops ; 6th, of
martyrs ; 7th, of saints ; 8th, of righteous kings ; 9th, of martyred or
solitary women. In pictures of the Last Judgment, these nine choirs are
grouped into three orders, corresponding to the three Angelic Hierarchies
(Didron's *Christian Iconography*, ii. 345, 346—Bohn). An example of this
division into choirs is seen in the mosaic of the Last Judgment in the
Cathedral of Torcello near Venice.

succession the souls of Peter, James, and John, who
examine Dante on Faith, Hope, and Love respectively,
—the three theological virtues without which he had
been unfit to ascend into the Empyrean and attain the
Beatific Vision. 'There is,' says Aquinas, 'a twofold
happiness of man : one proportionate to human nature,
whereunto man can arrive by the principles of his own
nature. Another happiness there is exceeding the nature
of man, whereunto man can arrive only by a divine
virtue involving a certain participation in the Deity,
according as it is said that by Christ we are made
"partakers of the divine nature" (2 Peter i. 4). And
because this manner of happiness exceeds the capacities
of human nature, the natural principles of human
action, on which man proceeds to such well-doing as is
in proportion with himself, suffice not to direct man
unto the aforesaid happiness. Hence there must be
superadded to man by the gift of God certain principles, whereby he may be put on the way to supernatural happiness. . . . Such principles are called
theological virtues : both because they have God for
their object, inasmuch as by them we are directed
aright to God ; as also it is only by divine revelation
in Holy Scripture that such virtues are taught.'[1] It is
therefore necessary for Dante to prove at this point of
his pilgrimage that he has the Faith which leads to
Sight, the Hope which fulfils itself in Comprehension,
and the Love whose Fruition is the perfect union of
the soul with God, its final end.

Now of these three virtues Peter, James, and John
became the representatives in mystical minds. Landino
derives the idea from their names. Peter, meaning a
stone, represents the firmness of faith. James or
Jacobus signifies supplantation, and therefore stands
for hope, because hope puts *under its feet* every adversity
and toil.[2] And John means grace, and thus represents
charity. But the idea has its root in the way in which,

---

[1] *Summa*, i-ii. q. lxii. a. 1 (Rickaby's trans.).
[2] Gen. xxvii. 36. *Supplant* is taken in its etymological sense—to put
under the soles of the feet.

as Dante puts it, 'Jesus gave greater clearness to the three': that is, by admitting them more intimately than the rest to the most sacred parts of His earthly experience, such as the raising of Jairus' daughter, His Transfiguration, and the garden of Gethsemane.[1] As thus by faith, hope, and love these three had been able to penetrate most deeply into the mystery of Revelation on earth, Dante regards them as the souls best fitted to examine him in these virtues, which open up the final mysteries of Heaven.

From out the sphere of the Apostles, then, Dante saw the soul of St. Peter come forth, its brightest fire, and circle round Beatrice with so Divine a song that the poet's imagination cannot recall it. Whereupon Beatrice asks him to test Dante concerning the faith by which he once walked upon the sea.[2] Not that the Apostle does not already see his faith, hope, and love in the mirror of the Divine Mind ; but that it is fitting Dante should glorify, by speaking out his faith, the kingdom whose citizens are made by faith. As a bachelor in the schools prepares himself for the question about to be proposed by the master, Dante arms himself for the encounter; and it must be confessed that, for three cantos, we have an almost purely scholastic discussion, in which it is not easy to see any gleam of poetic gold.[3] The substance is taken almost entirely

---

[1] *Par.* xxv. 31-33. Plumptre says 'the thought that the chosen witnesses of the Transfiguration (Matt. xvii. 1) were respectively the representatives of Faith, Hope and Love is found in Aquinas, *Summ.* iii. 45, 3.' This, however, is not so. Discussing the question whether a fitting choice was made of witnesses of the Transfiguration, Aquinas, quoting Chrysostom, says it was fitting to choose the greater Apostles : '"Nam Petrus excellens fuit in dilectione," quam habuit ad Christum, et iterum in potestate sibi commissa ; "Joannes vero in privilegio amoris, quo a Christo diligebatur propter suam virginitatem," et iterum propter praerogativam evangelicae doctrinae ; "Jacobus autem propter praerogativam martyrii."' In *Conv.* ii. 1 Dante says the *moral* significance of Christ's taking only three to the Mount of Transfiguration is that in the most secret things we should have but few companions.

[2] *Par.* xxiv. 34-39. Objection is sometimes made that Peter began to sink from lack of faith. True, but the question : 'wherefore didst thou doubt?' (Matt. xiv. 31) implies the faith which had enabled him to walk up to that point.

[3] Stopford A. Brooke thinks a definite creed incompatible with poetry. 'Art not only rejects, it abhors all attempts to bind down into unchang-

from Aquinas; and Dante has the great advantage of himself propounding the questions he is to answer. Some writers think the whole passage is a reminiscence of the poet's studies at Paris, Bologna, and elsewhere, but of this we have no proof.[1] The questions put by St. Peter are seven in number.

(1)   'Say, good Christian, make thyself manifest:
      Faith, what is it?'

Dante prepares himself for the answer by lifting his brow to the light of the Apostle who excelled in faith; by turning to Beatrice, perhaps in her character of the Ideal Church; and by prayer for grace, since the answer lies beyond the natural powers of man. He then quotes the exact words of St. Paul in Heb. xi. 1:

'Faith is the substance of things hoped for,
And the argument of things not seen;
And this appears to me to be its quiddity,'[2]

or essence. No definition could be got from St. Peter's writings; hence St. Paul is joined with him as the brother who aided him in 'setting Rome on the good path'—the path of faith.

(2) The second question carries us into the midst of scholastic subtleties which we find difficulty in associat-

ing forms the thoughts and emotions which play like lightning round the infinite horizons towards which the imagination sails, piloted by love, and hope, and faith. It has no creeds, no articles of faith, no schemes of salvation, no confessions; it cannot have them by its very nature. The unknowable, but the believable, is its country, its native land, its home. ... Even Dante, who was obliged to do something of this kind of work, does it only as a means by which he may launch himself forward into the infinite' (*Tennyson*, Introduction).

[1] Boccaccio says: 'This poet was of marvellous capacity and firmness of memory, and of piercing intellect, insomuch that when he was in Paris, and in a disputation *de quolibet* held there in the schools of theology fourteen theses had been maintained by divers men of worth on divers matters, he straightway gathered all together, with the arguments for and against urged by the opponents, and in due sequence, as they had been produced, recited them without break, following the same order, subtly solving and refuting the counter arguments; the which thing was reputed all but a miracle by them that stood by' (*Life of Dante*, viii., Wicksteed's trans.).

[2] *Par.* xxiv. 52-66. The Epistle to the Hebrews was attributed to Paul without hesitation. The verse in the Vulgate is exactly as Dante gives it: 'Est autem fides sperandorum substantia, rerum argumentum non parentium.'

ing with the simple Fisherman. St. Peter accepts the
definition, but asks why St. Paul has set Faith 'among
the *substances,* and then among the *arguments.*' The
answer turns on the contrast between Faith and Sight
—whether sight of the eyes, or of the mind through
first principles. The things which Dante is now *seeing*
in Paradise are on earth matters of mere *belief,* since
they lie beyond sense and reason alike. This belief in
their existence is the only foundation we have in this
world on which to build 'the high hope,' ' the hope of
glory'; and therefore, says Dante, ' it takes the intention of *substance*'—a very subtle statement. It is evident
that Dante takes *substance* partly in its etymological
sense—the thing that *stands under* something else : in
the present case, the foundation on which the theological virtue of Hope must be built. But the word
intention carries us far beyond this bare etymological
meaning. Aquinas says intention, as the word signifies,
means the tending towards some end—the stretching
out of the will towards it. Hence when Dante says
that faith ' takes the *intention* of substance,' he means
that faith contains this element of will, will reaching
out towards the substance, the eternal unseen reality,
and making it even here part of itself by a foretaste
and earnest of it.[1]

Dante now proceeds to explain why Paul placed
Faith among the *arguments.* Faith itself is not created

[1] *Summa,* i-ii. q. xii. a. 1. The usual interpretation of *intenza,* intention, in this passage is that faith carries the nature, or purport, or
designation of substance ; but, with Aquinas before him, Dante would
never have made this loose use of the word. His meaning runs into the
idea of ' substance' in *Summa,* ii-ii. q. iv. a. 1, where this definition of
Faith in Heb. xi. 1 is discussed. Aquinas there takes ' substance' as
equivalent to the first principle of anything, which contains virtually the
whole thing, as the first principles of knowledge contain all knowledge :
' Therefore in this fashion faith is said to be the substance of things hoped
for; because the first beginning of things hoped for is in us by the assent
of faith, which virtually contains all the things hoped for. Faith is a
habit of mind, by which eternal life is begun in us, making the intellect
to assent to things that are not apparent.' All this may seem confusing,
but the meaning is simple enough : faith involves the ' *intention* of the
substance'—the *reaching out* of the will to the unseen realities themselves, so that even here the beginnings and first principles of eternal
life are in the believer.

by arguments, for arguments are of the reason, and
the objects of faith are beyond the reason. It is
directly infused by God, and involves belief in the
things revealed by Him on the one sole ground that
they *are* revealed by Him : 'God is the motive of Faith
inasmuch as He is the First Truth.' But once this
supernatural basis is laid, the natural reason comes
into play, and we must 'syllogize' from it, as Dante
says, without further sight; and 'therefore it contains
the intention of *argument*.' 'Intention' bears the same
meaning as before—the power of an argument to
make the will *stretch towards* its end. 'Motives of
credibility' come in to give a reasonable certitude to
what we already believe on the motive of Faith. The
'intention' or tendency of the will is towards arguments which give this certitude. As Aquinas says :
'When a man has a prompt will to believe, he loves
the truth believed, and thinks it over, and embraces
any arguments that he can find in its favour.'[1] In
short, faith 'contains the *intention* of argument,' the
stretching of mind and will towards proofs and
evidences of the things believed. St. Peter welcomes
the answer as beyond the sophist's wit.[2]

(3) The third question drops these abstract subtleties
and becomes sharply personal :

> 'Right well has been gone over
> Of this coin now the alloy and the weight;
> But tell me if thou hast it in thy purse ?'[3]

The answer came with almost unexpected assurance :

> ' Yes have I, so shining and so round,
> That in its stamp to me there's no *perhaps*.'

This certainty is somewhat surprising when we remember the doubts concerning the Divine justice and
predestination which beset Dante in the lower Heavens.
He evidently means us to understand that at a certain
height of contemplation every doubt is lost: the coin

---

[1] *Summa*, ii-ii. q. ii. a. 10.   [2] *Par*. xxiv. 67-81.
[3] *Par*. xxiv. 83-85. According to Casini, the *coin* is faith, the *alloy* the
definition by which its essence appears (ll. 64, 65), the *weight* the demonstration of the agreement of the definition with the essence of faith
(ll. 70-78).

of faith is a perfect circle, and its image and superscription shining clear.   This absolute certainty on every point of the faith is necessary, according to the Church's teaching, to the very existence of faith: one doctrine doubted or denied invalidates the whole.[1]

(4) St. Peter's fourth question demands whence came to Dante 'this precious stone on which is founded every virtue.' The reply is—from the Divine inspiration of the Old and New Testaments:

> 'The plenteous rain
> Of the Holy Spirit, which is shed abroad
> Over the ancient parchments, and the new,
> A syllogism is, which brought it to a proof
> So keen for me, that, in comparison therewith,
> All demonstration seems to me obtuse.'

Since the objects of faith are above the power of the natural reason to discover, they must come through a revelation from God, and this is given through the Sacred Scriptures.   For the same reason, no 'demonstration' of their truth can be given by the natural faculties.   The only 'syllogism' that carries conviction is the inspiration of the Holy Spirit in the Scriptures themselves; and this carries with it a corresponding movement of the Spirit within the hearer's heart.   For, 'of those who hear the same preaching, some believe and some do not,' and therefore there must be an interior action of God convincing the soul of the

---

[1] *Summa*, ii-ii. q. v. a. 3: 'The formal object of faith is the First Truth, according as it is manifested in the Holy Scriptures and the teaching of the Church, which proceeds from the First Truth. . . . It is clear that he who adheres to the teaching of the Church, as to an infallible rule, assents to all the things which the Church teaches; else, if concerning what the Church teaches, he holds what he wishes, and does not hold what he does not wish, he does not adhere to the teaching of the Church as to an infallible rule, but to his own will.   And so it is clear that a heretic who pertinaciously disbelieves one article of faith is not ready to follow the Church's teaching in all points. . . . Such a heretic as to one article has not *faith* in regard to the other articles, but only a certain *opinion*, according to his own will.' 'The virtue of faith is destroyed by a single act of disbelief in revealed truth previously accepted on the authority of God. So that, e.g. if a Catholic ceases to believe in Transubstantiation but continues to believe in the Trinity, his acceptance of the latter is merely a natural assent and does not proceed from divine faith. This is the general, though not the universal, teaching of Catholic theologians' (Addis and Arnold's *Cath. Dictionary*, Art. 'Faith').

Divine inspiration of Scripture. It is a 'syllogism,' not of logic, but of the Spirit.[1]

(5) The next question brings us to those 'motives of credibility' spoken of a little ago. Dante bases his faith on the Word of God in the Old and New Testaments: St. Peter asks why he holds these to be a Divine Word at all. If his reason is simply a certain internal feeling that they are inspired, the proof is a mere subjective one, and may be delusive. There must be evidences outside the soul, fixed facts independent of individual thoughts and emotions, motives, not of faith itself, but of the credibility of the things proposed for faith. The chief of these 'motives of credibility' is the working of miracles. 'The proper criterion of the Divine origin of a verbal communication . . . consists in external, supernatural, and Divine facts or effects, which God intimately connects with the proposition of His Revelation, and by which He signifies to us His will that we should believe that He has spoken.'[2] This is precisely what Dante means in his reply:

'The proof which doth disclose to me the truth
Are the works that followed, for which nature
Ne'er iron heated yet, nor anvil beat.'[3]

(6) But the miracles themselves must be proved: how does Dante know that they are not fables?

'Say, who assureth thee
That those works were? That self-same thing
That would be proved, naught else, swears it to thee.'

---

[1] *Par.* xxiv. 88-96; *Summa*, ii-ii. q. vi. a. 1. Comp. *Contra Gentiles*, iii. 155: 'The invisible good things, the vision of which makes the happiness of the blessed, and which are the objects of faith, are first revealed by God to the blessed angels by open vision: then by the ministry of angels they are manifested by God to certain men, not by open vision, but by a certitude arising from divine revelation. This revelation is made by an inner light of the mind, elevating the mind to see such things as the natural light of the understanding cannot attain to' (Father Rickaby's trans.).

[2] Wilhelm and Scannell's *Manual of Catholic Theology*, i. 125.

[3] *Par.* xxiv. 97-102. In *Summa*, i. q. cx. a. 4 Aquinas argues that a miracle is something done beyond the *entire* course of nature, and therefore God alone can work it. A thing may be against nature in some particular point, as for a stone to rise in the air, but to throw up a stone is no miracle.

In other words, Dante is arguing in a circle: 'I believe in the Scriptures because of the miracles recorded in them; and I believe in the miracles because of the Scriptures which record them.' From this circle he escapes by an appeal to the greater miracle of converting the world without miracle:

> 'If the world was turned to Christianity,'
> Said I, 'withouten miracles, this one
> Is such, the rest are not the hundredth part;
> For thou didst enter poor and fasting
> Into the field to sow there the good plant,
> Which was once a vine, and now is grown a thorn.' [1]

The argument is taken from St. Augustine: 'If they (sceptics) do not believe that these miracles were wrought by Christ's apostles to gain credence to their preaching of His resurrection and ascension, this one grand miracle suffices for us, that the whole world has believed without any miracles.' [2] The assumption is that but for miracles the truths of Revelation would not have gained a hearing, or, at least, such a hearing as prepares for faith; and it is this assumption which makes it necessary for the Church to claim the continuance within it of miraculous power. Dante's answer is followed by the singing of *Te Deum laudamus* by the surrounding choirs of the Redeemed, in praise for that faith by which St. Peter

---

[1] *Par.* xxiv. 103-111.

[2] *De Civ. Dei*, Bk. XXII. 5. In this chap. St. Augustine argues the incredibility of the world's conversion, apart from miracles, by such men as the Apostles—'uninstructed in any branch of a liberal education, without any of the refinement of heathen learning, unskilled in grammar, not armed with dialectic, not adorned with rhetoric, but plain fishermen, and very few in number (Dods' trans.). Aquinas reproduces the argument in *Contra Gentiles*, i. 6: 'This so wonderful conversion of the world to the Christian faith is so certain a sign of past miracles, that they need no further reiteration, since they appear evidently in their effects. It would be more wonderful than all other miracles, if without miraculous signs the world had been induced by simple and low-born men to believe truths so arduous, to do works so difficult, to hope for reward so high. And yet even in our times God ceases not through His saints to work miracles for the confirmation of the faith' (Rickaby's trans.). Dante passes by Peter's humble birth and lack of learning: his poverty and hunger were a more pointed rebuke of his wealthy and luxurious successors, who changed the vine into a thorn.

went forth 'poor and fasting' to sow the good plant of which they themselves were the fruit.[1]

(7) We come now to the final question. St. Peter says it is fitting that Dante express his creed and tell how it presented itself for his belief : in fulfilment, evidently, of St. Paul's words : 'With the heart man believeth unto righteousness; and with the mouth confession is made unto salvation.'[2]   Dante begins his reply by a reference to a great act of faith on the part of St. Peter,—his entrance into Christ's empty sepulchre :

> 'O holy father, spirit who dost see
> What thou didst so believe that thou didst conquer
> Towards the sepulchre the younger feet.'

That is, Peter *sees* now the risen body of Christ, concerning which he had only *faith* as he ran to the sepulchre; but even faith made him conquer the younger feet of John, who at the time had no faith in the Resurrection. The difficulty is that it was John who outran Peter and came first to the sepulchre. It is not in the least likely that Dante forgot this. His meaning undoubtedly is that while the younger feet, through lack of faith, lingered at the entrance, Peter's faith carried him past his doubting companion to the inside.[3]   This does no injustice to John, since he himself

---

[1] *Par.* xxiv. 110-114.   It is perhaps worth while noting Dante's view of miracles in his other works.   In *Conv.* iii. 14 he says that through Philosophy 'one believes that every miracle may have a reason in a higher intellect.   Whence our good *faith* has its origin, from which comes *hope* of the foreseen desire, and from this is born the operation of *charity*.'   In *De Mon.* ii. 4 he argues the Divine right of Rome to the empire of the world from the miracles and portents wrought by God on her behalf, and winds up with a curious parallel between the miracles wrought for the temporal kingdom and those for the spiritual : 'It was fitting . . . that He who when visible [i.e. God when visible in the Incarnation] was to show miracles for the sake of things invisible [i.e. the invisible things of His spiritual kingdom], should, while invisible [i.e. before the Incarnation], show miracles for the sake of things visible [i.e. for the temporal and visible affairs of the Roman Empire].'

[2] Rom. x. 10.   Aquinas says confession of faith is necessary to salvation under certain circumstances—as when silence would withhold honour from God or profit from our neighbour, or leave the impression that the faith is false (*Summa*, ii-ii. q. iii. a. 2).

[3] In *De Mon.* iii. 9, however, the incident is given as an instance of Peter's impulsiveness rather than his faith : 'John says that he went in immediately when he came to the tomb, seeing the other disciple lingering at the entrance.'   Perhaps Dante wished to retract his former judgment.

says it was only after he entered and saw how the
grave-clothes were folded up, that he believed.[1] It is
somewhat strange, however, that Dante should choose
this incident as an example of Peter's faith; when he
was being asked for the confession of his own faith, it
would have been more natural to have referred to the
Apostle's great confession of Jesus as the Son of God
at Cæsarea Philippi.[2]

Dante's creed falls into two parts—the Unity and the
Trinity of God: the former a truth of the natural
reason as well as of Revelation, the latter of Revelation
alone. 'The truths that we confess concerning God,'
says Aquinas, 'fall under two modes. Some things
true of God are beyond all the competence of human
reason, as that God is Three and One. Other things
there are to which even human reason can attain, as
the existence and unity of God, which philosophers
have proved to a demonstration under the guidance
of the light of natural reason.'[3] Hence for the first
article of his creed Dante adduces philosophical as
well as Scriptural proofs:

> 'I believe in one God,
> Sole and eternal, who moveth all the heaven,
> Himself unmoved, with love and with desire.
> And for such faith not only have I proofs
> Physic and metaphysic, but 'tis given me also
> By the truth which from this place rains down
> Through Moses, through the Prophets and the Psalms,
> Through the Gospel, and through you who wrote
> After the burning Spirit made you nurses.'[4]

The opening words of this article are packed full of
scholastic subtleties. It would surprise me, for example,
if Dante in his own mind did not give the full scholastic

---

[1] John xx. 5-8.   [2] Matt. xvi. 16.
[3] *Cont. Gent.* i. 3. For the general principles of Sacred Doctrine, see
Summa, i. q. i.
[4] *Par.* xxiv. 115-138. I have translated *almi* in the last line *nurses* as
being much nearer the sense than 'blessed' or 'holy' or 'divine,' as many
render it. Dante remembers that he is speaking to the Apostle to whom
Christ gave repeated commands to feed His flock (John xxi. 15-17), and
that the power to obey descended in the fire of Pentecost, 'the burning
Spirit' that kindled them with inspiration. The idea is that of the
'nursing fathers' of Is. xlix. 23.

value to the word 'in' in 'I believe in one God.' Aquinas drew a distinction between *credere Deum*, belief in God as the subject-matter of faith—'I believe that God is'; *credere Deo*, belief on the authority of God—'I believe what God says'; and *credere in Deum*, including both the former meanings—'I believe in God on God's authority.' This last aspect of faith, according to Aquinas, involves the movement of the intellect by the *will*, and therefore the reaching of the will towards God as our final end.[1] It would be quite after the habit of Dante's mind to crowd all this into the statement: 'Io credo *in* uno Iddio'—the 'in' implying that his faith, while a thing of the intellect, involved a moral element, an 'intention' or reaching out of the will towards God as final end.

The 'proofs physical and metaphysical' run back undoubtedly to Aristotle's *Physics* and *Metaphysics*. According to 'the Philosopher,' as Aquinas and Dante loved to call him, Physics is the science of Nature, and Nature is existence in so far as it participates in *motion*.[2] The instinctive action of the human mind seeks to get behind the moving phenomena of Physics to some immovable reality or substance which is the source of their movement, and this gives rise to Metaphysics, the science of the first principles of all existence. These principles are four: Form or Essence, Matter or Substratum, Moving or Efficient Cause, and End; and these led Aristotle to the conception of God as pure Spirit, 'the first of all substances, the necessary first source of movement who is himself unmoved: a being with everlasting life, and perfect blessedness, engaged in never-ending self-contemplation: acting on the world as the primary object of love in which desire and reason fall into unity.'[3] This is what Dante

---

[1] *Summa*, ii-ii. q. ii. a. 2; Wilhelm and Scannell's *Manual of Cath. Theology*, i. 117.

[2] 'It is not the concern of physical science to study the first origin of all things: that study belongs to the metaphysician, who deals with being in general and realities *apart from motion*' (*Cont. Gent.* ii. 37).

[3] Wallace, *Outlines of the Philosophy of Aristotle*, 73; Ueberweg, *History of Philosophy*, i. 157-169.

means by 'proofs physical and metaphysical,' leading up by the natural action of human reason to the conception of one God, sole and eternal, the unmoved Mover of all the universe by the power of love, which makes all things desire Him as their final end. And this argument of natural reason is confirmed by the Revelation of Scripture.[1]

The second article of the poet's creed is the Trinity in Unity of God, and this being a truth of Revelation alone, proofs of reason are absolutely impossible : it must be received on the sole authority of the First Truth :

> 'And I believe in three Persons eternal, and these
> I believe one Essence, so One and so Trine,
> It bears to be conjoined with *are* and *is*.
> With the profound condition of Divinity
> Which I now touch, the evangelic teaching
> Full often sets its seal upon my mind.
> This is the Principle, this is the spark
> Which then dilates into a living flame,
> And, like a star in heaven, sparkles in me.'[2]

In the reference to *are* and *is* in line 141, we naturally suppose that *are* refers to the three Persons, and *is* to the one Essence; but the grammar of the sentence forbids this. It is the Essence alone that 'bears to be conjoined with *are* and *is*.' The question is discussed by Aquinas. Names that indicate the Essence of God, he says, may be used as substantives or as adjectives. If as substantives, they may be predicated of the Three Persons in the singular only; if as adjectives, they may be predicated of the Three Persons in the plural. The object of this law of language is so to preserve the unity of Essence and the distinction

---

[1] In *Summa*, i. q. ii. a. 3 Aquinas gives five proofs of the existence of God from the natural reason : (1) From the principle of motion—the mind demands some First Cause of motion, itself immovable ; (2) From the order of Efficient Causes in objects of sense—nothing can be its own efficient cause, and reason is forced to postulate a First Efficient Cause ; (3) From possible and necessary things—all things cannot be merely possible, some must be necessary, and of these there must be some one which is finally necessary, uncaused by any necessity beyond itself and the cause of all other necessary things ; (4) From degrees of goodness— there must be one final and perfect goodness, the source of all the inferior grades ; (5) From the idea of government—since some things are without understanding, and yet reach their end, there must exist one supreme directing Intelligence. [2] *Par.* xxiv. 139-147.

of the Persons as to avoid lapsing into Sabellianism on
the one hand, or Tritheism on the other. Aquinas gives
the Athanasian creed as an illustration of his meaning.
When Athanasius says: 'They are not three eternals,
but one eternal. As also there are not three incom-
prehensibles, nor three uncreated, but one uncreated,
and one incomprehensible,' he is using these words as
substantives; but when he adds: 'But the whole three
Persons are co-eternal together, and co-equal,' he is
using the words as adjectives.[1]

The closing words of the poet's creed seem to be
chosen with the same theological exactitude:

> 'This is the Principle, this is the spark
> Which then dilates into a living flame,
> And, like a star in heaven, sparkles in me.'[2]

There is dispute as to the reference of '*this*,' some
taking it to relate to 'the evangelic teaching' of the
preceding line, others more generally to the faith just
professed. Thus, according to Scartazzini, the lines are
equivalent to: 'This point of faith is the foundation
and the source from which emanate the other articles
of the Christian faith, which is in me as a star which
disperses the darkness.' Dante had probably a much
more exact theological idea before his mind. 'This is
the Principle' refers neither to 'the evangelic teaching'
nor to faith in general, but to the doctrine of the
Trinity just laid down. The word '*Principle*' directs
us to the doctrine known as the Temporal Mission of
the Divine Persons. The Father is the Principle
absolutely, since from Him proceed the Son and the
Holy Spirit. As Principle, He 'sends' the Son and the
Spirit to mankind on the temporal mission of salvation;
and this temporal mission being a continuation of

---

[1] *Summa*, i. q. xxxix. a. 3. The reason given by Aquinas is that 'a
substantive noun or name signifies something by mode of *substance*, but
an adjective only by mode of *accident* inhering in the subject.' Hence to
join a substantive noun with a plural verb in the case of God would be to
multiply the Substance, or to distribute it among the three Persons, and
thus make three separate Gods. See Augustine, *De Trin.* v. 10: 'Those
things which absolutely belong to God as His essence, are spoken of the
Trinity in the singular, not in the plural.'

[2] *Par.* xxiv. 145-147.

Their eternal 'procession' from the Father, implies no inferiority of those sent: They are of one substance with Their Principle, and therefore all Three co-operate in the effects which are the object of the Mission. Further, there is a twofold manner of this mission— one visible, of which the supreme example is the Incarnation, the other invisible, as in the entrance of the Son and the Spirit into a human soul in so intimate a way that They are united with it in a new and supernatural life. Now, I have no doubt that both forms of the mission were in Dante's mind, although, inasmuch as it is his personal faith he is here confessing, the main emphasis is laid on the invisible mission to his own soul—the spark of supernatural light created in him by the coming of Son and Spirit from their Principle, and its dilation into a living flame, sparkling within him like a star in heaven. What he means to say is that it is no mere light shed by a bare doctrine of the Trinity, from which he can infer logically the other doctrines of the faith. It is an irradiation of the soul by the very life of the Trinity being thus imparted to it from Him who is its Principle; in short, to use the words of the Apostle to whom he speaks, he is now 'partaker of Divine nature.' True, the supernatural light is but a star as yet, since faith is seeing Divine things 'in a mirror,' and not 'face to face'; nevertheless it is the spiritual beginning of the final vision, for, as Aquinas says, 'to the Blessed the invisible mission is made the very *principle* of their beatitude.'[1]

If to some readers the foregoing exposition seems too doctrinal, it must be remembered that Dante was a theologian of the first rank, and that at this time he had probably good reason to state his creed with the utmost theological exactitude. Among the early commentators, there is a persistent tradition that the poet was accused of heresy, and that this Canto is his defence.[2] There certainly seems to be a strong con-

---

[1] *Summa*, i. q. xliii. a. 6. The whole of this *Quaestio* should be read for the doctrine of the 'Mission of the Divine Persons.'

[2] For an account of this tradition see Wicksteed and Gardner's *Dante and Giovanni del Virgilio*, pp. 97-103. According to the story quoted

trast drawn between the honour shown him in Paradise
and the cruel contempt with which he was treated by
his native city — a contrast which he appears to
associate with this question of his faith. While
Florence refused him the laurel crown for his 'sacred
poem,' St. Peter, the first Pontiff, the supreme representative of Faith, on hearing his confession, made
himself, so to speak, into his laurel crown, encircling
him with his starry light three times, in symbol of the
Trinity. And remembering this high honour done
him by 'the greatest Peter,'[1] he resolves to accept the
laurel crown nowhere on earth save in his beautiful
St. John, over the font by whose waters he entered
into the faith he has just confessed. Canto xxv., as
Vernon says, ' opens with lines of infinite pathos and
beauty. Dante, about to be examined on Hope, breaks
forth in the very centre of Heaven, into the expression of what is his supreme hope and desire on earth,
namely, that his great poem may earn for him a recall
from banishment':[2]

> If e'er it happen that the Poem Sacred
> To which both heaven and earth have set their hand,
> So that it many a year hath made me lean,
> O'ercome the cruelty that bars me out
> From the fair sheepfold, where a lamb I slumbered,
> An enemy to the wolves that war upon it,
> With other voice forthwith, with other fleece
> Poet will I return, and at my font
> Baptismal will I take the laurel crown,
> Because into the Faith that maketh known
> All souls to God there entered I, and then
> Peter for her sake thus my brow encircled.[3]

---

from Papanti, Dante was in danger at Ravenna of the Inquisition, and
wrote a *Professione di Fede* to satisfy the Inquisitor. This Creed is given
in the Oxford edition of the poet's work, though, of course, Dr. Moore
takes care to make plain in the Preface that it is not genuine.

[1] *Inf.* ii. 24.   [2] *Readings on the Paradiso*, ii. 244.

[3] The reference to heaven and earth in l. 2 probably means that both
supplied the material of the poem, and that the study of both philosophy
and theology, which had made him lean for many years, entered into it.
The ' other voice' of l. 7 probably refers to the contrast between the poems
of his early life and his 'sacred poem' of the Christian Faith. The
' other fleece' of the same line is an allusion to his hair that had grown
grey in exile, as is evident from his own words in his First Eclogue to
Giovanni del Virgilio. This Eclogue, indeed, seems to have been written

It is obviously an appeal, not merely against the cruelty which prolonged his banishment, but also against some suspicion of heresy that had gathered round his name: his soul by faith is known to God, and in Heaven Peter has given him the crown refused on earth.[1]

at the very time when Dante was beginning these ten closing Cantos of the *Paradiso*, and the correspondence between the two poets casts a most interesting light on the present passage. About the year 1319 Giovanni del Virgilio, a professor of the humanities at Bologna, writes a pastoral song to Dante at Ravenna, urging him to write in Latin for scholars, and to choose as subject some of the stirring events happening in that day. This, he assures him, will bring him fame, and he, del Virgilio, will be delighted to present him for the laurel crown to the applauding schools of Bologna. To this Dante replies in the same playful pastoral style, gently declining to have his grey hairs crowned anywhere else than in his native city: ' Were it not better to trim my triumphal locks, and, should I e'er return to my ancestral Arno, to hide there the grey hairs, once yellow, under the twined leaves?' He then declares his purpose to accept the laurel only when the *Paradiso* is finished : ' When in my song shall be laid open the circumfluent bodies of the world (the revolving spheres of Paradise) and the star-dwellers (saints and Angels), even as are the nether realms, then shall it be my joy to bind my head with ivy and with laurel.' As yet ten Cantos of the *Paradiso* remain to be done (for there is no doubt that this is the meaning of the pastoral allegory), so that it was just at this time Dante was about to write these Cantos of Faith and Hope and the laurel crown : ' I have one ewe, the best-beloved (the *Paradiso*), so full of milk she scarce can bear her udders ; under a huge rock (? the protection of Dante's friend, Guido da Polenta of Ravenna) she chews the fresh-cropped grass (Dante's latest studies for this part of the poem); joined to no flock, accustomed to no fold (the poem had no model); of her own will is she wont to come to the milking-pail, ne'er driven by force (Dante waited for hours of inspiration). Her I am waiting to milk with ready hands ; from her ten vessels will I fill to send to Mopsus'—the pastoral name of del Virgilio, that of Dante being Tityrus. There is little doubt that the 'ten vessels' or measures are these ten closing Cantos of the *Paradiso*. At the moment Dante had not begun, apparently, the first of them, Canto xxiv.,—he was waiting for the inspiration to flow ; and the influence of this correspondence with his friend concerning the laurel passed into all the ten. It is as if Dante were gathering up all his powers in one final effort which would prove him worthy of the crown, if not on earth, at least in Heaven. Comp. Wicksteed and Gardner's *Dante and Giovanni del Virgilio*, 95-97; 119-125, etc. Boccaccio (*Life of Dante*, viii.) speaks of the poet's intense longing to receive the laurel crown beside his baptismal font,—perhaps only an echo of the present passage. See above,.pp. 47, 48 n. ; 192 n.

[1] Cf. his pathetic words in the Second Eclogue to del Virgilio (ll. 86, 87):

' Hoc illustre caput, cui iam frondator in alta
Virgine perpetuas festinat cernere frondes' :

' This illustrious head for which already the Pruner hastens to choose perpetual leaves from the exalted Virgin' (Daphne, the laurel).

CHAPTER XXIII

4. *St. James examines Dante on Hope*

WE come now to Dante's examination in Hope, the second of the theological virtues. As soon as his faith had received the crown, out of the Apostolic sphere there flashed another light which drew from Beatrice the joyful cry:

> 'Look, look, behold the Baron,
> For whom, below there, is visited Galicia!'[1]

The Baron is the Apostle James who, as we have seen, represents Hope; and the title suggests one reason why. According to the mediæval legends, St. James preached the Gospel in Spain. After his martyrdom by Herod Agrippa,[2] his body was placed on a ship, which was guided miraculously through the Pillars of Hercules to the coast of Galicia in the north-west corner of Spain, the land he had evangelized. During the barbarian invasions his tomb was lost, and it was only in the ninth century that it was discovered by a shepherd who saw a miraculous light hovering over the spot. From this the place may have received the name of Compostella or *Campus Stellae*, 'the Field of the Star,'—one of the most famous places of pilgrimage in the Middle Ages.[3] St. James, or Santiago, became

---

[1] *Par.* xxv. 13-18.   [2] Acts xii. 1, 2.

[3] Another derivation suggested is *Campus Apostoli.* 'One of the most remarkable phases or developments of this legend of St. James, is the *rediscovery* of the sacred body, which had been lost in the sixteenth century, after, and in some way on account of, the destruction of the Spanish Armada by the English; and the promulgation of the entire story as an Article of Faith by Pope Leo. XIII.' (Ulick R. Burke, *History of Spain*, i. 156 n.). In *Vita Nuova* § 41 a reference is made to pilgrims to the shrine at Compostella; and in *Conv.* ii. 15, the Milky Way or Galaxy (*Par.* xiv. 99) is called 'the Way of St. James.'

the patron saint of Spain, and sometimes led its armies to victory in visible form. The proud Spanish noblemen, however, unable to bear having a mere fisherman as their leader, transformed his father, Zebedee, into a baron of Galilee, who fished indeed, but only for his own pleasure.[1] It is possible that Dante alludes to this legend, but the meaning certainly goes much deeper. The idea of a celestial Empire runs through the passage. God, or perhaps Christ, is the Emperor, seated in 'the most secret hall' of His heavenly palace, surrounded by His 'princes,' 'barons,' 'counts,' the leaders of His armies, who 'jeoparded their lives unto the death in the high places of the field.'[2] This idea of warfare comes out again and again. James won the palm and issued from the field in martyrdom.[3] Dante is called a son of the Church Militant, and his life a warfare.[4] All this is intimately bound up with the very conception of Hope as a theological virtue, an essential part of which is the facing of arduous things. According to Aquinas, the object of Hope must have four marks: it must be good; must lie in the future; must be arduous, difficult to reach; yet not unattainable: all of which are found in 'the hope of glory.'[5] St. James, as the first martyr of the Apostolic band, gave the supreme proof of the power of his hope to face arduous things. This seems to be the special reason why he is chosen as the representative of Hope, which is a militant virtue nerving the soul for the endurance of every suffering for the sake of eternal bliss. His very name, as we saw, was understood in this sense—Jacob, the '*supplanter*,' the man who, like Hope, had power to tread *under foot* every toil, pain, and adversity.[6]

The meeting of the two Apostles is described in another of those bird similes in which Dante delights:

[1] Mrs. Jameson's *Sacred and Legendary Art*, i. 231.
[2] *Par.* xxv. 17; 23; 30; 41, 42.   [3] *Par.* xxv. 82-84.
[4] *Par.* xxv. 52-57.
[5] *Summa*, i-ii. q. xl. a. 1; ii-ii. q. xvii. a. 1: 'The object of hope is good in the future, arduous, possible to be had.'
[6] See above, p. 381.

> In the same way as when the dove alights
> Near his companion, and the one to the other
> Pours forth his love, circling round and murmuring,
> So did I see the one by the other great prince
> Of glory to be received with welcome,
> Praising the food whereon up there they feast.[1]

It might be thought that the meaning of the dove, the emblem of the Spirit that inspired the Apostles, could hardly be missed. Yet one writer sees nothing in the comparison but a delightful grotesqueness. 'It might be possible to imagine two exquisites of the Court of Louis XIV. strutting forward to meet each other, bowing their heads and preening themselves, perhaps even wheeling round with courtly etiquette, but we cannot conceive such a mode of greeting between two staid and dignified apostles. I think that Dante must have smiled as he wrote the words!'[2] It is possible, but not at their grotesqueness. Dante is simply bringing out by a simile the harmony between the two virtues which the two Apostles represent, faith being the substance of things hoped for. Since hope seeks happiness in God, its very existence depends on faith that God is; and faith, in its turn, completes itself in hope. It is this natural friendship between the two virtues which Dante means to indicate by the com

---

[1] *Par.* xxv, 19-24. In a very ancient mosaic in S. Clemente in Rome, the Twelve Apostles in the form of doves occupy the cross above and below the figure of their crucified Lord. The symbol was also applied to Christian preachers, and in the mediæval books which sprang from the *Physiologus*, the meaning is pursued into great detail. 'As the dove separates with its beak the choicest kernels of wheat from the chaff, so it is the office of the preacher to separate the pure grain of Christian doctrine from the husks of Judaism. Its two wings are love of man and love of God, compassion and contemplation, the active and the meditative life; the ring round its neck is the encircling sweetness of the Divine Word; the gold and silver of its plumage are the precious treasures of purity and innocence; its whiteness intermingled with changeable tints is the spirit of chastity in conflict with fickle and rebellious passions; its red feet are the feet of the Church stained with the blood of the martyrs; its two eyes survey the past and discern the future, looking in upon the soul and up to God; their yellowish lustre indicates maturity of thought and reflection, for yellow is the colour of ripe fruit' (Evans' *Animal Symbolism in Eccles. Architecture*, p. 76). See also 'Dove (as Symbol)' in *Dict. of Christian Antiquities*, Smith and Cheetham.

[2] Christopher Hare's *Dante the Wayfarer*, p. 149.

parison of the doves. It is 'grotesque' only when this allegorical element is ignored.[1]

When the friendly greeting was fulfilled, Beatrice asked St. James to examine Dante on the virtue of Hope, addressing him as the illustrious life by whom was written the liberality of the heavenly palace. The reference is to the Epistle of James, attributed here to the Apostle: 'If any of you lack wisdom, let him ask of God, that giveth to all men liberally, and upbraideth not; and it shall be given him. . . . Every good gift and every perfect gift is from above, and cometh down from the Father of lights, with whom is no variableness, neither shadow of turning' (i. 5, 17)— the liberality of God being, of course, a great quickener of hope. St. James bids Dante raise his head in the attitude of hope and take assurance to himself; whereupon the poet tells us that, in the words of Psalm cxxi., he 'lifted up his eyes to the hills,' that is, to the two Apostles, whose faith and hope towered so far above his own, or rather, whose faith and hope were now lost in sight and comprehension.[2]

St. James now proceeds to the examination, putting three questions concerning Hope in one:

> 'Say what it is, and how with it thy mind
> Enflowers itself, and say whence it came to thee.'[3]

Before Dante can open his lips, the second of the three questions is answered for him by Beatrice:

> 'The Church Militant hath not any son
> With greater hope, even as is written
> In the Sun who irradiates all our band;

---

[1] There is no intention, of course, to exclude the personal friendship which constitutes one of the joys of Paradise: that is taken for granted. Another meaning is perhaps not impossible. The Epistle of James, which Dante attributes to the Apostle James, *appears* to disparage faith (ii. 14-26): may not the affection here between Peter and James indicate that there was no real disparagement? This, however, is a mere suggestion.

[2] St. Bernard in his Sermons on Cant. ii. 8 interprets 'mountains' as the higher orders of Angels, and 'hills' as the lower orders; or 'mountains' as Angels generally, and 'hills' as 'Patriarchs and Prophets and other spiritual men.' Of the hills he gives a curious alternative interpretation—'the powers of the air,' fallen from their mountain altitudes as Angels, but not humbled to the valley of penitence: barren hills on which falls neither dew nor rain.   [3] *Par.* xxv. 46, 47.

> Therefore to him is granted that from Egypt
> He come into Jerusalem to see,
> Or ever yet his warfare be accomplished.'[1]

In other words, so strong is Dante's hope of glory
that it is changed to sight of the glory itself, while he
is still in the flesh. It is not easy to understand why
Beatrice gives this answer instead of Dante. The usual
solution is that had Dante said this of himself, it would
have been a piece of self-praise; and, of course, this
must be part of the meaning, since Beatrice expressly
says she leaves him to answer the other two questions
because this will involve no boastfulness.[2] It is difficult,
however, to see why it should be boastful for Dante
himself to say he had hope, when he has no hesitation
in saying he had faith and love. Indeed, in a few lines
further on he does say that he is full of hope to overflowing.[3] One cannot help suspecting that the true
reason lies in the attitude which Beatrice took up to
him in the Earthly Paradise on this very matter of
hope. There she drove Dante's sin against herself
home to his conscience so relentlessly that the Angels,
in pity of his pain, began to sing the opening verses of
Psalm xxxi.: 'In te, Domine, speravi': 'In thee, O Lord,
have I put my hope.' Beatrice, however, firmly sets
aside their interference, and refuses Dante the consolation of hope until he has drunk to the dregs the full
cup of sorrow for his sins.[4] It is difficult to think that
the two passages are unconnected, especially in view
of the Sperent in te of line 98 of this Canto. Dante

---

[1] *Par.* xxv. 49-57. The *militar* of the last line is an echo of the Vulgate
of Job xiv. 14: 'cunctis diebus, quibus nunc *milito*, expecto donec veniat
immutatio mea' (R.V. 'all the days of my warfare would I wait, till my
release should come'). Egypt, of course, is the bondage of this present
world, Jerusalem the liberty of the glory of Heaven (Heb. xii. 22). Comp.
Purg. ii. 46, where the souls chant Ps. cxiv. 1, 'In exitu Israel de
Aegypto'; *Conv.* ii. 1; and *Epis.* x. 7, where the anagogical sense of the
Psalm is given as 'the departure of the holy soul from the bondage of this
corruption to the liberty of the eternal glory.'
[2] *Par.* xxv. 58-63. For the folly of self-praise and self-blame on a man's
own lips, see *Conv.* i. 2.
[3] *Par.* xxv. 77. For Dante's claim to have faith and love, see xxiv. 85-
87 and xxvi. 16-18.
[4] *Purg.* xxx. 55-145. See my *Prisoners of Hope*, 445, 446.

wishes to tell us that she who once so sternly refused
him the comfort of hope now stands sponsor for him
in Heaven for this very virtue.   Indeed, it is to her he
traces his possession of it.   She is 'the compassionate
one who guided the feathers of his wings to so lofty a
flight.'[1]   At the very moment when she was most stern
to him, her green mantle, her olive wreath, her emerald
eyes, all spoke of hope;[2] and his last grateful words
to her are:

> 'O Lady, in whom my hope hath vigour.'[3]

With the eagerness of an expert scholar, Dante
proceeds to answer the master's questions:

> 'Hope,' said I, 'is a certain expectation
> Of future glory, which is the product
> Of grace divine and merit precedent'—

a definition taken almost word for word from Peter
Lombard.[4]   As we have seen so many times, Hope as
a theological virtue has the vision and enjoyment of
God as its final end.   As a habit of the soul, its origin
is the grace of God.   When, for instance, Dante says
it is the product in part of 'precedent merit,' he does
not mean that we can first do some meritorious act,
and thus earn the virtue of hope.   Hope is a virtue
'infused' by the Divine grace, and grace is not a
matter of merit.   The true connection is this.   First,
Divine grace creates within the soul the virtue of
hope—a supernatural virtue aiming at a supernatural
end.   This virtue urges us to acts in keeping with it,
and these acts being done in grace are accepted as
meritorious by God.[5]   Then the grace and the merit

---

[1] *Par.* xxv. 49, 50.   [2] *Purg.* xxx. 31, 32; xxxi. 116.
[3] *Par.* xxxi. 79.
[4] *Par.* xxv. 67-69.   Peter Lombard's words are (*Sentences*, iii. Dist. 26):
'Est enim spes certa expectatio futurae beatitudinis, veniens ex Dei
gratia et meritis praecedentibus, vel ipsam spem, quam natura praeit
charitas, vel rem speratam, id eᵗt, beatitudinem aeternam.   Sine meritis
enim aliquid sperare, non spes, sed praesumptio dici potest.'
[5] It is to be remembered that, according to the doctrine of the Roman
Catholic Church, the foundation of merit is grace.   Only works done in
grace merit eternal life; and they merit this only because God has
graciously promised to reward such works in this way.   Hence men in a
state of grace can claim this reward according to *justice*, since it is a

flowing from it create within the soul 'a sure expectation of future glory '—the 'precedent' having reference,
according to Aquinas, not to the grace but to the glory;[1]
and the *certitude* of the expectation has its root in that
knowledge of God which faith gives, for 'hope rests
principally on the Divine omnipotence and mercy, of
which every one is certain who has faith.'[2]

Hope being thus defined, Dante proceeds to answer
the Apostle's third question—from whence it came to
him. 'From many stars,' he says, the stars being the
souls in this Heaven of stars whose light had been to
him the prophecy of the eternal day. The first of
these stars of hope is David, 'the supreme singer of the
supreme Leader'—first, because he directs the soul to
Him who is the beginning and end of all hope:

> ' *Let them hope in thee*, in his Theody
> Saith he, *those who know thy name*: and who
> Doth not know it, if he hath my faith?'[3]

Since hope has for its object God Himself, and since
without His help we cannot reach Him, it is obvious
that we must know His name so far as to believe in His
existence and His willingness to grant us the necessary
aid: 'he that cometh to God must believe that he is,
and that he is a rewarder of them that diligently seek
him.' Faith in the goodness of God, therefore, is the

---

promise of God. Since everything thus runs back to grace, it becomes a
question whether ' merit' retains almost anything of its proper meaning.
Practically, merit is simply acting according to the grace of God and His
promises, which are also of grace.

[1] *Summa*, ii-ii. q. xvii. a. 1 ad 2.

[2] *Summa*, ii-ii. q. xviii. a. 4.   Bonaventura's description of Hope is :
' Spes est audacia mentis de largitate Dei concepta habendi vitam aeternam per bona merita.'   The certitude of Hope, he says, springs from
three things—the divine liberality, abundance of merits, and the foretaste
of things eternal. He distinguishes between various degrees of certitude.
The hope of souls in this world has certitude of *opinion*, that is, it holds
to its object, but with a certain fear of not reaching it.   That of souls in
Purgatory has certitude of *knowledge* (scientia).   And Stephen when he
saw the heavens opened, Paul when he said, 'I know whom I have
believed,' and Adam before his sin, had certitude of *vision*, though much
weaker than in heaven (*Compend. Theolog. Veritatis*, v. 22).

[3] *Par.* xxv. 73-75.   The Psalm quoted is ix. 10: ' Et sperent in te qui
noverunt nomen tuum.'

root of hope.[1] And this is probably the reason why
James himself is named as the second source of Dante's
hope, or rather as instilling it into him with David's
instilling—that is, presenting God as the fountain of
hope.   The reference seems to be to that liberality
of God in the first Chapter of the Epistle of James
already spoken of.

On hearing Dante's words the burning heart of the
Apostle quivered with a sudden flash as of lightning.
It is not the fire of hope, since the hope of the Blessed
is now fulfilled, but the dear memory of the virtue
which followed him

> 'Even to the palm and the issuing from the field.'[2]

He then asks one final question — what does hope
promise? The reply is a curious example of mediæval
interpretation of Scripture:

> 'Of the souls that God hath made His friends
> Isaiah saith that each one shall be clothed
> In his own land with double garments,
> And his own land is this sweet life.'[3]

Isaiah in the passage referred to (lxi. 7) says nothing
about garments: 'In their land they shall possess the
double,' though in v. 10 he speaks of 'the garments of
salvation' and 'the robe of righteousness.' The promise,
says Dante, is worked out with greater fulness by
James's brother in the passages in the Apocalypse
(vi. 11; vii. 9-17) where he speaks of 'the white robes.'
The double garments are the reunion of body and soul
in the Resurrection. The interpretation runs back to
St. Gregory the Great. In his *Dialogues* (iv. 25), speaking of this reunion he says: 'In respect of this their

---

[1] Heb. xi. 6; *Summa*, ii-ii. q. xvii. 7 : Faith precedes hope, because it
makes known to us the possibility of reaching eternal life, and that
divine help will be given us to reach it. In the dance of the three
theological virtues in the Earthly Paradise (*Purg.* xxix. 127-129), sometimes Faith led and sometimes Love, but never Hope.

[2] *Par.* xxv. 79-84. On the question whether the Blessed have hope, see
note on the following page.

[3] *Par.* xxv. 88-93. The reference in l. 90 is to James ii. 23: 'And he
was called the friend of God.'

double glory, the Scripture saith: "In their land they shall possess double things"; and it is written of the souls of the just, that before the day of resurrection, "to every one of them white robes were given: and it was said to them, that they should rest yet a little time, until the number of their fellow-servants and brethren were complete." They, therefore, that now receive but one robe, in the Day of Judgment shall every one have two: because now they rejoice only for the felicity of their souls, but then shall they enjoy the endless glory of body and soul together.'[1]

This is the close of the examination in Hope. Scarcely had Dante spoken of 'the white robes,' when he heard chanted the words he himself had just quoted from the Psalms: '*Sperent in te*.' It is generally assumed that the singers were one of the groups of souls in this Heaven, perhaps the choir of the Apostles. But Dante expressly says the sound came 'from above,' and that it was responded to by '*all* the carols.' 'From above,' therefore, seems to refer to the Angels in the next Heaven, the choirs of Angels above, and the choirs of saints below, singing the Psalm antiphonally. It is probably meant to be the reversal of the incident in the Earthly Paradise referred to a little ago. There, when the Angels, pitying Dante's distress, sang '*In te, Domine, speravi*,' they were promptly silenced by Beatrice—he had then no title to hope. Now every-

---

[1] According to the Church's teaching, the Blessed can have no hope, since they now possess the thing hoped for. Hence James says hope followed him 'to the palm and issuing from the field' (ll. 82-84), that is, to his martyrdom, and no farther. It might be thought, however, that, since the Blessed are still waiting for 'the redemption of the body' in the Resurrection, they would still be subject to the hope of that redemption. This, however, Aquinas denies for three reasons: (1) the principal object of hope is glory of the soul, not of the body; (2) the glory of the body, though 'arduous' to human nature, is no longer arduous to one who has already the glory of the soul; (3) he who has the glory of the soul has therewith that which is sufficient to produce the glory of the body (*Summa*, ii-ii. q. 18, a. 2). In spite of such arguments, the eager cry of *Amen* to Solomon's words about the Resurrection body (*Par.* xiv. 61-66) shows that the souls 'desire' their bodies, and therefore must have hope for them in some sense. Aquinas is bound by his own definition that the object of hope must be 'arduous' to reach; but it is surely possible to hope for things easy to reach.

thing is changed.   Beatrice herself proclaims him a
child of hope.   Dante passes his celestial examination
in the virtue.   And choirs of saints and Angels greet
him as one whose hope in God proves him worthy to
inherit the promises.

CHAPTER XXIV

5. *St. John examines Dante on Love*

WHEN the Psalm of Hope was ended, from the midst of the carols there beamed forth a light as bright as the sun.[1] It is the spirit of St. John, the representative of Love among the Apostles, as Beatrice tells Dante:

> ' This is he who lay upon the breast
> Of our Pelican, and this he who was
> From upon the cross to the great office chosen.'[2]

The words are meant to indicate the two great reasons why John is the symbol of Love. In the first place, he lay upon the breast of Love Himself. Christ is called ' our Pelican' because He shed His blood for our salvation. The red spot on the bill of this bird gave rise to the idea that, when it was pruning its feathers, it was thrusting its bill into its breast and feeding its young with its own blood. It became, therefore, one of the most familiar symbols of the love of Christ in laying down His life for sinners; and John, who lay on the breast of our Pelican, came nearest to that heart of Love which poured out its life-blood for the world.[3]

---

[1] This is the meaning of xxv. 100-102. During the winter month from middle of December to middle of January, while the sun is in Capricorn, the sign of Cancer opposite is in the sky at night. If during that time Cancer had a light as bright as St. John, winter would have a month of daylight—the sun shining by day and this ' crystal' of Cancer by night.

[2] *Par.* xxv. 100-114.

[3] John xiii. 23. There are many forms of the Pelican myth. One is that the young pelicans rebel against their father, and that he in self-defence strikes and kills them. Then in pity he strikes his bill into his breast, sprinkles his blood on them, and thus recalls them to life. Similarly, man rebels against his Creator, is doomed to death, and is

In the second place, Jesus from the very cross chose
this Apostle for 'the great office' of taking His own
place as a son to His Mother. When we remember the
almost boundless reverence which the Church pays to
the Virgin, we can understand what Dante thought of
the man worthy of so Divine a trust. Christ gave His
Mother into the charge of the disciple nearest to Himself in love.[1]

The burning soul of St. John drew near the other
two Apostles who were circling round under the im-

revived by the blood of Christ. For this reason the pelican was often
painted above the head of Christ on the cross, as in the Spanish Chapel
and in the Chapter House of St. Mark's in Florence. It was also used as
a lectern for the Gospels. The references in literature are numerous. In
Hamlet (Act iv. Sc. 5) Laertes, speaking of his dead father, says:

> 'To his good friends thus wide I'll ope my arms;
> And like the kind life-rendering pelican,
> Repast them with my blood.'

In Tennyson's *Holy Grail* Sir Bors has a pelican for the crest of his
helmet as he rides in quest of the cup that held his Redeemer's blood, the
idea being taken from Malory's Morte D'Arthur (Bk. XVI. chaps. vi., xiii.):
'He (Sir Bors) looked up into a tree, and there he saw a passing great
bird upon an old tree, and it was passing dry, without leaves; and the
bird sat above, and had birds, the which were dead for hunger. So
smote he himself with his beak, the which was great and sharp. And so
the great bird bled till that he died among his birds. And the young
birds took the life by the blood of the great bird.' An Abbot afterwards
showed him how this was a figure of the shedding of Christ's blood for
sinners. St. Augustine in his commentary on Ps. cii. 5 refers to the
myth. For other references, see Hulme's *Symbolism in Christian Art*,
188, 189, and Longfellow's note on the passage. In a hymn by Aquinas
occurs the following verse:

> Pie Pelicane, Jesu Domine,
> Me immundum munda Tuo sanguine,
> Cuius una stilla salvum facere
> Totum mundum quit ab omni scelere.

Two examples of the political use of the pelican myth may be given. In
a book written after the execution of Charles I. in 1649, the martyred king,
as the writer believed him to be, is called 'the Princely Pelican.' In the
following year the first Marquis of Montrose took up arms in Scotland to
avenge his death, but being captured and executed in Edinburgh, the
same name was applied to him. A medal was struck with his portrait on
one side, and on the other the legend:

> 'Treu Pellican who spilt his blood
> To save his King, do's Country good.'

[1] John xix. 25-27. Vellutello in his commentary says of this passage:
'This is he of whom the Church sings the antiphon: Iste est Johannes
Evangelista, qui in coena Domini supra pectus Jesu Christi recubuit,
cui Christus, in cruce pendens, matrem suam virginem virgini com-
mendavit.'

pulse of their glowing love, and put himself into the song and dance. His manner of doing this is compared to that of 'a joyous virgin' who rises to join the dance, 'to do honour to the bride, and not for any failing,' that is, not through any imperfect motive. The comparison is drawn from the virgin purity of the Apostle. The bride is generally taken to be Beatrice, who, in xxv. 110, 111, is said to have held her eyes like a bride fixed on the threefold light. If so, she represents the ideal Church, in contrast to the Papacy which St. Peter is soon to denounce. But there can be little doubt that Dante is thinking of the many references in the Apocalypse to the Church as 'the bride, the Lamb's wife.' The love which John represents signifies the eternal marriage, the final and absolute union, of the soul with God for Himself alone. And just here, perhaps, we may find the meaning of the clause in line 105 —'and not for any failing.' For, according to Aquinas, even faith and hope cling to God for the sake of something to be gained from Him, namely, truth and happiness; whereas love has no end save God Himself. Hence it is 'for the honour of the bride' that love should infuse itself into faith and hope, that all three virtues should have but one end—the Bridegroom Himself.[1]

Dante, on being told who this third 'splendour' was, did an unwise thing, for which he had to suffer: he strained his eyes so eagerly at the burning orb of the Apostle's soul that he was blinded, like a man who gazes at the sun's eclipse. To his alarm, he finds himself unable to see Beatrice:

> Ah, how much in my mind was I distressed,
> When I turned me round to look on Beatrice,
> That her I could not see, although I was
> Close at her side, and in the happy world![2]

I am unable to accept any of the allegorical interpretations of this blindness known to me. 'Benvenuto thinks,' says Mr. Gardner, 'that there is no meaning intended beyond the literal one, but mentions that

[1] *Par.* xxv. 100-111; *Summa*, ii-ii. q. xvii. a. 6.
[2] *Par.* xxv. 118-139.

many strive to expound the passage allegorically, as
that the poet was troubled by some doubt, or that, in
endeavouring to penetrate more deeply into the mysterious revelations of this Eagle of Christ, his intellectual sight was dazzled, and it needed the teaching of
theology to restore him from the blindness of error.
Others suppose that he cannot see Beatrice because
the glorious depths of Charity surpass and eclipse the
teachings of Theology; or that the meaning is that
the grace of God sometimes deprives man for a time
of spiritual sight, to then give it him again in fuller
measure (Scartazzini). It may perhaps be intended
as a warning against independent and unauthorized
interpretation of the Apocalypse, with a possible
reference to some of the errors of the later followers
of Joachim; but if, as is more probable, it is an
allegory of a period of gloom and want of spiritual
consolation, there would be a most beautiful fitness in
the utter trustfulness of Dante's discourse on the
Divine Love as long as the blindness lasts.'[1] Some of
the suggestions here are very interesting, but they all
suffer from one serious fault—they ignore Dante's own
words. The true cause of his temporary blindness was
that he did *not* gaze at 'the glorious depths of Charity'
in the Apostle of Love; probably, had he had the soul
to do this, he would have retained his sight and made
it clearer. But at the very moment when there appears before him the crowning virtue by which the
soul becomes one with God, what is Dante thinking
of? Of an old legend of the foolish earth below, which
had gathered round the body of St. John. He is consumed with curiosity to see if the story is true, and
that poor curiosity blinds him to higher things. The
very form of the story as given in the *Golden Legend*
reminds us of the passage before us. John, at the age
of ninety-nine, having received a message from Christ
that he was to be with Him the following Sunday, after
service on that day bade the people dig a sepulchre
in front of the altar. Descending into it he prayed,

---

[1] *Dante's Ten Heavens*, 182.

and 'anon came upon him great clearness and light, and so great brightness that none might see him, and when this light and brightness was gone and departed, there was nothing found in the pit or grave but manna, which came springing from under upward, like as sand in a fountain or springing well.' To use Dante's own comparison, he was not looking at the sun for the sake of its light, but in order to see the darkness of the eclipse. Hence John's rebuke:

> ' Why dost thou dazzle thee
> To see a thing which hath here no place?
> Earth in earth my body is, and there shall be,
> Together with the rest, until our number
> With the eternal purpose is made equal.
> With the two garments in the blessed cloister
> Are the two lights alone that have ascended;
> And this thou shalt bear back into your world.'[1]

In this rejection of the legend Dante differs from Aquinas, who held as a ' pious belief' that both Mary and John received the resurrection of the body immediately after death, not of merit, but of special privilege.[2] This John himself denies. Christ and His Mother, the two lights that had ascended from this Heaven, are the only ones clothed in the double garment of soul and body. Even Enoch and Elijah are excluded from this blessedness.[3]

St. John now quiets Dante's fears: his sight, like

---

[1] *Par.* xxv. 122-129. John probably refers to his own words in Rev. vi. 11: 'And white robes were given unto every one of them; and it was said unto them, that they should rest yet for a little season, until their fellow-servants also and their brethren, that should be killed as they were, should be fulfilled.'

[2] *Summa*, Suppl. q. lxxvii. a. 1, ad 2. John himself was regarded as the authority for the Assumption of the Virgin. The story is that St. Thomas was the only Apostle absent when she died. On his arrival, the tomb, being opened to show him the holy dust, was found empty; whereupon a revelation was given to St. John that Christ had taken His Mother's body, now united with her soul, to be with Him in Heaven.

[3] Wicksteed and Oelsner's note may be quoted: ' According to the conception prevalent in the Middle Ages, Enoch and Elijah, who were also taken up bodily from the earth, were not in heaven, but in the Earthly Paradise. Perhaps the present passage may be taken as indirect evidence that Dante too accepted the tradition' (*The Paradiso*, Temple Classics, 313). They were identified with the two witnesses of Rev. xi. 3 ff. ' Enoch no doubt was translated, and so was Elijah; nor did they experience death: it was postponed most certainly: they are reserved for the

Saul's, is bewildered, not dead—his Guide has in her glance the power of Ananias' hand. Meantime even in his blindness it were well to discourse of Love, and therefore the Apostle begins his examination of this virtue. The first question is somewhat vague: 'Say where thy soul centres itself'—brings itself to a point and focus. Dante replies:

> ' The Good that makes content this court is
> Alpha and Omega of whatso scripture
> Love readeth to me with light voice or strong.'[1]

Much difficulty is made of these words, but the meaning is quite simple: 'God is the beginning and the end of all my love.' The figurative form is taken from the Alpha and Omega of Rev. i. 8: God is the entire alphabet of the sacred writings which love reads to his soul —the scripture of the universe. Many meanings are suggested of ' *o lievemente o forte*,' 'with light voice or strong': such as reason and revelation, or human and Divine love, or God loved for Himself and for His benefits. Dante's own words which follow seem to me to give the answer. The *loud* voice corresponds to the arguments of Philosophy and the assurance of Revelation in ll. 25-45; and the *low* voice to the secondary causes of love in ll. 55-66. But whether low or loud, God is the one and only object of love. He is loved purely for His own sake, not for any benefit to be gained from Him. 'Even among theological virtues themselves,' says Aquinas, 'that one must be preferable which attains more to God. . . . Faith and hope attain to God, inasmuch as the knowledge of truth, or the obtaining of good, comes to us of Him: but charity attains to God Himself, to rest in Him, not that anything may accrue to us of Him. And therefore charity is more excellent than faith or hope.'[2]

---

suffering of death, that by their blood they may extinguish Antichrist' (Tertullian, *De Anima*, 50). This is probably the reason why they are omitted here: their death is only postponed.

[1] *Par.* xxvi. 1-18.

[2] *Summa*, ii-ii. q. xxiii. a. 5 (Rickaby); Matt. xxii. 36-38: ' Which is the great commandment in the law? . . . Thou shalt love the Lord thy God with all thy heart, and with all thy soul, and with all thy mind. This is the first and great commandment.'

This answer, however, is too general to please St. John: Dante 'must strain it through a closer sieve': 'Who directed thy bow to such a mark?' The poet's reply is that philosophic arguments and the authority of revelation alike led him to this love of God as the supreme good;[1] for, as he says in the *De Monarchia* (ii. 1), when the light of human reason and the ray of divine authority unite, needs must heaven and earth consent together. The philosophic argument is based on a first principle of the universe, that all created things seek some good for which they were made. Hence in an intelligence like man, good, so far as it is known as good, cannot but kindle love, the effort to reach it, and this in proportion to the goodness which it comprehends. It follows that whenever the intellect discerns this universal principle, its love must move to that Divine Essence of which every good beyond itself is but a ray. For, as Aquinas says, the object of the intellect being the essence of a thing, the intellect cannot rest until it reach the Essence of the First Cause and the First Good.[2] This truth, Dante proceeds, was made plain by him who showed him 'the first love of all the eternal substances.' If the reference is to Aristotle, as is generally supposed, 'the eternal substances' will probably be the heavenly bodies, the motions of which, he says, are caused by the First Mover, as the primary object of love;[3] with which, however, Dante must have joined the Orders of Angels and the souls of the Blessed. This philosophic argument is one of the *loud* voices of love, speaking, as it does, through what Dante calls *la conoscenza viva* (l. 61)—'the living consciousness,' the knowledge bound up with life itself, that our chief end is God.

And this 'living consciousness' is confirmed by revelation. Two passages are chosen, one from each of the Testaments. In discussing these, we must bear care-

---

[1] *Par.* xxvi. 19-45.

[2] *Summa*, i-ii. q. ii. a. 8 ; q. iii. a. 8.

[3] Dr. Moore (*Studies in Dante*, 1st series, 115) accepts Butler's reference to Aristotle's Metaphysics Λ. chaps. vii. and viii.

fully in mind what exactly it is of which these passages
are the confirmation, namely, that God is the one final
object of love. This is proved by the revelation of
what He is, given in Scripture. But Dante knew that
the revelation of God passed through varying degrees
of clearness. The passage which he quotes from the
Old Testament is Exod. xxxiii. 19, which reads in the
Vulgate: ' *Ego ostendam omne bonum tibi*,' the equivalent of Dante's 'I will make thee see all worth,' or
goodness (l. 42). It seems to me difficult to believe that
Dante, when quoting this, did not remember that God
proceeds to say: ' Thou canst not see my face: for there
shall no man see me and live. . . . Thou shalt see my
back parts: but my face shall not be seen.' And, as I
understand it, the passage which he takes from the
New Testament is chosen just because it is the fulfilment of the imperfect revelation given to Moses. It is
taken from St. John's writings, the particular reference
being much disputed:

> ' Thou too dost make it plain to me, beginning
> The high heralding, which cries aloud the secret
> Of this place down below, beyond all other edict.'

I do not think it necessary to discuss which of John's
writings is referred to. Dante is thinking of them all
as *one* proclamation of the secret of heaven to earth;
and if so, 'the *beginning* of the high heralding' is the Prologue to the Fourth Gospel. Now it happens that the
closing words of the Prologue allude to this very fulfilment of the imperfect revelation through Moses of
which I have spoken: ' The law was given by Moses;
grace and truth came by Jesus Christ. No man hath
seen God at any time; the only begotten Son, which is
in the bosom of the Father, he hath declared him.'
The evident connection of this with the passage quoted
from Moses seems to me conclusive. Moses saw the
back of God; Christ reveals the 'secret' of heaven—the
bosom of the Father.[1]

---

[1] *Par.* xxvi. 40-45. The reference is by many taken to be to the Apocalypse, and this may seem to be supported by the allusion in l. 17 to the
Alpha and Omega of Rev. i. 8. Others prefer the Prologue to the Fourth

St. John accepts this answer: human intellect and revelation agree in directing the highest of our loves to God. As Aquinas says, charity is a friendship with God, and exceeds all love to our neighbours and even to ourselves.[1] But the examination is not finished. 'The Eagle of Christ' pursues the subject into its secondary causes. We come at this point to the scripture which Love reads with a *low* voice (l. 18)—the collateral and subsidiary sources of charity, or as John puts it, the cords that draw, and the teeth that bite into the heart, from the outside:

> ' But say once more if thou feel other cords
> Draw thee towards Him, so that thou sound forth
> With how many teeth this Love is biting thee.'

In reply, Dante states the various motives and incentives which, in co-operation with 'the living consciousness' of his own intellect confirmed by revelation, drew him from the sea of distorted love and set him on the shore of right charity:[2]

> ' The being of the world, and my own being,
> The death which He sustained that I may live,
> And that which all the faithful hope, as I do.'

In other words, the creation of the world and man, the cross of Christ, and the hope of glory: these are 'the

---

Gospel, but without specifying any particular part. Mr. Butler takes the reference to be to 'God is love' in 1 John iv., but this is certainly not at the beginning of any of the Apostle's writings. Dr. Moore (*Studies in Dante*, 1st series, 86-89) fixes on John iii. 16, 'God so loved the world,' etc. His reason for setting aside both the Apocalypse and the Prologue to the Gospel is that they contain nothing specially relating to Love. He seems to forget that what Dante wants is a passage of Scripture in proof that God has revealed Himself as the supreme object of the love of man, and that is certainly not absent from the Prologue; it is indeed specially emphasized in v. 18 to which I refer. I lay stress on two points: (1) Dante is not singling out *one* of John's writings—they all constitute the highest proclamation of the secret of heaven; (2) the connection, to my mind very obvious, between Exod. xxxiii. 19-23 and John i. 17, 18. It is perhaps not a mere fancy to find some slight corroboration of this interpretation in the word '*grida*' of l. 44—'the high heralding which *cries* the secret' of heaven—an echo of John i. 15, where it is written that Christ's herald 'John bare witness and *cried*, saying, This was he,' etc.

[1] *Summa*, ii-ii. q. xxiii. a. i; q. xxvi.

[2] See Virgil's discourse on Love distorted, defective, and excessive in *Purg.* xvii. 91 ff.

teeth' with which the love of God bites into his heart,
for all are operations of that love. Yet it is to be
noted that they are not 'the interior act of charity,'
the clinging of the soul to God, but only cords to draw
men to the act. Aquinas, discussing the question
whether God is to be loved for His own sake alone,
gives his answer, in true scholastic fashion, through
Aristotle's four causes — final, formal, efficient and
material. As the first three of these causes, God must
be loved on account of Himself and nothing else. He
is the *final* cause of all things, therefore there is no
cause beyond Him on which the intellect can rest. He
is His own *formal* or essential cause: 'His substance is
His goodness': hence there is no higher goodness for
the will to seek. He is His own *efficient* cause, since
He owes His being to no other. Hence, when we think
of God in these three ways, we must love Him solely for
Himself. But under the fourth mode, the *material*
cause, it is possible to love Him on account of something else: 'because by certain other things we are
disposed to the love of God : as, for example, by benefits
received from Him, or by rewards hoped for, or even
by penalties which through Him we are eager to
escape.'[1] Through the scholastic form it is obvious
that the 'material cause' of Aquinas is identical with
Dante's cords and teeth-bites—the motives and incentives by which God is at first loved for the sake of
other things, in order that finally He may be loved for
Himself alone.[2]

The examination closes with Dante's declaration of
the *order* which his charity observes. Since God is the
principle of love, all things must be loved in their
relation to Him, in proportion to the good they hold of
Him. 'Diversity in the love of charity,' says Aquinas,
'must consist, so far as species goes, in loving different
neighbours differently according to the several ways
in which they stand to God ; wishing, that is, greater
good to him who is nearer to God'—a principle which
holds good even *in patria*:

[1] *Summa*, ii-ii. q. xxvii. a. 3.   [2] Hosea, xi. 4.

'The leaves wherewith enleaved is all the garden
Of the Eternal Gardener I love in measure
Of the good which from Him to them is borne.'[1]

---

[1] *Par.* xxvi. 64-66; *Summa,* ii-ii. q. xxvi. a. 7, 13. Comp. St. Bernard's sermon on Cant. ii. 4 : ' *Ordinavit in me caritatem* ' (Vulg.—in Eng. Bible : ' His banner over me was love '): ' Give me a man who, before all things, loves God with all his being; who loves both himself and his neighbour in the same degree in which each loves God ; who loves his enemy as one who may perhaps at some time in the future turn to the love of God ; who loves his relatives according to the flesh very tenderly, on account of nature, but his spiritual parents, that is, those who have instructed him, more abundantly on account of grace, and thus his love for all other things whatsoever is regulated by his love for God,' etc. (*Cantica Canticorum,* Serm. 1. Eales' trans.).

CHAPTER XXV

6. *Adam and the Fall*

No sooner was Dante silent than the Sanctus of Rev. iv. 8 resounded through Heaven: 'Holy, holy, holy, Lord God Almighty, which was, and is, and is to come,' —in thankfulness, perhaps, for the successful issue of the Pilgrim's examination, or, more probably, because the theological virtue of love is in proportion to the vision of the Divine holiness. Beatrice joined in the song, and by the piercing ray of her eyes so restored his sight that he saw more clearly than before : as it was through her eyes love first entered his soul (xxvi. 14, 15), so now that he is made 'perfect in love,' they raise him to a loftier power of vision. Yet, strange to say, this new power of vision is 'almost stupefied' by a fourth light which now joins the other three. It is 'the first soul the First Power e'er created.' It may seem an anticlimax thus to set Adam alongside the three chief Apostles of Christ; but this is the poet's way of summing up in one group the whole long history of Redemption, from the cause of 'the great exile' to the infusion of the three theological virtues by which the ban is lifted, and the natural man is raised to the supernatural life. The idea is repeated in the White Rose : Peter and John are seated on the Virgin's right, Adam on her left, Eve at her feet.[1] Several other reasons were no doubt present to Dante's mind. The

---

[1] *Par.* xxxii. 4-6 (Eve); 121-130 (Adam, Peter, John).

salvation of Adam, for example, had been denied:
Tatian, as we learn from the Fathers, held that the
Tree of Life is marriage, by the introduction of which
into the world Adam sinned beyond forgiveness.[1]
Against this stands Wisdom x. 1, 2: 'She preserved
the first formed father of the world, that was created
alone, and brought him out of his fall, and gave him
power to rule all things.' It is fitting too that the
first Adam should appear in this Heaven from which
the second Adam had just ascended—a Heaven which,
as we saw, is the celestial counterpart of the Earthly
Paradise which the first Adam lost. It is to be noticed
also that Adam is the last human soul whom Dante
meets before passing into the *Primum Mobile*, the
Heaven of the Angels, as if in allusion to Psalm viii. 5:
'Thou hast made him a little lower than the angels.'

On hearing who this fourth light is, Dante instinctively bent his head in reverence of the first
Father, and immediately raised it in a fire of eagerness to ask certain questions, which he does not utter
in order to have the answers sooner.[2] And here follows
a comparison which even lovers of the poet feel requires
some apology. The soul of Adam, in its joy at Dante's
request, moved within its garment of light as an
animal twists itself about under some covering of cloth
thrown over it:

[1] Irenæus (*Against Heresies*, iii. 23, Ante-Nicene Library) calls Tatian
and his followers 'patrons of the serpent and of death.' 'Inasmuch as
man is saved, it is fitting that he who was created the original man
should be saved. For it is absurd that he who was so deeply injured
by the enemy, and was the first to suffer captivity, was not rescued by
Him who conquered the enemy, but that his children were,—those whom
he had begotten in the same captivity.' Or, as Tertullian puts it : 'as if,
when the branches become salvable, the root were not!' The shame and
fear which followed their sin are regarded as proof of the repentance of
the first parents. In Christian Art they are represented as the first souls
rescued by Christ from Limbo. See *Inf.* iv. 55.

[2] Dante's address to Adam (xxvi. 92, 93) 'O ancient father, to whom
each bride is daughter and daughter-in-law,' is an echo of St. Augustine's
City of God, xv. 16 : ' "Father" and "father-in-law" are the names of
two relationships. . . . But Adam in his single person was obliged to
hold both relations to his sons and daughters, for brothers and sisters
were united in marriage. So too Eve his wife was both mother and
mother-in-law to her children of both sexes.'

Sometimes an animal, when covered, struggles
So that its impulse needs must be apparent,
By reason of the wrappage following it;
And in like manner the primeval soul
Made clear to me athwart its covering
How jubilant it was to give me pleasure.[1]

The comparison of the first soul to an animal is
certainly curious, but there is no need to be scandalized
by it, or to dismiss it as 'Dantesque' and therefore in-
explicable.   We may find the clue in the Vulgate of
1 Cor. xv. 44-46: 'Si est corpus animale, est et spiritale.
Sic et scriptum est: Factus est primus homo Adam in
animam viventem, novissimus Adam in spiritum
vivificantem.   Sed prius non quod spiritale est, sed
quod animale est; deinde quod spiritale.'   According
to Aquinas, the *anima rationalis* consists of two parts:
the *anima* or soul, which gives life to the body and is
common to man with the other animals; and *spiritus*
or spirit, that which is proper to man as an intellectual
being.   Now it seems to be this animal soul of which
Dante is thinking in this comparison.   Aquinas teaches
that it is an essential part of man, and will be re-united
with the body in the Resurrection, although in the
Redeemed its various senses will be spiritualized by the
predominance of the *spiritus*.[2]   Dante, then, standing
here before '*l'anima primaia*,' appears to see this
animal soul moving within its robe of light.   Elsewhere
he speaks of man as 'the noblest of animals' and 'the
divine animal'; and of Adam at his creation he says
that 'the earth was once made worthy of full animal

---

[1] *Par.* xxvi. 97-102 (Longfellow).   Plumptre's suggestion that Dante
was thinking of a cat as the animal adapted to 'the task of the scholar
and the thinker,' only makes commenting ridiculous.
[2] See the following passages in the *Summa*: i. q. xcvii. a. 3; Supp.
q. lxx. a. 1, 2; q. lxxxi. 4; q. lxxxii. 3, 4.   The general doctrine is (1) what
belongs to the 'first perfection' of man's animal life (i.e. its natural perfection in this life, as eating, drinking, sleeping, generating) has no
existence after the Resurrection, being no longer necessary; (2) the
sensitive powers remain, so far as they are necessary to allow the body to
participate in the beatitude of the soul; (3) the spirit so rules body and
soul that the risen body has four spiritual powers: *impassibilitas*, in-
capability of passion or suffering; *claritas* or splendour; *subtilitas*, the
power of penetrating other bodies; *agilitas*, the power of swift motion at
the will of the spirit.   See above, p. 226 n.

perfection.'[1] It is then this animal perfection, which
Adam alone of all men once possessed, which Dante
now sees move under its covering of light in the eagerness of its joy to do him pleasure.

Adam sees Dante's unspoken questions in the mirror
of the Divine Mind, and proceeds to answer them. They
are four in number. The first refers to 'the proper
cause of the great indignation'—God's anger for the
first sin, which shut the whole race out of Paradise.
The answer is that the real evil lay not in the mere
eating of the fruit, but in passing the bounds assigned
to human nature :—

> 'Now, son of mine, not the tasting of the tree
> Was of itself the cause of so great exile,
> But solely the o'erstepping of the mark.'[2]

This may mean that the eating of the fruit had been
innocent and harmless but for 'the mark,' the limit
laid down by the Divine command: one step beyond
this destroyed obedience, 'the mother and guardian,' as
Augustine calls her, 'of all the virtues in the reasonable creature.'[3] But the idea is probably more definite.
'The mark' is the limit assigned by God to human
nature. Aquinas traces the first sin to pride, according to Ecclus. x. 13: 'Pride is the beginning of sin.'
Adam's pride, however, did not seek equality with
God, which he knew to be an impossibility. It confined itself to seeking likeness to God in the knowledge of good and evil. Even this had been no
sin had it been sought according to the mark or
limit of man's nature, the limit being the dependence
of that nature upon God for all things. Adam broke
through these bounds by seeking the knowledge of
good and evil by virtue of his own natural powers,
apart from his Maker. Hence 'the first sin of man

---

[1] *De Vulg. Eloq.* i. 5; *Conv.* iii. 2; *Par.* xiii. 82, 83. In this last passage
Dante seems to imply that Christ also possessed this full animal perfection, but I cannot be sure that this is his meaning. See p. 219.

[2] *Par.* xxvi. 115-117.

[3] *City of God,* xiv. 12. Anselm (*Cur Deus Homo,* i. 21) argues that a
man ought not to take a single look contrary to God's command, to save
his own soul from perdition, or the whole universe from being destroyed.

consisted in this that he sought a spiritual good *supra suam mensuram*, which pertains to pride.'[1]

The second question is one of mere chronology—how long it was since God set Adam in the lofty garden where Beatrice had prepared Dante for the stairway of the Heavens, that is, of course, the Earthly Paradise. The answer follows the chronology of the age. The time of Adam's detention in Limbo was 4302 years. Add to this the 930 years of his life on earth, and we have from the Creation to the Crucifixion 5232 years; or to the birth of Christ, deducting the 34 years of His life, 5198. This added to the 1300 years of the Christian era makes the age of the world when Dante wrote 6498 years. I see no special reason for this answer beyond that of corroborating by the authority of Adam the received chronology. One can imagine much more interesting questions that the poet might have put to the first Father of our race.

The third question, as to the idiom which Adam used and made (l. 114), seems to be put in order to give Dante the opportunity of retracting his former views on the first language and its origin, and that in three particulars.

(1) In the *De Vulgari Eloquentia* (i. 6) it is held that a certain 'form' of speech was 'concreated' with the first soul to the very words, their grammatical construction, and the utterance of this construction. Now he holds that the power of speech is given by nature, but that the particular mode is left to reason :

> 'That man should speak is a work of nature,
> But thus or thus nature then doth leave
> To you to do as it seems best to you.'[2]

(2) In the same treatise (i. 6) Dante, following Augustine,[3] holds that the language of Adam was Hebrew, that it was the speech of all his descendants until the building of the Tower of Babel, and that after that it survived through the sons of Heber in order that

---

[1] *Summa*, ii-ii. q. clxiii. a. 1, 2. Lucifer's fall was due to the same passing beyond the bounds of his own nature. See *Par.* xix. 46-48, and p. 295 above.   [2] *Par.* xxvi. 127-132.   [3] *City of God*, xvi. 11.

our Redeemer should use not the language of confusion,
but of grace. All this is retracted in the passage before
us. The original language, whatever it was, Adam
declares was entirely extinct long before Nimrod began
the Tower. Language being a product of reason, and
the inclinations of reason being subject to the movements of the heavens, it is impossible that it should
retain the same form for ever.[1]

(3) Once more, in the *De Vulg. Eloq.* (i. 4) it is stated
that the first word uttered by Adam in Paradise was
El, the name of his Maker. Now, however, Adam declares that during his lifetime the name of God was *I*
(probably the Hebrew Jah or Jehovah), and that *El*
came later. Dante may have been thinking of Exod.
vi. 2, 3: 'And God spake unto Moses, and said unto
him, I am the Lord (*Jehovah*): and I appeared unto
Abraham, unto Isaac, and unto Jacob, as God Almighty
(*El Shaddai*), but by my name Jehovah was I not
known to them.'[2]

---

[1] Comp. *De Vulg. Eloq.* i. 9: 'Since every language of ours, except that
created by God with the first man, has been restored at our pleasure after
the confusion, which was nothing else but forgetfulness of the former
language, and since man is a most unstable and changeable animal, no
human language can be lasting and continuous, but must needs vary
like other properties of ours, as for instance our manners and our dress,
according to distance of time and place' (Temple Classics).

[2] If so, Dante must have had other means of getting at the Hebrew of
the passage than the Vulgate, which quite obscures it: 'Ego *Dominus*
(Heb. *Jehovah*) qui apparui Abraham, Isaac, et Jacob, in *Deo omnipotente*
(Heb. *El Shaddai*): et nomen meum *Adonai* (Heb. *Jehovah*) non indicavi
eis.' Plumptre thinks that 'the Hebrew *Yod* [the first letter of Jehovah,
represented by the I or J of line 134] had probably been shown to Dante by
some Jewish friend, such as Immanuel of Rome, as the symbol of the
sacred *Tetragrammaton*.' Aquinas in his discussion of the names of
God (*Summa*, i. q. xiii. a. 11) says that the *QUI EST* of Exod. iii. 14 (the
I AM of our version) is the name most proper to God since it signifies
His existence, and therefore His essence which is His existence. If Dante
identifies the names *Qui est* or *I Am* and *Jehovah*, he may have put this
essential name of God into Adam's mouth as the highest.

Salimbene narrates a curious linguistic experiment which Frederick II.
made on infants, 'bidding foster-mothers and nurses to suckle and bathe
and wash the children, but in no wise to prattle or speak with them;
for he would have learnt whether they would speak the Hebrew language
(which had been the first), or Greek, or Latin, or Arabic, or perchance
the tongue of their parents of whom they had been born. But he laboured
in vain, for the children could not live without clappings of the hands,
and gestures, and gladness of countenance, and blandishments' (Coulton's
From St. Francis to Dante, 242).

The final question is how long Adam remained in
Eden. The answer is, about seven hours—from the
first hour of the day to that which follows the
sixth (midday), 'when the sun changes quadrant.'
According to Hettinger, Dante follows the Greek
Fathers, the Latins allowing a longer stay. It is in
reality one of those idle questions which Dante himself denounces contemptuously in Canto xxix. 94-117.
It may, of course, have some symbolic meaning, but it
is not easy to discover it.[1]

Adam's speech was answered by a Doxology: 'Glory
be to the Father, to the Son, to the Holy Ghost,' in
which all Paradise joined, of such ineffable sweetness
that the poet was intoxicated by its beauty. At the
same time what seemed 'a smile of the universe' broke
over all Heaven, so that the intoxication of joy and
love and peace entered at once through ear and eye.
This 'joy unspeakable and full of glory' seems to have
a twofold purpose. On the one hand, this smile of a
universe redeemed is in contrast to the lost Eden of
which Adam has just spoken—the whole creation
groaning and travailing together in pain. On the
other, it throws into dark and terrible relief the
picture of the Papacy which St. Peter is about to paint—
the smile of the universe eclipsed by the blush of shame
which overspread the face of Heaven. As Dante looks
at 'the four torches,' he sees Peter change colour from

---

[1] One amazing symbolism for the whole passage has been put forward
confidently by Gabriele Rossetti in his *Disquisitions on the Antipapal
Spirit*. The leading idea is that the *Commedia* is a poem against Rome
in a secret language of which Dante is the creator. Hence the Adam here
and in the *De Vulg. Eloq.* is no other than Dante himself! 'He intended
to convey the information that, when the sectarian world [i.e. the various
heretical sects that had cast off allegiance to Rome] arose to a new life, *he*
was the Adam who fixed the value of each word in the reformed language.'
As Adam was nearly seven hours in Eden, so Dante was nearly seven
in the Earthly Paradise. The 4302 years of Adam's stay in Limbo are the
4302 verses of Dante's poem from his leaving Limbo (*Inf.* v. 1) to the rising
of the three symbolic stars (*Purg.* viii. 93). The *El* and the *I* stand for
Henry VII., whom Dante had hailed as a God: *El* for Enrico Lucem-
burghese, Henry of Luxembourg, and the *I* for *Imperadore* and *Iddio*,
Emperor and God!

white to red, and in the silence which followed the
Doxology, the Apostle spoke :

> ' If I my colour change,
> Marvel not at it ; for, while I am speaking,
> Thou shalt behold all these their colour change.
> He who usurps upon the earth my place,
> My place, my place, which vacant has become
> Before the presence of the Son of God,
> Has of my cemetery made a sewer
> Of blood and stench, whereby the Perverse One,
> Who fell from here, below there is appeased ! '[1]

Peter speaks, of course, in his character of the first
Pope. His cemetery, the Vatican, the holiest place of
pilgrimage in Christendom, had become a common
sewer down which rolled the blood shed by the ambition of the Papacy, and the filth of its vices, to gladden
the heart of Lucifer in the sink of the universe.
Peter's indignant repetition of 'my place, my place,
my place,' is sometimes explained by a reference to
Jer. vii. 4: 'Trust ye not in lying words, saying, The
temple of the Lord, the temple of the Lord, the
temple of the Lord, are these.' This, however, is a
mere accidental resemblance, and we must seek the
meaning somewhere in the Apostle's own life. The
threefold question put to him by Christ, 'Lovest thou
me?' and His threefold command, 'Feed my lambs,'
' Feed my sheep,' ' Feed my sheep,' are generally taken
as a threefold restoration of Peter to his place as chief
Apostle, which he had forfeited by his threefold denial.[2]
There can be little doubt that this is the reference.
What Dante means is that the guilt of Boniface VIII.
is revealed by the fact that he did not scruple to usurp
the place which even St. Peter did not dare to take,
until it had been thrice solemnly restored to him by
the Son of God Himself. Hence in *His* presence the
place is vacant. This, as we see from other passages,
does not mean that it was vacant on the earth. When,
for example, William of Nogaret and Sciarra Colonna
committed their dastardly outrage on Boniface at
Anagni, Dante regarded it as committed on Christ

[1] *Par.* xxvii. 1-27 (Longfellow).   [2] John xxi. 15-17.

Himself in the person of His Vicar, because for them, as Dr. Moore says, he was 'the Lord's Anointed,' and 'they outraged and insulted him *as such*, without any thought as to his title being invalid.'[1] In short, Dante's view is parallel to Paul's 'The powers that be are ordained of God,' written to Rome at the very time when Nero was Emperor.

At Peter's words all Heaven grew red with shame and indignation, Beatrice blushing like a modest lady at the mere mention of another's sin. The change in Heaven was such as that of the eclipse 'when the Supreme Power suffered': in other words, the crucifixion was virtually repeated by Boniface. Peter continues his invective by recalling some of the martyred Popes of the first three centuries,—himself, Linus, and Cletus in the first; Sixtus and Pius in the second; Calixtus and Urban in the third. For what purpose, he asks indignantly, was 'the Spouse of Christ' thus nurtured on their blood? To help their successors in the quest for gold? Or that they might divide the Christian people into sheep and goats—Guelphs on the right hand, and Ghibellines on the left? Or that the keys given to Peter should become the ensign on a banner of war against the baptized, as in the crusade of Boniface against the Colonnas?[2] Or, finally, that Peter's own image on the Papal seal should be used to stamp 'sold and lying privileges'—indulgences, decrees, and bulls bought and sold for fraudulent ends? But there is 'in the lowest deep a lower deep.' Boniface had, indeed, used the martyrs' blood 'for the acquest of gold'; but his successors would use it as their very drink:

> 'Of our blood the Caorsines and Gascons
> Prepare themselves to drink.'[3]

The reference is to John's words in Rev. xvii. 6 concerning Babylon: 'And I saw the woman drunken with the blood of the saints, and with the blood of the

---

[1] *Purg.* xx. 85-90; Moore, *Studies in Dante*, 2nd series, 31 n.
[2] *Inf.* xxvii. 85-90.   [3] *Par.* xxvii. 58, 59.

martyrs of Jesus.' From the point of view of 1300, it
forms a prophecy of the almost unspeakable corruption
of the Papal Court under the first two Popes of the
Babylonish captivity at Avignon. Clement V., a Gascon,
was a mere tool of Philip the Fair. His crowning crime
of blood was the destruction of the Order of the Templars. His final destination is the Bolgia of the Simon-
iacs, where he is to be thrust head foremost on the top
of Boniface.[1] 'The Caorsines' refers to John XXII., a
native of Cahors in the south of France, a town whose
very name was in the Middle Ages a synonym for
usury and usurers.[2] The insatiable avarice of this
Pope, his traffic in interdicts and excommunications,
and the almost incredible wealth which he accumulated, have been already described. He well deserved
his name of Caorsine. The vengeance of God may
seem to slumber, but Peter expresses his conviction
that He will send speedy succour to His Church even
as by the hand of Scipio He defended Rome, 'the glory
of the world,' from destruction. The denunciation
ends with a command to utter boldly on his return to
earth all he has heard of the corruption of the
Papacy:[3]

'Conceal not that which I do not conceal.'

Whereupon as our air snows down the frozen vapours,
the heavenly ether was made beautiful with the
upward flight of 'vapours triumphant'—the white
souls of the Church Triumphant ascending like a
shower of flakes of fire. Dante's eyes followed them
until they vanished in the distance; whereupon Beatrice
asks him to turn his eyes in the opposite direction, and
see how far he had rolled on since his last look downward. The meaning of both looks has been fully
discussed in Chap. XX. It is his last sight of the visible
world before passing into the invisible; for the next

---

[1] *Inf.* xix. 82-84; *Par.* xxx. 142-148. See below, 476 ff.
[2] *Inf.* xi. 49, 50.
[3] For the Pope's abandonment of Holy Land, see on *Par.* ix. 127-142,
p. 160 above; and his fraudulent use of excommunication, *Par.* xviii.
127-136, p. 290.

Heaven, the *Primum Mobile* or *Crystalline*, is imperceptible to the senses save by its motion.[1] His journey in Gemini, as we saw, had borne him, since his last downward look, from the meridian of Jerusalem to near that of. Gades on the Atlantic, thus showing him the entire world, from Palestine to Spain, evangelized by the three Apostles with whom he held converse. There it lay far below him, a little 'threshing-floor' which made men fierce for its possession, in their forgetfulness of the faith and hope and love for which these had lived and died. No wonder St. Peter burned red with indignation as he passed over his defiled and desecrated grave in Rome, and as he came within sight of the Babylon of Avignon, 'Mother of Abominations.'[2] From that low dark world Dante's 'enamoured mind' turned his eyes back with greater eagerness to his Lady's face, and found her smile fairer than anything Nature or Art ever wrought to take the eyes and hold the mind. One glance had power to pluck him from the constellation of his nativity, 'the fair nest of Leda,' and thrust him into the *Primum Mobile*, 'the swiftest Heaven.' We may regard this as the point at which 'speculation' passes into contemplation proper. As from a *specula* or watch-tower he has looked down on the whole universe of visible things; now, by the swift and piercing power of contemplation which Beatrice henceforward represents, he is caught up into the world that lies beyond the senses.

[1] *Conv.* ii. 4. The passage is quoted above, pp. 3, 4.
[2] Rev. xvii. 5. See p. 366 f.

CHAPTER XXVI

1. *The Nine Orders*[1]

BEATRICE appears to occupy a special relation to this Ninth Heaven. As its name, *Primum Mobile*, implies, it is the beginning of the movement of the universe, and the agents of this movement are the Angels. Hence in this Heaven Dante sees, as in a figure, the Nine Orders of Angels revolving round their Creator. Now, in all the lower Heavens the explanation of any subject connected with them is put into the lips of spirits belonging to them. Had Dante followed this method here, he must have chosen one of the Angels to explain the relations and powers of the various Hierarchies. Instead of this, he makes Beatrice the expositor of the Angelic life. She is the only speaker in this Heaven. Even the denunciations are put into her mouth. As, in the other Heavens, holy souls denounced corrupters of the order to which they themselves belonged—Peter avaricious Popes, Damiani luxurious Cardinals, Aquinas degenerate Dominicans, and so on—so Beatrice denounces those on earth who pervert and darken that Divine wisdom which flows down to the human race through the Angelic Orders. In giving her this position he means to indicate that she belongs specially to this Heaven of Angels and is its natural mouthpiece. It is, indeed, only the fulfilment of thoughts and feelings running through the whole of the *Vita Nuova*, in which she is constantly

---

[1] For the Dionysian doctrine of the Nine Orders and the Nine Heavens of which they are the movers, see Introduction.

associated with the Angels. During her earthly life, when people saw her pass 'crowned and clothed with humility,' they said: 'This is not a woman, but one of the most beautiful Angels of Heaven.'[1] In a dream of her death he saw Angels flying heavenward with her soul in the form of a little white cloud.[2] When she really dies, he sings:

> Beatrice is gone up into high Heaven,
> The kingdom where the Angels are at peace,
> And lives with them.[3]

And on the first anniversary of the day on which she was made 'of the citizens of life eternal,' he tells us that he drew in memory of her the resemblance of an angel.[4] If further proof is necessary, it may be found in the mystical use of the number *nine* in the *Vita Nuova*. At the nativity of Beatrice the nine Heavens were in conjunction; the number nine is in the hour, the day, the month, the year of her birth; he saw her for the first time when she was at the beginning, and he at the end, of their ninth year; and she herself is the number nine, 'a miracle whose only root is the Holy Trinity': 'And touching the reason why this number was so closely allied unto her, it may peradventure be this. According to Ptolemy, (and also to the Christian verity,) the revolving heavens are nine; and according to the common opinion among astrologers, these nine heavens together have influence over the earth. Wherefore it would appear that this number was thus allied unto her for the purpose of signifying that, at her birth, all these nine heavens were at perfect unity with each other as to their influence. This is one reason that may be brought: but more narrowly considering, and according to the infallible truth, this number was her own self: that is to say, by similitude. As thus. The number three is the root of the number nine; seeing that without the interposition of any other number, being multiplied merely by itself, it produceth nine, as we manifestly

---

[1] *Vita Nuova*, § 26.   [2] § 23.   [3] § 32.   [4] § 35.

perceive that three times three are nine. Thus, three
being of itself the efficient of nine, and the Great
Efficient of Miracles being of Himself Three Persons
(to wit: the Father, the Son, and the Holy Spirit),
which, being Three, are also One:—this lady was
accompanied by the number nine to the end that men
might clearly perceive her to be a nine, that is, a
miracle, whose only root is the Holy Trinity.'[1] After
all this, it was inevitable that she should hold some
special relation to the Ninth Heaven, ruled over by the
Ninth Order of Angels, the Seraphim who burn with
love, and that the exposition of the functions of the
Nine Orders should be put into her lips. It is, doubtless,
for the same reason that it is in her eyes, as in a
mirror, Dante first sees the Point of burning Light,
which represents God, as the centre of the nine Angelic
circles.[2]

Beatrice commences her exposition by explaining
that in this Heaven of the *Primum Mobile* the whole
system of ' Nature' has its origin:

> 'The nature of the world, which keepeth quiet
> The centre, and all the rest around it moves,
> From hence begins as from its starting-point.'[3]

Dante is here following Aristotle, who defines Nature
in terms of motion and rest: 'Nature is the first
principle of motion and of rest, *per se*, not *per
accidens.*'[4] The Tenth Heaven, the Empyrean, is
supernatural, because it is absolutely and eternally
above motion and mutation. Nature and motion are
identical,—motion in scholastic usage including every
form of alteration, sentient and intellectual as well as
spatial.[5] And since this motion is ever seeking a final
goal, a *bonum* in which to rest, Nature is also a principle

---

[1] *Vita Nuova*, § 30.　The quotations are from Rossetti's translation.
[2] *Par.* xxviii. 1-12.　　　　　　　　　[3] *Par.* xxvii. 106-108.
[4] *Physics*, ii. 3; see *Summa*, i. q. xxix. a. 1. Cornoldi illustrates the
distinction between *per se* and *per accidens* thus: ' When one billiard
ball is sent at another, the impulse is extrinsic and the motion forced (*per
accidens*); but when two drops of mercury, placed near each other,
approach and meet, their motion is from an intrinsic principle, and is
natural (*per se*)'—*Physical System of St. Thomas*, Eng. trans., p. 21.
[5] See above, p. 91 n.

of rest. This *bonum* is God; hence the entire system of Nature is one vast movement of desire for union with God as its final rest. As the sphere nearest to the motionless Empyrean, the Primum Mobile has the greatest longing, and therefore the swiftest movement. The reason is that its motive power is the highest Order of Angels, the Seraphim, whose fiery love wheels them round with a velocity greater still:

> ' Its movement is so swift
> By the burning love wherewith it is spurred on.' [1]

Beatrice proceeds to explain the spiritual origin of the Primum Mobile, and therefore of 'the nature of the world': it is, as it is called elsewhere, 'the royal mantle of all the volumes of the world,' [2] containing all the other spheres, but itself contained by nothing but the Mind of God:

> ' And this Heaven hath no other *Where*
> Than the Mind Divine, in which enkindled is
> The Love that turns it and the power it rains.
> Light and Love in one circle comprehend it,
> Even as it the others, and of that girdle
> He who engirds it is the sole Intelligence.' [3]

The meaning is that, as this is the last of the corporeal Heavens, it cannot be located by saying it is contained within any other material sphere: its only *Where* is the Mind of God. In that Mind are enkindled, first, the Love of the Seraphim by which the Ninth Heaven is moved, and, second, the virtue which it pours down upon the lower spheres. The Light and Love which in one circle comprehend it are the spiritual Heaven of the Empyrean, of which God alone is the Intelligence that comprehends and rules. Thus the entire system of·'Nature' is traced up to its origin in pure spirit. [4]

---

[1] *Par.* xxviii. 44, 45; *Conv.* ii. 4.   [2] *Par.* xxiii. 112, 113.
[3] *Par.* xxvii. 109-114. In the last line—'Colui che il cinge solamente intende,'—I follow Butler in translating '*intende*' 'is the Intelligence,' as in *Par.* viii. 37, to which he refers, where the Principalities are addressed as 'Voi che *intendendo* il terzo ciel movete'—'Ye who *by intellect* the third heaven move.' The ordinary translation 'governs' or 'controls' loses the main idea that the Empyrean is governed by the Divine Intellect.
[4] *Par.* ii. 112-114; xxx. 106-108; *Summa*, i. q. xliv., xlv.

It is only by bearing this carefully in mind that we shall understand the peculiar spiritual significance of what Beatrice proceeds to say concerning Time, as a necessary condition of that system of Nature. Time is measured by motion; and since all motion has its origin in the Primum Mobile, this Heaven measures the movements of all the other spheres, as exactly as ten is measured by its half and its fifth. Hence, says Beatrice in a striking figure,

> ' How time in such a vase
> May have its roots, and in the rest its leaves,
> Can now be manifest to thee.' [1]

In other words, the Primum Mobile is like a flower-pot in which the roots of Time are hidden, while its leaves are visible in the movements of the other Heavens. The spiritual idea in Dante's mind is contained in the phrase 'in such a vase'—such, namely, as he had just described. The Primum Mobile is a vase the *where* of which is the Divine Mind. It is encircled by the Light and Love of the Empyrean. Its movement and power flow from the Love of God through the Seraphim. Time, therefore, is infinitely more than a mere succession of corporeal movements. It is the procession of the Light and Love of Eternity into the temporal life of man. And thus Time becomes a thing of infinite value. It is man's great opportunity of yielding himself to this vast movement by which ' the nature of the world' yearns upward to its Source and End. That this spiritual conception of Time was in Dante's mind is proved by the way in which he immediately turns to the almost universal neglect of this great opportunity. That attraction of the Heavens of which Time is the visible sign, is rendered null by the counter-attraction of covetousness, which submerges men in the inordinate love of earth:

> ' O Covetousness, that mortals dost ingulf
> Beneath thee so, that no one hath the power
> Of drawing back his eyes from out thy waves !' [2]

---

[1] *Par.* xxvii. 115-120.   [2] *Par.* xxvii. 121-123.

And then he proceeds to show how the mere passage
of time, and a very short time, destroys the power of
yielding to the attraction of the Heavens. In the
spring-time of human life the will puts forth fair
blossoms, but 'the continual rain' of covetousness—
the constant beating of the surrounding worldliness on
the young soul, blasts its proper fruit. Faith and
innocence die with childhood.

'Heaven lies about us in our infancy'—

and only then. The child observes the fasts of religion,
and loves and honours his mother, only while he lisps:
when his speech is perfect he wishes her in her grave.
At the very first glance of the sun, which measures
Time, human nature begins to darken:

> 'Even thus is darkened, at the first glance,
> The white skin of the beauteous daughter
> Of him who bringeth morn and leaveth even.'

The meaning is much disputed; but the figure in
Dante's mind seems to be the change which the first
glance of the sun begins to make in his 'beauteous
daughter' Aurora—the whiteness of the dawn darkening on and on into the evening gloom.[1] Fused with
this figure is the idea of 'the beauteous daughter' of
the sun as human nature, as in *Par.* xxii. 116, where
the sun is called 'the father of all mortal life'; and in
De Mon. i. 9: 'The human race is the son of heaven,
which is most perfect in all its work; for "man and
the sun generate man," according to the second *De
Naturali Auditu.*'[2] The comparison is then to this
effect: as in the natural day the whiteness of dawn

[1] *Par.* xxvii. 124-138. Comp. the deepening of the colour on Aurora's
cheek from white to vermilion in *Purg.* ii. 7-9. I admit that Greek
mythology is against this view: Eos and Helios being sister and brother,
both children of Hyperion, the Titan. On the other hand, Helios from
his father is often called Hyperionides or Hyperion, a contraction for the
patronymic Hyperionion, and the poets have made us familiar with
Hyperion as the Sun. In any case, it seems plain to my mind that in this
passage Dante was drawing a parallel between the day of human life and
the natural day from dawn to the evening dark. Scartazzini's view that
'the beauteous daughter' of the Sun is the Church, seems to me quite
away from the context of thought in the passage.

[2] Aristotle, *Physics*, ii. 2: 11.

lasts but a moment, the very turning of the sun
changing morning into night: so in the day of human
life the white innocence of the soul passes with childhood, and the same turning of the sun darkens the
bright promise of the morning into the night of sin.
And yet Time, which works this ruin, has its roots in
a vase which is held in the very Light and Love of
God!

This frustration of the meaning and end of Time,
and of the motion of the Heavens which is 'the nature
of the world,' Dante traces to the absence of right
government on earth, temporal or spiritual, and
prophesies a speedy reformation:

> 'But ere that January be all unwintered
> By the centesimal neglected upon earth,
> Shall these supernal circles roar so loud
> The tempest that has been so long awaited
> Shall whirl the poops about where are the prows,
> So that the fleet shall run its course direct:
> And true fruit shall follow on the flower.' [1]

Since the subject under discussion is the abuse and
neglect of Time, Dante purposely uses, as an example
of it, an error in the Calendar, which, if uncorrected,
would carry January out of winter altogether. 'The
neglected centesimal' refers to the fact that, according
to the Julian Calendar, the year was too long by
almost the hundredth part of a day. In Dante's time,
this error had pushed January more than eight days
nearer the end of winter.[2] What Beatrice prophesies,

[1] *Par.* xxvii. 139-148. For this misgovernment, comp. *Purg.* vi. 76-151;
xvi. 82-132,

[2] Toynbee's note is: 'The allusion is to the error in the Julian Calendar, which put the length of the year at $365\frac{1}{4}$ days, and made every
fourth year a leap-year. This was, however, too long by somewhat less
than the hundredth part of a day ('la centesma negletta,' Par. xxvii.
143), so that in Dante's time the error was above eight days, and January
had been advanced by this amount nearer to the end of winter. This
error was not corrected until 1582, by which time it amounted to ten days,
when Gregory xiii. introduced the reformed or Gregorian Calendar (not
adopted in England until 1752), which provided that ten days should be
dropped and that three out of every four hundredth years should be
ordinary years, instead of every hundredth year being a leap-year as
under the old calendar. In this way began the new style (N.S.) as opposed
to the old style (O.S.).' Vellutello in his commentary adjures the Pope
of his day to undertake the reform and suggests a method.

then, is that before this error in the Calendar has
wholly unwintered this month—that is, 'before long,'
a long space being put ironically for a short one, as
when we say 'not a hundred miles hence'—the indignation of high Heaven would break out in a tempest
which would turn the fleet of the human race right
round, and set it on a straight course. It is obvious
that this cannot be a prophecy of Henry VII.'s descent
into Italy in 1310, since John XXII., the Caorsine referred
to in l. 58, was elected Pope in 1316, and therefore this
passage must have been written after the latter date.
'It may be doubted,' as Butler says, 'whether we have
not here a foreboding of greater, vaguer, and more
distant changes than those indicated in the "veltro"
and "DXV" passages,[1] with which it is usual to compare this. At any rate, with this passage the prophecies
of the poem may be said to end.'

Turning now to Cantos xxviii. and xxix., we find that
the great revelation of this Ninth Heaven is the unity
of God, while still remaining one, breaking itself up
into the nine mirrors of the nine Orders of Angels,
that through them the infinitude of His goodness
might be reflected to all the varied ranks of creation,
according to their power to receive it :

> 'Thou beholdest now the height and the breadth
> Of the Eternal Goodness, since it hath made
> Itself so many mirrors in which 'tis broken,
> One in itself remaining as before.'[2]

According to St. Bernard, 'height' is power and
'breadth' love. What Dante sees, therefore, in this
world of Angels is the Divine Goodness sharing its
power and love with all the creatures it has called into
being.

This unity of God is revealed to Dante as an atomic
Point of Light—so small that the smallest visible star
had seemed a moon beside it. 'The point by reason
of its indivisibility is immeasurable';[3] hence it is a
natural symbol of the immensity of the Deity. Hence

---

[1] *Inf.* i. 100-111 (*Veltro*); *Purg.* xxxiii. 40-45 (*DXV*).
[2] *Par.* xxix. 142-145.
[3] *Conv.* ii. 14.

also this Point which seems to be contained by the nine concentric circles of angelic fire which Dante sees revolving round it, in reality contains them :

Seeming enclosed by what itself encloses.[1]

On it hangs the entire universe of being : 'From that point,' says Beatrice,

'Dependent is the heaven and all nature.'[2]

The words are from Aristotle's *Metaphysics*, xi. 7. 5: 'Now on such a principle depends the heaven and nature' (ὁ οὐρανὸς καὶ ἡ φύσις)—the unity of the universe being implied in the unity of God.

Dante's eyes are even yet far from being strong enough to gaze directly at the Point of burning Light. His first vision of it is its reflection in 'the beauteous eyes of which Love made the cord to take him,' the unity of God being the unity of Love. Turning from the mirror of the eyes of Beatrice, he finds that he cannot yet rise beyond the mirrors of the nine Angelic Orders, which, in the form of rings of fire, circle round the burning Point. In these angelic mirrors the light of God is so broken up and divided that his eyes are able to bear its reflected brightness.

These nine circles differ in certain particulars. In the first place, in their rates of speed. As we have so often seen, motion means yearning for union with God, and the nearer the central Point the greater the yearning. Hence of the innermost circle, the Seraphim, Beatrice says :

'Its movement is so swift
By the burning love wherewith it is spurred on.'[3]

Its velocity surpasses that of the Primum Mobile itself, 'the movement that swiftest girds the world.'[4] The speed of the others diminishes according to their distance from the centre. It is to be noted that the circularity of their motion here has its symbolic significance. 'According to Dionysius, says St. Bonaventura,

---

[1] *Par.* xxx. 12.
[3] *Par.* xxviii. 43-45; *Conv.* ii. 4.
[2] *Par.* xxviii. 40-42.
[4] *Par.* xxviii. 25-27.

'the Angels have a threefold movement, circular, straight, and oblique. The circular is from the same to the same, and around the same immovable centre: this movement have the Angels, who receive illuminations immediately from God, and by means of these return to God.'[1] It is this noblest movement which Dante here sees; and he attributes it to the longing for likeness to God. Speaking of the Seraphim and Cherubim, Beatrice says:

> 'Thus swiftly follow they their bonds,
> To liken them unto the Point as most they can.'[2]

The idea seems to be that the swifter a circle revolves the more it resembles a point in appearance.

A second difference is in the degrees of brightness. The circle nearest to the central Point burns with the purest flame, and the clearness diminishes, like the velocity, in proportion to the distance. The reason is that the brightness of each circle varies according to its power of penetrating into the truth of God, 'the pure spark' of the Eternal Light.[3]

These differences give rise to a difficulty which Dante submits to Beatrice for solution. There seems to be no correspondence between these spiritual circles of Angels and 'the corporeal circles,' the Heavens over which they preside. In the case of the corporeal circles, the nine spheres grow Diviner as they recede from their centre, the earth. Whereas, in the case of the spiritual circles, the reverse holds: the nine rings of fire grow more Divine the nearer they approach *their* centre, the Point of burning Light. Thus pattern and copy seem to disagree: 'the world of sense' to contradict the world of spirit which governs it.

The reply of Beatrice is that Dante must not judge the nine Angelic circles by their 'appearance,' their visible size, but by the 'virtue' which each contains,

---

[1] *Compend. Theolog. Veritatis*, ii. 15.   Comp. Aquinas, *Summa*, ii-ii. q. clxxx. a. 6, and pp. 333-337 above.
[2] *Par.* xxviii. 100, 101.   Their 'bonds' are the love and yearning for God which hold them ever circling round the Point.
[3] *Par.* xxviii. 37-39.

their invisible spiritual power. For example, the smallest circle, the fire of the Seraphim, is the one that 'most loves and most knows'; and this greatness of love and knowledge naturally requires a great sphere for its exercise. Hence it is the Motor of this Ninth Heaven, 'the royal mantle of all the volumes of the world,' 'which sweepeth with it all the rest of all the universe.' And so with the other 'corporeal circles.' The size of each is determined by the amount of virtue diffused through it, and this in turn is in proportion of the greatness of the salvation each is intended to work out. Hence there exists the strictest correspondence of the virtue of each Order to the material Heaven of which it is the moving Intelligence. This explanation entirely satisfies Dante's mind: the truth shines like a star when the North-east wind has blown the whole heaven clear. When Beatrice ceased, the fiery circles broke like molten iron into innumerable sparks, each spark representing probably an individual Angel, and all following the flaming ring to which they belonged; while from choir to choir *Hosanna* rose

> To the fixed Point which holds them to the *Where*,
> And ever will hold, in which they have ever been.[1]

It is another reminiscence of his dream of his Lady's death: 'And I seemed to look towards Heaven, and to behold a multitude of angels who were returning upwards, having before them an exceedingly white cloud: and these angels were singing together gloriously, and the words of their song were these: " *Osanna in excelsis* ": and there was no more that I heard.'[2]

Beatrice proceeds to clear up certain 'dubious thoughts' which she saw rising in Dante's mind,—the uncertainty, apparently, as to whether Dionysius or Gregory was right concerning the order in which the Angelic Choirs stand to one another. Beatrice decides in favour of Dionysius, on the ground that he had received his knowledge, according to mediæval belief, from St. Paul:

---

[1] *Par.* xxviii. 46-96. [2] *Vita Nuova*, § 23 (Rossetti).

'For he who saw it up here disclosed it to him,
With much more of the truth about these circles.'

From St. Paul's statement that he was 'caught up to
the third heaven,'[1] we might infer that he had not
risen so far as this ninth, where the Angelic Orders
are revealed.   According to Aquinas, however, St.
Paul's third heaven is the same as Dante's tenth, the
Empyrean.   Counting upwards from the earth, the
first heaven is the Sidereal, divided into eight spheres
—the Fixed Stars and the Seven Planets; the second,
the Crystalline; and the third, the Empyrean.   Sometimes also three kinds of supernatural vision are called
three heavens,—corporeal, imaginary, and intellectual,
the intellectual being, according to St. Augustine, the
third heaven of St. Paul.[2]   So faithfully did the Apostle
reveal to Dionysius the order of the Angelic Choirs
that Gregory when he reached this heaven smiled at
his own error.   In reality, Dante is here correcting
himself even more than Gregory: in the *Convito* (ii. 6)
he had adopted an order which differs from that of
either theologian.[3]

Following the Areopagite, then, Beatrice names the
Nine Orders, beginning with those nearest God.   They

[1] 2 Cor. xii. 2.   [2] *Summa*, i. q. lxviii. a. 4.
[3] *Par.* xxviii. 130-139.   It may be of interest to give the different
arrangements as in Toynbee's Dante Dictionary, p. 265.

Dionysius and Dante (in the *Commedia*).	St. Gregory.	Dante in *Conv.* ii. 6.
	First Hierarchy.	
Seraphim.	Seraphim.	Seraphim.
Cherubim.	Cherubim.	Cherubim.
Thrones.	Thrones.	Powers.
	Second Hierarchy.	
Dominions.	Dominions.	Principalities.
Virtues.	Principalities.	Virtues.
Powers.	Powers.	Dominions.
	Third Hierarchy.	
Principalities.	Virtues.	Thrones.
Archangels.	Archangels.	Archangels.
Angels.	Angels.	Angels.

From this it is obvious that Dante had much greater cause to smile
at himself than Gregory had.   The latter merely transposed Virtues
and Principalities; whereas Dante utterly confused Principalities,
Powers, Dominions, and Thrones.   On the transposition of Thrones and
Principalities, see p. 136 f. above.

are divided into three Hierarchies of three each. Aquinas says the Orders of the First Hierarchy derive their names from their relation to *God*; those of the Second from their common office of *government*; and those of the Third from their function of *executing* the work.[1]

I. The First Hierarchy consists of Seraphim, Cherubim, and Thrones:

> 'The first circles
> Have shown to thee Seraphim and Cherubim.
> Thus swiftly follow they their bonds
> To liken them unto the Point as most they can.
> And they can as far as they are high in vision.
> Those other Loves that round about them go,
> Thrones of the Divine aspect are called,
> Because they terminated the first Triad.'[2]

It is difficult to understand this reason for the name of the Thrones. Perhaps it is something to this effect. The Thrones are, as they are called elsewhere, 'mirrors'[3] by which the Divine judgments are flashed throughout the universe. These judgments, however, descend to the Thrones through the Seraphim and Cherubim, that is, through love and knowledge. The Thrones, therefore, are the *terminus*, so to speak, of the love and knowledge of God issuing in judgment. 'The Seraphim,' says Bonaventura, 'contemplate the goodness of God, the Cherubim the truth, the Thrones the equity'[4]; and this equity contains the goodness and truth, the love and light, which flow down through the two higher Orders.

We now come to one of the great questions which

[1] *Summa*, i. q. cviii. a. 6.

[2] *Par.* xxviii. 98-105. Comp. Dionysius *On the Heavenly Hierarchy*, vii.; *Summa*, i. q. cviii. a. 5, 6: 'The name *Seraphim* is not given from charity alone, but from excess of charity, which the name of heat or burning implies. . . . Similarly the name *Cherubim* is given from a certain excess of knowledge; whence it is interpreted *plenitudo scientiae*. . . . The Order of *Thrones* has excellence over the inferior Orders in that they have power to know immediately in God the reasons of the Divine operations.' See also p. 6 f. above. For their powers of contemplation see *Conv.* ii. 6.

[3] *Par.* ix. 61-63.

[4] *Compend. Theol. Veritatis*, ii. 12; St. Bernard, *De Consideratione*, v. 4, 5.

divided the Schoolmen: whether the intellect or the will is the root of the blessedness of men and Angels. Duns Scotus, the famous Franciscan scholastic, took the latter view. To him the highest thing in God was will, not intellect: even good is good only because God commands it. And since in men and Angels the same relation exists between intellect and will, Scotus held that their blessedness consists in the attitude of the will to God, that is, in love,[1] and not in intellectual vision. Aquinas, on the other hand, as we have seen all through the poem, traces the blessedness of all spiritual creatures to the power of the intellect to see God. In the words of Beatrice here:

> 'And thou must know that they all have delight
> In measure as their vision sinketh deeper
> Into the Truth in which all intellect finds rest.
> Hence may be seen how the being blessed
> Is founded in the act which seeth,
> Not in that which loves, which follows after.'[2]

Aquinas lays down the principle that 'nothing is loved but what is known,' and argues with scholastic subtlety for the priority of intellect: 'For happiness two things are requisite, one which is the essence of happiness, another which is a sort of *proprium* of it, namely, the delight attaching to it. I say then that as for that which is the very essence of happiness, it cannot possibly consist in an act of will. For manifestly happiness is the gaining of the last end; but the gaining of the last end does not consist in any mere act of the will. The will reaches out both to an absent end, *desiring* it, and to a present end, resting in it with *delight*. But plainly the mere desire of an end is not the gaining of an end, but a movement in that direction. As for *delight*, that comes over the will from the fact

---

[1] The connection between love and will is this. Aquinas distinguishes *dilectio naturalis* and *dilectio electiva*. The former is the natural love or appetite which inclines every creature to seek *good* in general; the latter is the love which *elects* one particular good out of many as final end—as pleasure, money, God. The election, of course, involves will: indeed the word *dilectio* implies *electio* (*Summa*, i. q. lx. a. 1, 2).

[2] *Par.* xxviii. 106-111.

of the end being present, but not conversely, i.e., a
thing does not become present by the mere fact of the
will delighting in it. It must therefore be by something else than the act of the will that the end itself
becomes present to the will. And this manifestly
appears in the case of sensible ends; for if it were
possible to gain money by an act of the will, a covetous
man would have made his money from the first, the
instant that he wished to have it; but the fact is, at
first the money is away from him, and he gets it by
seizing it with his hand, or by some such means, and
then he is at once delighted with the money got. So
then it happens also in the case of an end of the
intellectual order. For from the beginning we wish to
gain this intellectual end; but we actually do gain it
only by this, that it becomes present to us by an act of
understanding, and then the will rests delighted in
the end already gained. So therefore the essence of
happiness consists in an act of understanding. But
the delight that follows upon happiness belongs to the
will.'[1] To our minds an argument like this produces
little conviction. Indeed, the whole dispute seems
futile, since both views are true in experience: vision
produces love, and love produces vision. Yet a real
issue lay beneath the controversy. The tendency of the
Scotist view that the will is superior to the intellect
in God and man, was to reduce omnipotence to the
arbitrary will of the Deity; whereas to Aquinas the
Divine will was simply the Divine intellect going forth
in action: His goodness is the reason for all He wills.[2]

The view, however, that blessedness 'is founded in
the act which sees,' and that love follows the intellect,
must not be taken as involving of necessity the inferiority of love. 'Love ranks above knowledge in
moving,' says Aquinas, 'but knowledge goes before

---

[1] *Summa*, i-ii. q. iii. a. 4 (Rickaby). The argument may be reduced to
this: to wish for a thing is not the same as to *have* it; and the organ by
which we actually *have* the vision of God is the intellect.

[2] *Summa*, i. q. xix. a. 4, 5; *Cont. Gent.* i. 86. For a comparison of
Aquinas and Scotus (died 1308), see Ueberweg, *History of Philosophy*,
i. 452-457; Alexander, *A Short History of Philosophy*, 169.

love in attaining.'¹ The proper name of the Holy Spirit
is Love.² The Seraphim are the highest of the Nine
Orders because they excel all the rest in love, the
Cherubim, who represent knowledge, being second.
'Of all human actions and affections, the last end is
the love of God' (*Dei dilectio*).³ And that which Dante
sets as the crown upon his poem is 'the Love that
moves the sun and the other stars.'⁴

One question remains: according to what law do the
various Orders of Angels possess their different degrees
of vision, on which their beatitude depends? The
answer is: vision is in proportion to 'merit':

> 'And of the vision merit is the measure,
> Which grace gives birth to and good will;
> Thus from rank to rank the process goes.'⁵

To understand this we must remember that, according
to the Church's teaching, there is no merit without
grace. The Angelic *nature* in itself has no power to
see God with that vision which constitutes beatitude.
Hence grace is necessary to lift even the highest Angel
above its nature to God, who is its *supernatural* end.
The acceptance of this grace by 'good will' constitutes
'merit,' the reward of which is the Beatific Vision.⁶

Before passing from this Hierarchy, we may look at
a difficulty which springs from the relation in which
the two highest Orders stand to each other. The
Cherubim, as we have seen, represent knowledge; yet
the Seraphim are described in l. 72 as 'the circle that
most loves *and most knows.*'⁷ In other words, it excels

¹ *Summa*, i-ii. q. iii. a. 4.   ² *Summa*, i. q. xxxvii. a. 1.
³ *Summa*, ii-ii. q. xxiii. a. 6; q. xxvii. a. 6.
⁴ *Par.* xxxiii. 142-145.   ⁵ *Par.* xxviii. 112-114.
⁶ *Summa*, i. q. lxii. a. 4. See *Par.* xxix. 58-66, and p. 455 below. The
argument of Aquinas is that beatitude is 'natural' to God only: to men
and Angels it lies above their nature. Since even Angels cannot rise
above their nature of themselves, the aid of Divine grace is necessary;
and when this grace is embraced by the will, merit follows. It was
debated whether Angels were created in grace; Aquinas holds that they
were, because without grace it had been impossible for them to *merit*
beatitude.
⁷ *Conv.* ii. 6 : 'The Father may be considered without respect to aught
save himself; and this contemplation the Seraphim do use, who see more
of the First Cause than any other angelic nature.' The whole passage
may be consulted for the purely fanciful way in which the mediæval
imagination apportioned the Persons of the Trinity, and their relations to

the Cherubim in knowledge as well as love. And although at first sight this seems an inconsistency, it is in reality the necessary consequence of what has just been said of knowledge and love. If love is in proportion to knowledge, then the Seraphim who love most, for that very reason must know most. And this relation holds through all the Angelic circles: each higher Order excels the one below it in the virtue proper to the lower. 'All spiritual perfections,' says Aquinas, 'are common to all Angels, and all exist more abundantly in the superior than in the lower. But since in the perfections themselves also there is a certain gradation, the superior perfection is attributed to the superior order *per proprietatem* (as the perfection proper to it), while to the inferior order it is attributed *per participationem* (i.e., as not found in it fully, but only partially), . . . and so the superior order is named from the superior perfection.'[1] As a Catholic poet beautifully paraphrases this passage:

> 'Think not the Spirits of Love
> Are less in knowledge than that Cherub Choir:
> Each loftier choir retains, yea, closelier clasps
> That special grace which names the choir beneath it,
> Retains, and lifts it to a higher heaven:
> The Spirits of Love in knowledge far transcend
> The Spirits of Knowledge, deeplier knowing this
> How worthy of love is God. Cherubs in turn
> Surpass in reverence for the Will Divine
> The Thrones who on their bosom throne that Will:
> Perchance such reverence for that Will it was
> Which made such Knowledge theirs. In all the Choirs
> The glories of all virtues co-exist
> Diverse in measure. Such diversity
> Not envy breeds in heaven, but Love's increase:
> The amplest Spirits possess no gift not held
> Implicitly by least. To choirs beneath
> Exulting they transmit it. Seraphs thus
> Fling fires of Love on Cherubs. These in turn
> Redound, subdued to milder lights of wisdom,
> Their kinglier knowledge on the Choir of Thrones:
> Thence down to humbler choirs.'[2]

---

one another, among the Hierarchies, as the special objects of their contemplation. [1] *Summa*, i. q. cviii. a. 5.

[2] From Aubrey de Vere's poem 'Saint Dionysius the Areopagite' in his *Legends and Records of the Church and the Empire.*

II. The Orders composing the Second Hierarchy are the Dominations, Virtues, Powers:

> 'The second Ternary which doth put forth buds
> In such wise in this sempiternal spring,
> Which no nocturnal Aries despoils,
> Perpetually *Hosanna* doth unwinter
> With three melodies, which resound in three
> Orders of joy, whereof it is intrined.
> In this Hierarchy are the three Divine:
> First Dominations, and then Virtues;
> And the third Order is of Powers.' [1]

The figure of the spring underlies this description—an eternal spring, not like that of earth, despoiled by the sign of Aries visible during the nights of winter. In this eternal spring this Hierarchy is ever putting forth new buds, ever breaking forth into new forms of life and action; and, like the songs of birds of spring, their *Hosanna* overflows in perpetual joy. This joyful praise is sung in three melodies which blend together. The reference may be to the threefold function of this Hierarchy. Its function is government, with this distinction, according to Aquinas: the *Dominations* distinguish the things to be done; the *Virtues* provide the faculty of fulfilling; while the *Powers* keep order that the precepts may be carried out. It is, perhaps, this threefold function of Divine government which unites in the threefold melody of their *Hosanna*.[2]

III. The Third Hierarchy consists of Principalities, Archangels, and Angels:

> 'Then in the dances twain penultimate,
> Principalities and Archangels circle round;
> The last is wholly of Angelic sports.' [3]

---

[1] *Par.* xxviii. 115-123. The 'unwintering of *Hosanna*' in l. 118 refers to the use of the verb *svernare* by the poets: in the spring-time the birds 'unwinter' themselves by beginning to sing. Here the 'unwintering of *Hosanna*' is perpetual—another way of saying that spring is eternal—its song is never stilled by winter as on earth.

[2] *Summa*, i. q. cviii. a. 6. According to Gregory, the Dominations are *Domini* over the rest, commanding the things to be done; the Virtues work miracles; the Powers restrain or repel the powers of evil. Comp. *Summa*, i. q. cviii. a. 5.   [3] *Par.* xxviii. 124-126.

These form, so to speak, the executive,—the execution
of angelic ministries consisting in the annunciation of
Divine things. This is initiated by the Principalities
as the head of the Hierarchy, communicated to the
Archangels as medium, and finally delivered by the
Angels as messengers.[1] The entire range of Angelic
being has a twofold action: all Orders gaze upward
in yearning and adoration, and, downward, all draw
and are drawn toward God.[2]

[1] *Summa*, i. q. cviii. a. 6. As pointed out in the Introduction, the
Angels are sometimes regarded as guardians of individuals, and Archangels of nations (Dan. x. 13, 21 ; xii. 1) ; while Principalities exercised a
kind of *international* control, so to speak, over the kings and kingdoms
of the earth (St. Bernard, Sermon xix. on the Song of Songs).

[2] *Par.* xxviii. 127-129.

CHAPTER XXVII

2. *The Angelic Life*

THIS Twenty-ninth Canto is occupied in answering certain questions concerning the Angels which greatly engaged the minds of mediæval theologians. If we find it difficult to understand their interest in such a subject, we must remember three things. First, they believed that the human soul was the great prize for which good and evil Angels carried on their age-long warfare, and it was not unnatural that they should desire to know something of the combatants. In the second place, it was their faith that in the future life the Redeemed would be 'equal unto the angels,'[1] and even fill the places of those who had fallen; and they could not but speculate concerning the higher nature of which they were to be partakers. Finally, they studied the Angelic nature as a means of knowing God. Since that nature contains more of its Cause than ours, the intellect which apprehends its essence sees God in a higher way than by speculations of science or philosophy. It may be impossible thus 'to pick the brains of angels,' to use Father Rickaby's phrase;[2] but the hope of doing it was the secret of half the speculations of the scholastics which provoke our smiles.

After her exposition of the Hierarchies, Beatrice gazed for a moment at the Point of burning Light, 'in which every *where* and every *when* is centred,' and there saw Dante's unspoken questions concerning the *where*

---

[1] Luke xx. 36.
[2] *Of God and His Creatures*, 214 n.

and the *when* of the creation of the Angels. Her
answer begins with God's motive in creation:

> ' Not to acquire some good unto Himself,
> Which cannot be, but that His splendour
> By its resplendency may say : *Subsisto.*'[1]

A selfish motive in creation is impossible to God,
morally, because He is Love, and metaphysically,
because His being possesses all goodness in itself, and
therefore cannot acquire more. 'Nothing else moves
God to the production of creatures but His own goodness, which He wished to communicate to other beings
according to the manner of their assimilation to Himself.'[2] The word 'splendour' in l. 14 must not be taken
in the vague general sense of 'glory.' We saw in the
Introduction[3] that Dante gives it a specific meaning.
Light as it exists in God its source, is *luce*, light ; as it
flows forth to objects, it is *raggio*, ray ; as it is reflected
from objects, it is *splendore*, splendour. Now, as the
Angelic nature is the first and clearest mirror of the
Divine light, that nature is *par excellence* the 'splendour'
of God—the reflection of His brightness throughout
the universe. It is by this reflection—*risplendendo*
(l. 15)—that the very subsistence of the Angels is maintained : if they could cease thus to receive and reflect
their Maker's light, they would thereby cease to subsist.
This, then, was the Divine motive : to create an order of
beings every one of whom could say *Subsisto* in receiving and communicating the Divine goodness to every
creature, according to its power to apprehend it.[4]

The question of the *when* and *where* of the creation
of Angels is almost unanswerable because, according
to the scholastics, following St. Augustine, neither time

---

[1] *Par.* xxix. 1-15.
[2] *Cont. Gentiles*, ii. 46 (comp. i. 87); *Summa*, i. q. l. a. 1. See also p. 122
above, on *Par.* vii. 64-66.
[3] P. 18.
[4] Comp. Dion. Areop., *De Coel. Hier.* iv. : 'It was through goodness
that the superessential Godhead, having fixed all the essences of things
being, brought them into being. For this is the peculiar characteristic of
the Cause of all things, and of goodness surpassing all, to call things being
to participation of Itself, as each order of things being was determined
from its own analogy' (Parker's trans.).

nor place could exist until some creature came into
being. 'If eternity and time,' says St. Augustine, 'are
rightly distinguished by this, that time does not exist
without some movement and transition, while in
eternity there is no change, who does not see that
there could have been no time had not some creature
been made, which by some motion could give birth to
change,—the various parts of which motion and
change, as they cannot be simultaneous, succeed one
another,—and thus, in these shorter or longer intervals
of duration, time would begin?'[1] Since, according
to Aquinas, four creations were simultaneous: the
Empyreal Heavens, Matter, Time, and the Angelic
nature,[2] it follows that all of these were created not
in time but in eternity.   Hence Beatrice says:

> 'In His eternity outside of time
> Outside all other limits, as it pleased Him,
> Into new Loves the Eternal Love unfolded.'[3]

St. Augustine says that while Moses omitted direct
mention of the creation of Angels, it must be regarded
as signified in the creation of light on the first day:
'For when God said, "Let there be light and there was
light," if we are justified in understanding in this
light the creation of the angels, then certainly they
were created partakers of the eternal light which is
the unchangeable Wisdom of God, by which all things
were made, and whom we call the only-begotten Son
of God,'[4]— a passage which Dante may have had in
mind when he calls the Angelic nature the '*splendour*'
of God, which has its subsistence in reflecting His
light.

---

[1] *City of God*, xi. 6 (Dods' trans.).   See also *Confessions*, xii. 15.
[2] *Summa*, i. q. xlvi. a. 3.
[3] *Par.* xxix. 16-18.   The 'new Loves' are the Angels (*Par.* xxviii. 103).
[4] *City of God*, xi. 9.   In *Summa*, i. q. xlvi. a. 3, Aquinas says the
words, 'In the beginning God created the heavens and the earth' refute
three errors.   (1) '*In the beginning*' denies that the world is eternal.
(2) '*In the beginning*' also refutes the error of a twofold creation—of
good and of evil: 'the beginning' being the Son, the entire creation was
good.   (3) '*God created the heavens and the earth*' excludes the error that
corporeal things were created through the medium of spiritual creatures.

Another question rises at this point: What was God doing before His Spirit went forth to move on the face of 'these waters'? In the infinite spaces of time before creation, was He resting inactive in some Divine torpor? Origen's answer that this world is only one of an endless succession of worlds,[1] is rejected by St. Augustine, who holds that it is as vain to ask why God chose a particular time as to speculate on his reasons for fixing on the particular part of space which the world occupies.[2] Beatrice takes another way. In the eternity of God is no *before* and *after*, eternity being, in the phrase of Boethius, *interminabilis vitae tota simul et perfecta possessio*—the entire, simultaneous, and perfect possession of endless life.[3] *Before* and *after* have meaning only in relation to this time-world; and, prior to its existence, God's being was going forth in other forms of activity.[4]

The question of *when* the Angels were created as compared with the rest of the universe was keenly debated from early times. The silence of Genesis was explained by the fear that the Israelites might fall into the worship of Angels, but the creation of these spiritual Intelligences was regarded by St. Augustine and others as included in the 'heaven' or the 'light' of Gen. 1. 1, 3, and therefore as simultaneous with that of the entire universe. On the other hand, as Beatrice says in ll. 37-39, St. Jerome held that the Angels had existed ages before the rest of the world: 'Six thousand years of our time are not yet completed; and how many times, and how many beginnings of ages, must we not believe to have been, in which Angels, Thrones, Dominations, and the other Orders have been serving God, and by God's command have stood without vicissitudes and

---

[1] *De Principiis*, iii. 5.

[2] *City of God*, xi. 5.

[3] *Consolation of Philosophy*, Bk. v. Prose 6. This definition of eternity is adopted by Aquinas in *Summa*, i. q. x. a. 1.

[4] Augustine in his *Confessions*, Books XI., XII., has a long discussion of the subject, but is obviously half inclined to sweep it aside as a vain prying into mysteries. He tells a story of some one who in reply to the derisive question, 'What was God doing before He made heaven and earth?' answered: 'He was preparing a hell for the inquisitive.'

measures of times.'[1] This view is rejected by Aquinas on the grounds here given by Dante—Scripture and reason. The special Scripture quoted is Gen. i. 1 ; and the argument from reason is, in the poet's words, that ' the motors' could not remain so long 'without their perfection.' In other words, the Angels, being the motors or governors of the nine corporeal Heavens, would have remained without the means of fulfilling the function for which they were made, had those Heavens not been created for ages after. The Angels, argues Aquinas, are but part of the universe, and the part finds its perfection only in the whole to which it belongs. Therefore it is not probable that God, whose works are perfect (Deut. xxxii. 4), created the angelic creature before all others.[2]

Hence Beatrice declares the simultaneousness of the creation of the universe, according to the saying of Ecclus. xviii. 1 : 'Qui vivit in aeternum creavit omnia *simul.*'[3] The three forms into which the scholastics divided creation came into existence at the one same instant :

> ' Form and matter, conjoint and in purity,
> Issued into being which had no defect,
> Even as from a three-stringed bow three arrows.
> And as in glass, in amber, or in crystal
> A ray re-flasheth so, that from its coming
> To its full being is no interval,
> So from its Lord did the triform effect
> Ray forth into its being all together
> Without discrimination of beginning.'[4]

The distinction here is between (1) *pure form*, (2) *pure matter*, and (3) *form and matter in conjunction.* The

---

[1] Comment on Titus i. 2.   Jerome is here following the Greek Fathers, Origen, Gregory Nazianzen, Chrysostom, etc.

[2] *Summa*, i. q. lxi. a. 3.

[3] The English rendering loses the idea of simultaneousness : ' He that liveth for ever created all things *in general.*' In reply to the objection that all things cannot have been made at once, since they are assigned to different days, Aquinas replies that the unformed substance of things was created *simul*, but that the formation by distinction and beauty was *non simul.* Hence the first day, according to Augustine, is called 'one day,' as involving all the other days (*Summa*, i. q. lxxiv. a. 2).

[4] *Par.* xxix. 22-30.

word *form* must, of course, be taken in its scholastic
sense—that which constitutes the essential being of a
thing. As the essential being of all spiritual creatures
is intellect, the intellect is the *form* of men and Angels.[1]
In men, this intellect is united with matter; in the
Angels, who are incorporeal, it is pure. Lower than
both is pure matter, the *materia prima*, the unknown
formless material substrate of the world, capable of
receiving 'substantial forms.' These three had no
distinction of beginning: pure form (Angels), pure
matter (*materia prima*), and the union of form and
matter (man as soul and body), issued forth at the same
instant from the creative hand of God, like three
arrows from a three-stringed bow.

In ll. 31-36, Beatrice states in mediæval phraseology
the powers inherent in these three forms of being, and
the order and relation in which they stand to each
other:

> 'Concreated was order and constructed
> In the substances, and those were summit
> In the world, in which pure act was brought forth.
> Pure potency held the lowest part;
> In the midst potency with act did twist
> Such bond that never shall it be unbound.'

The three scholastic terms, *pure act, pure potency,* and
potency with act, correspond respectively to the *pure
form, pure matter,* and *form and matter conjoined,* of
the preceding lines. *Pure act* refers to the intellectual
power of the Angels. The Angelic intellect, according
to Aquinas, differs from the human in this, that whereas the latter receives the *species* or images of things
from the world without, the former receives them from
its own nature. The species or images of things are

---

[1] *Summa,* i. q. lxxvi. a. 1: 'The intellect, which is the principle of
intellectual operation, is the *form* of the human body; for that by which
anything first operates is its form to which the operation is attributed.
. . . For the nature of a thing is manifested by its operation, and the
operation proper to man as man is to understand (*intelligere*), for by this
he transcends all other animals.' Spenser expresses the same idea in
his *Hymne in Honour of Beautie*:

> For of the soule the bodie forme doth take;
> For soule is forme and doth the bodie make.

'concreated' in the Angelic nature, and what they thus know by nature they understand directly and immediately. Being thus independent of the stimulus of external things, the Angelic intellect is always in a state of *pure act*—that is, its powers never lapse into mere potentiality, but are at every moment actualized. At the other extreme of creation, and therefore in the lowest place, is *pure matter*, the *prima materia*, which is *pure potentiality*—the possibility of becoming realized in some individual form. Midway between the two stands man, a union of both. Part of our powers goes forth intermittently in *act* or actuality; but part lies inactive as a mere *potentiality*, waiting to be called into play. And in man this union of *act* and *potentiality*, Beatrice declares, will never be dissolved. This is sometimes understood as the union of body and soul, which even death can dissolve only for a time; but it seems rather to imply that man even in the world to come will never attain to the *pure act* of the Angelic intellect—some part of his being will remain for ever *in potentia*.[1] Finally, these three forms of being were 'concreated' in this order and relation to each other— this order being inherent and necessary to the divine idea of the universe, which is its *form*.

The *where, when*, and *how* of the creation of Angels being answered, Beatrice turns to the question how some stood and some fell. The probation of the Angels was almost simultaneous with their creation: before one could count twenty, part of them 'disturbed the subject of your elements.' *Subject* is to be understood etymologically—that which is placed under something else: in the present case, the earth, which is the lowest of the four elements. The reference is to the fall of

---

[1] I give this interpretation of '*potentiality with act*' with some hesitation. It is difficult to give a reason for confining the phrase to man. Another interpretation may be given, as perhaps to be preferred: the Angels as *pure act* are 'the summit of the world'—in the Empyrean; the earth as *pure potentiality* 'holds the lowest place, a mere possibility of becoming'; and between the two lie the nine Heavens joined with their Angelic motors—*potentiality with act*—active and passive, receptive from above and active to those below (Landino, Vellutello, Vernon, Scartazzini, Casini, etc.).

Satan, before whose downward rush the land of the Southern hemisphere veiled itself with the sea and fled to the other side of the earth.[1] The reason why the probation of the Angels was decided in a moment of time lies in the fact that their nature is, as we have just seen, 'pure act.' Their whole intellectual being is so created that from the first moment of their existence it goes forth in actualization; hence its first movement is finally critical and decisive. Adam, whose nature was partly *in potentia*, and therefore did not rush so immediately into act, had the relatively much longer probation of six or seven hours.[2] The decisive test in the case of the Angels was the acceptance or non-acceptance of the Divine grace in which they were created, as the means of attaining glory and beatitude. Those whom Dante sees here in their joy circling round the Point of burning Light, were those who were 'modest' to acknowledge their dependence for their swift intellect on the Divine goodness; and this acceptance of grace was accounted to them for merit, and rewarded with the higher vision of God and the absolute confirmation of their wills in goodness:

> ' For the which their vision was exalted
> With grace illuminating and with their merit,
> So that they have a full and steadfast will.
> Nor would I have thee doubt, but certain be
> That to receive the grace is meritorious
> According as the affection opens to it.'[3]

In all this, Dante is simply following Aquinas. Grace, he holds, is as necessary for Angels as for men in the attainment of their beatitude; this beatitude is merited by their 'first act of charity,' that is, love to God; and this first act confirms their wills for ever, so that they cannot sin.[4] The reverse of all this happened in the

---

[1] *Inf.* xxxiv. 121-126. [2] *Par.* xxvi. 139-142. [3] *Par.* xxix. 61-66.

[4] *Summa*, i. q. lxii. a. 2-5 : ' An Angel after the first act of charity, by which he merited blessedness, was blessed at once. The ground of which is that grace perfects each nature according to its mode. But it is proper to the Angelic nature that it acquire its natural perfection not *per discursum* (by gradual processes), but that it have it immediately *per naturam* (by direct immediate intuition). Since, then, by its own nature an Angel is ordained to its natural perfection, so of merit it is ordained to

case of the fallen Angels. By one act of pride in the moment after their creation—seeking the beatitude of the Divine likeness by their own powers and apart from grace—the entire nature rushed in an instant into irrevocable ruin. 'For an Angel requires no delay of time for choice, or exhortation, or even consent, as a man does.' All is the work of an instant. 'An Angel has nothing to hold him back, but is moved to whatever he is moved to, whether good or evil, according to the whole power of his nature.'[1] Hence the irrevocable character of their fall. The will of man is flexible even after sin, and therefore recovery is possible for him; but the nature of the Angelic will is to adhere immovably to its first election. The first election, in short, is to Angels what death is to men—the end of all probation.[2]

At this point, says Beatrice, she might leave Dante to his own contemplation of the Angelic 'consistory,' were it not for certain errors which were being taught down below on earth. Plumptre and others think the errors relate only to the memory of Angels, and that Dante is venturing to condemn Aquinas himself. This seems to me a misunderstanding. The errors relate to all three of the powers named—understanding, memory, and will; and their source, as the word *equivocando* in l. 75 proves, is 'equivocation,' the use of these terms as if they meant the same in Angels as in men. So far from seeking to correct Aquinas, his purpose is to establish his views against the false teaching of certain schools. The passage is as follows:

> ' But since on earth throughout your schools
> 'Tis lectured that the angelic nature
> ·Is such as understands and remembers and wills,
> I will say on, that thou mayst see pure
> The truth that is confounded there below
> By the equivocations of such lecturing.

---

glory. And so, immediately after merit in an Angel beatitude was attained. . . . Separate instants (of an Angel's probation) must be recognized: in one of which he merited beatitude, and in the other he was *beatus*.'

[1] *Summa*, i. q. lxiii. a. 8.   [2] *Summa*, i. q. lxiv. a. 2.

These substances, since ever they were joyful
Of the face of God, have not turned their sight
From it, from which is nothing hid;
Hence they have not their vision intercepted
By a new object, and therefore have no need
To remember because of a divided thought.'[1]

The 'equivocation' was in supposing that understanding, memory, and will meant nothing more in the
Angelic nature than in the human; whereas all three
were lifted far above the human by the one fact that
the Angels saw all things in the face of God, from
which they never turned away. 'Man,' as Landino
says, ' pursuing discourse of reason, is often confronted
by something new and ill understood, which interrupts
the discourse; but to the Angel, seeing everything in
God, nothing can be new. And therefore "there is no
need to call back to memory because of a divided
thought." The Angel does not understand by means
of species [mental images] which he abstracts from the
things, either by composition and division, or by discourse of reason, as a man does; but he understands
by innate species [i.e. images of things not drawn from
the things themselves, but stamped by God on the
Angelic intellect at creation]." Further, there is not
in the Angel that will which is in man, though each is
called will; inasmuch as man wills the good through
discourse of reason, and the Angel in one instant. And
so, as he understands in a more excellent way than
man, he has a more excellent will.[3] Similarly, memory
cannot be said to be in the Angel, unless by equivocation; for the memory in us is founded on a bodily
organ, and the Angel has no body. Also memory in us
is of things past, and the Angel sees in God all things
present.' All this seems to me precisely what Aquinas
teaches. It is true, he admits memory in the Angels;
but it is in the sense of *retaining* the images of things
in the mind, not in the sense of *recalling* what has
been for the time forgotten.[4] In short, the very mode

---

[1] *Par.* xxix. 70-81.
[2] *Summa*, i. q. lvii. a. 2; lviii. a. 4, 5.   [3] *Summa*, i. q. lix. a. 3.
[4] In *Summa*, i. q. liv. a. 5, Aquinas ascribes to Angels memory in so far

of Angelic cognition—the vision of all things in God—
renders the understanding, memory, and will of these
great Intelligences of a far higher order than the
corresponding powers in man; and Dante is striking
at the equivocation which tended to identify them.

This error concerning the Angelic nature leads
Beatrice to a denunciation of false theological teaching
in general—the earthly perversion of the heavenly
wisdom which descends through the Angels, and of
which she herself is the symbol.[1] This false theology
is a kind of waking dream which some of its teachers
believe and some do not—the latter having the greater
sin and shame. Its source is twofold—false philosophy
and abuse of Scripture. In their vanity to strike out a
new system of thought, teachers go not 'by one pathway,' doubtless the philosophy of Aristotle. Still
worse is their treatment of the Holy Scriptures, sown
at so great a cost of blood. To make a show men
preach their own fancies, and the Evangel is dumb.
As an example of these vain speculations, Beatrice
gives the theories put forward to account for the
darkness at the Crucifixion from the sixth hour to the
ninth.[2] According to one, the moon, turning back on
her course, eclipsed the sun. According to another,
the sun eclipsed itself, producing darkness not over
Judæa alone, but over the entire habitable world
from Spain to India.[3] Such fables are as plentiful as

as it resides in the *mind*; but denies it as it resides in the *sensitive soul*;
and in *Summa*, q. lxxix. a. 6 he explains that memory in the sensitive
soul has the function of recalling things past. This is obviously impossible to Angels who, being without bodies, cannot have sensitive souls.

[1] *Par.* xxix. 82-126. See also p. 424 above.

[2] Matt. xxvii. 45.

[3] This criticism seems to be aimed at Aquinas, Jerome, and Dionysius.
In *Summa*, iii. q. xliv. a. 2 Aquinas holds that Christ wrought miracles
on the celestial bodies, the better to prove His Divinity. He quotes
Jerome on Matt. xxvii. 45, to the effect that the sun drew back his rays;
Origen, who attributes the darkness to clouds; and Dionysius, whose
opinion he favours, that it was due to a miraculous interposition of the
moon between the sun and the earth. Dante evidently regarded all this
as being wise above what is written; but the same criticism applied to
himself would eliminate a good many speculations from the *Commedia*.
On the 'glosses and pious embroideries' of mediæval preaching, see G.
G. Coulton, *From St. Francis to Dante*, p. 281.

Lapos and Bindos in Florence.[1] The ignorant sheep
are fed with wind;[2] yet does their ignorance not
excuse them, since Christ's own commands to His
Apostles might teach them better than to listen to the
jests which now pass for preaching. Could they but
see the evil bird that nests in the point of the
preacher's hood,[3] they would know how worthless are
the pardons given by such men—pardons of no authority, like unstamped coin, with which St. Anthony
fattens his swine and 'others more swinish far than
they.'[4]

Returning from this digression, Beatrice discusses a
question she had already touched on, the *number* of
the Angels. In *Par.* xxviii. 92, 93, she had declared
that they passed in thousands 'the doubling of the
chess-squares,'[5] and now she confirms this by Scripture:

---

[1] Lapo and Bindo, contractions for Jacopo and Aldobrando, were very
common names in Florence.

[2] Comp. Milton, *Lycidas*, 125-127:

> 'The hungry sheep look up and are not fed;
> But, swoln with wind and the rank mist they draw,
> Rot inwardly, and foul contagion spread.'

[3] As the dove was the emblem of the Divine Spirit, inspiring to holiness, so the crow represented the inspiration of Satan, who is here regarded as making his nest in the peak of the preacher's hood. For the
better symbolism of the crow, see *Par.* xxi. 34-42, p. 333 above. In *Purg.*
ii. 38 the Angel who ferried souls to Purgatory is called 'the Bird Divine.'

[4] St. Anthony is the famous Egyptian hermit who died in 356 at the age
of 105. Mrs. Jameson (*Sacred and Legendary Art*, ii. 750) says it is a
mistake to say that the pig is his symbol because he cured the diseases of
swine. 'The hog was the representative of the demon of sensuality and
gluttony, which Anthony is supposed to have vanquished by the exercises
of piety and by Divine aid. . . . The monks of the Order of St. Anthony
kept herds of consecrated pigs, which were allowed to feed at the public
charge, and which it was a profanation to steal or kill: hence the proverb
about the fatness of a "Tantony pig."' It is the pig in both literal and
symbolic sense that Dante means is fattened by the proceeds of unauthorized pardons.

[5] Longfellow's note is: 'The inventor of the game of chess brought it
to a Persian king, who was so delighted with it, that he offered him in
return whatever reward he might ask. The inventor said he wished only
a grain of wheat, doubled as many times as there were squares on the
chess-board; that is, one grain for the first square, two for the second,
four for the third, and so on to sixty-four. This the king readily granted;
but when the amount was reckoned up, he had not wheat enough in his
whole kingdom to pay it.'

> 'And if thou notest that which is revealed
> By Daniel, thou wilt see that in his thousands
> Number determinate is kept concealed.'[1]

The reference is to Daniel vii. 10: 'thousand thousands ministered unto him, and ten thousand times ten thousand stood before him.' As Dionysius says, their number surpasses the weak power of human thought.[2] In *Conv.* ii. 5 Dante attributes the vastness of their multitude to the greatness of their blessedness: the ampler the beatitude the greater the number of lofty Intelligences God creates to share in it. Plumptre is perhaps right in connecting the concealment of the 'determinate number' with the idea that the lost sheep of Luke xv. 4 was the human race, and the ninety and nine were the unfallen Angels. 'Their number was therefore that multiple of the whole family of man in all ages. With this was connected the thought that the "number of the elect" was identical with that of the rebel angels.' According to Dante, a tenth part of the Angels fell, and human nature was then created to fill up the broken ranks.[3] This question, however, is not directly raised in the *Paradiso*. Whatever the number of the countless Angelic host may be, the important point to mark is that each individual 'splendour' receives the primal light in a way peculiar to itself, its knowledge and the love it kindles being distinct and diverse from every other.[4] This is equivalent to the doctrine of Aquinas that every individual Angel

---

[1] *Par.* xxix. 130-135.   [2] *De Coel. Hier.* xiv.

[3] *Conv.* ii. 6: 'And here there is one word not to be passed in silence. I say that out of all these Orders some were lost as soon as they were created, perhaps to the number of a tenth part; for the restoration of which human nature was afterwards created.' Aquinas held that some Angels fell from every Order, and that therefore men are assumed into every Order to fill their places (*Summa*, i. q. lxiii. a. 9; q. cviii. a. 8). Augustine suggests that the creation of man may not merely fill up the broken ranks of the citizens of Heaven, but even give the city the joy of an 'overflowing population' (*City of God*, xxii. 1). Anselm refuses to make the salvation of men hang on the perdition of Angels for this among other reasons, that the joy of the Redeemed would then spring from the fall of those whose places they received. To remove all certainty as to whether they would have been saved had there been no Angelic fall, Anselm holds that the number of holy men will exceed that of the lost Angels (*Cur Deus Homo?* i. 18).   [4] *Par.* xxix. 136-141.

is a distinct species by himself. 'The perfection of the
Angelic nature'—that is, its separateness from matter
—'requires multiplication of species, but not multiplication of individuals in one species.'[1] The perfection
of the universe also demands it. 'The multiplication
of species adds more nobility and perfection to the
universe than the multiplication of individuals in the
same species. But the perfection of the universe consists principally in intelligences subsisting apart (i.e.
from matter). Therefore it makes more for the perfection of the universe that there should be many
intelligences different in species than many different
in number in the same species.'[2] Beatrice points to
this infinite diversity of Angelic species as a revelation
of the height and breadth of the Eternal Goodness,
which, remaining one in itself, breaks itself into so
many 'mirrors,' each of which receives and reflects it
in a distinct and separate way.[3]

[1] *Summa*, i. q. l. a. 4. Comp. i. q. xlvii. a. 2.
[2] *Contra Gentiles*, ii. 93. Father Rickaby, from whose version the
quotation is given, adds a characteristic note: 'A sort of canon of cosmic
architecture. And in the architecture of human hands it makes more for
the beauty of a frieze to have a procession of various figures, like the procession of Athenian knights in the frieze of the Parthenon, than to have
one cast reproduced all round, suggestive of so much a foot. It makes
for the beauty, and adds to the expense, but with the Creator there is no
question of expense.'
[3] *Par.* xxix. 142-145. Prof. Godet in his *Biblical Studies on the Old
Testament* (pp. 2-7) has an ingenious argument which corroborates the
view of Aquinas, though the phraseology is apparently reversed. In the
vegetable world individuality has no existence—the individual plant is
but a *specimen* of the species. In the animal world individuality does
appear, but it is still in a kind of bondage to the species. The human
world reverses completely this relation of the individual to the species:
species exists, but the individual can rise into moral superiority to the
mere race instincts. From this gradation—'species without individuality;
individuality under bondage to species; species overpowered by individuality'—he infers a fourth form of being to complete the chain,—
'individuality without species,' that is, Angels, who receive their being
directly from the hand of God, and not through the medium of parents.
'Individuality without species' is just what Aquinas means when he
says that each individual Angel is a species by himself.
    From this idea that each Angel is his own species, Anselm argues the
impossibility of those that fell being saved. They would need as Saviour
a God-angel, as man needs a God-man. But since Angels have no unity
of species, as man has, no God-angel could represent them all—hence
salvation is impossible for those who fell (*Cur Deus Homo?* ii. 21).

CHAPTER XXVIII

1. *The River of Grace and the White Rose of Glory*

WE are now about to enter the Paradise of God, the final and indeed the only true Heaven, the absolute and eternal Truth, and therefore the Divine peace, for which the lower spheres yearn in their ceaseless revolutions. For this reason, Dante represents his approach to it under the form of the dawn. As the stars fade and vanish before the sun, so before the Eternal Light the nine circles of Angelic fire pale and disappear, one by one, from the outermost to 'the most beautiful,' the Seraphim. Even the loftiest created Intelligences must veil their faces before the Uncreated Light.[1]

While the Angelic Circles fade away, the beauty of Beatrice so transcends all human measure that 'only its Maker may enjoy it all.' Never since Dante first saw her face 'in this life' has the increase of its beauty, as she rose from Heaven to Heaven, baffled his song until now. He is not thinking of her as a woman, but in her symbolic character of Theology or Divine Wisdom. She has now reached her most beautiful form of direct, immediate vision of the Divine; and

---

[1] *Par.* xxx. 1-13. This image of the dawn quenching the stars one by one is regarded by some as an indirect indication of the hour at which Dante entered the final Heaven; but as Paradise is a timeless world, it can scarcely bear this interpretation. See Moore's *Studies in Dante*, 3rd series, p. 58. In his *Time-References in the Divina Commedia* (pp. 59, 127), Dr. Moore thinks that 'Dante intends to give us generally to understand that though himself beyond the limits and conditions of time, still the time passing meanwhile on this earth was such that when he returned to it after his ecstatic vision of Paradise, it was found to be the evening of Thursday, April 14th'—the whole journey having occupied seven days, of which the last was spent in Paradise.

as Dante is as yet able to see only 'shadowy prefaces' of the truth, he is compelled to leave the proclamation of her loveliness to a greater trumpet.[1]

'With gesture and voice of a leader whose task is accomplished,'[2] Beatrice informs Dante that they are now arrived at the goal of all desire:

> ' We are issued forth
> From the greatest body to the Heaven which is pure light,
> Light intellectual fulfilled of love,
> Love of true good fulfilled of joy,
> Joy which transcendeth every sweetness.
> Here shalt thou see the one and the other soldiery
> Of Paradise, and the one in those aspects
> Which at the final judgment thou shalt see.'[3]

'Pure light' is light as it is diffused directly and immediately from God as its primal source, without admixture or intervention of any material medium. It is contrasted with 'the greatest *body*' from which they have issued—the Primum Mobile, the last of the corporeal Heavens, which folds in all the rest like a 'royal mantle.'[4]   Being thus independent of material media, it is 'light *intellectual*,' that is, no element of sense enters into it.   So long as we are in a material world, even the concepts of the intellect are formed only through corporeal things.   In the scholastic phraseology with which Dante was familiar, a material object striking on the senses produces a *species sensibilis*,

---

[1] *Par.* xxx. 14-36. The words 'in this life' in l. 29 do not refer to this earthly life in which Dante saw Beatrice for the first time in his ninth year (V.N. § ii.). The reference is to *Purg.* xxxi. 136-145, when she unveiled her face and showed him her 'second beauty' on the top of Mount Purgatory. 'This life' is therefore the spiritual life on which he then entered. The greater trumpet to which he leaves the proclamation of her beauty is taken by some as the trumpet of the last judgment (cf. *Purg.* xxx. 13)— only then will the full beauty of Divine Wisdom be displayed. But perhaps this is a straining of the sense.

[2] I take the *espedito* of line 37 as Butler does—'a leader *freed from his task*,' as in *Par.* xvii. 100: the gesture and voice of one who has successfully led him to the final revelation. If the ordinary rendering is taken— 'alert,' 'devoted,' 'perfect,' etc.—it would imply perfect familiarity with the secrets of this highest Heaven, and eagerness to reveal them in the fewest words.

[3] *Par.* xxx. 37-45. Mr. Tozer draws attention to the 'linkage' formed by the repetition in ll. 39-42 of the last word of each line as the first of the line following—the only example in the poem.

[4] *Par.* xxiii. 112, 113.

an *image* in the mind through the senses. The intellect lays hold of this sensible image, abstracts from it its particular and individual qualities, and thus reaches its *species intelligibilis*, the image of its universal essence, which is the proper object of the intellect. Dante's meaning therefore is that, being now in a world of pure light beyond the last of the corporeal Heavens, the intellect is independent of these sensible and material processes of knowledge. It needs no longer the old medium of body: in the pure light of God, it sees directly and immediately 'the universal form' and essence of all things.[1]

This 'light intellectual,' this immediate vision of all things in the 'pure light' of God, is full of love, because it is impossible to see God, the true good, without loving Him. This love in its turn is full of joy, joy which transcends every sweetness, because every other joy is in some lower end, but this rests only in the final end of all desire.[2]

In this 'Heaven of pure light' Beatrice promises Dante the vision of 'the one and the other soldiery'— the two hosts of Angels and redeemed souls, that have fought against the powers of evil and triumphed: the latter in the aspects which they shall wear at the last judgment. In the lower Heavens, as we have seen, the souls of the Blessed appear for the most part in the form of starry lights. Now, however, they are to be revealed, as St. Benedict promised,[3] in their own proper forms, as they shall appear when they have received their resurrection bodies after the final judgment. Since the great day is still to come, this vision must be in some sense prophetic. Perhaps to the 'light intellectual,' the future is as the present. Or Dante may be thinking of some intermediate body, which bears the image of that which is to be restored to them

---

[1] See Father Maher on the scholastic theory of knowledge, quoted above, p. 87 note.

[2] Vellutello interprets the passage in terms of the Trinity. The 'pure light' is the Father, the Light of the world; 'light intellectual' the Son, to whom Wisdom is attributed; and 'love' the Holy Spirit.

[3] *Par.* xxii. 58-63.

at last.[1] A corresponding change is implied in his
vision of the Angels. Hitherto he has seen them only
in symbolic forms: Gabriel as a crown of flame around
the Virgin, and the Nine Orders wheeling around the
Point of burning Light in the shape of concentric
circles of fire. Now he is to see them in their individual
and proper forms, each individual a separate species,
with his own distinct 'glow and art.'[2]

Before, however, this final vision of saints and Angels
can be given, the Pilgrim's eyes must receive a twofold
preparation. In the first place, the sight of the natural
man must be blinded, that a power of supernatural
vision may arise. 'A living light,' like a sudden flash
of lightning, so enswathed him in the 'veil of its glow'
that he saw nothing. The meaning is much debated.
We must put aside the idea that the sudden darkness
is an allegory of death, the separation of soul and
body, and the blinding of the spirit ushered in a
moment into the unutterable glory of Heaven. The
true explanation is given in the words of Beatrice:

> 'Ever the Love which quieteth this heaven
> Welcomes into itself with such salute,
> To make the candle ready for its flame.'

I have accepted the usual rendering of *salute* in l. 53,
as equivalent to *saluto*, 'salutation'; but I have the
feeling that its ordinary sense of 'salvation' is the key
to the meaning of the passage. Dante would naturally
feel this sudden blindness as a loss: Beatrice assures
him it is the *salvation* with which 'the Love that quiets
heaven' receives him into itself—gathers him into its
own peace, and fits the candle of his soul to be kindled
by Love's flame.[3] In other words, before Dante has

---

[1] Compare the intermediate body which the soul in Purgatory rays out
for itself: *Purg.* xxv. 88-108.   [2] *Par.* xxxi. 132.

[3] Casini thinks the image of the candle and its flame does not render
with the usual clearness the poet's thought. Dante, however, was thinking of Prov. xx. 27, 'The spirit of man is the candle (Vulg. *lucerna*, lamp)
of the Lord,' and the proper flame of that candle is the love of God.
Another reference to this text will be found in *Purg.* viii. 112-114, where
Conrad Malaspini prays that the wax in the lamp that leads the poet up
may not fail until he reach the summit of the Mount. Commentators
often impute their own misunderstanding to the author's want of
clearness.

power to enter into the peace of this Heaven, which is
at absolute rest because all its longings are satisfied in
the Divine Love, his eyes must be blinded to all lower
objects of desire. The blindness is therefore the
'salvation' by which his soul is prepared to be kindled
by the flame of the Love which gives eternal rest.
The moment he accepts this 'salvation,' he feels himself
raised above his own natural power, his blindness is
changed into a supernatural keenness of vision, capable
of gazing into the purest light. It is the clear and
piercing vision which comes only to the soul which is
blind to all lower objects of desire, because all desire is
quieted in the Eternal Love.[1]

Yet even so—uplifted beyond his own power, and his
eyes fortified against the purest light—Dante is not
able to bear all at once the promised vision of Angels
and glorified souls in their own proper forms : he must
be prepared for it by what Beatrice calls 'the shadowy
prefaces of their truth'—the last 'mask' of symbol
before the reality.[2]

> And I saw light, in fashion of a river
> Fulvid with effulgence, between two banks
> Depicted with a marvellous Spring.
> Out of this river issued living sparks
> And on every side settled in the flowers,
> Like unto rubies which gold circles round.
> Then, as if inebriate with the odours,
> They plunged again into the wondrous torrent,
> And, as one entered, another issued forth.[3]

The figure of a river is suggested by many passages
of Scripture.[4] That most frequently referred to by

---

[1] *Par.* xxx. 46-60.

[2] It is strange to find that even in this 'Heaven of pure light' there is
one more veil of figure and symbolism. The whole process of revelation
since Dante saw the Procession of the Spirit in the Earthly Paradise
consists of one long continuous penetration through symbol after symbol.
The poet was steeped in the mysticism of Dionysius the Areopagite :
'For it is not possible that the supremely Divine Ray should otherwise
illuminate us, except so far as it is enveloped, for the purpose of instruc-
tion, in variegated sacred veils, and arranged naturally and appropriately,
for such as we are, by paternal forethought' (*On the Heavenly Hierarchy*,
i. 2, Parker's transl.).

[3] *Par.* xxx. 61-69.

[4] In addition to those above referred to, Ps. xxxvi. 8, 9 ; xlvi. 4 ; Ezek.
xlvii. 1-12, etc.

commentators is Rev. xxii. 1: 'And he shewed me a
pure river of water of life, clear as crystal, proceeding
out of the throne of God and of the Lamb'; but the
colour of the river of Dante's vision—'fulvid with
effulgence'—reminds one rather of Dan. vii. 10: 'A
fiery stream issued and came forth before him'; while
the 'living sparks,' which issued from the river, and
which undoubtedly represent Angels, seem to have
been suggested by the continuation of the verse:
'thousand thousands ministered unto him, and ten thousand times ten thousand stood before him.' It is true
that this is understood by Aquinas as a river of Divine
judgment sweeping away the lost in its fiery torrent.[1]
To Dante, however, it is a river of light, of the illuminating grace of God. Its two banks are doubtless the
times of the Old and New Testaments, corresponding
to the vertical division of the Rose, of which this is the
symbol. The 'marvellous Spring'[2] upon the banks
consists of the souls of the saints in the form of flowers:
marvellous, not merely because the flowers never fade,
but because the river of Divine grace has quickened
them from the winter of sin and death into an eternal
life. From out the river, as parts of its glowing light
and love, issue Angels, bearing to the souls of the
saints the knowledge and grace of God. Their ministry
is its own reward: they plunge back into the river 'as
if inebriate with the odours' of the flowers. The
odours are the prayers of saints, or perhaps, since this
is Heaven, their praises, or, more generally, the sweet
perfume of their holiness. Once the Angels had joy
over their repentance as sinners; now their joy has
risen to an intoxication of delight in the fulfilment of
their salvation.

It can scarcely be by accident that the colours of red
and yellow are so prominent in this figure. The light

---

[1] *Summa*, Supp. q. lxxiv. a. 9.

[2] It is quite possible that Dante calls it *Primavera*, because it is 'the
shadowy preface,' the forerunner, of the truth. See *Vita Nuova*, § xxiv,
where he interprets 'Primavera,' the love-name of a certain lady,
Giovanna, as 'prima verra,' because she came before Beatrice, and was
therefore her forerunner.

of the river is *fulvido di fulgore*—'yellow with brightness,' the brightness, as the word implies, of lightning.[1] The Angel-sparks are called gems of topaz, and when they enter into the flowers they are compared to rubies set in gold. If, as Plumptre tells us, 'in the symbolism of gems the topaz represents the twofold love of God and man,' this would account for the comparison, the Angels being ministers and mediators of that twofold love. Gold or yellow is the symbol of the sun, which, in its turn, is 'the sensible image' of God; hence the appropriateness of picturing His illuminating grace as a river of yellow, golden light. As we shall see immediately, when the river changes into a circular sea, it retains its colour and becomes the golden heart of the White Rose of Paradise.

The river represents, as we have seen, the *lumen gratiae*, the light of grace; Beatrice now tells Dante that it is only by drinking of it that he can receive the *lumen gloriae*, the light of glory, 'which makes the Creator visible to the creature.' It is the light, according to mediæval theology, referred to in Ps. xxxvi. 8, 9, which, obviously, was in Dante's mind: 'Thou shalt make them drink of the river of thy pleasures. For with thee is the fountain of life: *in thy light shall we see light.*' The soul, being incapable of seeing God in His essence by its own natural powers, must be raised supernaturally above itself, and rendered in a certain sense deiform, by an ineffable union with God. The light by which this is accomplished is an effluence of that light in which God sees Himself.[2] To gain this

---

[1] I follow the reading of the Oxford edition. If we take that followed by Butler and others—*fulgido di fulgori* or *fulgore*—it would still more strongly support the derivation of the figure from Dan. vii. 10, which reads in the Vulgate: 'Fluvius igneus rapidusque egrediebatur a facie ejus.' Dante seems to echo the word 'rapidus' in the *gurge*, 'torrent,' of l. 68.

[2] *Summa*, i. q. xii. a. 5; *Cont. Gent.* iii. 53. 'Reason and Faith alike tell us that to see God face to face is (1) supernatural, at least inasmuch as it cannot be arrived at by the natural forces of the created mind, and is only possible to nature elevated and clarified by a supernatural light; (2) that it implies a participation in the Divine Nature, and a deification of the created nature. . . . This supernatural likeness to God may be resolved into the following elements: (*a*) the act and the object of vision

lumen gloriae Dante drank eagerly of the river of
grace with his eyelids' rim, and lo, in a moment the
last veil fell, the last 'mask' of symbolism was withdrawn, and the ultimate Heaven stood revealed *sub
specie aeternitatis.* Sight once for all took the place of
Faith with its shadows and similitudes, as is indicated
by making *vidi*, 'I saw,' rhyme three times with itself :

> Thus for me were changed to greater joys
> The flowers and the sparks, so that *I saw*
> Both the courts of Heaven made manifest.
> O splendour of God, by means of which *I saw*
> The lofty triumph of the realm of truth,
> Give me the power to tell how it *I saw* ! [1]

The first change wrought by sight is that the river
of grace turns in a moment into a circular sea, which
then forms the yellow heart of the great White Rose,
every petal of which is a white soul redeemed.[2] According to Landino and others, the meaning is that it
is only when the soul drinks deeply of the Divine grace
it is able to see how that grace circles round and
returns to its Source. The idea seems to me somewhat
different. Dante's great passion was to see unity in
all things. Standing beside the river of God's illuminating grace as it flows down the ages between the
banks of the Old Covenant and the New, the unity of
Divine truth is not easily discerned. It is a revelation
given 'by divers portions and in divers manners':[3]
only a part of the flowing river is seen at a time, and
the flowers on its margin are scattered here and there.
But in eternity, of which a circle is the symbol, that
river of time is seen rounding into its own inherent
and essential unity. The perfect circle of grace and
truth becomes a sea of light—the golden heart of the
great Rose which gathers into its eternal unity the

are of the same kind in God and in the creature, in as far as, in both, the
vision is an act of direct knowledge whose formal and material object is
the Divine essence ; (*b*) the likening of the created intellect to the Divine
is brought about by the infusion of a light proceeding from, and homo-
geneous with, the Divine Intellect' (Wilhelm and Scannell's *Manual of
Catholic Theology*, i. 456). [1] *Par.* xxx. 94-99.

[2] For the meaning of the colour of the Rose, see Introduction, p. 32.

[3] Heb. i. 1 (R.V.). In the Vulgate : 'multifarie et multis modis.'

scattered flowers of all generations of the saints. And
it is into the centre of that perfect circle of illuminating grace, sending up the splendour of its rays on all
the ranks of the souls redeemed by its power, that
Beatrice leads Dante to receive, in its light, his final
vision of the Church Triumphant.

It will be noticed that I speak of this central circular
sea as *lumen gratiae*, for it is still the light of grace
which once flowed in form of a river; but that light of
grace has now reached its perfect form of eternity, the
lumen gloriae. The change of the river into the circular
sea is Dante's symbolic way of stating that the grace
by which a soul is saved and strengthened to persevere
to the end of the earthly life, is not something different
in kind from the glory to which it leads. According to
Aquinas, 'grace is nothing else than a certain beginning
of glory in us,'[1] and the light of glory is simply the
perfected form of the grace of earth.[2] Hence Dante
goes on to say that the river of grace, changed now
into the perfect circle of a sea of glory, sends up its
light by which the souls of the Blessed see God—souls
that once grew like scattered flowers on the river-banks,
but now gathered into unity as petals of the White
Rose of Eternity:

> A light there is up yonder which doth make
> The Creator visible unto that creature
> Who only in the vision of Him hath its peace ;
> And it outspreads in figure of a circle

---

[1] *Summa*, ii-ii. q. xxiv. a. 3. 'Gratia et gloria ad idem genus referuntur ;
quia gratia nihil est aliud quam quaedam inchoatio gloriae in nobis.'
[2] *Summa*, i-ii. q. cxi. a. 3. Aquinas is here laying down the distinction
between *prevenient* and *subsequent* grace. There are, he says, five effects
of grace in us : (1) it heals the soul ; (2) it enables us to will the good ;
(3) and to perform effectually the good thus willed ; (4) it causes us to persevere in good ; (5) it thus secures that we attain to glory. The first is
called prevenient, as causing the second, which is thus subsequent; but
the second is also prevenient, as causing the third; and so on until you
reach the last, which leads to glory. He adds that because subsequent
grace pertains to the state of glory it is not therefore a numerically
different kind of grace from the prevenient grace by which we are now
justified; for just as the charity we have *in via* is not lost but perfected
in patria, so the light of grace is perfected in the light of glory, since
they do not differ in kind.

To such a bound, that its circumference
Would be too wide a girdle for the sun.
All that appears of it of a ray is made
Reflected on the summit of the First Moved Heaven,
Which takes therefrom its life and potency.
And as a hill in water at its base
Mirrors itself, as if to see itself adorned,
When it is richest in verdure and in flowers,
So standing above the light, around, around,
I saw mirror themselves in over a thousand tiers,
Whate'er of us have made return up yonder.[1]
And if the lowest step gather within itself
So great light, how vast then is the wideness
Of this Rose in its extremest leaves!
My vision in the breadth and in the height
Lost not itself, but comprehended all
The measure and the quality of that joy.
There near and far nor add nor take away,
For where God apart from means doth govern,
The natural law hath naught of relevance.[2]

This figure of the Church Triumphant in the form of a
White Rose takes the spiritual imagination with pure
loveliness. In one sense, doubtless, it sprang into being
full-formed in the poet's own creative soul. In another,
its roots sank deep into many beautiful and holy
associations. The chief of these is probably the thought
of the Virgin as the *Rosa Mystica* of the Litany,

　　　　the Rose in which the Word Divine
　　　　Made itself flesh.[3]

---

[1] The reference is to the doctrine of Creationism: the soul being a direct creation by God, these blessed spirits have but returned to their original source. 'All those souls which having come from God by creation, through their merits are now returned to God by beatitude' (Landino). Comp. *Purg.* xvi. 85-93; xxv. 61-78.

[2] *Par.* xxx. 100-123. Aquinas, discussing the question whether local distance hinders the knowledge of separated souls, decides that this is impossible. A separated soul has its knowledge, not through the medium of material objects and the senses, but by a direct influx of Divine light, to which far and near are equal (*Summa*, i. q. lxxxix. a. 7). This is what Dante means by God governing 'without medium': a direct influx of Divine light carries the *species* or images of things into the soul without the intervention of things sensible. Butler quite misunderstands when he says: 'How there can be a highest point where place does not exist, is a difficulty which does not seem to have occurred to Dante.' Highest and lowest are degrees of blessedness, not separations of space.

[3] *Par.* xxiii. 73, 74. See pp. 373, 374.

As such she became the Divinest symbol of the Church redeemed through the Incarnation,

> the saintly soldiery
> Whom Christ in His own blood did make His Bride.[1]

It was natural, therefore, to extend her mystical name to all the saints, to regard them as white petals of her pure loveliness, to gather together the scattered blossoms from the banks of Time into the unity of 'the Flower of glorious immortality.'[2] With this thought would mingle, doubtless, the symbolism of the Golden Rose blessed by the Pope every year on Laetare Sunday, and sent to some Catholic sovereign or nobleman, church or city. In the form of benediction the Rose is declared to be the symbol of the joy of Jerusalem triumphant and of the Church militant.[3]

This White Rose, it is to be noted, is rendered visible by a ray reflected from the outer surface of the Primum Mobile, the last of the corporeal Heavens, which draws thence 'life and potency': *life* for itself, the sign of which is motion, and *potency* for the other spheres, the power to transmit its influence to them. This seems to be Dante's way of indicating the connection between the White Rose, the great Church of the Redeemed in Paradise, and the Divine Light which is the source of its salvation. The order of the thought appears to be as follows. From the Eternal Light Himself flows

---

[1] *Par.* xxxi. 1-3.

[2] Bonaventura, *Speculum Beatae Mariae Virginis*, Lect. xii. One 'fruit of Mary,' according to the *Speculum* (Lect. xviii.), is 'the restoration of the ruin of the Empyrean Heaven,' by filling up with the saints the broken ranks of the Angelic host.

[3] Dean Church (*Dante*, p. 127) gives the form: 'Accipe rosam de manibus nostris . . . per quam designatus gaudium utriusque Hierusalem triumphantis scilicet et militantis ecclesiae per quam omnibus Christi fidelibus manifestatur flos ipse pretiosissimus qui est gaudium et corona sanctorum omnium.' The fourth Sunday in Lent, on which the Rose is blessed, is called Laetare Sunday, from the first word in the antiphon of the Introit, 'Rejoice, O Jerusalem, and come together, all ye that love her,' etc. Dante refers to the Golden Rose in *Conv.* iv. 29. Didron (*Christian Iconography*, i. 234 Bohn) traces the figure to the great 'rose-windows' of cathedrals such as Paris, Rheims, Chartres, which he thinks Dante saw in his travels in France ; but Plumptre asserts that the larger rose-windows belong to the end of the fourteenth, or to the fifteenth, century.

forth a ray which is the *lumen gloriae*. This ray, striking on the summit of the Primum Mobile with life and
potency, penetrates downwards from sphere to sphere,
until on earth it forms the *lumen gratiae* by which the
saints are saved. This light of grace then completes
the circle, returns from earth to heaven, and reflects
itself from the sea of light on the top of the Ninth
Heaven upon the Redeemed,—the ray of grace which
saved them now rendering them visible as the light of
glory. In other words, the light of glory by which the
saints *in patria* see God is not simply a direct ray from
Himself: it is a ray from Him *reflected* from all the
'life and potency' which it imparts to the nine corporeal Heavens, and therefore from all the experience
of Divine grace on earth by which they were redeemed.
This is why in ll. 97, 98 Dante invokes it as

> O *splendour* of God, by which I saw
> The lofty triumph of the realm of truth.

'Splendour,' as we have so often seen, is never a direct
but always a reflected ray.

It cannot be without purpose that Dante compares
the ascending ranks of the saints to a hillside mirroring
itself in water at its base, 'as if to see its own adornment' of verdure and flowers. We shall best get at
the meaning by contrasting this reflection with the
dream-vision of Leah and Rachel, Action and Contemplation, which Dante received the night before he
entered the Earthly Paradise.[1] In the dream, Leah
gathers flowers to make a garland for her own pleasure
and adornment at the glass. She represents, as Ruskin
says,[2] the Unglorified Active powers of man, rejoicing
only in the work of *her own hands*; and thus stands in
contrast to Matelda of the Earthly Paradise, the type
of Glorified Active Life, which finds its delight in the
work *of God's hands*. Similarly, Rachel stands for the
Unglorified Contemplative powers, and as such she sits

---

[1] *Purg.* xxvii. 94-108.
[2] *Modern Painters*, iii. Pt. IV. ch. xiv. §§ 37-39.

all day at her mirror, 'fain to see her own fair eyes,' rejoicing in her own demonstrations of the truth.[1] She is the dream-contrast to Beatrice, the Glorified Contemplative Life of the Earthly Paradise, who makes her eyes the mirror of the twofold nature of Christ. But even this Glorified Contemplation, it must be remembered, is under the forms and limitations of the Earthly Paradise: the vision is given under veils of types and shadows and similitudes.[2] Now, in the Celestial Paradise, all veils are withdrawn: the blessed souls see their own white purity, as they see all things, in the golden mirror of the light of the glory of God. Action and Contemplation of the dream of earth are over; type and symbol even of the Earthly Paradise have vanished away; and the souls of the Redeemed rejoice in the vision of their own beauty as part of the Divine glory. 'We all, with open face beholding as in a glass the glory of the Lord, are changed into the same image from glory to glory, even as by the Spirit of the Lord.'[3]

Nothing is more characteristic of Dante than the last words he puts into the lips of Beatrice. One expects something gentle and tender, reminiscent of the *Vita Nuova* of earth, prophetic of the New Life in God. Instead, we have a stern and indignant contrast between the eternal destiny of an Emperor and a Pope —the Emperor, faithful to his temporal task, exalted to Heaven; the Pope, false to his higher spiritual trust, cast down to Hell. Even in Paradise, Dante is still the patriot and politician. Beatrice draws him into the golden heart of the Rose which breathed forth 'odour of praise' to 'the never-wintering Sun,' and bids him cast his eyes round the vast amphitheatre of shining souls:

---

[1] *Conv.* ii. 16. 'The eyes of this Lady (Philosophy) are her *demonstrations*, which, directed to the eyes of the intellect, enamour the soul.'

[2] Christ in the form of a Gryphon, Lion and Eagle in one; the Church as a Chariot, Scripture as a Procession of Elders, the Gospels as animals, the Virtues as nymphs, etc. See closing Cantos of the *Purgatorio.*

[3] 2 Cor. iii. 18.

'Behold
How great the convent is of the white robes!
See our city how wide it circles round!
See those seats of ours that are so filled
That but few folk are now awaited there.' [1]

'Our city': one can surely imagine the thrill with
which the words passed through the heart of the poor
exile who had no city on this side of eternity. Florence,
the Flower-city of earth, had thrust him forth as unworthy of its citizenship, and now this Flower-city of
the heavens opens to receive him.[2] Once long ago,
when 'his lady was made of the citizens of eternal life,'
his grief had emptied his native city and hers of its
inhabitants: *Quomodo sedet sola civitas!*[3] In this
shining throng, that solitude of grief is past: she herself welcomes him into the citizenship of 'the city of
the living God, the heavenly Jerusalem.' Or, perhaps,
it were more in harmony with the passionate patriotism
of the poet to say the heavenly Rome. For Rome, as
the context shows, was certainly in his mind—the city
of sin and darkness down below, rebellious against the
Emperor appointed by God to lead her to the blessedness of earth, and betrayed and abandoned by her
spiritual head whose duty it was to lead her to this
felicity of eternal glory. The words, 'See our city,' are
the confirmation of the promise by which, in the
Earthly Paradise, Beatrice consoled Dante for the
ruin of Rome as both Church and Empire which she
was about to reveal to him in visions:

'And thou shalt be with me for evermore
A citizen of that Rome whereof Christ is Roman.'[4]

The reference to the fewness of the seats still vacant,
Casini thinks, is no indication that Dante regarded the
end of the world as at hand: it means only that times
of corruption had fallen on the world in which few
would be saved. Against this, however, we have
Dante's own statement in the *Convito*. Speaking of

---

[1] *Par.* xxx. 124-132. 'The convent of the white robes' refers to Rev.
vii. 13.
[2] See note on Florence on p. 486 below.
[3] *Vita Nuova*, § xxix; Lam. i. 1.   [4] *Purg.* xxxii. 101, 102.

the precession of the equinoxes—the slow movement from west to east of the Starry Heaven—he says: ' From the beginning of the world little more than the sixth part has revolved; and we are already in the last age of the world, and verily await the consummation of the celestial movement.'[1] This seems decisive. Dante believed he was living in the last times, and that the number of the elect was almost fulfilled.[2]

It is at this point Beatrice pronounces final judgment on Emperor and Pope. Dante's eye had been caught by one of the empty seats which had a crown placed above it, and she tells him it is the throne destined for the Emperor Henry VII.

> 'In that great seat where thou dost hold thine eyes
> For the crown's sake already placed above it,
> Ere at this wedding feast thyself do sup,
> Shall sit the soul, which down below will be Augustus,
> Of the high Henry, who to straighten Italy
> Shall come before that she is ready for it.
> The blind covetousness which bewitcheth you
> Has made you like unto the little child
> Who dies of hunger and drives off the nurse '[3]—

' because the Italians were always crying out for a deliverer, and refused him when he appeared.' The passage is, of course, written from the standpoint of 1300, and is therefore prophetic. In 1308 Henry, Count of Luxemburg, was elected Roman Emperor, and in the summer of 1310 crossed the Alps to overthrow and castigate, as Dino Compagni says, the tyrant lords of Lombardy and Tuscany, and thus create peace and order. Dino describes him as 'a wise man, of noble

---

[1] *Conv.* ii. 15.

[2] Dante makes no attempt to decide the number of the elect : it is known to God alone. See above, p. 320 on *Par.* xx. 130 ff. and note with quotation from Aquinas. Also note on p. 460.

[3] *Par.* xxx. 133-141. In his Epistle to the Florentines (Ep. vi. 5) Dante writes : ' The full-fledged and unspotted in the way see you, as if standing on the threshold of a prison, and driving away whosoever has pity on you, lest perchance he should free you from captivity and from the shackles which bind your feet and hands. Nor, because ye are blind, do ye perceive the covetousness which dominates you, soothing you with poisonous whisper, restraining you with vain threats, holding you captive in the law of sin, and forbidding you to obey the most sacred laws, which copy the image of natural justice.'

blood, just and famous, of great loyalty, proved in arms
and of noble race, a man of great ability of mind and of
great temperance.'[1]   Around Henry Dante's passionate
imagination threw a halo of religious veneration.   He
was not merely the 'bridegroom' of Italy, 'the solace
of the world, and the glory of her people, the most
clement Henry, Divus, and Augustus, and Caesar': he
was a second Moses leading a captive people to liberty,
a new David slaying the 'giant with the sling of his
wisdom and the stone of his strength'—nay, the Lamb
of God, taking away the sins of the world.[2]   Alas, he
came 'to straighten Italy before she was ready.'   Her
opposition changed his purposes of peace into incessant
war.   Soon all was over: in 1313 Henry died suddenly
at Buonconvento near Siena, and Dante's hopes of a
new heaven and a new earth died with him.   But the
Emperor who had striven so bravely and loyally to
fulfil his Heaven-appointed task remained in the poet's
heart as a sainted memory, and Beatrice now points
out his place in Paradise—the heavenly throne prepared
by God for him to whom men refused the earthly.
And Dante determines that the man to whom this
failure was chiefly due should not escape.   The last
words of Beatrice are a stern prophecy of the eternal
perdition of 'the Gascon who cheated the lofty
Henry':[3]

> 'And in the Court of God there then shall be
> A Prefect such, that openly and covert
> He will not go with him by the one path.
> But short time after shall God suffer him
> In the holy office; for he shall be thrust dow\
> There where Simon Magus is for his desert,
> And make him of Alagna lower go.'[4]

---

[1] *Cronica Fiorentina*, iii. 23.

[2] For Dante's extraordinary veneration for Henry, and his indignation
against Florence for rejecting him, see *Epistles* v, vi, vii.

[3] *Par.* xvii. 82.   See above, p. 273.

[4] *Par.* xxx. 142-148.   Beatrice foretells that Clement will survive
Henry but a short time.   Henry died Aug. 24, 1313 ; Clement, April 20 of
the following year.   Villani (ix. 59) tells a curious story which traces his
death indirectly to his besetting sin of simony and nepotism.   Wishing
to know the fate in the next world of one of his nephews, a cardinal, who
had died, a necromancer whom he employed caused one of the Pope's

The reference is to Clement v., who removed the
Papal Court from Rome to Avignon. It is difficult to
say what underlies the 'open and covert' of l. 143.
Villani tells us that Clement, fearing that Charles of
Valois, brother of Philip the Fair, should be elected
Emperor, and thus the lordship of the Empire as well
as of the Church should fall into the hands of the
French house, so contrived by secret plotting that
Henry was elected before he himself was pledged to
support the claims of Charles. Clement confirmed
Henry's election, sent his legates with him into Italy,
and wrote to the nobles and cities of that country an
extravagantly enthusiastic letter of commendation of
the King of the Romans. While thus outwardly sup-
porting Henry, the Pope, alarmed lest he should seize
the Papal territory, appointed King Robert of Naples,
the head of the Guelph party, Rector of the Church
in Romagna—obviously to act as a check upon the
Emperor. Henry found himself opposed and thwarted
at every turn by Robert, who prevented his coronation
at Rome.[1] It was in vain that he laid the ban of the
Empire upon him as a rebellious vassal; it did no harm
to a man who was carrying out the secret desires of
the Pope. Thus neither in his open policy nor in
his covert did Clement go with Henry 'in one path':
his aim was always to thwart his purpose of restoring
peace to distracted Italy. This is why Dante reserves
the last word of Beatrice for his stern condemnation.
Not only had he been unfaithful in his own spiritual

chaplains to descend to hell. This messenger reported that he found the
cardinal's soul in a palace on a bed of fire for his simony, and that another
palace near it was being built, the demons said, for Pope Clement. 'The
said chaplain brought these tidings to the Pope, which was never afterwards glad, and he lived but a short time longer; and when he was dead,
and his body had been left for a night in a church with many lights, his
coffin caught fire and was burnt, and his body from the middle downwards.'

[1] See Villani, ix. 39 for the arrangements made in April 1312 by King
Robert and the Guelph League of Tuscany to prevent the coronation of
Henry at Rome. 'It is beyond a doubt,' writes Gregorovius, 'that the
position which the Pope gave Robert in Italy was due to political foresight. He could not stand so far above parties as to survey with
indifference the entire enfeeblement of the Guelfs.'

office, but he had used all its resources, openly and in
secret, to hinder the wisest and best of Emperors from
fulfilling his Heaven-appointed task of creating peace
in the sphere of temporal things. It was an inevitable
moral judgment. 'For Dante,' as Mr. Gardner says,
'beholding the beatitude which God has prepared for
men, must naturally pass in thought to those ideal
guides, the Emperor and the Pope, that the ineffable
Providence has appointed to guide man to happiness
and bliss, and judge how each is fulfilling his lofty
mission.'[1]   And although at first we are startled to
find that the last words of Beatrice consist of this
terrible denunciation, yet in all the circumstances they
are perfectly natural, whether we regard her as the
symbol of Divine Wisdom or of the ideal Church. It is
not merely that Dante saw his country ruined by
French diplomacy and intrigue; it is that Beatrice
saw the heavenly Fatherland deprived of its citizens
by the very guide appointed by God to lead men to its
eternal bliss.

This heinous perversion of the spiritual office is
traced to 'the blind covetousness' already attributed
to Italy. In Clement it took the form of Simony, and
this determines his place among the lost. 'This was
a man,' says Villani, 'very greedy of money, and a
simoniac, who sold in his court every benefice for
money, and was licentious.'[2]   His place is in Bolgia III.
of the Eighth Circle of the Inferno. These simoniacal
Popes, who turned holy offices upside down by selling
them for money, are themselves turned upside down
and thrust head foremost into fissures in the rock, in
a long unholy and non-Apostolic succession that runs
down to Simon Magus, the rival of Simon Peter. When
Dante passed through this Bolgia, the last occupant of

---

[1] *Dante's Ten Heavens*, p. 225.

[2] *Chronicle*, ix. 59. 'He died shamefully rich,' says Milman. 'To his
nephew (nepotism had begun to prevail in its baleful influence) he be-
queathed not less than 300,000 golden florins, under the pretext of succour
to the Holy Land. He had died still more wealthy, but that his wealth
was drained by more disgraceful prodigality' (*Latin Christianity*, Bk.
XII. ch. v.). For the way in which his successor, John XXII., bettered his
example, see above, pp. 160-162; 289-292; 426, 427.

a certain opening, Nicholas III., informed him that the next comer, Boniface VIII., would thrust him further down into the rocky channel.[1] Soon, Beatrice here declares, Boniface in turn will be thrust down by Clement. One cannot help feeling that the reference to 'the man of Alagna' or Anagni is something more than one last savage blow aimed at the poet's enemy. Philip the Fair, after causing the death of Boniface by the outrage at Anagni, and after the short reign of his successor, had Clement elected to be his tool and instrument. Among the conditions by which he bound him were the annulling of the excommunication pronounced on him by Boniface; the absolution of his agents concerned in the outrage; and the destruction and condemnation of the memory of Boniface on charges of heresy and immorality. To save the memory of the dead Pope, Clement sacrificed the whole Order of Templars to Philip's rapacity.[2] Is it too ingenious to suppose that this is what was in Dante's mind when he introduced the allusion to 'him of Alagna'? Clement may in this world use every device and all the resources of his holy office to save the memory of Boniface from condemnation; but in the world to come the eternal justice will compel his own lost soul to thrust his predecessor in simony down to a darker deep of perdition. Such ironies of reversal and contrast between world and world seem to spring naturally out of Dante's stern and terrible imagination. The dark narrow fissure of rock into which these faithless Popes are thrust head foremost one on the top of the other, stands in his mind in awful contrast to the Divine light and amplitude of this White Rose, this vast amphitheatre of 'that Rome whereof Christ is Roman,' where every soul, 'ordered in its place among its peers,' shines with the *lumen gloriae*, 'the light of the knowledge of the glory of God.'

---

[1] *Inf.* xix. For a fuller exposition of this punishment, I may refer to my *Exiles of Eternity*, 276-291.

[2] *Purg.* xx. 85-96. For an account of the outrage on Boniface and the suppression of the Templars, see my *Prisoners of Hope*, 280-285.

CHAPTER XXIX

TENTH HEAVEN—THE EMPYREAN: GOD

2. St. Bernard and the White Rose

THE celestial intercourse of love is now revealed between 'the two courts'—the host of Angels and

> the saintly soldiery
> Whom Christ in His own blood did make His Bride.

The White Rose of the saints suggests the comparison of the Angels to a swarm of bees plying their busy task to and fro between the flowers and their hive. In like fashion Dante saw 'an innumerable company of Angels' descending into 'the great Flower,' and re-ascending to 'where their love abides for ever,' that is, God.[1] We must not fall into the error of regarding the Angels here as mediators through whom the saints hold intercourse with God; that would be to deny that they had received the Beatific Vision at all, since it consists in the sight of God face to face. We meet

[1] *Par.* xxxi. 1-12. Anselm says: 'Thousands of thousands pass to and fro continually between heaven and earth, like bees at their busy work between the hives and the flowers'; and Mr. Gardner quotes from St. Bernard's second Sermon on the Advent the comparison of Gabriel at the Annunciation to a bee entering the flower-like cup of Nazareth (see p. 161 above) and alighting on the lily of the Virgin's purity: 'The bee is that which feedeth among the lilies, that dwells in the flower-bearing land of the Angels. Hence it flew away to the city of Nazareth, which is inter-preted a Flower, and came to the sweet smelling flower of perpetual Virginity. Thereon it alighted, and therein it rested, and thereto it clung.' Doubtless Dante was familiar with the simile, but the form of the Rose would be enough to suggest it naturally and independently to his mind. The rearing of bees was a favourite occupation of the monks. The hive 'served as an example to the friars of an ideal life of communistic industry and cenobitic chastity.' The virgin bee-queen was a type of the Virgin, and the ascended Christ was called 'apis aetherea' (Evans' *Animal Symbolism in Eccles. Architecture*, p. 3).

here the distinction already noticed more than once between essential and accidental beatitude. The essential beatitude of saints and Angels alike is the immediate vision of God; but both may receive an accidental bliss in the eternal intercourse of spirit with spirit.[1]

The symbolism of the appearance of the Angels is not easy to determine:

> Their faces had they all of living flame,
> And the wings of gold, and all the rest so white
> No snow unto that limit doth attain.

The 'living flame' is obviously love, and it burns in the face, through which intelligence shines: to indicate, apparently, that their intellect is on fire with love. It is the 'light intellectual fulfilled of love' of which Beatrice spoke on Dante's entrance to this final Heaven. 'And I saw another mighty angel come down from heaven,' says St. John, 'and his face was as it were the sun.'[2] The wings may be taken to represent their obedience—the eagerness with which they fly forth on their errands of love; while the gold is a natural symbol of the pure and precious spirit of their service. The whiteness beyond snow of the rest of their forms seems to indicate the absolute purity of beings who never knew the stain of sin: even the white souls of the Rose were redeemed from a fallen race, but these had kept their first estate.[3]

---

[1] This is connected with the thought that the accidental bliss of Angels is increased by the number of souls their ministry has induced to do meritorious works: just as the misery of the fallen Angels grows greater with the ruin of every soul seduced by them to evil deeds. See above, p. 88, and *Summa*, Suppl. q. lxxxix. a. 8.

[2] Rev. x. 1. Bonaventura (*De Eccles. Hier.* chap. i.) says Angels are often compared to fire in Scripture (Ex. iii. 2; Cant. viii. 6; Ps. civ. 4, etc.) 'on account of the fixed and steady motion by which Angelic love, like a fire that is never consumed, is moved towards God.'

[3] *Par.* xxxi. 13-15. Mr. Gardner (*Dante's Ten Heavens*, 229) suggests that 'perhaps there is a reference in these colours to the three Persons of the Blessed Trinity, since Lucifer's three coloured faces are an infernal parody of their Divine attributes: the golden wings may refer to the Power of the Father, the white to the Wisdom of the Son, the flaming face to the burning Love of the Holy Spirit.'

The ministry of the Angels increases, as we have seen, the 'accidental' bliss of the saints:

> When they descended into the flower, from tier to tier,
> They proffered of the peace and of the ardour
> Which by the fanning of their sides they won.

According to one writer, this union of peace and ardour means that 'passion is here peaceful and peace passionate'; but we must remember that ardour does not mean passion in our sense, but love. Dante is thinking of that highest form of love whose burning ardour is full of peace because it has found its final resting-place, the end of all desire. The Angels win it 'by the fanning of their sides': by their flight up to God in contemplation and their flight down to the saints to share with them what they have received from Him. In other words, they win peace full of love and love full of peace by the union of the Active and Contemplative Life. This seems to be one of Dante's great discoveries in this Heaven—that when you reach the highest created Intelligences, the old earthly antagonism between action and contemplation has no existence. This is already indicated plainly near the beginning of the Canto, where the Angels are called the soldiery

> that flying sees and sings
> The glory of Him who doth enamour it
> And the goodness which created it so great.

'Flying sees and sings': no words can better describe the union of the two forms of life—the vision of God that is never lost in the swiftest flight of service, and the song of praise issuing from both, praise for what God is and for what He has created them to be. Great as Dante's power of condensation is, he has never crowded a more pregnant meaning into fewer words.

Further, just as they bring down to the saints something of their own peace and ardour, so, like bees, they carry to the presence of God some sweetness from the petals of the great Flower. The Angels are represented in Scripture as receiving through the Church a wider

revelation of God: 'to the intent that now unto the
principalities and powers in heavenly places might be
known by the church the manifold wisdom of God.'[1]
Within the circle of their own nature and life, the
Angels knew the wisdom of God in His dealings with
an order of beings, part of which remained sinless, and
part fell beyond recovery. In the Church, they saw
'the unsearchable riches of Christ'—a new and manifold revelation of that same wisdom in the salvation
of the elect spirits of another order of creatures, that
had fallen wholly away from Him. When, therefore,
they descended into the Rose they learned from the
saints some new knowledge of the manifold wisdom
which planned and fulfilled their redemption, and
carried the joy and sweetness of the vision back into
the presence of His face.

One last wonder Dante marks: the interposition of
'so great a flying plenitude'[2] of Angels causes no
hindrance either to the eyes of the saints as they gaze
up to the Fountain of Light, or to 'the splendour,'[3] the
lumen gloriae, the central sea of light reflected from
the summit of the Primum Mobile. The reason is that
the Divine light penetrates everything in the universe
according to its worth; and since, in these pure and
loving Intelligences, there is nothing that is unlike God
Himself, His light shines through them in its own unclouded clearness. They are, as it were, 'pure gold like
unto transparent glass': no cloud of sin or selfishness

[1] Eph. iii. 10.
[2] The word 'plenitude' in l. 20 has probably a much greater meaning
than that of mere multitude. It may be an echo of Lect. vii. of Bonaventura's *Speculum Virginis*, in which he explains what are 'the nine
plenitudes of Mary which represent the plenitudes of the nine Orders of
Angels in glory.' The plenitudes are drawn from Gabriel's salutation to
the Virgin, *Ave gratia plena* (Luke i. 28), and among them are the
perfection of the Church and fruition of eternal joy. Since Mary herself is
the type of the Church, Dante may mean to indicate by 'so great a flying
plenitude' of Angels the filling of the Church Triumphant with the plenitudes of the nine Orders which Bonaventura attributes to the Virgin.
[3] I take 'splendour' in l. 21 in the sense explained on p. 473—not a ray
shining directly on the saints, but the reflection upon them of the ray
from the top of the first corporeal sphere. The Angels, flying above the
circular sea of light, cast no shadow on it by intercepting the ray from
God.

obscures in them, as it so often does in earthly saints,
the pure light of God that shines through their service
of love.[1]

Suddenly, an overwhelming sense broke over the
poet's soul of the contrast between this 'secure and
joyous realm,' where every eye and heart was set upon
one mark, and the distracted and miserable earth from
which he came ; and a prayer bursts from his lips that
the Trinal Light, which shines in a single star, may look
down on the tempest of this lower world. He feels
like a barbarian from the uncivilized and savage North,
who for the first time sees 'Rome and her mighty
works' in the great days of her glory, 'when Lateran
transcended mortal things.'[2] Nay, far greater was his
stupefaction, for far greater was the contrast :

> I who to the Divine had from the human,
> From time unto eternity, had come,
> From Florence to a people just and sane,
> With what a stupor must I needs be filled !

This is his last and most bitter allusion to his native
city. Florence constitutes to his mind the very climax
of the unspeakable contrast between earth and
heaven. The Divine does not so far transcend the

---

[1] *Par.* xxxi. 19-24.

[2] This reference to the Lateran is not generally understood. Dante is
thinking of the ruin that had fallen on the Lateran Palace and Church
through the removal of the Papacy to Avignon. Soon after his conversion in 312, Constantine gave the Palace to Pope Sylvester, and for nearly
a thousand years it was the Papal residence. Near it the Emperor
erected the first Lateran Church, known as the *Basilica Aurea* on
account of its rich treasures and ornaments—gold and silver images,
cups, vases, precious stones. This basilica 'maintained, as the mother
church of Christendom, *Omnium Urbis et Orbis Ecclesiarum Mater et
Caput*, supremacy over all other churches in the world, and even claimed
to have inherited the sanctity of the temple at Jerusalem, the Ark of the
Covenant of the Jews being preserved beneath its altar.' When it was
replaced by another building in the tenth century, Roman tradition added
to its treasures the Tables of the Law, the Golden Candlesticks, the
Tabernacle, Aaron's priestly vestments, and the heads of the chief
Apostles, which Sylvester had preserved in the original basilica. Those
were the great times 'when Lateran transcended mortal things.' In 1305
the Lateran Palace and Church were deserted for Avignon. In 1308 the
beautiful Church with all its treasures was destroyed by fire. In 1312
Henry VII. was crowned amidst its ruins. It is the contrast of all this
with its ancient glory which is in Dante's mind. See Gregorovius, *Rome
in the Middle Ages*, i. 88, 213 ; vi. 10, 693, etc. (Eng. trans.)

human, or the Eternal time, as this 'secure and joyous
realm' transcends his fellow-citizens in justice and
sanity. Not even Rome can form so terrible a climax.
Doubtless, something of the bitterness of his own
personal wrongs entered into his judgment; but apart
from this altogether, to a man like Dante with a
passion for righteousness, the clear vision of the true
City of God could but throw into deeper darkness that
city of earth, whose injustice and insanity he had
greatest cause to know. If bitterness mingles with
his words, prayer also mingles.[1]

We have now reached the point at which Beatrice
hands over her task as guide to the great contemplative saint, Bernard of Clairvaux. Dante tells us how
he took a general survey of the great Flower, like a
pilgrim gazing around the temple of his vow:

> Faces I saw of charity persuasive,
> With Another's light adorned and their own smile,
> And gestures graced with every dignity.[2]

Having thus taken in 'the general form of Paradise,'
he turns eagerly to question his Lady, only to find
that she is gone and an old man in her place:

---

[1] *Par.* xxxi. 25-42. It is possible, as already suggested, that the contrast between the two Flower-cities was in his mind. 'The Roman
town was called *Florentia*, the Italian rendering of which, *Fiorenza*,
was evidently connected by the Florentines themselves with *fiore*, the
special flower adopted as their device being the lily (*giglio*); this appears
from the name of their coin, the florin (*fiorino*), which was stamped with
the lily on one side, as well as from the name of the Cathedral, *S. Maria
del Fiore*' (Toynbee's *Dante Dictionary*, 242). Such suggestions of
correspondence and contrast would rise instinctively in a mind like
Dante's.

[2] *Par.* xxxi. 43-51. Under these words lies the doctrine of the *dotes*
or marriage-gifts which Christ bestows on His Spouse, the Church in
Heaven. Aquinas defines thus: '*Dos* is a perpetual ornament of soul and
body, sufficient to the life, enduring continually in eternal beatitude.'
The three marriage-gifts of the *soul* in Paradise correspond to the three
theological virtues on earth—*vision* to faith, *comprehension* to hope,
fruition to charity. Those of the *body* spring from the glorified soul,
and are four in number—*subtlety*, the power to penetrate other bodies as
Christ's risen body did; *agility*, the power of swiftest motion; *clarity*,
by which the body becomes luminous or transparent; *impassibility*,
superiority to passion or suffering (*Summa*, i. q. xii. a. 7; iii. q. xlv. a. 1;
Supp. q. xcv.). See note on p. 226 above.

> One thing I purposed, and another answered me :
> I thought to see Beatrice, and saw an old man
> Clad in the vesture of the folk in glory.
> O'erspread he was in the eyes and in the cheeks
> With a benignant joy, in gesture kindly,
> As to a tender father is becoming.

In reply to Dante's agonized cry, 'Where is she?' the stranger says he has left his seat at the request of Beatrice to lead his desire to its end, and she herself is up yonder in the third rank, in the throne which her merits have assigned to her.   Without a word, Dante lifted his eyes and saw the woman he loved, crowned with the. eternal rays.   Though she was above him farther than the highest region of the thunder, her image came to him undimmed in that spiritual world where far and near are one.   And then 'the lover becomes the worshipper and pours out his gratitude' in one last prayer :

> 'O Lady, in whom my hope hath vigour,
> And who for my salvation didst endure
> In Hell to leave the imprint of thy feet,
> Of whatsoever things I have beheld,
> As coming from thy power and from thy goodness
> I recognize the virtue and the grace.
> Thou from a slave hast drawn me unto freedom
> By all those ways, by all the expedients,
> Whereby thou hadst the power of doing it.
> The great work thou hast wrought in me preserve,
> So that my soul, to which thou gavest health,
> Pleasing to thee be loosened from the body.'
> Thus did I pray ; and she, so far away
> As she appeared, smiled and looked back on me ;
> Then turned her to the Eternal Fountain.[1]

[1] *Par.* xxxi. 52-93.   The special virtue which Dante traces to Beatrice is Hope (l. 79)—Hope of this life of glory to which she has now brought him.   In the *Purgatorio* she wears a green mantle and is crowned with olive (xxx. 32, 68); her eyes are emeralds (xxxi. 116); she refuses to let him hope until he has fully confessed his sin (xxx. 82 ff.).   In. *Par* xxv. 49-57 she vouches for his Hope to St. James, the type of this virtue.   For the variety of ways and means by which she drew him from a slave to liberty, compare *Purg.* xxx. 121-141.

The words *la tua magnificenza* in l. 88 I have rendered with Butler ' the great work thou hast wrought.'   Such words as magnificence or munificence or bounteousness do not convey what was in Dante's mind ; he was thinking of the great working of Beatrice in his soul which he has just described, and asking her to guard it to the end.   Magnificence

This turning of her eyes to the Eternal Fountain is partly in contemplation and partly in intercession. In the Church's doctrine of the invocation of the saints, the two are most intimately united. The saints see in God the prayers of those who invoke them, their special needs, and the best ways and means of giving them aid. It is to see all this, that Beatrice lifts her eyes to God. Her turning away, therefore, does not mean that Dante is now parted from her. It is the answer to his prayer: in the Eternal Fountain she will see all his wants and how best to supply them out of its fulness.

We return now to Bernard, whose name is still unknown to Dante. 'The holy Elder' asks him, for the perfect fulfilment of his journey, to prepare his eye for 'mounting through the ray Divine,' by letting it range throughout the garden of souls; and promises him the special help of the Virgin:

> 'And the Queen of Heaven, for whom I am all
> On fire with love, will grant us every grace,
> Because that I her faithful Bernard am.'

On hearing the name, Dante gazed on the famous saint as in Rome he had seen some Croatian peasant looking eagerly at the Veronica, the legendary likeness of our Saviour, while the thought kept throbbing in his brain,

> 'My Lord Christ Jesus, God of very God,
> Now was your semblance made like unto this?' [1]

---

in the Aristotelian sense (*Ethics*, iv. 4; comp. *Conv.* iv. 17) is suitable expenditure on a great scale, such as is attributed to Can Grande in *Par.* xvii. 85, 86, and *Epis.* x. 1. In spiritual things, the expenditure of Beatrice had been on a grand scale: she had spared no effort, even to the leaving of her footprints in Hell.

[1] *Par.* xxxi. 94-111. Veronica, according to tradition, was a pious woman of Jerusalem who gave to Christ, while carrying His cross to Calvary, her veil or kerchief to wipe His brow. On receiving it back the likeness of His face was imprinted on it. It was preserved in St. Peter's in Rome, and Dante probably saw it exhibited to pilgrims during the Jubilee in 1300. 'The legend of the woman Veronica appears to have arisen from a confusion with another legend as to a *vera icon* or "true image," sent by Christ to Abgarus, King of Edessa in Mesopotamia' (Toynbee's *Dante Dictionary*, 553). On the Virgin's resemblance to her Son, see below, p. 509.

The appearance of St. Bernard in glory presents
some points of difficulty. Dante has already told us
that he wears the vesture of the folk in glory, the
form and appearance of the body he is to receive at
the Great Day; yet it is as an old man he sees him.[1]
Aquinas, following St. Augustine, teaches that in the
Resurrection the saints will rise, as Christ rose, *in aetate
juvenili*, the age which begins about the thirtieth year
when life is at its prime.[2] It is difficult to understand
why Dante did not so depict the saint whose personal
beauty shines so clear and life-like through the old
chronicles. 'Rather under middle height, with golden
yellow hair, darkening towards auburn in his beard,
very thin, and his skin so pure that he flushed very
easily, soft "dove-like" eyes, with a glance of quiet
power in them for all their softness, an expression of
grave cheerfulness, a clear musical voice.'[3] This is his
portrait at the age of twenty-two when he entered the
monastery of Citeaux. Add ten years, and one can
well imagine the form of immortal youth and beauty
with which the poet might have made Heaven itself
more fair. One can only suppose that Dante retained
the traditional picture of him as a kindly father out of
reverence for the Divine wisdom with which age had
invested him. For, says Aquinas, replying to the objec-

---

[1] *Par.* xxxi. 59, 60.

[2] *Summa,* iii. Supp. q. lxxxi. a. 1; *De Civ. Dei,* xxii. 15. This is drawn
from the Vulgate of Eph. iv. 13: 'Donec occurramus omnes . . . in virum
perfectum, in mensuram *aetatis* plenitudinis Christi.' If, says Augustine,
this does not refer to the fulfilling of the Body of Christ by the addition
of all the members to the Head, but to the resurrection of the body,
'the meaning is that all shall rise neither beyond nor under youth, but in
that vigour and age to which we know that Christ had arrived. For even
the world's wisest men have fixed the bloom of youth at about the age of
thirty; and when this period has been passed, the man begins to decline
towards the defective and duller period of old age. And therefore the
apostle did not speak of the measure of the body, nor of the measure of
the stature, but of " the measure of the age of the fulness of Christ."'

[3] 'Bernard of Clairvaux' by Principal Lindsay in *The Evangelical Succession,* 1st series, p. 176. Comp. Alan, Bishop of Auxerre: 'There
appeared in his flesh a certain grace, but spiritual rather than carnal; in
his face a clearness shone forth, not of earth but heaven; in his eyes
rayed a certain angelic purity and dove-like simplicity; also the
extreme delicacy of his skin showed the flush of modesty in his
cheeks.'

tion that age is necessary to man's perfection even in Heaven, 'old age has reverence not on account of the condition of the body, which is in defect, but of the wisdom of the soul, which is presumed to be there from ancientness of time. Hence in the elect will remain the reverence due to old age, on account of the fulness of Divine wisdom which will be in them, but there will not remain the defects of age.'[1] Dante probably gives Bernard the form of age, with the benignant joy and kindly gesture of a father, in symbol of this wisdom of the soul.[2]

We now come to the question why Bernard takes the place of Beatrice. The general assumption seems to be that there is in the symbolic character for which Beatrice stands some defect or limitation which made further guidance on her part impossible. She represents, it is said, Theology in its more scholastic sense, or the spiritual authority of the Church working by Theology; whereas Bernard is the highest representative of ecstatic contemplation, which alone is able, by excess of charity and the gracious aid of the Virgin Mother, to unveil the final secret of the Trinity. Plumptre states the theory somewhat more definitely. 'We can scarcely doubt, I think, that this somewhat startling change was meant to represent a like change in Dante's inner life. I venture to suggest that it indicates that he had passed, in his theological reading, from Aquinas to St. Bernard, and that, marvellous as was the dogmatic fulness and clearness of the former, he found in the latter that which raised him to a higher level of spiritual intuition. Throughout the *Paradise* Beatrice has been, as it were, the mouthpiece of the wisdom which Dante had learnt from St. Thomas, had answered every question, and drawn the lines of demarcation between truth and error. But there was something higher than even this, and in his case, as in that of a

---

[1] *Summa*, iii. Supp. q. lxxxi. a. 1.

[2] *Par.* xxxi. 61-63. The *benigna letizia* of l. 62 reminds us of Bonaventura's description of *Benignitas* as 'a certain sweetness of soul, excluding all iniquity, and disposing the soul to benevolence, forbearance (or endurance), and internal joy' (*Incendium Amoris*, ch. i.).

thousand others, St. Bernard had met a want which Aquinas had not met.'[1]

It requires some courage to question a theory supported by many great names, yet it has always seemed to me unsatisfactory. For example, a parallel is frequently drawn between the relation of Virgil to Matelda in the Earthly Paradise and that of Beatrice to Bernard in the Celestial. Just as Reason (Virgil) gives way to the Active Life (Matelda), so Theology (Beatrice) in turn gives way to Contemplation (Bernard). This assumes that Beatrice is Theology in some lower sense which excludes Contemplation. But of this limitation there seems to be little or no proof, apart from these closing Cantos. If she represents, as I think she does, Heavenly Wisdom in its widest sense, Contemplation can scarcely be excluded. If it were, the proper place for her to give way to Bernard would have been at the foot of the Golden Ladder of Contemplation in Saturn, the Heaven of contemplative saints. So far from showing any failure of power there, it is through her he is caught up with the other souls into the whirlwind of ecstatic rapture which lifted him above his own natural powers:

> The sweet Lady urged me on behind them
> With a single sign, up by that ladder,
> So did her virtue my nature overcome;
> Nor ever here below, where one mounts and descends
> By law of nature, was so swift a motion
> That it could be compared unto my wing.[2]

In the mysteries of the Heavens above the Ladder, her power of contemplation never fails up to this point; and, as if to indicate that her departure now is not due to any failure of her contemplative powers, Bernard points her out where she sits in the third rank of the Rose beside Rachel, the symbol of Contemplation. In

---

[1] *Dante*, ii. 181. Plumptre names Bernard's Sermons on Canticles and his *De Laudibus Virginis Matris* as the books which influenced Dante most; omitting the *De Consideratione*, to which Dante specially refers in connection with the *Paradiso* (*Epis.* x. 28).

[2] *Par.* xxii. 100-105.

face of all this, it seems to me impossible to establish any clear and definite contrast between Bernard and Beatrice as, respectively, Contemplation and Theology.

The truth is, Dante's primary purpose is simply that of setting the woman he had loved, long since 'ensky'd and sainted' in his soul, in her place in the Eternal Rose. Instead of contrasting her with Bernard, it is nearer the truth to say that he is chosen as the soul worthiest to carry on and complete the task of contemplation from which she is called away, not for any defect in her, but by the necessities of the poet's own heart. In three respects Bernard was indeed worthy to complete the task of Beatrice in her symbolic character of Contemplative Theology. He was, in the first place, the highest type of contemplative saint: one who, in Dante's words, by contemplation tasted of the peace of Paradise while still on earth.[1] In the second place, it was necessary for Dante to be raised beyond even Beatrice to her whose face is likest Christ's, the Queen of this kingdom of the saints; and no one was worthier to act as his intercessor with Mary than 'her faithful Bernard,' whose life and writings were on fire with love of her. In this, too, he but fulfilled the love and reverence in which Beatrice shared. When the city sat solitary, Dante's first thought was that she was with her to whom she gave her veneration: 'the Lord God of justice called my most gracious lady unto Himself, that she might be glorious under the banner of that blessed Queen Mary, whose name had always a deep reverence in the words of holy Beatrice'[2]—a reverence shared by Dante who daily invoked her name in his morning and evening prayers.[3] And finally, Bernard combined, if ever man did, the life of contemplation with that of action. He is Rachel and Leah in one, Mary and Martha, Beatrice and Matelda. This ecstatic mystic was the busiest man in Europe. His monasteries sprang up at the rate of four a year. He settled disputes of all kinds

---

[1] Lines 109-111.   [2] *Vita Nuova*, § xxix.   [3] *Par.* xxiii. 88, 89.

throughout Europe, as well as within his own convent.
'Struggling Christendom,' as Vaughan writes, 'sent
incessant monks and priests, couriers and men-at-arms,
to knock and blow horn at the gate of Clairvaux
Abbey; for Bernard, and none but he, must come out
and fight that audacious Abelard; Bernard must decide
between rival Popes, and cross the Alps time after
time to quiet tossing Italy; Bernard alone is the hope
of fugitive Pope and trembling Church; he only can
win back turbulent nobles, alienated people, recreant
priests, when Arnold of Brescia is in arms at Rome,
and when Catharists, Petrobrusians, Waldenses, and
heretics of every shade, threaten the hierarchy on
either side the Alps; and at the preaching of Bernard
the Christian world pours forth to meet the disaster
of a new crusade.'[1] This union of action and contemplation is the most wonderful thing in this most
wonderful man. He protested again and again against
their separation. 'For these two things,' he says, 'are
intimately related; they are chamber companions, and
dwell together. Martha is sister to Mary, and although
she comes forth from the light of contemplation, she
never suffers herself to fall into the darkness of sin, or
to subside into ignoble sloth, but remains still in the
light of good works. . . . I endure with patience the
being torn from the society of an unfruitful Rachel, to
obtain from Leah the plentiful fruits of your progress
in goodness.'[2] It is in this spirit he now leaves his
seat in the Rose and the direct vision of God, to
become the Pilgrim's guide. This union of Action and
Contemplation is one principal reason for his being
chosen for the office, for it is this union which constitutes the highest bliss of Paradise. The Angels
'flying see': their eternal joy is the contemplation of

---

[1] Vaughan, *Hours with the Mystics*, i. 134.
[2] Sermon li. on the Song of Songs. Such passages are frequent. In
Sermon ix. he exhorts his monks: 'The one (contemplation) is that
which maketh glad the heart of one man alone; but the other (action)
that which edifies many. For, although Rachel be the fairer, Leah is the
more fruitful. Do not, therefore, linger too much over the sweetness of
contemplation, for the fruits of preaching are the better' (Eales).

God in and through their ministry to the saints. St. Bernard seems to be the human soul in whom this angelic balance and harmony is most perfect, and as such, he is the highest form of that Divine Wisdom of which Beatrice is the symbol.

On hearing the name of Bernard, Dante gazed so intently on the great contemplative that the saint has to remind him that the only way to know 'this joyous being' is to see the entire company of the Redeemed, up to the Queen to whom the whole realm is subject. This, as we have seen, is regarded as a preparation of the eyes for the final vision of God : it is only 'with all saints' that we are able 'to comprehend what is the breadth, and length, and depth, and height; and to know the love of Christ, which passeth knowledge.'[1] It is not merely that it is only the vast multitude of the Redeemed that can reveal the infinitely varied power of Divine grace, as the diversities of flowers reveal the virtue of the sun. There is in the Church's faith the still deeper thought that the supernatural order— represented here in the form of the vital and organic unity of the White Rose—is an outward manifestation of the Blessed Trinity. 'The elevation of creatures to the godlike state of adoptive sons is an imitation and, therefore, a manifestation of the eternal generation of God the Son. Considered as a communication of Divine Nature by love, it is also an image and, as it were, an extension or ramification of the eternal procession of the Holy Ghost.'[2] This supernatural union and fellow-ship with the Divine Persons so constitutes the saints in glory a spiritual image of the Trinity, that to see them is a preparation for the vision of its mystery.

On one side of the White Rose, Dante's eyes were arrested at the far summit by the light of the Queen of Heaven which surpassed all the other lights, as the East, when the sun is about to rise, outshines all other parts of the heavens. Before that 'pacific oriflamme' of her brightness, more than a thousand Angels with

[1] Eph. iii. 18, 19.
[2] Wilhelm and Scannell, *Manual of Catholic Theology*, i. 494.

outspread wings made heavenly festival, each with his own distinct 'glow and art,' since each was a species by himself.[1] Mary made answer to their joy and songs by a smile whose beauty was gladness in the eyes of all the other saints. Powerless to tell the smallest part of her delightsomeness, Dante can only gaze; and Bernard, seeing his eyes fixed on her, turned his own eyes on her beauty with so much of love that he made him more ardent to behold her.

This is the very poetry of adoration, and it may seem to sin against it to attempt to fill it with definite meaning. If so, we sin in the good company of Bernard himself. These last three Cantos overflow with his burning devotion to the Virgin, and almost every phrase is an echo of something in his works. While still at school he had a vision of the Virgin. To her he dedicated all his monasteries. When writing his homilies on the Song of Songs, in which he sets forth the Virgin as the Spouse, the type of the Church on earth, the legend is that she appeared to him and, by moistening his lips with milk from her breast, imparted to him his irresistible eloquence.[2] Her praises pervade his works, though he set his face strenuously against the doctrine of her Immaculate Conception, which had been adopted by the Church of Lyons[3] It

---

[1] See p. 460 f.

[2] Murillo in a famous picture treats what is obviously a figure of speech as literal fact. Filippino Lippi's more restrained treatment of the legend in the Badia in Florence is more generally known. See Mrs. Jameson's *Legends of the Monastic Orders*, 139-148.

[3] This famous controversy lasted from Bernard's day down to Dec. 8, 1854, when Pius IX. 'defined that the Blessed Virgin Mary was, in the first instant of her conception, by a singular grace and privilege granted by Almighty God, in view of the merits of Christ Jesus, the Saviour of the human race, preserved free from all stain of original sin' (Father Hunter, *Outlines of Dogmatic Theology*, ii. 547). In his letter to the Canons of Lyons Bernard strongly opposes the doctrine. He gives her every honour but this. She was sanctified in the womb, born holy, sinless in life, chosen of God, foretold of prophets, reverenced by Angels, exalted above their highest Orders, the instrument of salvation and restorer of the ages; but she shared at the moment of her conception in the original sin of the race. Aquinas and the Dominicans supported Bernard's view, chiefly on the ground that if she had no stain of original guilt she could enter Paradise without the sacrifice of Christ, which is impossible, if He is the Saviour of the whole race (*Summa*, iii. q. xxvii. a. 1). The other side was

is therefore impossible to understand fully these closing
Cantos without constant reference to his writings. In
his life and works, Bernard is always to the poet the
saint

> who drew beauty from Maria,
> As from the sun the morning star.[1]

The comparison of the Virgin to the dawn means
more, according to Bernard, than light. It is the
symbol of humility. After quoting Canticles vi. 10 :
' Who is she that looketh forth as the morning?'—or
in his words, ' Quae est ista quae ascendit sicut aurora
consurgens'—he says : ' Aurora is the end of night, and
the beginning of light. But night signifies the life of
the sinner, light the life of the just. Hence aurora,
which drives away the darkness and announces the
light,- rightly denotes humility ; for as the one divides
day and night, so the other divides the just and the
sinful. For from this, that is, from humility, every
just man begins, and thence proceeds. Whence also she
is called *aurora consurgens*, that the structure of the
virtues rising from humility may be reared on its
proper foundation.'[2] This figure of Mary as aurora is
one of the commonest in the mystical writers of those
times.[3] In Bernard's view the Virgin wears this

led by Duns Scotus, the 'Subtle Doctor' of the Franciscans (d. 1308),
whose view prevailed at last after six or seven centuries of controversy.
(For the general subject see Father Hunter's work above quoted, pp. 545-
566 ; Wilhelm and Scannell's *Manual*, ii. 215-218 ; and for the attitude of
Dante, who follows Bernard and Aquinas, Liddon's *Essays and Addresses*,
174-175 ; Moore's *Dante Studies*, 2nd series, 60-65. A full account of the
long controversy will be found in Lea's *History of the Inquisition*, iii.
596-612.)

[1] *Par.* xxxii. 107, 108.

[2] *De Diversis*, Serm. xci. 3.

[3] Bonaventura almost surpasses Bernard in the elaboration of this
figure of the dawn. Mary in herself is like *aurora* because she drives
away the night of guilt; because she brings in the growing light of the
sun of justice ; because of ' her happy place in glory,' to which is applied
mystically the words in Job xxxviii. 12 : ' Numquid ostendisti aurorae
locum suum?' On our behalf she is a mediator to God, peacemaker to
the Angels, our defender from demons, and the illuminator of our souls
(*Speculum Virginis*, Lectio xi.). Bonaventura goes so far as to write a
Psalter of the Virgin in imitation of the Psalms, in which he frequently
substitutes *Domina* for *Dominus* : e.g., ' Domina mea in te speravi ' ;

celestial glory of the dawn surpassing that of all other creatures because she excelled all in humility : 'she ascends entirely above the human race, she ascends even to the Angels, nay, even them also she transcends, and rises above every celestial creature.' It is for this reason Dante sees more than a thousand Angels joying in the sunlight of her face, and singing songs of praise.

The 'pacific oriflamme' of l. 127 may mean nothing more definite than that 'Mary is the banner under which the Church wins her victories,' to use the words of Hettinger. The oriflamme was the name of the ancient scarlet banner of the French kings, used by them for war; Mary is the oriflamme of peace. But when we remember that it is in front of this banner that Dante sees more than a thousand Angels, it is possible that the peace has some reference to them. We find, for example, that Bonaventura in his praise of 'our aurora Mary,' calls her our peacemaker to the Angels. This is drawn from the story of Jacob's wrestling with the Angel, which meant discord between God, Angels, and men : for man's sin was an offence to God, and therefore to all His creatures, especially to those nearest to Him. It was only in the dawn the discord was stilled — the Angel blessed Jacob in the *aurora*, and our *aurora* is Mary, who brought this blessing of peace. 'Assuredly then,' says Bonaventura, 'by the aurora, by Mary, men are made at peace with the Angels, whereby the choirs of Angels are made whole again'[1]—that is, their ranks, broken by the Angelic fall, filled up by human souls redeemed through the Virgin's Son. It is under this 'pacific oriflamme' that Dante sees here men and Angels reconciled and gathered together into the unity of the peace of God, in

---

'Confitebor tibi Domina in toto corde meo'; 'Ad te Domina levavi animam meam'; 'Miserere mei Domina,' etc. The *Te Deum* is similarly adapted: 'Te Matrem Dei laudamus, te Mariam Virginem profitemur'; and also the Athanasian Creed: 'Quicumque vult salvus esse, ante omnia opus est ut teneat de Maria firmam fidem.'

[1] See the reference in the preceding note to Bonaventura's *Speculum Virginis*.

that world where all spirits find in Him their eternal
rest.[1]

[1] The interpretation of the 'oriflamme'—the *aurea flamma* or golden
flame—as the Virgin's throne between the gold and the flame, has no
foundation in Dante's words. Plumptre applies the word to the saints
surrounding the Virgin. This is a misunderstanding. Mary herself is
the oriflamme, and she is called 'pacific' because through her was
brought about that peace between God, Angels, and men which Dante
sees in the White Rose and its blessed interchange of love between the
three. If any one thinks the above interpretations too theological and
detailed, let him remember that just such passages as I have quoted from
Bernard and Bonaventura were familiar as household words to Dante's
mind, and that nothing is more characteristic of him than to condense in
one pregnant phrase or figure a whole train of thought from some
favourite theologian.

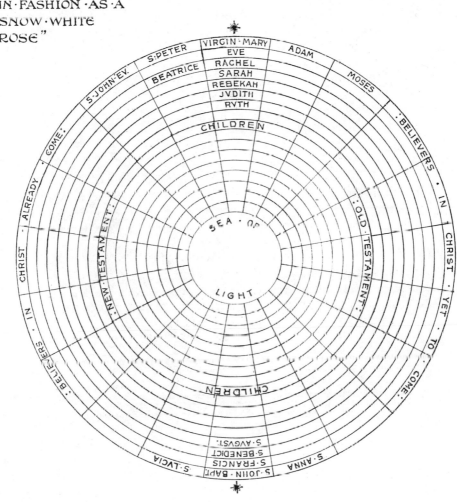

"IN·FASHION·AS·A
SNOW·WHITE
ROSE"

CHAPTER XXX

3. *The Plan of the White Rose*

ST. BERNARD, assuming now the 'free office of a teacher,' explains the plan of the mystic Rose. On one side it is divided vertically by a line of Hebrew women, beginning from Mary at the summit. Facing these on the opposite side, is a corresponding line of Christian men from John the Baptist downward. These lines divide the Flower into two equal portions: on Mary's left hand sit the Old Testament saints who believed on Christ before He came, and here every seat is filled; on her right hand are the New Testament believers, with a few seats still vacant. By 'the high Providence Divine,' the numbers on each side of the Garden are to be exactly equal.[1]

This vertical division is crossed by a horizontal one.[2] Midway down the Rose begin the ranks of the little children—babes who were 'hastened to the true life' before they were able to exercise 'true choices,' the freedom of their wills. As these ranks stretch down to the base, Dante apparently wishes us to understand that adults and children are in equal numbers.

So far as I am aware, there is no theological authority

---

[1] Sir Thomas Browne in his *Religio Medici* (i. 9) thinks the faith of O.T. saints surpasses ours, since we have history, while they had only prophetic signs: 'Nor is this much to believe; as we have reason, we owe this faith unto history: they only had the advantage of a bold and noble faith, who lived before his coming, who upon obscure prophecies and mystical types could raise a belief, and expect apparent impossibilities.' Dante, however, sets O.T. believers on Mary's left hand, the place of inferior honour.

[2] It is not likely to be accidental that the Rose is thus blessed with the sign of the Cross on each side.

for this arrangement and proportion of the souls redeemed.   It is probably due to the poet's passionate
love of unity: the very symmetry seemed to his mind
to make the unity more vivid.   The balance of equality
in number of souls from times before and after Christ,
and of adults and children, gave a new wonder and
glory to the Divine predestination which foresaw and
wrought with such exactness.   Further, as we saw in
the case of Bernard himself, Dante appears to ignore
the doctrine of Aquinas that in the Resurrection the
saints will rise at the age of thirty.   Bernard, himself
an old man, draws his attention to the child faces and
voices of the lower ranks.[1]   Each soul, apparently,
wears the form proper to the age it had attained on
earth, freed of course from weakness and defect of the
flesh.   Dante evidently felt that there would have been
something incongruous in making babes, who had never
exercised true choice, appear full-grown in the flower
of life.[2]   It is probably this absence of choice which
relegates them to the lower half of the Rose : the higher
ranks can be attained only when free will has had full
play and made its election of eternal life.   We may
compare their blessedness with the state of the unbaptized children whom his faith compelled Dante to
place in Limbo.   The latter, according to Aquinas, being
incapable of the vision of God, no more grieve for its
loss than does a wise man that he cannot fly as a bird ;
but they have a certain enjoyment of God by natural
knowledge and love.[3]   In the case of redeemed children,
then, we may suppose that this natural knowledge and
love will be raised to a certain supernatural power,
limited in some way by the immaturity of their wills.

Of the long line of Hebrew women forming the
division on one side, only seven are named : Mary, Eve,
Rachel (beside whom sits Beatrice, as near the Virgin
as Dante can place her), Sarah, Rebekah, Judith, Ruth.

---

[1] *Par*. xxxii. 46-48.

[2] Augustine thought otherwise : infants would receive 'by the marvellous and rapid operation of God that body which time by a slower process
would have given them' (*De Civ. Dei*, xxii. 14).

[3] *Summa*, App. q. i. a. 2.

As we shall see, they were all regarded as types of the
Church, and they are for the most part ancestresses of
Christ according to the flesh:[1] Ruth, for example, is
described as the *bisava*, the great grandmother, of
David, for the purpose, apparently, of indicating the
descent of the Virgin, and therefore of her Son, from
that king.[2] Chronological order is not observed: Rachel,
as at once the type of the Contemplative Life and of
Mary, sits nearer the Virgin than Sarah and Rebekah.
One point cannot be without meaning, although it is
passed over by the commentators—the fact that on
this side of the Rose it is *women* who constitute the
dividing line. St. Matthew and St. Luke trace the genealogy of our Lord chiefly through the fathers; it cannot
be without purpose that Dante, in so far as he traces
it at all, does so through the mothers. The entire line
of Hebrew women is simply his way of formally re-
instating woman in that Divine grace which through
a woman had been lost. It was a familiar thought in
mediæval theology. Anselm writes: 'It is most suitable that just as man's sin and the cause of our condemnation had its origin in a woman, so the medicine
for sin and the cause of our salvation should be born
of a woman. And lest women should despair of having
a share in the lot of the blessed, since so great evil
proceeded from a woman, it is fitting that for the
restoring of their hopes, so great good should proceed
from a woman.'[3] In a more impassioned strain
Bernard cries: 'Rejoice, father Adam, but more thou,

[1] Rachel and Judith alone are not in the direct line of our Lord's
ancestry. Judah, through whom the descent flows, was a son of Leah;
and Judith had no children (Jud. xvi. 22).

[2] The manner in which David is referred to—'the singer who for sorrow
of his sin said *Miserere mei*' (ll. 11, 12; Ps. li. 1)—while apparently
irrelevant to the question of descent, is in reality closely connected with
it. Matt. i. 6 states plainly that 'David the king begat Solomon of her
that had been the wife of Urias.' The reference therefore to David's
repentance for his great sin, so far from being irrelevant, suggests in the
most delicate way the continuation of the descent through Solomon. St.
Bernard lays stress on the *nobility* of the Virgin's descent. She is
crowned with the twelve stars of Rev. xii. 1, partly because something
starry shines through her generation—sprung from kings, of the seed of
Abraham, of the noble stock of David (Sermon on the Assumption).

[3] *Cur Deus Homo?* Bk. II. 8 (Prout's trans.).

O mother Eve, exult, who as ye have been parents of all, so have been destroyers of all; and, what is more miserable, destroyers before parents. Be consoled, both of you, I say, over a daughter, and such a daughter; but especially she from whom evil first sprang, whose reproach has passed forth to all women. . . . For this cause run, Eve, to Mary; run, mother, to the daughter; let the daughter answer for the mother, herself bear away the mother's reproach, herself make satisfaction to the father for the mother: for, behold, if man fell through a woman, now he is not raised save through a woman.'[1]

These quotations lead us directly to that antithesis between Mary and Eve which runs from Irenæus downward, and which is obviously Dante's reason for seating Eve at the Virgin's feet:

> 'The wound which Mary closed up and anointed,
> That one who is so beauteous at her feet,
> She it is who opened it and pierced it.'[2]

As Irenæus is the source of this famous antithesis, it may be of interest to quote the passage. After pointing out that before the Fall Eve was virgin as well as Mary, he proceeds: 'Just as the former was led astray by the word of an angel, so that she fled from God when she had transgressed His word; so did the latter, by an angelic communication, receive the glad tidings that she should sustain God, being obedient to His word. And if the former did disobey God, yet the latter was persuaded to be obedient to God, in order

---

[1] *De Laudibus Virginis Matris*, Hom. ii. 3. Bernard proceeds to rebuke Adam for the blame which he cast on Eve (Gen. iii. 12): through Mary the reproach against woman is rolled away.

[2] *Par.* xxxii. 4-6. The closing of the wound takes place in Mary's obedience and humility by which the Incarnation became possible. The anointing is with the 'unguent of pity': see note on p. 518 below. 'Opened it' refers to Eve's own act of disobedience; 'pierced it,' to her successful temptation of Adam by which she drove the wound of sin deep into him and all the race. According to Aquinas, if Eve alone had fallen, original sin, which is transmitted only through the father, would not have descended to posterity, nor would they have been subject to suffering and death (*Summa*, i. q. xcvii. a. 1, 2; i.-ii. q. lxxxi. a. 5). Eve is *tanto bella* (l. 5) because created by the immediate hand of God (*Summa*, i. q. xcii. a. 4).

that the Virgin Mary might become the patroness
(*advocata*) of the virgin Eve.   And thus, as the human
race fell into bondage to death by means of a virgin,
so is it rescued by a virgin; virginal disobedience
having been balanced in the opposite scale by virginal
obedience.'[1] The echo of this antithesis goes down the
ages with endless reverberations. St. Bernard, after
calling Mary a mediator, goes on: ' A cruel mediatrix
indeed was Eve, by whom the ancient serpent infused
his pestilential poison into the man himself: but
faithful is Mary, who to both men and women gave
to drink the antidote of salvation. For the former is
the ministress of seduction ; the latter, of propitiation :
the former prompted transgression ; the latter brought
in redemption.'[2] It might be thought that an antithesis
so unfavourable to Eve ought to exclude her from
salvation; but there were elements in the story of
Genesis which seemed to set her in a higher light.
Her origin from man constitutes her a type of the
Church which has its origin in Christ. The drawing
of her from Adam's side during sleep was regarded as
a figure of the blood and water which flowed from
Christ's side when He was asleep upon the cross, blood
and water being the sacraments by which the Church
is instituted.[3] Finally, she was in one sense a type of
Mary in that she also is a progenitrix of Christ ; though
the promise that the Seed of the woman should crush
the serpent's head could be fulfilled, according to the
Church's faith, only in a Virgin mother. For these
reasons, she who caused the wound of the human race
is seated at the feet of her who healed it, shining with
more than the beauty in which she left her Maker's

---

[1] *Against Heresies*, Bk. v. 19 (Ante-Nicene Library trans.). Compare
the echo in Tertullian (*On the Flesh of Christ*, xvii.): ' It was while Eve
was yet a virgin, that the ensnaring word had crept into her ear which
was to build the edifice of death. Into a virgin's soul, in like manner,
must be introduced that Word of God which was to raise the fabric of
life; so that what had been reduced to ruin by this sex, might by the self-
same sex be recovered to salvation. As Eve had believed the serpent,
so Mary believed Gabriel. The delinquency which the one occasioned
by believing, the other by believing effaced.'
[2] Sermon on the Assumption.   [3] *Summa*, i. q. xcii. a. 2, 3.

hand.[1] Rachel, as we have seen, is the symbol of Contemplation, and this is doubtless why she is set in the third rank, and above Sarah and Rebekah. The place of Beatrice beside her is probably connected with the number three, which in the *Vita Nuova* Dante mystically associates with her: 'this Lady was accompanied by the number nine to the end that men might clearly perceive her to be a nine, that is, a miracle, whose only root is the Holy Trinity'[2]— the great object of contemplation. Sarah, the freewoman, represents the Church repelling the son of Hagar the bondwoman—souls in slavery to sin—that her own freeborn children may be heirs of salvation, citizens of the Jerusalem above, 'which is the mother of us all.'[3] 'Rebekah is the type of the Church, chosen among the Gentiles to become the Spouse of Christ': in the continuation of the symbolism, Abraham represents God the Father; Isaac, Jesus Christ; Eliezer, the Apostles and all workers in the Gospel—so easily did the details lend themselves to allegory.[4] Judith stands for the Active Life, and specially for the Church Militant: her slaughter of Holofernes and rout of his

---

[1] On the general subject of the position which the Church gives the Virgin, see Father Hunter's *Outlines of Dogmatic Theology*, ii. pp. 545-587; Wilhelm and Scannell, *Manual of Cath. Theology*, ii. pp. 208-224; and, from the Protestant standpoint, Harnack's *History of Dogma*, vi. pp. 312-317 (Eng. Trans.). The antithesis between the first Eve and the second—for so Mary was named—is condensed in the reversal of *Eva* into the *Ave* of the Angel's salutation, as in the *Ave Maris Stella* hymn:

> Sumens illud Ave
> Gabrielis ore,
> Funda nos in pace
> Mutans Evae nomen.

Compare also Bonaventura's verse in his *Carmen* on the *Salve Regina*:

> Evae lapsus intulit damnum desperatum.
> Et a nobis abstulit gaudium beatum.
> Et post Evam contulit Virgini incarnatum.
> Quo modo mortem sustulit, diluit peccatum.

[2] *Vita Nuova*, § xxx.   [3] Gal. iv. 22-31.
[4] *Cathédrale d'Amiens*, p. 109, quoted in Mrs. Jameson's *History of our Lord*, i. 146. It is possible that Sarah and Rebekah are below Rachel, not as types but as women, because the former laughed at God's promise, and the latter helped Jacob to deceive his father.

host, representing the destruction of the enemies of the Faith. Ruth, like Rebekah, is a type of the Gentile Church becoming the Spouse of Christ; as a woman she is an ancestress of our Lord, thus weaving into His genealogy another strand of the Gentile world.

Of the line of Christian men dividing the Rose vertically on the opposite side, only four are named, John the Baptist, St. Francis, St. Benedict, and St. Augustine: it is possible that Bernard, in his humility, stops at this point because his own seat was next. The Baptist holds the highest place because of our Lord's words in Matt. xi. 11: as the greatest born of women he is counted worthy to sit in the seat opposite her who was blessed among women. His holy life in the desert, his martyrdom, and even, apparently, his endurance of Limbo for two years, constitute his claim to this loftiest throne. As the forerunner of Christ, he began the work of preparing the world for Him, which was carried on by the line of saints seated beneath him.[1] St. Francis holds the next rank as the saint who bore in his body 'the marks of the Lord Jesus,' who most nearly lived Christ's life over again, and who called the Church from the grave of sin and worldliness in which she lay, and inspired her with a new life.[2] In the third seat sits St. Benedict, 'The great contemplative monk,' to quote Mr. Gardner, 'is thus fitly placed opposite to Rachel, the type of contemplation itself.' Dante's desire to see him in his own proper form is now at last fulfilled.[3] The fourth seat is occupied by St. Augustine, either as the greatest theologian of the four Latin Fathers, or as the supposed founder of the Order that goes by his name. This line of Christian saints, as Hettinger says, 'bore Christ

---

[1] We may remind ourselves that the Baptist was the patron saint of Florence, as Lucia, on his left hand, was of Dante himself, and that it was in the Baptistery, *il mio bel San Giovanni* (*Inf.* xix. 17), that the poet's ancestors (*Par.* xv. 134, 135) and himself (*Par.* xxv. 8, 9), 'became Christian'—i.e. received that 'perfect baptism of Christ' without which they could not have entered Paradise.

[2] As we saw above (p. 201), the Franciscans gave their saint a still higher place—the throne from which Lucifer fell through pride.

[3] *Par.* xxii. 58-63. See above, p. 351 f.

spiritually, as the line of Hebrew women bore Him in the flesh.'[1]

Turning now to the ranks of the children, St. Bernard assures Dante that, since no 'point of chance' exists in this world of order, their places are fixed by the 'eternal law' of the good pleasure of the King. He does not pretend to explain it—'here let the effect suffice.' It is part of that mystery of predestination which 'the Seraph who hath his eye most fixed on God' cannot fathom. The fact of it is proved in Scripture by the twins whose anger was stirred within their mother's womb. This reference to Jacob and Esau seems to have suggested the peculiar form in which Bernard proceeds to state the different effects of the different degrees of grace in the appearance of these happy children:

> 'Therefore, according to the colour of the hair
> Of such a grace, 'tis fitting that the Most High Light
> Should garland them according to their worth.'[2]

The idea seems to be that as Jacob and Esau differed in complexion—one dark, the other red—by the mysterious decree of their Maker, and as this difference had its correspondence in their natures, so even here in Heaven the same mystery of predestination shows itself 'in the colour of the hair of such grace,' to use the poet's somewhat forced metaphor—the different degrees of light with which the different degrees of grace encircled the heads of the children as with crowns. Since they are here by no merit of their own —for merit comes only through the exercise of the will, which their age had made impossible—there is nothing

---

[1] *Dante's Divina Commedia*, p. 224. One of the most perplexing things about this line of Christian saints is the absence from it of the Apostle Paul. By every claim of right—character, work, martyrdom—he ought to have come immediately after the Baptist. Yet he is not mentioned even among 'the grand patricians' of the celestial Empire. In fact, we never meet him personally in the whole course of the poem. He is often quoted in Dante's works; referred to in all possible reverence; and is even seen for a moment in the Procession of writers of Scripture, not *in propria persona*, but as representing his Epistles (*Purg.* xxix. 134-141). But we never meet him as we do Aquinas or Bonaventura, Peter, James, John. It is difficult to forgive Dante this omission. Some of the symbolic and monastic shades might well have been spared for one look and word of the great Apostle of the Gentiles. He is worth a wilderness of Peter Damians, Romoaldos and Macarii.　　　　[2] *Par.* xxxii. 70-72.

to decide their rank and order in the Flower but 'the primal keenness' of their nature, which has its source only in the mystery of the Divine Will.[1]

Let us now look at the 'fixed conditions' under which they hold their seats. The most general condition is that, since Heaven is the reward of merit, and since they have none of their own, their salvation is due to 'the merit of another.'[2] Who 'another' is, has been made subject of dispute; but the teaching of the Church encourages us to give it a wide interpretation. Beneath everything, as foundation, are the merits of Christ, without which salvation is impossible for old or young. On this basis rise human merits—those of the parents, or, failing these, of the Church. 'Of what importance is it,' asks Bernard, 'that an infant is not able to speak for himself, while the voice of the Blood of his Brother, and of a Brother so great and prevailing, cries to God from the ground for him? The Church, which is his Mother, arises and lifts up her voice on his behalf also. . . . Let no one object to me that a child has not faith, for its Mother communicates to it her own, wraps it in this faith, so to speak, as in a cloak, in the Sacrament of Baptism, which she bestows upon it; so that it becomes worthy to receive and to develop that faith in its purity, if not by its own active powers, yet with its passive assent. Is it not a short and narrow cloak which cannot cover two? The faith of the Church is great. Surely it is not less than the faith of the Canaanitish woman, which we know was sufficient both for her daughter and herself.'[3]

---

[1] *Par.* xxxii. 52-75; Gen. xxv. 22-27; Rom. ix. 10-14.

[2] *Par.* xxxii. 40-45.

[3] Song of Songs, Serm. lxvi. 9, 10 (Eales). Comp. St. Augustine: 'Mother Church lends to children the feet of others, that they may come; the heart of others, that they may believe; the tongue of others, that they may confess'; and thus, adds Aquinas, 'children believe not by their own proper act, but through the faith of the Church, which is communicated to them; and by virtue of this faith grace and virtues are conferred upon them' (*Summa*, iii. q. lxix. a. 6). We must remember that the Church includes the Church Triumphant, whose merits supply anything that may be lacking in the Church Militant. For other references in St. Bernard, see *De Diversis*, Serm. xxviii. 2; *In Dominica Palmarum*, Serm. i. 3; *Tractatus de Baptismo*, ii. 9.

The special conditions vary according to the age of the world. In the earliest times, from Adam to Abraham, the faith of the parents alone, with the children's own innocence, was sufficient for salvation— the faith being specially faith in the Christ who was to come.[1] From Abraham to Christ, a second condition was added to the parents' faith—for that of course remained as necessary as before—namely, circumcision:

> 'After that the first ages were completed,
> 'Twas fitting that the males by circumcision
> Acquire virtue for their innocent wings.'

The necessity of circumcision arose from the fact that Abraham was the first to receive the promise of the Christ to come, and circumcision was instituted as a sign of that faith and of the separation from the heathen which it involved. It was preparatory to baptism, and was confined to males, according to Aquinas, because 'original sin, against which circumcision was specially ordained, is drawn from the father, not from the mother.'[2] From the time of Christ the third and final condition is baptism:

> 'But after that the time of grace was come,
> Without the perfect baptism of Christ
> Such innocence was held back there below'—

that is, in Limbo.[3] It is called 'perfect baptism' in contrast with circumcision, which is in type what baptism is in reality. The grace conferred in circumcision is in virtue of faith in the passion of Christ, of which it is but the sign; whereas that conferred in baptism is in virtue of the baptism itself, which is the instrument of the passion now accomplished. Hence baptism contains in itself the perfection of salvation, whereas circumcision is only a figure of it yet to be fulfilled.[4] It is strange to find a more severe attitude towards unbaptized children attributed to Bernard than he appears to take up in his own writings. In

---

[1] *Summa*, iii. q. lxx. a. 4: 'Before the institution of circumcision faith alone in Christ to come justified both children and adults.'
[2] *Summa*, i-ii. q. lxxxi. a. 5; iii. q. lxx. a. 2.
[3] *Par.* xxxii. 76-84; *Inf.* iv. 28-42.   [4] *Summa*, iii. q. lxx. a. 4.

his *De Baptismo* (i. 4; ii. 6) he suggests a hope that the faith of their parents may supply the lack of the sacrament. Perhaps Dante means to indicate that the saint now sees that such a hope was vain. He held to the strict doctrine of the Church that baptism is absolutely necessary for salvation; and while our sympathies are with St. Bernard's hope, we must remember, as already said, that in Dante's view the children in Limbo suffered no pain of sense and enjoyed the love and knowledge of God up to the measure of their natural powers.[1]

His teacher now directs Dante's eyes to their final preparation for the vision of God—the Virgin's face:

> 'Look now into the face that unto Christ
> Hath most resemblance; for its brightness only
> Is able to prepare thee to see Christ.'[2]

The leading thought is, of course, the spiritual likeness of the Virgin to her Son. 'Under Christ,' says Aquinas, 'who needed no salvation, seeing He is the universal Saviour, the greatest purity was that of the Blessed Virgin.'[3] But the corporeal resemblance must not be entirely excluded. It is the Virgin's glorified body that Dante sees. As the Son of a Virgin, Christ could derive his human lineaments from no other than herself. 'All the old legends assume that the resemblance between the Son and the Mother must have been perfect. The accepted type of the head of Christ [in Art] was to be taken as a model in its mild,

---

[1] See above, p. 500. St. Augustine's view is much harsher. Unbaptized infants suffer the eternal fire, though their pain is much less than that of those who die in mortal sin (Serm. 294; *De Peccal. Meritis et Remiss.* i. 20). One result of this Augustinian severity was that the administration of the sacrament could not be confined to priests. If no priest was available, was an innocent babe to go to eternal fire for lack of the saving rite? 'Since God wills all men to be saved, and has ordained baptism as a necessary means of salvation, it follows that this means should be at the ready disposal of all. Hence our Lord chose the common element water, and gave every human being, whether priest or layman, man or woman, Christian or pagan, the power of conferring valid baptism' (Wilhelm and Scannell's *Manual*, ii. 388. See also Harnack's *History of Dogma*, vi. 227-230; Cunningham's *The Growth of the Church*, 184-194).

[2] *Par.* xxxii. 85-87. Note in this *terzina* and the preceding the threefold rhyming of 'Christo' with itself.

[3] *Summa*, iii. q. xxvii. a. 2.

intellectual majesty, for that of the Virgin-mother, as far as difference of sex would allow.'[1] Since the brightness of the glorified body is the effluence of the inward purity of the soul, the two resemblances, corporeal and spiritual, blended into one another in the brightness of the Virgin to which Dante now lifted his eyes. Such joy rained down on her face through 'the holy minds,' the flying Angels, that all his previous vision, great and marvellous as it was, had not showed him 'so great a likeness of God.'

It is to be noted that there is a threefold vision of Mary, as there is of her Son; and the three form an ascending scale of glory. In Canto xxiii. she appears as one of the saints in her Son's Triumph, the most glorious fruit of His Passion, the Rose Divine in

'the garden beautiful
Which 'neath the rays of Christ enflowers itself'; [2]

for, as we saw, even the Virgin is saved by the merits of her Son. This first vision, therefore, shows her in her relation to Christ as her Saviour. The second (xxxi. 97 ff.) reveals her as *Regina Coeli*,

'the Queen
To whom this realm is subject and devoted.'

Here, therefore, we see her in her relation to saints and Angels, the crown of the entire spiritual creation. The third and crowning vision, to which Dante is now called, shows her in her relation to the Godhead. Through her the vision of the Trinity is given; and her face prepares for the final mystery of the union of the Divine and human in Christ.

---

[1] Mrs. Jameson, *Legends of the Madonna*, Intro. xli. Two views prevailed as to our Lord's likeness. The earliest, following such texts as Isa. lii. 14; liii. 2, 3, regarded Him as having no comeliness. That which prevailed in Dante's time was based on Ps. xlv. 2, 'Thou art fairer than the children of men,' from which sprang up the type of face now generally accepted. See Farrar's *Christ in Art*, 67-95, and 'History of the Portraits of the Son of God' in Didron's *Christian Iconography*, i. 242-278. Farrar (p. 85) quotes Epiphanius Monachus: 'His face resembled His mother's, and was slightly flushed, indicating dignity, wisdom, and unruffled gentleness. In all respects He reflected closely the semblance of His mother.' See also *Rex Regum*, by Sir Wyke Bayliss.

[2] *Par.* xxiii. 70-129. See above, pp. 372-378.

In front of the Queen of Heaven Dante sees the
Angel Gabriel with outspread wings, as when he
'brought the palm down to Mary' in Nazareth, and
glowing like a fire with love of her.   '*Ave Maria,
gratia plena*' is still his song, and all the blessed Court
responds.   St. Bernard tells Dante who he is :

> ' Boldness and gracefulness
> Much as can be in Angel and in soul,
> All is in him, and we would have it so ;
> Because he is the one who bore the palm
> Down unto Mary, when the Son of God
> Did will to load Him with our burden.' [1]

This is apparently a reference to a passage in St.
Bernard's *De Laudibus Virginis Matris* (Hom. i. 2).   The
'boldness' attributed to Gabriel refers to the meaning
of his name : 'Fortitudo Dei,' according to Bernard,
who infers from it that he was not one of the inferior
Angels sent, as is customary, by an Angel of higher
rank, but directly by God Himself.[2]   His name, which
implies power, is appropriate to one sent to announce
the coming of Him who is called ' the power of God.' [3]
All the saints rejoice in the courage and grace of
Gabriel because his annunciation ' brought down the
palm to Mary'—the symbol of this high Triumph of
Paradise, in the victory and glory of which they all
partake.[4]

[1] *Par.* xxxii. 109-114.

[2] Luke i. 26. 'The angel Gabriel was sent *from God*.' Bernard lays
emphasis on the words italicized as proof of the greatness of the
messenger and the importance of his errand.

[3] 1 Cor. i. 24. 'Christ, the power of God.' Compare St. Gregory : ' This
name (Gabriel) befits his office. For Gabriel is named "the fortitude of
God." Therefore by the fortitude of God He was announced who was
coming as the Lord of hosts (virtutum Dominus) and mighty in battle to
the casting down of the powers of the air' (quoted in *Summa*, iii. q. xxx.
a. 2).

[4] ' In general, the palm is given to the angel who announces the death
of Mary. In one or two instances only, I have seen the palm given to the
angel Gabriel, as in a predella by Angelico ; for which, however, the
painter had the authority of Dante, or Dante some authority earlier still'
(Mrs. Jameson, *Legends of the Madonna*, p. 180). Vernon is mistaken in
saying that in most of the representations of the Annunciation Gabriel
bears a palm. Sometimes he has a lily, a sceptre, a cross, an olive-branch,
and sometimes nothing at all. It is difficult to translate *leggiadria* in l.
109, but the dainty grace of Fra Angelico's Angel of the Annunciation
seems to me to convey the idea.

At this point Bernard directs Dante's eyes to

> 'the great patricians
> Of this most just and pious Empire,'

of which the Virgin is 'Augusta.' On the right hand
and the left, sit the 'two roots of the Rose'—spiritual
and natural—Peter and Adam. It is to be noted that
Adam is thus seated a rank higher than Eve, probably
in accordance with the view of Aquinas that his was
the lighter sin.[1] Beside Peter and Adam respectively
sit John and Moses, both described by the tribulation
they endured—John through his vision of the persecutions of the Church, Moses through the ingratitude
and rebellion of ancient Israel. On the opposite side
of the Rose, facing St. Peter, and therefore on the
Baptist's right, Anna, the mother of the Virgin, gazed
on her daughter so intently that she turned not away
her eyes even for the singing of *Hosanna*. On the
Baptist's other hand and opposite Adam was St. Lucia,
who moved Beatrice to go to Dante's help when he
was about to rush downhill from the terror of the She-
wolf. Her name brings us back to 'the three blessed
Ladies,' whose gracious help was the origin of Dante's
salvation.[2] The first movement began in Mary's pity
for his perilous state: she is therefore prevenient
grace, which does not wait for the sinner's will to
move towards goodness, but creates the motion.[3]
Mary called Lucia on the opposite side of the Rose to

---

[1] *Summa*, ii-ii. q. clxiii. a. 4.

[2] *Inf.* i. 49-61; ii. 49-126. In this last passage Mary is described as she
'who breaks the hard judgment there above'; and Lucia as 'the enemy
of all cruelty' (*Inf.* ii. 96; 100). Cruelty, according to Aquinas (*Summa*,
ii-ii. q. clix. a. 1), is excessive sternness in the exaction of penalties; and
since its opposite is clemency, Lucia may stand for that virtue. This does
not take away her symbolism as illuminative grace, since it is just the
light of grace which teaches clemency. The idea under it all seems to be
that Dante, when driven back by the three beasts in the savage wood, was
being punished beyond his deserving; and Lucia, the foe of such cruelty,
is sent by Mary, who breaks the sternness of Heaven's judgment, in pity
for the severity of his suffering.

[3] 'It is called *prevenient* grace, because it is not from free will, but is
infused by God Himself. But it is called *subsequent*, or co-operating
grace, in so far as it aids free will in respect to the eliciting of good works'
(Bonaventura, *Centiloquium*, iii. 35). See above, p. 470 n.

help her 'faithful one'—she being probably Dante's patron saint. From her name she stands for the illuminating grace of God, for which reason, perhaps, she is seated opposite 'the eldest Father of a household,' through whose sin grace was lost to all his race. So low, however, had Dante sunk in the darkness of evil, that illuminating grace could not impart the Divine light directly: Lucia has recourse to Beatrice, the symbol of Theology, and Beatrice in turn to Virgil, who stands for the natural Reason. From that comparatively low point, Dante has to work his way through Hell and Purgatory and Paradise into the knowledge of all that the three blessed Ladies represent. Nothing now remains but that she from whom the entire movement of his salvation had its beginning, should crown her work by that final gift of grace which would make his eyes strong to bear the vision of the Eternal Light.

From 'the great patricians of this most just and pious Empire,' and the application of the title 'Augusta' to the Virgin, Mr. Gardner draws the interesting significance that Dante wishes to make Mary the ideal of the Empire, as she is already of the Church. This Rose of Paradise is 'that Rome of which Christ is Roman'; and since the earthly Rome is the seat of both Church and Empire, it is natural to find the ideal of both in one whose kingdom is, in the poet's thought, the fruit of both. 'Perhaps, therefore, in this celestial Rome of eternal felicity and harmony, Dante would see in its most glorious Queen two types united, the Church and the Empire, the two ideals of his religious and political faith figured in Her who had taken pity upon him as he wandered lost and guideless in the dark wood, and who has been described by an illustrious Dante scholar as *la motrice di tutta la visione Dantesca*.'[1]

[1] *Dante's Ten Heavens*, 244-246. In support of this interpretation Mr. Gardner quotes the striking passage in *Conv.* iv. 5 (part of which will be found on p. 306 above) in which Dante aims at proving the Divine election of Rome as the seat of the Empire by the founding of the city being contemporaneous with the birth of David, from whom the Virgin sprang.

CHAPTER XXXI

TENTH HEAVEN—THE EMPYREAN : GOD

4. St. Bernard's Prayer to the Virgin

THE time for the breaking of the dream draws near. St. Bernard therefore urges Dante to lift up his eyes to ' the First Love '; and, that he may not look in vain, acts as his intercessor with Mary—' one who has power to aid thee '—for the grace necessary for the final vision.[1] The prayer to the Virgin which follows is one of the great passages of the *Commedia*, of surpassing beauty even to those who may be unable to give her the same intensity of devotion and veneration which breathes like a sweet odour through the lines. It falls into two parts—the praise of the Virgin (ll. 1-21); and the intercession for Dante (ll. 22-39). While Mr. Gardner is right in saying that the simple affection of the heart is a better interpreter of the prayer than ' the cold light of dogma,' it is to be remembered that with St. Bernard the light of dogma is never cold. When he speaks of Mary, his words glow and burn with the heart's own fire; and while I shall not interrupt the beauty and

---

[1] *Par.* xxxii. 139-151. There is something incongruous in Bernard's quotation in this lofty connection of the proverb of the tailor cutting the gown according to the cloth; but it is probably an echo of something in the writings of a saint who united the highest contemplation with the homeliest duties. Of the word *assonna* in l. 139 (' the time which *holds thee in sleep* ') Butler says that this is, so far as he is aware, ' the only instance in which Dante uses any phrase which would imply that what he has seen is of the nature of a dream.' May the meaning not be, however, that all he has seen up to this time is as a dream in sleep, and that now he is about to awake to the eternal reality of which it was but the shadow—the First Love Himself? For comparison of ecstasy to a sleep, and even to death—' the death which belongs to Angels '—see St. Bernard's *Cantica Canticorum*, Serm. lii. Cant. v. 2, ' I sleep, but my heart waketh,' was commonly taken to signify the state of contemplation.

devotion with comments, it may be of interest to give
in the footnotes parallel passages from the Saint's own
writings, in order to see how faithfully the poet reproduces his spirit. As an introduction, and to show the
power which Bernard believed Mary to possess, I may
quote the prayer with which he closes his second
sermon on the Advent: 'Let us also strive, most
beloved, to ascend through her to Him who through
her descended to us; through her to come into the
grace of Him who through her came into our misery.
Through thee may we have access to the Son, O blessed
finder of grace, author of life, mother of salvation[1]:
that through thee He may receive us, who through
thee was given to us. May thy integrity excuse before
Him the guilt of our corruption, and thy humility, pleasing to God, obtain the pardon of our vanity. May thy
abundant charity cover the multitude of our sins, and
thy glorious fecundity confer upon us fecundity of
merits. Our Lady, our Mediatrix, our Advocate,[2] reconcile us to thy Son, commend us to thy Son, represent us to thy Son. Obtain, O blessed one, by the
grace which thou hast found, by the prerogative which
thou hast merited, by the mercy which thou hast

---

[1] 'O benedicta inventrix gratiae, genetrix vitae, mater salutis.'
[2] 'Domina nostra, mediatrix nostra, advocata nostra.' It is to be remembered, of course, that the Church has no intention of setting the
mediation of Mary above that of Christ, or in any sense independent of
it. 'Evil, indeed, would this devotion be, if it diminished or obscured,
ever so little, that supreme devotion to God, who is over all, and to Jesus
Christ whom He has sent. But one who dared to put Mary on an
equality with God, or to deny that Christ is the "one mediator between
God and man"—i.e. the sole author of our redemption, the beginner and
the finisher of our faith—would, by that very fact, cease to be a Catholic'
(*Cath. Dictionary*, 607). Mary is a creature, though the highest, and is
herself dependent on the mediation of her Son for salvation. It is held,
however, that as she co-operated with Him in the work of Redemption
by consenting to become His mother, this co-operation is continued in
the distribution of His merits. Her position as mediatrix is therefore
that of the highest and holiest channel by which the benefits of His
salvation are conveyed to mankind. Apart from Him, there were no
benefits to convey. It is obvious that Dante had all this clearly before
his mind. Mary's position as one of the Redeemed in the Rose is proof.
He must have been familiar with the distinction of Aquinas between
latria, the worship due to God ; *dulia*, the veneration given to saints and
Angels ; and *hyperdulia*, the higher veneration given to Mary, as the
most exalted of creatures (*Summa*, ii-ii. q. ciii. a. 3, 4).

brought forth, that He who through thy mediation
deigned to become partaker of our infirmity and misery,
may also through thy intercession make us partakers
of His glory and blessedness, Jesus Christ, thy Son, our
Lord, who is over all God blessed for evermore. Amen.'
The position given to Mary in the poem shows that
Dante was in perfect sympathy with this prayer.
From her comes the first movement of his salvation in
the beginning of the *Inferno*; from her at the close of
the *Paradiso* comes the final grace by which his eyes
are strengthened to see God. She was his Lady, his
Mediatrix, his Advocate. I give Longfellow's rendering of the prayer he now puts in St. Bernard's lips:

> ' Thou Virgin Mother,¹ daughter of thy Son,²
> Humble and high beyond all other creature,³
> The limit fixed of the eternal counsel,⁴
> Thou art the one who such nobility
> To human nature gave, that its Creator
> Did not disdain to make Himself its creature.
> Within thy womb rekindled was the love,
> By heat of which in the eternal peace

---

¹ The virginity of Mary is an endless theme of wonder and praise with
Bernard. 'What tongue,' he asks, 'though it were that of an Angel,
could extol with worthy praises the Virgin Mother : mother not of
some one, but of God ? . . . What angelic purity may dare to be compared
to that virginity which was worthy to become the shrine of the Holy
Spirit and the habitation of the Son of God?' (*In Assumptione B.V.M.*,
Serm. iv.).

² Comp. Petrarch's prayer to the Virgin :

> ' Vergine pura, d'ogni parte intera,
>   Del tuo parto gentil figliuola e madre' ;

and Chaucer's rendering of ll. 1-21 in the *Second Nonne's Tale*.

³ Bernard regards humility as of greater value than even virginity :
'laudable is the virtue of virginity, but more necessary is humility. The
first is of counsel, the latter of precept. . . . Without humility (I dare to
say) the virginity of Mary had not been pleasing to God' (*De Laudibus
B.V.M.*, Hom. i). It was by humility she became the mother of the
Saviour : see *Purg.* x. 34-45. The perfect union of the two lifts her to the
supreme rank among creatures, human and Angelic (*In Nat. B.V.M.*).

⁴ The woman worthy to be the 'Mother of God' must have been elect
from the beginning. 'It was needful that the Maker of men, in order to
become man, should choose for Himself out of all, nay create, such a
mother as He knew to be worthy of Himself.' 'Not found recently or by
chance, but elect from eternity, foreknown and prepared for Himself by
the Most High, guarded by Angels, signified before by the patriarchs,
promised by the prophets.' The Scriptural proof of her election to this
great honour is Gen iii. 15, Prov. xxxi. 10, Is. xi. 1 (*De Laudibus Virginis*,
Hom. ii).

After such wise this flower has germinated.[1]
Here unto us thou art a noonday torch
Of charity,[2] and below there among mortals
Thou art the living fountain-head of hope.[3]
Lady, thou art so great, and so prevailing,
That he who wishes grace, nor runs to thee,
His aspirations without wings would fly.[4]
Not only thy benignity gives succour
To him who asketh it, but oftentimes
Forerunneth of its own accord the asking.[5]

---

[1] The 'love' of l. 7 probably refers to Luke i. 35: 'The Holy Ghost shall come upon thee'—love being the special attribute of the Spirit. The restoration of the 'supernal city' was attributed by Bernard to Mary: 'Through thee heaven is replenished, hell emptied, the ruins of the heavenly Jerusalem restored' (*In Assump. B.V.M.*, Serm. iv.). 'In thee the Angels evermore find joy, the just grace, sinners pardon. Rightly do the eyes of the whole creation look to thee, for in thee, and through thee, and for thee the bounteous hand of the Almighty has re-created what things soever He had created' (*In Festo Pentecostes*, Serm. ii.).

[2] In *Cant. Canticorum*, Serm. xxix. 8, Bernard uses another figure: 'There is also the elect arrow, the love of Christ, which not only pierced the soul of Mary, but transfixed it through and through, that it might leave no spot in that virgin breast empty of love, but that she should love with all the heart, and with all the soul, and with all the strength, and be full of grace. Or perhaps it transpierced her, that it might come even to us, and that of that fulness we might all receive, and that she might become the mother of charity, of which God who is charity is the Father, bringing forth and setting her tabernacle in the sun.'

[3] In his sermon *In Nativ. B.V.M.* Bernard calls Christ the fountain of living waters, and Mary the aqueduct by which the heavenly stream reaches us—an aqueduct whose summit, like the ladder which Jacob saw, touches the heavens, yea transcends the heavens, and reaches that most living fountain of the waters which are above the heavens. Dante seems almost to go beyond Bernard: Mary is more than the aqueduct, she is 'the living fountain' of the hope of glory.

[4] In this same sermon *De Aquaeductu*: 'Dost thou wish to have an Advocate with Christ? Fly to Mary. Without doubt the Son will hear the Mother, the Father will hear the Son. This is the ladder of sinners, this my greatest confidence, this the whole ground of my hope.' In Hom. ii. *De Laudibus Virg. Matris*, speaking of *Maria* as *Maris stella*, Bernard says: 'O thou, whoever thou be, who perceivest thyself to be tossed about in the flux and flow of this world among storms and tempests, rather than to walk on the earth: turn not away thine eyes from the shining of this star, if thou wish not to be overwhelmed by the storms. If winds of temptations arise, if thou run among rocks of tribulations, look to the star, call on Mary. If thou art tossed by waves of pride, of ambition, of detraction, of jealousy, look to the star, call on Mary,' etc. Elsewhere he says 'God wishes us to have nothing that does not pass through the hands of Mary.' God 'placed the plenitude of all good in Mary, that thus if there is anything of hope in us, if anything of grace, if anything of salvation, we might know that it redounds from her.'

[5] In *Conv.* i. 8 Dante quotes Seneca that 'nothing is bought so dear as that which is purchased with prayers': perfect liberality is to give without being asked, as the rose gives its fragrance (*Conv.* iv. 27; *Purg.*

In thee compassion is, in thee is pity,
In thee magnificence; in thee unites
Whate'er of goodness is in any creature.[1]
Now doth this man, who from the lowest depth
Of the universe as far as here hath seen
One after one the spiritual lives,[2]
Supplicate thee through grace for so much power
That with his eyes he may uplift himself
Higher towards the uttermost salvation.
And I, who never burned for my own seeing
More than I do for his, all of my prayers
Proffer to thee, and pray they come not short,
That thou wouldst scatter from him every cloud
Of his mortality so with thy prayers,
That the Chief Pleasure be to him displayed.
Still farther do I pray thee, Queen, who canst
Whate'er thou wilt, that sound thou mayst preserve
After so great a vision his affections.
Let thy protection conquer human movements;
See Beatrice and all the blessed ones
My prayers to second clasp their hands to thee!'

---

xvii. 59). As we saw, Mary, as prevenient grace, came to Dante's rescue through Lucia and Beatrice, not in answer to any prayer of his, but of her own pity and charity. See p. 512 above.

[1] Buti thinks *misericordia* (compassion), *pietate* (pity), and *magnificenza* (magnificence, the doing of great things) are singled out from the other virtues of the Virgin because of the lines preceding (16-18). Her *misericordia* is shown in succouring him who asks; her *pietate* in forerunning the asking; and her *magnificenza* in carrying the great things in which she succours to a perfect end. 'We praise thy virginity,' says Bernard, ' we marvel at thy humility : but thy compassion (misericordia) tastes sweeter to the wretched, we embrace thy compassion more lovingly, we remember it oftener, we call upon it more frequently' (*In Assump. B.V.M.*, Serm. iv.). In his *Cant. Canticorum*, Serm. xii. he says the perfume of piety (*unguentum pietatis*) is the most excellent of all, ' because it is made of the necessities of the poor, of the anxieties of the oppressed, of the unrests of the sad, of the faults of sinners, and finally of all the distresses of those who are wretched, though they should be our enemies. . . . Many miseries, therefore, gathered together, and looked on with the eye of pity (*oculo pietatis*), are the species from which the best perfumes are compounded, worthy of the bosom of the Bride, and pleasing to the senses of the Bridegroom.'

[2] The point of this reference is that it was by Mary's grace that Dante made his great journey down to 'the lowest lagoon of the universe' and up to the White Rose. She is not merely *Regina Coeli*, but, in Bonaventura's words, *Domina coelestium, terrestrium, et infernorum*. To her, says Bernard, 'look both those who dwell in heaven and those in hell . . . those who are in heaven, that their ranks may be restored; and those in hell, that they may be delivered' (*In Festo Pentecostes*, Serm. ii.). It was by Mary's authority and power as Domina infernorum that Beatrice was able to enter Limbo and send Virgil to guide Dante through the kingdom of the lost. I incline to think that we have here the solution of a most difficult passage in the *Inferno* (ix. 64-103)—the open-

Three petitions may here be distinguished. That 'every cloud of his mortality' may be scattered is regarded by some as a reminiscence of a passage in Virgil; and doubtless in form it is so.[1]   But Dante

ing of the gates of the City of Dis and the rebuke of the rebel angels by one 'sent from heaven.' In my *Exiles of Eternity*, p. 164, I suggested that this unnamed Messenger is Michael who hurled these rebel angels out of heaven, sent now on another errand of judgment.   I now suggest that it is Gabriel, for two reasons.   (1) He is described as *del ciel messo*, 'sent from heaven,' an echo, in my view, of the Vulg. of Luke i. 26, *Missus est* angelus Gabriel *a Deo* (comp. Bernard's Homilies 'Super *Missus est*,' which he himself preferred to call 'De Laudibus Virginis Matris').   (2) The second reason is more significant.   The 'sent from heaven' opened the gate of Dis with a rod—*una verghetta*.   What I suggest is that this *verghetta* is the *virga* which was universally regarded as a type or figure of the Virgo.   Aaron's rod that budded of itself was the Virgin; the rod from which Jesus, the Flower of Nazareth, bloomed (Is. xi. 1, Vulg. Et egredietur *virga* de radice Jesse, et *flos* de radice eius ascendet).   The writings of the mediæval mystics overflow with this play of piety on *virgo* and *virga*.   Now Bonaventura, in the passage just referred to, connects this play with Mary's power and authority as *Domina daemonum*: 'Consider how Mary is Domina daemonum in hell, so powerfully ruling over them that the passage of the Psalm (cx. 2) may be taken as referring to her: Virgam virtutis tuae emittet Dominus, etc.   *Virga virtutis est virgo Maria.* . . . Haec virga virgo Maria, virga virtutis est contra inimicos infernales, quibus magna virtute dominatur.'   In the light of such a passage it is not unnatural to suppose that the *verghetta* of the Messenger from heaven is the symbol of the *virga* of the Virgin—the rod of power by which she ruled the demons as their Domina.   Mary's name, like her Son's, is never mentioned in the *Inferno*, but Dante indicates here and elsewhere that the powers of darkness are subject to her.   E.g. In *Inf.* iii. 95 and v. 23 Virgil silences the opposition of Charon and Minos to Dante's journey by the words;

> 'It is so willed there where is power to do
> That which is willed.'

This is universally taken as meaning the will of God.   But in *Par.* xxxiii. 34 Bernard attributes the same power to Mary : 'Queen, who hast power to do that which thou wilt.'   It seems to me, therefore, that Virgil's words to Charon and Minos refer to Mary as *Domina daemonum* whose will has power behind it—the *virga virtutis*, of which the *verghetta* of the one 'sent from heaven' was the symbol.   If the Messenger was Gabriel, the storm with which he swept across the Stygian Fen shows how he fulfilled the meaning of his name, Fortitudo Dei, the Strength of God, armed as he was with the 'virga virtutis,' the rod of power of Virgo Maria.   He represents some intervention of the Virgin's grace to save Dante from the fiends of doubt that held the gate of the City of Heretics.

[1] *Aen.* ii. 604-606:

> 'Aspice, namque omnem, quae nunc obducta tuenti
> Mortales hebetat visus tibi, et humida circum
> Caligat, nubem eripiam.'

The speaker is Venus, the mother of Aeneas, and the cloud she promises to withdraw from his mortal sight is that which hides from him the deities who are aiding the Greeks in the destruction of Troy.

filled the heathen form with Christian contents. It is a petition that the last vestige of the darkness of original sin and its consequences be swept away from his soul. The loss of original justice through Adam inflicted, according to Aquinas, four wounds on our nature: ignorance in the intellect, badness in the will, weakness in things that require courage, and concupiscence, the rebellion of the senses against reason and Divine law[1]; and this wound of sin, overflowing the bounds of the soul, involved the body in diseases and death.[2] These are the clouds of mortality from which Dante must be freed before he could uplift his eyes to 'the last salvation'; and since the clouds had their rise in the sin of Eve, they could be dissipated only by the grace won through the prayers of her who closed the wound which she had made.

The second petition (ll. 34-36) has regard to the time when the great vision is past, and Dante must return to the earth and to himself. What will then be the effect of this supernatural vision of the intellect on the affections of the heart? Will they remain sound, sane, healthy; or will they be thrown by the reaction of the ecstasy into morbid disorder and confusion? In a Sermon on the right ordering of the affections, Bernard says the human soul cannot exist without four affections—love and joy, fear and sorrow. Rightly ordered, they sit as a crown of virtues on the soul; inordinate, they are confusions and perturbations. The prayer then is that when Dante returns to himself the very excess and rapture of intellect in 'so great a vision' may not throw the affections of his heart into an unhealthy disorder and confusion.[3] The last petition

---

[1] *Summa*, i-ii. q. lxxxv. a. 3: 'ignorantia in intellectu, malitia in voluntate, infirmitas in irascibili, et concupiscentia in concupiscibili.' Father Rickaby has a characteristic note on *irascible* and *concupiscible*: it will help an Englishman to understand if we call the former Pluck and the latter Passion. 'Pluck fails, and Passion runs to excess, till Pluck is formed to fortitude, and Passion to temperance' (*Moral Phil.* 86 n.).

[2] *Summa*, i-ii. q. lxxxv. a. 5.

[3] In *Cant. Canticorum*, Serm. xlix. 4, Bernard distinguishes two kinds of ecstasy: 'one in the intellect, the other in the affection; one in light, the other in heat; one in knowledge, the other in devotion: verily, pious

is that the guardianship of the Virgin may conquer
every movement that has its source in himself alone,
the mere natural man, that through her grace every
movement of his being may have a supernatural
beginning and end, from God to God. It is, as
Hettinger says, a prayer for perseverance, a virtue
that Bernard was never tired of urging on his hearers.[1]

The remainder of the Canto forms the answer to the
first petition of this prayer. Mary first fixed her eyes,
'beloved of God and venerated,' on St. Bernard, then
turned them to the Eternal Light in intercession. As
no other creature can pierce so far into that Light, so
none can see so clearly the soul's needs, or help so surely.
In a moment Dante felt all yearning die away, because
he now drew near the end of all desire. Since God is
'the good of the intellect,' and the intellect can rest
only in Him, desire itself fades away in the perfect
satisfaction of seeing Him as He is. Dante needed not
Bernard's smile and sign to make him look up: already
his purified vision was entering deeper and deeper into
'the high Light which of itself is true.'[2] From this
point onward he warns us again and again, as he did at
the very beginning of the poem, that his vision, being

affection, and the heart glowing with love, and the infusion of holy
devotion, yea, and a vehement spirit full of zeal: these assuredly are
brought back from no other where than the banqueting house; and
whoso can rise from prayer endowed with the fulness of these things, can
say with truth: 'The King hath brought me into his banqueting house'
(in cellam vinariam, Vulg. Cant. ii. 4).

[1] Perseverance is 'the image of the Divine eternity,' and it alone
receives the crown. 'Not he who begins, but he who perseveres, the
same shall be saved. Many can begin, few can persevere. Perseverance
is the daughter of the most high King, the fruit of virtues and their consummation, the storehouse of all good: a virtue without which no one
shall see God, nor by God be seen' (De Diversis, Serm. xli. 10). The 'four
horns' of the cross are continence, patience, prudence, humility; and
patience includes perseverance (In Festo S. Andreae Apos., Serm. ii.).

[2] Par. xxxiii. 46-54. In God, being and intellect are one, hence He is
truth in and of Himself, whereas all else is true only according to its
participation in the Divine intellect. 'His being is not only conformed
to His intellect, but it is His intellect itself; and His intellect is the
measure and cause of every other being and of every other intellect; and
He Himself is His own being and intelligence. Hence it follows that not
only is truth in Him, but that Himself is the sovereign and first truth'
(Summa, i. q. xvi. a. 5).

beyond the bounds of the natural powers, is of necessity
beyond the limits of both speech and memory. He is
like a man awaking from a dream who finds that the
clear outlines of the vision have vanished, and nothing
remains but the sweetness of the passion which it has
imprinted on the mind. As the snow unseals itself to
the sun and melts away; as on the leaves the oracle of
the Sibyl vanished light upon the wind,[1] so vanished
from his memory that which he had seen 'with open
face.' He can only invoke the Light Supreme to re-
lend to his mind a little of what He had appeared to
him, and to give his tongue power to leave one spark
of His glory to future generations, that even from the
spark they might conceive how far He transcended
'mortal thoughts.'[2]

Dante proceeds to tell how he gazed at the piercing
ray, until his vision became one with the Infinite Goodness, and he had boldness to look until he 'consumed
his sight upon it':

> I believe, by the keenness of the living ray
> Which I endured, I had bewildered been,
> If but mine eyes had been averted from it.

The reason is that, were it possible for a soul that sees
the Highest to turn to some lower good, the very conception of good would be darkened and confused. It is
not possible, as is expressly stated in ll. 100-105:

> In presence of that Light one such becomes,
> To turn from it to any other sight,
> It is impossible he e'er consent.
> Because the good which of the will is object
> Is gathered all in it, and outside it
> That is defective which is perfect there.[3]

---

[1] The reference is to *Aen.* iii. 441-452. The Cumaean Sibyl wrote her
oracles on the leaves of trees and left them in her cave; at the turning of
the hinge a breath of wind sets them flying, and she never gathers them
together again.

[2] *Par.* xxxiii. 55-75. 'Thy victory' in l. 75 is not, in the first instance,
the infinite greatness and excellence of God by which he conquers or
transcends the universe, though of course that is involved. But Dante's
immediate thought is what he is speaking of—the way in which the
vision of God conquered all his mortal powers, so that no more than a
spark of it remains in his memory.

[3] The good is the natural object of desire, however mistaken we may
be as to what it is. 'God in His goodness includes all goodnesses, and

' It is impossible,' says Aquinas, ' that any one seeing
the Divine Essence should wish not to see it: because
every good gift which one is willing to go without, is
either insufficient, so that something else more sufficing
is sought in its place, or has some inconvenience
annexed to it, whereby it comes to excite disgust. But
the vision of the Divine Essence fills the soul with
all good things, since it unites to it the Source of all
good. . . . In like manner that vision has no inconvenience annexed : as it is said of the contemplation of
wisdom: "Her conversation hath no bitterness, nor
her company any tediousness" (Wisd. viii. 16). Thus
it is evident that of his own will the happy being cannot forsake happiness.'[1] The feeling that could he turn
away all were lost, gave Dante boldness to endure the
keen ray to the utmost :

> And I remember that I was more bold
> On this account to bear so much that I united
> My aspect with the Goodness Infinite.
> O grace abundant, whereby I did presume
> To fix my sight upon the Light Eternal,
> So that my vision was consumed therein !

This last line is rendered by Vernon : ' I exhausted all
there was to be seen in it,' which is precisely what
Dante never could have meant. The teaching of
Aquinas is that the souls *in patria* see the Essence of
God by the union of that Essence with their intellect.

thus is the good of all good. God is good by essence : all other beings by
participation : therefore nothing can be called good except inasmuch as it
bears some likeness to the divine goodness. He is therefore the good of
all good' (*Cont. Gent.* i. 40, Rickaby's trans.). It follows that apart from
Him, all good is defective, as the part is, severed from the whole.

[1] *Summa*, i-ii. q. v. a. 4 (Rickaby's trans.). Comp. St. Bernard, *De
Consideratione*, v. 13 : 'When we shall see Him face to face, we shall
see Him as He is. When that blessed time shall come, the poor, weak
blade of our intellect, however hard it may strike, will not recoil, or be
broken to shivers. It will rather concentrate itself, and will conform
itself to His unity, or rather to that Unity, so that we shall have one
face corresponding to His one face' (Lewis' trans.). One is also reminded
of Tennyson's line already quoted :

> We needs must love the highest when we see it,

and the verse from Frederic Myers' *St. Paul* :

> Whose hath felt the Spirit of the Highest
>   Cannot confound nor doubt him nor deny :
> Yea with one voice, O world, tho' thou deniest,
>   Stand thou on that side, for on this am I.

Yet since God is what Dante here calls Him, the
Infinite Goodness, He is capable of being known to
infinity, and this is beyond the power of any created
intelligence. The Blessed see God more perfectly or
less according to the measure of their charity, and
Dante, of course, could see no more. He does not mean,
therefore, that he exhausted all there was to be seen in
the Eternal Light,—that would imply that the finite
creature was able to comprehend the infinitude of his
Creator. He means just what he says, that he consumed
his own sight: he gazed into the Light Eternal till he
reached the last limit of his power of vision, the limit
being determined by the measure of his charity.[1]

---

[1] *Summa*, i. q. xii. a. 5-8. In art. 6 Aquinas says : ' The intellect that
participates more in the *lumen gloriae* will see God more perfectly. But
he will participate more in the light of glory who has more of charity ;
because where is the greater charity, there is the greater desire ; and desire
makes him who desires in some fashion apt and prepared for the reception
of the thing desired. Hence he who will have the most of charity will see
God more perfectly, and will be more blessed.' This certainly seems to contradict the Thomist doctrine (see p. 442 above) that knowledge of God determines the love, and not conversely. The difficulty is solved, I understand,
by drawing a distinction between charity *in via* and *in patria*. Charity
on earth *merits* the vision of God ; but charity in Paradise is the *effect* of
the vision. There is unreality in such distinctions : the more we love
God the more we know Him, and the more we know Him the more we
love Him. Love and knowledge are mutually cause and effect.

CHAPTER XXXII

5. *The Beatific Vision*

IN the Beatific Vision which now breaks upon the intellect, Dante distinguishes three moments in an ascending scale. The first and lowest is the immediate and simultaneous knowledge of the entire created universe in God (ll. 85-93). It is the perfect celestial fulfilment of what Aquinas calls 'the ascent through creatures to the knowledge of God by the natural light of reason.'[1] Against those who held that the existence of God, being either a self-evident truth or one revealed to faith, is incapable of demonstration, Aquinas argues from Rom. i. 20: 'For the invisible things of him from the creation of the world are clearly seen, being understood by the things that are made, even his eternal power and Godhead.' That knowledge which begins thus in 'the natural light of reason' is now made perfect in the supernatural 'light of glory': 'the universal form' of the whole creation flashing on the intellect in one glance of direct, immediate vision. The second and infinitely higher moment is the vision of the Holy Trinity (ll. 106-126), from which the whole creation flows. 'The highest goodness of God,' says Aquinas, 'according to the mode in which it is at present known *by its effects*, can be known apart from the Trinity of persons; but according to the knowledge of it *in itself*, as it is seen by the Blessed, it cannot be known apart from the Trinity of persons.'[2] Beatitude

---

[1] *Cont. Gent.* iv. 1.

[2] *Summa*, ii-ii. q. ii. 8. St. Bernard (*In Festo Omnium Sanctorum*, Serm. iv. 3) says: 'In that eternal and perfect beatitude we shall enjoy God in a threefold way, seeing Him in all creatures, having Him in our-

consists in the vision of the Divine Essence as it exists in Father, Son, and Spirit. It is difficult to say whether Dante claims to have seen the very Essence. The Trinity appears to him under the similitude of three circles of light of different colours, and Aquinas declares that to say God is seen through a similitude is equivalent to saying that the Divine Essence is not seen at all.[1] The third and supreme moment is the vision of the Incarnation (ll. 127-141), which all mediæval theology regarded, in its union of Divine and Human, as the final mystery of all being.[2]

I. The vision of the universe in 'the Light Eternal' is told in terms of the scholastic philosophy with which Dante was familiar :

> I saw that in its depth far down is lying,
> Bound up with love together in one volume,
> What through the universe in leaves is scattered ;
> Substance and accidents and their operations,
> All interfused together in such wise
> That what I speak of is one simple light.
> The universal form of this knot
> Methinks I saw, since more abundantly
> In saying this I feel that I rejoice.[3]

---

selves, and (which is ineffably more joyful and blessed than all these) knowing the Trinity in itself, and contemplating that glory without any ænigma with the pure eye of the heart. For in this will be life eternal and perfect, that we know the Father and the Son with the Holy Spirit, and see God as He is: that is, not merely as He is in us, or in other creatures, but as He is in Himself.'

[1] *Summa*, i. q. xii. a. 2.

[2] Comp. *Par.* ii. 40-42; vii. 28-33; xiii. 25-27. 'The piety shown by Richard of St. Victor in the earlier period, by Bonaventura and others in the later, was able to attach itself most intimately to this intractable dogma of the Trinity, and also to the other dogma of the Incarnation. The infinite love must be contemplated in the Mystery of the Trinity, and the highest point of the spirit's enlightenment is reached when in prayer, in knowledge, and in vision, man becomes absorbed in the great mystery of the union of deity and humanity, and contemplates the indifference of opposites (indifferentia oppositorum), seeing how the Creator and the creature, the lofty and the lowly, the being and the not-being coalesce in one' (Harnack, *Hist. of Dogma*, vi. 103, Eng. trans.).

[3] *Par.* xxxiii. 85-93. The rendering is Longfellow's with the exception of one word. To translate *la forma universal* (l. 91) 'the universal fashion' is to betray the sense. *Forma* has a definite scholastic sense which is lost in 'fashion.' See above, p. 58, on *Par.* i. 103-105, where 'order' is defined as 'form, which makes the universe resemble God.' In our day this part of the vision has been called 'cosmic consciousness': 'The prime characteristic of cosmic consciousness is a consciousness of

The general meaning is, in the words of Aquinas, that he who sees the Divine substance sees in it 'the genera and species and capabilities of all things and the whole order of the universe.' In other words, what physical science in this life is ever laboriously seeking to spell out from the scattered leaves of the universe, and to reduce to one all-embracing principle of knowledge, is there seen at a glance in its unity, the 'one simple light' and 'universal form.' 'By "seeing all things that belong to the perfection of the universe,"' says Father Rickaby, 'St. Thomas would mean, in modern terminology, "having a comprehensive scientific view of the universe as a whole": this would include a knowledge of the constitution of matter, and of its working arrangements, molar and molecular; an understanding of electricity, of gravitation, of vegetable and animal life, of the genesis of nebulæ and stars, of the origin of species, animal and vegetable, of the workings of the mind, such as free will.'[1]

the cosmos, that is, of the life and order of the universe. Along with the consciousness of the cosmos there occurs an intellectual enlightenment which alone would place the individual on a new plane of existence— would make him almost a member of a new species. To this is added a state of moral exaltation, an indescribable feeling of elevation, elation, and joyousness, and a quickening of the moral sense, which is fully as striking, and more important than is the enhanced intellectual power. With these come what may be called a sense of immortality, a consciousness of eternal life, not a conviction that he shall have this, but the consciousness that he has it already' (Dr. R. M. Bucke, *Cosmic Consciousness: a Study in the Evolution of the Human Mind*, quoted by Prof. William James in his *The Varieties of Religious Experience*, p. 398. An instance of Dr. Bucke's experience of the cosmic consciousness is given. The whole of Lectures xvi. and xvii. on Mysticism should be read in connection with this closing vision of the *Paradiso*).

[1] Note in Father Rickaby's translation of *Contra Gentiles* (iii. 59, p. 231). Sir Oliver Lodge, mystic and man of science, seems to have reached the same idea as Aquinas, that a scientific knowledge of the universe is an essential part of the Beatific Vision. In an address, the reference to which I have mislaid, he holds that social reform must flow in the channel of the scientific study of Nature. Not, however, for the mere materialistic end of better physical life on earth, though that too will be 'added unto us.' His ultimate aim, he declares, 'is no less than to be able to comprehend what is the length and breadth and depth and height of this mighty universe, including man as part of it, and to know not man and nature alone, but to attain some incipient comprehension of what saints speak of as the love of God which passeth knowledge, and so begin an entrance into the fulness of an existence [I understand him to mean eternal life in another world] beside which the joy even of a

This is the general idea stated in terms of modern science, and we must not lose it under the mediæval phraseology which Dante employs. 'Substance' is that which exists *per se*, not as a mere quality in something else; 'accident' is that which apart from something else has no existence: the 'accidents,' e.g., of colour, hardness and softness, cold and heat, and so on, require some 'substance' in which they inhere, something that has a proper being of its own which persists, let the accidents vary as they may.[1] These variations and combinations are the *costume* of l. 88, the infinite relations and operations through which substance and accidents are continually passing. No longer are they seen as here, scattered in leaves throughout the universe. Dante now sees them not discursively and in succession, but simultaneously at one glance: as St. Augustine says: 'Our thoughts will no longer be in motion, going and returning from thing to thing; but we shall see all our knowledge at once, and at one glance.'[2] They form 'one simple light,' because God,

perfect earthly life is but as the happiness of a summer day.' The reform of mankind which leads to this comprehension of the universe which is thus part of the beatitude of heaven, is to begin by 'a study of nature and of mathematics, and of the facts at present studied under the conventional head "science."' It is interesting to see the modern man of science and the scholastic of the Middle Ages agree in holding that a scientific knowledge of the universe must be regarded as an essential element of man's final beatitude. The idea is eloquently drawn out in Father Joseph Rickaby's *Moral Philosophy*, 21-27.

[1] For a discussion of the mediæval doctrine of substance and accident, see Father John Rickaby's *General Metaphysics*, 221-297. A simple example is quoted to prove that the distinction is involved in ordinary experience: 'the wax which I handle is now warm, now cold; first hard, then soft, and finally liquid; by the pressure of the fingers it acquires first one shape, and afterwards another: yet throughout it is the same piece of wax. There is, therefore, a subject permanent under the successive changes: it is one while they are many; it can be without any particular set of them, they cannot be without it, for they are precisely its modifications' (p. 248). The doctrine that accidents cannot exist without a substance in which they inhere has one great exception. Transubstantiation means that the substance of the bread and wine of the Eucharist is changed into the substance of the body and blood of Christ. By a Divine miracle, however, the *accidents* of the bread and wine (extension, colour, taste, etc.) remain without any substance in which to inhere. This is in the realm of the supernatural; in the natural, the connection of substance and accident is constant.

[2] *De Trinitate*, xv. 16. Aquinas quotes and expands the saying in *Summa*, i. q. xii. a. 10.

in whom they are seen, is one simple light. The
relations in which He stands to the universe, though
manifold, in no sense prejudice the simplicity and
singleness of His Being, rather they are the attestation
of it.[1] Properly speaking, God is the one and only
Substance, and all other 'substances' are in relation
to Him mere 'accidents,' inasmuch as it is in Him they
have their being.[2] 'The universal form' which Dante
believes he saw is that order of the universe which
makes it, in its own measure, a likeness of its Maker.
The 'form' of anything is the archetypal idea of it in
the Divine Mind which gives it its essential nature.
Not only has each individual thing a form, but also
the universe as a whole. The universal form is that
by which every created thing participates, according
to the powers of its nature, in the likeness of God, and
by which all are so related to one another as to constitute an order and unity.[3] This universal form
Dante believed he saw, because the mere saying of it
gave him a more ample joy. Finally, this unity of
being is 'bound up in one volume with love.' Love in
God is the desire to communicate His own goodness as
widely as possible; when He loves He creates and
infuses goodness in things.[4] To sum up, what Dante
here sees is that Being, Unity, and Goodness are
essentially one: as he says in *De Monarchia* (i. 15):

---

[1] Comp. *Cont. Gent.* ii. 14. In i. 77 Aquinas argues that the multitude
of the objects of God's will is not inconsistent with the simplicity of His
substance, since they are all included under His goodness, and in His
goodness all things are one.

[2] Of course there is no such thing as an accident in God's own substance,
else His substance were composite. 'Accident is not of the essence of
the subject. But God *is* whatever He *has* in Himself. Therefore in God
there is no accident' (*Cont. Gent.* i. 23). Yet since God is the one
absolute substance, existing *per se* alone, and since all created substances
exist in Him, these substances in relation to Him are as accidents. To
mark this distinction the schoolmen confine *per se* to uncreated and
created substance, and apply *a se* to the self-existent substance which
is God (comp. Father John Rickaby's *General Metaphysics*, 251-253).

[3] *De Mon.* i. 8: 'It is of the intention of God that everything should
represent the Divine likeness, so far as its proper nature can receive it.'
Comp. *Summa*, i. q. iv-vi.

[4] *Summa*, i. q. vi. a. 4; xx. a. 2. See above, p. 122 on *Par.* vii. 64 f., and
p. 449 on xxix. 13 f.

'Being by nature precedes Unity, and Unity Good; for where Being is greatest, Unity is greatest, and where Unity is greatest, Good is greatest; and in proportion as anything is removed from Being in its supreme form, it is removed from being one, and by consequence from being good.'[1]

The comparison used by Dante to explain the effect on him of this vision of the universe in God has given rise to many interpretations :

> One moment only is to me more lethargy
> Than five-and-twenty centuries to the emprise
> That made Neptune wonder at the shade of Argo.[2]

The interpretation which seems now most generally accepted is that suggested by Scartazzini who takes the *letargo* of l. 94 not as forgetfulness of the vision the moment it was past, but as forgetfulness of all else in the absorbing admiration which the vision produced. This absorption in the vision, he thinks, is proved by the *terzina* immediately following (ll. 97-99), in which Dante says his mind was all suspended in the intensity of his gaze upon the Light; and he paraphrases accordingly : 'All the admiration which in five-and-twenty centuries men have given to the emprise of the Argonauts gathered together, would be less than mine in one single moment when I held my regard fixed on Divinity.' I confess that this does not seem to me the natural meaning of this strange comparison. To begin with, *letargo* can scarcely mean a wonder or admiration which made Dante forget all not included in his vision, for the simple reason that there was nothing not included in it. Dante has just been labouring to tell us that he saw the entire universe in God—the sum-total of things. In the second place, he has warned us

---

[1] In *Summa*, i. q. v. a. 1, 3 Aquinas identifies Being and Goodness, and in q. xi. a. 1, Being and Unity. The question is discussed by Boethius in Bk. III. of the *De Consolatione*. On 'Order' as the 'form' of the universe, see above, p. 58 on *Par.* i. 103-120.

[2] *Par.* xxxiii. 94-96. The expedition of the Argonauts was believed to have taken place about 1250 years B.C., and therefore fully twenty-five centuries before the ideal date of the poem. Neptune's wonder was to see the Argo, the first ship whose shadow fell upon his waves.

again and again that his memory is powerless to recall
his vision, and this is therefore likely to be a repetition
of this warning.   And finally, the comparison joins as
naturally with the preceding *terzina* as with the one
following.   In ll. 91-93, he cannot say positively that
he saw 'the universal form of this knot'—the union
of substance and accidents in the universe; all he
ventures to say is '*credo* ch' io vidi,' I *believe* that I saw.
The comparison seems to me to be a parenthetical
explanation thrown in to show why he could only say
he *believed* he saw: 'One moment after the vision was
past made me forget more of what I saw than five-
and-twenty centuries have made the world forget the
expedition of the Argonauts; hence I cannot go further
than "I believe I saw."'   After this parenthesis he
resumes the story of his vision in the following lines.

II. It is important to notice that, in order to receive
the vision of the Trinity, Dante has no need to turn
away his eyes from the 'one simple light' in whose
depth he saw the universe.   As we have seen, the
universe is a similitude of God, and since the three
Persons were concerned in its creation, Dante finds
that, by an absorbed continuance of his gaze upon it,
the Trinity itself begins to appear: though of the little
he remembers, he is able to tell less than an infant at
the breast.   The vision comes only by degrees: not
that the Living Light on which he gazed had more than
one simple semblance, the change was in himself.[1]   As

---

[1] We may compare the changing image of the two natures of Christ
which Dante saw in the eyes of Beatrice, Christ Himself remaining the
same:

> Think, reader, if within myself I marvelled,
> When I saw the thing in itself stay quiet,
> And in its image it transformed itself (*Purg.* xxxi. 124-126).

In *Summa*, i. q. ix. Aquinas holds the immutability of God (1) because He
is *Pure Act*—that is, His whole being is at every moment actualized, no
part of it in *potentiality*, which would imply that it was capable of
receiving more; (2) in every change there is something composite, the
substance remaining, the accidents varying, a thing impossible to God,
who is absolutely simple; (3) everything moved is moved to something it
had not before, and God having the plenitude of all perfections has no
need of anything, and therefore is absolutely unchangeable.

his sight gathered strength by what it looked upon,
' one sole appearance was winnowed out ' to him : [1]

> In the profound and clear subsistence
> Of the High Light appeared to me three circles,
> Of three colours and of one dimension ;
> And the one from the other, as Iris from Iris,
> Appeared reflected, and the third appeared fire
> From the one and the other equally breathed forth.
> O how short the speech is, and how faint,
> To my conception, and this to what I saw
> Is such, 'tis not enough to call it little ! [2]
> O luce eterna, che sola in te sidi,
>   Sola t'intendi, e da te intelletta
>   Ed intendente te, ami ed arridi !

As has been already pointed out, the mere fact that
Dante uses a figure to convey what he saw of the
Trinity is possibly his way of saying that he did not
see the Divine Essence, since the very idea of seeing
the Essence is face to face vision, without the need
of any similitude.[3] The word ' subsistence ' (l. 115) is
applied to the High Light in the strict scholastic sense,
as that which is absolutely self-existent.[4] The figure
chosen by Dante, since figure was necessary, is as full
of beauty and spiritual suggestion as it was possible to
find. The 'clear subsistence of the High Light' is the
symbol of the Unity of God, the First Truth 'unbroken
of the prism.' The three circles represent the Three
Persons of the Trinity, existing only in the Unity of the
Divine Light.[5] The three colours are the three attri-

---

[1] I follow Butler's rendering of *si travagliava* (l. 114). In the Glossary
to his translation of the *Paradiso* (p. 438) he says : ' I feel very little doubt
that in this place we must derive the word from *vaglio*, "a sieve," Lat.
vannulus, dim. fr. *vannus*.' The ordinary rendering implies mere
change or transformation.

[2] This refers back to ll. 67-69, where Dante had prayed for power to tell
' a little ' of his vision. Here he says it is not even ' a little.'

[3] Or, perhaps, that only in a similitude could he *report* what he saw.

[4] *Summa*, i. q. xxix. a. 2. ' As a thing exists *per se*, and not *in alio*, it
is called *subsistentia*.' It is not mere being, as it is sometimes rendered,
it is self-existent being.

[5] The circle is a natural symbol of Divine perfection. ' Many centuries
before,' says Landino, ' Hermes Trismegistus defined God as a circular
sphere, because the knowledge of God is the knowledge of Himself. And
so He is from Himself to Himself, like the circle, without beginning and
without end.' ' The circle,' says Didron, ' is considered as emblematic of
God, and three circles figure the three persons; but in order to mark the

butes specially connected in Dante's theology with the
several Persons : the Power of the Father, the Wisdom
of the Son, the Love of the Spirit. The unity of the
Persons and attributes is asserted in the 'one
dimension' of the three circles—the one substance of
Godhead.   The next *terzina* (ll. 118-120) gives what
Aquinas calls the Relations of Divinity according to
the Procession of Persons out of identity of substance
—the Relations of Paternity, Generation and Spiration.[1]
From the circle of the Father appeared reflected the
circle of the Son, as Iris from Iris ; and from both was
breathed forth equally the fire of Love which is the
Holy Spirit.[2]   We must not think of these in the form
of three rainbows one within another, or even as the
three colours of a rainbow, for these are also one
within another. The 'one dimension' shows that
Dante conceived of them as co-existing in the one
space, though he does not explain how he was able to
see the three colours distinct within each other.

In the following *terzina* (ll. 124-126) the scholastic
subtlety which pervades the whole passage reaches its
climax. I scarcely venture to translate it, and have
seen no interpretation which seems to me to reach
Dante's central thought, which is indeed the central
thought of the whole poem and of all Thomist theology,
namely, that the highest blessedness is an activity of
the intellect, and that it is from the intellect that love
springs. We have again and again seen the application
of this view to human blessedness ; in this *terzina*
Dante applies it to the supreme beatitude of the Trinity

indissoluble union in which those three persons are linked together, the
three circles are intertwined, one within the other, in such a manner that
one could not be severed or removed without at the same time severing
all the three' (*Christian Iconography*, ii. 45). Of course, in any visible
representation of this Tri-unity such as Didron gives from a French minia-
ture of the thirteenth century, this intertwining of the circles is the only
device possible ; but this is certainly not Dante's conception here. His
circles are ' of one dimension '—not intertwined, but, so to speak, occupying and containing the same space, though, of course, his vision is
intellectual and not spatial.

[1] *Summa*, i. q. xxviii.
[2] On the Procession of the Spirit from both Father and Son, and the
filioque-controversy, see above, p. 170 f. on *Par.* x. 1-3.

—the happiness of God within His own being, in the communion of Person with Person. Let us take the aspects of this happiness one by one. The first relates to God in His unity—His perfect rest in and knowledge of Himself:

> ' *O luce eterna, che sola in te sidi,*
> *Sola t'intendi.*'[1]

'O Light Eternal, who sole in Thyself abidest, sole understandest Thyself.' God alone abides in Himself: all other beings seek their rest beyond themselves. He rests in Himself because He is His own happiness, because He understands Himself. For perfect happiness is the perfect activity of a perfect intellect exercised upon a perfect object; and 'the activity of God,' says Aquinas, 'fulfils all these conditions: since it is (1) activity in the order of understanding; and (2) His understanding is the highest of faculties, not needing any habit to perfect it; and (3) His understanding is bent upon Himself, the highest of intelligible objects; and (4) He understands perfectly, without any difficulty, and with all delight. He is therefore happy.'[2] This perfect understanding of Himself is possible only to Himself, since no created intellect can equal His.[3]

The remainder of the *terzina* relates to what Catholic theology calls 'the inner fecundity of the Divine Life,' the productions of that Life within itself. According to Aquinas, the Eternal Wisdom in its own inner activity proceeds by two ways and only two: that of *intellect*, the procession of the Word, the Son, the Second Person; and that of *will*, the procession of Love, the Holy Spirit, the Third Person.[4] The words in ll. 125, 126: ' *da te intelletta ed intendente te,*' refer to the Word—'known of Thee and understanding Thee': the mutual knowledge of Father and Son of which Christ speaks: 'No man knoweth the Son but the Father;

---

[1] *Par.* xxxiii. 124, 125.
[2] *Cont. Gent.* i. 100; 47; *Summa,* i. q. xii.; xiv.; xxvi.
[3] *Cont. Gent.* iii. 56, 59.
[4] *Summa,* i. q. xxvii. a. 5; xxviii. a. 4; xxxvi. a. 2.

neither knoweth any man the Father save the Son,'
and 'As the Father knoweth me, even so know I the
Father.'[1] 'Wisdom in God is His knowledge of Himself.
But because He does not know Himself by any presenta-
tion of Himself other than His essence, and His act of
understanding is His essence, the wisdom of God . . .
is the very essence of God. But the Son of God is the
Word and Concept of God understanding Himself.
The Word of God, thus conceived, is properly called
"begotten Wisdom."'[2]

The final words, '*ami ed arridi*,' 'lovest and smilest,'
refer to the Third Person. As the Son proceeds by way
of intellect as Word, so the Holy Spirit proceeds by
way of will as Love, breathed forth equally by Father
and Son. This Love is here regarded, not in its outflow
upon creatures, but as the bond of communion and joy
between the Father and the Word. It is in the mutual
knowledge of Father and Son that the Spirit 'loves
and smiles,'—the smile representing the happiness with
which this activity of the Divine Life within itself is
for ever filled. 'The Father loves in the Son, as in the
resplendent image of His Goodness, the Supreme
Beauty; and the Son loves in the Father, as in the
principle of His Beauty, the Supreme Goodness.'[3]

III. We come now to the third and final moment of
the vision, the crowning mystery of the Incarnation:

---

[1] Matt. xi. 27; John x. 15.
[2] *Cont. Gent.* iv. 12.
[3] Wilhelm and Scannell, *Manual of Cath. Theol.*, i. 319. It is possible
that this exposition may cast little light on the mystery of the Trinity;
but we ought to be careful not to miss the great idea that was in Dante's
mind—the infinite activity and peace and joy which eternally fill the being
of God, an activity ever flowing through the intellect and the will. A
Trinity of Persons in the Divine unity was inferred from the beatitude of
God. Hettinger quotes the following from Richard of St. Victor on the
Trinity: 'The proof or argument for the plurality of persons, furnished by
the plenitude of the Divine Goodness, is obtained by a parity of reasoning
from the plenitude of the (divine) happiness. . . . As charity is ever
united with goodness and happiness, it must exist where the joy is
supreme. And as joyful love must be mutual, therefore in that sovereign
happiness, mutual love cannot but be found.' The above exposition is
based chiefly on *Summa*, i. q. xxvi-xlii. For exposition of other passages
relating to the Trinity, see above, p. 170 f. (*Par.* x. 1-3; 49-51); p. 392
(xxiv. 139-147).

> That circulation, which being thus conceived
> Appeared in Thee as a reflected light,
> When somewhat contemplated by mine eyes,
> Within itself, of its own very colour
> Seemed to me painted with our effigy,
> Through which my sight was all absorbed therein.
> As the geometrician who endeavours
> To square the circle, and discovers not,
> By taking thought, the principle he wants,
> Even such was I at that new apparition;
> I wished to see how the image to the circle
> Conformed itself, and how it there finds place;
> But my own wings were not enough for this,
> Had it not been that then my mind there smote
> A flash of lightning, wherein came its wish.[1]

It has been already pointed out that this is the third vision of Christ in the *Paradiso*. In the Heaven of Mars, Dante saw the outflash of His Sacrifice in the hosts who died as soldiers of the Cross (xiv. 103-108). In the Starry Heaven, His light shone forth in the souls of the Redeemed who formed His Triumph (xxiii. 25-45). Once before either of these, in the Earthly Paradise, he had a lower vision of the Divine and Human natures in the symbolic form of a Gryphon, half-eagle, half-lion,—the former representing the spiritual government on earth, the latter the temporal.[2] Now the time has come when all these indirect and partial modes of knowledge as in a glass are to give way to vision face to face, and the mystery be known of itself,

> In fashion of the first truth that man believes.[3]

It is to be noted that Dante, in common with all mediæval theologians, regarded the Incarnation as the final mystery, and the understanding of the union

---

[1] *Par.* xxxiii. 127-141 (Longfellow's trans., except *per che* in l. 132 which he renders *wherefore*. I take it as meaning that through the human nature, 'our effigy,' Dante was drawn into contemplation of the union of the two natures in the Person of the Son). The 'thus conceived' of l. 127 refers to the preceding *terzina*: the Word is begotten of the Divine Intellect. The 'measuring of the circle' in l. 134 is referred to as impossible in *Conv.* ii. 14 and *De Mon.* iii. 3.

[2] See my *Prisoners of Hope*, 421.

[3] *Par.* ii. 43-45. See p. 65.

of the Divine and Human in Christ as the crown of
the eternal beatitude.   'Of all the works of God,'
says Aquinas, 'the mystery of the Incarnation most
transcends reason.   Nothing more astonishing could
be imagined as done by God than that the true God
and Son of God should become true man.'[1]   And not
only is it the greatest mystery in itself: it is the fullest
revelation of the Divine Goodness, and therefore of
that interior life of the Trinity of which Dante has just
spoken.   To quote Aquinas once more, 'since the very
nature of God is the essence of goodness, and it belongs
to the idea of good to communicate itself to others, it
is clear that it is worthy of God to communicate Himself to creatures in the highest way, and this was
fulfilled in the work of the Incarnation.'   He quotes
John Damascene to the effect that the Incarnation
reveals at once the goodness and wisdom, the justice
and power of God: goodness, 'since He despised not
the infirmity of the work of His own hands; justice,
in that by the man conquered, and not another, He
conquered the tyrant, not snatching man from death
by force; wisdom, because He found the most fitting
payment of the heaviest price; and infinite power or
virtue, since nothing is greater than that God should
be made man.'[2]

To this final mystery Dante tells us his eyes were
specially drawn by the appearance of our effigy painted
within the circle in the very colour of the circle itself—
the human nature suffused with the Divine attribute
of Wisdom, and made one with it.   This union he found
as insoluble as the measuring of the circle.   Two
problems baffled all his thinking.   The first was 'how
the image conformed itself to the circle,' that is, how
human nature could be commensurate with the Divine.

---

[1] *Cont. Gent.* iv. 27.

[2] *Summa*, iii. q. i. a. 1.   In *Par.* vii. 85-120 (p. 122 f. above), Dante argues
similarly that the Incarnation was the way of salvation most honouring
to the *mercy* of God, since it was more generous for God to give Himself,
than to pardon of mere courtesy; and to His *justice*, since by becoming
incarnate, the Son of God humbled Himself as far as Adam had tried to
raise himself in pride : hence the atonement equalled the offence.

The fundamental thought of all scholastic theology is that the Divine nature is for ever beyond the human; before man can see God he must be raised above his natural powers.   Even when thus Divinized, he falls short of perfect union with all that is in God.   How then in Christ does the human image conform itself to the circle of Divinity?   How is the human nature commensurate with the Divine?   The second problem was 'how it there finds place,'—the mode of the union of the two natures.   Let any one read the discussion of this problem in the first twenty Quaestiones of the Third Part of the *Summa*, and he will not wonder that even Dante's 'wings were not enough for this.'   And then one lightning-flash of supernatural power smote his mind and gave him his wish.   The final secret of the union of God and Man lay open to his intellect.

The poet is too wise to attempt to tell us what he saw: it is, in St. Bernard's words, an *abyssus impenetrabilis*, and 'the rest is silence.'   There is no pressing with the Areopagite and many mystics into 'the darkness of the un-knowledge' behind the Trinity and beyond the intellect, in which one knows by knowing nothing.   Dante returns sanely, as St. Bernard always did, to the firm ground of the plain moral life.   In four lines, as simple as they are beautiful, he tells us the issue of the ineffable vision in his own nature and life, and so ends:

> Here to the high fantasy power failed;
> But now was turning my desire and will,
> Even as a wheel that equally is moved,
> The Love which moves the sun and the other stars.[1]

One cannot but feel the restrained and simple beauty of the words; yet if we examine them, they will discover to us Dante's strange power of fusing together the highest poetry and the most exact scholastic significance.   'The high fantasy,' for instance, is not, as

[1] Comp. the words of Boethius quoted in *De Mon.* i. 9:
> 'O felix hominum genus,
> Si vestros animos amor
> Quo coelum regitur, regat!'

many readers seem to suppose, the poem itself, as if
he were saying the high dream or vision failed and
broke. It is 'the shaping spirit of imagination.' The
phantasia in scholastic psychology is that interior
sense of the soul which has the power to form *images*
of things perceptible by the senses. The use of the
word does not mean that Dante regarded his crowning
vision of the Incarnation as having come to him
through sensible images: it was a lightning-flash of
pure supernatural intellect. For that very reason, he
means us to understand, his fantasy or imagination
failed in power to turn it into any image which would
give the reader some faint idea of what the pure
intellect saw. Even the mystery of the Trinity his
fantasy had been able to present under the sensible
image of three circles of colour; but now this is
beyond its highest power. When the pure intellect
attains the last reality of Being, it sends back no
report, no shadowy image, through any other power
of the soul, such as memory or imagination.

Nevertheless, this irrecoverable flash of intellect is
not without its issue in the other parts of his nature,
in accordance with that order by which, as we have so
often seen, vision and knowledge are the parents of
love,[1] Having once seen, if but for a moment, the
Incarnate Word, the Eternal Wisdom of the Father,
his desire and will are of necessity subdued to the
power of the Spirit of Love which is breathed equally
from both,

> The Love which moves the sun and the other stars.

For it seems to me that the entire context gives us no
option but to take Love here as the special attribute
of the Spirit. Within the Trinity itself, Dante's intellect had seen the love and smiling of the Spirit in
relation to the other Persons. It is the same Love
that moves like an axle, so to speak, the mighty wheel
of universal Nature. And in the equal and uniform

[1] *Par.* xxviii. 109-111.

motion of that wheel Dante feels that his desire and
will are carried round, that they are at last in harmony
with the Divine Love which is the Spirit of the universe. The comparison of the harmony between his
desire and will to the equal movement of a wheel in
its every part, has its own significance. As we have
many times seen, it is *desire* for God that 'moves the
sun and the other stars,' and keeps the Angelic Orders
circling round the Point of burning Light: 'He moves
the whole Heaven with love and with desire.'[1] The
desire, in short, is simply the Love of the Divine Spirit
drawing all creatures to itself, that there they may
find their rest. In this universal desire Dante shares;
but he was painfully conscious that oftentimes his *will*
was out of harmony with it, and went its own way.
His desire was for God, his will, alas, was too often
against Him. And now he knows that this inner contradiction is reconciled: desire and will move equally
together as a wheel moves, because they are one with the
Holy Spirit of Divine and universal Love that moves
the great wheel of Nature. It is the unity for which
Dante's whole being hungered, so far as it could be his
while the 'clouds of his mortality' hung around him—
unity with himself, with the universe, and with the
Spirit of God. It is impossible to read the passage
without feeling that Dante is drawing a contrast with
certain words which Love spoke to him in a sad and
troubled dream of his youth. Beatrice, he tells us in
the *Vita Nuova*, had just denied him 'her most sweet
salutation, in the which alone was his blessedness.' In
a passion of grief he fell asleep 'like a beaten sobbing
child,' and Love appeared to him, also weeping. 'Why
weepest thou, Master of all honour?' asked Dante; to
which the answer came: '*Ego tanquam centrum circuli,
cui simili modo se habent circumferentiae partes: tu
autem non sic*'—'I am as the centre of a circle, to
which the parts of the circumference bear a like relation: *but thou art not so.*'[2] In other words, Love is the

---

[1] *Par.* xxiv. 130-132; ii. 19, 20; *Conv.* iv. 12.
[2] *Vita Nuova*, § xii.

centre of the universe, the power that moves the sun
and the other stars in a perfect circle, but Dante was
not in right relation to that centre, his desire and
will did not move in the same circumference around it.
Now, at last, the disorder is removed. Though he is
powerless to recall his vision, it has left behind a great
unity of being; and he is content to wait 'until the
day break, and the shadows flee away,' and the little
moment's flash becomes the abiding vision of Eternity.

Meantime he has the mirrors of 'the sun and the
other stars.'[1] With that last shining word he closes
every stage of his pilgrimage, and every stage gives it
a higher meaning. To his mystic mind, as to that of
St. Bernard,[2] the stars stand for the bright virtues of
'the life which is life indeed,' and the entire poem is,
in Milton's phrase, 'a star-ypointing pyramid.' From
'the dead air' of the lost world 'where the light is as
darkness,' he 'issued forth to rebehold the stars.' In
the Paradise Regained on the summit of the Mount of
Cleansing, his will is made 'pure and disposed to
mount up to the stars.' And now, having climbed on
the shining stairway of all the starry virtues to the
Eternal Sun who is the fountain of their light, his
desire and will are carried round, as in the equal
motion of a wheel, by 'the Love that moves the sun

---

[1] 'What then? may I not everywhere behold the mirrors of the sun
and stars? Can I not everywhere under heaven meditate on the sweetest
truths?'—*Epis.* ix., in which Dante refuses to return to Florence on dishonourable terms.

[2] 'A holy soul is a heaven, having for *sun* the intellect, for *moon* faith, for
stars virtues. . . . A virtue, then, is a star, and a man of virtues a heaven'
(*Cantica Canticorum*, Serm. xxvii. 8). St. Bonaventura (*De Sept. Donis
Spiritus Sancti*, viii. ch. xi.) quotes from a sermon in which St. Bernard
explains the crown of twelve stars of Rev. xii. 1 as twelve beatitudes of
the souls *in patria*: 'Prima stella est memoria sine oblivione. Secunda
stella est ratio sine omni errore. Tertia stella est voluntas sine omni per-
turbatione. Quarta est impossibilitas moriendi, quia resurget corpus
incorruptibile. Quinta est claritas, quia configuramur claritati Christi
corporaliter. Sexta est agilitas, ut corpus sit agile secundum agilitatem
mentis. Septima est subtilitas, ut corpus nostrum penetret omnia cor-
pora. Octava est, ut quilibet diligat alium sicut seipsum. Nona est,
videre quod proximus quilibet diligit ipsum sicut seipsum. Decima est
Deum perfecte diligere, et plus quam seipsum. Undecima est diligere
seipsum tantummodo propter Deum. Duodecima est videre Deum diligere
se, diligentem plus quam ille homo diligat seipsum.'

and the other stars'—the Love of the Spirit which is the soul of every virtue. For 'God is love; and he that dwelleth in love dwelleth in God, and God in him.'

THOU SHALT MAKE THEM DRINK OF THE RIVER OF THY PLEASURES. FOR WITH THEE IS THE FOUNTAIN OF LIFE : IN THY LIGHT SHALL WE SEE LIGHT.

NOW UNTO HIM WHO IS ABLE TO KEEP YOU FROM FALLING, AND TO PRESENT YOU FAULTLESS BEFORE THE PRESENCE OF HIS GLORY WITH EXCEEDING JOY, TO THE ONLY GOD OUR SAVIOUR, THROUGH JESUS CHRIST OUR LORD, BE GLORY AND MAJESTY, DOMINION AND POWER, BEFORE ALL TIME, AND NOW, AND FOR EVERMORE. AMEN.

S'io torni mai, lettore, a quel devoto
Trionfo, per lo quale io piango spesso
Le mie peccata, e il petto mi percoto. . . .
Par. xxii. 106-108.

Starry amorist, starward gone,
Thou art—what thou didst gaze upon!
Passed through thy golden garden's bars,
Thou seest the Gardener of the Stars.
Francis Thompson.

Now just as the Gates were opened to let in the men, I looked in after them, and behold, the City shone like the Sun; the Streets also were paved with Gold, and in them walked many men, with Crowns on their heads, Palms in their hands, and golden Harps to sing praises withal. There were also of them that had wings, and they answered one another without intermission, saying, *Holy, Holy, Holy, is the Lord.* And after that they shut up the Gates. Which when I had seen, I wished myself among them. Bunyan, *The Pilgrim's Progress.*

Post Dantis paradisum nihil restat nisi visio Dei.
Cardinal Manning.

THE SUN SHALL BE NO MORE THY LIGHT BY DAY;
NEITHER FOR BRIGHTNESS SHALL THE MOON GIVE
LIGHT UNTO THEE: BUT THE LORD SHALL BE UNTO
THEE AN EVERLASTING LIGHT, AND THY GOD THY
GLORY. THY SUN SHALL NO MORE GO DOWN; NEITHER
SHALL THY MOON WITHDRAW ITSELF: FOR THE LORD
SHALL BE THINE EVERLASTING LIGHT, AND THE DAYS
OF THY MOURNING SHALL BE ENDED.

INDEX